Social
Issues
Primary
Sources
Collection

Gender Issues
and Sexuality

Essential Primary Sources

Social Issues Primary Sources Collection

Gender Issues and Sexuality

Essential Primary Sources

K. Lee Lerner, Brenda Wilmoth Lerner, and Adrienne Wilmoth Lerner, Editors

THOMSON

GALE

Detroit • New York • San Francisco • New Haven, Conn. • Waterville, Maine • London • Munich

THOMSON

★

GALE™

Gender Issues and Sexuality: Essential Primary Sources

K. Lee Lerner, Brenda Wilmoth Lerner, and Adrienne Wilmoth Lerner, Editors

Project Editors
Dwayne D. Hayes and John McCoy

Editorial
Luann Brennan, Grant Eldridge, Anne Marie Hacht, Joshua Kondek, Andy Malonis, Mark Milne, Rebecca Parks, Mark Springer, Jennifer Stock

Permissions
Shalice Shah-Caldwell, Tim Sisler, Andrew Specht

Imaging and Multimedia
Dean Dauphinais, Leitha Etheridge-Sims, Lezlie Light, Michael Logusz, Dan Newell, Christine O'Bryan, Kelly A. Quin, Denay Wilding, Robyn Young

Product Design
Pamela A. Galbreath

Composition and Electronic Capture
Evi Seoud

Manufacturing
Rita Wimberley

Product Manager
Carol Nagel

LIBRARY OF CONGRESS CATALOGING-IN-PUBLICATION DATA

Gender issues and sexuality : essential primary sources / K. Lee and Brenda Wilmoth Lerner, editors.
    p. cm. — (Social issues primary sources collection)
    Includes index.
    ISBN 1-4144-0325-9 (hardcover : alk. paper)
    1. Sex—Social aspects—History—Sources. 2. Sex role—History—Sources. 3. Sexual orientation—History—Sources. 4. Gender identity—History—Sources. 5. Sex customs—History—Sources. I. Lerner, K. Lee. II. Lerner, Brenda Wilmoth. III. Series.

    HQ21.G359 2007
    306.76—dc22   2006017445

This title is also available as an e-book.
ISBN 1414412614
Contact your Thomson Gale sales representative for ordering information.

Printed in the United States of America
10 9 8 7 6 5 4 3 2 1

Table of Contents

1 BEYOND FEMININITY AND MASCULINITY: PERSPECTIVES ON GENDER AND SEXUALITY

2 WOMEN'S RIGHTS MOVEMENT

6 GENDER AND SEXUALITY IN SCHOOL AND THE WORKPLACE

7 SEX, GENDER, AND SEXUALITY IN THE MEDIA

8 OBSCENITY, PORNOGRAPHY, AND SEX CRIMES

Advisors and Contributors

While compiling this volume, the editors relied upon the expertise and contributions of the following scholars, journalists, and researchers who served as advisors and/or contributors for *Gender Issues and Sexuality: Essential Primary Sources:*

Steven Archambault, Ph.D. Candidate
University of New Mexico
Albuquerque, New Mexico

Annessa Babic, Instructor and Ph.D. Candidate
SUNY at Stony Brook, Stony Brook, NY

James Anthony Charles Corbett
Journalist
London, UK

Bryan Davies, J.D.
Ontario, Canada

Sandra Galeotti, M.S.
S. Paulo, Brazil

Larry Gilman, Ph.D.
Sharon, Vermont

Amit Gupta, Ph.D.
Ahmedabad, India

Stacey N. Hannem
Journalist
Quebec, Canada

John Leblanc, Ph.D.
European Cultural Studies Institute
Paris, France

S. Layman, M.A.
Abingdon, MD

Adrienne Wilmoth Lerner (J.D. Candidate)
University of Tennessee College of Law
Knoxville, Tennessee

Pamela V. Michaels, M.A.
Forensic Psychologist
Santa Fe, New Mexico

Caryn Neumann, Ph.D.
Ohio State University
Columbus, Ohio

Nephele Tempest
Los Angeles, California

Jeremy Wimpfheimer, M.A.
Beit Shemesh, Israel

Melanie Barton Zoltán, M.S.
Amherst, Massachusetts

Gender Issues and Sexuality: Essential Primary Sources is the product of a global group of multi-lingual scholars, researchers, and writers. The editors are grateful to Ms. Christine Jeryan, Ms. Amy Loerch Strumolo, and Ms. Kate Kretschmann for their dedication and skill in copyediting both text and translations. Their efforts added significant accuracy and readability to this book. The editors also wish to acknowledge and thank Ms. Adrienne Wilmoth Lerner and Ms. Alicia Maria Cafferty for their tenacious research efforts.

The editors gratefully acknowledge and extend thanks to Mr. Peter Gareffa, Ms. Carol Nagel, and Ellen McGeagh at Thomson Gale for their faith in the project and for their sound content advice. Profound thanks go to the Thomson Gale copyright research and imaging teams for their patience, good advice, and skilled research into sometimes vexing copyright issues. The editors offer profound thanks to project managers Mr. Dwayne Hayes and Mr. John McCoy. Their clear thoughts and trusted editorial judgment added significantly to the quality of *Gender Issues and Sexuality: Essential Primary Sources.*

Acknowledgements

Copyrighted excerpts in *Gender Issues and Sexuality: Essential Primary Sources* were reproduced from the following periodicals:

American Journal of Orthopsychiatry, v. 70, October, 2000 for "National Lesbian Family Study" by Nanette Gartrell. © American Orthopsychiatric Association, Inc. Reproduced by permission of the publisher and author.—*Arizona Daily Star*, December 22, 2005. Reproduced by permission.—*The Boston Globe*, February 8, 1983; March 7, 1984; May 11, 1990. Copyright 1983, 1984, 1990, 2001 Globe Newspaper Company. All republished with permission of The Boston Globe, conveyed through Copyright Clearance Center.—*British Journal of Plastic Surgery*, v. 16, 1963. Copyright © 1963 The British Association of Plastic Surgeons. Reproduced with permission from The British Association of Plastic Surgeons.—*Christian Science Monitor*, v. 87, September 13, 1995. Copyright © 1995 The Christian Science Publishing Society. All rights reserved. Reproduced by permission from Christian Science Monitor, (www.csmonitor.com).—*Current Issues Brief*, 2002-2003. Reproduced by permission.—*Statistics Canada, The Daily*, May 3, 2005. Catalog number 11-001-XIE. The Daily is published under the authority of the Minister responsible for Statistics Canada. © Minister of Industry, 2003. Reproduced with permission.

The Economist, v. 349, October 17, 1998. © 1998 The Economist Newspaper Ltd. All rights reserved. Further reproduction prohibited. www.economist.com—*Fertility and Sterility*, September, 2001. Copyright © 2001 American Society for Reproductive Medicine. Reproduced with permission from American Society for Reproductive Medicine.—*Globe and*

"Parents and Friends of Ex-Gays and Gays," photograph. AP Images.—Afghan women attend a celebration on International Women's Day, Kabul, Afghanistan, photograph. © Syed Jan Sabawoon/EPA/epa/Corbis.—Anti-gay protestor standing outside the funeral of Matthew Shepard, photograph. Steve Liss/Time Life Pictures/Getty Images.—Arnaz, Desi, with Lucille Ball, photograph. CBS Photo Archive/Getty Images.—Barone, Judy, photograph. AP Images.—Benitez, Guadalupe, photograph. AP Images.—Bentham, Jeremy, mummified body, photograph. © Hulton-Deutsch Collection/Corbis.—Billboard displays a message of abstinence towards teen sex, Baltimore, MD, photograph. AP Images.—"Bloomerism Scandal," cartoon. Hulton Archive/Getty Images.—Bolton, Roxcy, and Mrs. Franklin D. Roosevelt, photograph. Courtesy of the State Library and Archives of Florida. Reproduced by permission.

Breast Cancer Awareness Stamp, photograph. AP Images.—Brown, Tiffany, photograph. AP Images.—Buckey, Peggy McMartin, photograph. AP Images.—Button from the 4th Annual Christopher Street Gay Pride Day, photograph. David J. and Janice L. Frent Collection/Corbis.—Chastity belt, photograph. ND/Roger Viollet/Getty Images.—Clinton, Hillary Rodham, photograph. AP Images.—Clubb, Travis, playing with his son Preston and daughter Jordan, photograph. AP Images.—Coleson, Nannie, sewing stockings at Crescent Hosiery, photograph. © Corbis.—Connors, Anne, photograph. AP Images.—Cuadra, Teresa, Dr., and Dr. Joan Waitkevicz, examining a mammogram, photograph. AP Images.—Customer looks at a display of vintage corsets at the Manhattan Vintage Clothing Show, photograph. AP Images.—Customers at a London bookshop read the

Mail (Toronto), January 10, 1941. Copyright 1941 Globe Interactive, a division of Bell Globemedia Publishing, Inc. Reproduced by permission.—*Human Rights Watch*, December, 1998; June, 2004. © Human Rights Watch 1998, 2004. Both reproduced by permission.—*Journal of Sex Research*, August, 2004. © 2004 by Society for the Scientific Study of Sexuality, Inc. Reproduced by permission.—*MacLean's*, v. 118, September 12, 2005. © 2005 by MacLean's Magazine. Reproduced by permission of MacLean's.—*National Post*, July 28, 2003. Copyright © 2003 CanWest Interactive Inc., and CanWest Publishing Inc. All rights reserved. Material reprinted with the express permission of National Post Company, a CanWest Partnership.

The New York Times, June 29, 1969; September 15, 2001. Copyright © 1969, 2001 by The New York Times Company. Both reprinted with permission.—*Psychology Today*, v. 26, January, 1993. Reproduced by permission.—*Science*, v. 220, May 20, 1983. Copyright © 1983 by AAAS. Reproduced by permission. http://www.sciencemag.org— *The Seattle Times*, July 16, 2005. Copyright © 2005 The Seattle Times Company. Reproduced by permission.—*St. Petersburg Times*, June 11, 2005. © Copyright, St. Petersburg Times. All rights reserved. Reproduced by permission.—*Time*, March 18, 1929. Copyright © 1929, renewed 1957 Time, Inc./January 7, 1935. Copyright © 1935, renewed 1963 Time, Inc./July 29, 2002. Copyright © 2002 Time, Inc. All reprinted by permission.—*The Village Voice*, November 14, 2001 for "Second Class Survivors" by Andy Humm. Copyright © 2001 Village Voice Media, Inc. Reproduced by permission of the author.

Copyrighted excerpts in *Gender Issues and Sexuality: Essential Primary Sources* were reproduced from the following books:

Bly, Robert. From *Iron John*. Copyright © 1990 by Robert Bly. Reprinted by permission of Da Capo Press, a member of Perseus Books, LLC.—Bornstein, Kate. From *Gender Outlaw: On Men, Women, and the Rest of Us*. Andover, Hampshire: Vintage Books, 1995. Copyright © 1994 by Routledge. Reproduced by permission of Routledge/Taylor & Francis Group, LLC.—Datnow, Amanda, Lea Hubbard, and Elisabeth Woody. From *Is Single Gender Schooling Viable in the Public Sector?* Ontario Institute for Studies in Education, University of Toronto, 2001. Reproduced by permission of the authors.—de Beauvoir, Simone. From *The Second Sex*. Translated by H. M. Parshley. Borzoi Book, 1993. © 1953. Original French edition © Gallimard 1949. Renewed 1980 by Alfred A. Knopf, a division of Random House, Inc. In the U. K.,

reprinted by permission of The Random House Group, Ltd. In the U. S. by Alfred A. Knopf, a division of Random House, Inc. A new English translation is due to be published in 2008 by Jonathan Cape (London) and Knopf (New York).

Friedan, Betty. From *The Feminine Mystique*. W. W. Norton, 1997. Copyright © 1983, 1974, 1973, 1963 by Betty Friedan. Used by permission of Victor Gollancz, a division of The Orion Publishing Group. In the U. K. by W. W. Norton & Company, Inc.— Gluck, Sherna B. From *Rosie the Riveter Revisited*. Twayne, 1987. Copyright 1987 Sherna Berger Gluck. All rights reserved. Reproduced by permission of the author.—Hanisch, Carol. From *Fight on Sisters and Other Songs for Liberation*. Reproduced by permission of the author.—Boston Women's Health Book Collective. From *Our Bodies, Ourselves*. Simon and Schuster, 1971. Copyright © 1971, 1973, 1976 by The Boston Women's Health Book Collective, Inc. New material for British edition copyright © Angela Phillips and Jill Rakusen, 1978. Abridged by permission of Simon & Schuster Adult Publishing Group. In the U. K. by the Penguin Group.—Kinsey, Alfred C. From *Sexual Behavior in the Human Male*. W. B. Saunders Co., Philadelphia and London, 1948. Copyright, 1948, by W. B. Saunders Company. Renewed 1975 by Mrs. Alfred C. Kinsey. All rights reserved. Reproduced by permission of The Kinsey Institute for Research in Sex, Gender, and Reproduction, Inc.

Le Guin, Ursula K. From *Dancing at the Edge of the World: Thoughts on Words, Women, Places*. © by Grove Press, 1989. Reproduced by permission.— Martin, Herbert W. From *All Shook Up*. University of Arkansas Press, 2001. Reproduced by permission of the author.—Millet, Kate. From *Sexual Politics*. University of Illinois Press, 2000. Copyright © 1969, 1970, 1990, 2000 by Kate Millet. Reprinted by permission of Georges Borchardt, Inc., for Kate Millet.— Nabokov, Vladimir. From *Lolita*. Borzoi Book, 1992. Copyright © 1955 by Vladimir Nabokov. Used by permission of Vintage Books, a division of Random House, Inc.—O'Hanlan, Katherine A., MD. From *Gay and Lesbian Medical Association*, 2002. Reproduced by permission.—Richards, Renee. From *Second Serve*. Stein and Day, New York, 1983. Reproduced by permission.—Spiro, Heather. From *Women's Roles and Gender Differences in Development Cases for Planners*. Population Council, 1983. Reproduced by permission.

Photographs and illustrations appearing in *Gender Issues and Sexuality: Essential Primary Sources* were received from the following sources:

Abercrombie and Fitch clothing displayed, photograph. Tim Boyle/Getty Images.—Ads by the group

controversial bestseller "Lolita" by Vladimir Nabokov, photograph. Keystone/Getty Images.—Dale, James, photograph. AP Images.—Davis, Debra, photograph. AP Images.—Dean, James, beside another actor in a scene from "Rebel Without a Cause," 1955, photograph. Copyright © Bettmann/Corbis.—Dixon, Jo-Ann C., photograph. AP Images.

Dorlester, Andrea, breastfeeding her son Emmett, photograph. Getty Images.—Drake, Harvey, Rev., talks with Ryan Olson, photograph. AP Images.—"Eighty Years and More," by Elizabeth Cady Stanton, frontispiece and title page, photograph.—Elementary school girls learning to cook, circa 1900, photograph. © Corbis.—Equal Rights Amendment Rally, New York City, NY, photograph. Peter Keegan/Hulton Archive/Getty Images.—Estradiol gel, photograph. © T and L/Image Point FR/Corbis.—Everts, Jeff, with his dog Cheyenne, photograph. AP Images.—Falwell, Jerry, Rev., photograph. Mark Meyer/Time Life Pictures/Getty Images.—Feet of an aristocratic Chinese woman deformed by binding, photograph. Hulton Archive/Getty Images.—Female member of Australia's Eastern Arrernte Aboriginal people, photograph. Medford Taylor/National Geographic/Getty Images.—Flint, Rob, and Kevin Burns, playing with their daughter Autumn Hope, photograph. David Friedman/Getty Images.—Flynt, Larry, photograph. AP Images.—Gardner, Penny, right, and William Colburn, talk outside the Ingham County courthouse, Lansing, MI, August 16, 2005, photograph. AP Images.

Gauthe, Gilbert, sits in a holding cell at Lafayette Parish Sheriffs Office, photograph. © Philip Gould/Corbis.—Gay demonstrators marching along Kings Road, London, England, photograph. David Ashdown/Keystone/Getty Images.—Girl following her wedding during the Hindu festival of Akha Teej, photograph. © Kate Brooks/Corbis.—Girl teaches other children and teenagers how to read and write outside a farmer's house, photograph. © Michael Philippot/Sygma/Corbis.—Girl with her mothers, photograph. © Ronnie Kaufman/Corbis.—Grable, Betty, and Jackie Coogan, cutting their wedding cake, photograph. AP Images.—Green, Tom, with his five wives and children, photograph. AFP/Getty Images.—Group of women and children, presumably slaves, photograph. Hulton Archive/Getty Images.—Hall, Marc, with his boyfriend Jean-Paul Doumond, photograph. © Reuters/Corbis.—Hall, Marguerite Radclyffe, photograph. Fox Photos/Getty Images.—Hand of Health Department technician pipetting blood in test for antibodies against AIDS virus, photo-

graph. James Pozarik/Time Life Pictures/Getty Images.—Hepburn, Thomas N., photograph. © Bettmann/Corbis.—Herbert, Austinite Phillip, at a rally with Texas gays and lesbians and their supporters, photograph, © Bob Daemmrich/Corbis.

Hester, Leigh Ann, Sgt., receiving the Silver Star, photograph. AP Images.—Hill, Margaret, and others at a rally on Capitol Hill, August 15, 1997, photograph. AP Images.—Holm, Paul, in front of a collection of photographs, photograph. AP Images.—Gay rights activists protest the verdict against Dan White, photograph. AP Images.—Indian eunuchs, photograph. Dibyanshu Sarkar/AFP/Getty Images.—Individual holds poster reading "Hijras are Women," photograph. Indranil Mukherjee/AFP/Getty Images.—Jackson, Janet, with Justin Timberlake during the Super Bowl halftime show, photograph. AP Images.—Japanese man converting to Judaism is circumcised in the Shaare Tzedez hospital, photograph. © David Rubinger/Corbis.—Javenella, Jiffy, and Donita Ganzon, photograph. AP Images.—Jorgensen, Christine, photograph. AP Images.—Judd, Ashley, marching on the Mall, photograph. AP Images.

Kato, Shizue, with her friend Margaret Sanger, photograph. Margaret Bourke-White/Time Life Pictures/Getty Images.—Katz, Mitchell, Dr., photograph. Justin Sullivan/Getty Images.—Kenny, Amber, rides Christmas the horse as Lady Godiva, photograph. Patrick Riviere/Getty Images.—Kinsey, Alfred C., Dr., with friends, photograph. Arthur Siegel/Time and Life Pictures/Getty Images.—Le Guin, Ursula K., photograph. Michael Buckner/Getty Images.—Leaves of Grass, cover of Walt Whitman's copy, photograph. Hulton Archive/Getty Images.—Lengila, Seita, photograph. Stephanie Welsh/Getty Images.—Lesbians participate in the International Dyke March, photograph. © Najlah Feanny/Corbis Saba.—Letter from Susan B. Anthony to Elizabeth Cady Stanton, November 5, 1872, photograph.—Mace, Nancy Ruth, left, with Petra Lovetinska, photograph. AP Images.—Mai, Mukhtar, photograph. AP Images.—Male and female Israeli soldiers carrying a wounded comrade, photograph. Getty Images.—"Man-Fishers on Sixth Avenue, New York City - Siren Games They Play to Rope in Trade," circa 1885, illustration. © Bettmann/Corbis.—Maquila workers insert electronic components at an assembly line for video turners, Tijuana, Mexico, photograph. AP Images.

Mark, Mimi, center, with Yu Ri, left, and Tiptantree Rujiranon, right, October 29, 2004, photograph. AP Images.—Matlovich, Leonard, Air Force Sgt., being buried at Congressional Cemetery, photograph. AP Images.—"Matrubhoomi - A Nation Without Women," film poster, photograph. © ADNAN ABIDI/Reuters/Corbis.—Mead, Margaret, photograph. © Bettmann/Corbis.—Men playing Dominoes, photograph. Nat Farbman/Time Life Pictures/Getty Images.—Midwife assisting home birth, photograph. © Royalty Free/Corbis.—Millet, Kate, left, and Gloria Steinem, December 17, 1970, photograph. AP Images.—Mitas, Betty, with her son Jordan and her friends Juliet Conroy and Shauna Carter, photograph by Gail Albert Halaban. © Gail Albert Halaban/Corbis.—Model wearing fashions by Jay Thorpe, photograph. © Conde Nast Archive/Corbis.—Models lay on a lower Manhattan street for artist Spencer Tunick, photograph. AP Images.—National Equal Pay Day rally, Montpelier, VT, photograph. AP Images. —Newborn baby is delivered at a Hiroshima hospital by Dr. Akiko Shikata, photograph. © Karen Kasmauski/Corbis.—Nightingale, Florence, at work in the Theapia Hospital, photograph. Rischgitz/Getty Images.—"Not Just a Medical Procedure" pamphlet issued by the Health Organizing Collective of Women's Health and Abortion Project, photograph. Health Organizing Collective of Women's Health and Abortion Project. Reproduced by permission.

Nurse collecting blood from a donor, photograph. China Photos/Getty Images.—Palestinian female suicide bomber trying to detonate her bomb, photograph. Getty Images.—Participants in New York's first Gay Pride parade gather at Christopher Street and Sixth Avenue in Greenwich Village, photograph. © JP Laffont/Sygma/Corbis.—Peak, Duncan, photograph. Greg Wood/AFP/Getty Images.—People gather outside Stonewall Inn in New York's Greenwich Village, photograph. AP Images.—Planned Parenthood Clinic leaders in New Haven, Connecticut, celebrating their victory in the Supreme Court's ruling on the Griswold vs. Connecticut case, photograph. © Bettmann/Corbis.—Plato's Retreat, photograph. © Bettmann/Corbis.—Postcards from the late nineteenth century, photograph. © Bettmann/Corbis.—Poster publicizing a syphilis sanitarium in Spain, by Roman Casas Carbo. © Archivo Iconografico, S. A./Corbis.—Poster urging women to vote, photograph. MPI/Getty Images.—Presley, Elvis, performing on the Ed Sullivan Show, photograph. © Bettmann/Corbis.—Prinsika, KMG, with her daughter Pujitha, photograph. AP Images.—Pro-Life activists and supporters of abortion rights during the 32nd Annual March for Life, Washington, D. C., photograph. © Micah Walter/Reuters/Corbis.

Protesters tussle with a policeman, Jammu, India, March 11, 2004, photograph. AP Images.—"Queer Eye for the Straight Guy" cast, from left to right: Ted Allen, Carson Kressly, Jai Rodriguez, Thom Filicia, and Kyan Douglas, photograph by Mary Altaffer. AP Images.—Race for the Cure participants, photograph. Neshan H. Naltchayan/AFP/Getty Images.—Ramona, Holly, photograph. John Storey/Time Life Pictures/Getty Images.—Reimer, David, photograph. © Reuters/Corbis.—Reshma, child prostitute, photograph. AFP/Getty Images.—Reward poster showing a girl laying on a couch playing a video game, photograph. AP Images.—Richards, Renee, at her match at the U. S. Open, photograph by Dave Pickoff. AP Images.—Robinah, Balidawa, standing in her backyard brick factory as her employees lay out mud bricks to dry, photograph. AP Images.—Sanger, Margaret, and her sister Ethel Byrne in court, photograph. AP Images.—Saraj, Shakeli Omar, putting on her Burka, photograph. AP Images.—Sarig, Robyn, and Lori Connors joined by their children as they exchange wedding vows, photograph. AP Images.—Schlafly, Phyllis, photograph. AP Images.—"She May Look Clean—But," photograph. Courtesy of the National Library of Medicine.

Shortz, Bob, dressed as Teletubby "Po," photograph. AP Images.—Sign warning of danger from a registered sex offender posted in the front of a residence, Corpus Christi, TX, May 22, 2001, photograph. AP Images.—"SpongeBob Squarepants" costume being worn by an actor, photograph. © Nancy Kaszerman/ZUMA/Corbis.—Stamp highlighting prostate cancer awareness, photograph. AP Images.—Steinem, Gloria, dressed as a Playboy Bunny, photograph. © Bettmann/Corbis.—Stratton, Barbara, left, Oretha Smith, center, and Lauren Nogle hold their brassieres during an Anti-Bra demonstration, September 5, 1969, photograph. © Bettmann/Corbis.—Students enjoy a class at Walt Whitman Community School, Dallas, TX, photograph. © Greg Smith/Corbis.—Suspect being led out of the Javits Federal Building, photograph. Robert Mecea/Getty Images.—Teacher conducts a family planning meeting, New Delhi, photograph. AP Images.—Teen with birth control pills, photograph. © LWA-Stephen Welstead/Corbis.—Teenage girl holding a condom, photograph. © Royalty Free/Corbis.—Teenagers with popsicles, photograph. © Ole Graf/zefa/Corbis.—Teletubbies, from left: Laa Laa, Dipsy, Tinky Winky, and Po, photograph. AP Images.—"The Lowell Offering," photograph. Courtesy of Harvard College Library. Reproduced by permission.

"The Mary Tyler Moore Show," still. © Corbis.—Theuner, Douglas E., right, presenting the incoming bishop, V. Gene Robinson, left, with a crosier, photograph. AP Images.—Thompson, Jim, displays a sign during a rally, photograph. Tim Boyle/Getty Images.—Torai, Masae, photograph. © Reuters/Corbis.—Tucker, Karla Faye, photograph. AP Images.—Two abortion supporters covered in red paint thrown at them by anti-abortion protestors, photograph. AP Images.—Upmeyer, Sue, photograph. AP Images.—Visitors sit at curbside tables outside a bar in a popular gay neighborhood, photograph. AP Images.—Warmack, Nathan, photograph. AP Images.—"We Can Do It!" poster by J. Howard Miller, illustration. © The National Archives/Corbis.—Wightman, Hazel, photograph. AP Images.—Wilde, Oscar, and Lord Alfred Douglas, photograph. Time Life Pictures/Getty Images.—Williams, Katherine, photograph. AP Images.—Winners of China's first beauty pageant for women who underwent plastic surgery, Beijing, China, photograph. AP Images.—Wollstonecraft, Mary, photograph. Hulton Archive/Getty Images.—Woman wearing a burqua votes on Afghanistan's Presidential Election Day, October 9, 2004, photograph. AP Images.—Women attending an Adult Literacy Course in The Gambia, photograph. © Liba Taylor/Corbis.—Women's Liberation Party member drops a brassiere in the trash barrel, Atlantic City, N. J., photograph. AP Images.—Yoruba Women, Nigeria, 1973, photograph. © Owen Franken/Corbis.—Zimbabwean women's pressure groups march, Harare, Zimbabwe, photograph. STR/AFP/Getty Images.

Copyrighted excerpts in *Gender Issues and Sexuality: Essential Primary Sources* were reproduced from the following websites or other sources:

"1931 Vagrants, Gaming, and Other Offences Act," *Queensland Parliamentary Council*, April 28, 1994. Copyright © 1994 Office of the Queensland Parliamentary Counsel, Queensland Australia. Reproduced by permission.—Cohen, Margot, "After the Tsunami, A Drive to Reverse Tubal Ligations in Tamil Nadu," *www.prb.org*. Population Research Bureau, 2005. Reproduced by permission.—"Kilt-wearing Missouri High School Boy Wins Apology," *www.Reuters.com*, January 11, 2006. © 2006 Reuters. Reproduced by permission.—Kincaid, James R., "Is This Child Pornography?" *Salon.com*, January 31, 2000. This article first appeared in Salon.com, at http://www.salon.com. An online version remains in the Salon archives. Reprinted with permission.—*Letter to Roxcy Bolton on her Campaign Against Men's Grills*, October 8, 1969. Reproduced by permission.—"Millenium Development Goals: National Reports—A Look Through a Gender Lens," *United Nations Development Programme*, 2003. Reproduced by permission.—O'Hanlan, Katherine A. From "Ten Things Lesbians Should Discuss with their Health Care Providers" in *Gay and Lesbian Medical Association*, 2002. Reproduced by permission.—Pope John Paul, II, "Educational Guidance in Human Love," November 1, 1983. Reproduced by permission.

Reddy, Helen, and Ray Burton. From *I am Woman*. Capitol Records, 1972. Reproduced by permission of Hal Leonard Corporation.—"Remembering Stonewall," *All Things Considered*, www.soundportraits.org, July 1, 1989. Copyright © 1989 Sound Portraits Productions. All rights reserved. Reproduced by permission.—Saletan, William, "The Media's Silence About Rampant Anal Sex," *www.slate.com*, September 30, 2005. © 2006 Washington Newsweek Interactive Co., LLC. Distributed by United Feature Syndicate, Inc.—Schlafly, Phyllis, "Feminism Meets Terrorism," *Townhall.com*, January 23, 2002. Copyright © 2002 Phyllis Schlafly. Reproduced by permission of the author.—Silenzio, Vincent B., MPH, MD. From "Ten Things Gay Men Should Discuss with their Health Care Providers" in *Gay and Lesbian Medical Association*, 2002. Reproduced by permission.

Smith, Tracy, "Only Fun for Stay at Home Dad," *CBS News*, August 3, 2005. Reproduced by permission.—"The Redstockings Manifesto," *Redstockings of the Women's Liberation*, 1969. Reproduced by permission. This first appeared as a mimeographed flier, designed for distribution at women's liberation events. A catalog containing ordering information for this and other documents is available from the Redstockings Women's Liberation Archives for Action.—*U. N. General Assembly Special Session on Women*, June 7, 2000 for "Focus on Women's Health Around the World" by Donna E. Shalala. Reproduced by permission of the author.—"UNFPA Saddened by U. S. Decision not to Rejoin Nations' Support for Multilateral Work to Protect Women's Health," *United Nations Family Planning Agency*, 2005. Reproduced by permission.

About the Set

Essential Primary Source titles are part of a ten-volume set of books in the Social Issues Primary Sources Collection designed to provide primary source documents on leading social issues of the nineteenth, twentieth, and twenty-first centuries. International in scope, each volume is devoted to one topic and will contain approximately 150 to 175 documents that will include and discuss speeches, legislation, magazine and newspaper articles, memoirs, letters, interviews, novels, essays, songs, and works of art essential to understanding the complexity of the topic.

Each entry will include standard subheads: key facts about the author; an introduction placing the piece in context; the full or excerpted document; a discussion of the significance of the document and related event; and a listing of further resources (books, periodicals, Web sites, and audio and visual media).

Each volume will contain a topic-specific introduction, topic-specific chronology of major events, an index especially prepared to coordinate with the volume topic, and approximately 150 images.

Volumes are intended to be sold individually or as a set.

THE ESSENTIAL PRIMARY SOURCE SERIES

- *Terrorism: Essential Primary Sources*
- *Medicine, Health, and Bioethics: Essential Primary Sources*
- *Environmental Issues: Essential Primary Sources*
- *Crime and Punishment: Essential Primary Sources*
- *Gender Issues and Sexuality: Essential Primary Sources*
- *Human and Civil Rights: Essential Primary Sources*
- *Government, Politics, and Protest: Essential Primary Sources*
- *Social Policy: Essential Primary Sources*
- *Immigration and Multiculturalism: Essential Primary Sources*
- *Family in Society: Essential Primary Sources*

Introduction

Gender Issues and Sexuality: Essential Primary Sources provides insight into the personal, social, and political issues of gender and sexuality—issues that range from what many hold as intimate matters of personal belief to matters that stir, shake, and thus profoundly shape modern society.

The women's rights and gay rights movements in the United States and Britain feature prominently in this volume. From the aftermath of the Senaca Falls Convention to present-day policies against sex discrimination, from the trial of Oscar Wilde to the legal recognition for same-sex marriages, these distinct movements share many of the same goals. Their struggle for social equity is a common movement for human rights: the right to own property, to live free of harassment and discrimination, to work, to enter into marriages, and to found families.

The primary sources contained in *Gender Issues and Sexuality: Essential Primary Sources* provide a global perspective and were chosen to highlight the complexity of gender and sexuality issues. The accompanying commentary with each primary source is intended as both thoughtful and thought-provoking.

As editors, it was our desire and goal that expert commentary exhibit both scholarly directness and sensitivity, always striving to present balanced commentary, while honoring the fundamental principles of the women's, gay, and human rights movements. Although we attempted to ensure that content (especially related to obscenity, pornography, and sex crimes) is suitable for a student and general readership, we did not wield a heavy hand with regard to opinion, however, nor did we attempt to parse words or censure opinion for what some would regard as simple political correctness. Accordingly, some of the more narrow and discordant views presented certainly do not reflect the personal opinions of the authors and editors. To ignore such opinions, however, or to pretend that they do not exist, does not serve the struggle for human equality and rights. With regard to knowledge, Einstein said, "As the circle of light increases, so grows the circumference of darkness about it." Accordingly, while basking in the light of reason and humanity, it is important to remember that the darkness exists at its edges.

Lastly, the intent of this collection of sources is not to provide the most vital sources of social theory, nor cover all facets of every issue. Many of the advanced sources in feminist or gender theory, for example, should be reserved for more advanced study. Our goal was more modest: To present the younger reader and interested general reader with a collection of sources and commentary that provoke critical thinking, while providing both a foundation and desire to investigate topics increasingly important in social and political discourse.

While encountering and considering the impacts of history, law, religious morality, globalization, shifting demographics—and even the biomedical aspects of sexuality and sexual practice—readers are encouraged to continually evaluate how issues of gender and sexuality continually challenge us to define ourselves, whether in terms of physiology or social convention and how, in turn, identity can be shaped by media and public opinion.

The editors sincerely hope that this book helps to foster respect for all individuals, and that readers gain from the sources and commentary offered an appreciation that the issues related to sexuality and gender are issues common to broad global struggles for human rights.

K. Lee Lerner, Brenda Wilmoth Lerner, & Adrienne Wilmoth Lerner, editors
Paris, France and Lisbon, Portugal
June, 2006

About the Entry

The primary source is the centerpiece and main focus of each entry in *Gender Issues and Sexuality: Essential Primary Sources*. In keeping with the philosophy that much of the benefit from using primary sources derives from the reader's own process of inquiry, the contextual material surrounding each entry provides access and ease of use, as well as giving the reader a springboard for delving into the primary source. Rubrics identify each section and enable the reader to navigate entries with ease.

ENTRY STRUCTURE

- Primary Source/Entry Title, Subtitle, Primary Source Type
- Key Facts—essential information about the primary source, including creator, date, source citation, and notes about the creator.
- Introduction—historical background and contributing factors for the primary source.
- Primary Source—in text, text facsimile, or image format; full or excerpted.
- Significance—importance and impact of the primary source related events.
- Further Resources—books, periodicals, websites, and audio and visual material.

NAVIGATING AN ENTRY

Entry elements are numbered and reproduced here, with an explanation of the data contained in these elements explained immediately thereafter according to the corresponding numeral.

Primary Source/Entry Title, Subtitle, Primary Source Type

[1] **Second-Parent Curbs Driving Same-Sex Couple from Arizona**

[3] Newspaper article

[1] **Primary Source/Entry Title:** The entry title is usually the primary source title. In some cases where long titles must be shortened, or more generalized topic titles are needed for clarity primary source titles are generally depicted as subtitles. Entry titles appear as catchwords at the top outer margin of each page.

[2] **Subtitle:** Some entries contain subtitles.

[3] **Primary Source Type:** The type of primary source is listed just below the title. When assigning source types, great weight was given to how the author of the primary source categorized the source.

Key Facts

[4] **By:** Stephanie Innes

[5] **Date:** December 22, 2005

[6] **Source:** Innes, Stephanie. "Second-Parent Curbs Driving Same-Sex Couple from Arizona." *Arizona Daily Star* (December 22, 2005).

[7] **About the Author:** *About the Author:* Stephanie Innes is a newspaper reporter with the *Arizona Daily Star*

and a professor of journalism at the University of Arizona. Her articles often focus on faith and values.

[4] **Author, Artist, or Organization:** The name of the author, artist, or organization responsible for the creation of the primary source begins the Key Facts section.

[5] **Date of Origin:** The date of origin of the primary source appears in this field, and may differ from the date of publication in the source citation below it; for example, speeches are often delivered before they are published.

[6] **Source Citation:** The source citation is a full bibliographic citation, giving original publication data as well as reprint and/or online availability.

[7] **About the Author:** A brief bio of the author or originator of the primary source gives birth and death dates and a quick overview of the person's work.. This rubric has been customized in some cases. If the primary source written document, the term "author" appears; however, if the primary source is a work of art, the term "artist" is used, showing the person's direct relationship to the primary source. For primary sources created by a group, "organization" may have been used instead of "author." Other terms may also be used to describe the creator or originator of the primary source. If an author is anonymous or unknown, a brief "About the Publication" sketch may appear.

Introduction Essay

[8] **INTRODUCTION**

In the 1980s and 1990s, as same-sex couples worked toward gaining more civil and social rights in the United States, the issue of gay adoption presented a complex issue for courts, legislatures, and individuals and families. The topic of gay parenting is not new. As a result of social pressures to conform to a heterosexual ideal, gay men and women (or persons struggling with their sexual orientation) have historically entered into heterosexual marriages, had children, and later divorced, parenting their children as a "gay parent" without fanfare. Until the past two decades, gay parents generally kept their sexuality a secret or treated it as a private matter disclosed only to close friends and family.

As homosexuality in the United States has gained greater acceptance, increasing numbers of gay couples openly choose to have children within a same-sex relationship. For lesbian couples this may involve artificial insemination of one of the partners, giving the child a biological mother with full parenting rights and a non-biological mother whose rights—depending on the state in which she resides—may vary from full parental rights to absolutely none.

Gay male couples generally use adoption of a non-biological child in their journey to parenthood, although surrogacy—hiring a woman to carry an egg fertilized with one male partner's sperm to term, at which time the baby is adopted by the male couple—is gaining popularity among gay male couples.

Each of these parenting processes presents legal and social challenges for the same-sex couples, the children in these families, and for society and governments. Opponents of gay adoption claim that the children in these families suffer from social and sexual problems, as a result of being raised by two parents of the same gender. Some research studies indicate that, although being raised by gay parents does not lead to higher rates of homosexuality among offspring, the children of gay couples do experiment with homosexuality to a greater extent than do children of heterosexual parents.

Same-sex adoption proponents point to a larger range of published research studies that show little or no difference in developmental and emotional health between children of gay parents and children of heterosexual parents. With endorsements from the American Psychiatric Association, American Academy of Pediatrics, American Academy of Family Physicians, and the American Psychological Association, gay parenting is gaining acceptance in the academic community and within general society.

[8] **Introduction:** The introduction is a brief essay on the contributing factors and historical context of the primary source. Intended to promote understanding and equip the reader with essential facts to understand the context of the primary source.

To maintain ease of reference to the primary source, spellings of names and places are used in accord with their use in the primary source. According names and places may have different spellings in different articles. Whenever possible, alternative spellings are provided to provide clarity.

To the greatest extent possible we have attempted to use Arabic names instead of their Latinized versions. Where required for clarity we have included Latinized names in parentheses after the Arabic version. Alas, we could not retain some diacritical marks (e.g. bars over vowels, dots under consonants). Because there is no generally accepted rule or consensus regarding the format of translated Arabic names, we have adopted the straightforward, and we hope sensitive, policy of using names as they are used or cited in their region of origin.

Primary Source

[10] PRIMARY SOURCE

Last week, Jeanine, Nichole and Isaac Soterwood left a home they loved, solid careers, and a wide circle of friends.

The state of Arizona does not allow them to be a legal family, so the Soterwoods moved from Tucson to California, where Nichole and Jeanine will file papers to become the legal parents of Isaac, who is 22 months old.

"This is tough for us. We love Tucson. And I had a great workplace and a promising, good career," said Nichole, 35, who was a systems engineer at Raytheon Missile Systems. "I was disappointed to leave and my co-workers at Raytheon were disappointed. But they understood that family comes first."

Like most other states, Arizona law does not allow unmarried couples to do what's known as second-parent adoption—when the non-biological parent adopts a partner's child. Stepparents in heterosexual unions can adopt the children of their spouses in Arizona. Gay couples can be foster parents. And gay people, as long as they are single, can adopt. But couples like the Soterwoods, who can't legally marry here, can't both be parents of a child.

SAME-SEX QUANDARY

Gay rights advocates say it's a growing issue because more same-sex couples are raising children. But challenging Arizona's law could backfire—lawmakers could react by passing laws prohibiting same-sex couples from adopting, as they did in Mississippi in 2000.

"Unfortunately, the political climate in Arizona is one that would not be welcoming of that change," said Amy Kobeta, director of public affairs for the Arizona Human Rights Fund. "We have a conservative Legislature, and the topic of gays and lesbians being parents is a very hot-button issue with the conservative movement."

Research by the city of Tucson's Urban Planning and Design Department, based on U.S. Census data, shows 1,253 same-sex male couples in Pima County, and 1,399 same-sex female couples, although many gay rights advocates believe those numbers are conservative because of underreporting.

At least one of three lesbian couples and one of five gay male couples are raising children nationwide, according to a 2004 research paper from the Washington, D.C.-based Urban Institute, based on an analysis of 2000 Census data. The research also says Pima County's numbers are higher than the national average for same-sex couples living with minor children.

The American Academy of Pediatrics issued a policy paper in 2002 endorsing second-parent adoption laws for same-sex couples, saying that children who are born to or adopted by one member of a same-sex couple deserve the security of two legally recognized parents.

Same-sex ballot measures

But at the moment, gay and lesbian rights advocates in Arizona are focused on preventing the passage of a proposed constitutional amendment that's slated to appear on the November 2006 general election ballot, rather than lobbying for second-parent adoption rights. The constitutional amendment, backed by a coalition that believes children should be raised in families with married, heterosexual parents, would prohibit same-sex couples from marrying and also would bar local governments from offering insurance benefits to domestic partners.

"I think the majority of Arizonans would agree that children being raised in a family of one man and one woman— a husband and a wife— is the environment we want to have in Arizona," said Nathan Sproul, a spokesman for Protect Marriage Arizona, the group backing the proposed amendment.

State Sen. Karen S. Johnson, the GOP chair of the Senate's Family Services Committee, did not return calls about second-parent adoption but sent a message through an assistant that she does not support same-sex couples. In her legislative biography, Johnson pledges to stand "resolutely against the homosexual agenda."

Kobeta noted there are alternatives same-sex parents in Arizona can use now to give the second parent power of attorney for emergency medical decisions and school record access. But she said the options are complicated and expensive, and schools and hospitals don't necessarily respect them.

Local attorney Amelia Craig Cramer knows the imperfection of those options too well. She is the former executive director of the Gay and Lesbian Alliance Against Defamation and former managing attorney for the Western office of Lambda Legal, a national group that works for the full recognition of the civil rights of lesbians, gay men, bisexuals and transgender people. She also is raising a 6-year-old child with her female partner.

"I'm the legal parent and it's in my will that my partner has guardianship, but that is not a guarantee," Craig Cramer said. "It terrifies me to think about what would happen if I were to die or become incapacitated."

2003 civil union in Vermont

The Soterwoods met as graduate students in applied mathematics at the University of Arizona in 1998. They had a commitment ceremony with 65 friends and family in 2001.

In 2003, they again exchanged vows, when they obtained a civil union in Vermont. That's when they also took the same last name, a combination of Nichole's surname, Soter, and Jeanine's last name, Smallwood.

They always knew they wanted a family and they wanted to live in Tucson, which they describe as a diverse and accepting community.

Nichole gave birth to Isaac in February 2004 and is his sole legal guardian. Every six months since his birth, she's had to fill out papers to give power of attorney to Jeanine, so Jeanine can legally make health and school decisions about Isaac.

"If, God forbid, we were to split up, I'd have no rights as a parent," said Jeanine, 31, who recently finished her doctorate at the UA, where she was an adjunct engineering instructor.

Jeanine and Nichole ultimately decided to move to Santa Clara, Calif., where Nichole already has a job and they will be near Jeanine's parents. One of the first things they'll do is sign on to California's domestic partner registry and find a lawyer to guide them through a second-parent adoption.

"I've heard of folks who have left Tucson and adopted children in another state. But they have to establish residency in that other state before they come back. It's a real hardship and it underscores the fact that we have a somewhat broken system in the United States," said Kent Burbank, executive director of Wingspan, Tucson's lesbian, gay, bisexual and transgender community center.

"If there are more people like Nichole and Jeanine leaving, it is a big loss, not just for the lesbian, gay, bisexual and transgender community, but for the community as a whole."

[9] **Primary Source:** The majority of primary sources are reproduced as plain text. The primary source may appear excerpted or in full, and may appear as text, text facsimile (photographic reproduction of the original text), image, or graphic display (such as a table, chart, or graph).

The font and leading of the primary sources are distinct from that of the context—to provide a visual clue to the change, as well as to facilitate ease of reading. As needed, the original formatting of the text is preserved in order to more accurately represent the original (screenplays, for example). In order to respect the integrity of the primary sources, content some readers may consider sensitive (for example, the use of slang, ethnic or racial slurs, etc.) is retained when deemed to be integral to understanding the source and the context of its creation.

Primary source images (whether photographs, text facsimiles, or graphic displays) are bordered with a distinctive double rule. Most images have brief captions.

The term "narrative break" appears where there is a significant amount of elided (omitted) material with the text provided (for example, excerpts from a work's first and fifth chapters, selections from a journal article abstract and summary, or dialogue from two acts of a play).

Significance Essay

[10] **SIGNIFICANCE**

In 1977, Florida's state legislature passed a law banning gay adoptions; in spite of recent challenges to the law, it stands, making Florida the only state in the United States to specifically ban gay adoption. Other states, including Mississippi, Oklahoma, and Utah, make it very difficult for same-sex couples to adopt. However, in all of these states, gay parents are permitted to act as foster parents. Gay adoption supporters point to this policy as hypocritical, asking why gay parents can act as substitute parents, but not as full legal parents.

More same-sex couples wishing to adopt and gain full legal protections are moving to the nine states that permit gay adoption. Part of a demographic shift, these gay couples seek out states with gay-friendly legal and social policies. While the raw number of gay couples who move for such reasons remains small as of 2006, the trend is of interest to sociologists, marketing experts, and economists, who point to a possible "brain drain" of mobile, higher-income couples with the means to move as needed and relocate based on gay-friendly policies.

At the same time, groups that oppose gay adoption, such as the Family Research Council, Concerned Women for America, and Focus on the Family, are working in sixteen states to put laws in place that would ban adoption by any gay person. The Ohio Restoration Project, a conservative Christian organization headed by Reverend Russell Johnson, seeks to ban all adoptions by gay individuals and families. Johnson is an activist who vigorously promoted passage of the Ohio Defense of Marriage Act ballot initiative in 2004. The Act defines marriage as a relationship between a man and a woman and makes any legal procedures created by same-sex couples in an imitation of marital rights (such as child custody or powers of attorney) illegal. Johnson currently is urging Ohio state legislators to pass a law banning gay adoption.

Gay rights groups, such as the Human Rights Council, claim that such laws punish many children within the foster care system, who are in need of loving, stable homes. The Child Welfare League of America, an umbrella organization representing more than 900 human services organizations, states that research shows gay parents to be as nurturing as heterosexual parents, and that decades of studies of gay parents and gay foster parents back up their claim. According to the CWLA, the crisis of the foster care system in the United States, with more than 500,000 children under state custody, would deepen if gay individuals and couples could no longer adopt or act as foster parents.

Adoptions by same-sex couples are currently legal in Andorra, Belgium, England, the Netherlands, Spain, Sweden, and Wales. Other countries permit "step-children" adoptions in which a partner in any couple can adopt a child.

[10] **Significance**: The significance discusses the importance and impact of the primary source and the event it describes.

Further Resources

[11] **FURTHER RESOURCES**

[11] **Further Resources**: A brief list of resources categorized as Books, Periodicals, Web sites, and Audio and Visual Media provides a stepping stone to further study.

Books

Gerstmann, Evan. *Same-Sex Marriage and the Constitution.* New York: Cambridge University Press, 2003.

Periodicals

Adam, Barry D. "The Defense of Marriage Act and American Exceptionalism: The 'Gay Marriage' Panic in the United States." *Journal of the History of Sexuality.* 12 (April 2003): 259–276.

Web sites

American Academy of Pediatrics. "AAP Says Children of Same-Sex Couples Deserve Two Legally Recognized Parents." <http://www.aap.org/advocacy/archives/febsamesex.htm> (accessed February 28, 2006).

American Psychiatric Association. "Adoption and Co-Parenting of Children by Same-Sex Couples." <http://www.psych.org/news_room/press_releases/adoption_coparenting121802.pdf> (accessed February 28, 2006).

Child Welfare League of America. <http://www.cwla.org> (accessed February 28, 2006).

Ohio Restoration Project. <http://www.ohiorestorationproject.com> (accessed February 28, 2006).

SECONDARY SOURCE CITATION FORMATS (HOW TO CITE ARTICLES AND SOURCES)

Alternative forms of citations exist and examples of how to cite articles from this book are provided below:

APA Style

Books:

Millet, Kate. (2000). *Sexual Politics,* Chicago: University of Chicago. Excerpted in K. Lee Lerner and Brenda Wilmoth Lerner, eds. (2006). *Gender Issues and Sexuality: Essential Primary Sources,* Farmington Hills, Mich.: Thomson Gale.

Periodicals:

Marx, Jean L. (1983, May 20). Human T-Cell Leukemia Virus Linked To AIDS. *Science,* vol. 220, no. 4599, p. 806–809. Excerpted in K. Lee Lerner and Brenda Wilmoth Lerner, eds. (2006) *Gender Issues and Sexuality: Essential Primary Sources,* Farmington Hills, Mich.: Thomson Gale.

Web sites:

Townhall.com. (2002, January 23) Feminism Meets Terrorism. Retrieved June 8, 2006 from http://www.townhall.com/opinion/columns/phyllisschlafly/2002/01/23/162218.html. Excerpted in K. Lee Lerner and Brenda Wilmoth Lerner, eds. (2006) *Gender Issues and Sexuality: Essential Primary Sources.* Farmington Hills, Mich.: Thomson Gale.

Chicago Style

Books:

Millet, Kate. *Sexual Politics.* Chicago: University of Chicago, 2000. Excerpted in K. Lee Lerner and Brenda Wilmoth Lerner, eds. *Gender Issues and Sexuality: Essential Primary Sources.* Farmington Hills, Mich.: Thomson Gale, 2006.

Periodicals:

Marx, Jean L. "Human T-Cell Leukemia Virus Linked To AIDS." *Scence.* 220 (May 20, 1983): 4599, 806–809. Excerpted in K. Lee Lerner and Brenda Wilmoth Lerner, eds. *Gender Issues and Sexuality: Essential Primary Sources.* Farmington Hills, Mich.: Thomson Gale, 2006.

Web sites:

Townhall.com. "Feminism Meets Terrorism." January 23, 2002. <http://www.townhall.com/opinion/columns/phyllisschlafly/2002/01/23/162218.html> (accessed June 8, 2006). Excerpted in K. Lee Lerner and Brenda Wilmoth Lerner, eds. *Gender Issues and Sexuality: Essential Primary Sources.* Farmington Hills, Mich.: Thomson Gale, 2006.

MLA Style

Books:

Millet, Kate.*Sexual Politics*, Chicago: University of Chicago, 2000. Excerpted in K. Lee Lerner and Brenda Wilmoth Lerner, eds. *Gender Issues and Sexuality: Essential Primary Sources*, Farmington Hills, Mich.: Thomson Gale, 2006.

Periodicals:

Marx, Jean L. "Human T-Cell Leukemia Virus Linked To AIDS." *Scence.* 220 (May 20, 1983): 4599, 806–809, Excerpted in K. Lee Lerner and Brenda Wilmoth Lerner, eds. *Gender Issues and Sexuality: Essential Primary Sources.* Farmington Hills, Mich.: Thomson Gale, 2006.

Marx, Jean L. "Human T-Cell Leukemia Virus Linked To AIDS." *Scence*, 20 May 1983, vol. 220, no. 4599, p. 806–809. Excerpted in K. Lee Lerner and Brenda Wilmoth Lerner, eds. *Gender Issues and Sexuality: Essential Primary Sources.* Farmington Hills, Mich.: Thomson Gale, 2006.

Web sites:

"Feminism Meets Terrorism. "*Townhall.com*, 23 January, 2002. 8 June 2006 <http://www.townhall.com/opinion/columns/phyllisschlafly/. Excerpted in K. Lee Lerner and Brenda Wilmoth Lerner, eds., *Gender Issues and Sexuality: Essential Primary Sources*. Farmington Hills, Mich.: Thomson Gale, 2006.

Turabian Style

Books:

Millet, Kate.*Sexual Politics*. (Chicago: University of Chicago, 2000). Excerpted in K. Lee Lerner and Brenda Wilmoth Lerner, eds.,*Gender Issues and Sexuality: Essential Primary Sources*. (Farmington Hills, Mich.: Thomson Gale, 2006).

Periodicals:

Ember, Lois R. "FBI Takes Lead in Developing Counterterrorism Effort." *Chemical & Engineering News*, 4 November 1996, vol.74, no. 27. Excerpted in K. Lee Lerner and Brenda Wilmoth Lerner, eds., *Terrorism: Essential Primary Sources*. (Farmington Hills, Mich.: Thomson Gale, 2006), 75.

Web sites:

Townhall.com. "Feminism Meets Terrorism" available from http://www.townhall.com/opinion/columns/phyllisschlafly/2002/01/23/162218.html; accessed 8 June, 2006. Excerpted in K. Lee Lerner and Brenda Wilmoth Lerner, eds., *Gender Issues and Sexuality: Essential Primary Sources*. (Farmington Hills, Mich.: Thomson Gale, 2006).

Using Primary Sources

The definition of what constitutes a primary source is often the subject of scholarly debate and interpretation. Although primary sources come from a wide spectrum of resources, they are united by the fact that they individually provide insight into the historical *milieu* (context and environment) during which they were produced. Primary sources include materials such as newspaper articles, press dispatches, autobiographies, essays, letters, diaries, speeches, song lyrics, posters, works of art—and in the twenty-first century, web logs—that offer direct, first-hand insight or witness to events of their day.

Categories of primary sources include:

- Documents containing firsthand accounts of historic events by witnesses and participants. This category includes diary or journal entries, letters, email, newspaper articles, interviews, memoirs, and testimony in legal proceedings.
- Documents or works representing the official views of both government leaders and leaders of terrorist organizations. These include primary sources such as policy statements, speeches, interviews, press releases, government reports, and legislation.
- Works of art, including (but certainly not limited to) photographs, poems, and songs, including advertisements and reviews of those works that help establish an understanding of the cultural milieu (the cultural environment with regard to attitudes and perceptions of events).
- Secondary sources. In some cases, secondary sources or tertiary sources may be treated as primary sources. In some cases articles and sources are created many years after an event. Ordinarily,

a historical retrospective published after the initial event is not be considered a primary source. If, however, a resource contains statement or recollections of participants or witnesses to the original event, the source may be considered primary with regard to those statements and recollections.

ANALYSIS OF PRIMARY SOURCES

The material collected in this volume is not intended to provide a comprehensive overview of a topic or event. Rather, the primary sources are intended to generate interest and lay a foundation for further inquiry and study.

In order to properly analyze a primary source, readers should remain skeptical and develop probing questions about the source. As in reading a chemistry or algebra textbook, historical documents require readers to analyze them carefully and extract specific information. However, readers must also read "beyond the text" to garner larger clues about the social impact of the primary source.

In addition to providing information about their topics, primary sources may also supply a wealth of insight into their creator's viewpoint. For example, when reading a news article about an outbreak of disease, consider whether the reporter's words also indicate something about his or her origin, bias (an irrational disposition in favor of someone or something), prejudices (an irrational disposition against someone or something), or intended audience.

Students should remember that primary sources often contain information later proven to be false, or contain viewpoints and terms unacceptable to future generations. It is important to view the primary source within the historical and social context existing at its creation. If for example, a newspaper article is written within hours or days of an event, later developments may reveal some assertions in the original article as false or misleading.

TEST NEW CONCLUSIONS AND IDEAS

Whatever opinion or working hypothesis the reader forms, it is critical that they then test that hypothesis against other facts and sources related to the incident. For example, it might be wrong to conclude that factual mistakes are deliberate unless evidence can be produced of a pattern and practice of such mistakes with an intent to promote a false idea.

The difference between sound reasoning and preposterous conspiracy theories (or the birth of urban legends) lies in the willingness to test new ideas against other sources, rather than rest on one piece of evidence such as a single primary source that may contain errors. Sound reasoning requires that arguments and assertions guard against argument fallacies that utilize the following:

- false dilemmas (only two choices are given when in fact there are three or more options)
- arguments from ignorance (*argumentum ad ignorantiam*; because something is not known to be true, it is assumed to be false)
- possibilist fallacies (a favorite among conspiracy theorists who attempt to demonstrate that a factual statement is true or false by establishing the possibility of its truth or falsity. An argument

where "it could be" is usually followed by an unearned "therefore, it is.")
- slippery slope arguments or fallacies (a series of increasingly dramatic consequences is drawn from an initial fact or idea)
- begging the question (the truth of the conclusion is assumed by the premises)
- straw man arguments (the arguer mischaracterizes an argument or theory and then attacks the merits of their own false representations)
- appeals to pity or force (the argument attempts to persuade people to agree by sympathy or force)
- prejudicial language (values or moral judgments—good and bad—are attached to certain arguments or facts)
- personal attacks (*ad hominem*; an attack on a person's character or circumstances)
- anecdotal or testimonial evidence (stories that are unsupported by impartial data or data that is not reproducible)
- *post hoc* (after the fact) fallacies (because one thing follows another, it is held to cause the other)
- the fallacy of the appeal to authority (the argument rests upon the credentials of a person, not the evidence)

Despite the fact that some primary sources can contain false information or lead readers to false conclusions based on the "facts" presented, they remain an invaluable resource regarding past events. Primary sources allow readers and researchers to come as close as possible to understanding the perceptions and context of events and thus, to more fully appreciate how and why misconceptions occur.

Chronology

So that the events in this volume may be placed in a larger historical context, the following is a general chronology of important historical, scientific, and social events along with specific events related to the subject of this volume.

1750–1799

1787: The Constitutional Convention in Philadelphia adopts the U.S. Constitution.

1789: The Declaration of the Rights of Man is issued in France.

1790: The first U.S. census is taken.

1791: The states ratify the Bill of Rights, the first ten amendments to the U.S. Constitution.

1800–1849

1800: World population reaches 1 billion.

1801: Great Britain and Ireland unite.

1803: Napoleonic Wars begin. Napoleon's army conquers much of Europe before Napoleon is defeated at Waterloo in 1815.

1803: The United States pays France $15 million for the Louisiana Territory extending from the Mississippi River to the Rocky Mountains.

1808: The importation of slaves is outlawed in the United States, but the institution of African slavery continues until 1864.

1812: The North American War of 1812 between the United States and the United Kingdom of Great Britain and Ireland begins. The war lasts until the beginning of 1815.

1814: The Congress of Vienna redraws the map of Europe after the defeat of Napoleon.

1819: South American colonial revolutions begin when Columbia declares its independence from Spain in 1819.

1820: The temperance movement begins in the United States.

1821: Mexico declares independence from Spain.

1821: Jean-Louis Prévost (1790–1850), Swiss physician, jointly publishes a paper with French chemist Jean-Baptiste-Andre Dumas (1800–1884) that demonstrates for the first time that spermatozoa originate in tissues of the male sex glands. In 1824 they also give the first detailed account of the segmentation of a frog's egg.

1822: American Colonization Society advocates the repatriation of freed African slaves to the Colony of Liberia.

1822: Jean-François Champollion (1790–1832), French historian and linguist, deciphers Egyptian hieroglyphics using the Rosetta Stone. He is the first to realize that some of the signs are alphabetic, some syllabic, and some determinative (standing for a whole idea or object previously expressed).

1822: William Church (c.1778–1863), American-English inventor, patents a machine that sets type. Patented in Boston, his machine consists of a keyboard on which each key releases a piece of letter type that is stored in channels in a magazine.

1829: Lambert-Adolphe-Jacques Quetelet (1796–1874), Belgian statistician and astronomer, gives the first statistical breakdown of a national census. He correlates death with age, sex, occupation, and economic status in the Belgian census.

1830: The Indian Removal Act forces the removal of Native Americans living in the eastern part of the United States.

1831: Charles Robert Darwin began his historic voyage on the H.M.S. *Beagle* (1831–1836). His observations during the voyage lead to his theory of evolution by means of natural selection.

1832: The advent of the telegraph.

1833: A washboard is patented in the United States. This simple wooden-framed device has a corrugated rectangular surface that is used for scrubbing clothes clean.

1835: Rubber nipples are introduced for infant nursing bottles.

1836: Johann Nikolaus von Dreyse (1787–1867), German inventor, patents the "needle" rifle with a bolt breech-loading mechanism. This gun is loaded through the rear of the barrel.

1838: More than 15,000 Cherokee Indians are forced to march from Georgia to present-day Oklahoma on the "Trail of Tears."

1838: Samuel Finley Breese Morse (1791–1872) and Alfred Vail (1807–1859) unveil their telegraph system.

1839: Theodore Schwann (1810–1882), German physiologist, extends the theory of cells from plants to animals. He states in his book, *Mikroscopische Untersuchungen*, that all living things are made up of cells, each of which contains certain essential components. He also coins the term "metabolism" to describe the overall chemical changes that take place in living tissue.

1840: John William Draper (1811–1882), American chemist, takes a daguerreotype portrait of his sister, Dorothy. This is the oldest surviving photograph of a person.

1840: Pierre-Charles-Alexandre Louis (1787–1872), French physician, pioneers medical statistics, being the first to compile systematically records of diseases and treatments.

1841: Horace Greeley (1811–1872), American editor and publisher, founds the *New York Tribune* which eventually becomes the *Herald Tribune* after a merger in 1924.

1842: John Benne Lawes (1814–1900), English agriculturalist, patents a process for treating phosphate rock with sulfuric acid to produce superphosphate. He also opens the first fertilizer factory this year, thus beginning the artificial fertilizer industry.

1842: Samuel Finley Breese Morse (1791–1872), American artist and inventor, lays the first underwater telegraph cable in New York Harbor. It fails due to a lack of proper insulation materials.

1842: The first shipment of milk by rail in the United States is successfully accomplished.

1844: Robert Chambers (1802–1871), Scottish publisher, publishes anonymously his *Vestiges of the Natural History of Creation*. This best-selling book offers a sweeping view of evolution and although incorrect in many specifics, it does pave the way for Darwin's theory by familiarizing the public with evolutionary concepts.

1845: The potato famine begins in Ireland. Crop failures and high rents on tenant farms cause a three-year famine. Millions of Irish immigrate to flee starvation.

1846: The Mexican War begins as the United States attempts to expand its territory in the Southwest.

1846: Oliver Wendall Holmes (1809–1894), American author and physician, first suggests the use of the terms "anaesthesia" and "anaesthetic" in a letter to William Thomas Green Morton (1819–1868), American dentist.

1847: Claude-Felix-Abel-Niepce de Saint-Victor (1805–1870) of France first uses light sensitive materials on glass for photographs. He coats a glass plate with albumen containing iodide of potassium which, after drying, is coated with aceto-silver nitrate, washed in distilled water, and exposed.

1847: John Collins Warren (1778–1856), American surgeon, introduces ether anesthesia for general surgery. It is soon taken up worldwide as an essential part of surgery.

1847: Richard March Hoe (1812–1886), American inventor and manufacturer, patents what proves to be the first successful rotary printing press. He discards the old flatbed press and places the type on a revolving cylinder. This revolutionary system is first used by the *Philadelphia Public Ledger* this same year, and it produces 8,000 sheets per hour printed on one side.

1848: Karl Marx publishes *The Communist Manifesto*.

1848: Delegates at the Seneca Falls Convention on Woman Rights advocate equal property and voting rights for women.

1848: A series of political conflicts and violent revolts erupt in several European nations. The conflicts are collectively known as the Revolution of 1848.

1848: A group of six New York newspapers form an association or news agency to share telegraph costs. It is later called the Associated Press.

1848: The first large-scale department store opens in the United States. The Marble Dry Goods Palace in New York occupies an entire city block.

1849: Elizabeth Blackwell becomes the first woman in the United States to receive a medical degree. She graduates this year from Geneva College (now a part of Syracuse University) in New York.

1849: John Snow (1813–1858), English physician, first states the theory that cholera is a water-borne disease and that it is usually contracted by drinking. During a cholera epidemic in London in 1854, Snow breaks the handle of the Broad Street Pump, thereby shutting down what he considered to be the main public source of the epidemic.

1850–1899

1851: James Harrison, Scottish-Australian inventor, builds the first vapor-compression refrigerating machinery to be used in a brewery.

1851: James T. King of the United States invents a washing machine that uses a rotating cylinder. It is hand-powered and made for home use.

1852: Harriet Beecher Stowe's novel *Uncle Tom's Cabin* is published. It becomes one of the most influential works to stir anti-slavery sentiments.

1854: Crimean War begins between Russia and allied forces of Great Britain, Sardinia, France, and the Ottoman Empire.

1854: Violent conflicts erupt between pro-and anti-slavery settlers in Kansas Territory. The "Bleeding Kansas" violence lasts five years.

1854: Florence Nightingale (1823–1910), English nurse, takes charge of a barracks hospital when the Crimean War breaks out. Through dedication and hard work, she goes on to create a female nursing service and a nursing school at St. Thomas' Hospital (1860). Her compassion and common sense approach to nursing set new standards and create a new era in the history of the sick and wounded.

1854: Cyrus West Field (1819–1892), American financier, forms the New York, Newfoundland and London telegraph Company and proposes to lay a transatlantic telegraph cable.

1855: Alfred Russel Wallace (1823–1913), English naturalist, publishes his paper "On The Law Which Has Regulated the Introduction of New Species." Although this is written before Wallace conceives of the notion of natural selection, it shows him in the process of anticipating Darwin.

1856: *Illustrated London News* becomes the first periodical to include regular color plates.

1857: Supreme Court of the United States decision in *Dred Scott v. Sanford* holds that slaves are not citizens and that Congress cannot prohibit slavery in the individual states.

1857: The Indian Mutiny revolt against British colonial rule in India begins.

1858: The transatlantic cable is first opened with an exchange of greetings between English Queen Victoria (1819–1901) and U. S. President James Buchanan (1791–1868). Several weeks later, a telegraph operator applies too much voltage and ruins the cable connection.

1858: Mary Anna Elson (1833–1884), German-American physician, is the first Jewish woman to graduate from the Women's Medical College of Philadelphia. She practices in Philadelphia and later in Indiana.

1859: Charles Robert Darwin (1809–1882), English naturalist, publishes his landmark work *On the Origin of Species by Means of Natural Selection*. This classic of science establishes the mechanism of natural selection of favorable, inherited traits or variations as the mechanism of his theory of evolution.

1859: Ferdinand Carre (1824–1900), French inventor, introduces a refrigeration machine that uses ammonia as a refrigerant and water as the absorbent. This method becomes widely adopted.

1860: The U. S. Congress institutes the U. S. Government Printing Office in Washington, D. C.

1861: The Civil War begins in the United States.

1861: The popular press begins in England with the publication of the *Daily Telegraph*.

1864: U.S. President Abraham Lincoln issues the Emancipation Proclamation, freeing the slaves in Union-occupied lands.

1865: The Civil War ends with the surrender of the secession states. The United States is reunified.

1865: President Lincoln is assassinated by John Wilkes Booth.

1865: The Thirteenth and Fourteenth Amendments to the U.S. Constitution are ratified. The Thirteenth Amendment outlaws slavery; the Fourteenth Amendment makes all persons born or naturalized in the United States to be U.S. citizens and extends equal protection under the law.

1867: Britain grants Canada home rule.

1869: The first transcontinental railroad across the United States is completed.

1870: The Franco-Prussian War (1870–1871) begins.

1871: The era of New Imperialism, or "empire for empire's sake," starts a multinational competition for colonies in Africa, Asia, and the Middle East.

1871: Charles Robert Darwin (1809–1882), English naturalist, publishes his *The Descent of Man, and Selection in Relation to Sex*. This work extends his theory of evolution by applying it to humans.

1874: Thomas Alva Edison (1847–1931), American inventor, perfects his quadruplex telegraph. It is able to transmit two messages over one telegraph line or four messages in each direction over two wires.

1875: Robert Augustus Chesebrough (1837–1933), American manufacturer, first introduces petrolatum, which becomes known by its product name of Vaseline. This smooth, semisolid blend of mineral oil with waxes crystallized from petroleum becomes useful as a lubricant, carrier, and water-proofing agent in many products.

1876: Alexander Bell files for a patent for the telephone.

1876: Robert Koch (1843–1910), German bacteriologist, is able to cultivate the anthrax bacteria in culture outside the body. He then studies its life cycle and learns how to defeat it. During the next six years, Koch isolates the tubercle bacillus and discovers the cause of cholera.

1876: The American Library Association is founded in Philadelphia, Pennsylvania by American librarian, Melvil Dewey (1851–1931), the founder of the decimal system of library classification.

1877: Reconstruction, the period of rebuilding and reunification following the U.S. Civil War, ends.

1879: Albert Ludwig Siegmund Neisser (1855–1916), German dermatologist, discovers gonococcus, the pus-producing bacterium that causes gonorrhea.

1879: John Shaw Billings (1838–1913), American surgeon, and Robert Fletcher (1823–1912) of England issue the first volume of *Index Medicus*. This massive medical bibliography is initially arranged by author and subject and continues today.

1880: Louis Pasteur (1822–1895), French chemist, first isolates and describes both streptococcus and staphylococcus (both in puerperal septicemia).

1883: *Journal of the American Medical Association* is first published.

1884: International conference is held in Washington, D. C., at which Greenwich, England, is chosen as the common prime meridian for the entire world.

1885: Karl Benz invents in automobile in Germany.

1885: Edouard van Beneden (1846–1910), Belgian cytologist, proves that chromosomes persist between cell divisions. He makes the first chromosome count and discovers that each species has a fixed number of chromosomes. He also discovers that in the formation of sex cells, the division of chromosomes during one of the cell divisions was not preceded by a doubling because each egg and sperm cell has only half the usual count of chromosomes.

1885: James Leonard Corning (1855–1923), American surgeon, is the first to use cocaine as a spinal anesthetic.

1885: Louis Pasteur (1822–1895), French chemist, inoculates a boy, Joseph Meister, against rabies. He had been bitten by a mad dog and the treatment saves his life. This is the first case of Pasteur's use of an attenuated germ on a human being.

1886: Richard von Krafft-Ebing (1840–1902), German neurologist, publishes his landmark case history study of sexual abnormalities, *Psychopathia Sexualis*, and helps found the scientific consideration of human sexuality.

1887: Theodor Boveri observes the reduction division during meiosis in *Ascaris* and confirms August Weismann's predictions of chromosome reduction during the formation of the sex cells.

1888: First incubator for infants in the United States is built by William C. Deming.

1888: Heinrich Wilhelm Gottfried Waldeyer-Hartz (1836–1921), German anatomist, first introduces the word "chromosomes."

1889: Francis Galton (1822–1911), English anthropologist, culminates his work on inheritance and variation with his book *Natural Inheritance*. It influences Karl Pearson and begins the science of biometrics or the statistical analysis of biological observations and phenomena.

1889: Pasteur Institute first opens in Paris.

1889: Richard Altmann (1852–1900), German histologist, isolates and names nucleic acid.

1890: The U.S. Census Bureau announces that the American frontier is closed.

1890: Herman Hollerith (1860–1929), American inventor, puts his electric sorting and tabulating machines to work on the U. S. Census. He wins this contract after a trial "run-off" with two other rival systems and his system performs in one year what would have taken eight years of hand tabulating. This marks the beginning of modern data processing.

1891: Maximilian Franz Joseph Wolf (1863–1932), German astronomer, adapts photography to the study of asteroids and demonstrates that stars appear as points in photographs while asteroids show up as short streaks. He makes the first discovery of an asteroid from photographs, and during his lifetime discovers over 500 asteroids in this manner.

1891: Hermann Henking (1858–1942), German zoologist, describes sex chromosomes and autosomes.

1892: Ellis Island becomes the chief immigration station of the eastern United States.

1893: Panic of 1893 triggers a three-year economic depression in the United States.

1893: Sigmund Freud (1856–1939), Austrian psychiatrist, describes paralysis originating from purely mental conditions and distinguishes it from that of organic origin.

1894: Thomas Alva Edison (1847–1931), American inventor, first displays his peep-show Kinetoscopes in New York. These demonstrations serve to stimulate research on the screen projection of motion pictures as well as to entertain.

1895: John Cox is the first U. S. physician to use x-rays an as adjunct to surgery.

1896: Landmark Supreme Court of the United States decision, *Plessy v. Ferguson*, upholds racial segregation.

1896: Edmund Beecher Wilson (1856–1939), American zoologist, publishes his major work *The Cell in Development and Heredity* in which he connects chromosomes and sex determination. He also correctly states that chromosomes affect and determine other inherited characteristics as well.

1897: Guglielmo Marconi (1874–1937), Italian electrical engineer, exchanges wireless messages across 3.5 miles of water in England.

1897: Havelock Ellis (1859–1939), English physician, publishes the first of his seven-volume work *Studies in the Psychology of Sex*. This contributes to the more open discussion of human sexuality and supports sex education.

1898: USS Maine sinks in harbor in Havana, Cuba; Spanish-American War begins.

1900–1949

1901: Guglielmo Marconi (1874–1937), Italian electrical engineer, successfully sends a radio signal from England to Newfoundland. This is the first transatlantic telegraphic radio transmission and, as such, is considered by most as the day radio is invented.

1902: Clarence Erwin McClung (1870–1946), American zoologist, isolates the "X" or sex chromosome which is combined with a "Y" chromosome in the male, as compared to two "X" chromosomes in the female.

1902: Ernest H. Starling (1866–1927) and William M. Bayliss (1860–1924), both English physiologists, isolate and discover the first hormone (secretin, found in the duodenum). Starling also first suggests a name for all substances discharged into the blood by a particular organ, and it is "hormones" from the Greek word meaning to "rouse to activity."

1902: The Horn & Hardart Baking Company of Philadelphia, Pennsylvania creates an early automat that offers food for a "nickel in a slot."

1903: Wright brothers make first successful flight of a controlled, powered airplane that is heavier than air.

1903: *The Great Train Robbery*, the first modern movie, debuts.

1903: Walter S. Sutton (1876–1916) of the United States writes a short paper in which he states the chromosome theory of inheritance. This important idea that the hereditary factors are located in the chromosomes is also offered independently by Theodor Boveri (1862–1915) of Germany.

1904: Russo-Japanese War (1904–1905): Japan gains territory on the Asian mainland and becomes a world power.

1904: First radical operation for prostate cancer is performed by the American urologist Hugh Hampton Young (1870–1945).

1904: Ivan Petrovich Pavlov (1849–1936), Russian physiologist, is awarded the Nobel Prize for Physiology or Medicine for his work establishing that the nervous system plays a part in controlling digestion and by helping to found gastroenterology.

1905: Albert Einstein (1879–1955), German-Swiss-American physicist, uses Planck's theory to develop a quantum theory of light that explains the photoelectric effect. He suggests that light has a dual, wave-particle quality.

1905: Fritz Richard Schaudinn (1871–1906), German zoologist, discovers *Spirocheta pallida*, the organism or parasite causing syphilis. His discovery of this almost invisible parasite is due to his consummate technique and staining methods.

1905: Albert Einstein (1879–1955), German-Swiss-American physicist, submits his first paper on the special theory of relativity titled "Zur Elektrodynamik bewegter Korpen." It states that the speed of light is constant for all conditions and that time is relative or passes at different rates for objects in constant relative motion. This is a fundamentally new and revolutionary way to look at the universe and it soon replaces the old Newtonian system.

1905: Albert Einstein (1879–1955), German-Swiss-American physicist, publishes his second paper on relativity in which he includes his famous equation stating the relationship between mass and energy is $E = mc2$. In this equation, E is energy, m is mass, and c is the velocity of light. This contains the revolutionary concept that mass and energy are only different aspects of the same phenomenon.

1905: Hermann Walter Nernst (1864–1941), German physical chemist, announces his discovery of the third law of thermodynamics. He finds that entropy change approaches zero at a temperature of absolute zero and deduces from this the impossibility of attaining absolute zero.

1905: Alfred Binet (1857–1911), French psychologist, devises the first of a series of tests (1905–1911) that make him the "father of intelligence testing."

1905: Edmund Beecher Wilson (1856–1939), American zoologist, and Nettie M. Stevens independently discover the connection between chromosomes and sex determination.

1905: Robert Koch (1843–1910), German bacteriologist, is awarded the Nobel Prize for Physiology or Medicine for his investigations and discoveries in relation to tuberculosis. He is one of the founders of the science of bacteriology.

1906: Marie Sklodowska Curie (1867–1934), Polish-French chemist, assumes her husband Pierre's professorship at the Sorbonne after he is killed in a traffic accident. She becomes the first woman ever to teach there.

1907: Alva T. Fisher of the United States designs the first electric washing machine. Manufactured by the Hurley Machine Corporation, it is the first washing machine that does not require an opera-tor to crank a handle to perform the washing action.

1907: Boris Rosing, a lecturer at the Technological Institute, St. Petersburg, Russia, first introduces the idea of using a cathode ray tube as a means of reproducing a television picture. Known as "Rosing's Apparatus," he names it the "electric eye." Although this system uses an electronic receiver, it still has a mechanical camera.

1907: Clemens Peter Pirquet von Cesenatico (1874–1929), Austrian physician, and Bela Schick, Austrian pediatrician, introduce the notion and term "allergy."

1907: The first powdered soap for home use is called "Persil" and is sold by Henkel & Co. in Germany.

1908: A. A. Campbell-Swinton of England first suggests the use of a cathode ray tube as both the transmitter (camera) and receiver. This is the first description of the modern, all-electronic television system.

1909: Phoebus Aaron Theodore Levene (1869–1940), Russian-American chemist, discovers the chemical distinction between DNA (deoxyribonucleic acid) and RNA (ribonucleic acid).

1910: Charles-Jules-Henri Nicolle (1866–1936), French bacteriologist, discovers the viral origin of influenza.

1910: Harvey Cushing (1869–1939), American surgeon, and his team present the first experimental evidence of the link between the anterior pituitary and the reproductive organs.

1912: The value of wireless at sea is demonstrated during the *S.S. Titanic* disaster as those who get to lifeboats are saved by rescuing vessels.

1913: Alfred Henry Sturtevant (1891–1970), American geneticist, produces the first chromosome map, showing five sex-linked genes.

1914: Archduke Franz Ferdinand of Austria-Hungary and his wife Sophie are assassinated; World War I begins.

1914: Panama Canal is completed.

1914: The massacre of 1.5 million Armenians by the Turkish government begins; it is later known as the Armenian Genocide.

1914: John Broadus Watson (1878–1958), American psychologist, launches his theory of behaviorism. This approach, which says that brain activity comprises responses to external stimuli, restricts psychology to the objective, experimental study of human behavior or human responses to stimuli.

1915: German U-boats sink the British passenger steamer RMS Lusitania.

1916: Easter Rising in Ireland begins the fight for Irish independence.

1917: The United States enters World War I, declaring war on Germany.

1917: The Russian Revolution begins as Bolsheviks overthrow the Russian monarchy.

1918: World War I ends.

1918: The Great Flu hits; nearly twenty million perish during the two-year pandemic.

1918: Thousands of political dissidents are tried and imprisoned during the Red Terror in Russia; five million die of famine as Communists collectivize agriculture and transform the Soviet economy.

1919: The ratification of the Nineteenth Amendment to the U.S. constitution gives women the right to vote.

1919: Mahatma Gandhi initiates satyagraha (truth force) campaigns, beginning his nonviolent resistance movement against British rule in India.

1920: The Red Scare (1920–1922) in the United States leads to the arrest, trial, and imprisonment of suspected communist, socialist, and anarchist "radicals."

1920: KDKA, a Pittsburgh Westinghouse station, transmits the first commercial radio broadcast.

1922: Twenty-six of Ireland's counties gain independence, while the remaining six become Northern Ireland and remain under British rule.

1922: Mussolini forms Fascist government in Italy.

1922: The British Broadcasting Company (BBC) is formed.

1922: The first canned baby food is manufactured in the United States by Harold H. Clapp of New York.

1923: Max Wertheimer (1880–1943), German psychologist, publishes *Untersuchungen zur Lehre der Gestalt*, which first originates the concept of Gestalt psychology. This school of psychological thought attempts to examine the total, structured forms of mental experience.

1925: Geneva Protocol, signed by sixteen nations, outlaws the use of poisonous gas as an agent of warfare.

1925: The Scopes Monkey Trial (July 10-25) in Tennessee debates the state's ban on the teaching of evolution.

1927: Charles Lindbergh makes the first solo nonstop transatlantic flight.

1927: Lemuel Clyde McGee, American biochemist, first obtains an active extract of the male sex hormone from bull testicles.

1927: Selmar Aschheim and Bernhardt Zondek, both German physicians, devise a pregnancy test in which the subject's urine is injected subcutaneously in immature female mice. A positive reaction is marked by congestion and hemorrhages of the ovaries in the mice.

1928: Alexander Fleming discovers penicillin.

1929: Black Thursday. The U.S. stock market crashes, beginning the Great Depression.

1929: Edward Adelbert Doisy (1893–1986), American biochemist, first isolates estrone from the urine of pregnant women.

1929: Adolf Friedrich Johann Butenandt (1903–1994), German chemist, isolates the first of the sex hormones, estrone. He obtains this female sex hormone from the urine of pregnant women.

1929: Casimir Funk, Polish biochemist, obtains active male hormone from male urine.

1930: Ronald Aylmer Fisher (1890–1962), English biologist, publishes *The Genetical Theory of Natural Selection* which, together with Sewall Wright's *Mendelian Populations* (1931), lays the mathematical foundations of population genetics.

1930: Rubber condoms made of a thin latex are introduced.

1932: Hattie Wyatt Caraway of Arkansas is the first woman elected to the U.S. Senate.

1932: Nazis capture 230 seats in the German Reichstag during national elections.

1932: Werner Karl Heisenberg (1901–1976), German physicist, wins the Nobel Prize for Physics for the creation of quantum mechanics, the application of which has led to the discovery of the allotropic forms of hydrogen.

1932: RCA (Radio Corporation of America) makes experimental television broadcasts from the Empire State Building in New York.

1933: Adolf Hitler named German chancellor.

1933: President Franklin D. Roosevelt announces the New Deal, a plan to revitalize the U.S. economy and provide relief during the Great Depression. The U.S. unemployment rate reaches twenty-five percent.

1933: U.S. President Franklin Delano Roosevelt (1882–1945) makes the first of his "fireside chats" to the American people. He is the first national leader to use the radio medium comfortably and regularly to explain his programs and to garner popular support.

1933: Christopher Howard Andrewes, English pathologist, Wilson Smith (1897–1965), English bacteriologist and virologist, and Patrick Playfair Laidlaw (1881–1940), English physician, demonstrate the viral nature of the human influenza agent by transmitting it to a ferret and then transferring the virus onto a suitable culture medium.

1934: George W. Beadle, working with Boris Ephrussi, in collaboration with A. Kuhn and A. Butenandt, worked out the biochemical genetics of eye-pigment synthesis in *Drosophila* and *Ephestia*, respectively.

1934: John Marrack begins a series of studies that leads to the formation of the hypothesis governing the association between an antigen and the corresponding antibody.

1935: Germany's Nuremburg Laws codify discrimination and denaturalization of the nation's Jews.

1935: Antonio Caetano de Abreu Freire Egas Moniz (1874–1955), Portuguese surgeon, performs the first lobotomy. This operation, which severs the patient's prefrontal lobes of the brain, opens a new field called psychosurgery. It is usually employed as a last resort and eventually is done away with once tranquilizers and other mind-affecting drugs are discovered.

1935: K. David and associates first isolate a pure crystalline hormone from testicular material and name it testosterone.

1936: Herbert McLean Evans (1882–1971), American anatomist and embryologist, and his group first isolate the interstitial cell stimulating hormone (ICSH). Also called luteinizing hormone, it is concerned with the regulation of the activity of the gonads or sex glands and is produced by the pituitary gland.

1938: Anti-Jewish riots begin across Germany. The destruction and looting of Jewish-owned businesses is know as *Kristalnacht*, "Night of the Broken Glass."

1938: Hitler marches into Austria; political and geographical union of Germany and Austria proclaimed. Munich Pact—Britain, France, and Italy agree to let Germany partition Czechoslovakia.

1938: Mass hysteria among American radio listeners is caused by a dramatic reenactment of H. G. Wells' (1866–1946) novel *War of the Worlds*. American actor, writer, and director George Orson Welles (1915–1985) leads many to believe that a "gas raid from Mars" is actually happening.

1939: The United States declares its neutrality in World War II.

1939: Germany invades Poland. Britain, France, and Russia go to war against Germany.

1939: The Holocaust (Shoah) begins in German-occupied Europe. Jews are removed from their homes and relocated to ghettos or concentration camps. The *Einsatzgruppen*, or mobile killing squads, begin the execution of one million Jews, Poles, Russians, Gypsies, and others.

1939: Television debuts at the World's Fair.

1940: George Wells Beadle, American geneticist, and Edward Lawrie Tatum (1909–1975), American biochemist, establish the formula "One gene = one enzyme." This discovery that each gene supervises the production of only one enzyme lays the foundation for the DNA discoveries to come.

1940: Ernest Chain and E.P. Abraham detail the inactivation of penicillin by a substance produced by *Escherichia coli*. This is the first bacterial compound known to produce resistance to an antibacterial agent.

1941: The U.S. Naval base at Pearl Harbor, Hawaii is bombed by the Japanese Air Force. Soon after, the United States enters World War II, declaring war on Germany and Japan.

1941: The first Nazi death camp, Chelmno, opens. Victims, mainly Jews, are executed by carbon monoxide poisoning in specially designed killing vans.

1942: Executive Order 9066 orders the internment of Japanese immigrants and Japanese-American citizens for the duration of World War II.

1942: Enrico Fermi (1901–1954), Italian-American physicist, heads a Manhattan Project team at the University of Chicago that produces the first controlled chain reaction in an atomic pile of uranium and graphite. With this first self-sustaining chain reaction, the atomic age begins.

1943: Penicillin is first used on a large scale by the U.S. Army in the North African campaigns. Data obtained from these studies show that early expectations for the new drug are correct, and the groundwork is laid for the massive introduction of penicillin into civilian medical practice after the war.

1945: Auschwitz death camp is liberated by allied forces.

1945: World War II and the Holocaust end in Europe.

1945: Trials of Nazi War criminals begin in Nuremberg, Germany.

1945: United Nations is established.

1945: Displaced Persons (DP) camps are established throughout Europe to aid Holocaust survivors. In the three years following the end of World War II, many DPs immigrate to Israel and the United States.

1945: First atomic bomb is detonated by the United States near Almagordo, New Mexico. The experimental bomb generates an explosive power equivalent to between 15 and 20 thousand tons of TNT.

1945: RCA Victor first offers vinyl plastic records to the public.

1945: The United States destroys the Japanese city of Hiroshima with a nuclear fission bomb based on uranium-235. Three days later a plutonium-based bomb destroys the city of Nagasaki. Japan surrenders on August 14 and World War II ends. This is the first use of nuclear power as a weapon.

1946: John von Neumann (1903–1957), Hungarian-American mathematician, begins work at the Institute for Advanced Study at Princeton, New Jersey to establish a digital computer project. He is soon joined by Julian Bigelow, American engineer, and American mathematician, Herman Heine Goldstein.

1948: Mahatma Gandhi is assassinated in New Delhi.

1948: The Soviets blockade Berlin. The United States and Great Britain begin airlift of fuel, food and necessities to West Berlin. The event, the first conflict of the Cold War, became known as the Berlin Airlift (June 26-Sept 30, 1949).

1948: The United Nations issues the Universal Declaration of Human Rights.

1948: Israel is established as an independent nation.

1948: American zoologist and student of sexual behavior, Alfred C. Kinsey (1894–1956) first publishes his *Sexual Behavior in the Human Male*.

1949: South Africa codifies apartheid.

1949: Soviets test their first atomic device.

1950–1999

1950: President Truman commits U.S. troops to aid anti-Communist forces on the Korean Peninsula. The Korean War lasts from 1950–1953.

1951: First successful oral contraceptive drug is introduced. Gregory Pincus (1903–1967), American biologist, discovers a synthetic hormone that renders a woman infertile without altering her capacity for sexual pleasure. It soon is marketed in pill form and effects a social revolution with its ability to divorce the sex act from the consequences of impregnation.

1952: First hydrogen bomb is detonated by the United States on an atoll in the Marshall Islands.

1953: Francis Harry Compton Crick, English biochemist, and James Dewey Watson, American biochemist, work out the double-helix or double spiral DNA model. This model explains how it is able to transmit heredity in living organisms.

1954: Sen. Joseph R. McCarthy begins hearings of the House Un-American Activities Committee, publicly accusing military officials, politicians, media, and others of Communist involvement.

1954: Landmark decision of the United States Supreme Court, *Brown v. Board of Education*, ends segregation of schools in the United States.

1954: The first frozen TV dinners become available in the United States.

1955: Emmett Till, age fourteen, is brutally murdered for allegedly whistling at a white woman. The event galvanizes the civil rights movement.

1955: Rosa Parks refuses to give up her seat on a Montgomery, Alabama, bus to a white passenger, defying segregation.

1955: Warsaw Pact solidifies relationship between the Soviet Union and its communist satellite nations in Eastern Europe.

1955: Chlorpromazine and lithium are first used to treat psychiatric disorders.

1957: President Eisenhower sends federal troops to Central High School in Little Rock, Arkansas, to enforce integration.

1957: Soviet Union launches the first satellite, Sputnik, into space. The Space Race between the USSR and the United States begins.

1958: Explorer I, first American satellite, is launched.

1960: African American students in North Carolina begin a sit-in at a segregated Woolworth's lunch counter; the sit-in spreads throughout the South.

1961: Soviet Cosmonaut Yuri Gagarin becomes the first human in space.

1961: Berlin Wall is built.

1961: Bay of Pigs Invasion: the United States sponsors an invasion to overthrow Cuba's socialist government but fails.

1962: *Silent Spring* published; environmental movement begins.

1962: Cuban Missile Crisis.

1963: Rev. Martin Luther King, Jr., delivers his "I Have a Dream" speech at a civil rights march on Washington, D.C.

1963: The United States and the Soviet Union establish a direct telephone link called the "hot line" between the White House and the Kremlin. It is intended to permit the leaders of both countries to be able to speak directly and immediately to each other in times of crisis.

1964: U.S. President Lyndon Johnson announces ambitious social reform programs known as the Great Society.

1964: Congress approves Gulf of Tonkin resolution.

1964: President Johnson signs the Civil Rights Act of 1964.

1965: March to Selma: state troopers and local police fight a crowd of peaceful civil rights demonstrators, including the Rev. Martin Luther King, Jr., as the group attempted to cross a bridge into the city of Selma.

1965: First U.S. combat troops arrive in South Vietnam.

1965: Voting Rights Act prohibits discriminatory voting practices in the United States.

1965: Watts Riots: thirty-five people are killed and 883 injured in six days of riots in Los Angeles.

1965: Francois Jacob, French biologist, André-Michael Lwoff, French microbiologist, and Jacques-Lucien Monod, French biochemist, are awarded the Nobel Prize for Physiology or Medicine for their discoveries concerning genetic control of enzyme and virus synthesis.

1965: Geoffrey Harris, British anatomist, shows that sexuality is built into the hypothalamus.

1966: Betty Friedan and other leaders of the feminist movement found the National Organization for Women (NOW).

1966: Choh Hao Li, Chinese-American chemist and endocrinologist, describes the structure of human growth hormone and first synthesizes it (1966–1971).

1967: The new fertility drug clomiphene is introduced. Although it can result in multiple births, it proves very successful in increasing a woman's chances of getting pregnant.

1968: Rev. Martin Luther King, Jr., is assassinated in Memphis, Tennessee.

1968: Cesar Chavez leads a national boycott of California table grape growers, which becomes known as "La Causa."

1969: Stonewall Riots in New York City spark the gay rights movement.

1969: The United States successfully lands a manned mission, Apollo 11, on the moon.

1970: Four anti-war demonstrators are killed when the National Guard fires into a crowd of protesters at Kent State University.

1972: Arab terrorists massacre Israeli athletes at the Olympic Games in Munich, Germany.

1973: Roe v. Wade: Landmark Supreme Court decision legalizes abortion on demand during the first trimester of pregnancy.

1973: The American Psychiatric Association removes the classification of homosexuality as a mental disorder.

1973: Last U.S. troops exit Vietnam.

1974: U.S. President Richard Nixon resigns as a result of the Watergate scandal.

1975: As the South Vietnamese government surrenders to North Vietnam, the U.S. Embassy and remaining military and civilian personnel are evacuated.

1976: Steve Jobs and Steve Wozniak invent personal computer.

1977: Earliest known AIDS (Acquired Immunodeficiency Syndrome) victims in the United States are two homosexual men in New York who are diagnosed as suffering from Kaposi's sarcoma.

1978: The Camp David Accord ends a three-decade long conflict between Israel and Egypt.

1979: Three Mile Island nuclear reactor in Pennsylvania suffers a near meltdown.

1979: Iran hostage crisis begins when Iranian students storm the U.S. embassy in Teheran. They hold sixty-six people hostage who are not released until 1981, after 444 days in captivity.

1980: 130,000 Cuban refugees flee to the United States during the Mariel Boatlift (April 4-October 31).

1980: President Carter announces that U.S. athletes will boycott Summer Olympics in Moscow to protest Soviet involvement in Afghanistan.

1981: Sandra Day O'Connor is sworn in as the first woman justice on the Supreme Court of the United States.

1981: Urban riots break out in several British cities, protesting lack of opportunity for minorities and police brutality.

1981: AIDS identified.

1982: Deadline for ratification of the Equal Rights Amendment to the Constitution; without the necessary votes the amendment failed.

1982: New surgical technique for prostate cancer that does not result in impotency is developed by Patrick Walsh.

1984: Steen A. Willadsen successfully clones sheep.

1986: U.S. space shuttle Challenger explodes seventy-three seconds after liftoff.

1986: Chernobyl nuclear disaster in the Soviet Union contaminates large swath of Eastern Europe with radioactive fallout. The disaster is the worst nuclear accident to date.

1987: U.S. President Ronald Reagan challenges Soviet leader Mikhail Gorbachev to open Eastern Europe and the Soviet Union to political and economic reform.

1988: Henry A. Erlich of the United States and colleagues develop a method for identifying an individual from the DNA in a single hair.

1989: The Berlin Wall falls.

1989: Tiananmen Square protest in Beijing, China begins.

1989: Oil tanker Exxon Valdez runs aground in Prince William Sound, spilling more than 10 million gallons of oil (March 24).

1989: Denmark becomes the first country to legalize same-sex partnerships.

1989: Tim Berners-Lee invents the World Wide Web while working at CERN.

1990: Human Genome Project begins in the United States.

1990: The U.S. Census includes questions about gay couples and families.

1991: The Soviet Union dissolves.

1991: Persian Gulf War (January 16-February 28): The United States leads "Operation Desert Storm" to push Iraqi occupying forces out of Kuwait.

1991: The sex of a mouse is changed at the embryo stage.

1991: U.S. FDA (Food and Drug Administration) announces it will speed up its process for approv-

ing drugs. This change in procedure is due to the protests of AIDS activists.

1992: U.S. and Russian leaders formally declare an end to the Cold War.

1992: L.A. Riots: The acquittal of four white police officers charged with police brutality in the beating of black motorist Rodney King sparks days of widespread rioting in Los Angeles.

1992: WHO (World Health Organization) predicts that by the year 2000, thirty to forty million people will be infected with the AIDS-causing HIV. A Harvard University group argues that the number could reach more than 100 million.

1993: A terrorist bomb explodes in a basement parking garage of the World Trade Center, killing six.

1993: Software companies introduce programs making the Internet easier to use, and several on-line information services open gateways into this "network of networks", making its popularity explode.

1993: After analyzing the family trees of gay men and the DNA of pairs of homosexual brothers, biochemists at the United States National Cancer Institute reported that at least one gene related to homosexuality resides on the X chromosome, which is inherited from the mother.

1993: The U.S. military adopts the "Don't Ask, Don't Tell" policy, permitting gay individuals to serve in the military only if they do not disclose their homosexuality and do not engage in homosexual acts; military recruiters and personnel are barred from inquiring about an individual's sexuality.

1994: The first all-race elections in South Africa are held; Nelson Mandela is elected President.

1996: The Federal Defense of Marriage Act (DOMA) is enacted; states permitted to enact legislation refusing to honor same-sex marriages entered into in another state.

1998: Terrorist attacks on U.S. embassies in Kenya and Tanzania.

1998: House of Representatives votes to impeach President William Jefferson Clinton. The Senate acquits President Clinton two months later.

1998: Matthew Shepherd, a gay college student, is tortured and murdered.

1999: NATO forces in former Yugoslavia attempt to end mass killings of ethnic Albanians by Serbian forces in Kosovo.

2000–

2001: Terrorists attack the World Trade Center in New York and the Pentagon in Washington, D.C. killing 2,752.

2001: The controversial Patriot Act is passed in the United States.

2001: United States and coalition forces begin War on Terror by invading Afghanistan (Operation Enduring Freedom), overthrowing the nation's Islamist Taliban regime in December of 2001.

2002: Slobodan Milosevic begins his war crimes trial at the UN International Criminal Tribunal on charges of genocide and crimes against humanity. He is the first head of state to stand trial in an international war-crimes court but dies before the trial concluded.

2002: After United States and coalition forces depose the Islamist Taliban regime in Afghanistan, girls are allowed to return to school and women's rights are partially restored in areas controlled by U.S. and coalition forces.

2002: The International Olympic Committee suspends gender verification procedures for the Olympics in Sydney, Australia citing potential harm to "women athletes born with relatively rare genetic abnormalities that affect development of the gonads or the expression of secondary sexual characteristics."

2002: The agricultural chemical atrazine, used in weed control, is thought to be partially responsible for the dramatic global decline in amphibians, as it is found to disturb male frog sex hormones, altering their gonads.

2003: U.S. space shuttle Columbia breaks apart upon re-entry, killing all seven crew members.

2003: The Supreme Court of the United States strikes down sodomy laws in the landmark decision, *Lawrence v. Texas*

2003: United States and coalition forces invade Iraq.

2003: The United States declares an end to major combat operations in Iraq. As of June 2006, U.S. fighting forces remain engaged in Iraq.

2003: American troops capture Iraq's former leader, Saddam Hussein.

2003: Studies indicate that women with a history of some sexually transmitted diseases, including the human papilloma virus, are at increased risk for developing cervical cancer.

2003: Canada recognizes same-sex marriages throughout the country.

2003: On November 18, the Massachusetts Supreme Judicial court rules that denying same-sex couples marriage rights violates the state constitution, legalizing same-sex marriages.

2004: Islamist terrorists bomb the commuter rail network in Madrid, Spain.

2004: Jason West, mayor of New Paltz, New York, defies state law and performs same-sex weddings. Later charged with twenty-four misdemeanor counts of performing illegal marriages, he was cleared of all charges in 2005.

2004: The California State Supreme Court, in a 5-2 decision, voids nearly 4,000 same-sex marriages performed in San Francisco earlier that year.

2005: Illinois outlaws sexual orientation discrimination.

2005: Massachusetts Supreme Court rules that same-sex couples who live in other states cannot marry in Massachusetts unless gay marriage is also legal in their home state.

Beyond Femininity and Masculinity: Perspectives on Gender and Sexuality

Beyond Femininity and Masculinity: Perspectives on Gender and Sexuality

When asked to define what makes one feminine or masculine, many people would respond with examples of dress, mannerisms, desires, or biological features. People may describe one man as more masculine than another, or a woman as less feminine. A man may also be described as more feminine and a woman more masculine. In this way, masculinity and femininity is used to describe and compare a person's mannerisms and features based on social expectations. For example, a girl may be said to be feminine if she wears a dress and plays with dolls. Alternatively, a girl may be described as a "tomboy" or more masculine for wearing pants and playing with toy cars. However, masculinity and femininity are more complex than stereotypes. They are cultural attributes of the intersection of one's sex, gender, and sexuality.

Sex is a biological determination. Our sex is male or female based on anatomy and genetics. Intersexed individuals, those born with reproductive organs of both sexes, are discussed in the chapter on *Gender and Sexuality Issues in Medicine and Public Health*.

Gender is a socially constructed idea of what is male and female, masculine and feminine. It is independent of sex; a biological male can choose to express a "female" gender (known as transgenderism). Furthermore, gender is evolving and culture-specific. The Chinese practice of foot binding, for example, was a marker of femininity and class status. The practice was unique to parts of Asia, and fell out of favor as notions of beauty, femininity, and the social status of women changed. Many cultures have very specific and sharply divided genders. Presented in this chapter are selected commentaries on femininity. Each represents a snapshot of gender and sexuality within a particular culture, at a particular time. Certainly, Western notions of femininity, womanhood, and women's gender roles have changed dramatically over the past two centuries. Though briefly addressed in this section of the book, this transformation is covered in depth in the *Women's Rights Movement* chapter.

Overall, most societies are gender divided. Most recognize two genders, male and female. Yet many cultures also recognize a fluidity of gender or even a third gender. A discussion of the hijras of India, individuals alternately thought of as men who became women or a distinct third gender, appears in the chapter *Transgendereds and Transsexuals*.

Sexuality is composed of our sexual activities with, and attractions towards, other individuals. It is possible for one individual to have dual sexualities or sexual behaviors. For example, one can be heterosexual (attraction) and celibate (activity). Sexuality issues appear throughout the book. Often, they are inextricably intertwined with issues of gender. Which sexualities are normative, and which are deviant, can be a social construct. Homosexuality, for example, is treated differently across cultures.

This chapter is an introduction to many of the issues more thoroughly discussed in subsequent chapters. International and historical perspectives on masculinity and femininity, gender, and sexuality illuminate the timelessness and globality of gender and sexuality issues in society.

Abigail Adams's Letters to John Adams

Letters

By: Abigail Adams

Date: March 31, 1776 and April 5, 1776.

Source: Adams, Abigail, and John Adams. *Adams Family Correspondence.* Vol. 1, edited by L. H. Butterfield. Cambridge, Mass.: Belknap Press.

About the Author: Abigail Adams was the first woman in American history to be both the wife and mother of a President. Born Abigail Smith in 1744 in Weymouth, Massachusetts, she married John Adams when she was twenty. She and Adams had five children, and she managed the couple's farm and affairs during the Revolutionary War, while John Adams worked toward independence for the thirteen British colonies. The couple exchanged over 1,100 letters during her lifetime.

INTRODUCTION

Abigail Smith Adams came from a well-established New England family. Her father was a Congregational minister, while her mother was a member of the prominent Massachusetts family, the Quincys. A sickly child, Abigail read voraciously and used this self-education as a substitute for formal instruction; born a female in the late 1700s, she was denied access to high school or college education. Her lack of formal schooling was always a source of frustration and embarrassment to her, and she was troubled by her lack of proper spelling and inability to speak or read French. Abigail Smith met John Adams, a Harvard graduate interested in pursuing a career in law, in 1759; the two were married when she was twenty years old, in 1764. John and Abigail Adams settled in Braintree, Massachusetts, and within ten years, Abigail gave birth to five children—three sons and two daughters.

As tensions between the American colonies and the mother country, Britain, erupted in the mid–1770s, John Adams felt called to the revolutionary cause. During his absences, Abigail Adams managed her children, the household, and the family farm at a time when financial matters were considered a male responsibility. John Adams placed his confidence in his wife; the two viewed their marriage as a partnership—unlike many couples of the era—in which the prevailing belief for the upper and middle classes held that the wife should be submissive, meek, and delicate.

A portrait of Abigail Adams, 1776. AP/WIDE WORLD PHOTOS. REPRODUCED BY PERMISSION.

John and Abigail Adams exchanged over 1,100 letters throughout her lifetime, touching on topics such as their children, farm finances, personal intimacy, slavery, the constitution and rights, her lack of a formal education, women's rights, the monarchy in Britain, and more. John Adams worked as a lawyer and a circuit judge. His work took him away from home for long stretches of time, leaving Abigail in charge of the farm long before the revolution ever began. In many ways, her letters read like those of any wife; she implores him to write more often, peppers him with questions on details of his daily life, and informs him of activities on the homestead. At the same time, her letters ask incisive questions and give strong opinions about the development of government just as the colonies were about to enter war with Great Britain.

In these two letters, dated March 31, 1776 and April 5, 1776, Abigail Adams implores John Adams to "remember the ladies" when writing law. She beseeches him to avoid placing too much power in the hands of husbands who might use it for tyrannical or cruel purposes against women.

PRIMARY SOURCE

Braintree, March 31, 1776

I wish you would ever write me a Letter half as long as I write you; and tell me if you may where your Fleet are gone? What sort of Defence Virginia can make against our common Enemy? Whether it is so situated as to make an able Defence? Are not the Gentery Lords and the common people vassals, are they not like the uncivilized Natives Brittain represents us to be? I hope their Riffel Men who have shewen themselves very savage and even Blood thirsty; are not a specimen of the Generality of the people.

I am willing to allow the Colony great merit for having produced a Washington but they have been shamefully duped by a Dunmore.

I have sometimes been ready to think that the passion for Liberty cannot be Eaquelly Strong in the Breasts of those who have been accustomed to deprive their fellow Creatures of theirs. Of this I am certain that it is not founded upon that generous and christian principal of doing to others as we would that others should do unto us.

Do not you want to see Boston; I am fearfull of the small pox, or I should have been in before this time. I got Mr. Crane to go to our House and see what state it was in. I find it has been occupied by one of the Doctors of a Regiment, very dirty, but no other damage has been done to it. The few things which were left in it are all gone. Cranch [Crane?] has the key which he never deliverd up. I have wrote to him for it and am determined to get it cleand as soon as possible and shut it up. I look upon it a new acquisition of property, a property which one month ago I did not value at a single Shilling, and could with pleasure have seen it in flames.

The Town in General is left in a better state than we expected, more oweing to a percipitate flight than any Regard to the inhabitants, tho some individuals discoverd a sense of honour and justice and have left the rent of the Houses in which they were, for the owners and the furniture unhurt, or if damaged suffcent to make it good.

Others have committed abominable Ravages. The Mansion House of your President [John Hancock] is safe and the furniture unhurt whilst both the House and Furniture of the Solisiter General [Samuel Quincy] have fallen a prey to their own merciless party. Surely the very Fiends feel a Reverential awe for Virtue and patriotism, whilst they Detest the paricide and traitor.

I feel very differently at the approach of spring to what I did a month ago. We knew not then whether we could plant or sow with safety, whether when we had toild we could reap the fruits of our own industry, whether we could rest in our own Cottages, or whether we should not be driven from the sea coasts to seek shelter in the wilderness, but now we feel as if we might sit under our own vine and eat the good of the land.

I feel a gaieti de Coar to which before I was a stranger. I think the Sun looks brighter, the Birds sing more melodiously, and Nature puts on a more chearfull countanance. We feel a temporary peace, and the poor fugitives are returning to their deserted habitations.

Tho we felicitate ourselves, we sympathize with those who are trembling least the Lot of Boston should be theirs. But they cannot be in similar circumstances unless pusilanimity and cowardise should take possession of them. They have time and warning given them to see the Evil and shun it.—I long to hear that you have declared an independency—and by the way in the new Code of Laws which I suppose it will be necessary for you to make I desire you would Remember the Ladies, and be more generous and favourable to them than your ancestors. Do not put such unlimited power into the hands of the Husbands. Remember all Men would be tyrants if they could. If perticuliar care and attention is not paid to the Laidies we are determined to foment a Rebelion, and will not hold ourselves bound by any Laws in which we have no voice, or Representation.

That your Sex are Naturally Tyrannical is a Truth so thoroughly established as to admit of no dispute, but such of you as wish to be happy willingly give up the harsh title of Master for the more tender and endearing one of Friend. Why then, not put it out of the power of the vicious and the Lawless to use us with cruelty and indignity with impunity. Men of Sense in all Ages abhor those customs which treat us only as the vassals of your Sex. Regard us then as Beings placed by providence under your protection and in immitation of the Supreem Being make use of that power only for our happiness.

April 5, 1776

Not having an opportunity of sending this I shall add a few lines more; tho not with a heart so gay. I have been attending the sick chamber of our Neighbour Trot whose affliction I most sensibly feel but cannot discribe, striped of two lovely children in one week. Gorge the Eldest died on wednesday and Billy the youngest on fryday, with the Canker fever, a terible disorder so much like the thr[o]at distemper, that it differs but little from it. Betsy Cranch has been very bad, but upon the recovery. Becky Peck they do not expect will live out the day. Many grown person[s] are now sick with it, in this [street?] 5. It rages much in other Towns. The Mumps too are very frequent. Isaac is now confined with it. Our own little flock are yet well. My Heart trembles with anxiety for them. God preserve them.

I want to hear much oftener from you than I do. March 8 was the last date of any that I have yet had.—

You inquire of whether I am making Salt peter. I have not yet attempted it, but after Soap making believe I shall make the experiment. I find as much as I can do to man-ufacture cloathing for my family which would else be Naked. I know of but one person in this part of the Town who has made any, that is Mr. Tertias Bass as he is calld who has got very near an hundred weight which has been found to be very good. I have heard of some others in the other parishes. Mr. Reed of Weymouth has been applied to, to go to Andover to the mills which are now at work, and has gone. I have lately seen a small Manuscrip de[s]cribing the proportions for the various sorts of pow-der, fit for cannon, small arms and pistols. If it would be of any Service your way I will get it transcribed and send it to you.—Every one of your Friend[s] send their Regards, and all the little ones. Your Brothers youngest child lies bad with convulsion fitts. Adieu. I need not say how much I am Your ever faithfull Friend.

SIGNIFICANCE

On April 18, 1776, British General Thomas Gage sent 700 British troops to Concord, Massachusetts, to destroy munitions stored by rebel colonists; the first shots of the Revolutionary War were fired at Lexing-ton, Massachusetts. Abigail Adams's words, penned just weeks before these first shots were fired, noted issues of substance that formed the core of questions about self-government and rights for the emerging United States.

The April 5, 1776 letter refers to "the various sorts of powder, fit for cannon, small arms and pistols. If it would be of any Service your way I will get it tran-scribed and send it to you." This short note shows her understanding of the cause, how deeply the tensions between Britain and the colonies were, and the meas-ures needed to fight should war erupt. Her comments about the question of whether to plant crops, for fear of being forced away from the sea coast and missing the harvest, further demonstrate her understanding of the pending danger. In her letter she reassures John Adams that she has decided to stay, and that fellow vil-lagers believe that remaining on their farms is a safe course. Her discussions of Boston and the danger that city dwellers experienced refers to the Boston Mas-sacre of the previous year, the Boston tea party, and British soldiers demanding to be quartered in various homes in the city.

Her desire to hear that "independency" be declared is followed by a discussion of the relationship between male rights and the oppression of women. In this passage, Abigail Adams makes her famous "remember the ladies" statement. Using revolutionary political rhetoric, such as "remember that all men would be tyrants if they could," Abigail Adams takes a statement applied to King George III and turns it toward men in general. In addition, by threatening a ladies' rebellion, which would result from being ruled "without Representation," she co-opts the "No Taxa-tion Without Representation" cry that formed a cru-cial part of the colonies' rebellion against Britain.

Her words made an impression on John Adams, though female enfranchisement was not made law in the United States until 1920, some 144 years later. In 1784, after the colonies won independence, John Adams was assigned to diplomatic work in France; Abigail joined him until the two returned to the United States in 1788.

Abigail Adams continued to argue for greater freedoms for women and for literacy rights for slaves and free blacks. When John Adams was elected Vice President in 1789 and then President in 1797, Abi-gail's poor health forced her to spend much of her time in Quincy, Massachusetts, away from her hus-band. In spite of this distance, she was very much a part of his inner circle of advisors; critics of Abigail Adams dubbed her "Her Majesty" for her influence on her husband. After John Adams left the presidency in 1801, the two retired to Braintree. Abigail Adams died in 1818; her husband outlived her by eight years.

FURTHER RESOURCES

Books

Adams, Abigail and John Adams. *The Letters of John and Abi-gail Adams.* New York: Penguin Classics, 2003.

Levin, Phyllis Lee. *Abigail Adams: A Biography.* New York: St. Martin's Griffin, 2001.

Web sites

PBS, The American Experience. "John & Abigail Adams." <http://www.pbs.org/wgbh/amex/adams/filmmore/index.html> (accessed March 29, 2006).

Small Feet of the Chinese Females

Remarks on the Origin of the Custom of Compressing the Feet; the Extent and Effects of the Practice; with an Anatomical Description of a Small Foot

Journal article

By: Anonymous

Date: 1835

Source: "Small feet of the Chinese females: remarks on the origin of the custom of compressing the feet; the extent and effects of the practice; with an anatomical description of a small foot." *Chinese Repository.* 3 (1835): 537–539.

About the Author: The article was written without author acknowledgement for *Chinese Repository*, a Protestant missionary journal that operated from 1832 through 1851. Its readership was composed of missionaries, ministers, and lay persons with an interest in international issues surrounding mission work.

INTRODUCTION

The Chinese practice of footbinding has been traced back as far as the Shang era (1600–1046 B.C.E.), but gained popularity during the Han Dynasty (206 B.C.E.–A.D. 220). The procedure, outlawed in China in 1911, was part of Chinese upper class and imperial society for more than 2000 years.

A properly bound foot involved breaking the arch of the foot and curling the toes inward and under the insole; the result was a foot that resembled a "golden lotus," a symbol of the perfect, delicate and feminine foot. Mothers performed the footbinding in most cases. During infancy, young girls of the upper and imperial class would begin to have their feet bound. First the foot was soaked in hot water and then massaged; the mother molded the toes under and wrapped the foot with bandages. A proper binding broke the four small toes, leaving the big toe in place to permit balance while walking. As the foot grew, the bindings continued, with the goal of creating a foot no longer than four inches when the girl reached full growth as a woman.

A painful process, footbinding also left the girl prone to infection, gangrene, and severe joint problems. Approximately ten percent of all girls subjected to the procedure died from infection.

Footbinding was a class-based procedure; peasant women generally did not have bound feet, although there were exceptions. Once the footbinding process was complete, the woman could take tiny steps and was incapable of field work, shopping, or walking distances of more than a few hundred feet at a time. Decorative, delicately bound feet were a status symbol for the rich and those families who served at court. A wife with bound feet was considered a source of pride and an example of wealth and prosperity for many Chinese men.

By the 1600s, footbinding was accepted practice in the upper classes, and at times peasant families chose to follow the practice with the hope that their daughters could marry into the higher classes. When the expected marriage did not come through, however, these peasant women were disabled and experienced great difficulty caring for themselves or others. Peasant men did not want them, for they could not work or walk. Only those men who could afford to support a woman who provided no assistance to the household could have a wife with bound feet.

Westerners who entered China in the 1800s, and especially Christian missionaries, considered the practice of footbinding to be barbaric. Footbinding reached its peak in the 1800s, converging with the influx of Christian missionaries. In this passage, from a journal devoted to Chinese missionary work, a Christian missionary in China in 1835 gives his account of footbinding from a western perspective.

■ PRIMARY SOURCE

Art. I. Small feet of the Chinese females: remarks on the origin of the custom of compressing the feet; the extent and effects of the practice; with an anatomical description of a small foot.

Ample evidence of the inefficiency of the ethical systems of the Chinese, is found in their national and domestic customs. Not only the minds of the people, but their bodies also, are distorted and deformed by unnatural usages; and those laws, physical as well as moral, which the Creator designed for the good of his creatures, are perverted, and, if possible, would be annihilated. The truth of these remarks is presented to our view in a clear light by the anatomical description, which forms a part of this article. Historians are not agreed as to the time or place in which the practice of compressing the feet originated. Du Halde states, but on what authority he does not inform us, that the practice originated with the infamous Take, the last empress of the Shang dynasty, who perished in its overthrow, B.C. 1123. "Her own feet being very small, she bound them tight with fillets, affecting to make that pass for a beauty which was really a deformity. However, the women all followed her example; and this ridiculous custom is so thoroughly established, that to have feet of the natural size is enough to render them contemptible." Again, the same author remarks, "The Chinese themselves are not certain what gave rise to this odd custom. The story current among us, which attributes the invention to the ancient Chinese, who, to oblige their wives to keep at home, are said to have brought little feet into fashion, is by some looked upon as fabulous. The far greater number think it to be a political design, to keep women in continual subjection. It is certain that they are extremely confined, and seldom stir out of their apartments, which are in the most retired place in the house; having no communication with any but the women-servants." Others state that the custom originated in the time of the woo tae, or "five dynasties," about A.D. 925. According to the native historian, quoted in Morrison's View of China, "it is not known when the small feet of females were introduced. It is said that the custom arose in the time of the five dynasties. Le Howchoo ordered his concubine, Yaou, to bind her feet with silk, and cause them to appear small, and in the shape of the new moon. From this, sprung the imitation of every other female."

In regard to the extent and effects of the practice, there is not the same degree of uncertainty. It prevails more or less throughout the whole empire, but only among the Chinese. The Tartar ladies do not yield to the cruel custom, but allow their feet to retain their natural form. In the largest towns and cities, and generally in the most fashionable parts of the country, a majority of the females have their feet compressed. In some places, as many as seven or eight in ten are tormented in this way; in other places, the number is not more than four or five in ten. The operation of compressing the feet is commenced in infancy; and so closely and constantly are the bandages applied, in the most successful cases, as to prevent almost entirely the growth and extension of the limb. Ladies of rank and taste, who are fashioned in this manner, are rendered quite unable to walk. The effects of this process are extremely painful. Children will often tear away the bandages in order to gain relief from the torture; but their temporary removal, it is said, greatly increase the pain by causing a violent revulsion of the blood to the feet. This violent compression of the limbs, moreover, is injurious to health, and renders the victim a cripple through life. In some cases the compression is very slight, and consequently the effect is less hurtful. It is no marvel that the Chinese ladies never dance; it is rather a matter of surprise that they can move at all on such ill shaped and distorted members; some of which, scarcely if at all, exceed two and a half inches in length. Those who can avoid it, seldom appear abroad except in sedans; (we speak of those in the neighborhood of Canton;) but there are frequent cases, among the poorer classes, where the unhappy victims of this barbarous custom are compelled to walk on their little feet. Their gait appears exceedingly awkward to others, and must be painful to themselves. Generally, in attempting to walk any considerable distance, they find a stick, or the shoulder of a matron or servant girl, a necessary support. In walking, the body is bent forwards at a considerable inclination, in order to place the centre of gravity over the feet; and the great muscular exertion required for preserving the balance is evinced by the rapid motion of the arms, and the hobbling shortness of the steps. The form of these "golden lilies," kin leën, as the Chinese call them, is accu-

rately described in the following paper, from the Transactions of the Royal Society of London. It was written by Bransby Blake Cooper, esq., surgeon to Guy's hospital; and was communicated to the society by the secretary, P.M. Roget, M.D., March 5th, 1829.

"A specimen of a Chinese foot, the account of which I have the honor to lay before the Royal Society, was removed from the dead body of a female found floating in the river at Canton. On its arrival in England, it was presented to sir Astley Cooper, to whose kindness I am indebted for the opportunity of making this curious dissection. Without entering into an inquiry whether this singular construction, and as we should esteem it hideous deformity, of the Chinese female foot, had its origin in oriental jealousy, or was the result of an unnatural taste in beauty; I shall content myself with describing the remarkable deviations from the original structure, which it almost every-where presents."

SIGNIFICANCE

Nineteenth century western attitudes toward the Chinese included the supposition that Chinese civilization was backwards and cruel in its treatment of women. Many missionaries viewed footbinding as a character deformity, a cultural tradition that demonstrated Chinese brutality and oppression.

Women of the upper classes with bound feet often lived in cloistered sections of the household, surrounded by female servants, and were expected to partake in activities deemed feminine, such as painting, reading light verse, and memorizing poetry. Their formal education was limited to Confucian basics, and these women, largely ornamental, were trained to be models of restraint and obedience.

The first western missionaries were Catholic Jesuits, who arrived during the 1600s. By the early 1800s, Protestant missionaries entered China, though it was not until the Opium Wars ended in 1842 that Protestants were able to go to China in large numbers.

This article, published four years before the Opium Wars began, therefore, gave western readers one of the few written accounts of Chinese society and footbinding available in the West. The description of the process of footbinding accurately explains in detail the suffering girls experienced with the procedure. Meant to shock, this account reinforces the missionary writer's assertion that "Not only the minds of the people, but their bodies also, are distorted and deformed by unnatural usages; and those laws, physical as well as moral, which the Creator designed for the good of his

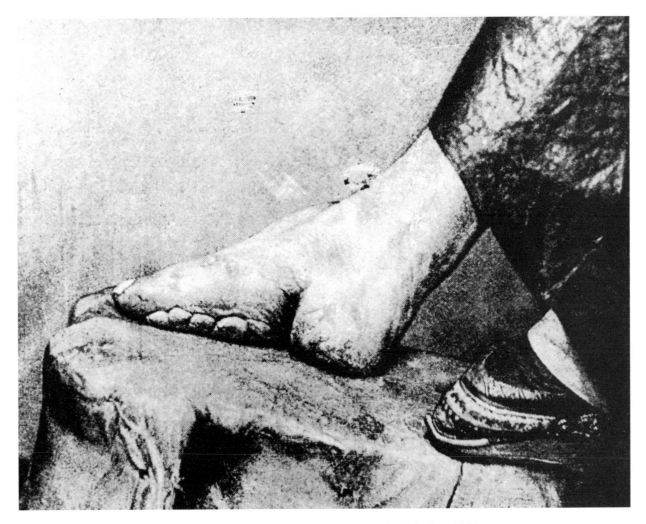

A close-up of the foot of an aristocratic Chinese woman, deformed by foot binding, 1900. PHOTO BY HULTON ARCHIVE/GETTY IMAGES

creatures, are perverted, and, if possible, would be annihilated."

Characterizing Chinese minds and morality as "deformed" and using footbinding as a physical manifestation of this deformity set the stage for western beliefs of Chinese barbarity. In the 1840s, as Chinese immigrants to the United States flooded the west coast during the Gold Rush in California, anti-Chinese sentiment emerged. By the 1880s, after decades of Chinese immigration and the use of Chinese labor to build railroads, the United States Congress passed the Chinese Exclusion Act, which barred Chinese laborers from coming to the United States.

Many male Chinese immigrants who found financial success in the United States married Chinese women with bound feet and brought them to the United States. Having such a wife was considered to be a sign of prestige, though in many cases the husband could not afford to hire servants to help the footbound wife. In cities such as San Francisco, the inability to walk, coupled with little or no household help, made these women isolated prisoners in their own homes.

In 1895, in Shanghai, an anti-footbinding society formed. Its members registered their children with the society to find mates from families who did not adhere to the practice. As China moved away from the imperial system, the practice of footbinding fell further out of favor. China declared footbinding illegal in 1911, though the practice continued in some isolated areas.

FURTHER RESOURCES

Books

Ping, Wang. *Aching for Beauty: Footbinding in China.* New York: Anchor, 2002.

Ko, Dorothy. *Cinderella's Sisters: A Revisionist History of Footbinding* . Berkeley: University of California Press, 2005.

Web sites

Virtual Museum of San Francisco. "Chinese Girl With Bound Feet." <http://www.sfmuseum.org/chin/foot.html> (accessed April 3, 2006).

A Letter About Old Maids

Letter

By: Betsey

Date: 1840

Source: Betsey. "A Letter About Old Maids." in *The Lowell Offering.* Lowell, Mass.: A. Watson, 1840.

About the Author: Betsey was a female factory worker in the textile mills in Lowell, Massachussetts, during the 1840s.

INTRODUCTION

The social legacy of the Old Maid and Spinster is steeped in tradition. Originally, spinsters appeared as widows (young and old), orphans, and young unwed girls who performed tasks of spinning, weaving, and the making of clothes within the home. As technology and industry developed, these women moved from the home to the factory and, once there, their social role began to take a different character.

In the United States, particularly New England in the 1820s, the first wave of industrialization was underway, and textile mills heavily recruited young women. Young women were deemed ideal candidates for textile work because these new factory tasks were not drastically different from what they were doing at home. Within their homes, women were already spinning cotton, and other fibers, into thread to weave into cloth, and they were the primary creators of clothing and other textile products. In addition to sewing and weaving, women regularly worked in the fields as part of farm labor, and they were known to do "outwork." Outwork consisted of making goods that could be sold for cash or bartered. Sometimes outwork is also called "piecework," but the second term really refers to a later period when women would be contracted to sew clothing that would then be bought by factories and larger companies.

The mills and factories of this period were sexually segregated operations. Men held supervisory positions, and women worked the spinning wheels and sewing machines and handled the cloth and cloth products. These divisions stem from social expectations on the relations between men and women, and they derived from the fact that sewing, spinning, and weaving were traditionally deemed "woman's work." These women often considered factory work to pay well, especially in light of the fact that much of their work within the home was unpaid. Letters and fiction from the first wave of mill employees shows a great deal of pride in their work and financial independence.

Just as these women took pride in their financial independence and work, they also grappled with the issue of being a single working girl and wanting to get married. The mills in Lowell, Massachusetts—one of the earliest factory towns in the United States—set up boardinghouses for their female employees. They did this as a way to accommodate society's expectations that women would (and should) get married and stay within the home, and that men earned the family income. But, a growing population, advances in technology (like Eli Whitney's cotton gin in the late 1790s), and a need for increased production of goods caused many women to continue to work in mills and factories. More importantly, a growing number of women did not get married. They remained spinsters, and social dichotomies created lively and intense discussions, writings, and debates on the role of the female—particularly the spinster—in society.

These spinsters, most often, did not intend to become Old Maids. Rather, they were young girls who entered factories looking for a bit of financial gain, independence, and pride. Women like Betsey, the author of the letter excerpted below, aptly captured their dismay at, and sometimes disdain of, society's scornful attitude towards them. Betsey wrote her letter in 1840, when local and state governments were being forced to examine working conditions, women began organizing protests against their employers, and society was facing the reality that more and more women were not getting married.

PRIMARY SOURCE

Mr. Editor:—

I am one of that unlucky, derided, and almost despised set of females, called spinsters, single sisters,

Letter about Old Maids....Recollections of an Old Maid. 5

that it is an institution ordained by the All-wise Disposer of human affairs, for the promotion of the happiness of mankind in general; but I think it was a part of that wise design, that there should be *Old Maids.*

The first reason I shall give in support of this opinion, is, that they are not only very useful, but even extremely necessary; for how many homes are rendered happy, after the departure from them of sons and daughters into the wide world, by the continuance of the old maid?—she who is now to be the light, life and joy of those who would otherwise be sad and solitary. How many parents are cheered and consoled, in the decline and departure of life, by her who remains to repay their care of her early years, by the constant and much needed attentions which can only be rendered by the old maid! How many married sisters, when trial and sorrow come to their homes and hearts, look for help and consolation from the one of their number who remains free from such cares, the ever ready and sympathizing old maid! How many widowed brothers have, with perfect confidence, consigned their motherless children to the love and care of the trusty old maid! Oh, many a little orphan has never felt its mother's loss, while sheltered by the kindly affection of some soft-hearted old maid! And who is usually the nurse in sickness, the friend in affliction, the help in every time of need, but the old maid?

These have ever been her duties and her pleasures; but in later times, old maids have taken a more conspicuous part. They form a large proportion of our authoresses ; they are the founders and pillars of Anti-Slavery, Moral Reform, and all sorts of religious and charitable societies; and last, (though not least,) in country towns where no weekly sheet is published, they are extremely useful in carrying the news.

For these reasons, I think we must all acknowledge that there is a great need of old maids; and this want has been provided for by the greater number of females who outlive the years of infancy, than of males. Some assert that more are *born* ; but at all events they do not *die* so easily. Of the males who arrive at years of manhood, some die on the high seas, or in battle, or in foreign climes, or in distant parts of their own land, where they have been attacked by disease, and died for want of the judicious care of an old maid. So that all will allow, there must be quite a surplus of the female sex, who can be nothing more or less than *old maids.*

But all this reasoning in favor of *them* goes directly against old bachelors; for I do not see that they are either useful or necessary, at least not more useful for remaining single, (present company always excepted—) and had they been *needed*, more

males would have been allowed to arrive at years of bachelorship.

Having thus introduced myself, and shown the utility of the tribe to which I belong, I reveal it as my design to furnish certain recollections of my youthful days. They are chiefly recollections of simple country girls, the companions of my earlier years, of whom the greater number are now wives and mothers. I shall care but little what opinions are entertained or expressed in relation to the style of composition, if the *moral* be remembered and regarded.   BETSEY.

——o——

RECOLLECTIONS OF AN OLD MAID.
NUMBER I.

THERE was but one young lady in our village: —I mean by this, that there was but one young female who did no work. The word *lady* has now a very indefinite signification. It means, sometimes, merely a female; sometimes, a female distinguished from most of her sex by elegance of mind, or appearance; and sometimes again, one whose claims to distinction are those of birth or wealth. But those of every class and character who can contrive to worry away their lives without being of any benefit to "that vulgar herd," the world in general, have a great desire to appropriate this cognomen to themselves; and as people are apt to designate others by the names which they assume, so those are often called ladies (*par excellence*) who do no work.

Widow A. had but one pretty little daughter, and as she had also a pretty little house and farm, she thought these were very sufficient reasons for making herself a slave to her child. She early discovered that her little girl had a very delicate constitution; and instead of invigorating it by work and exercise, she pampered and nursed her, till she looked as though she was indeed *born* (to use her mother's expression) *to be a lady.*

Ruth A. had been sheltered from the morning breeze, the midday sun, and the evening dew; till she was as pale and slender as the lily of the vale, and her little soft white hands would of themselves have been a sufficient guarantee for her claims to ladyship.

Now though I in my young days was about as broad as I was long, with a face as round as the full moon, and cheeks as red as peony, and owned a pair of hands which had been lengthened and widened, thickened and roughened, reddened and toughened, by long and intimate acquaintance with the wash-tub, scouring-cloth, and broom-stick ; though I was as tough as a squaw, and could not have been persuaded that I had a nerve about me, yet I never looked at Ruthy without blessing my stars that I was not "a natural born lady." I

Page 5 from "The Lowell Offering," 1840. COURTESY OF HARVARD COLLEGE LIBRARY.

lay-nuns, etc., but who are more usually known by the appellation of Old Maids. That I have never been married, is not my own fault, for I never refused an offer in my life, neither have I by disdain, coldness, or indifference, kept my male acquaintance at a distance. I have always had, and still retain, a great respect for the marriage state, and for those of my friends who, from right motives, have entered into it. I believe, what I presume will not here be doubted, that it is an institution ordained by the All-wise Disposer of human affairs, for the promotion of the happiness of mankind in general; but I think it was apart of that wise design, that there should be *Old Maids*.

The first reason I shall give in support of this opinion, is, that they are not only very useful, but even extremely necessary; for how many homes are rendered happy, after the departure from them of sons and daughters into the wide world, by the continuance of the old maid?— she who is now to he the light, life, and joy of those who would otherwise be sad and solitary. How many parents are cheered and consoled, in the decline and departures of life, by her who remains to repay their care of her early years, by the constant and much needed attentions which can only be rendered by the old maid! How many married sisters, when trial and sorrow come to their homes and hearts, look for help and consolation from the one of their number who remains free from such cares, the ever ready sympathizing old maid! How many widowed brothers have, with perfect confidence, consigned their motherless children to the love and care of the trusty old maid! Oh, many a little orphan has never felt its mother's loss, while sheltered by the kindly affection of some soft-hearted old maid! And who is usually the nurse in sickness, the friend in affliction, the help in every time of need, but the old maid?

These have ever been her duties and her pleasures; but in later times, old maids have taken a more conspicuous part. They form a large proportion of our authoresses; they are the founders and pillars of Anti-Slavery, Moral Reform, and all sorts of religious and charitable societies; and last, (though not least,) in country towns where no weekly sheet is published, they are extremely useful in carrying the news.

SIGNIFICANCE

Single women, like Betsey, represented then, and continue to comprise, a significant sector of society. They enabled industry and society to grow and flourish through their labor, helped establish roles for women outside of the home, and paved the way for future female activists. The Betseys, spinsters, and Old Maids of society provided role models for future generations of women who chose (or were forced to

assume) lives other than the standard expectations of marriage and keeping a traditional home. Instead of remaining passive, the words and actions of these working women who remained unmarried,—in eras when marriage was the normal course of a woman's life—paved the way for the liberation movements of the late twentieth century.

FURTHER RESOURCES

Books

Amireh, Amil. *The Factory Girl and the Seamstress: Imaging Gender and Class in Nineteenth Century Fiction.* New York: Garland, 2000.

Isreal, Betsy. *Bachelor Girl: The Secret History of Single Women in the Twentieth Century.* New York: William Morrow, 2002.

Moran, William. *The Belles of New England: The Women of the Textile Mills and the Families Whose Wealth They Wove.* New York: St. Martin's Griffin, 2004.

Web sites

Robinson, Harriet Hanson. "The Lowell Mill Girls Go on Strike, 1836." *History Matters,* <http://historymatters.gmu.edu/d/5714/> (accessed March 24, 2006).

Sun Associates. "Lowell Mill Girls Webquest." <http://www.sun-associates.com/mercer/handouts/millgirls.html> (accessed March 24, 2006).

Ain't I a Woman?

Speech

By: Sojourner Truth

Date: December 1851

Source: Truth, Sojourner. "Ain't I a Woman?" Speech delivered to the Women's Convention, Akron, Ohio, December 1851. Available at: < http://www.fordham.edu/halsall/mod/sojtruth-woman.html> (accessed February 5, 2006).

About the Author: Sojourner Truth, born Isabella Baumfree, traveled throughout the United States from the 1840s through the 1870s, giving public speeches denouncing slavery and restrictions on women's rights. In 1850, she published *The Narrative of Sojourner Truth.* The proceeds from sales of the book supported her for the rest of her life. She died in Battle Creek, Michigan, in 1883.

Sojourner Truth, circa 1864. THE LIBRARY OF CONGRESS

INTRODUCTION

Isabella Baumfree was born into slavery in Ulster County, New York, in 1797. One of thirteen children born to slave parents, Baumfree spent the first eleven years of her life living with her parents on a farm with Dutch immigrant masters. She spoke only Dutch until she was eleven, when she was sold to a new master and forced to learn English.

Baumfree was sold to a number of masters before reaching the Dumont family, where she met Thomas, whom she "married" (legal marriage was not permitted for slaves) and with whom she had five children between 1810 and 1826. New York emancipated slaves as of the year 1828; Baumfree's owner promised to free her and her youngest child one year early as part of a private agreement. When the owner reneged on this promise, Baumfree fled to New York City with her youngest child, leaving Thomas and her other children behind. Shortly after her escape, Baumfree learned that her son Peter had been sold illegally into slavery in Alabama. She fought a court battle and won Peter's freedom—the first time a black woman had won a court case against a white man.

In 1843, Isabella Baumfree took the name Sojourner Truth and left New York City. She traveled throughout Long Island and Connecticut, eventually settling in Florence, Massachusetts, in a utopian community called The Northampton Association, which was devoted to abolition, pacifism, and equality. She met abolitionists such as Frederick Douglass (c. 1817?–1895), Olive Gilbert (1801–1884), and William Lloyd Garrison (1805–1879). Olive Gilbert transcribed Truth's dictated autobiography, which was published in 1850 under the title *The Narrative of Sojourner Truth*.

As Truth gained more notoriety among abolitionists, she also turned her attention to the cause of women's rights. Following the publication of her book, Truth was popular on the lecture circuit, speaking of the dual problems of slavery and female oppression. Her speech at a women's rights convention in Akron, Ohio, in December 1851, is her most famous public appearance.

■ PRIMARY SOURCE

Well, children, where there is so much racket there must be something out of kilter. I think that 'twixt the negroes of the South and the women at the North, all talking about rights, the white men will be in a fix pretty soon. But what's all this here talking about?

That man over there says that women need to be helped into carriages, and lifted over ditches, and to have the best place everywhere. Nobody ever helps me into carriages, or over mud-puddles, or gives me any best place! And ain't I a woman? Look at me! Look at my arm! I have ploughed and planted, and gathered into barns, and no man could head me! And ain't I a woman? I could work as much and eat as much as a man—when I could get it—and bear the lash as well! And ain't I a woman? I have borne thirteen children, and seen most all sold off to slavery, and when I cried out with my mother's grief, none but Jesus heard me! And ain't I a woman?

Then they talk about this thing in the head; what's this they call it? [member of audience whispers, "intellect"] That's it, honey. What's that got to do with women's rights or negroes' rights? If my cup won't hold but a pint, and yours holds a quart, wouldn't you be mean not to let me have my little half measure full?

Then that little man in black there, he says women can't have as much rights as men, 'cause Christ wasn't a woman! Where did your Christ come from? Where did your Christ come from? From God and a woman! Man had nothing to do with Him.

If the first woman God ever made was strong enough to turn the world upside down all alone, these women together ought to be able to turn it back, and get it right side up again! And now they is asking to do it, the men better let them.

Obliged to you for hearing me, and now old Sojourner ain't got nothing more to say.

SIGNIFICANCE

Sojourner Truth's plain speech, matched with her life experience and publishing success, brought large audiences to her speeches. Both men and women alike flocked to her public appearances. Her comment "Ain't I a Woman?" took the core of the anti-women's rights arguments—that women were delicate and in need to great protection and care—and turned it on its head. If women were indeed such delicate creatures, Sojourner Truth asks, then what about black female slaves? If black female slaves plowed and worked fields and bore children taken from them, where was the delicacy and protection offered to them as women?

The plaintive and simple cry in Truth's short speech resounded with those present to witness the speech and with readers of the text as printed in newspapers throughout the country. Women's rights activists such as Harriet Beecher Stowe (1811–1896; author of *Uncle Tom's Cabin*) and Lucretia Mott (1793–1880) befriended Truth and helped her to gain more appearances on the lecture circuit. Stowe wrote about Truth in an article published in *Atlantic Monthly*, a major publication in the United States with wide circulation. Truth partnered with fellow escaped slave Frederick Douglass, a noted author and anti-slavery speaker, on the lecture circuit at times, drawing enormous crowds. Truth tied slavery to the cause of women's rights, considering both to be equal rights issues.

Emancipation for most slaves came in 1863 with Abraham Lincoln's Emancipation Proclamation, and Sojourner Truth organized supplies for black volunteer regiments that fought during the Civil War. In 1864, President Lincoln received Truth at the White House, and after all slaves gained their freedom in 1865, Truth campaigned for programs that would help former slaves adjust to their freedom. She worked for a year as a counselor within the Freedman's Bureau, a short-lived federal program designed to help slaves with resettlement and adjustment.

When Congress considered the question of voting rights for former slaves, Truth split with Frederick Douglass. Douglass wanted to press for male black suffrage only, advocating a gradualist approach. White and black women's rights supporters split on the issue; Truth wanted female suffrage—for all races—to be

part of what became the Fifteenth Amendment. In the end, the amendment extended the vote only to male black citizens.

Truth's "Ain't I a Woman?" speech appealed to women's rights advocates, abolitionists, and mothers. The timing of her speech—just one year after The Missouri Compromise had literally drawn a slavery line through the United States—was a crucial part of her rise as a public speaker. Truth continued to work to promote the cause of black and female rights through 1875, until the age of 78. She spent her remaining years in Battle Creek, Michigan, where she died in 1883.

FURTHER RESOURCES
Books

Jacobs, Harriet. *Incidents in the Life of a Slave Girl*. Mineola, N.Y.: Dover Publications, 2001.

Truth, Sojourner. *The Narrative of Sojourner Truth*. Mineola, N.Y.: Dover Publications, 1997.

Web sites

NPR.org. "Ruby Dee Gives Voice to Sojourner Truth." <http://www.npr.org/templates/story/story.php?storyId=4492096> (accessed February 5, 2006).

Breastfeeding Manual for Slaves

Manual excerpt

By: James Hammond

Date: 1857

Source: Hammond, James. "Plantation Manual." James Henry Hammond Papers (container 43). Manuscript Division, Library of Congress, 1857–58.

About the Author: James Hammond was a plantation owner and United States Senator, representing the state of South Carolina from 1857 to 1860.

INTRODUCTION

In writing about African slave women in the antebellum south in the United States, researchers and historians often examine such issues as manual labor, rape by the plantation master and other white authority figures, attempts by mothers to keep their children from being sold, differences between female field hands and household slaves, and pregnancy, childbirth, and slave conditions.

Discussions of African slave women as wet nurses are also part of the scholarship on this time period. Slave women, across historical periods and regions, often acted as wet nurses—women who breastfeed the children of other mothers for money or as part of a slave's labor. From ancient Greece to imperial Rome to modern day America, which puts a scientific spin on wet nurses with the creation of human milk banks—in which breast milk donors give their pumped milk to banks for use by premature babies in hospitals—wet nursing has played a strong role in infant growth and development.

In the pre-Civil War south, African female slaves acted as wet nurses for the white owner's children as well as the children of fellow slaves for cultural as well as practical reasons; older female slaves often acted as wet nurses to the children of younger slaves, freeing the young mother for labor in the fields. From the owner's standpoint, this was a wise use of labor sources, while keeping the infant, a future source of labor, alive and healthy.

In the manual entry below, James Hammond, the owner of plantations outside of Savannah, Georgia and a United States Senator who represented the state of South Carolina, documents his rules for slaves and the issue of breastfeeding. He outlines a series of breastfeeding policies, regulating the amount of time a nursing slave mother could spend breastfeeding, and dictating a weaning schedule. His discussion of pregnant, nursing, and old and infirm women slaves displays his view of the roles and value of slave women in his household.

PRIMARY SOURCE

BREASTFEEDING MANUAL FOR SLAVES

Sucklers

Sucklers are not required to leave their houses until sun-rise, when they leave their children at the children's house before going to field. The period of suckling is 12 months. Their work lies always within 1/2 mile of the quarter. They are required to be cool before commencing to suckle—to wait 15 minutes, at least, in summer, after reaching the children's house before nursing. It is the duty of the nurse to see that none are heated when nursing, as well as of the overseer and his wife occasionally to do so. They are allowed 45 minutes at each nursing to be with their children. They return 3 times a day until their infants are three months old—in the middle of the forenoon, at noon, in the middle of the afternoon; 'til the 12th month but twice a day, milking at noon during the twelfth month at noon only. On weaning, the child is removed entirely from its mother for two weeks, and placed in charge of some careful woman without a child during which time the mother is not to nurse it at all.

Remarks: the amount of work done by a suckler is about 3/5 of that done by a full hand, a little increased toward the last.

Old and Infirm

Those, who from age infirmities are unable to keep up with the prime hands are put in the sucklers gang.

Pregnant

Pregnant women at 5 months are put in the suckler's gang. No plowing or lifting must be required of them. Sucklers, old and infirm and pregnant receive the same allowances as full work hands.

SIGNIFICANCE

Hammond's manual for slaves grants female slaves work breaks for breastfeeding on an average of every three to four hours, with a fifteen minute rest, then a forty-five minute nursing session, far in excess of breaks provided by most modern corporations for female employees who breastfeed. The breaks Hammond provided allowed for slave infants to survive, though he could have required that wet nurses, and not the mothers, nurse the children. He makes no mention in his diary of reasons for eschewing wet nurses for slave children.

At the same time, Hammond provided full rations to "sucklers" in spite of the fact that they provided approximately sixty percent of the work of a non-suckling mother. Hammond's benevolence toward his slaves, compared to other masters, was progressive. In a speech before the U.S. Senate, Hammond noted that "In all social systems there must be a class to do the menial duties, to perform the drudgery of life. That is, a class requiring but a low order of intellect and but little skill. Its requisites are vigor, docility, fidelity." Hammond, like many owners, viewed African slaves as child-like and in need of protection. At the same time, Hammond never pulled away from harsh punishment of slaves who disobeyed, but his "sucklers" manual sets him apart in his treatment of female slaves as mothers by providing them with time to nurture and breastfeed their infants.

Nursing to the age of one and beyond, in a time before artificial baby milk, provided babies with nutritionally complete food and with liquids that were filtered through the mother's body, protecting the infant

A group of slave women and children in the Southern United States during the mid 19th Century. PHOTO BY HULTON ARCHIVE/GETTY IMAGES

or toddler from disease. Therefore, James Hammond's approach focused on infant survival; slave children were an investment, and the more children who survived the first year of life at a time when infant mortality rates for slave children neared fifty percent, the more future slaves Hammond could cultivate.

As women in the Western world strive for breastfeeding rights that include breaks from work patterned after the three to four hour interval suggested for optimal milk supply, Hammond's manual provokes questions about how breastfeeding is valued in modern-day culture in which artificial baby milk is widely available, while at the same time public health campaigns designed to reduce infant mortality and morbidity promote breastfeeding as the optimal form of infant nutrition.

FURTHER RESOURCES

Books

Burton, Annie L. *Women's Slave Narratives*. Mineola, N.Y.: Dover Books, 2006.

Golden, Janet. *A Social History of Wet Nursing in America: From Breast to Bottle*. Cambridge, U.K.: Cambridge University Press, 1996.

Stuart-Macadam, P., and K. Dettwyler. *Breastfeeding: Biocultural Perspectives*. New York: Haworth Books, 1995.

Web sites

La Leche League <http://www.lalecheleague.org/NB/ NBpublic.html> (accessed March 7, 2006).

A Lay Sermon by a Young Lady

Speech

By: Rachel "Ray" Frank

Date: 1890

Source: Frank, Rachel. "A Lay Sermon by a Young Lady." *American Hebrew*. (October 1890).

About the Author: Rachel "Ray" Frank was born in San Francisco in 1861. She taught public school in Nevada before moving to Oakland, California, to teach Sabbath School (classes on Jewish religion and history). After the congregation's rabbi and school's superintendent resigned Frank became the school's principal. In addition to teaching, she also worked as a journalist throughout the Northwest. In 1890, Frank addressed a congregation in Spokane Falls, Washington, during the High Holy Days. Her sermon made her a sought-after orator and preacher; newspapers dubbed her "the maiden in the temple" and "girl rabbi of the golden West."

INTRODUCTION

Traveling through the American Northwest as a journalist in 1890, Rachel "Ray" Frank reached Spokane Falls, Washington, during the Jewish High Holy Days (the ten days between Rosh Hashana and Yom Kippur). Because of ongoing strife between Orthodox and Reform Jews, she learned, the town had no synagogue. Voicing her dismay at such a state of disunity, she agreed to address the community. In doing so, she became the first Jewish woman to preach in the United States. The Spokane community asked her to stay and continue to speak throughout the High Holy Days. She soon became a preacher and lecturer to diverse audiences throughout the country and continued her public speaking role for the next decade.

Frank's oratory challenged the role of women in traditional Judaism, which offered few leadership roles to women during this period. Women could not read from the *Torah* and were segregated from men when attending synagogue. During this period, however, some American Jews had begun to reform these traditions, introducing mixed-sex choirs and family pews, which helped increase the presence of women within Jewish communities.

At the same time, the role of women in society was beginning to shift. The American West, which lacked the social structure of the Eastern states, gave women more opportunities. In 1890, the same year as Frank's sermon, Wyoming joined the Union as the first state to grant full suffrage to women. Colorado, Utah, and Idaho followed soon afterward. As a result, the frontier states symbolized opportunities for women and political equality.

Although Jewish communities in the West lacked the established institutions and communities of the East, the very fact that Frank spoke from the pulpit was unusual. As she later noted, "I know that it is unusual, and that in the history of our people no woman except Deborah spoke in the synagogue, yet the experience did not seem strange."

Frank spoke wherever she traveled along the Pacific coast, covering such diverse topic as culture, history, and art. She spoke at B'nai B'rith lodges as well as women's groups and synagogues, and even officiated at services. Some of her speeches, such as "The Prayers That are Heard," "Jewish Women in Fact and History," and "Nature—The Supreme Teacher" are infused with deep spirituality. Although her speeches challenged the role of women in religious leadership, she held to traditional views. In 1893 she wrote, "Nothing can replace the duty of the mother in the home." Upon her marriage in 1901, she retired from public life.

Frank gave this speech on the eve of Yom Kippur in 1890, speaking from the pulpit—the first Jewish woman in America ever to do so.

■ PRIMARY SOURCE

Ladies and Gentleman, and considering—this is Yom Kippur eve, I know you will permit me to say—friends, brothers, and sisters; for surely to-night is one of the most solemn and sacred periods in the lives of Israelites, for to-night, at least, we must be brother and sister in letter and spirit. My position this evening is a novel one. From time immemorial the Jewish woman has remained in the background of history, quite content to let the fathers and brothers be the principals in a picture wherein she shone only by a reflected light. And it is well that it has been so; for while she has let the stronger ones do battle for her throughout centuries of darkness and opposition, she has gathered strength and courage to come forward in an age of progressive enlightenment and do battle for herself if necessary, or prove by being a noble helpmeet how truly she appreciates the love which shielded her past.

I can scarcely tell you how much I feel the honor you have this evening conferred upon me in asking me to address you. For a woman to be at any time asked to give counsel to my people would be a mark of esteem; but on this night of nights, on Yom Kippur eve, to be requested to talk to you, to advise you, to think that perhaps I am to-night the one Jewish woman in the world, mayhap the first since the time of the prophets to be called on to speak to such an audience as I now see before me, is indeed a great honor, an event in my life which I can never forget.

The time is short, and the story have to tell a long one; I most therefore do as a young friend of mine did who was once called upon for a narrative—that is—"begin in the middle."

I have been requested to speak to you concerning the formation of a permanent congregation. On Rosh Hashana I was surprised to find such a large number of you assembled here for worship, and at that time the idea of a *permanent congregation* first occurred to me. Mentioning the matter to some of the prominent Jewish gentleman of Spokane, I was informed that the number of Hebrews and their financial standing was sufficient to warrant an established congregation. "Then," said I, "how is it you are content to go on this way having neither *schule* nor a Sabbath School? Do you think you are doing right towards yourselves, towards your children who are growing up without a creed of any kind, a most dangerous thing for society and a most ungrateful way of paying tribute to God." I was answered that such a difference of opinion existed among you, so many were prejudiced against reform, the remainder stubborn for orthodoxy, that it would be hopeless task to organize a permanent congregation. Think of it, ye Israelites, the "*chosen of the earth,*" so divided as to how you will worship Jehovah that ye forget to worship at all! You who have received divine protection through centuries of danger and oppression, you whom the prophets say are to survive for the grandest destiny of man, you to whom has been vouchsafed every blessing—because you cannot agree as how you will do this or that, how you will say *thank you, Almighty,* therefore you do not say it at all. O, you intend saying it all in good time! There maybe be repentance at the eleventh hour, but who can say which hour may not be the eleventh one? This is the time for action—*right now,* and our solemn Yom Kippur is the right now of our existence.

Now is a most excellent time for you to consider the question. It is the time for you to decide whether you will effect a permanent organization or whether you will continue to go on and hold only one or two services a year. There are here, I know, certain disagreements as to the form of worship, whether we should cling to the old orthodox style or take up the reform that has gradually been instituted in the Jewish church. This is a progressive age, and some of the customs of two or three thousand years ago will not do for to-day, and at the same time many customs which were good then are just as good now, and can be just as appropriately used. It would be well for you to throw aside all little disagreements and unite in the one cause—that of upholding the creed of our religion. Do not persuade yourself that coming to schule once or twice a year, or fasting for twenty-four hours, will make you a good Jew. Do not comfort yourself with the belief that God will, at the eleventh hour, accept your tithe, which you pay because you must. For three hundred and sixty-three days you are content to go your own way, doing as you please, piling up the coin of the United States, and congratulating yourself that your credit is good. You give never a thought to the One from whom all blessings come until reminded that Rosh Hashanah is here and Yom Kippur will follow. O, the growls that come because the store must remain closed two days; perhaps you refuse to close it at all! O, the shameful ungrateful sneers and remarks by the *too reformed to be good ones!* Friends, you are making a mistake. For such as I have mentioned it would be better to keep the store open—the sin would not be so great.

Religion is not compulsory. God wants not grudgingly that which you give; keep it, you cannot be poorer that you are.

Whatever you do for religion, or whatever you give, must be voluntary and sincere. Coming here because your neighbor does is not religion; neither is it religion to give certain amount because some one else has done the same. True religion is true repentance for our many sins and mistakes.

I have before me one of the most intelligent audiences of my people I have ever addressed. It would make the best congregation on the Pacific Coast. I can tell by your faces, and the little that I have conversed with you. You have always said that in union there is strength, therefore it is necessary that you should unite, giving help to each other through the creed you all believe in. Drop all dissension about whether you should take off your hats during the service and other unimportant ceremonials, and join hands in one glorious cause. We are all Israelites, and anxious to help one another. Look up to our creed and live up to it. It is not necessary to build a magnificent synagogue at once; that can be done in time. The grandest temples we have ever had or the world has ever known were those which had the blue sky for a roof, and the grandest psalms ever sung were those rendered under the blue vaults of heaven.

It is absolutely necessary for a man to be something. A cipher or a million of ciphers all count naught. One must have fixed value or be looked upon as a nothing. This holds as true in religion as in the other things. Your neighbors of various creeds and denominations would as soon think of avowing themselves cannibals as of disavowing their religion. They have no respect for the man who is nothing; neither do they trust him. If you would stand well in the eye of the community, uphold your faith and teach your children the glory of perpetuating a grand old creed.

Form yourselves into a permanent congregation as soon as possible, and organize a Sabbath school. Unless one is established soon your children will grow up without any creed at all. One must believe in something, and one must have faith in something or become a menace to society. Keep one day holy, and teach your children to do the same. It isn't good for you to do as you are doing. We are no longer a nation of people, although we are often spoken as such. We have no ruler, but are simply citizens of the country we live in. We are loyal to the civil rule that governs us, and we should be loyal to the religious rule that we all bow to.

Friends, I thank you for your patience with which you have listened to me, and in the name of all we Hebrews hold most dear, I ask you to be patient with each other. Drop all personal feeling in this matter, and meet each other half way over your differences; give each other a hearty handshake for the sake of the cause, and I prophesy Heaven will crown your efforts with peace and prosperity.

From to-night on *resolve to be something.*

SIGNIFICANCE

Frank took advantage of the opportunities afforded by the lack of societal constraints in the West to confront the traditional role of women in Judaism, openly challenging conventions within its leadership. Her actions broke barriers not only for Jewish women, but for other women as well. During this time, women's public speech was severely restricted. In legal matters, women could not sue, stand as witness, or enter into contracts. Following in the paths of other women orators of the time, such as Susan B. Anthony, Frank helped propel women into leadership within the religious and political communities.

FURTHER RESOURCES

Periodicals

Nadell, Pamela S. "Opening the Blue of Heaven to Us. Reading Anew the Pioneers of Women's Ordination." *Nashim.* (April 1, 2005) 88.

Web sites

Jewish Women 's Archive. "Exhibit: Women of Valor—Ray Frank." <http://www.jwa.org/exhibits/wov/frank> (accessed March 13, 2006).

We Two Boys Together Clinging

Portraits of Masculinity

Poem

By: Walt Whitman

Date: 1855

Source: Whitman, Walt. "We Two Boys Together Clinging." in *Leaves of Grass*, 1855.

About the Author: Walt Whitman (1819–1892) born on Long Island, New York was a quintessential American poet, known for such poems as "Oh Captain, My Captain" (1866), on the subject of Abraham Lincoln. His most famous work is *Leaves of Grass*, a book that originally consisted of twelve poems, and after many editions, eventually included 293 poems. Whitman was also a skilled journalist and essayist.

INTRODUCTION

Walt Whitman's poem "We Two Boys Together Clinging" is often identified as a poem of homosexual

Walt Whitman. THE LIBRARY OF CONGRESS.

love, a label breeched from its title and the history of its author. Other scholars insist the poem represents a unique concept of the brotherhood of two young men, forged by the experiences of war. In either interpretation, the poem paints a portrait of masculinity through its setting of soldiering during the Civil War (1861–1865). Whitman's poetry, including "We Two Boys Together Clinging", was written before the "unspoken love" of homosexuality had a name to be spoken of. The context of the poem recalls the camaraderie of men through the challenges and ruggedness of this American war. Enveloping the romance of soldiering, the lines of the poem easily echo the ancient wars of the Romans as much as modern and contemporary wars through which notions of pride, glory, and masculinity are still associated. Whitman's portrayal of this intense companionship developed from "excursions making" and "sailing, soldiering, thieving, threatening…" often leaves the reader with notions of survival, learned (or inherited) skill, manipulating the enemy, strength of body and intelligence, and the pursuit of adventure—all aspects society traditionally perceive as masculine.

PRIMARY SOURCE

WE two boys together clinging,
One the other never leaving,
Up and down the roads going, North and South excursions making,
Power enjoying, elbows stretching, fingers clutching,
Arm'd and fearless, eating, drinking, sleeping, loving.
No law less than ourselves owning, sailing, soldiering, thieving,
threatening,
Misers, menials, priests alarming, air breathing, water drinking, on
the turf or the sea-beach dancing,
Cities wrenching, ease scorning, statutes mocking, feebleness
chasing,
Fulfilling our foray.

SIGNIFICANCE

Masculinity throughout literature's history has been portrayed in similar respects to Whitman's poem. For instance, Stephen Crane's Civil War novel *The Red Badge of Courage* uses its title to convey the idea of a wound made during battle to be part of the glory and honor of war. The main character, Henry Fleming, does not find peace within himself until he has "rid himself of the red sickness of battle." Towards the conclusion of Crane's story, Henry reflects on his abandonment of a fellow "tattered soldier," but can rest his conscience now that he has been a full participant in fighting the enemy:

> With this conviction came a store of assurance. He felt a quiet manhood, nonassertive but of sturdy and strong blood. He knew that he would no more quail before his guides wherever they should point. He had been to touch the great death, and found that, after all, it was but the great death. He was a man.

Masculinity is celebrated through trial and error in this book—discovering what makes one "a man" after realizing one's cowardice. Because he has found his inner masculinity, he can reap the fruits of his glory:

> He had been an animal blistered and sweating in the heat and pain of war. He turned now with a lover's thirst to images of tranquil skies, fresh meadows, cool brooks—an existence of soft and eternal peace. This portrait of natural rewards is reminiscent of those described by Whitman: "air breathing, water drinking, on the turf or the sea-beach dancing;" although simple, these life aspects are seen in a new light after playing on the edge of death. *The Red Badge of Courage* leaves the reader

The cover of American poet Walt Whitman's own copy of the first edition of his 1855 collection, *Leaves of Grass.* PHOTO BY HULTON ARCHIVE/GETTY IMAGES

the dance did not arouse lecherous desires. Nudity, partial or complete, is not in itself lewd.'"

A high New York State court, peering through a knothole in a legal fence, decided fortnight ago that Nudist Vincent Burke was not guilty of "indecent exposure and openly outraging public decency" when he gave a nudist party in an uptown Manhattan gymnasium. Believing that the court approved the contention of all high-minded nudists that their cult is a matter of Health, Mr. Burke put his head through the legal knothole and crowed: "The court has declared Nudism is legal in New York State and inasmuch as the laws in all the other States are patterned closely after the New York State law, this decision will undoubtedly serve as a model and precedent for the rest of the States"

The crowing reached the alert ears of Alfred Emanuel Smith on the 32nd floor of the Empire State Building. As chairman of the advisory committee of the Legion of Decency which is making cinema companies toe the mark, Mr. Smith called for a copy of the law Mr. Burke considered so exemplary. It read: "A person who willfully and lewdly exposes his person, or the private parts thereof, in any public place or in any other place where others are present, or procures another so to expose himself is guilty of a misdemeanor."

Exclaimed pious Catholic Smith: "The present penal law is not adequate to prevent public mingling and exhibitions of naked men and women. If such action is not an offense against public decency, this league will ask the Legislature to speedily remedy this defect in the law and make it so. It seems to us inconsistent to take a stand for decency on the screen and ignore this latest challenge to the enforcement of decency in reality, We cannot overlook indecency in the substance while condemning it in the shadow."

Thereupon the four-time Governor of New York proposed a new law which he expected the New York Legislature to pass and other State Legislatures to imitate. The Smith proposal: "A person who in any place willfully exposes his person...in the presence of two or more persons of the opposite sex whose persons...are similarly exposed, or who aids or abets any such act, or who procures another so to expose his person...or who as owner, manager, lessee, director, promoter or agent, or in any other capacity, hires, leases or permits the land, building or premises of which he is the owner, lessee or tenant, or over which he has control, to be used for any such purposes, is guilty of a misdemeanor."

At this moment the Rev. Dr. Ilsley Boone, onetime minister of a Dutch Reformed church at Oakland, N. J. stepped forward. Dr. Boone is executive secretary of the International Nudist Conference which publishes an illustrated "health" magazine called The Nudist.*

While the ear of the nation was attuned to Nudism, Dr. Boone tried to fill it with rebuttal against Mr. Smith and with arguments for Nudism. Cried he: "There is more social danger to our young folks in a quart of gin than in three miles of State-censored movie film. There is a striking inconsistency between the removal of prohibition from liquor [for which Mr. Smith fought] and the placing of prohibition upon a movement which by actual results, has everywhere been hailed as a blessing and in no instances has been cited as the source of immorality or illicit relations, or disruptive of conjugal happiness."

In what amounted to a notably bold editorial in the lay press, the New York Herald Tribune declared: "In this controversy it is much easier to go part way with Dr. Boone than it is to go anywhere at all with the League of Decency....The exhibitionists among these folk who would go through the world as they came into it are a trifling minority.... All testimony goes to show that the great majority of these latter-day Edenites take their antics in the altogether solemnly, if not sadly....All non-nudist reporters on the life at a nudist camp find it insufferably dull. They are diverted by nothing about it so much as the quiet but firm sway of the proprieties over groups that affect to live like nymphs and fauns. The truth of the matter seems to be that the average nudist is a puritan....He notes with triumph that he experiences no wicked reactions to visions that are allegedly wicked. This indulgence may seem thoroughly absurd; but when the League of Decency sets out to have it pronounced immoral, is it not simply compounding an absurdity?"

*Circulation, 50,000. Last week buyers of Dr. Boone's The Nudist from Manhattan newsstands were obliged to secure the February issue clandestinely. Charged with obscenity, the publishers had to limit circulation until New York courts decide whether The Nudist's modestly retouched pictures of naked men, women and children violate the law. Complained Dr. Boone last week: "We might tone down the illustrations. We do not desire to break the law. But we feel we should have the right and the privilege to publish unless it can be proved that Nudism is provocative of immorality."

SIGNIFICANCE

The conflict that exists between the rights of nudists to practice their lifestyle and the general public to be removed from social behavior they view as immoral or disrespectful lies at the center of the debates over privacy and freedom of expression. While in some parts of the world little room exists for the types of expression like that practiced by nudists, in Western democracies including the United States, laws promoting freedoms of speech and expression have served to

Approximately 150 models pose nude for a photo shoot by artist Spencer Tunick, in Manhattan on June 4, 2000. Tunick's right to conduct the shoot was challenged by city officials but he ultimately prevailed in court. AP IMAGES

defend the rights of nudists. This article, written in 1935 at a time when public standards were more conservative than they are today, demonstrates that even when society was largely dedicated to preserving moral codes of conduct, the legal systems of the United States protected the rights of groups like nudists.

At the center of the controversy over nudism, is that unlike pornography, prostitution and strip clubs, nudism is not driven by a desire to be lewd or sexual. Even while certain acts of sexual exhibitionism, including pornography have been sanctioned as legal in some areas, they have generally been associated with deviancy and lawlessness, something that has not been attached to nudism, as this article demonstrates. Adherents of the lifestyle claim it as a personal choice not to be ashamed of their bodies and avoid connecting the lives they lead with sexuality. It is the acceptance of this position that stands behind the judgments of courts in the United States that the behavior is acceptable in private locations.

This article largely presents nudists as a group that is interested in protecting their freedoms of privacy as opposed to criminals who are threatening to demoralize society. It suggests that nudism is a personal choice that is practiced by a small fraction of the society and represents little danger in a moral sense but is rather a fringe group.

Even as decades later the justice system has continued to protect the rights of nudists to practice their lifestyles in certain specified locations, the movement has little recognition in broader society and continues to be portrayed, as it was in 1935, as eccentric but mostly harmless. This article is most significant for displaying that even decades ago when social norms were far more opposed to perceived acts of lewdness and immorality, nudism was viewed as a legitimate form of expression when practiced in private. In today's world where liberal approaches have been attached to these types of issues, nudism, while an eccentric lifestyle, would be allowed to continue to be practiced.

FURTHER RESOURCES

Books

Selth, Jefferson P. *Alternative Lifestyles: A Guide to Research Collections on Intentional Communities, Nudism, and Sexual Freedom.* Wesport, Conn.: Greenwood, 1985.

Web sites

National Geographic. ""The Skinny on Nudism in the U.S." <http://news.nationalgeographic.com/news/2004/07/0 721_040721_tvnude.html> (accessed March 1, 2006).

The Objects of Marriage

Book excerpt

About the Author: Havelock Ellis

Date: 1937

Source: Ellis, Havelock. "The Objects of Marriage" in *On Life and Sex: Essays of Love and Virtue*. New York: Garden City, 1937.

About the Author: Havelock Ellis (1859–1939) was an English physician, sexual psychologist, and social activist.

INTRODUCTION

While the definitions of marriage differ greatly between religions and societies, the institution of marriage is generally understood as one wherein two people, traditionally a man and a woman, enter into a contract to begin a family. In certain societies, mostly non-Western cultures, marriage can exist between a man and more than one woman, referred to as polygamy. In recent years, marriages between two people of the same gender, known as same-sex marriage, has become increasingly recognized in some areas of the world. The marriage contract has religious, legal and social ramifications and is perceived as a formal recognition of commitment between spouses.

Marriage in most modern cultures in Western society is entered into by the parties voluntarily. In other parts of the world, as was the case prior to modernity, marriages are arranged with little or no consultation with the spouses who will be entered into the contract. Throughout history, marriages in royal courts existed only between other members of royal dynasties and the choice of spouse was an issue of honor and thus required the choice of a respected spouse with the proper lineage. These strong traditions remain in many cultures, social arenas, and religions today. The concept of intermarriage, defined as a marriage between two different groups, whether religious, cultural, ethnic, or social, is seldom seen in cultures where marriage is arranged.

In Western culture, marriage is often preceded by a period of courtship where the parties can become acquainted with one another and decide whether marriage is appropriate. Most religions consider marriage to be a prerequisite for sexual intercourse between husband and wife, and extra-marital sexual relations by one of the parties in a marriage can be used as the grounds for divorce.

The widely accepted custom of exchanging wedding rings between the spouses finds its origins in biblical mandates requiring the exchange of items of value to consecrate a marriage. Even while alternative coupling arrangements in modern society have evolved, marriage remains the most popular form of social contract between two people for the purposes of building a life together within a new family.

PRIMARY SOURCE

WHAT are the legitimate objects of marriage? We know that many people seek to marry for ends that can scarcely be called legitimate, that men may marry to obtain a cheap domestic drudge or nurse, and that women may marry to be kept when they are tired of keeping themselves. These objects in marriage may or may not be moral, but in any case they are scarcely its legitimate ends. We are here concerned to ascertain those ends of marriage which are legitimate when we take the highest ground as moral and civilized men and women living in an advanced state of society and seeking, if we can, to advance that state of society still further.

The primary end of marriage is to beget and bear offspring, and to rear them until they are able to take care of themselves. On that basis Man is at one with all the mammals and most of the birds. If, indeed, we disregard the originally less essential part of this end—that is to say, the care and tending of the young—this end of marriage is not only the primary but usually the sole end of sexual intercourse in the whole mammal world. As a natural instinct, its achievement involves gratification and well-being, but this bait of gratification is merely a device of Nature's and not in itself an end having any useful function at the periods when conception is not possible.

This is clearly indicated by the fact that among animals, the female only experiences sexual desire at the season of impregnation, and that desire ceases as soon as impregnation takes place, though this is only in a few species true of the male, obviously because, if his sexual desire and aptitude were confined to so brief a period, the chances of the female meeting the right male at the right moment would be too seriously diminished; so that the attentive and inquisitive attitude towards the female by the male animal—which we may often think we see still traceable in the human species—is not the outcome of lustfulness for personal gratification ("wantonly to satisfy carnal lusts and appetites like brute beasts," as the *Anglican Prayer Book* incorrectly puts it) but implanted by Nature for the benefit of the female and the attainment of the primary object of procreation. This primary object we may term the animal end of marriage.

This object remains not only the primary but even the sole end of marriage among the lower races of mankind generally. The erotic idea, in its deeper sense, that is to say the element of love, arose very slowly in mankind. It is found, it is true, among some lower races, and it appears that some tribes possess a word for the joy of love in a purely psychic sense. But even among European races the evolution was late. The Greek poets, except the latest, showed little recognition of love as an element of marriage. Theognis compared marriage with cattle-breeding. The Romans of the Republic took much the same view. Greeks and Romans alike regarded breeding as the one recognizable object of marriage; any other object was mere wantonness and had better, they thought, be carried on outside marriage. Religion, which preserves so many ancient and primitive conceptions of life, has consecrated this conception also, and Christianity—though, as I will point out later, it has tended to enlarge the conception—at the outset only offered the choice between celibacy on the one hand and on the other marriage for the production of offspring.

Yet, from an early period in human history, a secondary function of sexual intercourse had been slowly growing up to become one of the great objects of marriage. Among animals, it may be said, and even sometimes in man, the sexual impulse, when once aroused, makes but a short and swift circuit through the brain to reach its consummation. But as the brain and its faculties develop, powerfully aided indeed by the very difficulties of the sexual life, the impulse for sexual union has to traverse ever longer, slower, more painful paths, before it reaches, and sometimes it never reaches, its ultimate object. This means that sex gradually becomes intertwined with all the highest and subtlest human emotions and activities, with the refinements of social intercourse, with high adventure in every sphere, with art, with religion. The primitive animal instinct, having the sole end of procreation, becomes on its way to that end the inspiring stimulus to all those psychic energies which in civilization we count most precious. This function is thus, we see, a by-product. But, as we know, even in our human factories, the by-product is sometimes more valuable than the product. That is so as regards the functional products of human evolution. The hand was produced out of the animal forelimb with the primary end of grasping the things we materially need, but as a by-product the hand has developed the function of making and playing the piano and the violin, and that secondary functional by-product of the hand we account, even as measured by the rough test of money, more precious, however less materially necessary, than its primary function. It is, however, only in rare and gifted natures that transformed sexual energy becomes of supreme value for its own sake without ever attaining the normal physical outlet.

For the most part the by-product accompanies the product, throughout, thus adding a secondary, yet peculiarly sacred and specially human, object of marriage to its primary animal object. This may be termed the spiritual object of marriage.

By the term "spiritual" we are not to understand any mysterious and supernatural qualities. It is simply a convenient name, in distinction from animal, to cover all those higher mental and emotional processes which in human evolution are ever gaining greater power. It is needless to enumerate the constituents of this spiritual end of sexual intercourse, for everyone is entitled to enumerate them differently and in different order. They include not only all that makes love a gracious and beautiful erotic art, but the whole element of pleasure in so far as pleasure is more than a mere animal gratification. Our ancient ascetic traditions often make us blind to the meaning of pleasure. We see only its possibilities of evil and not its mightiness for good. We forget that, as Romain Rolland says, "Joy is as holy as Pain."' No one has insisted so much on the supreme importance of the element of pleasure in the spiritual ends of sex as James Hinton. Rightly used, he declares, Pleasure is "the Child of God," to be recognized as a "mighty storehouse of force,"' and he pointed out the significant fact that in the course of human progress its importance increases rather than diminishes. While it is perfectly true that sexual energy may be in large degree arrested, and transformed into intellectual and moral forms, yet it is also true that pleasure itself, and above all, sexual pleasure, wisely used and not abused, may prove the stimulus and liberator of our finest and most exalted activities. It is largely this remarkable function of sexual pleasure which is decisive in settling the argument of those who claim that continence is the only alternative to the animal end of marriage. That argument ignores the liberating and harmonizing influences, giving wholesome balance and sanity to the whole organism, imparted by a sexual union which is the outcome of the psychic as well as physical needs. There is, further, in the attainment of the spiritual end of marriage, much more than the benefit of each individual separately. There is, that is to say, the effect on the union itself. For through harmonious sex relationships a deeper spiritual unity is reached than can possibly be derived from continence in or out of marriage, and the marriage association becomes an apter instrument in the service of the world. Apart from any sexual craving, the complete spiritual contact of two persons who love each other can only be attained through some act of rare intimacy. No act can be quite so intimate as the sexual embrace.

Betty Grable and Jackie Coogan cut their wedding cake in Los Angeles on November 20, 1937. AP IMAGES

SIGNIFICANCE

Within the institution of marriage, the act of sexual intercourse is considered as the ultimate display of affection and intimacy and has therefore been an act which within traditional and religious circles is reserved for marriage. As this excerpt displays, sex is not simply an act that takes place during marriage, but is rather at the center of what two humans being married is all about. While sex is in itself a physical act driven by hormonal desires and physical attraction, it is directly linked to emotional and spiritual issues including love, which acts as a central factor in bringing people together in marriage.

This excerpt identifies that sex in marriage has two principle roles, the functional and the spiritual. From the functional perspective, it achieves the goal for which the institution of marriage exists, to allow for procreation. On a spiritual level, the act of sex produces emotions of love that further fosters attraction between spouses and encourages marriages to succeed. It is this distinction whereby humans are able to transmit the physicality of sex to the emotions of love that differentiates people from all other living things that reproduce sexually.

Sexuality need not be recognized as something that is only linked to eroticism and attractions between people. Rather, as this excerpt contends, sex has been proven to have an impact upon human emotions that enable the person to fully appreciate many of the interactions that people deal with on a daily basis, including art and religion.

This excerpt is most significant because it argues that sex is a prerequisite for a healthy life and marriage in the sense that some degree of sex is necessary to enable the type of love that fosters in successful marriages. Sex in the context of marriage therefore is an element that is necessary for the development of the union that defines the institution of marriage. Without sex in a marriage, it should be assumed it would be difficult if not impossible to preserve a sense of intimate unity that often exists between spouses.

While the excerpt reflects a traditional view in it's depiction of marriage in the 1930s, the reality of today's objects of marriage are more varied. Some modern couples choose not to have children, and families in developed countries have fewer children than in the 1930s. While China has an official one-child policy, married couples in other countries including Spain, Italy, and the Czech Republic have, on average, only one child, thus de-emphasizing the object of marriage as mainly to bear and raise children. Americans are also waiting longer to marry and start their families than young people in the 1930s. Whereas the median age for a bride in 1930s America was barely twenty years old, by 2006, the average age for a woman marrying for the first time had risen to 25 years.

FURTHER RESOURCES
Books

Coontz, Stephanie. *Marriage, a History: From Obedience to Intimacy, or How Love Conquered Marriage.* New York, N.Y.: Viking, 2005.

LaHaye, Beverly and Tim LaHaye. *The Act of Marriage: The Beauty of Sexual Love.* Grand Rapids, Mich.: Zondervan, 1998.

Feminine Sports Reel

Newspaper article

By: Bobbie Rosenfeld

Date: January 10, 1941

Source: *Jewish Women's Archive.* "Resource Information for Feminine Sports Reel." <http://www.jwa.org/archive/jsp/presInfo.jsp?resID=24> (accessed March 1, 2006).

About the Author: Fanny "Bobbie" Rosenfeld (1903-1969) was a pioneer in female athletics—a dominant force in a number of sports at a time when the concept of organized, high-level competition in women's sport was a novelty. Born in what is now the Ukraine in 1903, as a child Rosenfeld immigrated to Canada with her family. In the early 1920s, Rosenfeld established herself as a talented, all-around athlete, excelling in team sports such as basketball, ice hockey, and softball, while winning championships in individual pursuits

such as tennis and speed skating. Rosenfeld added track and field to her athletic repertoire, first competing as a sprinter in events in Toronto, and she soon gained acclaim as the fastest female sprinter in Canada. At the 1928 Summer Olympics, the first games to sanction female athletics competition, Rosenfeld won both a gold medal with the Canadian team in the 4 × 100 m relay, and a silver medal in the 100 m sprint event. Arthritis ended Rosenfeld's competitive sports career in 1933. From 1937 to 1957, she wrote a regular newspaper column for the Toronto *Globe and Mail* entitled "Feminine Sports Reel," through which Rosenfeld shared with her readership her views concerning the world of sports at large. Rosenfeld was voted Canada's Female Athlete of the Half Century in 1950, and she also was posthumously inducted into the International Jewish Sports Hall of Fame.

INTRODUCTION

The 1928 Summer Olympic Games was the first great watershed in the modern history of female athletics. With a limited number of track and field events the primary focus of female competition, these Games represented the first time that women were welcomed as athletes into the Summer Olympics. Prior to 1928, no female sports of any kind occupied a place of prominence within any of the world's sports cultures. In North America, female athletes were not encouraged to participate in sport; where women did form teams or establish leagues, the public and prevailing media sentiment was to regard such sports as a novelty act.

The 1928 Olympics made a star of Bobbie Rosenfeld, whose double medal performance at the Games was a natural extension of the superb athletic talents that she exhibited over a range of sports throughout her adult life. However, the brief period in the international spotlight that followed the 1928 Olympics did not suddenly elevate women's sports to a position of equality with male athletic pursuits. With the exception of individual competitors such as figure skater Sonja Henie (1912–1969) and tennis player Althea Gibson (1927–2003) garnering a measure of media attention, female track and field competitors remained the most significant and the most visible international example of female athletes until the 1970s.

The Toronto of 1941 was not a city that encouraged female sports. "Toronto the Good" was the quintessential WASP (white, Anglo-Saxon, Protestant) haven, with an overwhelming air of decorum and sobriety. In 1941, Toronto had its notorious "blue laws," which prohibited sports of any kind being played on Sunday. Ice hockey, baseball, and football

Hazel Wightman talks to members of the women's American Wightman Cup team, practicing in England on June 8, 1932. The players will participate in the ladies international tennis challenge. They are, from left to right, Mrs. Fabian, Dorothy Bundy, Helen Wills, Alice Marble, and Helen Jacobs. AP IMAGES

were the prominent sports, and there was very little room on either the playing fields or within the public consciousness for female athletes of any kind. Thirteen years after her Olympic triumphs, Bobbie Rosenfeld and her views concerning athletic equality remained decidedly outside the mainstream.

The Feminine Sports Reel of January 1941 was published against a societal backdrop in which there were few, if any, facilities dedicated to female sports. There were no organizations or administrative structures to assist female athletes. To place the attitudes of a superlative athlete such as Bobbie Rosenfeld in perspective, the National Collegiate Athletic Association (NCAA), the governing body of American college athletics and the largest such organization in the world, did not formally sanction women's athletic championships until 1980. The Boston Marathon did not have

a female participant until 1967 (and then only through the subterfuge of Kathryn Switzer, who entered the race using a man's name); the first women's Olympic marathon competition took place in Los Angeles in 1984, fifty-six years after the triumphs of Bobbie Rosenfeld and the first female Summer Olympians.

PRIMARY SOURCE

One of those periodic diatribes against Eve has burst into print again. Its author is Jack Miley, chivalrous two-fisted scribbler with the *New York Post,* who once earned himself a black eye from the fist of the Dizzy Dean in an encounter in Florida. It's the same old malarkey flavoring most all misogynistic articles levelled at women athletes. Just in case you're not familiar with the trend of thought, we print typical paragraphs: "A female flushed face over a hot stove is not only prettier but more practical than a purple face produced by puffing and panting from participation in some masculine sport for which nature never intended her." "Women's place is in the home, and I never saw a girl yet who didn't look a sight better with a frying pan than a tennis racquet." And more about girl athletes' legs looking like turkey gobblers' and the fact that girls in sport never get any place.

Why these gentleman of the press insist on taking a few cobwebby tales about women competitors, giving them new twists and endowing them with universality and delivering them as proof that women are physically, mentally and morally unfit to traverse the field of sport with their boy scout brothers beats us. What is more beautiful in sport than this: Colored ice surface, a blazing beam light spotlighting the whirling figure of a human doll, spinning in rhythmic perfection, effortless, without strain, a symphony of grace. What is more beautiful in sport than a graceful figure poised atop a high diving board, leaning forward, arms arched, and floating off into space, coming down to the water like a great sea bird, a thing of infinite grace, striking smoothly, without a splash, and streaking into the depths, leaving hardly a ripple? Or watching Alice Marble gliding over tennis courts, or the sight of some graceful girl golfer swing with precise rhythm and a certain power on a teed-up ball.

Having offered, for the umpteenth time, our defense of women athletes, to Jack Miley we say: "Aw nerts!" (This is for the want of something more expressive.)

SIGNIFICANCE

The comments of Jack Miley that so stirred Bobbie Rosenfeld in 1941 sound hopelessly old fashioned to the modern ear. The image of the harried housewife toiling over a hot stove has been replaced variously by the modern "Super Mom", or more accurately, by the working mother who battles to balance the obligations of career, home, and family. The dynamics of the modern North American family make female sports participation a difficult proposition for many adult women.

There is an irony in the Rosenfeld argument that is the product of war, not sport. Women's sport may have been either scorned or ignored by the general population, but, in January 1941, Canada was at war with Germany, a worldwide conflict in which the United States would be joined less than one year later. Until 1945, North American women would take employment by the tens of thousands in the munitions factories and arms manufacturing industries, work of tremendous societal importance that was previously as secure a male preserve as the sports fields. Women

demonstrated through the war effort that they were entirely capable of driving rivets into the frame of an aircraft and other essential work; as in the business world, women have never attained equality in either compensation or management representation in the over sixty years since the end of World War II; women similarly continue to strive for athletic equality today. The proverbial "glass ceiling" is as evident in the public recognition of the accomplishments of female athletes as it is apparent in business.

The sports equality desired by Rosenfeld and other female athletes found its first legal manifestation in the 1972 passage of Title IX to the United States Civil Rights Act. On one level, Title IX has achieved much for female athletics in terms of greater participation; at the NCAA level alone, by 2006, over 825 percent more women played intercollegiate sports in the Unites States than in 1972.

The greater significance of the desire for equality in sport is whether there has been an accompanying increase in the ever ephemeral respect for the physical abilities of the female athlete. Bobbie Rosenfeld writes from the perspective of one who seeks an equality of respect for the relative abilities of women and men, not a comparison of their absolute levels of achievement. It is for this reason that Rosenfeld points to the sports of figure skating and diving to counter sports chauvinism—each sport the ultimate in subjective judgment, where the traditional attributes of grace and form are essential to competitive success. In 1941, these sports were the closest to male mainstream acceptance achieved by female athletic pursuits.

Rosenfeld's individual sport examples were also a product of the era. Tennis and golf were primarily the preserve of private clubs and were not popular pursuits of typical citizens in 1941. Golf entered the mainstream of North American and then world sports in the 1960s, in part due to dominant professionals Arnold Palmer and Jack Nicklaus. However, while the Ladies Professional Golf Association has organized a professional tour for over fifty years, it has never captured the golf fan's imagination or the sponsors' check books to the same extent that the male PGA tour has.

The American war effort and the resulting mobilization of millions of servicemen after 1941 also prompted the formation of the first women's professional baseball league. The All American Girls Baseball League (AAGBBL), which operated from 1943 to 1954 and was popularized in the film *A League of Our Own*, was the first prominent exception to the exclusively male control of organized team sports in North America.

The title of the Rosenfeld column is also of significance. In modern parlance, the word "feminine" is synonymous with ladylike, soft, and womanly, images distinct from those associated with the word "female", the more clinical term that would no doubt headline the Rosenfeld column today.

FURTHER RESOURCES

Books

Dublin, Anne. *Bobbie Rosenfeld: The Olympian Who Could Do Everything.* Toronto: Second Story Books, 2004.

Web sites

International Jewish Sports Hall of Fame. "Fanny 'Bobbie' Rosenfeld." <http://www.jewishsports.net/BioPages/FannyRosenfeld.html> (March 1, 2006).

Sports in Canada. "Bobbie Rosenfeld." <http://www.histori.ca/sports/rosen.html> (March 1, 2006).

Cassandra

Essay

By: Florence Nightingale

Date: 1852

Source: Nightingale, Florence. *Cassandra: An Essay.* Old Westbury, NY: Feminist Press, 1979. Originally written in 1852.

About the Author: Florence Nightingale (1820–1910) the daughter of prosperous British parents, is the founder of modern nursing. Believing that she had a calling from God to become a nurse, she defied her family to pursue a nursing career. She became famous during the Crimean War for dramatically reducing the death rate in hospitals by eliminating filth and establishing order. After founding a nursing school in England, she spent the remainder of her life working to better nursing education.

INTRODUCTION

In the nineteenth century, the idea of separate spheres for men and women dictated that women should devote their lives entirely to the home and family. This ideology, enormously popular in industrialized nations, including Great Britain and the United States, dramatically restricted women's lives.

The public arena of work and politics was reserved for men only. The notion of a separate domestic realm for women prevented them from pursuing higher education, having a professional career, or participating in politics by voting or holding office. Distinctions between men and women were most noticeable in the privileged classes. While boys attended secondary schools, most middle- and upper-class girls were educated at home, where they were taught to be religious, obedient, and accomplished in music and languages. Women dressed for decorative effect in long, cumbersome skirts that restricted freedom of movement and wore long hair that required hours of brushing and styling.

Laws everywhere defined the subordination of women. Many countries followed the model of the French Napoleonic Code, which classified married women, children, the insane, and criminals as legally incompetent. In England, British common law upheld a husband's complete control over his wife.

Florence Nightingale chafed at these restrictions. An upper-middle-class woman of extraordinary intellectual gifts, her ambition to become a nurse was thwarted for many years by opposition from her parents and sister, who believed firmly that proper women simply did not work for a living. Nightingale's frustration was mirrored by other women of her class, who were trapped in an oppressive atmosphere that did not permit them to engage in fulfilling intellectual activity. As Nightingale angrily wrote, they were expected to fritter away their days doing needlework, reading, and taking drives in the country. To Nightingale, work was the means by which every individual could achieve self-fulfillment and serve God. Nightingale wrote *Cassandra* in 1852 but did not publish it in her lifetime.

■ PRIMARY SOURCE

Is discontent a privilege?

Women often try one branch of intellect after another in their youth, *e.g.* mathematics. But that, least of all, is compatible with the life of "society." It is impossible to follow up anything systematically. Women often long to enter some man's profession where they would find direction, competition (or rather opportunity of measuring the intellect with others), and, above all, time.

In those wise institutions, mixed as they are with many follies, which will last as long as the human race lasts, because they are adapted to the wants of the human race; those institutions which we call monasteries, and which, embracing much that is contrary to the

British hospital reformer and nurse Florence Nightingale at work in the Therapia Hospital. PHOTO BY RISCHGITZ/GETTY IMAGES

laws of nature, are yet better adapted to the union of the life of action and that of thought than any other mode of life with which we are acquainted; in many such, four and a half hours, at least, are daily set aside for thought, rules are given for thought, training and opportunity afforded. Among us, there is *no* time appointed for this purpose, and the difficulty is that, in our social life, we must be always doubtful whether we ought not to be with somebody else or be doing something else.

Are men better off than women in this?

If one calls upon a friend in London and sees her son in the drawing-room, it strikes one as odd to find a young man sitting idle in his mother's drawing-room in the morning. For men, who are seen much in those haunts, there is no end of the epithets we have: "knights of the carpet," "drawing-room heroes," "ladies' men." But suppose we were to see a number of men in the morning sitting round a table in the drawing-room, looking at prints, doing worsted work, and reading little books, how we should laugh! A member of the House of Commons was once known to do worsted work. Of another man was said, "His only fault is that he is too good; he drives out with his mother every day in the carriage, and if he is asked anywhere he answers that he must dine with his mother, but, if she can spare him, he will come in to tea, and he does not come."

Now, why is it more ridiculous for a man than for a woman to do worsted work and drive out every day in the carriage? Why should we laugh if we were to see a parcel of men sitting round a drawing-room table in the morning, and think it all right if they were women?

Is man's time more valuable than woman's? or is the difference between man and woman this, that woman has confessedly nothing to do?

Women are never supposed to have any occupation of sufficient importance *not* to be interrupted, except "suckling their fools"; and women themselves have accepted this, have written books to support it, and have trained themselves so as to consider whatever they do as *not* of such value to the world or to others, but that they can throw it up at the first "claim of social life." They have accustomed themselves to consider intellectual occupation as a merely selfish amusement, which it is their "duty" to give up for every trifler more selfish than themselves.

A young man (who was afterwards useful and known in his day and generation) when busy reading and sent for by his proud mother to shine in some morning visit, came; but, after it was over, he said, "Now, remember, this is not to happen again. I came that you might not think me sulky, but I shall not come again." But for a young woman to send such a message to her mother and sisters, how impertinent it would be! A woman of great administrative powers said that she never undertook anything which she "could not throw by at once, if necessary."

How do we explain then the many cases of women who have distinguished themselves in classic, mathematics, even in politics?

Widowhood, ill-health, or want of bread, these three explanations or excuses are supposed to justify a woman in taking up an occupation. In some cases, no doubt, an indomitable force of character will suffice without any of these three, but such are rare.

SIGNIFICANCE

Although chiefly known for her work as a nurse, Nightingale was also a social reformer. She supported feminist principles for the same reasons that many other women did: they were frustrated by the restrictions that prevented them from living a full life. They wanted to enjoy the same liberty and equality granted to men.

Opponents of women's rights argued that feminist demands would threaten society by undermining marriage and the family, which they saw as a woman's profession. In addition, nineteenth-century commentators often argued that women had a small capacity to reason, could not calculate consequences, and behaved in a reckless fashion—in short, they needed male assistance to survive.

In their struggle for equality, feminists had to overcome deeply ingrained beliefs about female inferiority, a battle that took decades to win. Although women's rights had become a major issue by the turn of the century, women in most industrialized countries, including Great Britain, did not win full legal rights until the mid- to late twentieth century.

FURTHER RESOURCES
Books

Burstein, Miriam Elizabeth. *Narrating Women's History in Britain, 1770–1902*. Burlington, VT: Ashgate, 2004.

Dossey, Barbara Montgomery. *Florence Nightingale: Mystic, Visionary, Healer*. Springhouse, PA: Springhouse, 2000.

Purvis, June, ed. *Women's History: Britain, 1850–1945: An Introduction*. New York: St. Martin's Press: Ashgate, 1995.

Web sites

Florence Nightingale Museum. <http://www.florence-nightingale.co.uk/centre.htm> (accessed April 10, 2006).

A Left-Handed Commencement Address

Speech

By: Ursula K. Le Guin

Date: May 1983

Source: Le Guin, Ursula K. "A Left-Handed Commencement Address" in *Dancing at the Edge of the World*. New York: Grove Press, 1989. Available at <http://gos.sbc.edu/l/leguin.htm> (accessed March 20, 2006).

About the Author: Ursula K. Le Guin (1929–) is an award-winning science fiction author.

INTRODUCTION

"A Left-Handed Commencement Address" is the text of a commencement address delivered at Mills College in Oakland, California, in 1983 by Ursula K. Le Guin. Mills College was founded in 1852 as a women's college and is still women-only at the undergraduate level.

Le Guin's speech encapsulates the branch of feminism that emphasizes the essential peacefulness of women as compared to men. This school of thought stresses that men have historically tended to fight wars and think in terms of opposites—true/false, strong/weak, win/lose, succeed/fail—while women have, as Le Guin puts it, "lived, and have been

Author Ursula K Le Guin receives an award at the PEN USA Annual Litfest Awards Gala November 9, 2005. PHOTO BY MICHAEL BUCKNER/GETTY IMAGES

despised for living, the whole side of life that includes and takes responsibility for all that is obscure, passive, uncontrolled, animal, unclean—the valley of the shadow, the deep, the depths of life." Since our culture has been dominated by men for thousands of years, it has become, in this view, a "man's world of institutionalized competition, aggression, violence, authority, and power," a "psychopathic social system." Le Guin urges the women and men in her audience to reject the competitive, either/or world of "Machoman" and choose to live "without the need to dominate, and without the need to be dominated."

"Left-handed" is a reference to Le Guin's 1969 science fiction novel *The Left Hand of Darkness*, which won the Nebula Award in 1969 and Hugo Award in 1970. *The Left Hand of Darkness* is one of the earliest explicitly feminist works of science fiction, and it helped establish Le Guin's reputation as a feminist

thinker. Many of the ideas presented in compressed, declarative form in the address are worked out in imaginative terms in the novel.

In 1983, when Le Guin addressed the graduates of Mill College, the changes made by feminism in the 1970s were under various forms of cultural counterattack. The presidency of Ronald Reagan, a former movie actor once known for portraying cowboys, football players, soldiers, and other archetypically masculine roles, coincided with a political resurgence of political, gender, and religious conservatism and heightened global military tensions. In 1982, the year before Le Guin's address, Reagan called the Soviet Union an "evil empire" in a speech to the British House of Commons, fanning global fears of all-out nuclear war. Only two months before Le Guin's address, Reagan had called for the U.S. to deploy a vast complex of orbital weaponry known as the Strategic Defense Intitiative or "Star Wars", hence LeGuin's reference, in the address, to a "sky full of orbiting spy-eyes and weaponry." The intersection of archetypical heterosexual maleness with military aggression was probably particularly stark for Le Guin in this context.

Despite apparently blaming men for most of what is wrong with the world, Le Guin is not anti-man. In her address and in many other essays, she speaks hopefully to and about men. As of 2006, she had been married to her first husband, historian Charles Le Guin, for over fifty years. And the protagonist of *The Left Hand of Darkness* is a heterosexual man.

The reference to left-handedness in the titles of both the book and the address is somewhat cryptic: the inhabitants of Gethen are not particularly left-handed, and in actuality men are slightly more likely to be left-handed than women. Left-handedness is apparently cited as a metaphor for that disapproved (or less-approved), non-dominant side of human nature that Le Guin identifies as particularly female. In many societies, the left hand is used for personal hygiene after defecation, and it is a social offense to present the left hand in greeting or to use it while taking food from a common dish. Our word "sinister" is from the Latin for left.

PRIMARY SOURCE

I want to thank the Mills College Class of '83 for offering me a rare chance: to speak aloud in public in the language of women.

I know there are men graduating, and I don't mean to exclude them, far from it. There is a Greek tragedy where the Greek says to the foreigner, "If you don't understand Greek, please signify by nodding." Anyhow, commencements are usually operated under the unspoken agreement that everybody graduating is either male or ought to be. That's why we are all wearing these twelfth-century dresses that look so great on men and make women look either like a mushroom or a pregnant stork. Intellectual tradition is male. Public speaking is done in the public tongue, the national or tribal language; and the language of our tribe is the men's language. Of course women learn it. We're not dumb. If you can tell Margaret Thatcher from Ronald Reagan, or Indira Gandhi from General Somoza, by anything they say, tell me how. This is a man's world, so it talks a man's language. The words are all words of power. You've come a long way, baby, but no way is long enough. You can't even get there by selling yourself out: because there is theirs, not yours.

Maybe we've had enough words of power and talk about the battle of life. Maybe we need some words of

weakness. Instead of saying now that I hope you will all go forth from this ivory tower of college into the Real World and forge a triumphant career or at least help your husband to and keep our country strong and be a success in everything—instead of talking about power, what if I talked like a woman right here in public? It won't sound right. It's going to sound terrible. What if I said what I hope for you is first, if—only if—you want kids, I hope you have them. Not hordes of them. A couple, enough. I hope they're beautiful. I hope you and they have enough to eat, and a place to be warm and clean in, and friends, and work you like doing. Well, is that what you went to college for? Is that all? What about success?

Success is somebody else's failure. Success is the American Dream we can keep dreaming because most people in most places, including thirty million of ourselves, live wide awake in the terrible reality of poverty. No, I do not wish you success. I don't even want to talk about it. I want to talk about failure.

Because you are human beings you are going to meet failure. You are going to meet disappointment, injustice, betrayal, and irreparable loss. You will find you're weak where you thought yourself strong. You'll work for possessions and then find they possess you. You will find yourself—as I know you already have—in dark places, alone, and afraid.

What I hope for you, for all my sisters and daughters, brothers and sons, is that you will be able to live there, in the dark place. To live in the place that our rationalizing culture of success denies, calling it a place of exile, uninhabitable, foreign.

Well, we're already foreigners. Women as women are largely excluded from, alien to, the self-declared male norms of this society, where human beings are called Man, the only respectable god is male, the only direction is up. So that's their country; let's explore our own. I'm not talking about sex; that's a whole other universe, where every man and woman is on their own. I'm talking about society, the so-called man's world of institutionalized competition, aggression, violence, authority, and power. If we want to live as women, some separatism is forced upon us: Mills College is a wise embodiment of that separatism. The war-games world wasn't made by us or for us; we can't even breathe the air there without masks. And if you put the mask on you'll have a hard time getting it off. So how about going on doing things our own way, as to some extent you did here at Mills? Not men and the male power hierarchy—that's their game. Not against men, either—that's still playing by their rules. But with any men who are with us: that's our game. Why should a free woman with a college education either fight Machoman or serve him? Why should she live her life on his terms?

Machoman is afraid of our terms, which are not all rational, positive, competitive, etc. And so he has taught us to despise and deny them. In our society, women have lived, and have been despised for living, the whole side of life that includes and takes responsibility for helplessness, weakness, and illness, for the irrational and the irreparable, for all that is obscure, passive, uncontrolled, animal, unclean—the valley of the shadow, the deep, the depths of life. All that the Warrior denies and refuses is left to us and the men who share it with us and therefore, like us, can't play doctor, only nurse, can't be warriors, only civilians, can't be chiefs, only indians. Well, so that is our country. The night side of our country. If there is a day side to it, high sierras, prairies of bright grass, we only know pioneers' tales about it, we haven't got there yet. We're never going to get there by imitating Machoman. We are only going to get there by going our own way, by living there, by living through the night in our own country.

So what I hope for you is that you live there not as prisoners, ashamed of being women, consenting captives of a psychopathic social system, but as natives. That you will be at home there, keep house there, be your own mistress, with a room of your own. That you will do your work there, whatever you're good at, art or science or tech or running a company or sweeping under the beds, and when they tell you that it's second-class work because a woman is doing it, I hope you tell them to go to hell and while they're going to give you equal pay for equal time. I hope you live without the need to dominate, and without the need to be dominated. I hope you are never victims, but I hope you have no power over other people. And when you fail, and are defeated, and in pain, and in the dark, then I hope you will remember that darkness is your country, where you live, where no wars are fought and no wars are won, but where the future is. Our roots are in the dark; the earth is our country. Why did we look up for blessing—instead of around, and down? What hope we have lies there. Not in the sky full of orbiting spy-eyes and weaponry, but in the earth we have looked down upon. Not from above, but from below. Not in the light that blinds, but in the dark that nourishes, where human beings grow human souls.

SIGNIFICANCE

The Left Hand of Darkness, to which the title of Le Guin's address refers, is a science fiction story of the social thought-experiment type. In the book, a male ambassador from an interstellar human civilization where heterosexuality is the norm arrives on the planet Gethen. The ambassador's job is to see if the Gethenians would like to join the network of cultural exchange that is the primary activity of his civilization. The

Gethenians are neither male nor female but androgynous. All individuals can sire children or bear them, and many have done both. They are gender-neutral most of the time but periodically shift into a sexually active phase that may be either male or female. Individuals are thus neither "men" nor "women."

By positing a world without maleness (or femaleness) as we know it, Le Guin can work out what she sees as the consequences of gender in our own world. The most notable consequence, war, she also emphasizes in her commencement address. On Gethen, violence occurs only on small scales.

In the larger discussion about whether behavioral differences between men and women are "programmed" by biology or learned by cultural immersion—the longstanding "nature versus nurture" debate—Le Guin occupies an ambiguous position. Since Gethen's warlessness arises from a biological cause, Le Guin seems to be saying that Earth's wars also arise from a biological cause—male sexuality. Yet the two-gendered civilization represented by her book's protagonist is nonviolent. Le Guin's position therefore appears to be mixed: aggression and war arise from biological causes, but do not arise from them inevitably. In this view, nurture can modify nature.

FURTHER RESOURCES
Books
Ridley, Matt. *Nature via Nurture: Genes, Experience, and What Makes Us Human.* New York: HarperPerennial, 2004.

Inglehart, Ronald and Norris, Pippa. *Rising Tide: Gender Equality and Cultural Change Around the World.* New York: Cambridge University Press, 2003.

Web sites
Justice, Faith L. "Ursula K. Le Guin." *Salon*, January 23, 2001. <http://www.salon.com/people/bc/2001/01/23/le_guin/> (accessed March 2, 2006).

The Effect of an Early Association of Ideas on the Character

Book excerpt

By: Mary Wollstonecraft

Date: 1792

Source: Wollstonecraft, Mary. *A Vindication of the Rights of Woman.* Penguin Books, 1992.

About the Author: Mary Wollstonecraft (1759–1797) was an English writer, philosopher, translator, and vocal advocate of educational equality for women. Best known as a feminist author, Wollstonecraft produced a full range of work on topics such as religion, philosophy, sexuality, education, travel, history, and politics. An autodidact and former educator, Wollstonecraft immersed herself in London's intellectual culture in the late 1880s and published several books, most notably *Thoughts on the Education of Daughters* and *A Vindication of the Rights of Woman*, the latter of which is considered one of the first great feminist manuscripts. She died shortly after the birth of her daughter Mary Godwin, who would grow up to become Mary Wollstonecraft Shelley, celebrated author of the classic Gothic novel *Frankenstein*.

INTRODUCTION

A Vindication of the Rights of Woman, by Mary Wollstonecraft was first published in 1792. It is often cited as the founding text of feminism, that school of modern thought which emphasizes the equality of men and women. Wollstonecraft's *Vindication* has influenced feminist thinkers in all succeeding periods, including the suffragettes (women seeking the right to vote) of the late nineteenth and early twentieth centuries, Virginia Woolf (author of the equally famous *A Room of One's Own*, 1929), and thinkers of the "second wave" of feminism from the late 1960s onward.

Mary Wollstonecraft grew up in England. Her family started out wealthy but was steadily impoverished by her father's business errors. Her first fifteen years were spent on farms; her family then moved to London, where Mary educated herself by reading newspapers and library books. She also received some instruction from friends of the family. Later, the education of women was to be her major theme as a writer.

Starting in 1787, only a decade before her death, she published a series of works on subjects including philosophy, politics, religion, fiction, and travel. Wollstonecraft was an ardent Protestant Christian with liberal theological views (she avowed in *Vindication* that she could not take the story of Genesis literally even "were an angel from Heaven" told her to). Her first major work was *Thoughts on the Education of Daughters*, which outlined a rationalist system for producing reasonable and virtuous girls. In 1790, she published *A Vindication of the Rights of Man*, a book-length rebuttal of a recent book by Edmund Burke that had criticized

The English feminist and writer Mary Wollstonecraft.
PHOTO BY HULTON ARCHIVE/GETTY IMAGES

the recent egalitarian revolution in France. She began working on *A Vindication of the Rights of Woman* even before finishing *A Vindication of the Rights of Man*, completing it in a mere six weeks.

In *A Vindication of the Rights of Woman*, Wollstonecraft advanced many arguments that were to become basic principles of feminism in the centuries to come. Her effort was spent largely in rebutting claims, which were frequently made by male writers of her day, that women are mentally less capable of men by nature: obsessed with physical appearance, unreliable in judgment, unfit for intellectual work such as business or science. She admitted the reality of female character flaws but denied that innate female nature was the cause.

In the 1700s, writers pointed to behavioral differences between young children as evidence for innate mental differences between the genders. Jean-Jacques Rousseau (1712–1788), philosopher of the French Revolution, wrote that "Boys love sports of noise and activity; to beat the drum, to whip the top, and to drag about their little carts: girls, on the other hand, are fonder of things of show and ornament; such as mirrors, trinkets, and dolls; the doll is the peculiar amusement of the females; from whence we see their taste plainly adapted to their destination… Here then we see a primary propensity firmly established." Wollstonecraft quoted this passage and counter-asserted that gender differences of taste and behavior arise from education. "Girls," she wrote, are "forced to sit still, play with dolls, and listen to foolish conversations; the effect of habit is insisted upon as an undoubted indication of nature." Prefiguring modern views of acculturation, she wrote that "Everything that [children] see or hear serves to fix impressions, call forth emotions, and associate ideas, that give a sexual character to the mind."

If women were eductated better throughout life, Wollstonecraft argued, they would grow up more virtuous and rational. "Asserting the rights which women in common with men ought to contend for, I have not attempted to extenuate their faults; but to prove them to be the natural consequence of their education and station in society. If so, it is reasonable to suppose, that they will change their character, and correct their vices and follies… Let woman share the rights, and she will emulate the virtues of man." This, according to Wollstonecraft, would be manifested especially in a correction of women's tendency to choose unworthy, exploitative men ("rakes") as mates, which she attributes to the schooling of women in vanity: "Rakes know how to work on their sensibility, whilst the modest merit of reasonable men has, of course, less effect on their feelings…"

Ironically, Wollstonecraft's own first choice of a mate met with exactly the disaster that she hoped all women would someday be able to avoid. In 1793, she began an affair with Gilbert Imlay; she had a daughter by him in 1794 and in 1795, after learning of his unfaithfulness to her, she attempted suicide twice. She married the more stable William Godwin in 1797 and died that same year from medical complications arising from the birth of their daughter Mary.

PRIMARY SOURCE

This habitual slavery, to first impressions, has a more baneful effect on the female than the male character, because business and other dry employments of understanding, tend to deaden the feelings and break associations that do violence to reason. But females, who are made women of when they are mere children, and brought back to childhood when they ought to leave the go-cart for ever, have not sufficient strength of mind to efface the superinductions of art that have smothered nature.

Everything that they see or hear serves to fix impressions, call forth emotions, and associate ideas, that give a sexual character to the mind. False notions of beauty and delicacy stop the growth of their limbs and produce a sickly soreness, rather than delicacy or organs; and thus weakened by being employed in unfolding instead of examining the first associations, forced on them by every surrounding object, how can they attain the vigour necessary to enable them to throw off their factitious character?—where find strength to recur to reason and rise superior to a system of oppression that blasts the fair promises offspring? This cruel association of ideas, which everything conspires to twist into all their habits of thinking, or, to speak with more precision, of feeling, receives new force when they begin to act a little for themselves; for they then perceive that it is only through their address to excite emotions in men, that pleasure and power are to be obtained. Besides, the books professedly written for their instruction, which make the first impression on their minds, all inculcate the same opinions. Educated then in worse than Egyptian bondage, it is unreasonable, as well as cruel, to upbraid them with faults that can scarcely be avoided, unless a degree of native vigour be supposed, that falls to the lot of the very few amongst mankind.

For instance, the severest sarcasms have been leveled against the sex, and they have been ridiculed for repeating 'a set of phrases learnt by rote,' when nothing could be more natural, considering the education they receive, and that their highest praise is to obey, unargued—the will of man.

And when all their ingenuity is called forth to adjust their dress 'a passion for a scarlet coat,' is so natural, that it never surprised me; and, allowing Pope's summary of their character to be just, 'that every woman is at heart a rake,' why should they be bitterly censured for seeking a congenial mind, and preferring a rake to a man of sense?

Rakes know how to work on their sensibility, whilst the modest merit of reasonable men has, of course, less effect on their feelings, and they cannot reach the heart by the way of understanding, because they have few sentiments in common.

It seems a little absurd to expect women to be more reasonable than men in their *likings*, and still to deny them the uncontrolled use of reason. Why do men *fall in love* with sense? When do they, with their superior powers and advantages, turn from the person to the mind? And how can they then expect women, who are only taught to observe behaviour, and acquire manners rather than morals, to despise what they have been all their lives labouring to attain? Where are they suddenly to find judgement enough to weigh, patiently the sense of an awkward virtuous man, when his manners, of which they are made critical judges, are rebuffing, and his conversation cold and dull, because it does not consist of pretty repartees, or well-turned compliments? In order to admire or esteem anything for a continuance, we must, at least, have our curiosity excited by knowing, in some degree, what we admire; for we are unable to estimate the value of qualities and virtues above our comprehension. Such a respect, when it is felt, may be very sublime; and the confused consciousness of humility may render the dependent creature an interesting object, in some points of view; but human love must have grosser ingredients; and the person very naturally will come in for its share—and, an ample share it mostly has!

Love is, in a great degree, an arbitrary passion, and will reign like some other stalking mischiefs, by its own authority, without designing to reason, and it may also be easily distinguished from esteem, the foundation of friendship, because it is often excited by evanescent beauties and graces, though, to give an energy to the sentiment, something more solid must deepen their impression and set the imagination to work, to make the most fair—the first good.

Common passions are excited by common qualities. Men look for beauty and the simper of good-humoured docility: women are captivated by easy manners; a gentleman-like man seldom fails to please them, and their thirsty ears eagerly drink the insinuating nothings of politeness, whilst they turn from the unintelligible sounds of the charmer—reason, charm he never so wisely. With respect to superficial accomplishments, the rake certainly has the advantage; and of these females can form an opinion, for it is their own ground. Rendered gay and giddy by the whole tenor of their lives, the very aspect of wisdom, or the severe graces of virtue, must have a lugubrious appearance to them; and produce a kind of restraint from which they and love, sportive child, naturally revolt. Without taste, excepting of the lighter kind, for taste is the offspring of judgement, how can they discover that true beauty and grace must arise from the play of the mind? And how can they be expected to relish in a lover what they do not, or very imperfectly, possess themselves? The sympathy that united hearts, and invites to confidence, in them is so very faint, that it cannot take fire, and thus mount to passion. No, I repeat it, the love cherished for such minds, must have grosser fuel!

The inference is obvious; till women are led to exercise their understandings, they should not be satirized for their attachment to rakes; or even for being rakes at heart, when they who live to please—must find their enjoyments, their happiness, in pleasure! It is a trite, yet true remark, that we never do anything well, unless we love it for its own sake.

SIGNIFICANCE

The ideas put forward by Mary Wollstonecraft long remained those of a tiny minority. Throughout the nineteenth century, the view that men are innately more rational than women actually became more prevalent, gaining the endorsement of mainstream scientific opinion. For example, Gustave Le Bon, a respected French psychologist, wrote in 1879 that "All psychologists who have studied the intelligence of women, as well as poets and novelists, recognize today that they represent the most inferior forms of human evolution and they are closer to children and savages than to an adult, civilized man. They excel in fickleness, inconstancy, absence of thought and logic, and incapacity to reason." These are exactly the charges that Wollstonecraft was answering in the 1790s.

In the late nineteenth century, however, Wollstonecraft's ideas began to gain wider currency. Suffragettes fought for and won the vote for women early in the twentieth century. Starting in the 1960s, a new wave of feminists began to take Wollstonecraft's radical egalitarianism with renewed seriousness. Although her religious beliefs and her emphasis on the "virtues of man" (which women, she thought, could hope to emulate) were largely dropped, her belief that girls and women could be equally capable in all departments if given equal education became standard for millions of women and men, as did her demand of equal pay for equal work.

However, the belief that human behaviors are to some large extent programmed by inheritance regained credence in parts of the scientific community starting with the rise of sociobiology in 1975. Rousseau's belief that boys' and girls' play habits reflect innate mental differences is being seriously researched today; in 2005, a widely cited study announced that male vervet monkeys are more likely to play with balls and toy trucks and female monkeys with pots and dolls. Thus, controversy continues over precisely the nature/nurture debate in which Wollstonecraft participated over two hundred years ago. However, it is very rare today for any scientist to insist that male/female differences, even if partly or mostly biological in origin, imply female inferiority; Wollstonecraft's once-revolutionary insistence on the equal merit, "virtue," and reasonableness of the sexes has now become nearly universal in Western society.

FURTHER RESOURCES

Books

Feminist Interpretations of Mary Wollstonecraft, edited by Maria J. Falco. University Park, Pa.: Pennsylvania State University Press, 1996.

Kelly, Gary. *Revolutionary Feminism: The Mind and Career of Mary Wollstonecraft*. New York: St. Martin's Press, 1995.

Web sites

Todd, Janet. *BBC.* "Mary Wollstonecraft: A Speculative and Dissenting Spirit." <http://www.bbc.co.uk/history/society_culture/protest_reform/wollstonecraft_01.shtml> (accessed April 1, 2006).

Iron John: A Book About Men

Book excerpt

By: Robert Bly

Date: 1990

Source: Bly, Robert. *Iron John: A Book About Men*. Reading, Mass.: Addison-Wesley, 1990.

About the Author: Robert Bly (1926–) is an American poet, translator, and author. Born in Minnesota, Bly graduated from Harvard University in 1950, and in 1956 received a Fulbright grant to travel to Europe and translate Norwegian poetry into English. While abroad, Bly discovered a number of major poets whose influence had not yet reached the United States, resulting in *The Fifties*, *The Sixties*, and *The Seventies*, a series of literary magazines of translated poetry. While Bly is most well-known for his award-winning poetry, his most influential nonfiction work, *Iron John: A Book About Men*, was an international bestseller credited as the foundation of the Mythopoetic Men's Movement. Bly frequently leads workshops for men and women throughout the United States.

INTRODUCTION

Iron John: A Book About Men is both an influential and controversial nonfiction book about masculine depth psychology. In it, Bly diagnoses a type of American man that he says developed in the 1960s and 1970s, the "soft male" (later in the book he also calls this figure "the Sixies-Seventies man"). The soft male, Bly says, developed when men reacted too simplistically to the feminist movement, which declared women's strength, independence, and equality; many young men defined their maleness around being eager to please, gentle, nonviolent, passive, and emotionally full of light. This type of man was preceded by the "Fifties man," whose maleness was more energetic but also more brittle, and potentially more violent: he was "supposed to like football, be aggressive, stick up for the United States, never cry, and always provide."

Bly proclaims a "third possibility for men, a third mode" or way of individuating, that is, of becoming an adult. He visualizes a balanced male person who is capable of both quietness and loudness, tears and laughter, civility and wildness—unlike the Fifties man, who was supposed to be a one-sided worker and patriot, never "weak," or the Sixties-Seventies man, who was supposed to be always soft, never angry, never wild. This third mode, Bly argues, can be discerned in the story "Iron John" or "Iron Hans," a Northern European folk tale first collected into print around 1820 by the Grimm brothers. The book *Iron John* is Bly's at-length, in-depth interpretive read of this story.

In the tale, the servants of a king find a large, hairy man lying at the bottom of a pond in a nearby forest. The wild man is brought back to the castle, imprisoned by the King in an iron cage, and called Iron John. The King gives the cage's key into the keeping of his wife, the Queen. One day, the eight-year-old son of the King and Queen is playing with a golden ball. The precious ball rolls into Iron John's cage. Iron John says the boy can only have the ball back if he opens the cage. The boy is reluctant, but greatly desires the golden ball. Iron John informs him that the key is hidden under the Queen's pillow, and the boy gets it and lets him out. Bly interprets this much of the story in his first chapter, hence its title ("The Pillow and the Key").

Afraid of being beaten for releasing the wild man, the boy accompanies him back to the woods, and a complex series of adventures ensues. By the end of the tale, a number of years have passed. At the very end, a stately King appears at the boy's marriage-feast and says, "I am Iron Hans, and was by enchantment a wild man, but you have set me free; all the treasures which I possess, shall be your property."

Bly was greatly influenced by the psychological theories of Carl Jung (1875–1961). Jungian analysis of fairy tales seeks to relate their events to recurrent or universal aspects of human feeling called "archetypes." Thus, Bly interprets the golden ball in the story as "that unity of personality we had as children—a kind of radiance, or wholeness" that is lost as we approach adulthood. He then argues that a man can recover this sense of wholeness in its proper adult-male form only

James Dean, an icon of 1950s masculinity, in a scene from the 1955 film *Rebel Without a Cause.* © BETTMANN/CORBIS. REPRODUCED BY PERMISSION.

by separating from his mother (stealing the key from under her pillow) and freeing the wild man within himself—in story terms, by letting Iron John out of his cage and going off with him to the forest. This "wild" self is not, in Bly's system, an uncontrolled, vicious, or evil self, but an instinctive one—a peculiarly male psychological mode that Bly calls the "deep masculine." Recovery of right relationship with the deep masculine or Wild Man self might, Bly teaches, occur at any time of life, not necessarily in youth.

■ PRIMARY SOURCE

IRON JOHN: A BOOK ABOUT MEN

The Pillow and the Key

We talk a great deal about "the American man," as if there were some constant quality that remained stable over decades, or even within a single decade.

The men who live today have veered far away from the Saturnian, old-man-minded farmer; proud of his intro-

version, who arrived in New England in 1630, willing to sit through three services in an unheated church. In the South, an expansive, motherbound cavalier developed, and neither of these two "American men" resembled the greedy railroad entrepreneur that later developed in the Northeast, nor the reckless I-will-do-without culture settlers of the West.

Even in our own era the agreed-on model has changed dramatically. During the fifties, for example, an American character appeared with some consistency that became a model of manhood adopted by many men: the Fifties male.

He got to work early, labored responsibly, supported his wife and children, and admired discipline. Reagan is a sort of mummified version of this dogged type. This sort of man didn't see women's souls well, but he appreciated their bodies; and his view of culture and America's part in it was boyish and optimistic. Many of his qualities were strong and positive, but underneath the charm and bluff there was, and there remains, much isolation, deprivation, and passivity. Unless he has an enemy, he isn't sure that he is alive.

The Fifties man was supposed to like football, be aggressive, stick up for the United States, never cry, and always provide. But receptive space or intimate space was missing in this image of a man. The personality lacked some sense of flow. The psyche lacked compassion in a way that encouraged the unbalanced pursuit of the Vietnam war, just as, later, the lack of what we might call "garden" space inside Reagan's head led to his callousness and brutality toward the powerless in El Salvador, toward old people here, the unemployed, schoolchildren, and poor people in general.

The Fifties male had a clear vision of what a man was, and what male responsibilities were, but the isolation and one-sidedness of his vision were dangerous.

During the sixties, another sort of man appeared. The waste and violence of the Vietnam War made men question whether they knew what an adult male really was. If manhood meant Vietnam, did they want any part of it? Meanwhile, the feminist movement encouraged men to actually look at women, forcing them to become conscious of concerns and sufferings that the Fifties male labored to avoid. As men began to examine women's history and women's sensibility, some men began to notice what was called their *feminine* side and pay attention to it. This process continues to this day, and I would say that most contemporary men are involved in it in some way.

There's something wonderful about this development—I mean the practice of men welcoming their own "feminine" consciousness and nurturing it—this is important—and yet I have the sense that there is something wrong. The male in the past twenty years has become more thoughtful, more gentle. But by this process he has not become more free. He's a nice boy who pleases not only his mother but also the young woman he is living with.

In the seventies I began to see all over the country a phenomenon that we might call the "soft male." Sometimes even today when I look out at an audience, perhaps half the young males are what I'd call soft. They're lovely, valuable people—I like them—they're not interested in harming the earth or starting wars. There's a gentle attitude toward life in their whole being and style of living.

But many of these men are not happy. You quickly notice the lack of energy in them. They are life-preserving but not exactly life-giving. Ironically, you often see these men with strong women who positively radiate energy.

Here we have a finely tuned young man, ecologically superior to his father, sympathetic to the whole harmony of the universe, yet he himself has little vitality to offer.

The strong or life-giving women who graduated from the sixties, so to speak, or who have inherited an older spirit, played an important part in producing this life-preserving, but not life-giving, man.

I remember a bumper sticker during the sixties that read "WOMEN SAY YES TO MEN WHO SAY NO." We recognize that it took a lot of courage to resist the draft, go to jail, or move to Canada, just as it took courage to accept the draft and go to Vietnam. But the women of twenty years ago were definitely saying that they preferred the softer receptive male.

So the development of men was affected a little in this preference. Nonreceptive maleness was equated with violence, and receptive maleness was rewarded.

Some energetic women, at that time and now in the nineties, chose and still choose soft men to be their lovers, and, in a way, perhaps, to be their sons. The new distribution of "yang" energy among couples didn't happen by accident. Young men for various reasons wanted their harder women, and women began to desire softer men. It seemed like a nice arrangement for a while, but we've lived with it long enough now to see that it isn't working out.

Part of their grief rose out of remoteness from their fathers, which they felt keenly, but partly, too, grief flowed from trouble in their marriages or relationships. They had learned to be receptive, but receptivity wasn't enough to carry their marriages through troubled times. In every relationship something *fierce* is needed once in a while: both the man and the woman need to have it. But at some point when it was needed, often the young man came up short. He was nurturing, but something else was required—for his relationship, and for his life.

The "soft" male was able to say, "I can feel your pain, and I consider your life as important as mine, and I will take care of you and comfort you." But he could not say what he wanted, and stick by it. *Resolve* of that kind was a different matter.

The journey many American men have taken into softness, or receptivity, or "development of the feminine side," has been an immensely valuable journey, but more travel lies ahead. No stage is the final stop.

SIGNIFICANCE

Because of *Iron John*'s emphasis on maleness and Bly's involvement in the "men's movement," some writers have interpreted him as antifeminist or male supremacist. However, this is inaccurate. Bly claims, rather, that women and men have distinctive forms of deep psychology; consequently (he says), girls need to be initiated into the distinctively female form of wholeness by women, boys into the distinctively male form of wholeness by men. Properly initiated or grown-up men and women can then relate successfully to each other as partners. (Recall that Iron John reappears at the end of the fairy tale to bless the marriage feast.) Yet proper initiation is rare for men, Bly argues, leading to imbalanced men and defective relationships. Bly's concerns are not limited to male figures such as Iron John: some of his earliest writing on mythological and fairytale figures was devoted not to the Wild Man but the Great Goddess. By 2006, Bly had hosted thirty-one annual conferences devoted to interpretation of the Great Goddess or Great Mother figure in religion, mythology, and literature (broadened, in later years, to include "the Great Mother and the New Father").

Iron John enhanced Bly's not-entirely-willing status as an intellectual leader of the men's movement, a very loosely related set of efforts to further male self-understanding that developed starting in the late 1980s. The men's movement includes groups as diverse as the evangelical Christian "Promise Keepers," mythopoetic drumming circles, and father's-rights advocates.

FURTHER RESOURCES
Periodicals
"Interview with Robert Bly." *M.E.N. Magazine* (November 1995). <http://www.menweb.org/bly-iv.htm> (accessed March 27, 2006).

Websites
GreatMotherConference.com. "Robert Bly's 32nd Annual Conference on the Great Mother and the New Father."

<http://www.greatmotherconference.com> (accessed March 27, 2006).

RobertBly.com. <http://www.robertbly.com> (accessed March 27, 2006).

Sexual Politics

Book excerpt

By: Kate Millet

Date: 1969

Source: Millet, Kate. *Sexual Politics*. Chicago: University of Illinois Press, 2000.

About the Author: Kate Millet is a feminist revolutionary whose groundbreaking theories and writings helped launch the feminist movement during the 1970s.

INTRODUCTION

Kate Millet's *Sexual Politics* began as her doctoral thesis at Columbia University. The volume examines the various ways in which traditional gender roles have undermined women's power and roles in society, and how men have used marriage, family structure, wage discrimination, and sexual relations to keep women from attaining their true potential. Her criticism of the patriarchal society and her ideas about the rights of women, which were considered radical when first published, helped form the foundation for basic theories of feminism. Millet posited that natural differences between the genders had been twisted to imply

Kate Millet (left) author of the best selling feminist tract "Sexual Politics" at a news conference given by women's liberation activists on December 17, 1970 in New York City. AP IMAGES

superiority and inferiority, with men capitalizing on their greater physical strength to give themselves power. This structure carries over into male homosexual relationships, where one partner is traditionally considered the dominant, more powerful or "male" partner, while the weaker, less forceful or dominant partner is ascribed the "female" role. These labels are derived from the traditional structure of a male-dominated society.

■ PRIMARY SOURCE

Sexual Politics

I IDEOLOGICAL

Hannah Arendt has observed that government is upheld by power supported either through consent or imposed through violence. Conditioning to an ideology amounts to the former. Sexual politics obtains consent through the "socialization" of both sexes to basic patriarchal polities with regard to temperament, role and status....

II BIOLOGICAL

Patriarchal religion, popular attitude, and to some degree, science as well assumes psycho-social distinctions to rest upon biological differences between the sexes, so that where culture is acknowledged as shaping behavior, it is said to do no more than cooperate with nature. Yet the temperamental distinctions created in patriarchy ("masculine" and "feminine" personality traits) do not appear to originate in human nature, those of role and status still less.

The heavier musculature of the male, a secondary sexual characteristic and common among mammals, is biological in origin but is also culturally encouraged through breeding, diet, and exercise. Yet it is hardly an adequate category on which to base political relations *within civilization*. Male supremacy, like other political creeds, does not finally reside in physical strength but in the acceptance of a value system which is not biological. Superior physical strength is not a factor in political relations—vide those of race and class. Civilization has always been able to substitute other methods (technic, weaponry, knowledge) for those of physical strength, and contemporary civilization has no further need of it. At present, as in the past, physical exertion is very generally a class factor, those at the bottom performing the most strenuous tasks, whether they be strong or not.

It is often assumed that patriarchy is endemic in human social life, explicable or even inevitable on the grounds of human physiology. Such a theory grants patriarchy logical as well as historical origin. Yet if as some anthropologists believe, patriarchy is not of primeval origin, but was preceded by some other social form we shall call pre-patriarchal, then the argument of physical strength as a theory of patriarchal *origins* would hardly constitute a sufficient explanation—unless the male's superior physical strength was released in accompaniment with some change in orientation through new values or new knowledge. Conjecture about origins is always frustrated by lack of certain evidence. Speculation about prehistory, which of necessity is what this must be, remains nothing but speculation....

VI FORCE

We are not accustomed to associate patriarchy with force. So perfect is its system of socialization, so complete the general assent to its values, so long and so universally has it prevailed in human society, that is scarcely seems to require violent implementation. Customarily, we view is brutalities in the past as exotic or "primitive" custom. Those of the present are regarded as the product of individual deviance, confined to pathological or exceptional behavior, and without general import. And yet, just as under other total ideologies (racism and colonialism are somewhat analogous in this respect) control in patriarchal society would be imperfect, even inoperable, unless it had the rule of force to rely upon, both in emergencies and as an ever-present instrument on intimidation....

Patriarchal force also relies on a form of violence particularly sexual in character and realized most completely in the act of rape. The figures of rapes reported represent only a fraction of those which occur, as the "shame" of the event is sufficient to deter women from the notion of civil prosecution under the public circumstances of a trial. Traditionally rape has been viewed as an offense one male commits upon another—a matter of abusing "his woman." Vendetta, such as occurs in the American South, is carried out for masculine satisfaction, the exhilarations of race hatred, and the interests of property and vanity (honor). In rape, the emotions of aggression, hatred, contempt, and the desire to break or violate personality, take a form consummately appropriate to sexual politics. In the passages analyzed at the outset of this study, such emotions were present at a barely sublimated level and were a key factor in explaining the attitude behind the author's use of language and tone.

Patriarchal societies typically link feelings of cruelty with sexuality, the latter often equated both with evil and with power. This is apparent both in the sexual fantasy reported by psychoanalysis and that reported by pornography. The rule here associates sadism with the male ("the masculine role") and victimization with the female ("the feminine role"). Emotional response to violence against women in patriarchy is often curiously ambivalent; references to wife-beating, for example, invariably produce laughter and some embarrassment. Exemplary atrocity, such as the mass murders committed by Richard Speck, greeted at one level with a certain scandalized, possibly hypocritical indignation, is capable of eliciting a mass response of titillation at another level. At such times one even hears from men occasional expressions of envy or amusement. In view of the sadistic character of such public fantasy as caters to male audiences in pornography or semi-pornographic media, one might expect that a certain element of identification is by no means absent from the general response. Probably a similar collective *frisson* sweeps through racist society when its more "logical" members have perpetrated a lynching. Unconsciously, both crimes may serve the larger group as a ritual act, cathartic in effect....

SIGNIFICANCE

"Sexual politics" does not refer to any organized form of government or delineation along party lines, but to the power structure of relationships and how one group is controlled by another, in this case according to gender roles. Often, power is maintained through superior physical strength and the threat of violence, with sexual assault used as an extreme measure of force (either in actuality or as an implication). Even in societies where violence appears to have been eliminated, the threat is still implicit in that the more powerful person can always use force against the weaker. That idea itself is a motivator.

Historically, patriarchal societies have been the norm. While there have been female-dominated societies, they are traditionally small, agricultural peoples living in remote areas, such as the Nagovisi of Bougainvillea in the South Pacific or the Machinguenga of Peru. Because men have the physical ability to take power by force, they take the more dominant role as a matter of supposed right. Though this appears to be a natural advantage, there is nothing to say that physical prowess is more important than the qualities women possess, such as the ability to bear children. Nature has separated the roles of the sexes, but mankind has labeled certain abilities superior and allowed them to justify male dominance.

In modern society, men still maintain control over women, though their methods have diversified. Beyond purely physical superiority, men have established themselves in controlling positions in family, business, and the law. Prior to the mid-twentieth century, most women stayed at home and cared for their homes and family while their husbands worked, keeping women at the financial mercy of men. Even after they entered the work force in significant numbers, their salaries were kept low in comparison to their male counterparts, with men rationalizing that women were not required to support a family, and so were in less need of the money.

Though women took jobs similar to men, their work was often undervalued simply due to their gender and preconceived roles in society. As women spent more time in the work force, they found it difficult to earn promotions that were far more likely to go to men. The "glass ceiling", the point at which women ceased to climb the corporate ladder, became one more way to control women and make it impossible for them to gain power.

Reminders of male physical superiority appear in the media on a daily basis, through reports of violent crimes like rape and domestic abuse. Their existence promotes constant awareness of the possibility of violence, even in a society where women have grown more powerful. Outside the Western world, many societies continue to subjugate women, forcing them to stay in traditional roles, as well as less secure positions of prostitute, concubine, and so on. Some religious teachings help encourage male dominance and remove women from any part of the power hierarchy.

Many modern women have taken control over their lives with substantial jobs, financial independence, a voice in government, and raising children on their own rather than within the traditional family structure. But society as a whole is still patriarchal in nature, and in certain communities, male supremacy is not even questioned. Although arguments over traditional gender roles often center on natural capabilities and reasons why women deserve to choose their role in society on an individual basis, the underlying issue is power, and who will ultimately control the way society functions.

FURTHER RESOURCES

Books

Koven, Seth. *Slumming: Sexual and Social Politics in Victorian London.* Princeton, NJ: Princeton University Press, 2004.

Web sites

Alice Paul Institute and National Council of Women's Organizations. "Equal Rights Amendment." <http://www.equalrightsamendment.org/> (accessed March 16, 2006).

JoFreeman.com. Henley, Nancy, and Jo Freeman. "The Sexual Politics of Interpersonal Behavior." <http://www.jofreeman.com/womensociety/personal.htm/> (accessed March 16, 2006).

Salon.com. Crawford, Leslie. "Kate Millet, the Ambivalent Feminist." <http://www.salon.com/people/feature/1999/06/05/millet/> (accessed March 18, 2006).

Women on the Verge of Power and Other Incredible Stories. "Matriarchy: History or Reality?" <http://www.saunalahti.fi/penelope/Feminism/matriarchy.html> (accessed March 16, 2006).

Child Marriage

Photograph

By: Kate Brooks

Date: May 1, 2001

Source: Brooks, Kate. "Child Marriage." Corbis, May 1, 2001.

About the Photographer: Kate Brooks is an award-winning photographer who began her career in the Soviet Union focusing on child abuse in state-run institutions. After the terrorist attacks of September 11, 2001, Brooks moved to Pakistan to photograph the impact of the war on terror in that part of the world. She has worked in Afghanistan as well as Iraq and countries all over the Middle East and is involved with photography of both political and human rights issues with a specific concentration on women's rights and exposing injustices and violence against women.

INTRODUCTION

Throughout history, marriage has long been viewed as an institution designed for the purpose of producing a family. Traditionally accomplished through sexual reproduction, to enter into marriage the spouses ideally would need to have reached sexual maturity recognized with the onset of puberty. Yet, in many parts of the world, primarily in third-world countries, children are forced by their parents into marriage even before they are able to sexually reproduce. Girls are the ones most often forced into marriage at young ages and in some developing countries of Africa and Asia, more than twenty percent of girls are entered into marriages before they are fifteen.

Young girls regularly marry far older men. The girl's parents are often provided with large gifts for the sale of their daughters that come either in the form of monetary payments or material goods. The girls usually have little or no part in the decision-making process as to when and with whom they will be married, and often the wedding ceremony will be the first time they will be meeting their new husbands.

Child marriage is practiced against the law in most of the countries where it is prevalent. The minimum age for marriage in most countries as well as under several international agreements is eighteen. Yet traditional and tribal practices ensure that children, some as young as three or four years old, are being entered into marriages. Beyond the emotional traumas that can result from people at young ages being forced to adopt the responsibilities of marriage, young girls can become very ill and even die as a result of the physical conditions resulting from sexual activity at an early age. Children rarely have any education about sexual health issues like contraception, pregnancy or sexually transmitted diseases. In many cultures, young girls are sold into marriage to men far older than them who often have had sex with many other partners, greatly increasing the chance that these young girls will contract diseases such as HIV/AIDS, which is rampant in many parts of the world.

Controlling the spread of child marriage has largely fallen onto national human rights and women's rights organizations who have tried to lobby national governments to more strictly enforce their laws. However, in many of these countries where child marriage is strongly linked with deeply held traditions, governments are lenient and marriages at very young ages continue for tens of millions of couples each year.

■ PRIMARY SOURCE

CHILD MARRIAGE

See primary source image.

SIGNIFICANCE

Religion combined with traditional and societal norms continue to serve as the primary bases that allow marriage between children at very young ages to remain popular. The primary source photograph indicates the religious dedication with which families associate marriage, and while the prospect of marriage is daunting for such a young child, it is combined with a sense of religious and cultural fulfillment.

India is one of the world's largest centers of child marriage, as it is encouraged within many segments of Hinduism, the country's largest religion. While it is officially illegal, marriage between children sometimes as young as four years old continues, spurred on by the gifts or dowries that are arranged between the parents.

PRIMARY SOURCE

Child Marriage: Gita, a 10-year-old girl from northern India, dressed for her wedding on May 1, 2001. Her groom, Bribal, is 12. Child marriage has been illegal in India for decades but remains a common practice. © KATE BROOKS/CORBIS

Marrying off a daughter can be a critical source of income in an Indian society, where desperate poverty requires parents to search for unique forms of income to support their families.

According to local legend, the practice of child marriage in India is believed to be connected to a desire by parents to protect their daughters from predators looking to have relations with unmarried girls. Nevertheless, the practice of child marriage can rob a young girl of the normal sense of innocence and enjoyment that comes with childhood and places adulthood responsibilities on their shoulders at an early age.

Even while young girls often are able to abstain from living with their older spouses until they reach puberty, they can be required to work for the groom's family and are typically asked to move out of their childhood homes. Because of the fact that Indian communities frown on marriage within villages, young girls frequently are asked to move far away from their homes at very young ages, losing any regular contact with their families.

In India, as in many nations around the world, girls in the poorest regions often receive very minimal—if any—educational training. When they are entered into marriages at such young ages, they are often deprived of any opportunities to be educated or to be exposed to any other types of lifestyle. Despite the efforts of national governments and international organizations to curtail the frequency of child marriage, it continues in large numbers in many parts of the world.

FURTHER RESOURCES
Books

Sagade, Jaya. *Child Marriage in India: Socio-Legal and Human Rights Dimensions*. Oxford, U.K.: Oxford University Press, 2005.

Periodicals

Burns, John F. "Child Marriages, Though Illegal, Persist in India." *New York Times* (May 11, 1998).

Web sites

International Women's Health Coalition. "Factsheet: Child Marriage." <http://www.iwhc.org/resources/childmarriagefacts.cfm> (accessed April 1, 2006).

After the Attacks: Finding Fault; Falwell's Finger-Pointing Inappropriate, Bush Says

Newspaper article

By: Laurie Goodstein

Date: Sep. 15, 2001

Source: Goodstein, Laurie. "After the Attacks: Finding Fault; Falwell's Finger-Pointing Inappropriate, Bush Says." *New York Times*, Sep. 15, 2001.

About the Author: This article is by staff writer Laurie Goodstein at the *New York Times*.

Fundamentalist Rev. Jerry Falwell holds the Bible as he teaches at Thomas Road Baptist Church. PHOTO BY MARK MEYER/TIME LIFE PICTURES/GETTY IMAGES

INTRODUCTION

On September 11, 2001, terrorists hijacked four American passenger jets. Two were flown into the World Trade Center towers in New York, killing 2,986 people. One was flown into the Pentagon, killing 174, and a third crashed in a Pennsylvania field after a heroic passenger revolt prevented the hijackers from reaching yet another target in Washington, D.C.

Two days after the attacks, Baptist ministers Jerry Falwell (1933—) and Pat Robertson (1930—) made controversial remarks on Robertson's Christian television program *The 700 Club*, which claims one million viewers daily in the United States alone.

Falwell and Robertson blamed people "who try to secularize America" for distancing the nation from God. Falwell went even further, stating, "I point the finger in their face and say, '[Y]ou helped this happen.'"

A few days after the broadcast, Falwell apologized, saying that "This is not what I believe and I therefore repudiate it and ask for God's forgiveness and yours." A few weeks later, however, he indicated to the *Washington Post* that the only problem with his remarks was that the list of blameworthy groups had not been long enough: "I didn't complete what I was going to say. If I added the church as one of the offenders—a sleeping church that is not praying enough—it would have been acceptable."

PRIMARY SOURCE

After the Attacks: Finding Fault

Falwell's Finger-Pointing Inappropriate, Bush Says

Did God allow the terrorist attacks?

The Rev. Jerry Falwell and Pat Robertson set off a minor explosion of their own when they asserted on television on Thursday that an angry God had allowed the terrorists to succeed in their deadly mission because the United States had become a nation of abortion, homosexuality, secular schools and courts, and the American Civil Liberties Union.

Liberal groups and commentators denounced their remarks yesterday, as did President Bush, who has long enjoyed the political support of the two evangelists.

"The president believes that terrorists are responsible for these acts," said a White House spokesman, Ken Lisaius. "He does not share those views, and believes that those remarks are inappropriate."

Yet Mr. Falwell's and Mr. Robertson's remarks were based in theology familiar to and accepted by many conservative evangelical Christians, who believe the Bible teaches that God withdraws protection from nations that violate his will.

Several conservative theologians and evangelists said in interviews yesterday that they agreed with the basic notion but rejected the idea that mere humans can ever know which particular sins lead to which particular tragedies.

The Rev. R. Albert Mohler Jr., president of the Southern Baptist Theological Seminary in Louisville, Ky., and a friend of Mr. Falwell's, said, "There is no doubt that America has accommodated itself to so many sins that we should always fear God's judgment and expect that in due time that judgment will come. But we ought to be very careful about pointing to any circumstance or any specific tragedy and say that this thing has happened because this is God's direct punishment."

Mr. Falwell, chancellor of Liberty University in Lynchburg, Va., and senior pastor of Thomas Road Baptist Church there, was in Washington yesterday in a service at the National Cathedral at Mr. Bush's invitation, a spokesman for Mr. Falwell said.

Mr. Falwell released a statement yesterday on the controversy, saying, "Despite the impression some may have from news reports today, I hold no one other than the terrorists and the people and nations who have enabled and harbored them responsible for Tuesday's attacks on this nation."

"I sincerely regret that comments I made during a long theological discussion on a Christian television program yesterday were taken out of their context and reported and that my thoughts—reduced to sound bites—have detracted from the spirit of this day of mourning."

Mr. Robertson yesterday defended Mr. Falwell. "In no way has any guest on my program suggested that anyone other than the Middle East terrorists were responsible for the tragic events that took place on Tuesday," he said in a written statement.

What Mr. Falwell said on Thursday on "The 700 Club," while chatting with the program's host, Mr. Robertson, was this:

"What we saw on Tuesday, as terrible as it is, could be minuscule if, in fact, God continues to lift the curtain and allow the enemies of America to give us probably what we deserve."

Mr. Robertson responded, "Jerry, that's my feeling. I think we've just seen the antechamber to terror. We haven't even begun to see what they can do to the major population."

A few moments later Mr. Falwell said, "The abortionists have got to bear some burden for this because God will not be mocked. And when we destroy 40 million little innocent babies, we make God mad. I really believe that the pagans, and the abortionists, and the feminists, and the gays and the lesbians who are actively trying to make that an alternative lifestyle, the A.C.L.U., People for the American Way, all of them who have tried to secularize America, I point the finger in their face and say, 'You helped this happen.'"

To which Mr. Robertson said, "Well, I totally concur, and the problem is we have adopted that agenda at the highest levels of our government."

Mr. Robertson also issued a press release on Thursday saying that in a country rampant with materialism, Internet pornography, and lack of prayer, "God almighty is lifting his protection from us."

James Robison, a well-known evangelist in Euless, Tex., and host of the Christian television program "Life Today," concurred but emphasized a different catalog of what he saw as sins: arrogance in relationships with Third World and foreign countries, plundering other countries for resources while supporting their despots, and indifference to others' poverty and pain.

"Any time you get away from God, you do become vulnerable," Mr. Robison said. "If it is a parent who stays out all night, the children become vulnerable and are left to fend for themselves. Bad judgment always leaves the door open to perpetrators of pain."

Mr. Robison is one pastor called on for advice and prayer by the president. Mr. Robison said that in August, he spent morning praying with Mr. Bush at the president's Texas ranch, and counseled that "love can break the conspiracy of terrorism."

Among evangelicals, the terrorist attacks have unleashed renewed calls for repentance, prayer, and spiritual revival. A nationwide prayer vigil planned for Saturday is to be broadcast by satellite into 1,500 churches. Next week will bring newspaper advertisements by evangelical groups calling for the nation to unite in prayer.

"Many people are calling this a wake-up call, and yet it doesn't help us respond to God to somehow feel that we've been chastised by this," said Steve Hawthorne, director of WayMakers, a prayer ministry in Austin, Tex. "It might be wise for us to examine our lives and our hearts and our practices."

SIGNIFICANCE

Despite the media furor that erupted after his appearance on *The 700 Club*, the Rev. Falwell said that many religious conservatives approved of his controversial remarks. "As a matter of fact," he told the *Washington Post* in November 2001, "most of the heat I've taken has not been because of the statement. It's from people who are upset that I apologized. Thousands of people of faith in America unfortunately agreed with the first statement.... They were incensed that I apologized." But many conservatives disapproved of the original statements: Conservative publisher William F. Buckley, Jr., called them "ignorant" and proof that ordained ministers are "able terribly to misteach Christian thought."

It should be noted that Falwell and Robertson did not apologize for saying that God is "lifting his protection" from the United States, a claim that Robertson reiterated in writing soon after the controversial broadcast. What they retracted was the claim that a specific disaster or attack could be attributed to God's wrath at particular sins or sinners. Robertson, however, has repeatedly warned that disasters may be visited by God upon, or permitted by God to befall, specific groups or geographical areas in response to specific sins, especially sexual sins.

In 1998, Robertson warned that because Disneyland had rented its facilities for a privately sponsored "Gay Day," Florida might be visited by disastrous weather, earthquakes, terrorist bombings, or even a meteor strike. In 2005, he warned that the people of Dover, Pennsylvania, had "rejected" God by voting out school board members who supported the anti-evolutionary concept of Intelligent Design, and that if disasters befell the town its people should not expect divine assistance. In 2006, he claimed that Israeli Prime Minister Ariel Sharon's stroke was God's punishment for Sharon's order that Israel end its occupation of the Gaza Strip. He later apologized for the remark.

The belief—not held by all Christians—that God sends disasters to punish cities, regions, or groups for sinful behavior is based on Old Testament narratives such as the story of the destruction of Sodom and Gomorrah. Many conservative Christians interpret this story as saying that God destroyed these cities for their practice of homosexuality. On the other hand, many religious scholars say that inhospitality, not homosexuality, was the sin that doomed the cities. There is no independent historical or archaeological basis for the narrative.

Conservative evangelists like Falwell and Robertson are influential among one of the most powerful voting blocs in the United States—conservative Christians—many of whom believe that American society is threatened by liberals, feminists, and homosexuals. The danger of homosexuality is a particularly common theme in the social thinking of some fundamentalist or evangelical American Christians. In the mid-1980s, Falwell called homosexuals "brute beasts" and said that a gay-oriented group of California churches constituted "a vile and Satanic system" that would "one day be utterly annihilated," after which there would "be a celebration in Heaven."

The political clout wielded by televangelists such as Falwell and Robertson could be seen when President Bush, despite his repudiation of the remarks made on Robertson's show, met privately with Robertson shortly before the United States war with Iraq began in early 2003.

FURTHER RESOURCES

Web sites

CNN.com. "Falwell Apologizes to Gays, Feminists, Lesbians." Sep. 14, 2001. Available at <http://archives.cnn.com/2001/US/09/14/Falwell.apology/> (accessed March 16, 2006).

Harris, John F. "God Gave U.S. 'What We Deserve', Falwell Says." *Washington Post*, September 14, 2001. Available at <http://www.astr.ua.edu/white/worldviews/falwell911.html> (accessed March 17, 2006).

Carlson, Peter. "The Televangelist's Awkward Apology: What Did He Mean and When Did He Mean It?" *Washington Post*. November 26, 2001. Available at <http://www.washingtonpost.com/ac2/> (accessed March 17, 2006).

Buckley, William Jr. "Invoking God's Thunder: on the Rev. Jerry Falwell." *National Review Online*, November 26, 2001. Available at <http://www.people.vcu.edu/~dbromley/jerryfalwellspeaksLink.htm> (accessed March 17, 2006).

Changing Faces

Magazine article

By: Lisa Takeuchi Cullen

Date: July 29, 2002

Source: Cullen, Takeuchi Lisa. "Changing Faces." *Time, Asia*. (July 29, 2002).

About the Author: Lisa Takeuchi (née Reilly) Cullen is a staff writer for *Time* magazine in New York. She joined the magazine in 2001 as a Tokyo-based correspondent.

INTRODUCTION

For much of history, cosmetic surgery was essentially the repair of battle wounds. In the twentieth century, surgeons also began fixing protruding ears, receding chins, and large noses. As standards of beauty rose, the list of physical attributes perceived to be defective expanded dramatically. This labeling of certain nose shapes and types as deformities helped to cement standards of normality and acceptability.

Cosmetic surgery first became widely popular in the United States. Much of the favorable publicity that such surgery has received over the years has attempted to place it within the American tradition of self-improvement as part of an American cultural tendency to change rather than cope. Entertainers have been particularly enthusiastic about altering features that they believed would limit their careers or their chances for happiness. Many sought to minimize or remove physical signs of race or ethnicity that they believed marked them as an "other."

Race and ethnicity-based surgery has always focused on the most identifiable and most caricatured features. Jews, Italians, and others of Mediterranean or eastern European heritage made the "nose job" a household word. Later in the twentieth century, African Americans began slimming their lips and noses, while Asians pursued larger noses and folded eyelids. Cosmetic surgery pioneers were content to fix just one feature. Modern plastic surgeons have expanded their repertoires to fulfill a wider range of requests.

PRIMARY SOURCE

At 18, Saeko Kimura was a shy, sleepy-eyed university student. Until she discovered a secret weapon: if she applied a strip of glue to her eyelids, her eyes became wider, rounder, and prettier. "Men noticed me," she says. "I became outgoing. Suddenly, I had a life." Her new looks also landed her part-time work as a hostess in an upmarket bar, where she gets top dollar on a pay scale determined by beauty.

But Kimura lived in fear of discovery, rushing off to the bathroom several times a day to reapply the glue and never daring to visit the beach. And so, at twenty-one, she finds herself in a doctor's office in a Tokyo high-rise, lying on an operating table with her fists nervously clenched. Plastic surgeon Katsuya Takasu breezes in

wielding a cartoonishly enormous needle. "This will hurt a little," he says cheerfully. Once the anesthetic is administered, Takasu brandishes another hooked needle and threads it through Kimura's upper eyelids, creating a permanent crease. He then injects a filler fluid called hyaluronic acid into her nose and chin and pinches them into shape. Takasu inspects his handiwork. "The swelling will go down in a few days," he says. "But even if you went out tonight in Roppongi, you'd be a hit." A nurse hands Kimura a mirror. Though red and puffy, she now has the face she's always dreamed of: big, round eyes, a tall nose, a defined chin. The entire procedure took less than ten minutes. But Kimura collapses with an ice pack on her face and moans, "Oh, the pain."

What we won't do for beauty. Around Asia, women—and increasingly, men—are nipping and tucking, sucking and suturing, injecting and implanting, all in the quest for better looks. In the past, Asia had lagged behind the West in catching the plastic surgery wave, held back by cultural hang-ups, arrested medical skills and a poorer consumer base. But cosmetic surgery is now booming throughout Asia like never before. In Taiwan, a million procedures were performed last year, double the number from five years ago. In Korea, surgeons estimate that at least one in ten adults have received some form of surgical upgrade and even tots have their eyelids done. The government of Thailand has taken to hawking plastic surgery tours. In Japan, noninvasive procedures dubbed "petite surgery" have set off such a rage that top clinics are raking in $100 million a year.

Elsewhere in Asia, this explosion of personal re-engineering is harder to document, because for every skilled and legitimate surgeon there seethes a swarm of shady pretenders. Indonesia, for instance, boasts only forty-three licensed plastic surgeons for a population of about 230 million; yet an estimated four hundred illicit procedures are performed each week in the capital alone. In Shenzhen, the Chinese boomtown, thousands of unlicensed "beauty-science centers" lure hordes of upwardly mobile patients, looking to buy a new pair of eyes or a new nose as the perfect accessory to their new cars and new clothes.

The results are often disastrous. In China alone, over 200,000 lawsuits were filed in the past decade against cosmetic surgery practitioners, according to the *China Quality Daily*, an official consumer protection newspaper. The dangers are greatest in places like Shenzhen that specialize in cut-price procedures. "Any Tom, Dick or Harry with a piece of paper—genuine or not—can practice over there," says Dr. Philip Hsieh, a Hong Kong-based plastic surgeon. "They use things that have not been approved, just for a quick buck. And people in China don't know that they're subjecting themselves to this kind of risk."

Of course, Asians have always suffered for beauty. Consider the ancient practice of foot binding in China, or the stacked, brass coils used to distend the necks of Karen women. In fact, some of the earliest records of reconstructive plastic surgery come from sixth century India: the Hindu medical chronicle *Susruta Samhita* describes how noses were recreated after being chopped off as punishment for adultery.

The culturally loaded issue today is the number of Asians looking to remake themselves to look more Caucasian. It's a charge many deny, although few would argue that under the relentless bombardment of Hollywood, satellite TV, and Madison Avenue, Asia's aesthetic ideal has changed drastically. "Beauty, after all, is evolutionary," says Harvard psychology professor Nancy Etcoff, who is the author of *Survival of the Prettiest: The Science of Beauty*—not coincidentally a best seller in Japan, Korea, Hong Kong and China. Asians are increasingly asking their surgeons for wider eyes, longer noses and fuller breasts—features not typical of the race. To accommodate such demands, surgeons in the region have had to invent unique techniques. The number one

procedure by far in Asia is a form of blepharoplasty, in which a crease is created above the eye by scalpel or by needle and thread; in the U.S., blepharoplasty also ranks near the top, but involves removing bags and fat around the eyes. Likewise, Westerners use botox, or botulinum toxin, to diminish wrinkles—while in Korea, Japan and Taiwan, botox is injected into wide cheeks so the muscle will atrophy and the cheeks will shrink. Just as Asian faces require unique procedures, their bodies demand innovative operations to achieve the leggy, skinny, busty Western ideal that has become increasingly universal.

The cultural quirks of the plastic surgery business in Asia also extend to sexuality. In China, Korea and Indonesia, where virginity is highly prized, young women go in for hymen reconstruction in time for their wedding night. In Japan, Indonesia and Korea, men ask for penis-enlargement procedures, in part to avoid shame when bathing en masse. In Thailand, with its sizable population of so-called "lady boys," a thriving industry has sprung up to provide male-to-female sex-change operations.

Traditionally, most Asians going under the scalpel were women. But a mutant strain of male vanity has

Winners of China's first beauty pageant for women who have undergone plastic surgery celebrate after being crowned during the finals in Bejing, on December 18, 2004. AP IMAGES

back, and hurt him a lot, and I told him it was the first and last time he would ever hurt me. After that we separated." She said she did not seek out the police because her boyfriend was a police officer.

Abused men are very similar to abused women, experts say. They arrive at shelters or special police stations here with low self-esteem and are afraid their wives or girlfriends will discover that they have sought help. At one shelter, a social worker recounted the story of a prominent union leader who was being physically abused by his wife.

At the women's shelter in Sao Goncala, officials reported the experience of a 50-year-old businessman they call "X." He came to see social workers complaining his wife was verbally abusing him, and throwing things at him. "He was completely in love with his wife, who was having an extramarital affair," said the co-ordinator of shelter, Mariza Gaspary. "The curious thing was that after they separated, the wife hooked up with a new boyfriend who started to abuse her physically."

SIGNIFICANCE

Domestic abuse transcends national, cultural, class, and religious barriers. In most poor countries, women are more likely to be assaulted by a husband or boyfriend than by a stranger outside the home. Men also are victims of domestic violence but less frequently. Figures on the relative frequency of male and female domestic victimization are not readily available for Brazil, but in the United States, according to the U.S. Bureau of Justice Statistics, eighty-five percent of those violently victimized by "intimate partners" in 2003 were women and seventy-four percent of those killed by an intimate partner were women. In the United States, intimate partners committed twenty percent of all violent crimes against women and three percent of all violent crimes against men.

The article reproduced above gives no quantitative information about the growth of domestic abuse of men in Brazil as a whole; it uses nonspecific phrases that give the impression that the phenomenon of increasing male victimization in Brazil is revolutionary in scope, the "death of machismo." For instance, in its first paragraph it states that a "significant portion" of those seeking help at government domestic abuse centers are men but never defines "significant." In its second paragraph, it notes that in one suburb the number of men seeking help for abuse doubled from 108 to 259 over a one-year period, but it does not say how many women sought help in the same period. Without such context, there is no way to assess the significance of the figures given. Morever, figures for one suburb

are of little value in establishing the extent or even the existence of a national trend. Other vague language appears in the fourth paragraph: after the article states that women are still the "biggest sufferers of domestic violence throughout Brazil" (how much bigger is "biggest"?), it goes on to state that women are now "more likely" (how much more?) to "lash out" in abusive situations and that "in many cases" (how many?) social workers find that men are "just as much a victim" as the wife or girlfriend. The article quotes a Brazilin study as finding that in "many" (how many?) cases women respond with physical violence to verbal abuse. Finally, although the piece speaks of "the recent violence against men," it cites no data to support its claim that violence against men is increasing ("soaring", in fact) in Brazil.

It should also be noted that while the article speaks repeatedly of the "abuse" of men by women, the only detailed anecdote related—the story of Fatima, a woman skilled in Thai martial arts who was attacked by her boyfriend and fought back, injuring him—is an instance of self-defense, not abuse of a man by a woman. In that story, Fatima's boyfriend is not legally a "victim" at all. This would apply to all women who "lash out" violently when attacked violently. Fighting back against violent attack is not considered to be a form of domestic abuse.

Conclusions about sweeping changes in social psychology cannot be drawn from data as fragmentary as those given in this source. Nevertheless, the article draws attention to a group often omitted from discussions of domestic violence—whether in Brazil or elsewhere—namely male victims.

FURTHER RESOURCES

Periodicals

Nelson, Laura Sue. "The Defense of Honor: Is It Still Honored in Brazil?" *Wisconsin International Law Journal.* 11 (1992–93): 531. Available at: <http://www.law-lib. utoronto.ca/Diana/fulltext/nels.htm> (accessed March 13, 2006).

Web sites

BBC News. "Two in Three Women Abused." <http://news. bbc.co.uk/1/hi/health/1992915.stm> (accessed March 14, 2006).

BBC News. "Women 'Face Worst Abuse at Home'." <http://news.bbc.co.uk/2/hi/europe/4465916.stm> (accessed March 14, 2006).

U.S. Department of State. "Brazil: Country Reports on Human Rights Practices, 1999." <http://www.state. gov/g/drl/rls/hrrpt/1999/377.htm> (accessed March 14, 2006).

Women in Aboriginal Societies

Photograph

By: Taylor Medford

Date: November 4, 2004

Source: Taylor, Medford. *Northern Territory, Australia.* National Geographic/Getty, 2004.

About the Photographer: Medford Taylor has photographed the natural world for publications such as *National Geographic* and Fodor's travel guides.

INTRODUCTION

Aboriginal people arrived in Australia between 30,000 and 50,000 years ago, where they created a thriving and diverse society. By the time European colonization began in the late 1700s, there were over 270 languages and 600 dialects among the estimated 300,000 to one million Aborigines.

In traditional Aboriginal society, both men and women had well defined cultural and religious roles that were disrupted by colonization. Many Aboriginal people were killed by new diseases or as a result of fighting as the British forced them from their traditional lands. Today, the majority of Aboriginals live on the periphery of modern Australian society, making up just over two percent of the country's approximately 19.5 million people. By the end of the twentieth century, only twenty of the original Aboriginal languages were still spoken. High rates of unemployment, crime, alcoholism, domestic abuse, and other ills plague the indigenous culture, which continue to exist in a reduced form.

Women in traditional Aboriginal culture were respected for their role as life givers. They often carried out healing ceremonies and dances and told stories to carry on social traditions. Women generally looked after children, cooked, and took on the role of gatherers, collecting vegetables, eggs, shellfish, and small animals. In many cases, they were the primary providers of food, since chances were great that men who went hunting would be unsuccessful. Women also made hand tools and clothing.

Aboriginal culture centers around Ancestral Spirit Beings, who are believed to be the origin of all existence and guides that tell Aboriginals how to live their lives. Connection with the Ancestral Spirits, or "dreaming," comes through the land, water, animals, and other aspects of the natural world. Dreaming stories are said to help people in the past, present, and in some cases the future. Access to sacred locations and participation in traditional ceremonies is often restricted to those who have the prerequisite levels of spiritual knowledge. Although both men and women have special secret ceremonies and duties, women are generally less involved in ceremonies than men and are often controlled by threats that they will not be allowed to participate in ceremonies.

PRIMARY SOURCE

WOMEN IN ABORIGINAL SOCIETIES

See primary source image.

SIGNIFICANCE

As European settlers came to Australia, Aboriginal people were pushed off their traditional lands, which compromised their ability to be hunter-gathers and limited their access to sacred sites. This disrupted the entire social and religious structure of many Aboriginal clans. Both women and men began to work for Europeans in the early 1800s, relying on labor for wages and food. The patriarchal society that Europeans brought to Australia diminished the prominent role Aboriginal women traditionally held, and they began to lose rights as they became second-class citizens even to Aboriginal men.

Since Australia began as a British penal colony, there was a disproportionate ratio of men to women. This led to a somewhat high rate of sexual interaction between Aboriginal women and white men. Many Europeans considered this wrong, and in the late 1800s and 1900s they enacted rules and regulations to limit such relationships and encourage more white women to move to parts of Australia where their numbers were low, particularly in the Northern Territory.

Change in cultural norms has led to increased violence in Aboriginal communities, with women particularly victimized. Aboriginal women are more likely than non-Aboriginal women to be victims of homicide, rape, and assault. In addition, cultural taboos dissuade them from bringing such problems to light in their communities. The Australian government and national organizations have worked to improve conditions for Aboriginal people, particularly women.

PRIMARY SOURCE

Women in Aboriginal Societies: A member of Australia's Eastern Arrernte Aboriginal people sits next to Corroboree Rock in the Simpson Desert. The circular carvings were made by her ancient ancestors. PHOTO BY MEDFORD TAYLOR/NATIONAL GEOGRAPHIC/GETTY IMAGES

FURTHER RESOURCES

Books

Keen, Ian. *Aboriginal Economy and Society: Australia at the Threshold of Colonisation.* Oxford University Press, 2000.

Periodicals

Hannah, Mark. "Aboriginal Workers in the Australian Agricultural Company, 1824–1857." *History Cooperative* No. 82 (2002). <http://www.historycooperative.org/journals/lab/82/hannah.html> (accessed March 15, 2006).

Web sites

Andrews, Penelope. *University of Toronto Bora Laskin Law Library: Women's Human Rights Resources Programme.* "Violence against Aboriginal Women in Australia: Possibilites for Redress within the International Human Rights Framework." <http://www.law-lib.utoronto.ca/Diana/fulltext/andr.htm> "accessed March 15, 2006".

Australian Human Rights & Equal Opportunity Commission. "Racial Discrimination." <http://www.hreoc.gov.au/racial_discrimination/index.html> (accessed March 15, 2006).

Australia's Centenary of Federation: Birth of the Nation, Growth of the Commonwealth. "Aboriginal Australia: The Unfinished Business—Institutions." <http://www.abc.net.au/federation/fedstory/ep4/ep4_institutions.htm> (accessed March 15, 2006).

Bloodworth, Sandra. *Australian National University/* "Gender Relations in Aboriginal Society. What Can We Glean from Early Explorers' Accounts?" <http://www.anu.edu.au/polsci/marx/interventions/gender.htm> (accessed March 15, 2006).

Matrubhoomi—A Nation Without Women

Photograph

By: Adnan Abidi

Date: July 13, 2005

Source: Corbis Corporation

About the Photographer: This photograph was taken by photographer Adnan Abidi, a photographer who specializes in covering events in India for Reuters, a worldwide news organization based in London.

INTRODUCTION

In 2003, Manish Jha released the film "Matrubhoomi," which translated means "motherland" at the Venice Film Festival where it won the International Critics Prize. The movie tells the story of a fictional village in India in the future. After generations of female infanticide and dowry deaths, the village is populated completely by men. Society in the village is unstable due to the physical, emotional, and psychological absence of women on the men. The men of the village become debased and brutish, turning to pornography, homosexuality, and bestial violence to release their sexual frustrations.

The village chief, Ramcharan, discovers Kalki, a young girl from a nearby village. Kalki's father enters into a negotiation with Ramcharan to marry his daughter to all five of Ramcharan's sons. As a result of the polyandrous marriage, all five of the sons and Ramcharan engage Kalki in conjugal relations with the girl. The youngest of the sons, Sooraj, treats Kalki with kindness and the two become close. In a fit of jealousy, the oldest son kills his brother. After turning to her father for help and being refused, Kalki attempts to escape with Raghu, a low caste family servant. Raghu is killed and Kalki is shackled with iron chains in a cow shed where she is repeatedly raped by her married family and townspeople. When she becomes pregnant, everyone claims paternity and a caste war destroys the village.

▌ PRIMARY SOURCE

MATRUBHOOMI—A NATION WITHOUT WOMEN

See primary source image.

▌ PRIMARY SOURCE

Matrubhoomi—A Nation Without Women: A women walks past movie poster for *Matrubhoomi* in New Delhi, on July 13, 2005. The film highlights India's problems with female infanticide and foeticide by depicting a future where women are extremely rare. © ADNAN ABIDI/REUTERS/CORBIS

SIGNIFICANCE

A UNESCO (United Nations Educational, Scientific, and Cultural Organization) report estimates that 50 million women are missing from India's population due to gender discrimination. Jha asserted that he wrote the movie to address the universal theme of the exploitation of women and the phenomenon of missing women in India. He suggests that some women run away to escape oppression, while others have been murdered, many before their first birthday. India's patriarchal society perceives sons as a source of economic security and preservation. Daughters, on the other hand, are often viewed as a burden to the family due to the lack of educational and employment opportunities for women and the dowry system (the dowry tradition involves women bringing money or property into a marriage). Although the dowry system is prohibited by law, it continues to be practiced.

The first reported cases of female infanticide date back to reports from the British during the nineteenth century, who reported its occurrence in the region of Tamil Nadu. However, India's government denied the practice occurred until 1985. In 1985, the news magazine *India Today* reported the existence of female infanticide in the Usilampatti, Madurai district of Tamil Nadu. The report asserted that the practice was prevalent primarily among Kallars, the dominant caste. Between 1994 and 1997, almost three thousand girls died immediately after birth in the Tamil Nadu districts of Dindigul and Madurai. A *Christian Science Monitor* report found that in the Salem district of Tamil Nadu, sixty percent of girls are killed within three days of birth. Mothers refuse to nurse the newborns and the midwives or mothers-in-law administer oleander sap which poisons the girl.

A review of demographic data by the British medical journal *The Lancet* reveals that the number of women in India is, in fact, decreasing. The number of girls to boys over the last three decades has particularly diminished. In 1981, there were 962 girls to every one thousand boys. That number decreased by 1991 to 945 girls to every one thousand boys. And by 2001, the number of girls continued to fall to 927 girls to every one thousand boys. In a 1995 study of 1320 newly delivered babies, the number of girls who died during the neo-natal period was three times that of the boys. The country's 2000 National Family Health survey revealed that between the ages of one and five, a female child has a forty-three percent higher risk of dying than a boy.

In recent years, the practice of sex determination during pregnancy in India has led to an increase in abortions of girl fetuses. Although the gender determination is illegal, it is rarely enforced and a law that would ban ultrasound and other genetic testing lack the support of India's medical community. However, one gynecologist, Puneet Bedi at the Apollo Hospitals in New Delhi asserts that "Abortions are a low-risk, high-profit business. As a specialist in fetal medicine, I can tell you that no pregnant woman would suffer if the ultrasound test were banned. Right now, it is used to save one out of 20,000 fetuses and kill twenty out of every one hundred because [it reveals that the baby] is the wrong gender." Approximately 11.2 million illegal abortions are performed every year in India. One advertisement reads, "Pay five hundred rupees now and save 50,000 rupees later," suggesting that aborting a female fetus would save in future wedding expenses.

Although infanticide is illegal, it is rarely prosecuted. Similarly, prenatal gender determination is also illegal, but it is also rarely prosecuted. As a result, the population of girls in India is declining. In addition to government actions, nongovernmental organizations are working to curb these practices. The Community Service Guild has been working to discourage female infanticide for at least twenty years. The group teaches mothers and daughters skills that can contribute to their families' income in an attempt to shift the cultural view that girls are a burden to the family.

FURTHER RESOURCES

Periodicals

Sabu, George, M. "Female Infanticide in Tamil Nadu, India—From recognition back to denial." *Reproductive Health* (November 1, 1997).

Jha, Prabhat; Kumar, Rajesh; Vasa, Priya; Dhingra, Neeraj, et al. "Low male-to-female sex ratio of children born in India: A national survey of 1.1 million households." *The Lancet* (January 21, 2006).

Web sites

Christian Science Monitor. "For India's daughters a dark birthday." http://www.csmonitor.com/2005/0209/p11s01-wosc.html (Accessed March 25, 2006).

Rediff.com. "I was scared to see so many Indian's get upset with Matrubhoomi." http://in.rediff.com/movies/2003/oct/16jha.htm (Accessed March 25, 2006).

Webster Universtiy. "Female Infanticide." http://www.webster.edu/~woolflm/femaleinfanticide.html (Accessed March 25, 2006).

Kilt-wearing Missouri High School Boy Wins Apology

News article

By: Anonymous

Date: January 12, 2006

Source: "Kilt-wearing Missouri High School Boy Wins Apology." Reuters (January 12, 2006).

About the Author: This article was published without a byline and was written by a contributor to Reuters, a global news reporting agency.

INTRODUCTION

In November 2003, an exhibition opened at the Metropolitan Museum of Art's Costume Institute in New York City. The exhibition was entitled "Bravehearts: Men in Skirts" and documented the asymmetry in men's and women's fashion. The exhibition identifies that although women have, through the ages, borrowed men's fashions, the taboo is greater for a man to borrow from women's fashions. Therefore, the display examines the designers and individuals who have challenged these societal norms by injecting the skirt into men's fashions. The curator for the exhibition, Andrew Bolton, noted that "Since 'the great masculine renunciation' of the late eighteenth and early nineteenth century, men have tended to follow a more restricted code for appearance... From the 1960s, with the rise of countercultures and an increase in informality, men have enjoyed more sartorial freedom, but they still lack access to the full repertoire of clothing worn by women."

After centuries of flamboyant attire, men's fashions began to change at the turn of the nineteenth century, when a tailored black suit in the managerial style ended the colorful trends in men's fashions. However, throughout the centuries, subtle skirt wearing has been deemed acceptable in certain arenas of men's dress. A man's caftan is a long-sleeved, floor-length robe worn by men in the Middle East and Africa and has been adopted by Western clergy. Tailcoats and aprons can be viewed as partial skirts and are acceptable attire for men. Popular culture also provides examples of men borrowing women's fashions. For example, hip-hop jeans, worn extremely loose and below the hips, are viewed in Bolton's exhibition at the Metropolitan Museum as a variation on a skirt. The curator also identifies the black floor-length soutane worn by Keanu Reeves in *The Matrix Reloaded* as another example of borrowing women's fashion.

The kilt, however, is the most well-known men's fashion borrowed from women's attire. The original kilts consisted of a piece of tartan (or patterned) cloth—two yards wide and four yards long—intended to be drawn around the waist and adjusted with folds and a tightly buckled belt. Kilts reached the knees and the upper part attached to the left shoulder and intended to cover the shoulder and body in wet weather. The kilt was once viewed as a symbol of nationalist rebellion, and in 1745, following a Jacobite uprising, the dress was considered politically subversive and banned by the British government. The Dress Act, which banned the wearing of kilts by all Scots except those in the army, was repealed in 1783. The ban had successfully affected the popularity of the kilt, which after the ban shifted from a traditional Highland attire to a nationalist statement.

PRIMARY SOURCE

KANSAS CITY, Missouri (Reuters)—A Missouri high school student who was barred from a school dance because he was wearing a Scottish kilt has received an apology from school officials after the action sparked outrage among Scottish heritage supporters.

In a letter dated January 9, Jackson School District Superintendent Ron Anderson apologized to Jackson High School senior Nathan Warmack and said the district would train staffers how to properly apply the school dress code.

The letter came after more than two months of debate and discussion about the actions of school officials when they asked Warmack, who is of Scottish descent, to change into trousers before entering the dance on November 5.

News of the event sparked an Internet petition, which was ultimately signed by more than 10,000 supporters and championed by the Clan Gunn Society of North America, which promotes Scottish heritage and traditions.

"Individual members felt like there had been an injustice to the young man," said society president Rich Gunn.

SIGNIFICANCE

Nathan Warmack was not the first young man to wear a kilt to a school dance and receive a negative response from his school's administration. In 2001, Matt McCarl received in-school suspension for wearing a kilt to his junior prom at Lakeview high school in Stoneboro, Pennsylvania.

Nathan Warmack was considered an average student who became interested in his Scottish heritage after seeing the 1995 Mel Gibson movie *Braveheart*. Warmack, a defensive lineman on his Jackson, Missouri high school football team, bought a kilt online to wear to his schools "Silver Arrow" dance. He showed the kilt to his school's vice principal, who jokingly advised him to wear something underneath the skirt. Warmack did wear shorts underneath the skirt and to complete the ensemble wore a white dress shirt and tie.

After being ejected from his high school dance, the school's District Superintendent Ron Anderson issued a statement in support of principal Rick McClard's decision. Anderson asserted that McClard had the authority to judge "appropriate dress" under the district's dress code, which covers extracurricular activities such as dances. The authority stems from McClard's responsibility "to protect from the possibility of a disruption or something that could be viewed as a disruption." By

Nathan Warmack poses in his living room in Jackson, Mo., on December 17, 2005. AP IMAGES

January 6, 2006, however, a lawyer for the Jackson School District announced that kilt wearing is allowed unless it creates a disruption. As a result, Warmack received an apology during a school board meeting and the district superintendent promised to train school staff on the proper interpretation of the dress code.

FURTHER RESOURCES

Periodicals

Heinhold, Jenn. "Scot Student's Kilt is Crux of Controversy." *The Herald* (May 20, 2001).

Muschamp, Herbert. "Design Review: In the Land of the Free, Who Wears the Skirts?" The *New York Times* (November 7, 2003).

Taylor, Betsy. "Missouri Student Receives Apology over Kilt." Associated Press (January 10, 2006).

Web sites

Metropolitan Museum of Art. "Bravehearts: Men in Skirts." <http://www.metmuseum.org/special/se_event.asp?Oc currenceId={823731F9-6846-4D66-AFF5-AB57B 724C97A}> (accessed April 1, 2006).

Women's Rights Movement

2

Women's Rights Movement

The struggle for women's rights extends beyond the right to own property or vote. It is the fight for woman to be considered a individual in her own right, defined on her own terms, by her own intellect and accomplishments, afforded the same opportunities as her male peers. While not by any means an exhaustive or exclusive definition of the movement for women's rights, it encompasses the victories secured by two centuries of activism: the recognition of women as legal and political entities separate of their fathers or husbands; the rights to own property in their own name, to secure an education, to vote and hold office, to enter the workforce, and to plan their families and control their reproductive lives.

More than just the procurement of a bundle of rights, the women's movement also pushed for a rethinking of gender roles. Feminists asserted that housework was not intrinsically womanly, rather social norms had constructed what was considered "woman's work." Furthermore, many claimed that society did not value "women's work" as much as it did men's. Traditional housekeeping and childrearing are largely accomplished in the confines of the house. The work is unpaid, and women are dependent on a breadwinner, typically their husband. This social structure is especially difficult for widowed or divorced women. Advocating "partnership marriages" and cooperative parenting duties changed the family structure for men as much as for women.

The women's movement transformed society as well as the home. Most of the major feminist issues of the past 40 years were sparked by tensions created as women ventured further from the traditional roles in the home. Working women demanded equal pay and promotion opportunities. Women pressed for the right to control their reproductive lives, to use birth control or obtain a legal abortion, whether married or single. Articles on the landmark U.S. Supreme Court decision of *Roe v. Wade* focus on this still-controversial issue.

Criticism of feminism and the effects of the women's movement also appear in this chapter.

Finally, the women's movement strives for social acceptance of a variety personal and professional choices that women make. An ideal goal is the death of social stigmas for female sexuality, for women who choose not to marry or have children, and for women who work outside the home as well as those who choose to be stay-at-home mothers.

Letter to Elizabeth Cady Stanton on Her (Susan B. Anthony's) Illegal Vote

Letter

By: Susan B. Anthony

Date: November 5, 1872

Source: Anthony, Susan B. "Letter to Elizabeth Cady Stanton on Her (Susan B. Anthony's) Illegal Vote." Image of letter from Ida Harper Collection, November 5, 1872.

About the Author: Susan B. Anthony (1820–1906) was one of the foremost women's rights activists of the late nineteenth century. She focused on women's suffrage as the key to other social and political advances. Born in Adams, Massachusetts in 1820, the future organizer took up schoolteaching in Canajoharie, New York. Dissatisfied with the limits of teaching and frustrated that she only received a quarter of a man's salary for the exact same work, Anthony dedicated herself to reform in 1848. She met Elizabeth Cady Stanton in 1851 and the two would become lifelong friends as well as the leading lights of the woman suffrage movement.

INTRODUCTION

In the first half of the nineteenth century, the abolition and temperance movements consumed the attention of reform-minded Americans. Women played a role in both movements, but custom dictated that women remain in seclusion. Proper women did not speak in public, permit their names to appear in print, or engage in any other kind of activity in the male sphere of politics.

Women chafed at the restraints placed upon them. Elizabeth Cady Stanton began her activism as an abolitionist. She deeply resented that male abolitionists would not allow women to speak at an abolitionist convention, instead forcing them to sit in a curtained balcony as the men debated. Stanton dedicated herself to women's rights. Along with other women, she saw a parallel between the lives of women and the lives of slaves.

Anthony was active in the temperance movement (a public effort to moderate alcohol consumption). She was frustrated by the refusal of male temperance advocates to welcome women as equals. In 1852, Anthony and Stanton founded the Women's New York State Temperance Society, which addressed temperance but

also ventured into the controversial realm of women's rights by advocating the right to vote and to divorce drunken husbands. Beginning as an agent for this society, Anthony became a full-time reformer. Witty, down-to-earth, and seemingly tireless, Anthony traveled throughout New York in the 1850s to speak on behalf of coeducation, equal pay, mothers' custody rights, and liberalized divorce laws.

After the Civil War, Anthony still promoted the same causes but increasingly she came to see women's suffrage as the only way to establish economic equality, abolish racism, remove the ills caused by industrialization, and rid government of corruption. Other concerns fell by the wayside as Anthony and Stanton founded the National Woman Suffrage Association in 1869 to promote a federal suffrage amendment.

Anthony believed that her primary responsibility was to educate society of the importance of the ballot and she did this through cross-country lecture tours, the lobbying of state legislatures and members of Congress, petition drives, and state suffrage campaigns. She emphasized the humiliation of disfranchisement, noting that the laws also prohibited the mentally challenged, the insane, and convicted criminals from casting ballots.

In 1872, Anthony attempted to vote in the hope that, as a citizen, she could not be deprived of rights protected by the U.S. Constitution. Indicted by New York authorities for "knowingly, wrongfully, and unlawfully" casting a ballot in Rochester for a representative to the U.S. Congress, Anthony was not permitted by the judge to speak at her trial or to request a poll of the jurors. Found guilty and fined $100, she refused to pay. The fine remained uncollected. Since she had not been ordered to jail, a frustrated Anthony could not take her case to the Supreme Court on a writ of habeas corpus.

■ PRIMARY SOURCE

LETTER TO ELIZABETH CADY STANTON ON HER (SUSAN B. ANTHONY'S) ILLEGAL VOTE

See primary source image.

■

SIGNIFICANCE

It took a very long time for women's rights to win any popular support, even among women. Most people, male and female, approved of separate spheres for men and women. Anthony and Stanton believed that women failed to support the vote for women because they did not realize what its absence cost them.

PRIMARY SOURCE

Letter to Elizabeth Cady Stanton on Her (Susan B. Anthony's) Illegal Vote: A Letter from Susan B. Anthony to Elizabeth Cady Stanton, November 5, 1872. In it, Anthony describes her attempt to vote in the 1872 presidential election. This attempt eventually led to the case United States v. Susan B. Anthony, which detrmined that citizenship did not give women the right to vote. PUBLIC DOMAIN.

Since the founding of the country, American women had complained about their lot in life. Women were excluded from public office, denied an education equivalent to that provided to males, oppressed by religious rules, given a subordinate role in society, and forced to be dependent on men who were not always dependable providers and husbands. Such protests, however, were likely to be infrequent, private, and voiced only when some particular humiliation compelled a woman to violate the command that she remain silent and subservient.

Anthony and Stanton helped change this situation. Despite harassment, Anthony's arrest, and pub-lic ridicule, they spearheaded the feminist movement. While Stanton remained at home with her large family, the single Anthony traveled to virtually every state and territory in the Midwest and West to organize women in support of women's suffrage. The Nineteenth Amendment to the Constitution, ratified in 1920 and granting women the right to vote, was often called the "Anthony Amendment" in honor of the woman who insisted that "Failure is Impossible." Anthony and Stanton left a legacy of social, political, legal, and educational reforms that improved the status of all the women who came after them.

FURTHER RESOURCES

Books

Barry, Kathleen. *Susan B. Anthony: Biography of a Singular Feminist*. New York: New York University Press, 1988.

DuBois, Ellen Carol. *Feminism and Suffrage: The Emergence of an Independent Women's Movement in America, 1848–1869*. Ithaca, N.Y.: Cornell University Press, 1978.

The Elizabeth Cady Stanton—Susan B. Anthony Reader: Correspondence, Writings, Speeches, edited by Ellen Carol DuBois. Boston: Northeastern University Press, 1981.

One Woman, One Vote: Rediscovering the Woman Suffrage Movement, edited by Marjorie Spruill Wheeler. Troutdale, Ore.: New Sage Press, 1995.

Comstockery in America

Newspaper article

By: Margaret Sanger

Date: July 15, 1915

Source: Sanger, Margaret. "Comstockery in America." *International Socialist Review* (1915): 46–49.

About the Author: Margaret Sanger (1879–1966) was a nurse who fought for public access to information on contraception in the early part of the twentieth cen-

During a birth control class in 1953, Mrs. Shizue Kato, Japan's leading feminist, birth control expert and disciple of friend Margaret Sanger, holds a model of female sex organs, and demonstrates how to insert a pessary. PHOTO BY MARGARET BOURKE-WHITE//TIME LIFE PICTURES/GETTY IMAGES

tury. Her efforts to disseminate birth control information led to her repeated arrest for violating the Comstock Act in the United States. She helped to found Planned Parenthood, an organization that helps provide health and gynecological care for women in the United States.

INTRODUCTION

In 1873, Anthony Comstock, the Postmaster General of the United States, succeeded in persuading the U.S. Congress to pass legislation that became known as the Comstock Act. The Comstock Act stated, in part, that it was illegal "to sell, or to lend, or to give away, or in any manner to exhibit, or shall otherwise publish or offer to publish in any manner, or shall have in his possession, for any such purpose or purposes, an obscene book, pamphlet, paper, writing, advertisement, circular, print, picture, drawing or other representation, figure, or image on or of paper or other material, or any cast instrument, or other article of an immoral nature, or any drug or medicine, or any article whatever, for the prevention of conception, or for causing unlawful abortion, or shall advertise the same for sale, or shall write or print, or cause to be written or printed, any card, circular, book, pamphlet, advertisement..."

Critics of the Comstock Act claimed that Anthony Comstock—under the impetus of his religious convictions (he was a conservative Congregationalist)—was imposing his own brand of morality on others. When the law passed in 1873 there was little opposition. However, by the early 1900s, as women's rights activism increased in the United States, critics began to voice their dissent.

Margaret Sanger was one of eleven children. Her mother was pregnant eighteen times and died at the age of fifty. Sanger was strongly affected by her mother's health struggles related to childbirth and childrearing. As a nurse, she visited the tenement houses and slums of the Lower East Side of New York City. Urbanization, immigration, and industrialization converged in the first decade of the twentieth century, and Sanger's experiences working in public health with the poor convinced her that access to family planning information was crucial for poor women and men. According to Sanger's own writings, her patients frequently asked her how to stop having babies; husbands and wives alike begged for such knowledge.

By 1912, Sanger resigned from nursing and took up the cause of what she called "birth control," the use of a basic understanding of natural family planning and conception to control family size. In 1913, she founded the publication *Woman Rebel*, which published information on birth control. She was indicted for mailing "obscene" material and violating the Comstock Act, but left for Europe before a trial could take place.

In this excerpt from her article "Comstockery in America," Sanger discusses some of these events and also expresses her contempt for an industrial system that she perceives to be corrupt and in collusion with the government to oppress the poor and working class urban citizens. Sanger adopted the Socialist cause and published this article in a Socialist publication.

■ PRIMARY SOURCE

There have been many publications during these years which have been suppressed by the orders of Comstock, and the publisher imprisoned, but one of the latest, and most flagrant disregard of Press Freedom was in the suppression and confiscation of the monthly publication, "The Woman Rebel." This was a working woman's paper, the first of its kind ever issued in America. It had for its motto: "Working Women, build up within yourselves a conscious fighting character against all things which enslave you," and claimed that one of the working woman's greatest enslavements was her ignorance of the means to control the size of her family. The editor promised to defy the existing law and to impart such information to the readers of "The Woman Rebel" and urged all working women to rally to its support.

The first issue in March, 1914, was suppressed. The May, July, August, September and October issues were suppressed and confiscated, and three indictments, on the March, May and July issues, covering twelve counts, were returned against me, as the editor, by the Federal Grand Jury. One of the counts against me was for an article called "Open Discussion." This was a discussion of the subject of birth control and was considered "obscene." Another was an article announcing the organization of The Birth Control League, setting forth its object and methods of organization. All the indictments were returned and counts were made on all articles which discussed the idea of the Working Woman keeping down the number of her family.

"The Woman Rebel" did not advocate the practice of this knowledge as a "panacea" for the present economic enslavement, but it did urge the practice of it as the most important immediate step which should be taken toward the economic emancipation of the workers. Thousands of letters poured in to me from all over the country. I was besieged with requests for the information from all kinds and classes of people. Nearly every letter agreed with me that too long have the workers produced the slave class, the children for the mills, the soldiers for the wars, and the time had come to watch the masters produce their own slaves if they must have them. We know the capitalist class must have a slave class, bred in poverty and reared in ignorance. That is why it is quite consistent with their laws that there should be a heavy penalty of five years' imprisonment for imparting information as to the means of preventing conception. Industry in the U.S.A. is fairly new; it is reaching out in foreign lands to capture trade and to undersell its rival competitors. They have only one way to do this, and that is to get labor cheap. The cheapest labor is that of women and children; the larger the number of children in a family, the earlier they enter the factory. We need only to look to our mill towns to see the truth of this statement; so the conditions in the cotton mills of the South where little boys and girls, eight, nine and ten years of age, wend their sleepy way to the mills in the morning before the winter sun has risen, to work at a killing tension for twelve hours as helper to the mother, and return again when the sun has set.

We, who know the conditions there, know that the father cannot get a man's wage, because a child's labor can be had. There is an average of nine children to every family in these and in other industrial sections where child labor exists and wages run low and infant mortality runs high.

Many of the stockholders of these mills are legislators and congressmen who have to do with the making of the laws. Naturally it is to their interest that child slaves be born into the world and their duty is to enforce the laws to that end.

"The Woman Rebel" told the Working Woman these things, and told her that a large family of children is one of the greatest obstacles in the way to obtain economic freedom for her class. It is the greatest burden to them in all ways, for no matter how spirited and revolutionary one may feel, the piteous cry of hunger of several little ones will compel a man to forego the future good of his class to the present need of his family.

It is the man with a large family who is so often the burden of a strike. He is usually the hardest to bring out on strike, for it is he and his who suffer the most through its duration. Everywhere, in the shop, in the army of the unemployed, in the bread line where men are ready to take the place of a striker, it is the large family problem which is the chief of the multitudes of miseries that confront the working class today.

"The Woman Rebel" told the Working Woman that there is no freedom for her until she has this knowledge which will enable her to say if she will become a mother or not. The fewer children she had to cook, wash and toil for, the more leisure she would have to read, think and develop. That freedom demands leisure, and her first freedom must be in her right of herself over her own body; the right to say what she will do with it in marriage and out of it; the right to become a mother, or not, as she desires and sees fit to do; that all these rights swing around the pivot of the means to prevent conception, and every woman had the right to have this knowledge if she wished it.

As editor and publisher of "The Woman Rebel," I felt a great satisfaction and inspiration in the response which came from working men and women all over America. For fourteen years I have been much in the nursing field, and know too well the intolerable conditions among the workers which a large family does not decrease.

I saw that the working women ask for this knowledge to prevent bringing more children into the world, and saw the medical profession shake its head in silence at this request.

I saw that the women of wealth obtain this information with little difficulty, while the working man's wife must continue to bring children into the world she could not feed or clothe, or else resort to an abortion.

I saw that it was the working class women who fill the death list which results from abortion, for though the women of wealth have abortions performed too, there is given them the best medical care and attention money can buy; trained nurses watch over them, and there is seldom any evil consequence. But the working woman must look for the cheapest assistance. The professional abortionist, the unclean midwives, the fake and quack— all feed upon her helplessness and thrive and prosper on her ignorance. It is the Comstock laws which produce the abortionist and make him a thriving necessity while the lawmakers close their Puritan eyes.

I saw that it is the working class children who fill the mills, factories, sweatshops, orphan asylums and reformatories, because through ignorance they were brought into the world, and this ignorance continues to be perpetuated.

I resolved, after a visit to France, where children are loved and wanted and cared for and educated, to devote my time and effort in giving this information to women who applied for it. I resolved to defy the law, not behind a barricade of law books and technicalities, but by giving the information to the workers directly in factory and workshop.

This was done by the publication of a small pamphlet, "Family Limitations," of which one hundred thousand copies were distributed in factories and mines throughout the U.S.

Women's rights advocate Margaret Sanger (left) , and her sister, Ethel Byrne are in court in Brooklyn, N.Y., January 1917. Sanger was charged with maintaining a "public nuisance" after opening the first birth-control clinic in the United States. AP IMAGES

SIGNIFICANCE

Like many essays written by activist women during this time, Sanger's work appealed to the reader's sense of humanity. She discussed the poor mothers' health, the toll on children, the pleadings from husbands and wives for information on the prevention of conception so that parents could give their existing children a better life. This theme—appealing to the reader's emotions regarding the plight of the poor—was a common Progressive Era theme.

Sanger's theory concerning industry, government, and the intentional suppression of information on birth control, however, was a shocking concept to the middle class of that era. Socialists argued that contraception information would lead to "economic emancipation" for the poor. The bearing of nine, ten, eleven, or more children by a woman who worked twelve hour days, six days a week, led to the continuation of cycles of poverty. In addition, it could lead to an early death for the mother—leaving her children orphaned and deepening the need for child labor to help support the family. Sanger connected the government's regulation of birth control information with industrial development; her writings claimed that the Comstock Act had become a tool to force the poor to continue to produce the workers that fed industrial growth, while limiting the poor worker's ability to rise out of the slums and achieve personal progress.

In addition to her own arrest for various articles and actions, Sanger's husband William was arrested in 1915 after a postal agent, pretending to be a Socialist friend of Margaret Sanger's, requested a pamphlet on birth control called "Family Limitation." William Sanger was arrested, convicted, and sentenced to thirty days in jail for this violation of the Comstock Act.

In October 1916, Margaret Sanger opened the first birth control clinic in the United States in Brooklyn, New York. In addition to offering counseling and written materials on family planning, the clinic provided condoms and diaphragms. It was shut down within nine days and Sanger was charged with "maintaining a public nuisance." She served thirty days in jail and appealed her case, also arguing for the right for doctors to distribute birth control information and devices to patients. The appellate court ruled for her conviction but did permit doctors the right—when medically necessary—to dispense birth control information and supplies.

In 1921, Sanger founded the American Birth Control League, which eventually became the Planned Parenthood Federation of America, the largest organization in the United States devoted to women's health and contraception.

In 1936, the U.S. Congress repealed the Comstock Act.

FURTHER RESOURCES

Books

Sanger, Margaret. *The Autobiography of Margaret Sanger.* Mineola, N.Y.: Dover Publications, 2004.

Sanger, Margaret. *The Selected Papers of Margaret Sanger.* Champaign: University of Illinois Press, 2002.

Web sites

Michigan State University Libraries. "What Every Girl Should Know." <http://digital.lib.msu.edu/collections/index/> (accessed February 6, 2005).

Sophia Smith Collection, Smith College. "Margaret Sanger Papers 1761–1995." <http://asteria.fivecolleges.edu/findaids/sophiasmith/mnsss43_main.html> (accessed February 6, 2005).

Convention on the Nationality of Women (Inter-American)

Treaty

By: Governments of Twenty Pan American Nations

Date: 1933

Source: Convention on the Nationality of Women (Inter-American). *Treaties and Other International Agreements of the United States of America 1776–1949,* edited by Charles I. Bevans. Washington D.C.: Government Printing Office, 1969.

About the Author: The Convention on the Nationality of Women consisted of an assembly of representatives from the following nations: Argentina, Bolivia, Brazil, Chile, Colombia, Cuba, Dominican Republic, Ecuador, El Salvador, Guatemala, Haiti, Honduras, Mexico, Nicaragua, Panama, Paraguay, Peru, United States of America, Uruguay, and Venezuela.

INTRODUCTION

The representatives of twenty nations, at the Seventh International Conference via the Pan American Union, all signed a treaty acknowledging that a woman's citizenship would not be jeopardized if she married a man that was not a national of her country. Furthermore, the treaty established that a woman's citizenship rights would not be based upon her gender.

The Convention on the Nationality of Women convened in December 1933, and the delegates signed the treaty on December 26, 1933. The United States Senate acknowledged the signing on May 24, 1934; the U.S. president ratified it on June 30, 1934; and the signed treaty was deposited into the binding records of the Pan American Union on July 13, 1934. After its

During a protest against a proposed law, in India's Jammu-Kashmir state, protesters tussle with a policeman, while shouting anti-government slogans. The proposed law will not allow women local citizenship rights if they marry a man from another state. AP IMAGES

deposit into official record, the treaty became force (meaning law), and U.S. President Franklin D. Roosevelt publicly proclaimed its establishment, success, and significance on October 11, 1934.

The signing and enactment of this treaty—which directly addresses citizenship rights of women—acts a measure to help facilitate peaceful relations between nations. The nations involved are those aligned with the Pan American Union, which was originally established as the Organization of American States in 1889–1890 and renamed in 1910. The building of such an alliance, and the name Pan American, showed respect and levels of trust between these nations—those of North, South, and Central America. The creation of the Union coincided with territorial expansion efforts, particularly those of the United States with its occupation of Puerto Rico, the annexation of Hawaii, and the Spanish-American War in 1898. With the annexation and occupation of additional territories (by the United States and other countries), cultural misconceptions occurred, and with expanded communication and travel ability, many individuals began leaving their native countries and settling elsewhere. Hence, marriages between people from different nations were not uncommon, and in an act of good faith treaties like this one attempted to bridge boundaries between cultures and races. Interestingly, the delegates who signed this treaty were predominantly male—ninety-nine delegates signed the treaty and only three were female. The female representatives came from the United States, Uruguay, and Paraguay.

PRIMARY SOURCE

CONVENTION ON THE NATIONALITY OF WOMEN (INTER-AMERICAN)

ARTICLE 1

There shall be no distinction based on sex as regards nationality, in their legislation or in their practice.

ARTICLE 2

The present convention shall be ratified by the High Contracting Parties in conformity with their respective constitutional procedures. The Minister of Foreign Affairs of the Republic of Uruguay shall transmit authentic certified copies to the governments for the aforementioned purpose of ratification. The instrument of ratification shall be deposited in the archives of the Pan American Union in Washington, which shall notify the signatory governments of said deposit. Such notification shall be considered as an exchange of ratifications.

ARTICLE 3

The present convention will enter into force between the High Contracting Parties in the order in which they deposit their respective ratifications.

ARTICLE 4

The present convention shall remain in force indefinitely but may be denounced by means of one year's notice given to the Pan American Union, which shall transmit it to the other signatory governments. After the expiration of this period the convention shall cease in its effects as regards the party which denounces but shall remain in effect for the remaining High Contracting Parties.

ARTICLE 5

The present convention shall be open for the adherence and accession of the States which are not signatories. The corresponding instruments shall be deposited in the archives of the Pan American Union which shall communicate them to the other High Contracting Parties.

In witness whereof, the following Plenipotentiaries have signed this convention in Spanish, English, Portuguese and French and hereunto affix their respective seals in the city of Montevideo, Republic of Uruguay, this 26th day of December, 1933.

SIGNIFICANCE

While treaties advocating the equal citizenship rights of women may have not altered the quality, stability, or equality of a woman's life on a daily basis, they certainly helped pave the way for future international and national legislation. Permitting women the right to vote, as well as guaranteeing that they would not lose their citizenship rights if they married a non-national, has allowed women to prosper on local and national levels. Women have staged strikes, fought in war, served as nurses, acted as international liaisons, and have worked alongside men to promote equality, justice, and harmony. The United Nation's Millennium Development Goals and its conventions on women are just a few examples of the progress, and attempted progress, that the world community is making to elevate the status of women and alleviate gender divisions that exist throughout the world.

FURTHER RESOURCES

Books

Peters, Julie Stone, and Andrea Wolper. *Women's Rights, Human's Rights: International Feminist Perspectives*. New Brunswick, N.J.: Routledge, 1994.

Williams, B. *Women Out of Place: The Gender of Agency and the Race of Nationality*. New Brunswick, N.J.: Routledge, 1996.

Web sites

Amnesty International. "Women's Human Rights and the Stop Violence Against Women Campaign." <http://www.amnestyusa.org/women/index.do> (accessed March 27, 2006).

Bora Laskin Law Library. "Women's Human Rights Resources Programme." <http://www.law-lib.utoronto.ca/Diana> (accessed March 27, 2006).

Redstockings Manifesto

Article

By: Redstockings

Date: 1969

Source: Redstockings. *Redstockings Manifesto*. Stuyvesant, NY: Redstockings of the Women's Liberation Movement, 1969.

About the Author: The Redstockings were a short-lived radical women's liberation organization that formed in 1969 and died in the early 1970s. The organization challenged male supremacy in the political system and in American culture. Although the group, centered in New York City, remained fairly small throughout its existence, it did influence the debate on abortion reform.

INTRODUCTION

The Redstockings, part of the radical feminist movement of the late 1960s and early 1970s, were founded in 1969 by Ellen Willis and Shulamith Firestone. The group was committed to militant public actions as well as to raising consciousness of women's oppression. They chose the name Redstockings in tribute to the insulting nickname of "bluestockings" given to nineteenth-century feminists and because red is the color of revolution. The Redstockings printed the first "SISTERHOOD IS POWERFUL" button, which inspired a host of other buttons proclaiming women's rights that became symbols of the early 1970s.

For their first public action, the Redstockings focused on abortion. New York, which was among the states then considering legalizing the procedure, had convened an expert hearing on the topic and invited fourteen men and a nun to be its only expert witnesses. The Redstockings interrupted the proceedings and offered impromptu testimony from "real experts" (sexually active women) about the need to repeal all abortion laws. The hearing was forced to be adjourned.

Encouraged by this success, the Redstockings decided to hold their own public hearings on abortion. The subsequent "speak-out" in 1969 was so successful that it inspired other feminists, including those in France, to voice their opinions on the issue. To challenge the assumption that abortion was not political, women told of the abortions that they had undergone. To keep attention focused on abortion, the Redstockings considered hanging a banner that would read "Liberty for Women, Repeal All Abortion Laws" from the Statue of Liberty, but disagreements within the organization stopped this plan. They were never again so action oriented.

The Redstockings Manifesto was an attempt to raise the consciousness of women about the impact of male supremacy. It reflects Marxist thinking about the oppression of women as a class. Unlike many other feminists, the Redstockings saw women's behavior as the result of resistance and accommodation to male supremacy. They rejected as false all psychological explanations of women's conduct. The Redstocking ideology saw all women as united by common oppression with class and race far less significant.

PRIMARY SOURCE

REDSTOCKINGS MANIFESTO

I. After centuries of individual and preliminary political struggle, women are united to achieve their final liberation from male supremacy. Redstockings is dedicated to building this unity and winning our freedom.

II. Women are an oppressed class. Our oppression is total, affecting every facet of our lives. We are exploited as sex objects, breeders, domestic servants, and cheap labor. We are considered inferior beings, whose only purpose is to enhance men's lives. Our humanity is denied. Our prescribed behavior is enforced by the threat of physical violence.

Because we have lived so intimately with our oppressors, in isolations from each other, we have been kept from seeing our personal suffering as a political condition. This creates the illusion that a woman's relationship with her man is a matter interplay between two unique personalities, and can be worked out individually. In reality, every such relationship is a *class* relationship, and the conflicts between individual men and women are *political* conflicts that can only be solved collectively.

III. We identify the agents of our oppression as men. Male supremacy is the oldest, most basic form of domination. All other forms of exploitation and oppression (racism, capitalism, imperialism, etc.) are extensions of male supremacy: men dominate women, a few men dominate the rest. All power structures throughout history have been male-dominated and male-oriented. Men have controlled all political, economic and cultural institutions and backed up this control with physical force. They have used their power to keep women in an inferior position. *All men* receive economic, sexual, and psychological benefits from male supremacy. *All men* have oppressed women.

IV. Attempts have been made to shift the burden of responsibility from men to institutions or to women themselves. We condemn these arguments as evasions. Institutions alone do not oppress; they are merely tools of the oppressor. To blame institutions implies that men and women are equally victimized, obscures the fact that men benefit from the subordination of women, and gives men the excuse that they are forced to be oppressors. On the contrary, any man is free to renounce his superior position provided that he is willing to be treated like a woman by other men.

We also reject the idea that women consent to or are to blame for their own oppression. Women's submission is not the result of brainwashing, stupidity, or mental illness but of continual, daily pressure from men. We do not need to change ourselves, but to change men. The most slanderous evasion of all is that women can oppress men. The basis for this illusion is the isolation of individual relationships from their political context and the tendency of men to see any legitimate challenge to their privileges as persecution.

V. We regard our personal experience, and our feelings about that experience, as the basis for an analysis of our common situation. We cannot rely on existing ideologies as they are all products of male supremacist culture. We question every generalization and accept none that are not confirmed by our experience.

Our chief task at present is to develop female class consciousness through sharing experience and publicly exposing the sexist foundation of all our institutions. Consciousness-raising is not "therapy," which implies the existence of individual solutions and falsely assumes that the male–female relationship is purely personal, but the only method by which we can ensure that our program for liberation is based on the concrete realities of our lives.

The first requirement for raising class consciousness is honesty, in private and in public, with ourselves and other women.

VI. We identify with all women. We define our best interest as that of the poorest, most brutally exploited woman.

We repudiate all economic, racial, educational or status privileges that divide us from other women. We are determined to recognize and eliminate any prejudices we may hold against other women.

We are committed to achieving internal democracy. We will do whatever is necessary to ensue that every woman in our movement has an equal chance to participate, assume responsibility, and develop her political potential.

VII. We call on all our sisters to unite with us in struggle.

We call on all men to give up their male privileges and support women's liberation in the interest of our humanity and their own.

In fighting for our liberation we will always take the side of women against their oppressors. We will not ask what is "revolutionary" or "reformist," only what is good for women.

The time for individual skirmishes has passed. This time we are going all the way.

SIGNIFICANCE

As in the first wave of the women's movement in the nineteenth century, the second wave, in the mid-twentieth century, was divided between those favoring reform of the existing political structure and those favoring a complete overthrow. The Redstockings, part of the radical wing, saw the existing system as too corrupted by male supremacy to be worth keeping.

Radical feminists wanted to render gender irrelevant. They believed that gender, not class or race, was the primary concern and that all other forms of social domination originated with male supremacy. To radical feminists, liberal feminist's narrow focus on formal equality with men not only ignored the fundamental problem—women's subordination within the home—it assumed that equality in an unjust society was worth fighting for.

The women's movement redefined leadership because of the feminist conception of power. For women fighting male domination, the concept of having power over another person was unacceptable. Therefore, rather than seeking power over others, the leaders of the women's movement wanted to empower one another to seek leadership. The nonhierarchal, shared leadership style of the women's movement has influenced many other organizations, including those in the business world. The shift from the idea of a single leader who issues top-down directives and toward team leadership reflects the legacy of the women's movement.

Radical feminism gradually gave way in the early 1970s to cultural feminism, a countercultural movement that celebrated the value of women. Despite the collapse of radical feminism, many of the ideas of the radicals were adopted by moderate reformers. Abortion rights and the notion that the personal is political have since become part of the American mainstream.

FURTHER RESOURCES

Books

Echols, Alice. *Daring to Be Bad: Radical Feminism in America, 1967–1975*. Minneapolis: University of Minnesota Press, 1989.

Ezekiel, Judith. *Feminism in the Heartland*. Columbus, OH: Ohio State University Press, 2002.

Rosen, Ruth. *The World Split Open: How the Modern Women's Movement Changed America*. New York: Viking, 2000.

Roxcy O'Neal Bolton, an equal rights activist, meets with Eleanor Roosevelt (right) in 1953. COURTESY OF THE STATE LIBRARY & ARCHIVES OF FLORIDA.

Roxcy Bolton's Campaign Against Men's Grills

Letter

By: Anonymous

Date: October 8, 1969

Source: Letter to Roxcy Bolton on her campaign against men's grills, October 8, 1969.

About the Author: In 1969, Roxcy Bolton protested the establishment of "men's grills" in Miami restaurants—public eating areas set aside for men only. This letter, not originally anonymous, was written in rebuttal.

INTRODUCTION

Roxcy O'Neal Bolton was born in Mississippi in 1926 and became a pioneer of feminism in Florida. She helped found the Florida chapter of the National Organization for Women in 1966 and founded a nonprofit women's aid organization called Women in Distress. In 1974, she was instrumental in establishing one of the first rape treatment centers in the United States, the Rape Treatment Center at the Jackson Memorial Hospital in Miami, Florida, now called the Roxcy Bolton Rape Treatment Center.

In 1969, Bolton began a campaign to end the practice of "men-only" lunch sections in Miami restaurants. She wrote letters and met with business owners, arguing that the practice was discriminatory. Her actions were successful, and eventually, the men's grills disappeared. The document below was written by a woman who argued that Bolton's opposition to the men's-only lunch businesses was excessive and improper.

■ PRIMARY SOURCE

Roxcy Bolton's Campaign against Men's Grills

Florida

8 October 1969

Dear Mrs. Bolton

I have been watching the progress of this NOW organization with some misgivings, and feel I must speak out against some of your activities.

"Persuading" Jordan Marsh [a department store chain] to open its Men's Grill to women strikes me as highly ridiculous, and very unwise. This is the kind of move that simply gives rise to resentment among men, without being a significant gain to women.

There are many areas of life, in which separation of the sexes is desirable—I very much enjoy the female atmosphere of a beauty shop, and feel men are entitled to their Barber Shops to themselves. With four sons I have had occasion to intrude on this little masculine world, and much prefer to do some shopping or otherwise occupy myself while the boys are having their hair cut.

I have attended the Plaine Powers studio, and all of us were discomfited when an electrician was working in the studio—not that we were so modest, just that that is a woman's place.

Now I realize that eating lunch is not something which requires separation of the sexes, but men ENJOY being special, just as they enjoy their all-male poker games and hunting trips. Why should we try to snatch this away from them?

A parallel situation would seem to me to be the relationship between parents and their growing children. There are things my children do which I simply find no pleasure in, front lawn football games, loud rock music sessions, even slumber parties. There is no reason why I must intrude myself on their pleasures, nor why they must intrude on my more quiet pastimes. We are Different, with different tastes and different interests, and we can both benefit from time spent apart, pursuing our separate lives, discussing with our own friends the things that interest us.

While I myself have never felt that I was treated as an inferior by men, I realize that there are probably some injustices in hiring practices (though I can even see reasons for much of that—I wouldn't want to be a jockey, or

try to fulfill some other traditionally male role, and a female minister simply leaves me cold).

The point I am trying to make is just this: we should not confuse discrimination with a mere and harmless desire on the part of men to be separate and a little special.

Sincerely yours,

SIGNIFICANCE

Opposition to feminism has taken a number of forms over the centuries. Some men have argued outright for male superiority, often with the support of temporarily fashionable scientific arguments, including that women are less intelligent than men because they have smaller brains. (On average, they do, but only in proportion to their body size; smaller men also have smaller brains. Human body size does not correlate with intelligence.) It was also acceptable for many decades to argue that women are inherently more childlike, emotional, and irrational than men, hence unsuited for political leadership and other traditional male roles. This is the brand of antifeminism sometimes known as "male chauvinism."

Another type posits that men and women have innate differences that are properly reflected in various forms of segregation, such as different professions for men and women. Both women and men have argued for such a position, believing that there was value in social role differences, whether in dress, profession, segregated eating or socializing spaces, or the like. In the late nineteenth and early twentieth centuries, some influential writers (for example, G. K. Chesterton) argued that women would lose some part of the peculiarly feminine purity or dignity properly belonging to them if given the right to vote, which would involve them in the rough-and-tumble sphere of practical politics—which they could influence anyway by telling their husbands what to do. The letter given here is an expression of a related view: It argues that essential differences between men and women properly give rise to different roles, including the separation of women (and possibly men, though the writer does not specify this) in some otherwise public places or activities.

The belief that some activities or spaces can and should be segregated by gender, is, in fact, almost universal; the issue is how many activities and what sort. Contrary to some panicky claims made in the 1970s, for example, few if any feminists have ever advocated the elimination of gender-segregated toilet and shower facilities in public buildings, gymnasia, and the

Members playing dominos at a men's luncheon club in San Francisco. PHOTO BY NAT FARBMAN//TIME LIFE PICTURES/GETTY IMAGES

like. Also, many feminists support the existence of women's colleges in addition to coeducational institutions, also the free and private formation of men- or women-only groups. It would be difficult to find a feminist, in 1969 or today, who would disagree with the letter writer's contention that both men and women can "benefit from time spent apart with friends." The letter writer, however, implies that the "mere and harmless desire on the part of men to be separate and a little special" may rightly be served by the formal exclusion of women from some public businesses, such as restaurants.

In contast, most feminists would contend that all professional and political roles and general-purpose public spaces should be open equally to men and women. Both men and women can—and, despite the lack of men-only eateries post-1969, still do—form all-male or all-female dining parties.

In any case, by the time Bolton conducted her campaign to open up the men-only eateries to women, the Civil Rights Act of 1964 had already removed the question from the realm of personal opinion. The Act explicitly banned discrimination in public facilities on the basis of sex, race, religion, or ethnicity. Banning women from a public restaurant was, therefore, illegal in 1969, as it is today. The nondiscrimination provisions of the Act do not necessarily apply to private facilities and clubs, so men-only organizations remain an option for those who desire them.

FURTHER RESOURCES

Websites

The Florida Memory Project. "Roxcy Bolton, Pioneer Feminist." <http://www.floridamemory.com/OnlineClassroom/RoxcyBolton/index.cfm> (accessed March 26, 2006).

Our Changing Sense of Self

Book excerpt

By: Boston Women's Health Book Collective

Date: 1971

Source: "Our Changing Sense of Self," from *Our Bodies, Ourselves*, the Boston Women's Health Book Collective, New England Free Press, 1971.

About the Author: The Boston Women's Health Book Collective is an association of feminist women centered in Boston, MA. The group has been publishing updated editions of the book since 1971, most recently in 2005.

INTRODUCTION

Our Bodies, Ourselves (OBOS) is a basic text of modern feminism. It has been adapted or translated into over twenty languages and sold over four million copies. The eighth edition, greatly expanded, appeared in 2005; the excerpt given here is from the first edition (1971).

The Boston Women's Health Book Collective was founded in 1969, when twelve women met at a workshop on "women and their bodies" at a feminist conference in Boston. As a followup to the workshop, the women decided that they would each research a women's health topic; the essays were meant to empower women to learn about their bodies, be active in guiding their own medical treatment rather than passively submitting to the authority of doctors, and, in the words of the Collective, "challenge the medical establishment to change and improve the care that women receive." One revolutionary feature of the book was that none of its authors were doctors or nurses.

In 1970, the collection of essays was issued as a 193-page booklet, *Women and Their Bodies*, printed on newsprint, stapled, and sold for thirty cents a copy. In 1971, the title was revised to be more emphatic—*Our Bodies, Ourselves*—and the essays were printed as a bound book. Around 1980, the informal, consensus-governed "collective" structure of the original group was replaced as the group became a non-profit group. Today, the Boston Women's Health Book Collective (still its official name) states that it is "a nonprofit, public interest women's health education, advocacy, and consulting organization."

For a non-medical textbook, *Our Bodies, Ourselves* was and remains unusually frank about women's sexuality. For example, it contains photographs and drawings of female genitalia, instructs users on how to become familiar with the appearance of their own genitalia by using mirrors, and (in early editions) offered sketches of six different types of hymens. Its most controversial photograph, which showed the naked corpse of a woman who bled to death in a hotel room after an attempted illegal abortion, has been retained in all editions. Frankness about anatomic and social realities was the book's original goal: it sought to demystify women's bodies and to enable them to make informed decisions about health and behavior. This goal remains unchanged: in 2005, a board member of the organization explained that "Our aim is to empower women with accurate information about health, sexuality, and reproduction."

■ PRIMARY SOURCE

OUR CHANGING SENSE OF SELF

This book was written by many women. Those responsible for seeing its completion form the Boston Women's Health Book Collective. This, in part, is who we are: we are in our mid-twenties and early thirties, mostly married or in (or have been in) some long-term relationship with a man. Some of us have had children recently. We are college educated (some of us have gone to graduate school), and all of us have spent a number of years living away from home either with female roommates, with men, alone, or in some varying combination. We have worked or are working. Most of us feel that unlike what we were promised in childhood, we were not totally fulfilled by marriage (a man), and/or motherhood (a child), and/or a (typically feminine) job. This is not to say that we have not grown a lot within marriages and with our children or in our work. Most of us see these relationships as continuing. But just being wife or wife and mother and viewing our work as secondary was too limiting for us. We needed space to do our own work or find out what work we wanted to do. We also needed space to discover who we were separate from these primary relationships so that we could become autonomous adult people as well as have important relationships with others.

We can talk only for ourselves, although we consider ourselves part of a larger movement of women in the Boston area—a group of great variety. We realize that the development of the ideas presented in this book comes from many women we know from other women's collectives as well as our own.

Coming together with women was exciting. We were individual women coming together out of choice and strength. Since we had patterned and focused much of our life around men, this was liberating. It was also liberating because we were legitimizing our need for one another. Most of us had gone to college, had lived with women, and so had had close female friendships with women, but viewed this as a transitional stage leading up to a male-centered life. That was the traditional pattern, and that is what we expected of our lives. We felt that as young adult women we had missed close female friendships. Traditionally, the extended family provided close female contacts—women in unself-conscious ways providing support, sharing experience and wisdom with each other. Most of us were not living in cities where our families lived, and needed to create for ourselves a place and occasion for women to come together.

Coming together to do something about our lives was scary. It was admitting that we were not completely satisfied with the lives we were leading. We knew we would be standing back and taking a hard look at ourselves, and this aroused anxiety, fear of the unknown. Some of us fantasized that commitment to the women's movement and pressure from the group would weaken our ties with our men, children, jobs, life styles—we would lose control over our lives. We came to realize that this fear was unrealistic. No one could take from us what we did not want to give up. We were coming together out of choice. Our hope was to come to feel ourselves to be fuller, more integrated female persons....

From our beginning conversations with each other we discovered four cultural notions of femininity which we had in some sense shared: woman as inferior, woman as passive, woman as beautiful object, woman as exclusively wife and mother. In our first discussions we discovered how severely those notions had constricted us, how humanly limited we felt at being passive, dependent creatures with no identities of our own. As time passed, with each other's support we began to rediscover ourselves. The passion with which we did this came from getting in touch with human qualities in ourselves that had been taboo.

We all went through a time when we rejected our old selves and took on the new qualities exclusively. For a while we became distortions, angry all the time or fiercely independent. It was as though we had partly new selves and we had to find out what they were like. But ultimately we came to realize that rejecting our "feminine" qualities was simply another way of going along with our culture's sexist values. So with our new energy came a desire to assert and reclaim that which is ours.

In no way do we want to become men. We are women and we are proud of being women. What we do want to do is reclaim the human qualities culturally labeled "male" and integrate them with the human qualities that have been seen as "female" so that we can all be fuller human people. This should also have the effect of freeing men from the pressure of being masculine at all times—a role as equally limiting as ours has been. We want, in short, to create a cultural environment where all qualities can come out in all people....

What was exciting through all this talking together was learning that what each of us had thought was a personal sense of inferiority was in fact shared by many women. This reflected a larger cultural problem: that power is unequally distributed in our society; men, having the power, are considered superior and we, having less power, are considered inferior. What we have to change are the power relationships between the sexes, so that each sex has equal power and people's qualities can be judged on their own merits rather than in terms of power. Although this problem is not easily solvable, at least the situation is changeable, since it is not based on biological facts. We know we will feel daily tension in recognizing the gap between our ideology and the realities of our everyday life caused by our resistance of change, male resistance, and external social structures not supportive of our ideology. Still, we have a direction we want to move in.

We looked at our present lives and realized how we were perpetuating unequal power relationships between ourselves and men. Many of the instances, which are numerous, are explored in this book. We never expected enough time and pleasure in sex, we never respected the questions we asked our doctors, we never expected men to adjust their lives to parenthood as we bore the child for both of us, we never expected men to take on some of the worry about birth control, we didn't take care of our bodies as if they/we mattered, we never respected the support and comfort other women gave us when we needed it. The list is endless. We began to see our relationships with ourselves. Men, other women, and the social institutions in this country in a new way. To be able to see and feel the strength, beauty and potential in women was exhilarating. We began to feel prouder and prouder of ourselves....

SIGNIFICANCE

Our Bodies, Ourselves, although occasionally denounced for its feminist attitude—or, more recently, for not being feminist enough, or not feminist in the right way—has apparently never been accused of medical inaccuracy. Controversy has arisen, rather, around its attitudes. It is passionately pro-abortion, pro-sex education, and pro-birth control and openly discusses and illustrates terms such as clitoris, menstruation, hymen, menopause, and orgasm. A number of public and high school libraries have banned the book, and the fundamentalist Baptist minister Jerry Falwell denounced it as "obscene trash" during an interview with the *Seattle Times* in May 2005.

Our Bodies, Ourselves claims credit for having started the women's health movement, the push by

During an Anti-Bra demonstration Barbara Stratton, Oretha Smith and Lauren Nogle hold out their bras in protest prior to discarding them, September 5, 1969. © BETTMANN/CORBIS

women for health care that responds to their desires, cares competently for health problems particular to women, does not treat childbirth, menstruation, or menopause as disease processes, and does not implicitly consider the male body the default or normal "human" body. At the time *Our Bodies, Ourselves* was conceived, breast-feeding was abnormal in the United States, fathers were generally not permitted in delivery rooms, the administration of drugs was standard during birth rather than optional, and babies were usually separated from their mothers immediately after birth. Today, new standards of care have replaced these older approaches.

Yet controversy continues about other *Our Bodies, Ourselves* subjects—abortion, birth control, sex education, and what the 2005 edition calls "the beauty culture," the system of assumptions about female bodies, beauty, desirability, and sexuality that circulates throughout the advertising, clothing, "beauty," and entertainment industries. The first chapter of *Our*

Bodies, Ourselves 2005 begins, "For women, life can often seem like a beauty pageant. Throughout every phase of our lives, from childhood to maturity, our appearance is judged and critiqued. Our looks are compared to those of our peers, our sisters, the women in the media, or imaginary ideals. We're rated pretty, ugly, plain—or just plain average. No one has ever asked us if we want to compete in this lifelong beauty contest. Being born female automatically makes us contestants, whether we like it or not."

Recently, *Our Bodies, Ourselves* has been criticized for these views. A major review of the book in the *Atlantic* by a self-identified feminist complained that "this women's health classic has become a compendium of the curses and clichées that feminism must discard or else render itself obsolete....That women's interest in their appearance lies largely in wanting to please men is a myth, and one that should be retired without further ceremony." Most other reviews were more positive.

FURTHER RESOURCES

Periodicals

Jacobs, Alexandra. "A Feminist Classic Gets a Makoever.". *New York Times*. July 17, 2005. Available at <http://www.nytimes.com/2005/07/17/books/review/> (accessed March 26, 2006).

Song, Kung M. "New edition of *Our Bodies, Ourselves* updates the groundbreaking feminist book.". *Seattle Times*. May 4, 2005.

Websites

Boston Women's Collective. *Our Bodies Ourselves Companion Website*. <http://www.ourbodiesourselves.org/book/default.asp> (accessed March 26, 2006).

London, Sarai. "I (Heart) Book Critics." *International Journal of Psychosomatic Disorders*. Nov. 18, 2005. Response by associate and photo editor of 2005 edition of *Our Bodies, Ourselves* to critical reviews in *The New York Times* and *The Atlantic* <http://anglofille.blogspot.com/2005/11/i-heart-book-critics.html> (accessed March 26, 2006).

Roe v. Wade

Legal decision

By: U.S. Supreme Court

Date: January 22, 1973

Source: *Roe v. Wade* 410 U.S. 113 (1973). Available at: <http://supreme.justia.com/us/410/113/case.html> (accessed April 12, 2006).

About the Author: At the time of the *Roe v. Wade* decision, the U.S. Supreme Court was composed of Justices Warren Burger (Chief), William Douglas, William Brennan, Potter Stewart, Byron White, Thurgood Marshall, Harry Blackmun, Lewis F. Powell, and William Rehnquist.

INTRODUCTION

Roe v. Wade 410 U.S. 113 (1973) was a landmark case in the debate over a woman's right to terminate an unwanted pregnancy. Brought forward by attorney Sarah Weddington in 1970, on behalf of Norma McCorvey, a young woman from Texas whose identity was protected by the pseudonym "Jane Roe," the case was argued before the U.S. Supreme Court in 1971, again in 1972, and finally decided on January 22, 1973. District Attorney Henry Wade of Dallas County, Texas, was the defendant in the case. In a seven-to-two decision in favor of the plaintiff, the U.S. Supreme Court agreed that most existing state laws regulating abortion violated a woman's constitutional right to privacy. As a result of this ruling, Texas's abortion laws and all legislation outlawing or restricting abortion in the United States was overturned.

The following excerpt from the text of the court's decision discusses the point at which it is appropriate for the state to regulate and intervene in the decision to abort a human fetus.

■ PRIMARY SOURCE

X

In view of all this, we do not agree that, by adopting one theory of life, Texas may override the rights of the pregnant woman that are at stake. We repeat, however, that the State does have an important and legitimate interest in preserving and protecting the health of the pregnant woman, whether she be a resident of the State or a nonresident who seeks medical consultation and treatment there, and that it has still another important and legitimate interest in protecting the potentiality of human life. These interests are separate and distinct. Each grows in substantiality as the woman approaches term and, at a point during pregnancy, each becomes "compelling."

With respect to the State's important and legitimate interest in the health of the mother, the "compelling" point, in the light of present medical knowledge, is at approximately the end of the first trimester.... It follows that, from and after this point, a State may regulate the abortion procedure to the extent that the regulation reasonably relates to the preservation and protection of maternal health. Examples of permissible state regulation in this area are requirements as to the qualifications of the person who is to perform the abortion; as to the licensure of that person; as to the facility in which the procedure is to be performed, that is, whether it must be a hospital or may be a clinic or some other place of less-than-hospital status; as to the licensing of the facility; and the like....

XI

To summarize and to repeat:

1. A state criminal abortion statute of the current Texas type, and that excepts from criminality only a life-saving procedure on behalf of the mother, without regard to pregnancy stage and without recognition of the other interests involved, is violative of the Due Process Clause of the Fourteenth Amendment.

(a) For the stage prior to approximately the end of the first trimester, the abortion decision and its effectuation must be left to the medical judgment of the pregnant woman's attending physician.

(b) For the stage subsequent to approximately the end of the first trimester, the State, in promoting its interest in the health of the mother, may, if it chooses, regulate the abortion procedure in ways that are reasonably related to maternal health.

(c) For the stage subsequent to viability, the State in promoting its interest in the potentiality of human life may, if it chooses, regulate and even proscribe, abortion except where it is necessary, in appropriate medical judgment, for the preservation of the life or health of the mother.

SIGNIFICANCE

At the time of *Roe v. Wade*, Texas law stated that the abortion of a human fetus was a crime, except when medically advised for the purpose of saving the life of the mother. Norma McCorvey, who claimed to be pregnant as the result of a rape, challenged the law that prevented her from obtaining an abortion by arguing that it was vague and violated the rights guaranteed by the First, Fourth, Fifth, Ninth, and Fourteenth Amendments to the U.S. Constitution. The case was eventually expanded to include two other plaintiffs: James Hubert Hallford, a doctor who had been charged with violations of Texas abortion laws and John and Mary Doe, aliases for a married couple whose doctor had advised them against pregnancy.

The district court that first heard the case in Dallas County, Texas ruled in favor of "Jane Roe," but refused to grant an injunction allowing McCorvey to have an abortion in violation of Texas law. Both Roe and Wade appealed the district court decision and the case was heard by the Supreme Court in December 1971. Justice Harry Blackmun wrote a decision striking down the Texas abortion law, but Chief Justice Warren Burger proposed that the case be held over for rehearing, allowing two newly appointed justices, William Rehnquist and Lewis F. Powell, Jr., to participate in the decision.

The Supreme Court rendered its final decision on December 22, 1973, voting seven to two to strike down the Texas law prohibiting abortion. In that decision, the court defined the limits of state power and individual freedom with respect to each of the trimesters of pregnancy. As stated above, abortion during the first trimester of pregnancy must be left to

the sole discretion of the woman and her medical counsel, effectively ending state power to intervene in first trimester abortions. Following the end of the first trimester, the state may regulate abortion in ways that reasonably relate to the "preservation and protection of maternal health." During the final stage of pregnancy in which a fetus is a viable life that can survive outside of the womb (third trimester), the state reserves the right, if it chooses, to regulate or even prohibit abortion, unless it is necessary to protect the health and life of the mother.

In its decision, the court addressed three historical justifications for the criminalization of abortion. First, it considered the notion that the availability of abortion would make women more likely to be sexually promiscuous. The court criticized the lack of evidence to support this notion and noted that this idea failed to differentiate between married and unmarried mothers. According to the court, this justification for denying access to abortion appears to be nothing more than an ill-informed attempt to regulate women's sexuality. Second, the court addressed the idea that the abortion procedure was a risky one prior to the development of antibiotics and remains risky in the later stages of pregnancy. Third, the court considered the interest that the state has in protecting life. The court held that the latter two points are valid concerns and justify the possibility of state regulation and limitation of abortion for health reasons in the second and third trimesters, given current knowledge about the progression of pregnancy.

Roe v. Wade was also an important case for its discussion of standing and mootness, although these issues received very little attention in the public debate. Generally in legal proceedings, the resolution of the issue at stake renders the case moot—no longer having bearing or reason to proceed in the court. The U.S. Supreme Court does not render decisions of law in hypothetical cases to guide policy. In this case, the legal challenge to Texas abortion law took longer to resolve than the term of Roe's pregnancy. Given that the issue—her desire for an abortion, contrary to Texas law—had been resolved by the birth of her baby, the court could have deemed the case moot and dismissed the proceedings, since the ruling would not be applicable to Roe herself. However, the U.S. Supreme Court found that the appeal should be allowed to proceed for two reasons. First, because Roe could potentially become pregnant again, necessitating a ruling on the matter, and second, because any legal discussion having bearing on pregnancy was likely to outlast the duration of the specific pregnancy in question. The court reasoned that to rule the case moot at the con-

Different viewpoints are shown as pro-life activists and supporters of abortion rights hold up signs during the 32nd Annual March For Life in Washington on January 24, 2005. The march marked the anniversary of the Roe v. Wade Supreme Court decision that legalized abortion. © MICAH WALTER/REUTERS/CORBIS

clusion of the pregnancy would effectively stymie any potential litigation on such issues and would be contrary to the constitutional rights of women.

The *Roe v. Wade* decision was highly controversial in the United States and was opposed by vocal pro-life and religious organizations. In response to *Roe v. Wade*, and within its scope, many states enacted new abortion legislation. In some cases, these laws limit access to abortions in varying degrees, including requiring parental consent for the procedure to be performed on a minor, and prohibiting most late-term abortions that use intact dilation and extraction—so-called partial-birth abortions. In November 2003, President George W. Bush signed a federal law banning the practice of partial-birth abortion in the United States. However, the Partial Birth Abortion Ban Act did not take immediate effect, as it awaited the outcome of appeals and challenges filed by pro-choice advocates. Then, on January 31, 2006, the law was declared unconstitutional by two separate appeals

courts—one in New York and the other in California. The legislation was found to be unconstitutional because, contrary to *Roe v. Wade* decision, the law did not allow exceptions in the interest of the mother's health. In February 2006, the legislation was reintroduced before the U.S. Supreme Court and a decision on the case is pending. *Roe v. Wade* continues to impact judicial decision and abortion policy in the United States to the present day.

FURTHER RESOURCES

Books

Critchlow, Donald T. *Intended Consequences: Birth Control, Abortion and the Federal Government in Modern America.* New York: Oxford University Press, 2001.

Garrow, David J. *Liberty and Sexuality: The Making of Roe v. Wade.* Berkeley: University of California Press, 1998.

Hull, N. E. H. *Roe v. Wade: The Abortion Right Controversy in American History.* Lawrence, Kans.: University Press of Kansas, 2000.

Periodicals

Devins, Neal. "Liberty and Sexuality: The Right to Privacy and the Making of Roe v. Wade." *Michigan Law Review* 93 (1995): 1433–1459.

Farr, Kathryn Ann. "Shaping Policy Through Litigation: Abortion Law in the United States." *Crime and Delinquency* 39 (1993): 167–183.

Garrow, David J. "Abortion Before and After Roe v. Wade: An Historical Perspective." *Albany Law Review* 62 (1999): 833.

Web sites

Cornell Law School. Supreme Court Collection. "410 U.S. 113, Roe v. Wade: Appeal from the United States District Court for the Northern District of Texas." <http://www.law.cornell.edu/supct/html/historics/USSC_CR_0410_0113_ZS.html> (accessed February 22, 2006).

I Am Woman

Song lyrics

By: Helen Reddy and Ray Burton

Date: 1972

Source: Reddy, Helen. "I Am Woman," from *I Don't Know How to Love Him*. Capital Records, 1972.

About the Author: Helen Reddy is an Australian native who moved to the United States in 1966. She signed a contract with Capital Records in 1970 and had numerous number-one hits throughout the 1970s. She is the first Australian-born singer to have won a Grammy. In 1974, she became a U.S. citizen.

INTRODUCTION

The history of the women's movement is long and expansive, and by the 1970s, pop culture connections like Betty Freidan's *The Feminine Mystique* and Helen Reddy's number-one song "I Am Woman" had given the movement a renewed sense of cultural awareness, action, and visibility.

Historians mark the beginnings of the women's movement in July 1848 with "The Seneca Falls Statement," written by Elizabeth Cady Stanton. The document, which called for equal rights and treatment of women, used the Declaration of Independence as its framework. During the American Civil War (1861–1865), Clara Barton created the American Red Cross organization, bringing women's wartime contributions into the public spotlight. Women changed the culture of medicine by becoming nurses and working alongside doctors under intense and horrific conditions.

Acts of war led to calls for action within the movement. The campaign for woman suffrage began long before the First World War (1915–1918), but upon the war's completion women received the right to vote (in 1920). Additionally, world leaders like President Woodrow Wilson praised women for their wartime service in factories, nursing, and other areas. The 1960s brought the second wave of feminism into the public spotlight, and the movement took on a very public role.

Women like Gloria Steinem challenged social beliefs that feminists could not be beautiful, and public protests like the 1968 Miss America Pageant Protest forced the public to acknowledge the demands of women. Helen Reddy's song "I Am Woman" gave the movement a way to express itself through mainstream media and entertainment.

"I Am Woman" appeared on Reddy's first album; it became a number-one hit and the women's movement unofficial anthem. Reddy said that she (co)wrote the song (with Ray Burton) to portray a positive self-image for women and young girls.

PRIMARY SOURCE

I Am Woman

I am woman, hear me roar
In numbers too big to ignore
And I know too much to go back an' pretend
'cause I've heard it all before
And I've been down there on the floor
No one's ever gonna keep me down again.

Refrain:

Oh yes I am wise
But it's wisdom born of pain
Yes, I've paid the price
But look how much I gained
If I have to, I can do anything
I am strong (strong)
I am invincible (invincible)
I am woman

You can bend but never break me
'cause it only serves to make me
More determined to achieve my final goal
And I come back even stronger
Not a novice any longer
'cause you've deepened the conviction in my soul

Refrain

I am woman watch me grow
See me standing toe to toe
As I spread my lovin' arms across the land
But I'm still an embryo
With a long long way to go
Until I make my brother understand

Oh yes I am wise
But it's wisdom born of pain
Yes, I've paid the price
But look how much I gained
If I have to I can face anything
I am strong (strong)
I am invincible (invincible)
I am woman
Oh, I am woman
I am invincible
I am strong

(fade)
I am woman
I am invincible
I am strong
I am woman

SIGNIFICANCE

The lyrics of "I Am Woman" may not completely capture the nature, feeling, and ambiance of the women's movement, but they do represent a substantial portion of the cause. Women who fought for their liberation from social stereotypes encouraged others to celebrate themselves for who they were. In the current era, women and young girls still face conflicting notions of how they should look and act, and a variety of organizations still teach women on how to grow beyond the norms and expectations of society.

Today, the National Organization for Women (NOW) is the largest organization for feminist activism in the United States, with over 500,000 members in all fifty states. NOW defines the most pressing issues facing women in the United States involve the possibility of restricted access to abortion, the continuing need for a constitutional amendment for equality, the elimination of racism towards women of color, ending violence against women, fighting discrimination based on sexual orientation, and advocating for economic justice for women.

FURTHER RESOURCES
Books

Buechler, Steven M. *Women's Movements in the United States: Woman Suffrage, Equal Rights, and Beyond.* New Brunswick, NJ: Rutgers University Press, 1990.

Douglas, Susan J. *Where the Girls Are: Growing up Female with the Mass Media.* New York: Three Rivers Press, 1994.

Web sites

National Women's History Project. "History of the Movement" <http://www.legacy98.org/move-hist.html> (accessed April 15, 2006).

People Hold Signs in Favor of the Equal Rights Amendment

Photograph

By: Peter Keegan

Date: November 3, 1975

Source: Keegan, Peter. "People Hold Signs in Favor of the Equal Rights Amendment to the New York Constitution at a Rally in Bryant Park, New York City." Getty Images, 1975.

About the Photographer: Peter Keegan is a contributing photographer to the Hulton Archive at Getty Images, a leading world provider of visual content materials to such communications groups as advertisers, broadcasters, designers, magazines, new media organizations, newspapers, and producers.

INTRODUCTION

The late 1960s and early 1970s brought forth a wide array of protest movements in the United States and throughout the world. Scholars continually debate which, if any, movement can be considered the most influential, but all agree that one of the more significant movements from the era was Women's Liberation. Women's Liberation sought a variety of reforms for the treatment of women, and one of the movement's more heated battles concerned the passage of the Equal Rights Amendment.

The premise of the Equal Rights Amendment (ERA) is that equal rights could and would not be abridged because of a person's sex. The ERA passed in the U.S. Congress on March 22, 1972, after decades of struggle. The U.S. Constitution maintains that three-fourths of the states must ratify an amendment before it can be added to the U.S. Constitution. Congress placed a deadline of March 22, 1979 for ratification, which was later extended to June 30, 1982. Even though Hawaii ratified the amendment within thirty-

PRIMARY SOURCE

People Hold Signs in Favor of the Equal Rights Amendment: People rally in New York City to show support for the Equal Rights Amendment, November 3, 1975.   PHOTO BY PETER KEEGAN/HULTON ARCHIVE/GETTY IMAGES

two minutes of Congress registering its approval, and several other states passed the ERA shortly thereafter, it failed to achieve ratification by the necessary thirty-eight states. By the time the deadline passed, only thirty-five states had ratified the ERA.

A wide array of Hollywood actors and actresses publicly supported the amendment, and they sought to counter sensationalized claims that the ERA would force men and women to have to use the same bathrooms, take away maternity leave, and other extreme

beliefs. At the heart of the movement to prevent the ERA from ratification was female lawyer Phyllis Schlafly. Schlafly adamantly campaigned against the amendment by stating that it would lead to women being drafted into the military, increased federal power, increased taxpayer expense, and that it would lead to state-funded abortions. She took the same social beliefs that had permeated society since women began publicly voicing their opinions, demanding rights, obtaining the vote, and forcibly creating social change. Many critics argue, however, that Schlafly captured the American public with her claims because she was well educated (a Master of Arts Degree from Harvard and a Juris Doctorate in 1978). How and why she obtained enough support to stop the ERA's passage can not be fully qualified, but the fact remains that her actions—combined with others—stirred controversy, outrage, and stopped an amendment.

Feminist organizations, men and women, and some male organizations joined the fight for the ERA. They carried signs declaring their support, and some added to the contemptuous atmosphere surrounding the ERA. Groups like the National Gay Task Force and the Feminist Communist Coalition fought for the ERA, and their presence also increased the fears that counter-activists like Schlafly conveyed to the public. These groups threatened the perceived moral authority of the United States, and communist-affiliated groups still were associated with the Red Scares of the 1950s and the fight in Vietnam.

■ PRIMARY SOURCE

PEOPLE HOLD SIGNS IN FAVOR OF THE EQUAL RIGHTS AMENDMENT

See primary source image.

SIGNIFICANCE

The ERA has been reintroduced into Congress every session since the 1982 expiration, and on March 15, 2005, both houses of Congress nodded at the passage of the ERA by sending it to the Committee of the Judiciary for consideration, but as of June 2006 Congress had not reenacted the ERA. Some supporters of the ERA argue that even though the deadline for its ratification has passed, the ERA should become part of the Constitution if it is ratified by three more states. They point to a precedent set in 1992 when the "Madison Amendment" passed 203 years after its presentation to the states. The Madison Amendment concerns congressional pay raises.

FURTHER RESOURCES

Books

Becker, Susan D. *The Origins of the Equal Rights Amendment: American Feminism Between the Wars.* Westport, Conn.: Greenwood Press, 1981.

Masbridge, Jane J. *Why We Lost the ERA.* Urbana and Chicago, Ill.: University of Chicago Press, 1986.

Web sites

The Equal Rights Amendment. <http://www.equalright-samendment.org> (accessed March 18, 2006).

National Organization for Women. "Equal Rights Amendment." <http://www.now.org/issues/economic/era-text.html> (accessed March 18, 2006).

Fight on, Sisters

Song lyrics

By: Carol Hanish

Date: 1978

Source: Hanish, Carol. "Fight on Sisters," in *Fight on Sisters: And Other Songs for Liberation.* Franklin Printing, 1978.

About the Author: Carol Hanish, who coined the phrase "the personal is the political," was one of the key organizers of the 1968 Miss America protest by feminists. Her song "Fight on Sisters" was published in 1978 as part of a larger collection of protest songs—all paying homage to the feminist movement.

INTRODUCTION

Like Helen Reddy's 1972 song "I Am Woman," the lyrics for "Fight On Sisters" celebrate the triumphs and milestones of the feminist movement, such as the 1968 Miss America Pageant Protest and the vocal disruption of a government panel discussing abortion. The song reminds the listener that not every fight for women's rights has been peaceful, dainty, or within standard social guidelines of feminine behavior.

■ PRIMARY SOURCE

Fight on, Sisters

When we started this movement 'bout ten years ago
Men laughed and said that it never would grow
But we raised up our voices and we let 'em know
Fight on, sisters, fight on.

CHORUS:

Fight on sisters, fight on
Fight on sisters, fight on

Our power will grow and our dreams will be won
If we fight on, sisters, fight on.

CHORUS

Our foremothers visions would not let them rest
They fought for their freedom from the east to the
    west
They won some hard battles; we must win the rest
So fight on, sisters, fight on.

CHORUS

Telling the truth about sex, love, and men
We examined our lives and again and again
It was male supremacy we found we must end
So fight on, sisters, fight on.

CHORUS

The bosses claim women just aren't qualified
To work at the good jobs for which we applied
But we talked to each other and found out they lied
Fight on, sisters, fight on.

The Miss America Pageant we did protest
The curlers, the girdles, high heels and the rest
That torture a woman—our real self is best
Fight on, sisters, fight on.

CHORUS

We disrupted a hearing on abortion reform
Telling the panel—14 men and a nun
That WE are the experts; our bodies our own
We fight on, sisters, fight on.

CHORUS

We know as we knew we must do it alone
The war for our freedom can never be won
Unless we grasp hold and make it our own
Fight on, sisters, fight on.

CHORUS

We've made some mistakes now and don't get it
    wrong
The forces against us are wily and strong
But we're getting' smarter as we go along
And fight on, sisters, fight on.

CHORUS

Now some say the problem is all in our head
While others proclaim that our movement is dead
But we'll rise up again, our anger still red
And we'll fight on, sisters, fight on.

CHORUS

SIGNIFICANCE

As the lyrics state, women were frequently criticized for protesting, speaking out in public, and challenging accepted social roles. At the time this song was written, women were expected to be diligent wives and mothers, and any work outside the home should be for charity or community gain—most certainly not for political, educational, or economic gain.

In 1972, the Equal Rights Amendment was passed by Congress, but it failed to be ratified by a majority of states and never became law. The Women's Movement did not end with the failure of the ERA, however. Labor groups like the Glass Ceiling Commission, for example, drafted plans to encourage corporations place women in leadership roles. And just as women have made significant social and political strides, gay and transgender individuals have begun to demand equality as well. Thus, the fight for equal treatment has given voice to a number of gender and lifestyle orientations.

FURTHER RESOURCES

Books

Kerber, Linda K. *No Constitutional Right to be Ladies: Women and the Obligations of Citizenship.* New York: Hill and Wang, 1999.

Evans, Sara M. *Born for Liberty: A History of Women in America.* New York and London: The Free Press, 1989.

Pinello, David R. *Gay Rights and American Law.* Cambridge and New York: Cambridge University Press, 2003.

Web sites

Equal Rights Advocates. "Equal Rights and Economic Opportunities for Women and Girls" <http://www.equalrights.org> (accessed April 16, 2006).

Human Rights Campaign. "Working for Lesbian, Gay, Bisexual, and Transgender Equal Rights" <http://www.hrc.org> (accessed April 16, 2006).

Since the French Revolution: The Job and the Vote

Book excerpt

By: Simone De Beauvoir

Date: September 1989

Source: De Beauvoir, Simone. *The Second Sex.* New York: Vintage Books, 1989.

"Liberty Leading the People" by French artist Eugene Delacroix, 1830. © ARCHIVO ICONOGRAFICO, S.A./CORBIS. REPRO-DUCED BY PERMISSION.

About the Author: Simone De Beauvoir was born in 1908, the eldest of two daughters. De Beauvoir graduated from the Sorbonne in 1929 and taught high school while she developed her philosophy on feminism and existentialism. Her writings were influenced by her friend, philosopher Jean-Paul Sartre, and focuses on the historical oppression of women. Her works include, "The Second Sex," "The Mandarins," and "The Coming of Age."

INTRODUCTION

In 1788, economic hardships in France caused unrest among the middle class. As a result, King Louis XVI was forced to summon the Estates General, the medieval legislative body which had not met since 1614. The Estates General opened at Versailles on May 5, 1788, to address the "cahiers de doleances," or list of grievances compiled by citizens. However, controversy erupted at the Estates General over the representation of the commoners in the body. The First Estate consisted of clerical representatives; the Second Estate represented the nobility. The Third Estate represented the commoners. Traditionally, members of

the First and Second Estates unified and overlooked the concerns of the Third Estate. By June 17, 1789, continued conflict over whether deliberations should take place by estate and how each estate's vote would be tallied led to the Third Estate separating itself to declare the National Assembly. The National Assembly invited members from the other two estates to join and enough defected to the assembly to force the King to acknowledge its existence.

The revolution in France took a violent turn on July 14, 1789 as Parisians stormed and destroyed the Bastille, an old prison. The act was viewed as an attack on feudalism. However, it also set off a period of unrest throughout France. By August 4, 1789, the nobility voluntarily surrendered all feudal rights and privileges. This period also contributed to the creation of the "Declaration of the Rights of Man," a document written in the same spirit as the American Bill of Rights. The declaration states, "Men are born and remain free and equal in rights" and that "liberty, property, security and resistance to oppression" are within the natural rights of man.

In 1791, Olympe de Gouge published the "Declaration of the Rights of Women and the Female Citizen" in response to the absence of women's stated rights and equality under the law in the "Declaration of the Right's of Man." During the 1790s, women began to form clubs to discuss politics and inject themselves into the political revolution. Women sought equal rights within marriage, the right to divorce, property rights for widows and parental rights for widowed mothers. In de Gouges' declaration, she writes, "Man, are you capable of being just?" She states, "woman is born free and lives equal to man in her rights." However, "Having become free, [man] has become unjust to his companion."

Shortly after the death of the king, the second phase of the French Revolution placed Maximilien Robespierre into dictatorial power over the country. Working class men and women held that they had gained little benefit from the revolution. They demanded both universal suffrage and participatory democracy. However, the period became known as the "Reign of Terror" as thousands of protesters were put to death at the guillotines. Olympe de Gouges was one of those executed during the Reign of Terror. Women during this period became identified with extreme violence in images of women knitting while watching executions at the guillotines or by firing guns near their children. In February of 1792 and again in February of 1793, women led protests and riots over rising food prices. In May 1793, the Society of Revolutionary Republic Women formed as a women's club. The group was created to gain political education and voice for women. However, the Jacobins, led by Robespierre, asserted that women did not belong in the political debate and that their influence belonged in the home. As a result, the organization, along with all other political women's clubs, were outlawed and many of their participants arrested.

▮ PRIMARY SOURCE

It might well have been expected that the Revolution would change the lot of woman. It did nothing of the sort. That middle-class Revolution was respectful of middle-class institutions and values and it was accomplished almost exclusively by men. It is important to emphasize the fact that throughout the Old Regime it was the women of the working class who as a sex enjoyed the most independence. Woman had the right to manage a business and she had all the legal powers necessary for the independent pursuit of her calling. She shared in production as seamstress, laundress, burnisher, shopkeeper, and so on; she worked either at home or in small places of business; her material independence permitted her a great freedom of behavior; a woman of the people could go out, frequent taverns and dispose of her body as she saw fit almost like a man she was her husband's associate and equal. It was on the economic, not on the sexual plane that she suffered oppression. In the country the peasant woman took a considerable part in farm labor; she was treated as a servant; frequently she did not eat at the table with her husband and sons, she slaved harder than they did, and the burdens of maternity added to her fatigue. But as in ancient agricultural societies, being necessary to man she was respected by him; their goods, their interests, their cares were all in common; she exercised great authority in the home. These are the women who, out of the midst of their hard life, might have been able to assert themselves and demand their rights; but a tradition of timidity and of submissiveness weighed on them. The *cahiers* of the States-General contained but few feminine claims, and these were restricted to keeping men out of women's occupations. And certainly women were to be seen beside their men in demonstrations and riots; these women went to seek at Versailles "the baker, his wife, and his little journeyman." But it was not the common people who led the Revolution and enjoyed its fruits.

As for the middle class women, some ardently took up the cause of liberty, such as Mme Roland and Lucile Desmoulins. One of them who had a profound influence on the course of events was Charlotte Corday when she assassinated Marat. There was some feminist agitation. Olympe de Gouges proposed in 1789 a "Declaration of the Rights of Woman," equivalent to the "Declaration of the Rights of Man," in which she asked that all masculine privilege be abolished; but she perished before long on the scaffold. Short-lived journals appeared, and fruitless efforts were made by a few women to undertake political activities.

In 1790 the right of the eldest and the masculine prerogative in inheritance were abolished; girls and boys became equals in this respect. In 1792 a law was passed establishing divorce and thus relaxing matrimonial bonds. But these were only insignificant victories. Middle-class women were too well integrated in the family to feel any definite solidarity as a sex; they did not constitute a separate caste capable of imposing claims: economically they led a parasitic existence. Thus it was that while women who, in spite of their sex, could have taken part in events were prevented from doing so on account of their class, those belonging to the active class were condemned to stand aside as being women. When economic power falls into the hands of the workers, then it will become possible for the workingwoman to win rights and privileges that the parasitic woman, noble or middle-class, has never obtained.

During the liquidation of the Revolution woman enjoyed a liberty that was anarchic. But when society underwent reorganization, she was firmly enslaved anew. From the feminist point of view, France was ahead of other countries; but unfortunately for the modern French woman, her status was decided during a military dictatorship; the Code Napoleon, fixing her lot for a century, greatly retarded her emancipation. Like all military men, Napoleon preferred to see in woman only a mother; but as heir to a bourgeois revolution, he was not one to disrupt the structure of society and give the mother preeminence over the wife. He forbade the investigation o paternity; he set stern conditions for the unwed mother and the natural child. The married woman herself, however, did not find refuge in her dignity as mother; the feudal paradox was perpetuated. Girl and wife were deprived of the attribute of citizenship, which prevented them from practicing law and acting as guardian. But the celibate woman, the spinster, enjoyed full civil powers, while marriage preserved the old dependency. The wife owed *obedience* to her husband; he cold have her condemned to solitary confinement for adultery and get a divorce from her; if he killed her, caught in the act, he was excusable in the eyes of the law; whereas the husband was liable to penalty only if he brought a concubine into the home, and it was in this case only that the wife could obtain a divorce from him. The man decided where to live and had much more authority over the children than did the wife; and except where the wife managed a commercial enterprise, his authorization was necessary for her to incur obligations. Her person and property were both under rigorous marital control.

During the nineteenth century jurisprudence only reinforced the rigors of the Code. Divorce was abolished in 1826, and was not restored until 1884, when it was still very difficult to obtain. The middle class was never more powerful, but it was uneasy in its authority, mindful of the menaces implied in the industrial revolution. Woman was declared made for the family, not for politics; for domestic cares and not for public functions. Auguste Comte declared that there were radical differences, physical and moral, between male and female which separated them profoundly, especially in the human race. Femininity was a kind of "prolonged infancy" that set woman aside from "the ideal of the race" and enfeebled her mind. He foresaw the total abolition of female labor outside the home. In morality and love woman might be set up as superior; but man acted, while she remained in the home without economic or political rights.

Balzac expressed the same ideal in more cynical terms. In the *Physiologie du mariage* he wrote: "The destiny of woman and her sole glory are to make beat the hearts of men...she is a chattel and properly speaking only a subsidiary to man." Here he speaks for the antifeminist middle class, in reaction against both eighteenth-century license and the threatening progressive ideas of the time. Blazac showed that bourgeois marriage where love is excluded naturally leads to adultery, and he exhorted husbands to keep a firm rein, deny their wives all education and culture, and keep them as unattractive as possible. The middle class followed this program, confining women to the kitchen and the home, closely watching their behavior, keeping them wholly dependent. In compensation they were held in honor and treated with the most exquisite politeness. "The married woman is a slave whom one must be able to set on a throne," said Balzac. She must be yielded to in trifles, given first place; instead of making her carry burdens as among primitives one must rush forward to relieve her of any painful task and of all care—and at the same time of all responsibility. Most bourgeois women accepted this gilded confinement, and the few who complained were unheard. Bernard Shaw remarks that it is easier to put chains on men than to remove them, if the chains confer benefits. The middle-class woman clung to her chains because she clung to the privileges of her class. Freed from the male, she would have to work for a living, she felt no solidarity with workingwomen, and she believed that the emancipation of bourgeois women would mean the ruin of her class.

SIGNIFICANCE

Women participated in many facets of the French Revolution. Women organized marches, participated in debates, petitioned for rights and ran schools. However, most 18th Century activists and philosophers viewed women as biologically and socially different than man. Women worked as shopkeepers and seamstresses, defined by their sex not their occupation. Activists sought the primary right of education for women over rights to vote or own property. As a result, women never gained the political rights achieved by men during the revolution. In fact women in France did not gain the right to vote until 1944. Ironically, the images of the French revolution are largely female figures in Roman togas. The image of liberty is embodied in "Marianne," the most famous symbol of the revolution.

FURTHER RESOURCES

Web sites

California State University, Fullerton. "The French Revolution." <http://faculty.fullerton.edu/nfitch/history110b/rev.html> (accessed March 18, 2006).

Center for History and New Media at George Mason University. "Women and the Revolution." <http://chnm.gmu.edu/revolution/chap5a.html> (accessed March 18, 2006).

Women's Rights Are Human Rights

Speech

By: Hilary Rodham Clinton

Date: September 5, 1995

Source: Clinton, Hilary Rodham. "Women's Rights Are Human Rights." Remarks to the United Nation's Fourth World Conference on Women. September 5, 1995.

About the Author: Hilary Rodham Clinton was the forty-second First Lady of the United States. She has been married to former President Bill Clinton since 1975. Clinton earned her Bachelor of Arts degree from Wellesley College and a law degree from Yale University. Before becoming First Lady, she was a prominent lawyer in Arkansas, and she was the First Lady there when her husband was Governor. In 2000, Clinton won the New York Senate race, and she continues to serve in the U.S. Senate.

INTRODUCTION

In 1995, Hilary Rodham Clinton spoke before the United Nations Fourth World Conference on Women. Her speech "Women's Rights Are Human Rights" addressed issues that have concerned women for centuries. In the tradition of second and third-wave feminism, Clinton did not place blame for the weak placement of women in politics and business. Instead, she called for collective actions by world governments.

Her speech, which called for women "to come together" the way they do "every day in every country," reflected the politics of the 1990s. The decade began with Sadam Husein's invasion of Kuwait and the subsequent deployment of United States troops to the region. In 1993, U.S. troops were sent to Somalia to overthrow the warlord General Adid, in 1994, Haiti saw itself overrun by a military dictatorship, in 1996, a NATO peace keeping force sent troops to Bosnia, and in 1999, NATO sent air strikes on Yugoslavia to prevent genocide in Kosovo. These international acts of force and cohesion with the sending of joint world troops, represented a world community demanding the equal and fair treatment of individuals. Media coverage from Somalia, the Middle East, and Kosovo showed women in subjugation. In some instances, they were required to cover their entire bodies with fabric, were flogged and stoned in public, and raped and brutalized.

In conjunction with international politics, before and after Clinton's speech, other areas of political debate give poignancy and pertinence to her words. The 1995 Glass Ceiling Commission reported, in November, that women still held fewer positions of power in the U.S. and world markets, and in 1991, Anita Hill testified before the U.S. Senate about acts of sexual harassment. Also, in 1991, the U.S. Navy endured the Tailhook scandal, in which several female Naval officers made public claims of sexual misconduct by fellow male Navy officers. In addition to these events, Clinton's husband came under fire for alleged acts of sexual misconduct. Initially, he was deemed not guilty of these actions, but in 1998, an impeachment trial occurred against the President. Here, a former White House intern acknowledged having sexual relations with the President. The impeachment trial did not remove Clinton from office, and the Clinton's kept their marriage intact, but the issues of women and their relation to men in power dominated media attention throughout the decade.

Hillary Rodham Clinton addresses a panel during the U.N. Fourth World Convention on Women in Beijing, China, September 5, 1995. AP IMAGES

These continual actions concerning male and female behavior perplexed much of the American public, and the international community. In Hilary Clinton's United Nation's address she indirectly and directly addressed these concerns by asking men and women to come together for the benefit of the larger community—issues of family, education, health care, employment, and basic rights and enjoyments of life.

■ PRIMARY SOURCE

I would like to thank the Secretary General of the United Nations for inviting me to be a part of the United Nations Fourth World Conference of Women. This is truly a celebration—a celebration of the contributions women make in every aspect of life: in the home, on the job, in their communities, as mothers, wives, sisters, daughters, learners, workers, citizens and leaders.

It is also a coming together, much of the way women come together every day in every country.

We come together in fields and in factories. We come together in village markets and supermarkets. We come together in living rooms and board rooms.

Whether it is while playing with our children in the park, or washing clothes in a river, or taking a break at the office water cooler, we come together and talk about our aspirations and concern. And time and again, our talk turns to our children and our families. However different we may be, there is far more that unites us than divides us. We share a common future, and are here to find common ground so that we may help bring new dignity and respect to women and girls all over the world. By doing this, we bring new strength and stability to families as well.

By gathering in Beijing, we are focusing world attention on issues that matter most in the lives of women and their families: access to education, health care, jobs and credit, the chance to enjoy basic legal and human rights and participate fully in the political life of their countries.

There are some who question the reason for this conference.

Let them listen to the voices of women in their homes, neighborhoods, and workplaces.

There are some who wonder whether the lives of women and girls matter to economic and political progress around the globe.

Let them look at the women gathered here and at Huairou—the homemakers, nurses, teachers, lawyers, policymakers, and women who run their own businesses.

It is conferences like this that compel governments and people everywhere to listen, look, and face the world's most pressing problems.

Wasn't it after the women's conference in Nairobi ten years ago that the world focused for the first time on the crisis of domestic violence?

Earlier today, I participated in a World Health Organization forum, where government officials, NGOs, and individual citizens are working on ways to address the health problems of women and girls.

Tomorrow, I will attend a gathering of the United Nations Development Fund for Women. There, the discussion will focus on local—and highly successful—programs that give hard-working women access to credit so they can improve their own lives and the lives of their families.

What we are learning around the world is that if women are healthy and educated, their families will flourish. If women are free from violence, their families will flourish. If women have a chance to work and earn as full and equal partners in society, their families will flourish.

And when families flourish, communities and nations will flourish.

That is why every woman, every man, every child, every family, and every nation on our planet has a stake in the discussion that takes place here.

SIGNIFICANCE

Hilary Clinton's speech before the United Nation's shows the continual struggle of women in the world community. Even though most developed nation's have granted women the right to vote, obtain higher education, and complete and hold the same jobs as men, women in many developing nations have not achieved equality. For example, over half of all women in the Arab world are unable to read, are unable to vote or own property, and face severe restrictions in dress and movement. In parts of Asia and Africa, a growing number of young women (and female children) are kidnapped, taken far from their homes, and forced into marriage or to work in sweatshop factories, as prostitutes, or domestic servants. Organizations such as Amnesty International and Human Rights Watch work to document and expose such practices and to publicize the need for laws and cultural change to prevent them.

The World Health Organization also estimates that over 500,000 women still die in childbirth every year due to lack of access to adequate medical facilities and maintains that every pregnant woman has the right to basic education about childbirth, a clean environment to deliver her child, and skilled care during pregnancy and birth. Among it's Millennium Development Goals, the United Nations lists maternal health and women's human rights as two of the world's eight most important targets for significant improvement by the year 2015.

FURTHER RESOURCES

Books

Clinton, Hilary Rodham. *Living History*. New York: Scribner, 2004, reprint.

Cook, Rebecca J. *Human Rights of Women: National and International Perspectives*. Philidelphia: University of Pennsylvania Press, 1994.

Peters, Julie Stone and Andrea Wolper, eds. *Women's Rights, Human Rights; International Feminist Perspectives*. New York: Routledge, 1994.

Web sites

Amnesty International USA. "Women's Human Rights." <http://www.amnestyusa.org/women/index.do> (accessed April 13, 2006).

Human Rights Watch. "Women's Rights." <http://www.hrw.org/women/> (accessed April 13, 2006).

The Feminine Mystique

Book excerpt

By: Betty Friedan

Date: 1963

Source: Friedan, Betty. *The Feminine Mystique*. New York: W.W. Norton, 1997.

About the Author: Betty Friedan, the author of four books chronicling her experiences as a woman in 20th century America and the forces shaping gender relations and women's rights, was the co-founder of the National Organization for Women (NOW), the National Women's Political Caucus, and the National Association for the Repeal of Abortion Laws (NARAL).

INTRODUCTION

Betty Friedan was born Betty Naomi Goldstein in Peoria, Illinois, in 1921. Friedan attended Smith College from 1938–1942, graduating with a degree in psychology. She went on to study psychology at the graduate level at the University of California, Berkeley, but left graduate school. She moved to New York City and became a freelance writer and journalist, working for three years with Federated Press, a news service that provided articles to union newspapers nationwide. In 1947, she married Carl Friedan and continued to write and publish articles in a variety of magazines and newspapers.

In 1952, Friedan was fired during her second pregnancy from her position as a writer for UE News, a publication of the United Electrical, Radio, and Machine Workers of America. Her articles often focused on gender rights and minority rights, using a socialist viewpoint. Friedan believed she was fired as a result of asking for maternity leave, while UE News claimed that the anti-Communist and anti-Socialist atmosphere in American society, embodied by McCarthyism, forced them to lay her off.

At her 15th college reunion, Friedan distributed a survey to fellow members of the Smith College class of 1942, asking questions about their daily lives, work pursuits, and general satisfaction with the lives they'd created for themselves fifteen years out of college. Friedan had become dissatisfied with domestic life and the expectations placed on a post-war, well-educated class of women; the results of her survey revealed that she was not alone.

Friedan wrote an article about the results and attempted to publish it in 1958 in a wide range of women's magazines. Editors rejected the article repeatedly. Unable to publish the results of her survey, Betty Friedan shaped the information into a book, titled *The Feminine Mystique*. In it she discusses the role of women in 20th century America, leading to the late 1940s and 1950s, in which college-educated women were expected to stay home and care for the domestic sphere of house, children, and husband. She noted a "problem that has no name," the dissatisfaction and even depression experienced by stay-at-home mothers and wives of the middle class, suburban, and largely white group of which she was part.

In the passage excerpted here, Friedan discusses the ideas held about women's sexuality in the field of clinical psychology and psychiatry in the late 1950s.

PRIMARY SOURCE

A psychiatrist states that he has often seen sex "die a slow, withering death" when women, or men, use the family "to make up in closeness and affection for failure to achieve goals and satisfactions in the wider community." Sometimes, he told me, "there is so little real life that finally even the sex deteriorates, and gradually dies, and months go by without any desire, though they are young people." The sexual act "tends to become mechanized and depersonalized, a physical release that leaves the partners even lonelier after the act than before. The expression of tender sentiment shrivels. Sex becomes the arena for the struggle for dominance and control. Or it becomes a drab, hollow routine, carried out on schedule."

Even though they find no satisfaction in sex, these women continue their endless search. For the woman who lives according to the feminine mystique, there is no road to achievement, or status, or identity, except the sexual one: the achievement of sexual conquest, status as a desirable sex object, identity as a sexually successful wife and mother. And yet because sex does not really satisfy these needs, she seeks to buttress her nothingness with things, until often even sex itself, and the husband and the children on whom the sexual identity rests, become possessions, things. A woman who is herself only a sexual object, lives finally in a world of objects, unable to touch in others the individual identity she lacks herself.

Is it the need for some kind of identity or achievement that drives suburban housewives to offer themselves so eagerly to strangers and neighbors—and that makes husbands "furniture" in their own homes?

Author and activist Betty Friedan speaking on the topic of sexual discrimination, November 21, 1966. AP/WIDE WORLD PHOTOS.

SIGNIFICANCE

Friedan's critique of the 1950s housewife's sexuality, and her encouragement by magazine editors, husbands, fellow housewives, media advertisements, and society as a whole to identify herself in terms of her function as a mother and wife only, focused on psychological theory. The "problem that has no name," according to Friedan, left women with a hollow feeling, an emptiness that needed to be filled. Society told middle-class white women in the suburbs that this emptiness could be filled with wifehood, motherhood, the care of the house, the purchase of new appliances and clothes, and with the creation of oneself as a sexual being, pleasing to one's husband. As Friedan notes in this passage, these messages led to a form of sexual dysfunction, for a focus on "feminine mystique" is elusive, ever-changing, reliant on sexual objectification, and drove women to create an identity that inherently separated them from their partners and themselves.

Sigmund Freud, whose theories of the psyche dominated American thoughts about social and sexual desire at the time, did not escape Friedan's ire concerning this sexual issue: "The fact is that to Freud, even more than to the magazine editor on Madison Avenue today, women were a strange, inferior, less-than-human species. He saw them as childlike dolls, who existed in terms only of man's love, to love man and serve his needs." Connecting magazine editors who provided women with articles on decorating, skin care, and "How to Please Your Husband" rather than foreign policy, philosophical thought, and literary analysis, with a Freudian approach to women that infantilized them, Friedan built an argument that the logical result of such a series of events and attitudes was depression and disaffection.

Three years after publishing *The Feminine Mystique*, which became a national bestseller, Friedan cofounded the National Organization for Women in 1966. The organization fought for greater women's rights in the areas of labor, education, and reproductive rights, among others. Between the publication of *The Feminine Mystique* and helping to found NOW, Friedan was at the heart of the "second wave" of feminism, which took voting rights from the first wave and extended those rights to fight for equal wages, freedom from workplace harassment, credit rights, and birth control and abortion access. With Gloria Steinem and Bella Abzug, Friedan helped to organize the National Women's Political Caucus, and championed the Equal Rights Amendment.

The Feminine Mystique provoked a national discussion about gender roles in a thin sliver of American society; Friedan did not address the issues faced by the working class, minorities, immigrants, and homosexual women. Critics from the political left and right debated Friedan's thesis, and the ripple effects of her book and her ideas about sexuality helped to launch a national women's rights movement.

FURTHER RESOURCES

Books

de Beauvoir, Simone. *The Second Sex*, translated and edited by H.M. Parshley. New York: Knopf, 1993.

Millet, Kate. *Sexual Politics*. Champaign, Ill.: University of Illinois Press, 2000.

Steinem, Gloria. *Outrageous Acts and Everyday Rebellions*. New York: Henry Holt & Co., 1987.

Web sites

Ms. Magazine. <http://www.msmagazine.com/about.asp> (accessed March 27, 2006).

National Organization for Women. <http://www.now.org> (accessed March 27, 2006).

National Women's Political Caucus. <http://www.nwpc.org> (accessed March 27, 2006).

Actress Ashley Judd taking part in an abortion rights rally and march on April 25, 2004. The event focused on protecting women's reproductive rights. AP IMAGES

Feminism Meets Terrorism

Article

By: Phyllis Schlafly

Date: January 23, 2002

Source: Phyllis Schlafly. "Feminism Meets Terrorism" January 23, 2002. <http://www.townhall.com/opinion/columns/phyllisschlafly/2002/01/23/162218.html> (accessed March 14, 2006).

About the Author: Phyllis Schlafly is a Phi Beta Kappa graduate of Washington University. She holds a master's degree in political science from Harvard University, as well as a J.D. degree from Washington University Law School. A lawyer and syndicated columnist, she founded the national volunteer organization Eagle Forum in 1972. A best-selling author since 1964, Schlafly is considered a founding member of the national conservative movement. She has written over twenty books and was named one of the 100 most influential women of the twentieth century by *Ladies Home Journal*. Schlafly is an opponent of the radical feminist movement.

INTRODUCTION

Feminism is a movement of diverse approaches that collectively focus on gender issues such as equal opportunities for men and women, promoting women's rights, and protecting women's interests. The roots of feminism in the United States can be traced to 1848, when the first Seneca Falls Convention was held in Seneca Falls, New York. The assembly produced a "declaration of sentiments" that called for full legal equality for women, including equal educational and commercial opportunities, the right to collect wages, equal compensation, and, most contentiously, the right to vote.

The feminist movement gained momentum in the United States and other countries. In 1919, the Nineteenth Amendment to the Constitution was ratified, giving women the right to vote. In the 1960s, the Equal Pay Act of 1963 ensured that men and women doing similar work would be paid equal wages; the Civil Rights Act of 1964 prohibited discrimination against women in companies that employed more than twenty-five people.

As time went on, feminists began to demanded abortion rights, occupational upgrading of women, scrapping of all legal and social barriers to education, political influence, and economic power. In 1972, Congress passed Title IX of the Educational Amendments to the United States Code, which prohibited gender discrimination in federally funded education programs. Additionally, the law required colleges to award sports scholarships proportionally based on the number of male and female athletes in their programs.

Feminists have been criticized for many of these demands. One opponent of radical feminism—Phyllis Schlafly, condemns feminists who demand equal representation in positions that require considerable physical strength, in an article called "Feminisim Meets Terrorism."

PRIMARY SOURCE

One of the unintended consequences of the terrorist attack on the World Trade Center on September 11, 2001, was the dashing of feminist hopes to make America a gender-neutral or androgynous society. New York City's fireMEN dared to charge up the stairs of the burning Twin Towers, and the firefighters' death tally was: men 343, women 0.

It is a testament to their courage and skill that many thousands of people were successfully evacuated despite mass confusion. The fewer than 3,000 office workers who died were mostly trapped above the explosions and could not have been evacuated under any scenario.

The feminists had made repeated attempts to sex-integrate New York's fire department through litigation, even though the women could not pass the physical tests. They even persuaded a judge to rule that upper body strength is largely irrelevant to firefighting.

September 11th called for all the masculine strength that strong men could muster. Firefighting is clearly a job for real men to do the heavy-lifting, not affirmative-action women.

President George W. Bush sent our Special Forces to the rugged and remote Afghan hills and caves to get the terrorists, dead or alive. Fighting the Taliban is a job for real men.

When the national media interviewed some of our Marines, one of our guys said, "There's no place I'd rather be than here." America is fortunate that the warrior culture has survived 30 years of feminist fantasies and that some men are still macho enough to relish the opportunity to engage and kill the bad guys of the world.

Watching the war pictures on television, we almost expected to see "High Noon" sheriff Gary Cooper or John Wayne riding across the plains. I suggest the feminists go to see the new movie "Black Hawk Down" and reflect on the reality that women could not have done what our men did in Somalia.

For several decades, the feminists have been demanding that we terminate the discrimination that excludes women from "career advancement" in every section of the U.S. armed forces, assuring us that hand-to-hand combat is a relic of the past and that all our wars will now involve only pulling triggers and pushing buttons. Tell that to our troops who trudged over land mines and jagged rocks where there are not even any roads.

In the eighties and nineties, the feminist assault on the right to be a masculine man became increasingly obvious and hostile. It was not just a semantic parlor game when they insisted that the words manly, masculine, and gentleman be excised from our vocabulary.

The feminists are playing for keeps. They attacked the right to be a masculine man in the U.S. armed services, the kind of man who would rush into a burning building to save a woman or search the Afghan caves for Osama bin Laden.

The feminists have intimidated our military into using a training system based on gender-norming the tests, rewarding effort rather than achievement, and trying to assure that females are not "underrepresented" in officer ranks. It's bad enough that men are forbidden to question the double standards or preferential treatment given to women; it is dishonorable to induce them to lie about it.

The feminists have used the courts to try to criminalize masculinity. Feminist lawyers first created judge-made law to expand the statutory definition of sex discrimination to include sexual harassment, and they now prosecute sexual harassment on the basis of how a woman feels rather than what a man does.

The feminists' attack on the right to be a masculine man is in full swing at colleges and universities. Feminism is a major tenet of political correctness, and the female faculty are the watchdogs of speech codes.

Subservience to feminist orthodoxy on campuses is not only mandatory, it is nondebatable. Women's studies courses and many sociology courses are tools to indoctrinate college women in feminist ideology and lay a guilt trip on all men, collectively and individually.

The feminists use Title IX, not as a vehicle to ensure equal educational opportunity for women, but as a machete to destroy the sports at which men excel. Since 1993, 43 colleges have eliminated wrestling teams, 53 have eliminated golf, 13 have eliminated football, and the number of colleges offering men's gymnastics has dropped from 128 to 23.

The feminist battalions are even on the warpath against the right to be a boy. In elementary schools across America, recess is rapidly being eliminated, shocking numbers of little boys are drugged with psychosomatic drugs to force them to behave like little girls, and zero-tolerance idiocies are punishing boys for indulging in games of normal boyhood such as cops and robbers.

Of course, when you wipe out masculine men, you also eliminate gentlemen, the kind of men who would defend and protect a lady—like the gentlemen who stepped aside so that, of the people who survived the sinking of the Titanic, 94 percent of those in first-class and 81 percent of those in second-class were women.

Phyllis Schlafly during a nationwide campaign to stop the Equal Rights Amendment in January 1977. AP IMAGES

SIGNIFICANCE

Phyllis Schlafly notes above that after the World Trade Center attacks on September 11, 2001, no female firefighters died, while 343 male firefighters did. Such statistics, she posits, prove that women are not physically capable of enduring a firefighter's responsibilities. According to the Fire Department of New York (FDNY), fewer than 0.3 percent of fire fighters employed by them are women, which explains why there were no female casualties after the September 11 attacks. As of 2005, only 2.5 percent of fire fighters in the United States were women. Media reports indicated that soon after the attacks, women volunteers inundated ground zero to offer their services. Many of these—nurses, doctors, emergency medics, construction workers, and chaplains—contributed in the rescue efforts.

Schlafly also pointed out that women were not sent into combat against the Taliban in Afghanistan—because this is prohibited by law. However, women have served in the United States armed forces for over

a hundred years. The Army Nurse Corps was created in 1901, marking the beginning of female enlistments in the army. Till the 1950s, women were mostly employed as nurses, telephone operators, or ground support staff. It was only during the Korean conflict that the military began to recruit women for active duty posts in the army, navy, and air force. Ten percent of U.S. soldiers serving in Afghanistan and Iraq in 2006 are women. They include engineers, medical personnel, truck drivers, pilots, weapon experts, and intelligence experts—positions that are considered extremely important. Several female army veterans emphasize that women must be considered at par with men in the armed forces—a practice that is rarely followed. They argue that women do not get as many opportunities to fight in a war as they are not provided with similar training, guidance, and counseling as male recruits.

Schlafly also argues that Title IX has destroyed a number of male collegiate wrestling, golf, football, and gymnastics teams. However, a March 2001 study undertaken by the Government Accountability Office (GAO) found that the Title IX does not require schools to abolish male athletic programs to add female teams. The report found that about eighty percent of schools added one or more women's sports teams in the 1990s, and more than two-thirds did so without discontinuing any existing teams. Experts claim that lack of interest has led to the elimination of male teams in colleges.

In February 2002, the National Wrestling Coaches Association, College Gymnastics Association, U.S. Track Coaches Association, and several other groups representing male athletes filed a lawsuit against the Department of Education alleging that Title IX regulations and polices were unconstitutional and unfair. However, on May 14, 2004, the District of Columbia Circuit Court dismissed the case, stating that there were no grounds for suing the Department of Education. The court observed that men's sports teams were not eliminated as a result of Title IX, or under pressure from female students. It also claimed that there was no reason to believe that the teams would be reinstated if Title IX was amended.

FURTHER RESOURCES

Web sites

American Association of University Women. "Equity in School Athletics" <http://www.aauw.org/issue_advocacy/actionpages/positionpapers/titleix_athletics.cfm> (accessed March 14, 2006).

Education Update Online. "Title IX Comes of Age: Eliminating Gender Discrimination" <http://www.educationupdate.com/archives/2004/apr04/issue/spot_titleix.html> (accessed March 14, 2006).

Maryland Institute for Technology in the Humanities. Facts about Women in the Military, 1980—1990" <http://www.mith2.umd.edu/WomensStudies/GovernmentPolitics/Military/factsheet> (accessed March 14, 2006).

United States Department of Education. "Title IX: A Sea Change in Gender Equity in Education" <http://www.ed.gov/pubs/TitleIX/part3.html> (accessed March 14, 2006).

United States General Accounting Office. "Intercollegiate Athletics" <http://www.gao.gov/new.items/d01297.pdf> (accessed March 14, 2006).

Women in the Fire Service. "Beyond Ground Zero" <http://www.wfsi.org/resources/archive/article_archive.php?article=4> (accessed March 14, 2006).

Women's International Center. "Women's History in America" <http://www.wic.org/misc/history.htm> (accessed March 14, 2006).

Women's eNews, Inc. "Record Number of Female Soldiers Fall" <http://www.womensenews.org/article.cfm/dyn/aid/2226/context/cover> (accessed March 14, 2006).

What Does Sex Discrimination Include?

Newspaper article

By: Jane Howard-Martin

Date: December 19, 2002

Source: Howard-Martin, Jane. "What Does Sex Discrimination Include?" *USA Today.* (December 19, 2002).

About the Author: Jane Howard-Martin holds a degree from Harvard Law School, and has practiced employment law for over a decade.

INTRODUCTION

Growing numbers of people are seeking gender reassignment (sex change) operations. In order to do so, doctors and psychologists insist that a candidate for gender-change surgery live as the desired sex for a year (for example, a man awaiting surgery to become a woman must dress and act like a woman for a year or more prior to surgery and vice versa). Individuals like Julieanne Goins and Reagan Kirkpatrick who underwent the surgery lived like women beforehand, but faced workplace discrimination because they chose to act, dress, and live their lives outside of expected sexual boundaries. Hence, this type of workplace harassment is different from that of the mainstreamed view of sexual harassment. Recent court cases have shown that men and women are facing scrutiny at work based on their life choices. Some of these choices center upon sex change operations, some rest on employers learning that employees cross-dress on occasion (but normally adhere to standard social expectations for their sex), and some cases revolve around individuals who act and "fit" some traditional gender codes, but not enough.

Title VII of the Civil Rights Act of 1964 states that an employer is not allowed to discriminate against someone based on his or her gender—which means that a woman cannot be turned down for a traditionally male position and vice versa. But, this narrow reading of the act allows for discrimination to occur

During the Out & Equal Workplace Summit in Minneapolis on October 2, 2003, Debra Davis, who is transgender and executive director of a Gender Education Center, checks out a Chevron Texaco booth. AP IMAGES

for people who do not fit within traditional gender roles. For instance, men and women who choose to change their biological sexual markers, and persons who do not dress in traditional manners for their gender, do not fit within the boundaries of the legislation.

In the Goins and Kirkpatrick cases, they reported gender stereotyping at work, but as neither had completed their sex change operations, they did not fall into what society considers a woman. Instead, their behavior and lifestyle choices are sometimes considered deviant, and the responses they encountered highlight societal conceptions on how men and women are expected to act. They cited co-worker and management complaints that they were upsetting other employees, and in both cases, the individuals were either fired or resigned. The question of why Goins and Kirkpatrick, and countless others, encountered workplace turmoil about their lifestyle choices remain unanswered.

Other instances of persons encountering workplace harassment mirror the instances of Goins and Kirkpatrick. Ann Hopkins won a court case contesting her failure to be promoted because she did not dress "womanly enough." Here, in much the same manner

that Goins and Kirkpatrick received criticism for not dressing and acting like men, Hopkins was told to wear more jewelry, make-up, and dresses, traditional feminine attire.

■ PRIMARY SOURCE

A number of courts and civil rights commissions have begun to expand the view of what constitutes gender discrimination under Title VII. Instead of limiting the analysis to whether a person was mistreated because of his or her gender, these courts are considering whether a person was discriminated against because he or she failed to conform to societal expectations for how his or her gender looks, lives or acts.

One of the earliest cases involved Ann Hopkins, a female senior manager at a professional accounting partnership. Though the partners deciding on promotions praised her work, they criticized her appearance and demeanor. They noted that she was brusque and used profanity. They decided to delay her candidacy for partnership. One partner explained that to improve her chances for promotion, Hopkins should "walk more femininely, talk more femininely, dress more femininely, wear makeup, have her hair styled and wear jewelry." A court found discrimination because the decision to delay her consideration for partner was based, in part, on comments that reflected sexual stereotyping. The remarks were evidence that her gender played a role in the promotion decision.

Recently, a number of employees have claimed "gender identity" discrimination. Cases are being brought by transgender individuals, cross dressers and effeminate but heterosexual males—all of whom claim they are being discriminated against because they don't fit a stereotype of their gender.

Influenced by the rationale in Ann Hopkins' case, they argue that it is gender discrimination when they are discharged for not acting sufficiently male. While some cases are successful, others have been dismissed. Many courts still hold a traditional view of gender discrimination.

Since the scope of Title VII is unclear, a number of states and municipalities have passed laws or ordinances specifically prohibiting discrimination on the basis of gender identity or gender expression. The cities of Portland, Tucson, New Orleans, and Iowa City and the state of Rhode Island are among the jurisdictions prohibiting gender identity discrimination.

However, the federal government and most jurisdictions still do not prohibit discrimination on the basis of gender identity.

One of the biggest barriers to such legislation is the restroom issue. Although most restrooms have stalls that provide privacy, many Americans are uncomfortable with the idea of sharing a restroom with someone of the opposite sex. Without broad public support, legislation cannot be passed.

Interestingly, corporate America may lead the trend to prohibit gender identity discrimination. Several large corporations have amended their nondiscrimination policies to include a prohibition on discrimination based on gender identity. According to the Human Rights Campaign Foundation, these companies include Apple Computers, Lucent Technologies, and Xerox.

One reason may be that companies doing business in a jurisdiction that prohibits gender identity discrimination already have to comply in that locality, and it is easier to have one policy for all of the corporate locations.

Another reason may be the recognition that talent comes in many different packages. By creating a more inclusive environment, these companies are attracting the broadest cross section of applicants and retaining valued employees, which gives them a competitive edge. Still other companies may have decided that as a matter of corporate values, they are more concerned with an employee's work than with his or her dress, appearance or out-of-work activities.

SIGNIFICANCE

Recent legislative debates concerning same-sex marriage and heightened media attention about transgendered persons, cross-dressers, and sex change operations have prompted industry and communities, as well as state governments to reexamine their policies concerning sex discrimination. Yet, even though some states and industries have reworded their sex and gender discrimination policies to attempt to show a balance between societal beliefs, events, and codes, occurrences of gender discrimination still occur. Hence, the question still permeates society on what really constitutes discrimination based upon sex.

Discrimination in it's most extreme form, hate crimes, are also a problem for people in unconventional gender roles. A study from the Harvey Milk Institute in San Francisco found that transgendered people living in the United States today have an estimated eight in 100 chance of being a victim of murder, compared to the general population risk of about five in 100,000 persons. Publicized cases, such as the murder of twenty-one-year-old Brandon Teena in 1993 on which the film "Boys Don't Cry" was based, have helped bring the issue into the public consciousness.

By 2003, a national opinion poll commissioned by the Human Rights Commission, a Washington, D.C.-based organization that campaigns for equal rights for homosexual, bisexual, and transgendered people, showed that the majority of Americans are familiar with the term transgender and support the inclusion of transgendered people in anti-discrimination laws.

FURTHER RESOURCES

Books

Lenhart, Sharyn. *Sexual Harassment and Gender Discrimination: Psychological Consequences and Clinical Interpretations.* New York: Routledge, 2004.

Web sites

U.S. Equal Employment Opportunity Commission. "Sex-Based Discrimination."<http://www.eeoc.gov/types/sex.html> (accessed April 10, 2006).

Australian Human Rights and Equal Opportunity Commission. "Sex Discrimination." <http://www.hreoc.gov.au/sex_discrimination/index.html> (accessed April 11, 2006).

Corsets and Restrictive Clothing

Photograph

By: Frank Franklin II

Date: January 31, 2003

Source: Franklin, Frank II. "Vintage Clothing Show." Associated Press, January 31, 2003.

About the Photographer: Frank Franklin II is a New-York-based photographer for the Associated Press, an international news agency providing syndicated coverage to thousands of newspapers, television stations, and radio stations around the world.

INTRODUCTION

Corsets first appeared in the sixteenth century, and into the modern era they can still be found in both high-end and low-end clothing stores. Popular belief holds that the corset is uncomfortable and binding for women, but that is a matter of some dispute. Nineteenth-century corsets, with their tightly laced system of support, are the center of this misconception. Corsets are still used by women, and the basic principle of the corset—support—is used for orthopedic materials such as back braces.

Corsets represent a shift in clothing manufacturing and styles—that is, while clothing was previously shaped to the body, the corset allowed the body to be shaped for clothing. The fashion trends of the late 1500s to middle 1600s saw women wearing empire waistlines, where the dress gathered just below the chest and the shirt fabric flowed downward in a multitude of layers and gathers. This type of dress did not need a woman to wear a tightly laced, or restrictive, corset because most of her body was hidden under layers of fabric. But, as fashion evolved, waistlines were lowered, narrowed, and the need for the corset was perceived.

PRIMARY SOURCE

CORSETS AND RESTRICTIVE CLOTHING
See primary source image.

SIGNIFICANCE

The removal of multiple layers of clothing, yards of fabric from gathered skirts and shirtsleeves, and the corset all reinforced changing social and political fronts. For instance, removal of the corset had been on the fringes of feminist thought since the mid-nineteenth century. The corset, and the wearing of, represented core feminine attributes. A woman with a corset was respectable, clean, and pure. She would never disregard her "womanly" and "wifely" duties by asserting herself in public, demanding social change in the name of womankind. Most importantly, a corset represented a certain type of woman—the marrying kind. These beliefs may appear to be harsh and misconstrued, but in the light of "radical" feminist movements, forced social changes of World War I, and the continually increasing role of modernity on culture, they act as metaphors for the era.

Removing the corset coincided with the transformation of industrial work, the utilization of efficiency and rationalization, and with the young women reformers of the Great War. These were the women who were coming of age with gyms, sports clothes, and a body image of slender and curvy versus hidden under multiple layers of clothing. Manufacturers desperately attempted to encourage women to dismiss any desires for the corset's removal, but pressures for comfort and freedom coerced the industry to redesign and use science to "enhance" the corset. Hence, the girdle emerged on the U.S. consumer market. Women

PRIMARY SOURCE

Corsets and Restrictive Clothing: A customers looks at a display of vintage corsets at the Manhattan Vintage Clothing Show in Manhatten on January 31, 2003. AP IMAGES

were then metaphorically expressing themselves in public with their dress and makeup. Furthermore, newspapers and popular culture heightened the fear and mystique of the "New Woman" by calling them spinsters, homeless (meaning a life without a man), and adrift. Older generations abhorred the "modern" image of women, and the younger generations entertained the newer images, acted upon them, or merely dreamed of them.

FURTHER RESOURCES
Books

Fields, Jill. "Fighting the Corsetless Evil: Shaping Corsets and Culture, 1900–1930." In *Beauty and Business: Commerce, Gender, and Culture in Modern America*, edited by Phillip Scranton. New York and London: Routledge, 2001.

Koda, Harold. *Extreme Beauty: The Body Transformed*. New York: Metropolitan Museum of Art, 2004.

Steele, Valerie. *The Corset: A Cultural History*. New Haven, Conn. and London: Yale University Press, 2003.

A Look through a Gender Lens

Report

By: United Nations

Date: 2003

Source: Bureau for Development Policy, United Nations Development Programme, "Millenium Development Goals: National Reports — A Look Through a Gender Lens," 2003.

About the Author: The United Nations (UN) was founded in 1945 when fifty nations met to draft the organization's charter. Initially established to prevent war, the UN has evolved into a 191-member organization working for human rights around the world.

INTRODUCTION

The twentieth century saw much progress toward women's equality. The passage of the Nineteenth Amendment gave American women the right to vote, and the feminist movement of the 1960s and 1970s forced social notions about gender and sexuality to change. Women began to demand equal pay, benefits, and access to higher education.

Supreme Court decisions like *Roe v. Wade*, which legalized abortion, and *Griswold v. Connecticut*, which held that no state could intrude on a person's right to privacy, gave women additional choices in their reproductive decisions. But these did not eradicate gender bias. Instead, it continued to exist, and as society progressed so did its forms.

In the 1990s, the Glass Ceiling Commission encouraged businesses to place women in positions of power, and public figures like Hilary Rodham Clinton urged United Nations member states to elevate the

Afghan women in burquas, covering their entire bodies, during the International Women's Day in Kabul, Afghanistan on March 4, 2005. © SYED JAN SABAWOON/EPA/EPA/CORBIS

status of women worldwide. As the issue of gender equality continued to dominate political discussions, the United Nations set forth its own directive for the new millennium.

The May 2003, Millennium Development Goals (MDG) report, signed by 191 countries, called for the eradication of poverty; universal primary education (through high school); gender equality and empowerment of women; reduction of child mortality; better maternal health; increasing the fight against malaria, HIV/AIDS, and other deadly diseases; environmental reforms; and the development of a global partnership for development. Although only some of the MDG goals concern gender equality, the issue took center stage in discussions about the international agenda for human rights. The report set a 2015 deadline to meet its goals, and it encouraged each country to develop programs to work toward that end.

■ PRIMARY SOURCE

1.2 Gender and the MDGs

Goal 3—"Promote gender equality and empowerment of women"—is the culmination of years of determined advocacy and action by the international women's movement. The high priority accorded to Goal 3 represents a global affirmation of women's rights and gender equality as core values of development.

This hard-won recognition that "development, if not engendered, is endangered" was also an outcome of debates and discussions at the UN Conferences of the 1990s, including the World Conference on Human Rights (Vienna 1993), the International Conference on Population and Development (Cairo, 1994), the World Summit on Social Development (Copenhagen, 1995) and the Fourth World Conference on Women (Beijing, 1995). Growing recognition of the gender dimensions of development paradigms and policies during the 1990s created the momentum for a consensus on gender mainstreaming—the incorporation of gender perspectives into all aspects of development theory and practice—as a key strategy to achieve gender equality.

There is a clear correspondence between the MDGs and other global instruments related to gender equality, such as the Beijing Platform for Action and CEDAW. However, unlike the other goals, Goal 3 is not specific to any particular sector or issue, since gender equality and women's rights underpin all the other goals. It has been pointed out that attempting to achieve the MDGs without promoting gender equality will both raise the costs and decrease the likelihood of achieving the other goals. (1) The reverse is equally true—achievement of Goal 3

depends on progress made on each of the other goals. The implication is clear—while accurate reporting against Goal 3 is critical, tracking gender gaps and inequalities against each of the other MDG targets and indicators is no less important.

At the national level, MDGRs [Millenium Development Goals Reports] and the process of MDG reporting represent a new opportunity for gender advocates to enlarge the space for dialogue and build a broad national commitment to women's rights and gender equality. Apart from their role in monitoring and tracking key indicators of women's empowerment, national MDGRs are also aimed at facilitating systematic policy dialogue on critical development challenges and building a supportive environment for translating commitments into actual results on the ground. Ideally, MDGRs are expected to reach out to a range of national actors including communities, civil society groups, and the media, initiating wider debate and dialogue around key development choices and enabling citizens to demand accountability from their governments. ...

Given the above, it is important for women's organizations and gender equality advocates to use the opportunity created by the MDGRs and the MDG reporting process to ensure greater public visibility and awareness of gender inequality, and demand a stronger policy commitment for gender equality.

■ SIGNIFICANCE

The goals set forth by the MDG are intended to bring a larger social awareness, concern, and action for basic human rights. They are not necessarily the rights of life, liberty, and the pursuit of happiness that are considered integral to American culture. Rather, the basic human (and gender) rights discussed in the MDG concern the right to be treated equally and fairly, the guarantee of an education, and access to modern medical treatment.

Critics debate whether the MDGs can be achieved at any point, but the global agenda is clear and certain—a united community can help alleviate some of the world's injustices. More importantly, the document proclaims the underlying belief that trying to improve the status of women can lead to a stronger global community.

FURTHER RESOURCES
Books

Jain, Devaki. *Women, Development, and the UN: A Sixty-Year Quest For Equality And Justice.* Bloomington: Indiana University Press, 2005.

Weiss, Thomas G., David P. Forsythe, and Roger A. Coate. *United Nations and Changing World Politics.* Boulder, CO, and San Francisco: Westview Press, 2004.

Web sites

Schwentker, Lee. "The Millennium Goals and Gender Equality." *American Association of Colleges and Universities: On Campus with Women* <http://www.aacu.org/ocww/volume33_3/global.cfm> (accessed April 14, 2006).

United Nations Development Programme. "Gender Equality" <http://www.undp.org/gender> (accessed April 14, 2006).

United Nations Millennium Campaign. "Voices against Poverty" <http://www.millenniumcampaign.org/site/> (accessed April 14, 2006).

Chile: High Court Discriminates Against Lesbian Mother

Report

By: Human Rights Watch

Date: June 2, 2004

Source: *Human Rights Watch.* "Chile: High Court Discriminates Against Lesbian Mother." <http://hrw.org/english/docs/2004/06/02/chile8722.htm> (accessed February 22, 2006).

About the Author: Human Rights Watch is an international, non-governmental organization devoted to monitoring human rights issues. Founded in 1978 as Helsinki Watch, the organization currently has over 150 journalists, lawyers, academics, and field experts documenting and analyzing situations related to human rights abuses.

INTRODUCTION

In February 2002, Karen Atala, a government-appointed judge from the town of Villarrica in the South American country of Chile, separated from her husband, Jaime Lopez. The couple had three daughters, then seven, three, and two years old. Atala openly admitted to Lopez that she was a lesbian and gave this as the reason for the separation. She was granted custody of the children when the couple split and sought therapy for herself and her daughters to aid in the family's transition.

Jaime Lopez, a lawyer, appealed in the Chilean courts for custody of the couple's daughters. In a second court ruling, Atala was granted custody again; the court found her to be a stable, loving mother who provided well for the girls. The father was granted non-custodial parental visitation rights.

The girls' father argued that Atala should not receive custody based on the fact that she was gay. Chile is one of the most socially conservative countries in South America. It is a devoutly Catholic country and one in which the right-wing, conservative policies of General Augusto Pinochet—the military commander who seized power in 1973 and who ruled until 1990—persist in civil and social society. The influence of the Catholic Church in Chilean politics runs very deep. Sodomy laws were repealed in 1999, and Chile did not have a divorce law on the books until 2004, long after other developed South American nations had enacted divorce reforms.

Jaime Lopez appealed his custody case to the Chilean Supreme Court, and, on May 31, 2004, the Supreme Court issued a stunning reversal of the two lower court decisions. On a three-to-two vote, the Supreme Court stated that custody should go to Mr. Lopez based solely on the fact that Karen Atala's choice to live openly as a lesbian was a sign that she placed her own interests above those of her children. Citing concerns about social, sexual, and emotional development in the children, the court did not use any other criteria, such as abuse or neglect, in removing the girls from Atala's custody.

■ PRIMARY SOURCE

(Santiago, June 2, 2004)—The Chilean Supreme Court has discriminated against a lesbian mother in denying her custody of her daughters on the basis of her sexual orientation, Human Rights Watch said today.

"The court deprived this mother of custody of her children only because she refused to hide her lesbian relationship from them," said José Miguel Vivanco, executive director of the Americas division of Human Rights Watch. "Lesbians should not be forced to choose between their sexuality and motherhood."

Karen Atala, a judge from the town of Los Andes, had been awarded custody of her three daughters by an appeal court. Her former husband appealed, arguing that the court had wrongfully put Atala's rights before those of her children. Accepting the appeal by 3 votes to 2, a Supreme Court panel on Monday held that Atala's open lesbian relationship disqualified her from the right to custody that separated mothers in Chile enjoy unless barred by exceptional circumstances. The decision is final, and she has no other avenue of appeal.

The panel considered that the children's emotional and sexual development could be harmed by the absence of a father in the home and "his replacement by another person of the female gender." It also expressed concern that Atala's children could suffer from discrimination and rejection since "their exceptional family situation is significantly different from that of their classmates and neighborhood peers." The justices also criticized the lower court for "a serious fault or abuse" because it chose not to uphold "the preferential right of the children to live and grow up in a normally structured and socially reputable family, according to the proper traditional model."

The type of appeal used in this case is known in Chile as a recurso de queja (complaint appeal). For the appeal to be successful, the appellant must establish that the sentencing court committed a serious fault or abuse. This invalidates the sentence and makes the judges responsible for it liable to disciplinary action.

"To add insult to injury, the Supreme Court is telling us that the lower court did wrong even though it resolved this issue on solid legal argument and principle," said Vivanco.

The two dissenting justices stressed that the sentencing judges had proceeded correctly. They argued that Atala's sexual orientation was not a ground for depriving her of the custody she would normally enjoy as a separated mother under Chilean law. Denying her custody would impose on her daughters as well as her "an unnamed punishment, outside the law as well as discriminatory."

The Atala case has stimulated debate in Chile about the right of gays and lesbians to express their sexual orientation without prejudice or discrimination. Human Rights Watch in May published an article and a letter in the prominent Chilean newspaper, El Mercurio, urging the Supreme Court to study recent jurisprudence of the European Court of Human Rights condemning discrimination on the basis of sexual orientation.

Article 26 of the International Covenant on Civil and Political Rights prohibits discrimination based on "race, color, sex, language, religion, political or other opinion, national or social origin, property, birth or other status." In 1994 the Human Rights Committee—the U.N. expert body charged with interpreting the Covenant—ruled that the reference to "sex" in the treaty should be interpreted as including sexual orientation. The Convention on the Rights of the Child requires states to "take all appropriate measures to ensure that the child is protected against all forms of discrimination or punishment on the basis of the

status, activities, expressed opinions, or beliefs of the child's parents, legal guardians, or family members."

Sodomy was decriminalized in Chile in 1999, but prejudice against gays and lesbians is still rife.

SIGNIFICANCE

Chile has a history of blending social conservatism with economic liberalism. One of the most developed South American nations, in recent years it has experienced annual economic growth near six percent and the development of a flourishing middle class as the country moves away from the extreme political conservatism of the Pinochet years. At the same time, the human rights abuses experienced under Pinochet's regime—which included more extreme cases of torture as well as curbs on freedom of speech, curtailment of women's rights, and repression of homosexuals—have come under scrutiny as more people speak out about past experiences and civil society moves toward a more progressive tone.

Karen Atala's occupation as a respected judge in Chile placed her in a difficult position when testifying in the custody trials. Unlike many lesbian mothers in Chile, who often lie about their homosexuality in order to preserve their custody rights, Atala could not lie. As an officer of the court, she believed that she needed to be open and honest under oath. Ninety-nine percent of all child custody cases in Chile are found in the mother's favor.

Atala appealed the Chilean Supreme Court's decision to the the Inter-American Commission of Human Rights (IACHR) and its judicial branch, the Inter-American Court of Human Rights, both with oversight from the Organization of American States. The IACHR is designed to enforce the American Convention on Human Rights, a treaty which Chile ratified in 1990.

Karen Atala claims that her rights were violated under Article 1 to the convention, which states that citizens in member countries should have the full rights and freedoms of all others "without any discrimination for reasons of race, color, sex, language, religion, political or other opinion, national or social origin, economic status, birth or any other social condition." The case is ongoing between the IACHR and the Chilean government as of February 2006.

On December 11, 2005, Chilean presidential elections were held. Michelle Bachelet, a self-described divorced socialist agnostic won forty-six percent of the vote. Bachelet had been tortured under General Augusto Pinochet's military rule in the early

1970s and her father, a military commander under Socialist President Salvador Allende, was killed in the 1973 coup. Her return to Chile and popularity in the election alarmed social conservatives. A run-off election on January 15, 2006, confirmed Bachelet's presidency when she received fifty-three percent of the total vote.

Bachelet campaigned on the issue of gender equality and used her status as a mother and a pediatrician to appeal to Chilean progressives. The election of a female socialist to the highest office in Chile bolstered hopes in the Chilean gay and lesbian community for an expansion of gay rights. However, as of February 2006, Karen Atala's children remained in the custody of their father.

FURTHER RESOURCES

Books

Power, Margaret. "Right Wing Women, Sexuality, and Politics in Chile During the Pinochet Dictatorship, 1973–1990," in *Right Wing Women: From Conservatives to Extremists Around the World*, edited by Paola Bacchetta and Margaret Power. New York: Routledge, 2002.

Stephen, Lynn. *Women and Social Movements in Latin America: Power from Below*. Austin, Tex.: University of Texas Press, 1997.

Web sites

Inter Press New Service Agency. "RIGHTS-CHILE: Gay Community Guardedly Optimistic About Future." <http://www.ipsnews.net/news.asp?idnews=32016> (accessed February 22, 2006).

3 Gay Rights Movement

Gay Rights Movement

Jeremy Bentham was one of the first Western legal scholars to suggest reform of laws banning homosexuality. His *Offenses Against Oneself*, an excerpt of which is included in this chapter, was written at a time in England when homosexual sex was a crime punishable by hanging. Bentham thought his ideas too scandalous for his own time and the essay was not widely published until 1978—almost two hundred years after it was written. Indeed, sodomy laws lingered on the books in the United States long after the gay rights movement was a vocal and present social force. An article on *Lawrence, et al. v. Texas* chronicles the landmark U.S. Supreme Court decision that struck down a Texas sodomy law.

While decriminalizing homosexual sex is an important step, the struggle for gay rights is founded upon a larger struggle for social equity. In 1969, the Stonewall Riots launched the current movement for gay rights in the United States. The first Gay Pride Day and parade was held on its first anniversary. Pride events marked a significant turn in the gay rights movement. The struggle was taken to the streets, the media, and the public. The emphasis on pride sought to foster tolerance and combat stigma and shame, but in an uncompromising manner that encouraged gay individuals to be open and honest about their sexuality. The movement grew more inclusive and broadened its predominantly male focus. Espousing lesbian, bisexual, and transgendered rights, the gay rights movement often prefers the acronym LGBT (Lesbian, Gay, Bisexual, and Transgendered).

The appearance of AIDS unmistakably altered the gay rights movement. Activists asserted that silence about gay issues could literally be fatal. The AIDS crisis in may ways solidified various factions of the gay rights movement, uniting the community—and society at large—in the struggle to combat not only AIDS, but the culture of fear, panic, intolerance, and misinformation surrounding the disease. Today, AIDS is no longer a gay issue. The disease does not discriminate on the basis of gender, sexuality, or ethnicity. Accordingly, AIDS is addressed in the chapter on Gender and Sexuality Issues in Medicine and Public Health.

A significant portion of this chapter is devoted to current issues in the LGBT community, especially marriage and family. Articles on the Defense of Marriage Act (DoMA) and the recognition of civil partnerships and same-sex marriages frame the debate over gay marriage in the United States. Several articles explore issues associated with the increasing number of LGBT households with children, such as adoption and child custody.

The Trials of Oscar Wilde

Book excerpt

By: H. Montgomery Hyde

Date: 1973

Source: Hyde, H. Montgomery. *The Trials of Oscar Wilde*. New York: Dover,1973.

About the Author: H. Henry Hyde first published the *Trials of Oscar Wilde* in 1948, adding commentary and appendices in 1962 and 1973. A scholar of criminal law, Hyde published a wide range of books including a biography of Lord Alfred Douglas and a biography of Oscar Wilde.

INTRODUCTION

On February 14, 1895, writer Oscar Wilde's latest play, *The Importance of Being Earnest*, premiered in London at the St. James Theater. Wilde, in his early forties and a literary sensation, learned that the Marquess of Queensberry, John Douglas, was prepared to disrupt the play's premiere.

The Marquess was livid after learning that Wilde and the Marquess's son, Lord Alfred "Bosie" Douglas, had been homosexual lovers. At a time when English law declared homosexuality a crime against nature, and the 1885 Labouchere Amendment definied homosexual sex as "gross indecency," the Marquess planned to reveal Wilde's relationship with his son, placing the writer in a precarious, if not potentially criminal, position.

The Marquess was blocked from entering St. James Theater but left a calling card for Oscar Wilde, on which the Marquess wrote: "To Oscar Wilde posing Somdomite [sic]." Wilde was angered by the public insult and Bosie encouraged him to file a libel suit against the Marquess.

Wilde was known in his circle of literary friends to have homosexual affairs with younger men; Bosie was twenty-four and Wilde forty at the time of the Marquess's card and insult. Wilde filed the lawsuit and a trial was held in April 1895. As part of his defense, the Marquess and his lawyer, Edward Carson, found approximately ten young men with whom Wilde had either had sexual relations or whom he had solicited for sexual relations. Wilde went forward with his suit. By the third day of the trial, Wilde, as the plaintiff, found himself in the odd position of defending his actions.

The judge found that not only was the Marquess's note acceptable, but that in effect, the defense had shown that the note was justified, for Wilde most likely was, the court said, a homosexual. On April 6, 1895, the day after the libel trial was dismissed, Wilde was himself arrested and detained for "gross indecency" under the Criminal Law Amendment Act of 1885.

The excerpts from Wilde's criminal trial that follow demonstrate Wilde's wit, the prosecutor's arguments, and how English law handled the issue of homosexual acts between consenting males in the latter nineteenth century.

■ PRIMARY SOURCE

G—:

Listen, Mr. Wilde, I shall keep you only a very short time in the witness box. Counsel, read the following poem from *The Chameleon*.

"Last night unto my bed methought there came
Our lady of strange dreams, and from an urn
She poured live fire, so that mine eyes did burn
At sight of it. Anon the floating flame
Took many shapes, and one cried: I am Shame
That walks with Love, I am most wise to turn
Cold lips and limbs to fire; therefore discern
And see my loveliness, and praise my name.
And afterwards, in radiant garments dressed
With sound of flutes and laughing of glad lips,
A pomp of all the passions passed along
All the night through; till the white phantom ships
Of dawn sailed in. Whereat I said this song,
"Of all sweet passions Shame is loveliest."

G—: Is that one of the beautiful poems?

Sir Edward Clarke—: That is not one of Mr. Wilde's.

G—: I am not aware that I said it was.

Sir Edward Clarke—: I thought you would be glad to say it was not.

Mr. Justice Charles—: I understand that was a poem by Lord Alfred Douglas.

G—: Yes, my lord, and one which the witness described as a beautiful poem. The other beautiful poem is the one that follows immediately and precedes "The Priest and the Acolyte."

G—: Your view, Mr. Wilde, is that the "shame" mentioned here is that shame which is a sense of modesty?

W—: That was the explanation given to me by the person who wrote it. The sonnet seemed to me obscure.

Anglo-Irish author Oscar Wilde (1854-1900) and companion Lord Alfred Douglas posing in a studio, 1893. PHOTO BY TIME LIFE PICTURES/MANSELL/TIME LIFE PICTURES/GETTY IMAGES

G—: During 1893 and 1894 You were a good deal in the company of Lord Alfred Douglas?

W—: Oh, yes.

G—: Did he read that poem to you?

W—: Yes.

G—: You can, perhaps, understand that such verses as these would not be acceptable to the reader with an ordinarily balanced mind?

W—: I am not prepared to say. It appears to me to be a question of taste, temperament, and individuality. I should say that one man's poetry is another man's poison!

G—: I daresay! The next poem is one described as "Two Loves." It contains these lines:
"'sweet youth,
Tell me why, sad and sighing, dost thou rove
These pleasant realms? I pray thee tell me sooth,
What is thy name?' He said, 'My name is Love,'
Then straight the first did turn himself to me,
And cried, 'He lieth, for his name is Shame.
But I am Love, and I was wont to be
Alone in this fair garden, till he came
Unasked by night; I am true Love, I fill
The hearts of boy and girl with mutual flame.'
Then sighing said the other, 'Have thy will,
I am the Love that dare not speak its name'."

G—: G—Was that poem explained to you?

W—: I think that is clear.

G—: There is no question as to what it means?

W—: Most certainly not.

G—: Is it not clear that the love described relates to natural love and unnatural love?

W—: No.

G—: What is the "Love that dare not speak its name"?

W—: "The Love that dare not speak its name" in this century is such a great affection of an elder for a younger man as there was between David and Jonathan, such as Plato made the very basis of his philosophy, and such as you find in the sonnets of Michelangelo and Shakespeare. It is that deep, spiritual affection that is as pure as it is perfect. It dictates and pervades great works of art like those of Shakespeare and Michelangelo, and those two letters of mine, such as they are. It is in this century misunderstood, so much misunderstood that it may be described as the "Love that dare not speak its name," and on account of it I am placed where I am now. It is beautiful, it is fine, it is the noblest form of affection. There is nothing unnatural about it. It is intellectual, and it repeatedly exists between an elder and a younger man, when the elder man has intellect, and the younger man has all the joy, hope, and glamour of life before him. That it should be so the world does not understand. The world mocks at it and sometimes puts one in the pillory for it.

G—: Then there is no reason why it should be called "Shame"?

W—: Ah, that, you will see, is the mockery of the other love, love which is jealous of friendship and says to it, "You should not interfere."

G—: I wish to call your attention to the style of your correspondence with Lord Alfred Douglas?

W—: I am ready. I am never ashamed of the style of my writings.

G—: You are fortunate, or shall I say shameless? I refer to passages in two letters in particular?

W—: Kindly quote them.

G—: In letter number one you use the expression "Your slim gilt soul," and you refer to Lord Alfred's "red rose-leaf lips." The second letter contains the words, "You are the divine thing I want," and describes Lord Alfred's letter as being "delightful, red and yellow wine to me." Do you think that an ordinarily constituted being would address such expressions to a younger man?

W—: I am not happily, I think, an ordinarily constituted being.

G—: It is agreeable to be able to agree with you, Mr. Wilde.

W—: There is nothing, I assure you, in either letter of which I need be ashamed. The first letter is really a prose poem, and the second more of a literary answer to one Lord Alfred had sent me.

G—: And these witnesses have, you say, lied throughout?

W—: Their evidence as to my association with them, as to the dinners taking Place and the small presents I gave them, is mostly true. But there is not a particle of truth in that part of the evidence which alleged improper behaviour.

G—: Why did you take up with these youths?

W—: I am a lover of youth.

G—: You exalt youth as a sort of god?

W—: I like to study the young in everything. There is something fascinating in youthfulness.

G—: So you would prefer puppies to dogs and kittens to cats?

W—: I think so. I should enjoy, for instance, the society of a beardless, briefless barrister quite as much as that of the most accomplished Q.C.

G—: I hope the former, whom I represent in large numbers, will appreciate the compliment.

G—: You made handsome presents to all these young fellows?

W—: Pardon me, I differ. I gave two or three of them a cigarette case: Boys of that class smoke a good deal of cigarettes. I have a weakness for presenting my acquaintances with cigarette cases.

G—: Rather an expensive habit if indulged in indiscriminately, isn't it?

W—: Less extravagant than giving jewelled garters to ladies.

SIGNIFICANCE

At the time of his trial, Oscar Wilde had been married to Constance Lloyd Wilde for nearly eleven years; the couple had two young sons. Constance Wilde changed her last name to Holland and refused to see Wilde or let him see his children.

The prosecution's discussion of the "love that dare not speak its name" as well as Wilde's letters to Lord Alfred Douglas showcased what many considered to be Wilde's homosexual inclinations. Testimony from young men concerning Wilde's propositions, gifts of cigarette cases and rings, and the prosecution's ability to present many different men with similar reports of Wilde's companionship with younger men in the hotel built a case against Wilde.

Wilde was found guilty of gross indecency on May 25, 1895 and sentenced to two years labor in prison at Reading Gaol. He later published *The Ballad of Reading Gaol*, in which he describes the desperation of fellow inmates, the imprisoned children, and the horrid conditions; prison reforms came about after his death, in part due to his writings. He died on November 30, 1900, three years after his release.

English law continued to treat homosexual acts as criminal offenses throughout the next six decades. Mathematician and early computer science pioneer Alan Turing was tried for homosexuality in 1952 under the same law, Section 11 of the Criminal Law Amendment Act of 1885, under which Oscar Wilde had been tried. Turing, like Wilde, was convicted of the crime of homosexual acts with another man, but unlike Wilde, Turing did not receive prison as a sentence. The court ordered Turing to undergo hormonal treatment that would control or destroy his homosexual desires. Turing lost government security clearance for his job on a cryptography project with the British government. Forced hormonal injections of estrogens were considered an appropriate treatment

for homosexuality under English law at the time; Turing's health and mental stability suffered as a result of the treatments. In 1954, Turing died after ingesting cyanide; his death was ruled a suicide.

Private sexual acts between two members of the same sex were decriminalized in England in 1967 with the passage of the Sexual Offences Act of 1967.

FURTHER RESOURCES
Books

Brady, Shawn. *Masculinity and Male Homosexuality in Britain, 1861–1913*. London: Palgrave MacMillan, 2005.

McKenna, Neil. *The Secret Life of Oscar Wilde*. New York: Basic Books, 2005.

Oscar Wilde. *The Complete Works of Oscar Wilde*. New York: HarperCollins, 2003.

Bisexuality

Book excerpt

By: Alfred C. Kinsey

Date: 1948

Source: Kinsey, Alfred C. *Sexual Behavior in the Human Male*. Philadelphia: W.B. Saunders, 1948.

About the Author: Alfred C. Kinsey (1894–1956) is one of the most influential American sexologists. Kinsey earned an entomology doctorate from Harvard University in 1920 and became a professor of zoology at Indiana University. During the late 1930s, having become interested in human sexual behavior and impressed by the lack of information in the field, he began interviewing people about their sexual experiences. His subsequent best-selling books, on the sexual behaviors of males and females, were the first scientific studies of sexuality. He also founded the Institute for Sex Research in Bloomington, Indiana.

INTRODUCTION

Alfred Kinsey was the first investigator in sex research in the United States to have a major impact on American thinking. No one before Kinsey had scientifically studied sexual behavior. He applied to humans the same techniques that he had learned in graduate school at Harvard University while studying gall wasps. These techniques called for the collection of large masses of data through fieldwork, the classification of data, statistical analysis of the findings, and summarization of the findings.

Kinsey published his results in *Sexual Behavior of the Human Male* (1948) and *Sexual Behavior of the Human Female* (1953). The books, each based on over five thousand personal interviews, were popularly known as the Kinsey Reports. They quickly became bestsellers. However, Kinsey was faulted for treating behavior in isolation. He paid little attention to the meanings that sexual behaviors had for the individuals involved. Such an omission limited the significance of some of his findings and made other results incomplete. Humans were not the same, after all, as gall wasps.

The Kinsey Reports were important, as well as shocking, because they documented the existence of wide variations in human sexual behavior including the prevalence of bisexuality. Most experts interpreted bisexuality as a form of psychological and social deviance, often as a stage preceding the formation of a mature heterosexual identity. The bisexual man was stigmatized as an incomplete man. This attitude prevailed through the mid-twentieth century until Kinsey produced his results on male bisexuality.

PRIMARY SOURCE

The term bisexual has been used in biology for structures or individuals or aggregates of individuals that include the anatomy or functions of both sexes. They are universal species which are exclusively female and reproduce parthenogenetically (from eggs that are not fertilized). In contrast, there are bisexual species which include both males and females and which commonly reproduce through fertilization of the eggs produced by the females. Among plants and animals which have an alternation of generations, there are unisexual or parthenogenetic generations in which there are only females, and bisexual generations in which there are both males and females. In regard to the embryonic structures from which the gonads of some of the vertebrates develop, the term bisexual is applied because these embryonic structures have the potentialities of both sexes and may develop later into either ovaries or testes. Hermaphroditic animals, like earthworms, some snails, and a rare human, may be referred to as bisexual, because they have both ovaries and testes in their single bodies. These are the customary usages for the term bisexual in biology.

On the other hand, as applied to human sexual behavior, the term indicates that there are individuals who choose to have sexual relations with both males and

females; and until it is demonstrated, as it certainly is not at the present time, that such a catholicity of taste in a sexual relation is dependent upon the individual containing within his anatomy both male and female structures, or male and female physiologic capacities, it is unfortunate to call such individuals bisexual. Because of its wide currency, the term will undoubtedly continue in use among students of human behavior and in the public in general. It should, however, be used with the understanding that it is patterned on the words heterosexual and homosexual and, like them, refers to the sex of the partner, and proves nothing about the constitution of the person who is labelled bisexual.

There has been a very considerable confusion of the concept of bisexuality and the concept of intersexuality by persons who are unacquainted with the exact nature of the work that has been done on intersexual forms among animals. As the term was originally used by Goldschmidt, and subsequently among geneticists and students in other fields of biology, and individual is recognized as an intersex if it shows secondary sexual characters that are intermediate between those of the typical male and the typical female in the population. Where a single individual combines in its one person the primary sex characters of two sexes (namely, the ovaries and the testes), it is recognized as a *hermaphrodite*. Where the secondary sexual characters of an individual are in part the unmodified characters of one sex, and in part the characters of the other sex, the individual is known as a *gynandromorph*. A gynandromorphic insect may have the head coloration that is typical of one sex and the thoracic coloration that is typical of the other sex. An *intersex*, on the contrary, has a portion or the whole of its structures intermediate in character between the structures of the typical male or the female of the species. In the case of Goldschmidt's gypsy moths, the females are typically large, the males typically smaller. The intersexual individuals show gradations in size between the larger female and smaller male. The typical female of the gypsy moth is buff yellow, the male is white. The intersexes show various grades of color between yellow and white. A gynandromorphy might have one wing yellow and one wing white, one wing large and one wing small, but the intersexes have wings that are intermediate in size and color.

In spite of the fact that Goldschmidt himself (1916) accepted the idea that the homosexual human male or female was an intersex, there is no adequate basis for reaching any such conclusion. Those who have accepted this interpretation have assumed without asking for specific evidence that an individual's choice of a sexual partner is affected by some basic physiologic capacity. No work that has been done on hormones or on any other

Sexual researcher Dr. Alfred C. Kinsey with friends at home, June 1953. PHOTO BY ARTHUR SIEGEL/TIME & LIFE PICTURES/GETTY IMAGES

physiologic capacities of the human animal justifies such a conclusion (Kinsey 1941). Goldschmidt and others, who have thought of the homosexual individual as an intersex have relied upon incidence figures which were pure guesses and which, as the data in the present chapter will show, bear little relation to the fact as it has now been ascertained.

There are a few males in whom the urethra opens on the under surface of the penis. Such a condition is known as a *hypospadia*. The most extreme confusion of biological ideas has come from the identification of these hypospadiac males and intersexes who are predisposed to be homosexual in their behavior. However, an investigation of the embryonic development of the male penis (Arey 1924, 1946, Patten 1946) will show that a hypospadia is nothing more than a failure in the closure of the ure-

thra at the end of normal embryonic development, and has no relation whatsoever to the genetic maleness or femaleness of the individual, nor to the endocrine constitution of the individual. As our own histories of hypospadiac individuals definitely show, such malformations have nothing to do with their choice of sexual partners unless, as in some extreme cases among ignorant and uneducated persons, the sexual identity of the individual is confused and he is raised in the clothing and the traditions of the opposite sex. In popular parlance such individuals are commonly called "morphodites," but the designation is incorrect, for a true hermaphrodite, as we have already pointed out, has functioning gonads of both sexes within its one body. It is, of course, in the same way that a female with a large clitoris is sometimes called a hermaphrodite. Sometimes the term intersex has been applied to such females (Dickinson 1933); but until more is known about the biological basis of this situation, it is not certain that the term intersex should be applied even in these cases.

SIGNIFICANCE

Kinsey's research contributed substantially to the general liberalization of attitudes toward sexuality. Most Americans before the mid-twentieth century identified bisexuality as a form of homosexuality, which they then defined as being abnormal. His work prompted scholars to discuss bisexuality as a common phenomenon and a normal one. He had less impact on the general public, which continued to see bisexuality as a variation of homosexuality.

The heterosexual-homosexual notion that structured American understandings of sexual identity left bisexuals without a clear place. The emergence of the gay rights movement in the late 1960s helped the development of a bisexual identity. Bisexual activists formed their own organizations, including the National Bisexual Liberation Group in 1972, the Bisexual Center in San Francisco in 1976, BiPol in 1983, and BiNet USA in 1990. Bisexual activists worked with gay and lesbian organizations to increase awareness of distinctive bisexual identities and to reduce tensions between members of the queer communities.

Despite such efforts, discrimination against bisexuals and misunderstandings of bisexuality persisted. In the 1980s, popular women's magazines such as *McCall's* and *Ladies' Home Journal* portrayed bisexual men as a threat to heterosexual women and as conduits by which AIDS could pass from gay communities to the nuclear family. While the stigmatization of bisexual men has dropped, cultural conservatives continue to view bisexuality as a social evil in the same category as homosexuality.

FURTHER RESOURCES
Books

Irvine, Janice M. *Disorders of Desire: Sexuality and Gender in Modern American Sexology.* Philadelphia: Temple University, 2005.

Jones, James H. *Alfred C. Kinsey.* New York: W.W. Norton, 1997.

Pomeroy, Wardell B. *Dr. Kinsey and the Institute for Sex Research.* London: Thomas Nelson and Sons, 1972.

Four Policemen Hurt in 'Village' Raid

Newspaper article

By: Anonymous

Date: June 29, 1969

Source: "Four Policemen Hurt in 'Village' Raid." *New York Times* (June 29, 1969).

About the Author: This article was written by an anonymous staff writer at the *New York Times.*

INTRODUCTION

The Stonewall Riots in New York City in 1969 ignited the gay civil rights movement. The riots reflected widespread anger at long-standing police harassment of gay, lesbian, bisexual, and transgendered people.

Shortly after midnight on June 27, 1969, nine plainclothes detectives entered the Stonewall Inn at 53 Christopher Street in Greenwich Village. This part of New York City was well-known for attracting a gay crowd. Police had visited the Stonewall Inn in the past to arrest and harass patrons. Those arrested were booked and held overnight, and their arrests were announced in the newspapers for neighbors and relatives to see. Homosexuals often lost their jobs when they were exposed as gay.

On this day, the police intended to close the bar for selling liquor without a license. As the bartender, doorman, and three male-to-female transgendered individuals were arrested and led to a police wagon, an unexpectedly angry crowd gathered. The crowd soon swelled to over 400 people. People in the crowd started to throw coins, a reference to the payoffs that police historically accepted from gay men threatened with arrest. They also threw beer bottles and bricks.

The arresting officers retreated and tried to remain inside the bar. However, the mob, now chanting "Pigs" and "Faggot cops," smashed down the door. A detective threatened to shoot the first man through the door. One of the protesters then tried to set the bar on fire using lighter fluid and matches. Another protester was grabbed by the detectives and beaten on the head. Meanwhile, the barrage of bottles, cans, and rocks continued. One group of protesters uprooted a parking meter and hurled it towards the police. When police reinforcements arrived, the crowd gradually faded away.

Button from the 4th Annual Christopher Street Gay Pride Day held in Greenwich Village, NYC, shows an illustration of the Stonewall Inn, where a police raid resulted in a riot that helped launch the gay pride movement. DAVID J. & JANICE L. FRENT COLLECTION/CORBIS

A second consecutive night of rioting in Greenwich Village began when a crowd gathered outside the Stonewall Inn to protest the previous night's police raid. Police units poured into the area in response. The mostly male protesters set fires, threw bottles, and shouted "Legalize gay bars," "Gay is good," and "We are the Stonewall girls/We wear our hair in curls/We have no underwear/We show our pubic hair." One group of gay men formed a chorus line and did a can-can routine down the street until they were dispersed by police with billy clubs. The riot lasted about two hours.

The final Stonewall riot occurred on July 3. Five hundred protesters gathered to chant gay pride slogans and march down Christopher Street. Police broke up the protest with nightsticks, leaving many protesters bleeding on the sidewalk.

The riots initially attracted little attention from both the straight and gay communities. A brief report of the first confrontation appeared on page 33 of the *New York Times* two days later.

▮ PRIMARY SOURCE

MELEE NEAR SHERIDAN SQUARE FOLLOWS ACTION AT BAR

Hundreds of young men went on a rampage in Greenwich Village shortly after 3 A.M. yesterday after a force of plainclothes men raided a bar that the police said was well known for its homosexual clientele. Thirteen persons were arrested and four policemen injured.

The young men threw bricks, bottles, garbage, pennies and a parking meter at the policemen, who had a search warrant authorizing them to investigate reports that liquor was sold illegally at the bar, the Stonewall Inn, 53 Christopher Street, just off Sheridan Square.

Deputy Inspector Seymour Pine said that a large crowd formed in the square after being evicted from the bar. Police reinforcements were sent to the area to hold off the crowd.

Plainclothes men and detectives confiscated cases of liquor from the bar, which Inspector Pine said was operating without a liquor license.

The police estimated that 200 young men had been expelled from the bar. The crowd grew to close to 400 during the melee, which lasted about 45 minutes, they said.

Arrested in the melee, was Dave Van Romk, 33 years old, of 15 Sheridan Square, a well-known folk singer. He was accused of having thrown a heavy object at a patrolman and later paroled in his own recognizance.

The raid was one of three held on Village bars in the last two weeks, Inspector Pine said.

Charges against the 13 who were arrested ranged from harassment and resisting arrest to disorderly conduct. A patrolman suffered a broken wrist, the police said.

Throngs of young men congregated outside the inn last night, reading aloud condemnations of the police.

A sign on the door said, "This is a private club. Members only." Only soft drinks were being served.

▮

SIGNIFICANCE

The alternative press spread the news of the Stonewall Riots over the next few months to people who understood the significance of the uprising. By 1969, there were dozens of gay and lesbian organizations that were working for civil rights for homosexuals. Yet none of these groups captured the imagination of large numbers of gays and lesbians. Stonewall became an iconic moment because it provided enough drama to inspire gays and lesbians to resist discrimination.

The riots started a widespread movement to remove the stigma from homosexuality. Gays and lesbians engaged in conduct that was criminal according to law. They could be arrested, prosecuted, and jailed for dressing in the clothing of a member of the opposite sex. They were commonly seen as being seriously disturbed, with the American Psychiatric Association labeling homosexuality as a mental illness. In this climate, queers typically lost custody of their children, lost jobs, and lost homes because of discrimination that was legal.

The Stonewall Riots are a part of the 1960s drive for minority civil rights. The Gay Revolution or the Gay Liberation Movement, as it was commonly called, came on the heels of the Black Revolution, the Chicano Revolution, and the Women's Liberation Movement. Primed by a decade of militant movements for other minorities, gays and lesbians developed their own militancy. The riots helped them see themselves as another unjustly oppressed minority.

FURTHER RESOURCES
Books

Carter, David. *Stonewall: The Riots That Sparked the Gay Revolution.* New York: St. Martin's Press, 2004.

Thompson, Mark, editor. *Long Road to Freedom: The Advocate History of the Gay and Lesbian Movement.* New York: St. Martin's Press, 1994.

Web sites

Stonewall and Beyond: Gay and Lesbian Culture. <http://www.columbia.edu/cu/lweb/eresources/exhibitions/sw25/> (accessed March 31, 2006).

Conviction of *Gay News* for Blasphemous Libel

Photograph

By: David Ashdown

Date: July 30, 1977

Source: Getty Images

About the Photographer: David Ashdown is an award-winning English photographer whose work has been published in the London *Independent*.

INTRODUCTION

England in 1977 was a very different place from the hip image portrayed by the Beatles and London's fashionable Carnaby Street in the "Swinging 60s". Traditional English society felt itself under siege, with its twin bulwarks the Church of England and the class system waning in influence. Immigration was changing the face of the nation, and a young, frustrated underclass was finding its voice in the primal sounds of punk rock. In addition, the British economy was in a slump and the country was divided by the question of Common Market membership.

It was in this depressed social and economic environment that an informal amalgam of religious conservatives and elements of traditional English society began to coalesce around the efforts of Mary Whitehouse, founder of the National Viewers and Listeners Association (NVLA), a group that sought to eradicate all references to sexuality or perceived blasphemy from media. "Mrs. Whitehouse," as she was known, was a tireless crusader who managed to ban two songs by the Sex Pistols—"Anarchy in the U.K" and "God Save the Queen"—from the public airwaves. Like any forbidden fruit, however, the Sex Pistols sold more records than ever after drawing the NVLA's ire.

The greatest battle waged by Mary Whitehouse and the NVLA was a criminal prosecution brought against the *Gay News*, a biweekly London newspaper published by Denis Lemon. In 1976, the *Gay News* published James Kirkup's poem "The Love That Dares to Speak Its Name", in which Jesus Christ is portrayed as a homosexual who engaged in sexual relations with his apostles, a characterization of Jesus that was profoundly offensive to many Christians.

Under English law, a private citizen can launch a criminal prosecution, subject to compliance with a number of procedural steps. Mary Whitehouse retained counsel to advance her charge of blasphemous libel against both Lemon and the *Gay News*. The defendants were represented by John Mortimer, famed as both a libel law expert and as a writer, creator of the fictional barrister Horace Rumpole and author of the screenplay for the television series *Brideshead Revisisted*.

Before the *Gay News* case, the last blasphemous libel prosecution in England had occurred in 1922; it was widely held in English legal circles that such cases could no longer be tried. Despite this, the Whitehouse jury found the *Gay News* guilty, and the judge fined the paper £1,000 (approximately $2,500). Lemon was assessed a suspended jail sentence of nine months.

The *Gay News* conviction was upheld in England's highest court, the House of Lords, in February 1979. By 1983, the *Gay News* had ceased publication.

PRIMARY SOURCE

CONVICTION OF *GAY NEWS* FOR BLASPHEMOUS LIBEL

See primary source image.

SIGNIFICANCE

The *Gay News* trial was a flashpoint in the conflict between traditional English society, as represented by Mary Whitehouse, and the forces of a modern liberal and more permissive English society.

Blasphemy remains grounds for criminal prosecution in Great Britian, and although the last blasphemy trial resulting in imprisonment there was in 1921, various political efforts to legislate it out of existence have failed. It may be that technology has trumped such proceedings, since Internet-based communications, especially those that originate from offshore servers blur jurisdictional lines.

The prosecution was a concerted effort by Whitehouse and the NVLA to sway public opinion. It was also a "civil" war in every sense: the rule of law, the cornerstone of English justice, reigned in every aspect of the proceedings. The protests, such as those depicted in the photograph, were peaceful and orderly. The defendants attempted to redress what they perceived as a wrong in the appeal courts, without ever resorting to violence.

The trial and its aftermath stand in stark contrast to the events that followed the 2005 publication of a series of cartoons in a Danish newspaper that were deemed blasphemous by the European Muslim community. In reaction, violent demonstrations erupted throughout Europe and in the Middle East, with Danish embassies and other government property destroyed. Throughout the controversy, it was evident that the Muslims who reacted with violence in response to the offending cartoons did so with the belief that God sanctioned their actions and that even the most extreme acts of destruction were justified. None of the parties in the *Gay News* prosecution took similar action or claimed similar divine authority.

There are also a number of parallels between the *Gay News* trial and the Scopes "Monkey" trial in Day-

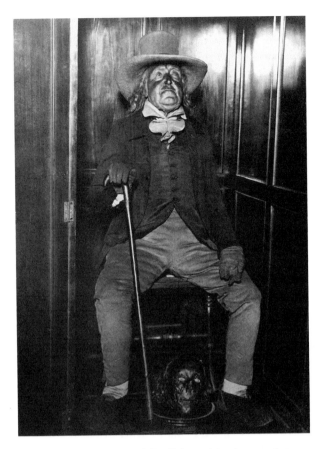

The mummified body of English social reformer Jeremy Bentham (1748-1832) is kept at University College London. © HULTON-DEUTSCH COLLECTION/CORBIS

It was in this environment that Bentham wrote, over a period of fifty years, about "paederasty," working to reconcile the harsh British treatment of homosexuality with his own philosophical beliefs.

■ PRIMARY SOURCE

To what class of offences shall we refer these irregularities of the venereal appetite which are stiled unnatural? When hidden from the public eye there could be no colour for placing them anywhere else: could they find a place anywhere it would be here. I have been tormenting myself for years to find if possible a sufficient ground for treating them with the severity with which they are treated at this time of day by all European nations: but upon the principle utility I can find none.

Offences of impurity—their varietys

The abominations that come under this heading have this property in common, in this respect, that they consist in procuring certain sensations by means of an improper object. The impropriety then may consist either in making use of an object:

1. Of the proper species but at an improper time: for instance, after death.
2. Of an object of the proper species, and sex, and at a proper time, but in an improper part.
3. Of an object of the proper species but the wrong sex. This is distinguished from the rest by the name of paederasty.
4. Of a wrong species.
5. In procuring this sensation by one's self without the help of any other sensitive object.

Paederasty makes the greatest figure

The third being that which makes the most figure in the world it will be proper to give that the principal share of our attention. In settling the nature and tendency of this offence we shall for the most part have settled the nature and tendency of all the other offences that come under this disgusting catalogue.

Whether they produce any primary mischief

1. As to any primary mischief, it is evident that it produces no pain in anyone. On the contrary it produces pleasure, and that a pleasure which, by their perverted taste, is by this supposition preferred to that pleasure which is in general reputed the greatest. The partners are both willing. If either of them be unwilling, the act is not that which we have here in view: it is an offence totally different in its nature of effects: it is a personal injury; it is a kind of rape.

As a secondary mischief whether they produce any alarm n the community

1. As to any danger exclusive of pain, the danger, if any, must consist in the tendency of the example. But what is the tendency of this example? To dispose others to engage in the same practices: but this practice for anything that has yet appeared produces not pain of any kind to any one.

Reasons that have commonly been assigned

Hitherto we have found no reason for punishing it at all: much less for punishing it with the degree of severity with which it has been commonly punished. Let us see what force there is in the reasons that have been commonly assigned for punishing it.

The whole tribe of writers on English law, who none of them knows any more what they mean by the word "peace" than they do by many other of the expressions that are most familiar to them, reckon this among offences against the peace. It is accordingly treated in all respects as an offence against the peace. They likewise reckon forgery, coining, and all sorts of frauds among offences against the peace. According to the same writers it is doubted whether adultery be no a breach of the peace. It is certain however that whenever a gallant accepts an invitation of another man's wife he does it with force and arms. This needs no comment.

SIGNIFICANCE

The eighteenth and early nineteenth century attitude in Britain toward homosexuality largely ignored Greek and Roman acceptance of sexual and intimate relationships between men. British students studied leaders such as Julius Caesar and Alexander the Great, known to have engaged in homosexual relationships, but discussion of homosexuality was taboo in English society. In the margins of Bentham's writings he notes his fear of airing his views publicly, and his use of classical literature in discussing homosexuality throughout history is part of an effort to lend legitimacy to his arguments.

Bentham applies a utilitarian argument to homosexual behavior: if paederasty causes pleasure between two willing participants and causes no pain to others, then it is not an offense and therefore should not be punished. If one partner is unwilling, Bentham labels it rape, but between two consenting partners homosexual activity, in and of itself, without moral or religious context, he argues, is neutral behavior that brings pleasure and therefore he sees "no reason for punishing it at all."

Bentham viewed homophobia as a form of moral and religious superiority; by condemning paederasty and assigning it capital crime status, the condemner could view himself as somehow less sinful, ignore his own violations of religious law, and elevate himself above his own sin. Sexual sins such as adultery, Bentham argued, produced greater harm than paederasty; adultery could produce illegitimate children, for instance. This application of utilitarian thought to a morally-charged subject was unique in its time.

In 1883, the publication of John Addington Symonds' *A Problem in Greek Ethics*, which defended homosexuality, caused a controversy in England, although the author's first print run was only ten copies. British doctor and writer Havelock Ellis's writings on "sexual inversion" were banned from public reading until 1935; only medical students and doctors could access his works.

Sexual acts between two consenting adult males were finally made legal in Britain in 1967. Bentham's "Offences Against One's Self" was first published nearly two hundred years after it had been written, in 1978.

FURTHER RESOURCES

Books

Bayer, Ronald. *Homosexuality and American Psychiatry*. Princeton: Princeton University Press, 1987.

Crompton, Louis. *Homosexuality and Civilization*. Belknap Press, 2003.

Web sites

University College London "UCL Jeremy Bentham Project." <http://www.ucl.ac.uk/Bentham-Project/info/jb.htm> (accessed March 31, 2006).

NYC Moscone Milk Verdict Protest

Photograph

By: David Karp

Date: May 22, 1979

Source: Karp, David. "NYC Moscone Milk Verdict Protest." Associated Press Worldwide Photos, May 22, 1979.

About the Photographer: David Karp is a freelance photographer and author.

INTRODUCTION

The murder of gay rights activist Harvey Milk in 1978 is regarded as an event that equals the 1969 New York City Stonewall Riots for mobilizing the homosexual community to oppose anti-gay discrimination.

Harvey Milk (1930–1978) served in the United States Navy before being dismissed for being homosexual. His dishonorable discharge prevented him from pursuing a teaching career and instead, Milk became a prosperous Wall Street financial analyst. He was not openly homosexual until he moved to San Francisco in 1969 to take a job as a securities analyst. He subsequently opened a camera shop on Castro Street, in the gay section of San Francisco. Known as the Mayor of Castro Street, Milk won election to the San Francisco Board of Supervisors in 1977. His election made him both the first openly gay supervisor in the city and the highest openly gay government official in the United States.

Milk's major political achievement was the passage of a citywide gay rights ordinance that forbade discrimination on account of sexual orientation in

PRIMARY SOURCE

NYC Moscone Milk Verdict Protest: Hundreds of gay rights activists in New York City protest the "diminished capacity" verdict in the prosecution of Dan White for the killings of San Francisco mayor George Moscone and San Francisco's first openly gay Supervisor, Harvey Milk. AP IMAGES

employment, housing, and public accommodation. The only San Francisco supervisor to oppose the bill was Dan White, a former fireman and policeman. White resigned from office on November 10, 1978 claiming that the $9,600 part-time salary was not sufficient to support his family. Milk urged Mayor George Moscone (1929–1978) not to reappoint White when he requested a few weeks later that the supervisor seat be returned to him. (Moscone, a heterosexual man, was known for being gay-friendly and had appointed a number of homosexuals to various city commissions.) On November 27, 1978, White got revenge by fatally shooting both Moscone and Milk in their City Hall offices. Over 25,000 San Franciscans attended the memorial service for the men.

In White's trial, defense lawyers mounted the infamous "Twinkie" defense. They claimed that their client consumed so much junk food that it impaired

his judgment. In May 1979, White, who faced the death penalty, was found guilty of the lesser charge of voluntary manslaughter. He received a sentence of seven years and eight months. The sentence triggered enormous anger in the gay and lesbian community, who perceived that the judge and jury were putting little value on the life of a gay man. In San Francisco, the White Night Riots erupted with three thousand protesters converging on City Hall and causing over $1 million in damages. After White's release from prison in 1984, he took his own life.

PRIMARY SOURCE

NYC MOSCONE MILK VERDICT PROTEST

See primary source image.

SIGNIFICANCE

As the first openly homosexual public official in the United States, Harvey Milk was a pioneer. His charisma, his speeches, and his entrance into the heterosexual power base of San Francisco gave the homosexual community hope that they would someday live in a world free of persecution. Milk never tolerated low self-esteem, and he supported gay pride efforts by stressing the need for homosexuals to make themselves known in the community.

Compared to other historic figures, Milk's legend has remained mostly intact. Given his brief time in office and his refusal to sanitize his personal life, there have been few revelations since the 1982 publication of a biography of Milk by Randy Shilts.

In the years since his murder, Milk has become a martyr of the gay rights movement. He is far better known now than he was in his lifetime. He has been immortalized in a Broadway play, a made-for-TV movie, in the first gay-themed film to win an Academy Award ("The Times of Harvey Milk" in 1984), in a New York City high school for gay and lesbian children, in an opera, and in books. In San Francisco, an elementary school, a civic plaza, a restaurant, a queer cultural institute, and library bear Milk's name. He is invoked as a symbol of the gains that gay men and lesbians have made and their continuing struggle for equality.

FURTHER RESOURCES

Books

Hinkle, Warren. *Gayslayer!: The Story of How Dan White Killed Harvey Milk and George Moscone and Got Away With Murder*. Virginia City, NV: Silver Dollar, 1985.

Periodicals

Shilts, Randy. *Mayor of Castro Street: The Life and Times of Harvey Milk*. New York: St. Martin's Press, 1982.

Web sites

Time. "The *Time* 100: Harvey Milk." <http://www.time.com/time/time100/heroes/profile/milk01.html> (accessed April 2, 2006).

Remembering Stonewall

Radio transcript

By: National Public Radio

Date: July 1, 1989

Source: Sound Portraits Productions, Dave Isay, Executive Producer. "Remembering Stonewall." *Weekend All Things Considered*. National Public Radio, July 1, 1989.

About the Author: Sound Portraits Productions is an independent production company dedicated to telling stories that bring neglected American voices to a national audience. Most Sound Portraits Productions are broadcast on National Public Radio. The participants in the Stonewall riots interviewed for the program included Sylvia Rivera, Seymour Pine, and Howard Smith.

INTRODUCTION

The Stonewall, often a term used to denote a larger group of social rebellions, was the name of a popular New York City gay bar. Located in Greenwich Village (in lower Manhattan), an eclectic section of the city known for its vibrant culture celebrating homosexuals, writers, artists, and a younger crowd, the Stonewall Inn was not unique nor alone in its cultural appeal.

On June 27, 1969, police raided the local hangout, and shortly after one A.M., (June 28) rioting began. The initial start of the conflict is uncertain—some say that a burly patron lunged a garbage can filled with empty liquor bottles at a police car, and others note that a drag-queen (a man dressed in women's clothing) resisted arrest. The central point, however, remains clear. On this Friday night, the atmosphere in New York's gay community would change, and in succeeding years, the nation would see the after-effects of this event and demand change in social attitudes and decorum.

Prior to the initial night of riots, police would normally enter a known gay arena, declare a raid, and patrons would show their identification and leave, not show ID and be arrested, or sometimes those with ID were arrested. There is no clear direction in how these arrests and raids took place, but prior to Stonewall, they were generally quiet and non-resistant. Yet, in June 1969, patrons forcefully acted out against the police, and within five days over 1000 people were gathered in front of Stonewall Inn. An active gay resistance movement to social policy had begun.

Throughout the United States, protest groups publicly voiced their concerns and aspirations for gay rights, and Stonewall represents a smaller part of that chaotic picture. Prior to Stonewall, police frequently would arrest gay couples for indecent exposure. These acts of indecent exposure often involved gay couples merely holding hands or kissing in public places, but social codes and understandings allowed police to apply the law liberally. Police departments often tar-

People gather outside the Stonewall Inn in New York's Greenwich Village, June 24, 1994. AP IMAGES

geted gay communities because the larger community demanded that action be taken to remove the gay subculture, and many individuals feared anyone that did not fit the social norm.

Many religious and political groups aligned to support gay rights, just as many similar organizations united to denounce gay culture and life choices. Frequently, gay communities were targeted as unclean, harbors for child-molesters, social deviants, and some individuals feared that being homosexual was a disease. Hence, Stonewall was an intense reaction to a society that (up to this point) forced individuals to hide their identities and live in fear. Gay persons feared loosing their homes, jobs, and families if their sexual choices were discovered.

■ PRIMARY SOURCE

RIVERA: People started gathering in front of the Sheridan Square Park right across the street from Stonewall.

People were upset — "No, we're not going to go!" and people started screaming and hollering.

PINE: One drag queen, as we put her in the car, opened the door on the other side and jumped out. At which time we had to chase that person and he was caught, put back into the car, he made another attempt to get out the same door, the other door, and at that point we had to handcuff the person. From this point on, things really began to get crazy.

PINE: Well that's when all hell broke loose at that point. And then we had to get back into Stonewall.

HOWARD SMITH: My name is Howard Smith. On the night of the Stonewall riots I was a reporter for the *Village Voice,* locked inside with the police, covering it for my column. It really did appear that that crowd— because we could look through little peepholes in the plywood windows, we could look out and we could see that the crowd—well, my guess was within five, ten minutes it was probably several thousand people. Two thousand easy. And they were yelling, "Kill the cops! Police brutality! Let's get 'em! We're not going to take this anymore! Let's get 'em!"

PINE: We noticed a group of persons attempting to uproot one of the parking meters, at which they did succeed. And they then used that parking meter as a battering ram to break down the door. And they did in fact open the door—they crashed it in—and at that point was when they began throwing Molotov cocktails into the place. It was a situation that we didn't know how we were going to be able control.

SIGNIFICANCE

Expressions of protest at Stonewall mirrored the concurrent protests against U.S. involvement in the Vietnam conflict and those of the civil rights movement (most commonly remembered from the late 1950s and early 1960s with Martin Luther King Jr. and Birmingham). As the heated social atmosphere of 1969 quickly turned into the turbulent decade of the 1970s, protesters continually used these expressions. In each instance, the protests shouted may have stood for a different social agenda, but with each use they still maintained the same overall meaning—freedom of choice and rights.

Stonewall forced the nation to reexamine its interaction with homosexual communities, and the riots are still commemorated each year with Gay Pride Day. This celebration is usually the last Sunday in June, when cities across the United States host parades and other festivities honoring gay lifestyles.

FURTHER RESOURCES

Books

Carter, David. *Stonewall: The Riots That Sparked the Gay Revolution.* New York: St. Martin's Griffin, 2005.

Web sites

American Civil Liberties Union. "Lesbian and gay Rights." <http://www.aclu.org/lgbt/index.html> (accessed April 10, 2006).

Stonewall Revisited. <http://www.stonewallrevisited.com/> (accessed April 10, 2006).

The Lesbian

Book excerpt

By: Simone de Beauvoir

Date: 1949

Source: de Beauvoir, Simone. *The Second Sex*, translated and edited by H.M. Parshley. New York: Knopf, 1993.

About the Author: The French feminist writer and philosopher Simone de Beauvoir (1908–1986) is one of the most important figures in twentieth-century thought. She is the author of *Le Deuxième Sexe* (*The Second Sex*), one of the founding texts of modern Western feminism.

INTRODUCTION

Simone de Beauvoir authored *The Second Sex* (1949) and other existential books exploring sexuality and the gender roles of women in history. One of the few female intellectuals of the twentieth century to achieve international fame and a pioneering feminist, de Beauvoir is a widely read and highly controversial figure.

The elder of two daughters, de Beauvoir was born in Paris on January 9, 1908. She met existentialist Jean-Paul Sartre when both were philosophy students at the University of Paris, Sorbonne. The two were together for more than fifty years but never married, lived in separate apartments, and frequently had affairs with younger partners. Sartre was jealous of de Beauvoir's greater intellectual reputation, one that she earned with a series of philosophical books as well as essays, novels, and plays. Although she did not identify as a feminist at the time that she wrote *The Second Sex*, de Beauvoir became a women's rights activist and remained active in radical feminist causes until her death in 1986.

The Second Sex, a two-volume work, is de Beauvoir's groundbreaking study of the situation of women from prehistory to the late 1940s. It famously introduced the idea that "one is not born, but rather becomes, a woman." De Beauvoir argued that there is no natural feminity or masculinity or any maternal instinct. A woman becomes her gender by learning to conform to patriarchal society's requirements that she exist inauthentically.

De Beauvoir approached women's oppression from a materialist viewpoint. She believed that women could only achieve freedom by becoming economically free. She saw patriarchy as a social system in which women and men formed different classes with different interests. Critics of de Beauvoir's work believe that *The Second Sex* is fundamentally flawed by an oppositional conception of male and female, an inadequate understanding of the structure of the social world, and a commitment to the existentialist belief in the possibility of absolute free choice.

Simone de Beauvoir sitting with Jean Paul Sartre, 1967. AP/WIDE WORLD PHOTOS. REPRODUCED BY PERMISSION.

PRIMARY SOURCE

We commonly think of the lesbian as a woman wearing a plain felt hat, short hair, and a necktie; her mannish appearance would seem to indicate some abnormality of the hormones. Nothing could be more erroneous than this confounding of the invert with the 'viriloid' woman. There are many homosexuals among harem inmates, prostitutes, among most intentionally 'feminine' women; and conversely a great many 'masculine' women are heterosexual. Sexologists and psychiatrists confirm the common observation that the majority of female 'homos' are in constitution quite like other women. Their sexuality is in no way determined by any anatomical 'fate.'

A man is more annoyed by an active and independent heterosexual woman than by an unaggressive lesbian; only the first assaults the masculine prerogatives; sapphic love affairs by no means run counter to the traditional distinction of the sexes; they involve in most cases an acceptance of femininity, not its denial. We have seen that they often appear among adolescent girls as a substitute for the heterosexual relations that such girls as yet have neither the opportunity nor the hardihood to enter

upon. The homosexual affair represents a stage, an apprenticeship, and a girl who engages in it most ardently may well become tomorrow the most ardent of wives, mistresses, or mothers. What must be explained in the female invert is not, then the positive aspect of her choice, it is the negative; she is distinguished not by her taste for women but by the exclusive character of this taste.

Two types of lesbians are often distinguished (as by Jones and Hesnard); the 'masculine,' who 'wish to imitate the male,' and the 'feminine,' who 'are afraid of the male.' It is true that one can, on the whole, discern two tendencies in inversion; certain women decline passivity, whereas others choose feminine arms in which to abandon themselves passively. But these attitudes reach the one on the other; the relations to the object chosen, to the object rejected, are explained the one by the other. For many reasons, as will appear, the distinction made above seems to me to be rather arbitrary.

To define the 'masculine' lesbian by her will to 'imitate the male' is to stamp her as inauthentic. I have already noted how many ambiguities the psychoanalysts create by accepting the masculine/feminine categories as society currently refines them. The truth is that man today represents the positive and the neutral— that is to say, the male and the human being—where as woman is only the negative, the female. Whenever she behaves a human being, she is declared to be identifying herself with the male. Her activities in sports, politics, and intellectual matters, her sexual desire for other women, are all interpreted as a 'masculine protest'; the common refusal to take account of the values toward which she aims, or transcends herself, evidently leads to the conclusion that she is, as subject, making an inauthentic choice.

The chief misunderstanding underlying this line of interpretation is that it is *natural* for the female human being to make herself a *feminine* woman: it is not enough to be a heterosexual, even a mother, to realize this ideal; the 'true woman' is an artificial product that civilization makes, as formerly eunuchs were made. Her presumed 'instincts' for coquetry, docility, are indoctrinated, as is phallic pride in man. Man, as a matter of fact, does not always accept his virile vocation; and woman has good reasons for accepting with even less docility the one assigned to her. The concepts of the 'inferiority complex' and the 'masculine complex' remind me of the story told by Denis de Rougemont in the *Part du Diable*; a woman believed that the birds attacked her when she strolled in the country; after some months of psychoanalytic treatment, which failed to cure the obsession, the doctor went into the garden of the clinic with his patient and saw that the birds actually *did* attack her! Woman feels inferior because, in fact, the requirements of femininity *do* belittle her. She spontaneously chooses to be a complete person, a subject and a free being with the world and the future open before her; if this choice has a virile cast, it is so to the extent that femininity today means mutilation. Various statements made by female inverts to physicians clearly show that what outrages them, even in childhood, is to be regarded as feminine. They feel contempt for girlish pursuits, demand boys' games and playthings; they feel sorry for women, they are afraid of becoming effeminate, they object to being put in girls' schools.

This revolt by no means implies a predetermined homosexuality; most little girls feel the same sense of outrage and the same desperation when they learn that the chance conformation of their bodies renders their tastes and aspirations blameworthy. Colette Audry was enraged to discover at twelve that she could never become a sailor. It is perfectly natural for the future woman to feel indignant at the limitations imposed upon her by her sex. The real question is not why she should reject them: the problem is rather to understand why she accepts them. She conforms through docility and timidity; but this resignation will easily become transformed into revolt if the compensations offered by society seem

inadequate. This is what will happen in cases where the adolescent girl feels she is unattractive, as a woman; it is in this way particularly that anatomical endowments are important; ugly of face and figure, or believing herself to be so, woman rejects a feminine destiny for which she feels poorly equipped. But it would be erroneous to say that a mannish bent is acquired in order to compensate for a lack of feminine attributers; the truth is rather that the opportunities offered to the adolescent girl seem too meager to be a fair exchange for the required sacrifice of masculine advantages. All little girls who are brought up conventionally envy the convenient clothing worn by boys; their reflections in the mirror and the promising futures they foresee for themselves are what make them come little by little to value their furbelows; if the harshly truthful mirror reflects an ordinary face, if it holds no promise, laces and ribbons continue to seem an irksome livery, even a ridiculous one, and the *'garcon manque'* stubbornly retains her boyishness.

SIGNIFICANCE

Feminism would not have exploded worldwide in the mid-twentieth century without de Beauvoir's *The Second Sex*. The book set off shock waves upon its publication in France in 1949, with the first edition selling twenty-two thousand copies. However, in a deeply traditional France, most people only read summaries of the book. De Beauvoir analyzed the effects of patriarchal power in everyday life in a France in which women had only just won the right to vote in 1944 and where a woman could not work outside the home without her husband's formal consent. At the time of the book's publication, abortion and contraception were illegal, making de Beauvoir's exploration of sexuality all the more shocking. To many in France, *The Second Sex* was indecent and scandalous.

Following the appearance of an edited English translation in 1953, English-speaking feminists began to explore de Beauvoir's ideas. As time passed, her ideas seemed less shocking. The work was eventually translated into forty-nine languages. Key feminist theorists such as Shulamith Firestone of Canada, Germaine Greer of Australia, and Betty Friedan and Judith Butler of the United States have acknowledged their intellectual debt to de Beauvoir's work even as they moved in radically different directions. Although there are few explicit references to de Beauvoir in the publications of these women, her work helped establish a framework for their subsequent arguments about women's liberation.

The feminists inspired by the French feminist theory that developed in the 1970s, such as Luce Irigaray and Monique Wittig, have tended to either ignore de Beauvoir or to treat her as a theoretical dinosaur. De Beauvoir worked with these feminists in the 1970s on such issues as abortion and violence against women. Although she never retracted any of her original arguments in *The Second Sex*, de Beauvoir also acknowledged that she had underestimated the political significance of women's sexuality.

FURTHER RESOURCES

Books

Bauer, Nancy. *Simone de Beauvoir: Philosophy and Feminism.* New York: Columbia University Press, 2001.

Duran, Jane. *Eight Women Philosophers: Theory, Politics, and Feminism.* Urbana, Ill.: University of Illinois Press, 2006.

Tidd, Ursula. *Simone de Beauvoir.* New York: Routledge, 2004.

International Dyke March in Manhattan

Photograph

By: Najlah Feanny-Hicks

Date: June 25, 1994

Source: Feanny-Hicks, Najlah. "International Dyke March in Manhattan." Corbis, 1994.

About the Photographer: Photojournalist Najlah Feanny-Hicks is best known for founding New Jersey's Heart Gallery, a photographic exhibit that helps children find adoptive parents.

PRIMARY SOURCE

International Dyke March in Manhattan: Lesbians participate in the International Dyke March, which is on the eve of the 25th anniversary of the Stonewall Riots. The Stonewall Riots in New York marked the beginning of the modern gay and lesbian rights movement. © NAJLAH FEANNY/CORBIS SABA

INTRODUCTION

The International Dyke March is a New York City event that began in 1992 as a political protest. Organized by the Lesbian Avengers, the march attacks discrimination against lesbians. It is an illegal parade, held in June close to the anniversary of the 1969 Stonewall Riots that began the gay and lesbian rights movement.

Commonly known simply as the Dyke March, the parade involves lesbians from around the world. The marchers move down Fifth Avenue from Central Park to Worthington Square Park. Unlike the five-hour Gay Pride marathon held earlier in the week, the Dyke March is messy and militant. Groups do not march in any organized fashion and organizers traditionally refuse to apply for parade permits. New York City police provide no opposition to the march and no longer attempt to enforce the permit law.

The protesters cover the spectrum of lesbians from radical activists to stroller-pushing two-mommy families. The groups that have participated in the past include the National Organization for Women, Lesbian Avengers, Lesbian Social Workers, and female members of the AIDS Coalition to Unleash Power (ACT-UP). The New York City Gay and Lesbian Anti-Violence Project, a regular participant, always issues a call for a moment of outrage to protest attacks on women with the crowd urged to scream, screech, howl, yell, shriek, wail, and stomp feet.

INTERNATIONAL DYKE MARCH IN MANHATTAN

See primary source image.

SIGNIFICANCE

The International Dyke March is a chance for lesbians to step out of the shadow of gay men. With greater financial resources and a more aggressive style than women, gay men have typically dominated gay and lesbian organizations. Although these groups are ostensibly for both women and men, comparatively few women hold positions of leadership.

In response to this male domination of the gay and lesbian rights movement, lesbians have turned to other venues for activism. In the 1970s and 1980s, they founded lesbian feminist collectives, women's studies programs at colleges, and feminist newspapers. By the 1990s, lesbians were more willing to aggressively and publicly demand lesbian rights. The Lesbian Avengers, almost entirely formed of young women in their teens and twenties, formed in 1992 to promote lesbian visibility through such actions as marches.

The gay pride parades that are held across the United States around the anniversary of the Stonewall Riots do not give lesbians the same sense of solidarity as the Dyke March. The presence of so many men, often with radically different agendas than lesbians, tends to draw attention away from lesbian concerns such as violence against women and child custody. The Dyke March draws considerable notice from the media, which helps to publicize lesbian issues.

FURTHER RESOURCES

Books

Carter, David. *Stonewall: The Riots the Sparked the Gay Revolution*. New York: St. Martin's Press, 2004.

Schulman, Sarah. *My American History: Lesbian and Gay Life During the Reagan/Bush Years*. New York: Routledge, 1994.

Web sites

NCLR—National Center for Lesbian Rights. <http://www.nclrights.org> (accessed April 1, 2006).

New York City Dyke March. <http://www.nycdykemarch.org> (accessed April 1, 2006).

1931 Vagrants, Gaming, and Other Offenses Act

Legislation

By: Queensland Parliamentary Council

Date: 1931

Source: Queensland Parliamentary Council. Vagrants, Gaming, and Other Offenses Act. 1931.

About the Author: The Queensland Parliamentary Council is part of the elected representative form of government in Queensland, a north-eastern state in Australia.

INTRODUCTION

In an effort to legislate morality, the government of Queensland, Australia passed the Vagrants, Gaming, and Other Offenses Act in 1931. The law targeted a wide range of behaviors that were believed to pose a threat to society, including prostitution and public nudity as well as gambling. Violators were subject to a fine of 50–100 Australian dollars (about 68.5–137 American dollars) and imprisonment of up to two years.

The Vagrants, Gaming, and Other Offenses Act punished women for using premises for the purposes of prostitution. The aim of the legislation was not to suppress prostitution entirely. Australia had a long history of tolerating prostitution, in part because the vast majority of the first European immigrants to the country were male. Australian legislators generally accepted prostitution as a necessary evil that kept men from seducing or raping respectable women. Instead, the Queensland government sought to control the more offensive side-effects of prostitution. They did not want prostitution to be carried out in an open and flagrant manner. Police typically gave women sex workers summonses under the act but did not harass the patrons of prostitutes.

The legislation did target pimps. Changes to vagrancy laws across Australia in the early twentieth century made living off the proceeds of prostitution a criminal offense. The targets of these laws were white slavers, men who were assumed to have tricked innocent white girls into a life of prostitution. Concern about this practice was worldwide, fueled by sensationalist newspaper and magazine reports of an international white slave traffic. In most cases, these stories had racist overtones, with the white slavers typically portrayed as Asian or immigrant men who corrupted virtuous Anglo-Saxon females.

PRIMARY SOURCE

PART 2—VAGRANTS AND DISORDERLY PERSONS

4.(1) Any person who—Vagrants

(a) having no visible lawful means of support or insufficient lawful means, does not, on being charged before a court, give to its satisfaction a good account of the person's means of support;

(b) is the occupier of a house frequented by reputed thieves or persons who have no visible lawful means of support;

(c) being an habitual drunkard, behaves in a riotous, disorderly, or indecent manner in any public place;

(d) habitually consorts with reputed criminals or known prostitutes or persons who have been convicted of having no visible lawful means of support;

(e) in a house or place frequented by reputed thieves or persons who have no visible lawful

means of support, is found in company with reputed thieves or such persons, and does not, on being charged before a court, give to its satisfaction a good account of the person's lawful means of support, and of the person being in such house or place on a lawful occasion;

(f) plays or bets at any unlawful game, or plays or bets in any street, road, highway, or other public place at or with any table or instrument of gaming at any game or pretended game;

(g) without lawful excuse (the proof of which shall be upon the person)—

(i) is found in any dwelling house, warehouse, coach-house, stable, or outhouse, or in any enclosed yard, garden, or area, or on board any vessel in any port, harbour, or place, or in or upon any mine or claim as defined by the *Mining Act 1898* or any Act amending or in substitution for the same;

(ii) has in the person's custody or possession any picklock key, crow, jack, bit, or other implement of housebreaking, or any dangerous or explosive substance;

(iii) has in the person's custody or possession any instrument of gaming or any instrument which, in the opinion of the court, is constructed or kept or used as a means of gaming or cheating;

(iv) willfully exposes his or her person in view of any person in any public place;

SIGNIFICANCE

The Vagrants, Gaming, and Other Offenses Act of 1931 had became obsolete and the subject of mockery by the new millennium. While the legislation primarily targeted vagrants and gaming, it also made it illegal for Queenslanders to wear slippers outside the home at night, to carry dark lanterns, vomit in public, walk home while drunk, use offensive language in public, and make too much noise while in a park at night. Some of the provisions were regarded as unjust in a modern society while other parts of the legislation were phrased in language that needed to be amended to suit the modern era.

The segment of the act that came under the heaviest attack banned nude sunbathing and nude swimming in public areas. Both the Australian Tourism and Police Ministers worried about the effects of the law on tourism, especially on international tourism. The Australian Tourist Commission (ATC) and the Queensland Government spent considerable sums to induce foreigners to visit Australian beaches. In 2000,

Model Amber Kenny rides Christmas the horse as Lady Godiva in Sydney, NSW, on October 19, 2005 to attend the opening of LushART Gallery, the first nude art gallery to open in Australia. PHOTO BY PATRICK RIVIERE/GETTY IMAGES

ATC promoted Australia as a free-spirited country and included shots of nude bathing on a Sydney beach in its advertisements. In response to demand, ATC also produced a fact sheet in reference to nudist vacations and advised potential tourists of the availability of clothing optional beaches. No one told visitors that Queensland police might arrest them, take them to court, and fine them for sunbathing in the nude. The other Australian states and territories had long legalized nude bathing at certain beaches.

Accordingly, the 1931 act was replaced by the Summary Offenses Bill of 2004 that sought to allow police to prevent serious crime by tackling lower-level offenses. Under the new law, willful exposure, begging, being drunk in a public place, and piercing the nipples or genitals of a child all remained illegal. The new legislation was part of the Australian government's child protection reforms. The additional new legislation that aimed to protect children required registered nurses to report suspected child abuse and expanded the monitoring powers of the Child Guardian.

FURTHER RESOURCES

Books

Daniels, Kay. *So Much Hard Work: Women and Prostitution in Australian History.* Sydney: Fontana, 1984.

Perkins, Roberta, Garrett Prestage, Rachel Sharp, and Francis Lovejoy, eds. *The History of Female Prostitution in Australia.* Sydney: University of New South Wales, 1994.

Hate Groups and Religious Intolerance

Photograph

By: Steve Liss

Date: October 16, 1998

Source: Liss, Steve. "Hate Groups and Religious Intolerance." Getty Images/Time Life Pictures, 1998.

About the Author: Steve Liss has been a photographer for *Time* magazine since 1976. He has won numerous awards from the World Press Organization and the National Press Photographers' Association. In 2004, Liss was the recipient of the Soros Criminal Justice Journalism Fellowship for his work on *No Place for Children: Voices from Juvenile Detention*, a photo-journal examination of incarcerated children.

INTRODUCTION

On October 7, 1998, Matthew Shepard, a twenty-one-year-old student at the University of Wyoming, was attacked by Russell Henderson and Aaron McKinney. He was robbed, beaten, tied to a fence, and left to die. Some eighteen hours later, Shepard was discovered by a passing cyclist, unconscious, but still alive. Shepard died of his injuries in the hospital on October 12, 1998. The photograph depicts a protestor picketing outside Shepard's funeral.

Shepard, a gay man, was believed to have been targeted in the attack for his sexual preference. Friends, family, and gay rights activists were vocal in calling the murder a "hate crime," even though United States federal law and state law in Wyoming did not consider crimes perpetrated on the basis of sexual orientation to be "hate crimes." In 1999, President Bill Clinton introduced legislation to add sexual orientation to the federal hate crimes law. The bill was defeated.

■ PRIMARY SOURCE

HATE GROUPS AND RELIGIOUS INTOLERANCE

See primary source image.

■ PRIMARY SOURCE

Hate Groups and Religious Intolerance: An anti-gay protester stands outside of Matthew Shepard's funeral in Casper, Wyoming on October 16, 1998 with signs reading FAGS DOOM NATIONS and MATT IN HELL. Shepard was beaten and left to die by two local men because he was gay. PHOTO BY STEVE LISS/TIME LIFE PICTURES/GETTY IMAGES

SIGNIFICANCE

Matthew Shepard's murder brought the victimization and discrimination faced by gays and lesbians in the United States into public consciousness. While Shephard lay critically injured in hospital, candlelit vigils were held around the world. Media coverage of the incident and the outpouring of support for Shephard focused on the issue of his sexuality and brought gay-bashing and homophobia into the arena of public debate. Gay rights activists and other supporters argued the need for tougher legislation against hate crimes and the inclusion of homosexuals as a protected group.

However, the coverage of Shepard's murder also brought out anti-gay activists and conservative sentiments. Fred Phelps, the controversial leader of Westboro Baptist Church in Topeka, Kansas, and his supporters picketed at vigils and at Shepard's funeral, holding anti-gay placards like the ones depicted here. Phelps is best known for preaching that "God hates gays," and outside of the church where Shepard's funeral was held, he delivered a sermon informing mourners that Matthew Shepard was in hell and that everyone in attendance at the funeral would be going to hell for being "fag-enablers."

When Henderson and McKinney were arrested and charged with Shepard's murder, Phelps and his supporters protested at their trials. Citing biblical references against homosexuality and declaring gays and lesbians to be "an abomination," Phelps and his group have been accused of inciting hate but never prosecuted due to a lack of legislation in the United States. Phelps has been vocally opposed to hate crime legislation in Canada, which protects gays and lesbians and prevents his group from legally picketing and protesting the 2005 legalization of gay marriage. In 1999, when President Bill Clinton proposed the addition of sexual orientation to U.S. federal hate crime legislation, the bill was defeated by a Republican majority in the House of Representatives.

Although not all Christians are as vocally or vehemently opposed to homosexuals as Phelps' group, Republican supporters tend to hold conservative views of sexuality, based in biblical theology, that do not look positively on homosexuality. While they do not support the express protection of homosexuals under hate crime law, most Christians in the United States also do not agree with the violent persecution of gays and lesbians, preferring instead to believe that judgment for homosexuality will come from God in the afterlife. Groups such as Fred Phelps' supporters are an active and vocal minority in singling out homosexuals as "evil." Phelps continues to protest actively at gay rights rallies and Pride parades. The Ku Klux Klan and Neo-Nazi organizations are also staunchly opposed to gay rights and have been involved in the persecution of homosexuals in the United States and elsewhere. However, the actions of these groups are generally given much less legitimacy than Christian organizations.

Attitudes toward the propagation of anti-gay hate speech in the United States are beginning to shift. In a recent response to the actions of Fred Phelps' supporters and other such groups, as of February 7, 2006, thirteen states are considering banning protests near funeral sites immediately before, during, and after the ceremonies. Phelps and his supporters have held "God hates fags" rallies near the funerals of U.S. soldiers killed in Iraq, prompting Wisconsin, Indiana, and South Dakota to institute bans on such gatherings in early 2006.

Although crimes motivated by sexual orientation are not prosecuted under hate crime legislation in the United States, they are recognized and recorded by the Federal Bureau of Investigation (FBI) under the auspices of the 1990 Hate Crime Statistics Act. This act acknowledges that hate crimes are not, in fact, a separate class of crimes, but rather that the designation "hate crime" refers to the motive behind the offence. In 1995, 1,019 incidents of victimization prompted by sexual orientation were recorded in the United States. In 2000, there were almost thirteen hundred such incidents, 1,244 in 2002, and in 2004, nearly twelve hundred incidents. While the number fluctuates from year to year, there has not been a significant decrease, despite increased awareness and pleas for tolerance from gay and civil rights activists.

Statistics such as these indicate that more work needs to be done in building understanding and tolerance for differences of sexual orientation and lifestyle in the United States. Anti-gay messages rooted in religious intolerance only contribute to misunderstanding and hatred for homosexual people and can lead to more violent incidents like the murder of Matthew Shepard. Henderson and McKinney are each serving two consecutive life sentences for his killing.

FURTHER RESOURCES

Books

Loffreda, Beth. *Losing Matt Shepard: Life and Politics in the Aftermath of Anti-Gay Murder*. New York: Columbia University Press, 2000.

Periodicals

Boeckmann, Robert J., and Carolyn Turpin-Petrosino. "Understanding the Harm of Hate Crime." *Journal of Social Issues* 58, 2 (2002): 207–226.

Levin, Brian. "Extremism and the Constitution: Hate Speech and Freedom of Speech." *American Behavioral Scientist* 45, 4 (2001): 714–755.

Web sites

Federal Bureau of Investigation. "Uniform Crime Reports: Hate Crime Statistics." <http://www.fbi.gov/ucr/ucr.htm> (accessed April 1, 2006).

Left on a Fence

Magazine article

By: Anonymous

Date: October 17, 1998

Source: Anonymous. "Left on a Fence." *The Economist* 349, no. 8090 (October 17, 1998).

About the Author: The article was written by an anonymous staff writer for the British magazine *The Economist*.

INTRODUCTION

The brutal 1998 murder of gay college student Matthew Shepard in Wyoming shocked the United States and prompted calls to add sexual orientation to hate crimes legislation. While Shepard was not the first or last homosexual to be killed because of his sexual orientation, the sheer ugliness of the crime made him the poster child for the gay rights movement.

Shepard (1977–1998), a slightly built blond who stood only 5 feet, 2 inches tall, had traveled the world with his father, who worked in the oil business. Educated in Switzerland and Denver, he spoke English, German, Italian, and some Arabic. He attended Casper (Wyoming) Junior College before transferring to the University of Wyoming in Laramie in the fall of 1998 as a political science major. Shepard had worried about how his homosexuality would be perceived at the university and was hesitant to tell others that he was gay.

He was lured from a campus bar on October 6, 1998, by two men who told him they were gay. He was then robbed, beaten, and lashed to a split-rail fence in near-freezing temperatures. The bicyclists who found him at first mistook him for a scarecrow. Shepard died on October 12 in a Colorado hospital. He had been beaten so badly that his mother was able to recognize him only by his eye color, a bump on his ear, and his braces. His skull was so badly smashed that doctors could not perform surgery.

A cross of stones marks the spot where gay student Matthew Shepard was tied and beaten into a fatal coma, a hate crime committed by homophobes. AP/WIDE WORLD PHOTOS. REPRODUCED BY PERMISSION.

Russell Arthur Henderson, 21, and Aaron James McKinney, 22, were originally charged with attempted murder, kidnapping, and aggravated robbery and jailed on $100,000 bail each. With Shepard's death, the charges were upgraded to first-degree murder, which carried a possible death sentence. Their girlfriends, Chastity Vera Pasley, 20, and Kristen Leann Price, 18, were charged as accessories after the fact for dumping bloody clothing and initially lying about Henderson and McKinney's whereabouts. Both men are serving life in prison; the women received short jail sentences.

In a 2004 interview with television news show *20/20*, McKinney and Henderson claimed that they killed Shepard for reasons that had nothing to do with his sexuality. They said that he died as the result of a robbery gone wrong. McKinney, who had been strung out on methamphetamines for days, decided to rob a drug dealer. Henderson thought that if he kept McKinney drinking that he would forget the plan. Shepard, well-dressed and with a wallet full of money, said that he was too drunk to go home from the bar, asked for a ride, and then asked for sex in return for giving the pair drugs. McKinney struck Shepard with a gun in his truck and demanded money. Shepard handed over his wallet but McKinney continued to beat him. The pair then decided to dump Shepard in a secluded area and McKinney decided to tie him to a fence. When Shepard purportedly stated that he would report McKinney, he was beaten some more. While the credibility of convicted killers is somewhat questionable, the prosecutor in the Shepard case said that people had overlooked the drug and robbery aspects of the crime in an effort to find an easy answer.

PRIMARY SOURCE

Left on a Fence

Dateline: Big Horn, WYOMING

"IT AIN'T the Wyoming way," the locals say. They are talking of homosexuality. Yet almost all of them are horrified by last week's fatal beating of Matthew Shepard, a homosexual student at the University of Wyoming.

The police have charged two men, Russell Henderson and Aaron McKinney, with luring Mr Shepard away from a bar in Laramie on the night of October 6th. The accused are said to have taken him to the outskirts of town, tied him to a split-rail fence of lodgepole pine, and repeatedly fractured his skull with the butt end of a .357 Magnum. He hung there for 18 hours before being discovered by a passing cyclist. At first, he was thought to be a scarecrow. He died four days later.

Senator Craig Thomas called the attack "the most violent, barbaric thing I've ever heard happening in Wyoming." The state, a place of ranchers and miners, has a tough reputation, but Mr Thomas may be right. By and large, Wyoming is tolerant. Although Indians have occasionally had a difficult time, Wyoming, unlike Montana and Idaho, has not attracted right-wing militiamen or end-of-the-worlders. The Ku Klux Klan, too, has never gained a foothold.

But rural Wyoming is also conservative, and reluctant to address what it thinks of as "big-city problems". After the Shepard murder, President Bill Clinton called for the passage of a hate-crimes bill that would give federal officials greater powers to intervene when people are attacked because of their race or their sexual orientation. Similar legislation has never got far in the state legislature in Cheyenne, though Mr Shepard's death may change that.

More than anything, it has violated the western credo: mind your own business, and tolerate the behaviour of others no matter how strange it seems. The neighbours of Theodore Kaczynski behaved like that as he passed his days hunting and bomb-building in his cabin in the woods. So, too—up to a point—did the ranchers who lived next door to the militant Freemen in Jordan, Montana.

John Edgar Wildeman was once asked what it was like to be a black professor at the University of Wyoming. He replied: "I'm an object of curiosity, not animosity. The frontier ethic still applies in this state. If somebody messes with me, they know that some day they're going to have car trouble way out on Route 287 and the only driver in sight is going to be me."

SIGNIFICANCE

The Matthew Shepard case put a face on issues surrounding anti-gay sentiment and violence. It initially led to a strong push for hate crime legislation to cover attacks made on the grounds of sexual orientation. Shepard's mother Judy and human rights activists used the case to publicize the need for protections for gays. The Shepard murder became the subject of a popular play and television movie called *The Laramie Project* that urged tolerance.

However, no national hate crime legislation that includes sexual orientation has become law. As of 2006, Wyoming remains one of four states, including Arkansas, Indiana and South Carolina, that have not passed a single piece of hate crime legislation. Legislation periodically introduced in the Wyoming legislature would enhance penalties for those convicted of a misdemeanor in which bigotry was a motivating factor. Supporters argue that the distinction needs to be made clear because not all crimes are equal and that the intent to impose fear on a population should be punished. Rather than pass a law listing particularly vulnerable groups, opponents prefer to focus on evil intent and malice, which already are on the books. Such aspects of a crime can be considered by judges as aggravating factors and can encourage them to take a closer look at defendants whose crimes are motivated by bigotry or the intentional selection of a person because of their association with a group. Additionally, opponents of hate crime legislation fear that ministers who condemn homosexuality on biblical grounds could face sanctions.

FURTHER RESOURCES

Books

Ingebretsen, Edward J. *At Stake: Monsters and the Rhetoric of Fear in Public Culture.* Chicago: University of Chicago Press, 2001.

Patterson, Romaine. *The Whole World Was Watching: Living in the Light of Matthew Shepard.* New York: Advocate, 2005.

Swigonski, Mary E., Robin S. Mama, and Kelly Ward, eds. *From Hate Crimes to Human Rights: A Tribute to Matthew Shepard.* New York: Harrington Park Press, 2001.

Audio and Visual Media

Kaufman, Moises. *The Laramie Project.* HBO Home Video, 2002.

Gay Tinky Winky Bad for Children

Photograph

By: Bob Esposito

Date: February 11, 1999

Source: Bob Esosito. "Bob Shortz, of Luzerne, Pa., dressed as the Teletubby 'Po.'" Associated Press, February 11, 1999.

About the Photographer: Bob Esposito is a photographer based in Pennsylvania who has contributed photographs to several Pennsylvania newspapers as well as the Associated Press.

INTRODUCTION

Muppets Bert and Ernie, from the long-running children's show Sesame Street, have been the targets of rumor since the 1980s, when *Spy* magazine founder Kurt Anderson, in his 1980 book *The Real Thing*, stated that "Bert and Ernie conduct themselves in the same loving, discreet way that millions of gay men, women and hand puppets do. They do their jobs well and live a splendidly settled life together in an impeccably decorated cabinet." At the time the creators of the Muppets, Henson Productions, did not reply to the statement, but the rumor persisted.

By 1993, the rumors had reached a point where Children's Television Workshop received a steady stream of letters complaining about Bert and Ernie's alleged homosexual relationship. Conservative leaders and religious figures, concerned about children's exposure to homosexuality through cartoon and puppet characters, began to scrutinize children's programming, prompting the Children's Television Workshop to issue a 1993 statement concerning Bert and Ernies' sexual orientation: "Bert and Ernie, who've been on Sesame Street for twenty-five years, do not portray a gay couple, and there are no plans for them to do so in the future. They are puppets, not humans."

A Charlotte, North Carolina Pentacostal preacher, Reverend Joseph Chambers, railed against Bert and Ernie in a religious radio program hosted in early 1994. Reverend Chambers stated that "They're two grown men sharing a house and a bedroom. They share clothes. They eat and cook together. They vacation together, and they have effeminate characteristics…. In one show, Bert teaches Ernie how to sew. In another, they tend plants together. If this isn't meant to represent a homosexual union, I can't imagine what it's supposed to represent."

In February 1999, the Reverend Jerry Falwell, a conservative Christian leader in the United States and founder of the Moral Majority, released a statement concerning the sexual orientation of a fictional character on the British children's television show "Teletubbies." "Tinky Winky," a stuffed purple asexual character on the popular toddler television show, according to Falwell, spoke with a female affect, was purple (a color sometimes associated with gay pride), carried a purse, and on the top of his stuffed head he wore an upside-down triangle, a symbol of homosexuality.

PRIMARY SOURCE

GAY TINKY WINKY

See primary source image.

SIGNIFICANCE

Falwell's critique generated ridicule and scorn from cultural critics, late-night television talk show hosts, and newspaper columnists in the United States and abroad. The creators of "Teletubbies" issued statements negating Falwell's accusations while Falwell stood by his original assertion, claiming that "As a Christian, I believe that role-modeling the gay lifestyle is damaging to the moral lives of children. I find the flat denials of such a portrayal by "Teletubbies" producers to be disingenuous and insufficient in answering the questions that have been raised about the Tinky Winky character since the series premiered in England in 1997."

This pattern of finding homosexual undertones in children's programming emerged again in 2005 when Dr. James Dobson, head of Focus on the Family (a conservative religious organization) accused the founders of We Are Family Foundation, a foundation formed after September 11, 2001 to promote cultural understanding, of using the popular children's cartoon character and television show "SpongeBob

PRIMARY SOURCE

Gay Tinky Winky: Bob Shortz, dressed as the Teletubby "Po" holds a sign in reaction to the comments made by Rev. Jerry Falwell that "Tinky Winky," another teletubby character, is a homosexual role model. AP IMAGES

The Teletubbies children's television characters, from left to right: Laa Laa, Dipsy, Tinky Winky, and Po. Rev. Jerry Falwell has claimed that Tinky Winky is a homosexual role model. AP IMAGES

SquarePants" to support pro-homosexuality messages in curriculum designed for multiculturalism programs. The videotape Dobson critiques is one in which cartoon characters such as Clifford the Big Red Dog, Barney, Bob the Builder, and others appear, discussing tolerance and diversity. There are no references to sexual orientation or sexuality in the video.

According to Dobson, in a newsletter to members of Focus on the Family, the We Are Family Foundation website included lessons plans for teachers with questions such as "Do you know of any people in your school whose sexual orientation differs from yours?" "How do you know?" "Are you comfortable with that person or those people?" Dobson stated that his remarks about the video were "about the way in which those childhood symbols are apparently being hijacked to promote an agenda that involves teaching homosexual propaganda to children."

Characterizing his SpongeBob reference as one that was taken out of context, Dobson went on the say "I'm sure you can see, now, why I expressed great con-

cern about the intention of the We Are Family Foundation in using SpongeBob and company to promote the theme of 'tolerance and diversity,' which are almost always buzzwords for homosexual advocacy." Other conservative organizations in the United States, such as Traditional Family Values and the American Family Association echoed Dobson's concerns.

Nile Rodgers, founder of the We Are Family Foundation and writer of the 1979 hit song "We Are Family," denies that his video or website contain a homosexual agenda.

According to a statement from Jerry Falwell ministries, "Dr. Falwell has never seen the 'Teletubbies' TV program."

FURTHER RESOURCES
Books

Day, Frances Ann. *Lesbian and Gay Voices: An Annotated Bibliography and Guide to Literature for Children and Young Adults.* Westport, Conn.: Greenwood Press, 1997.

Web sites

BBC News Online. "Gay Tinky Winky Bad for Children." <http://news.bbc.co.uk/2/low/entertainment/276677.stm> (accessed March 31, 2006).

Focus on the Family. "Dr. Dobson's Newsletter: Setting the Record Straight." <http://www.family.org/docstudy/newsletters/a0035339.cfm> (accessed March 31, 2006).

Jerry Falwell's National Liberty Journal. "Tinky Winky Comes Out of the Closet." <http://www.nljonline.com/index/> (accessed March 31, 2006).

NYTimes.com "Conservatives Pick Soft Target: A Cartoon Sponge." <http://www.nytimes.com/2005/01/20/politics/20sponge.html/> (accessed March 31, 2006).

The National Family Lesbian Study

Journal article

By: Nanette Gartrell

Date: October 2000

Source: Gartrell, Nanette, Amy Banks, Nancy Reed, Jean Hamilton, Carla Rodas, and Amalia Deck. "The National Lesbian Family Study: Interviews with Mothers of Five-year-olds." *American Journal of Orthopsychiatry* 70, 4 (October 2000): 542–548.

About the Author: American psychiatrist and researcher Nanette K. Gartrell is the main study investigator for the National Lesbian Family Longitudinal Study. She worked at Harvard Medical School from 1976–1987 and is considered to be the institution's first openly lesbian faculty member. From 1988–2005, Gartrell served as associate clinical professor of psychiatry at the University of California, San Francisco. She is a widely published author in the field of lesbian parenting and a frequent reviewer of several major psychiatry journals.

INTRODUCTION

The National Lesbian Longitudinal Family Study (NLLFS) is the largest and longest-running study in the United States on children of lesbians. Nanette Gartrell initiated the study in 1986 after her psychiatry practice, which catered to a large lesbian population, revealed that there was limited data regarding the effect of parenting on lesbian couples. Gartrell began to seek answers for the most commonly posed questions such as whether lesbian couples remained together after they had children and if motherhood impacted their romantic lives.

NLLFS researchers launched the study by first gathering information on lesbian mothers who became pregnant by donor insemination. They continued to document the mothers' lives and partner relationships as the children grew older. Study investigators interviewed the mothers prior to the child's birth and again at different points in the child's life. The information garnered from NLLFS has been used to evaluate the overall dynamic of the entire non-traditional family as well as the social, psychological, and emotional development of the child of lesbian parents.

The first stage of the longitudinal study found that lesbian partners give considerable thought to conceiving a child, and that the prospective children are much desired. The lesbian couples identified in the initial phase of the NLLFS appeared well-educated about the challenges of raising a child in a same-sex setting but had access to appropriate support groups. They tended to have flexible schedules that allow for more child rearing time.

Interviews conducted when the children were toddlers showed that the lesbian mothers equally shared an active parenting role, and that most of them had publicly revealed their lesbianism. The new parents showed concern regarding the impact of homophobia on their children, and spent considerable time educating their co-workers, families, babysitters, and health care providers about lesbian families and enacting legal protection such as a will and powers of attorney. This phase of the study also found that child rearing had a positive impact on the lesbian mothers' feelings toward her own family of origin. Most reported feeling closer to their parents. Although the 156 women interviewed said that having a child put stress on their romantic relationship and delayed their careers, their children were thriving. Most described the first two years of mothering as the most enjoyable, yet most exhausting, time of their lives.

Researchers conducted the third set of NLLFS interviews when the children of the lesbian mothers were five years old. Questions evaluated six primary issues: health of the mothers and child, parenting experiences, relationships, support systems, education, and discrimination concerns. At this time, the majority of the original lesbian couples remained together and felt that their child had bonded equally to both parents. Thirty-one percent of the original lesbian couples had split up. The respondents said the breakup caused considerable stress on the non-traditional

Lesbian partners spending time with their daughter. © RONNIE KAUFMAN/CORBIS

family. Less than half of the divorced couples shared joint custody of the child. In some cases, the child's attending parent had re-partnered, further enhancing the non-traditional family with step-mom's and, perhaps, step-children.

The evaluations revealed that many of the mothers attended counseling, most often because of relationship conflicts. However, among the couples that stayed together, thirty-seven percent of birthmothers and twenty-nine percent of co-mothers said that having a child strengthened their relationship.

Some children (eighteen percent) face homophobia from friends and teachers. Overall, however, the children of lesbian parents seemed to be happy, healthy, and well adjusted. Most were honest when asked about their family and had grandparents who did the same.

■ PRIMARY SOURCE

THE NATIONAL FAMILY LESBIAN STUDY

This third report from a longitudinal study of lesbian families presents data obtained from interviews with mothers of five-year-old children conceived by donor insemination. Results indicated that 87% of the children related well to peers, 18% had experienced homophobia from peers or teachers, and 63% had grandparents who frankly acknowledged their grandchild's lesbian family. Of the original couples, 31% had divorced. Of the remainder, 68% felt that their child was equally bonded to both mothers. Concerns of lesbian families are discussed.

In the past two decades increased access to donor insemination (DI) has resulted in what might be termed a baby boom among North American and European lesbians. However, relatively little information is available about lesbian family life at the various stages of their children's growth and development. The National Lesbian Family Study (NLFS), launched in 1986, was designed to develop a database on a population of U.S.-based lesbian families whose children had been conceived by DI. The NLFS is a longitudinal, descriptive survey documenting the lifestyles of these families. By following this cohort from the children's conception until their adulthood, it seeks to broaden our understanding of lesbian families and communities (Gartrell et al., 1996, 1999).

The first NLFS interview with prospective birthmothers and co-mothers was conducted during insemination or pregnancy (T1). It found that the children were highly desired and thoughtfully conceived (Gartrell et al., 1996), and that participants were well educated about the potential difficulties of raising children in a homophobic society. The second interview took place when the children were toddlers (T2). It found that most of the couples shared parenting, and that nurture was as strongly associated as biology with mother-child bonding (Gartrell et al., 1999). The literature on DI suggests that by elementary school, children of lesbians are typically as well adjusted as the children of heterosexuals (Chan, Raymond, Raboy, & Patterson, 1998). Patterson, Hurt, and Mason (1998) found that the psychological adjustment of children did not differ whether they had one or two parents, and that most had regular contact with their grandmothers and grandfathers and with other adult males. In another study of DI children. Mitchell (1998) reported that children of lesbians, who often felt special about having two mothers, tended to bond with other nonmajority classmates.

Several investigators have examined lesbian family life from the perspective of mothers conceiving through DI. Having a child was found to strengthen the relationships of couples in one study (Nelson, 1996) and ties to their family of origin in another (Dunne, 2000). Lesbian mothers tended to be honest with their children about the DI and about their own lesbianism, and many felt an ongoing obligation to educate their communities about lesbian families (Nelson, 1996; Mitchell, 1998).

The present NFLS report (T3) is based on interviews with the birthmothers and, if co-parenting, with the co-mothers, when the index children were five years old. The interviews were constructed to generate data that could assist professionals in health care, family services, sociology, feminist studies, education, ethics, and public policy on matters pertaining to lesbian motherhood. In addition, the research objectives at T3 included exploration of topics that might be helpful to future generations of lesbians raising preschool-age and elementary school-age children.

METHOD

Participants

Eighty-four families with children conceived by DI have been followed since the mothers were pregnant with the 85 index children (one set of twins). Interviewing began in 1986, and the study was closed to new participants in 1992. At T1, 70 households consisted of a prospective birthmother and a co-mother, and 14 were headed by a prospective single mother.

At the time of the index child's birth, 73 of the families had both a birthmother and a co-mother. By the third interview (T3), 23 of the 73 couples (31.5%) had split up, one co-mother had died, and one single mother had acquired a partner who assumed the role of stepmother. Six participants were unavailable for interview, two divorced birthmothers had acquired male partners, and one birthmother was transitioning to become a man. Consequently, with six missing interviews, one dropout (the deceased co-mother), and one addition (the new stepmother), 150 mothers of 85 children participated at T3.

At T1, lesbians who were in the process of insemination or already pregnant by a donor, whether known or unknown, and any partners who planned to share parenting, were eligible for study participation. Recruitment was solicited via announcements at lesbian events, in women's bookstores, and in lesbian newspapers. To sample racial-ethnic subgroups of the lesbian community, study flyers were distributed at multicultural events. Prospective participants were asked to contact the researchers by telephone, and the nature of the study, including the importance of planning for long-term participation, was discussed with each caller. Interviewers were trained mental health professionals, representing the fields of psychiatry, psychology, public health, and social work.

The participants originally resided in the metropolitan areas of Boston, Washington, D.C., and San Francisco. By T3, 17 of the families had moved to other areas of the United States.

They were predominantly college-educated (67%), professionals or managers (82%), middle- and upper-middle class (82%), and Christian (56%) or Jewish (33%) (Gartrell et al., 1996). Racially, 93% of the mothers described themselves as white, 3% as African American, 2% as Native American, 1% as Latina, and 1% as Asian/Pacific Islander. The children demonstrated slightly greater heterogeneity, with 89% described as white, 4% as Latino, 2.5% as African American, 2.5% as Asian/Pacific Islander, 1% as Native American, and 1% as "other."

By T3, 29 of the index children had one or more younger siblings; 16 had been delivered by the birthmother and nine by the co-mother, while eight had been adopted. The birthmothers' age range was 29-47 years (M=39.4, SD=4.1), and that of the co-mothers 29–54 years (M=40.9, SD=5.4, p=.057, NS). Median household income was $75,000 (25th percentile=$50,000; 75th percentile=$102,000); 64% of families said they had sufficient income to cover their expenses, the rest reported that they were struggling financially. Eighty-eight percent of families occupied single-family dwellings, and 12% shared housing.

Procedure

The T3 interview was conducted when the index children were five years old. Birthmothers and co-mothers were interviewed separately in their homes or by telephone. The research protocol calls for subsequent interviews with the mothers when the index child is 10 years (T4), 17 years (T5), and 25 years (T6) old. If permission is granted, the children, too, will be interviewed at T4, T5, and T6. Since continuity is critical to a longitudinal study of this nature, participants are contacted twice annually to verify their addresses and telephone numbers. They are also sent copies of NLFS publications, and encouraged to provide feedback about each phase of the project.

Semi-Structured Interview

The semi-structured, 184-item T3 interview was modified from the T2 instrument so that questions appropriate for mothers of five-year-old children could be included. The questions were open-ended and began with the least sensitive material (e.g., demographic), and proceeded to more affective material (e.g., family conflicts). Because most participants had difficulty finding time for the interviews once their children were born, efforts were made to limit the number of questions after T1. The average duration of the T3 interviews, which were yet more streamlined than those of T2, was one hour.

The T3 questionnaire assessed six areas of motherhood experience: health status, parenting experiences, relationship issues, support systems, educational choices, and discrimination concerns. Under the topic of health concerns, the mothers were asked to comment on the index child's health and development, family health status, their own utilization of mental health services, and their own substance use history. Questions concerning parenting experiences and relationship issues focused on the pleasures and stresses of raising children with continuous partners, with divorced co-parents, or alone. Regarding support systems, participants provided information about acceptance by their family of origin, their neighborhood, and the lesbian community. In the section on secular and spiritual education, the mothers discussed school choices and spiritual training for their children. Finally, they were queried about the impact of homophobia on their families.

At the end of the interview, the interviewers rated each family's overall level of functioning on a scale of 1–5 (with 1=low, 5=high), based on a quality of life assessment, since T2. For assigning a score to each family, the interviewers were instructed to utilize diagnostic skills comparable to those reporting a Global Assessment of Functioning score (DSM-IV) in an individual mental health evaluation.

Data Analysis

Most questions (92%) lent themselves to precoding, such that categories could be checked off during the interview itself. For the remaining questions, categories for qualitative data were developed from the text itself rather than imposed upon it. Trained raters achieved inter-rater reliability of 95% in coding the qualitative data (Cohen's Kappa). McNemar's test was used for the significance of difference between matched pairs of birth- and co-mothers on categorical-level data.

RESULTS

Physical and Mental Health Status

Most (83%) of the 150 mothers had no concerns about their child's health or development at age five. Most (87%, N=74) of the children were described as relating well to their peers. Questions about their conception had been asked by 43% (N=37) of the children by T3, and their mothers said they had answered honestly. Similarly, most (68%, N=58) of the children were reported to answer matter-of-factly when queried by peers about their families.

The great majority (96%) of the mothers described themselves as healthy; the remaining 4% had been coping with major illnesses between T2 and T3. Alcohol abuse, as determined by the CAGE questionnaire (Seppa, Lepisto, & Sillanaukee, 1998), was confined to 5% of participants; three participants abused alcohol at both T2 and T3. At T3, 7% of mothers smoked cigarettes and 5% used other substances.

Between T2 and T3, 65% of the mothers had sought counseling. Among motivations for doing so, relationship conflict was the most frequently cited (25%). Other motivators included parental illness or death—between T2 and T3, 11% of the mothers had lost a parent, and at T3, 17% had a seriously ill parent. Overall level of functioning was rated at 4 or 5 for 82% of the families. Those receiving lower scores had experienced divorce, illness, or death between T2 and T3.

Parenting Experiences

At T3, the mothers were uniformly enthusiastic about participating in their child's growth and reported loving the child deeply. Of the 50 original couples who were still together at T3 (hereafter referred to as continuous couples or families), 29 were sharing child rearing responsibilities equally, 17 had allocated more responsibilities to the birthmother, and 4 had allocated more to the co-mother. Of the original co-mothers, 35 had adopted their children by T3, thereby enhancing their "official" parenting role. Among continuous couples, 68% reported that the child was equally bonded to both mothers, while all but two felt that their child was more bonded to the birthmother. In 92% of the continuous families, the birthmother and co-mother had similar child-rearing philosophies. When they disagreed, most (84%) of the continuous couples discussed their differences rather than fighting over them.

By T3, 23 (31%) of the original 73 couples had divorced, with 15 of the divorces occurring between T2 and T3. The mean relationship duration for all divorced couples was 8.2 years (SD=3.6). Divorced couples had been together a significantly shorter time before the index child's birth than had continuous couples (t=-2.53, df=63.5, p=.014). Those couples who acknowledged competitiveness around bonding at T2 were no more likely to have divorced by T3 than were the other couples. All divorced participants described the breakup as very stressful to their families. Child custody was shared in ten of these families, while the birthmothers retained sole custody in seven, and primary custody in six. No co-mother had adopted the index child in any of the families in which the birthmother retained primary or sole custody.

Relationship Issues

Of the continuous couples, 37% of birthmothers and 29% of co-mothers felt that having a child had strengthened their relationship. Fewer continuous couples were experiencing jealousy or competitiveness around bonding with the child at T3 than at T2, with 70% acknowledging jealousy at T2, and 48% at T3. However, 94% of the continuous couples indicated that having children significantly reduced their time and energy for one another. Before pregnancy, 12% of the continuous couples reported a sexual frequency of more than once a week, and 50% a frequency ranging from once a week to once a month. By T3, that frequency was more than once a week for 4%, between once a week and once a month for 26%, and less than once a month for the remaining 70%.

Single and divorced participants discussed the difficulties of juggling motherhood and dating. Several indicated frustration when their child and date (or new partner) competed for their attention: "It's hard now that [my child] is old enough to have his own opinions about the women I see," said a divorced participant. "I met one woman I really liked, but [my child] didn't hit it off with her at all. It was really difficult." Participants who had or were seeking new partners assumed that the new partner's role in the family would develop over time.

Support Systems

By T3, 63% of the index children's grandparents were "out" about their grandchild's lesbian family. However, 14% of birthmothers in continuous relationships (N=50) said that their parents did not acknowledge their partners as co-mothers. In addition, 17% of birthmothers

and 13% of co-mothers in continuous families indicated that their parents did not relate to the index child as a fully fledged grandchild.

Among the 21 children with known donors, 29% saw their fathers regularly, and 71% saw them occasionally. Although 76% of mothers (N=150) wanted their children to have contact with good, loving men, only 53% felt by T3 that they had successfully incorporated such men into their children's lives. The possibility that a single donor might sire multiple children (who would therefore be half-siblings of their own children) in their community gave rise to some discomfort in 37% of the mothers.

By T3, 68% of the mothers felt that their lesbian family had been accepted by their neighbors. By this time, too, 76% reported that most of their close personal friends were parents themselves, and that social outings involved other lesbian or gay families 76% of the time.

Seventy-five percent of the mothers were active participants in the lesbian community, and 87% felt that the lesbian community played an important role in their child's life. As one mother put it, "[My child's] two favorite events each year are Halloween and Lesbian/Gay Pride day. She loves dressing up, and she loves being in the parade. San Francisco's lesbian community is the perfect place to raise a kid who likes dressing up!"

Education

A slight majority (52%) of the index children were enrolled in public schools; the remainder were being schooled privately. Commenting on their school choices, the mothers were unanimous in their belief in public education, but ultimately chose the system that offered the best educational opportunity for their child: 74% of the schools chosen were multicultural; 33% had some lesbian or gay staff; and 40% had incorporated lesbian/gay lifestyle awareness into the curriculum. Although many participants had commented on being the first lesbian family to be treated by a particular pediatrician, or the first lesbian family to enroll in a particular preschool, by the time the index children entered elementary school, they were less unusual. Nearly half (49%) of the index children at T3 attended schools in which children from other lesbian families were also enrolled.

A slightly larger majority (54%) of families participated in religious or spiritual communities. Each such family had chosen a temple, church, or spiritual community on the basis of its willingness to accept and embrace lesbian lifestyles.

Concerns With Discrimination

All participants were concerned about the impact of homophobia on their children and their families. Despite their mothers' efforts to shield them from the harsh realities of discrimination, 8% of the index children had experienced some form of homophobia on the part of their peers or teachers by T3. Anticipating such prejudice, most mothers had done their best to prepare their children. Preparation involved discussing different kinds of families, the importance of appreciating diversity, and sometimes role-playing responses to homophobic comments. Mistaken assumptions of heterosexuality were a common occurrence for the mothers, and 25% reported that they felt quite distressed when their child witnessed such "heterosexism."

Thirty percent of the mothers acknowledged the importance of keeping their own homophobia in check. For example, one birthmother said, "It's so tempting to just let it go when other moms in the park assume I'm straight [when I am there with my daughter], but I feel obligated to maintain our integrity by explaining that we're a lesbian family. It's scary to be so honest with people I don't even know, because you never know what they'll do with that information. But I would feel far worse having [my daughter] grow up thinking that there is anything shameful about being a lesbian."

At T3, as at the previous interviews, the mothers were asked which sexual orientation they would choose for their child, if such a choice were possible; 65% declined to answer (up from 50% at T2), stating that their children needed to find their own paths. Fewer mothers at T3 than at T2 hoped their children would become heterosexual (21% at T3, down from 28% at T2).

The mothers' struggle to reduce the level of homophobia in their communities continued at T3, with 75% actively engaged in political and educational efforts to foster public acceptance of diversity. "For us, the choice to have a child represents a lifelong commitment to make the world a safer place for him to grow up," said a typical birthmother. "That means we have to find a nonhomophobic doctor, teacher, school, temple, neighborhood-a nonhomophobic whatever our child needs. We've got our work cut out for us!"

DISCUSSION

According to their mothers, most of the children in this study were healthy and well-adjusted. The mothers described their own lives as very child-focused, with limited time and energy left over for their adult relationships. Such constraints were voiced by mothers in all family constellations, regardless of the number of children in the household. Other indications that the mothers were less attentive to their partners included reports of sexual infrequency and relationship conflict. Although many of the mothers had sought counseling between T2 and T3, the psychotherapy utilization rates in this study were much lower than in other surveys of lesbians (Morgan, 1992; Morgan & Eliason, 1992).

Between the birth of the index child and T3, one-third of the couples had divorced. In Blumstein and Schwartz's (1983) landmark survey of American couples, lesbians had a higher break-up rate than had heterosexual or gay male couples. Interestingly, their survey found no association between how much (or little) sex a couple had and how long they stayed together. They hypothesized that complaints about sexual infrequency might actually reflect unhappiness with the quality of affection between partners. This survey, which took place before the lesbian "baby boom" of the mid 1980s, did not include a separate variable about parenting as a predictor of relationship longevity.

Of heterosexual couples marrying in the 1980s, over 20% dissolved their marriages within five years, and nearly one-third within ten years (Chadwick & Heaton, 1999). Heterosexual marriages ending in divorce last an average of seven years. Recent estimates suggest that over one-half of all children born to heterosexual parents will experience marital disruption (Chadwick & Heaton, 1999). Data from the NLFS suggest a comparable divorce rate among lesbian mothers.

In the present study, the children of divorced lesbians spent equal time with both mothers in 43% of the cases. The birthmother was more likely to retain sole or primary custody if the co-mother had not officially adopted the child. These findings suggest that co-parent adoptions not only enhance the legitimacy of the parenting role for co-mothers, but also increase the likelihood of shared custody in the event of relationship dissolution. However, at T3, co-parent adoptions were available only in a few progressive counties in the U.S.

For the most part, the mothers in continuous relationships at T3 were sharing child rearing, and finding that their child was equally bonded to both mothers. Although many of the co-mothers at T2 had talked about feeling left out of the birthmother-child bonding that occurred with breast feeding (Gartrell et al., 1999), by T3 they were feeling less jealous and competitive.

Most couples reported compatibility in their child-rearing philosophies, and many felt that having a child strengthened their relationships. Children in continuous families at T3 still had two actively-involved parents-a finding that distinguishes these lesbian families from traditional heterosexual families, in which fathers are less involved in parenting (Dunne, 1998; Golombok, Tasker, & Murray, 1997; Tasker & Golombok, 1997, 1998). Tasker and Golombok (1997, 1998) and Golombok et al. (1997) reported that adolescents were more likely to be accepting of their mothers' lesbianism if their mothers had had continuous, long-term relationships when the children were six years old. It will be interesting to see if the NLFS data at T4 and T5 corroborate these reports.

Most of the families in this study had strong support systems at T3. To the extent that they had the option, the mothers chose to live in neighborhoods where they would not be the only lesbian family. In addition, more grandparents were "out" about their grandchild's lesbian family at T3 (63%) than at T2 (29%) (Gartrell et al., 1999). However, a sizable minority of grandparents still did not acknowledge their daughter's partner as a co-mother or relate to the index child as a fully fledged grandchild. Experiencing such homophobia from their own parents was an ongoing source of sadness and hardship for these mothers.

The elementary schools selected by the mothers were almost evenly divided between public and private. In keeping with the mothers' expressed preferences at T1 for exposing their children to diversity (Gartrell et al., 1996), most of the schools were multicultural, and many had either lesbian/ gay staff or lesbian/gay lifestyle awareness in their curriculum. Because most of the mothers at T3 lived in metropolitan areas heavily populated with other lesbian families, the responsibility of eradicating homophobia in the schools was more likely to be shared with other lesbian or gay parents. Those mothers who had moved to more rural or conservative communities carried a heavier load in protecting their children from discrimination. Some children had already experienced homophobia from peers or teachers by age five; advance preparation for the possibility of discrimination, especially role-playing healthy responses to homophobia, helped these children cope with such adversity. These findings suggest that a child who is likely to experience any form of discrimination might benefit from parental preparation.

At T3, the mothers were continuing their efforts to reduce the level of homophobia in their communities. Tasker and Golombok (1997, 1998) and Golombok et al. (1997) found that children of lesbian mothers had more positive attitudes about their mothers' lesbianism if the mothers were politically active in lesbian/gay organizations. Herek, Cogan, Gillis, and Glunt (1998) also found an association between decreased internalized homophobia in lesbians and increased contact with the lesbian/gay community. The participants in the present study had become even more openly lesbian after their children were born: for example, 55% were out at work at T1, and 93% at T2 (Gartrell et al., 1996, 1999). By T3, most of the mothers declined to state a preference for their child's eventual sexual orientation, perhaps as a result of their increased comfort with their own lesbianism.

The study participants are self-selected and not necessarily demographically representative of the lesbian population as a whole (Gartrell et al., 1996). Nevertheless, the participant pool has remained very consistent since the study began in 1986. The participants appreci-ated the limited time commitment required for the T3 interview, since their days were very tightly scheduled. Although it was tempting to incorporate standardized tests along with the oral interview at T2 and T3, participants' expectations of longer interviews might have resulted in a greater dropout rate. Hopefully, this longitudinal overview of lesbian family life will stimulate further in-depth studies of lesbian mothers and their children at different stages of the children's development.

The T3 findings of the NLFS suggest that children conceived by DI and raised in lesbian families are healthy and well-adjusted. At five years old, most children in continuous two-mother families were equally bonded to both mothers. Acceptance by families of origin had increased, and most mothers were actively participating in the lesbian community. As this study of 84 lesbian families progresses, it is expected to provide ongoing information about the life experiences of children conceived by DI and raised in a homophobic world.

SIGNIFICANCE

The availability of donor insemination to lesbian couples in the late 1980s helped radically change the face of the American family. Today, the traditional mother-father family structure is being complemented with alternative, lesbian-parented households. Political factors, including legislation that allows same-sex marriages in various states, have also made non-traditional families an integral part of our social landscape.

Society has questioned whether children of alternative families, particularly lesbian parents, face more hardships than those who are raised by heterosexual parents. However, information regarding the successes and failures of these alternative families has been slight. One study released in 2002 by the Free University of Brussels in Belgium found that children born to lesbian women using donor sperm seem to be as well-adjusted as those brought up by heterosexual couples. By following lesbian mothers from conception through their child's adulthood, the NLLFS will help broaden the public's understanding of lesbian parenting, and reveal its overall impact on children. Results from NLLFS thus far have shown that lesbian parents are no more stable than traditional couples. The findings have surprised study researchers, who had theorized that lesbian mothers would stay together longer. However, that surprise has no bearing on the happiness of the children from alternative families. Data from NLLFS strongly shows that lesbian parents raise happy children, who are unaffected by the lack of a traditional father figure.

Robyn Sarig and Lori Conners, surrounded by their children, exchange vows, during a mass wedding held before the New York Lesbian, Gay, Bisexual and Transgender Pride March on June 27, 2004. AP IMAGES

The NLLFS will continue until the children of the lesbian parents reach age twenty-five. Documenting the child's journey through life will help illustrate the challenges and realities faced by non-traditional families. The findings are expected to help raise awareness of alternative parenting and reduce the impact of homophobia. They will be used to educate healthcare providers, social and public policy makers, educators, ethicists, and family service workers.

FURTHER RESOURCES

Books

Everyday Mutinies: Funding Lesbian Activism, edited by Nanette Gartrell and Esther Rothblum. Binghamton, N.Y.: Haworth Press, 2002.

Periodicals

Gartrell, Nanette. "Not Tonight Dear, The Kids Have Earaches." *Girlfriends Magazine* (May 2005).

Web sites

The National Longitudinal Lesbian Family Study. <http://www.nllfs.org> (accessed April 1, 2006).

Boy Scouts of America v. Dale

Legal decision

By: Supreme Court of the United States

Date: June 8, 2000

Source: *Boy Scouts of America v. Dale* (99–699) 530 U.S. 640 (2000).

About the Author: The Supreme Court of the United States is the nation's highest court, with eight associate justices and one chief justice. The opinion in the *Boy Scouts of America v. Dale* case was delivered by Chief Justice William Renquist.

INTRODUCTION

The Boy Scouts of America was founded in 1910 as a not-for-profit organization with the expressed mission to, "prepare young people to make ethical and moral choices over their lifetimes by instilling in them the values of the Scout Oath and Law." The Scout Oath states, "On my honor I will do my best to do my duty to God and my country and to obey the Scout Law; To help other people at all times; To keep myself physically strong, mentally awake and morally straight." The organization is broken into small troops, consisting of fifteen to thirty scouts and led by a scoutmaster and assistant scoutmaster, and approximately sixty-five percent of these troops are sponsored by religious entities. Much of the activities of the scouts is considered instructional in nature. As a result, the scoutmaster performs the role of teacher and role model to his scouts and is expected to exemplify the ideology found within the Scout Oath and Scout Law. Although the Boy Scouts of America does not posses an explicit anti-homosexual stance, the organization advises its Scoutmasters to "instruct sexual abstinence until marriage in accordance with the 'morally straight' provision of the Scout's Oath."

Since its inception, over ninety million boys have entered into the Boy Scouts of America and the organization currently maintains a membership over five million. James Dale was one such member. Dale began as a Cub Scout at age eight and then entered the Boy

Scouts. Throughout his membership, he earned twenty-five merit badges, was elected to the society of honor campers—Order of the Arrow, and was awarded the Scout's highest honor of Eagle Scout. In 1989, Dale's application to become Assistant Scoutmaster for Troop seventy-three in Monmouth, New Jersey was accepted. However, sixteen months later, Dale's membership into the Boy Scouts was revoked. Dale's position as assistant scoutmaster coincided with his entry into college at Rutgers University. While at school, Dale began to openly identify himself as a homosexual and became the co-president of the Rutgers University Lesbian/Gay Alliance in 1990. On July 8, 1990, an interview with Dale along with his photograph accompanied an article in the *Newark Star Ledger* entitled, "Seminar Addresses Needs of Homosexual Teens." As a result of this article, Dale was dismissed from his leadership role within the Scouts.

Dale sued the Boy Scouts of America under New Jersey's Anti-Discrimination laws and, in 1999, won his case for reinstatement under the New Jersey Supreme Court. Initially, the state superior court, chancery division, identified the Boy Scouts as a "distinctly private group" and therefore was exempt to New Jersey's public accommodation laws. The court asserted that by forcing the Scouts to accept Dale as a leader would be an infringement on the organization's freedom association. The Appellate Court unanimously overturned that decision and declared that the Boy Scout's widespread membership constituted a "public accommodation" similar to a hotel or restaurant and therefore must comply to state anti-discrimination laws. As a result, the U.S. Supreme Court heard the argument of *Boy Scouts of America v. Dale* on April 26, 2000.

PRIMARY SOURCE

"The Boy Scouts of America has always reflected the expectations that Scouting families have had for the organization. We do not believe that homosexuals provide a role model consistent with these expectations. Accordingly, we do not allow for the registration of avowed homosexuals as members or as leaders of the BSA....

The Boy Scouts publicly expressed its views with respect to homosexual conduct by its assertions in prior litigation. For example, throughout a California case with similar facts filed in the early 1980's, the Boy Scouts consistently asserted the same position with respect to homosexuality that it asserts today. See *Curran v. Mount Diablo Council of Boy Scouts of America*, No. C-365529 (Cal. Super.

Ct., July 25, 1991); 48 Cal. App. 4th 670, 29 Cal. Rptr. 2d 580 (1994) Cal. 4th 670, 952 P.2d 218 (1998). We cannot doubt that the Boy Scouts sincerely holds this view.

We must then determine whether Dale's presence as an assistant scoutmaster would significantly burden the Boy Scouts' desire to not "promote homosexual conduct as a legitimate form of behavior." Reply Brief for Petitioners 5. As we give deference to an association's assertions regarding the nature of its expression, we must also give deference to an association's view of what would impair its expression See, *e.g., La Follette, supra,* at 123–124 (considering whether a Wisconsin law burdened the National Party's associational rights and stating that "a State, or a court, may not constitutionally substitute its own judgment for that of the Party). That is not to say that an expressive association can erect a shield against antidiscrimination laws simply by asserting that mere acceptance of a member from a particular group would impair its message. But here Dale, by his own admission, is one of a group of gay Scouts who have "become leaders in their community and are open and honest about their sexual orientation." App. 11. Dale was the copresident of a gay and lesbian organization at college and remains a gay rights activist. Dale's presence in the Boy Scouts would, at the very least, force the organization to send a message, both to the youth members and the world, that the Boy Scouts accepts homosexual conduct as a legitimate form of behavior.

Hurley is illustrative on this point. There we considered whether the application of Massachusetts' public accommodations law to require the organizers of a private St. Patrick's Day parade to include among the marchers an Irish-American gay, lesbian, and bisexual group, GLIB, violated the parade organizers' First Amendment rights. We noted that the parade organizers did not wish to exclude the BLIB members because of their sexual orientations, but because they wanted to march behind a BLIB banner. We observed:

"[A] contingent marching behind the organization's banner would at least bear witness to the fact that some Irish are gay, lesbian, or bisexual, and the presence of the organized marchers would suggest their view that people of their sexual orientations have as much claim to unqualified social acceptance as heterosexuals.... The parade's organizers may not believe these facts about Irish sexuality to be so, or they may object to unqualified social acceptance of gays and lesbians or have some other reason for wishing to keep GLIB's message out of the parade. But whatever the reason, it boils down to the choice of a speaker not to propound a particular point of view, and that choice is presumed to lie beyond the government's power to control." 515 U.S., at 574–575.

Here, we have found that the Boy Scouts believes that homosexual conduct is inconsistent with the values it seeks to instill in its youth members; it will not "promote homosexual conduct as a legitimate form of behavior." Reply Brief for Petitioners 5. As the presence of BLIB in Boston's St. Patrick's Day parade would have interfered with the parade organizers' choice not to propound a particular point of view, the presence of Dale as an assistant scoutmaster would just as surely interfere with the Boy Scout's choice not to propound a point of view contrary to its beliefs.

The New Jersey Supreme Court determined that the Boy Scouts' ability to disseminate its message was not significantly affected by the forced inclusion of Dale as an assistant scoutmaster because of the following findings:

> "Boy Scout members do not associate for the purpose of disseminating the belief that homosexuality is immoral; Boy Scouts discourages its leaders from disseminating *any* views on sexual issues; and Boy Scouts includes sponsors and members who subscribe to different views in respect of homosexuality." 160 N. J., at 612, 734 A. 2d, at 1223.

We disagree with the New Jersey Supreme Court's conclusion drawn from these findings.

First, associations do not have to associate for the "purpose" of disseminating a certain message in order to be entitled to the protections of the First Amendment. An association must merely engage in expressive activity that could be impaired in order to be entitled to protection. For example, the purpose of the St. Patrick's Day parade in *Hurley* was not to espouse any views about sexual orientation, but we had that the parade organizers had a right to exclude certain participants nonetheless.

Second, even if the Boy Scouts discourages Scout leaders from disseminating views on sexual issues—a fact that the Boy Scouts disputes with contrary evidence— the First Amendment protects the Boy Scouts' method of expression. If the Boy Scouts wishes Scout leaders to avoid questions of sexuality and teach only by example, this fact does not negate the sincerity of its belief discussed above.

Third, the First Amendment simply does not require that every member of a group agree on every issue in order for the group's policy to be "expressive association." The Boy Scouts takes an official position with respect to homosexual conduct, and that is sufficient for First Amendment purposes. In this same vein, Dale makes much of the claim that the Boy Scouts does not revoke the membership of heterosexual Scout leaders that openly disagree with the Boy Scouts' policy on sexual orientation. But if this is true, it is irrelevant. The presence of an avowed homosexual and gay rights activist in an assistant scoutmaster's uniform sends a distinctly different message from the presence of a heterosexual assistant scoutmaster who is on record as disagreeing with Boy Scouts policy. The Boy Scouts has a First Amendment right to choose to send one message but not the other. The fact that the organization does not trumpet its views from the housetops, or that it tolerates dissent within its ranks, does not mean that its views receive no First Amendment protection.

Having determined that the Boy Scouts is an expressive association and that the forced inclusion of Dale would significantly affect its expression we inquire whether the application of New Jersey's public accommodations law to require that the Boy Scouts accept Dale as an assistant scoutmaster runs afoul of the Scouts' freedom of expressive association. We conclude that it does.

State public accommodations laws were originally enacted to prevent discrimination in traditional places of public accommodations —like inns and trains. See, *e.g., Hurley, supra,* at 571–572 (explaining the history of Massachusetts' public accommodations law); *Romer v. Evans,* 517 U.S. 620, 627–629 (1996) (describing the evolution of public accommodations laws). Over time, the public accommodations laws have expanded to cover more places. New Jersey's statutory definition of "[a] place of public accommodation" is extremely broad. The term is said to "include, but not be limited to," a list of over 50 types of places. N.J. Stat. Ann. 10:5-5(l) (West Supp. 2000); see Appendix, *infra,* at 18–19. Many on the list are what one would expect to be places where the public is invited. For example, the statute includes as places of public accommodation taverns, restaurants, retail shops, and public libraries. But the statute also includes places that often may not carry with them open invitations to the public, like summer camps and roof gardens. In this case, the New Jersey Supreme Court went a step further and applied its public accommodations law to a private entity without even attempting to tie the term "place A" to a physical location. As the definition of "public accommodation" has expanded from clearly commercial entities, such as restaurants, bars, and hotels, to membership organizations such as the Boy Scouts, the potential for conflict between state public accommodations laws and the First Amendment rights of organizations has increased.

We recognized in cases such as *Roberts* and *Duarte* that States have a compelling interest in eliminating discrimination against women in public accommodations. But in each of these cases we went on to conclude that the enforcement of these statutes would not materially interfere with the ideas that the organization sought to express. In *Roberts,* we said, "[I] indeed, the Jaycees failed to demonstrate...any serious burden on the male members' freedom of expressive association. " 468 U.S., at 626. In *Duarte,* we said:

"[I]impediments to the exercise of one's right to choose one's associates can violate the right of association protected by the First Amendment. In this case, however, the evidence fails to demonstrate that admitting women to Rotary Clubs will affect in any significant way the existing members' ability to carry out their various purposes." 481 U.S. at 548 (internal quotation marks and citations omitted.)

We thereupon concluded in each of these cases that the organizations' First Amendment rights were not violated by the application of the States' public accommodations laws.

In *Hurley,* we said that public accommodations laws "are well within the State's usual power to enact when a legislature has reason to believe that a given group is the target of discrimination, and they do not, as a general matter, violate the First or Fourteenth Amendments." 515 U.S., at 572. But we went on to note that in that case "the Massachusetts [public accommodations] law has been applied in a peculiar way" because "any contingent of protected individuals with a message would have the right to participate in petitioners' speech, so that the communication produced by the private organizers would be shaped by all those protected by the law who wish to join in with some expressive demonstration of their own." Id, at 572–573. And in the associational freedom cases such as *Roberts, Duarte,* and *New York State Club Assn.,* after finding a compelling state interest, the Court went on to examine whether or not the application of the state law would impose any "serious burden" on the organization's rights of expressive association. So in these cases, the associational interest in freedom of expression has been set on one side of the scale, and the State's interest on the other.

Dale contends that we should apply the intermediate standard of review enunciated in *United States* v. *O'Brien,* 391 I/S/ 367 (1968), to evaluate the competing interests. There the court enunciated the four-part test for review of a governmental regulation that has only an incidental effect on protected speech—in that case the symbolic burning of a draft card. A law prohibiting the destruction of draft cards only incidentally affects the free speech rights of those who happen to use a violation of that law as a symbol of protest. But New Jersey's public accommodations law directly and immediately affects associational rights, in this case associational rights that enjoy First Amendment protection. Thus *O'Brien* is inapplicable.

In *Hurley,* we applied traditional First Amendment analysis to hold that the application of the Massachusetts public accommodations law to a parade violated the First Amendment rights of the parade organizers. Although we did not explicitly deem the parade in *Hurley* an expressive association, the analysis we applied there is similar to the analysis we apply here. We have already concluded that a state requirement that the Boy Scouts retain Dale as an assistant scoutmaster would significantly burden the organization's right to oppose or disfavor homosexual conduct. The state interests embodied in New Jersey's public accommodations law do not justify such a severe intrusion on the Boy Scouts' rights to freedom of expressive association. That being the case, we hold that the First Amendment prohibits the State from imposing such a requirement through the application of its public accommodations law.

Justice Stevens' dissent makes much of its observation that the public perception of homosexuality in this country has changed. See *post,* at 37–39. Indeed, it appears that homosexuality has gained greater societal acceptance. See *ibid.* But this is scarcely an argument for denying First Amendment protection to those who refuse to accept these views. The First Amendment protects expression, be it of the popular variety or not. See *e.g., Texas v. Johnson,* 491 U. S. 397 (1989) (holding that Johnson's conviction for burning the American flag violates the First Amendment); *Brandenburg v. Ohio,* 395 U.S. 444 (1969) (holding that a Ku Klux Klan leaders' conviction for advocating unlawfulness as a means of political reform violates the First Amendment). And the fact that an idea may be embraced and advocated by increasing numbers of people is all the more reason to protect the First Amendment rights of those who wish to voice a different view.

SIGNIFICANCE

In its petition to the U.S. Supreme Court, the Boy Scouts of America readdressed their argument that being forced to readmit Dale into a leadership role within the Scouts constituted a violation in the organization's First Amendment freedom of speech and freedom of association. The group cited that although homosexuality is not forbidden, the Scout's Oath calls for scouts to be "morally straight." The brief submitted by the Boy Scouts asserts that, "a society in which each and every organization must be equally diverse is a society which has destroyed diversity."

On the other hand, Dale argued that the organization's large, non-selective membership and lack of explicit language in its mission statement, oath, and law banning homosexuality required them to accept his membership under anti-discrimination laws. Dale asserted that "First Amendment rights are not absolute" and "the state has a compelling interest in eradicating invidious private discrimination." Dale cited past cases, such as a 1984 case in which the U.S. Supreme Court

James Dale. AP IMAGES

upheld the Minnesota Human Rights Act which prohibited private organizations (in particular, a Jaycees club) from discriminating on the grounds of gender. At the time, the court declared that the organization's First Amendment interests yielded to the state's compelling interest to end discrimination toward women.

In a five-to-four decision, the U.S. Supreme Court decided on behalf of the Boy Scouts of America, stating that the First Amendment protects private groups from complying with state anti-discrimination laws and allows them to exercise their right to association by excluding homosexuals. The court asserted expressive groups are free to deliver a discriminatory message and that the organization is to be the judge of its membership.

FURTHER RESOURCES
Periodicals

Richey, Warren and Kris Axtman. "Scouts Can Control Membership." *Christian Science Monitor.* (June 29, 2000): 92, 153.

"Discrimination and the Law." *Economist* (April 29, 2000): 335, 8168.

O'Quinn, John C. "How Solemn is the Duty of the Mighty Chief: Mediating the conflict of Rights in *Boy Scouts of America v Dale.*" *Harvard Journal of Law and Public Policy.* (Fall 2000): 24,1.

H.B. 272: Ohio Defense of Marriage Act

State law

By: Bill Seitz

Date: November 2001

Source: Ohio House. 2001. Ohio Defense of Marriage Act. 124th General Assembly, regular session. H.B. 272.

About the Author: Ohio state representative Bill Seitz of Green Township is the Assistant Majority Whip for the Ohio House of Representatives. He authored and sponsored Ohio's Defense of Marriage Act.

INTRODUCTION

In the mid-1990s, Defense of Marriage Acts began to appear on the state legislative dockets of various states in the United States. These acts, referred to as DOMAs, came about as a reaction to judicial decisions that granted same-sex couples some of the benefits and rights of heterosexual married couples. Although the issue of granting marriage licenses to same-sex couples reaches back to the 1970s, where such licenses were granted in rare exceptions in Minnesota, Colorado, and Arizona (and subsequently struck down by the courts), DOMA legislation did not gain political momentum until the mid-1990s.

A Hawaiian Supreme Court decision in 1993, *Baehr v. Miike*, stated that the prohibition against same-sex marriage violated the state's Equal Protection clause in the Hawaiian state constitution; the state needed to prove a compelling reason for preventing same-sex marriage. This decision alarmed same-sex marriage opponents, who feared that a "domino effect" could take place; if one state approved same-sex marriage, would the Full Faith Clause of the United States Constitution force other states to recognize same-sex marriage via the traditional reciprocity and recognition that each state gave to another?

A federal Defense of Marriage Act, sponsored by Republican Congressmen such as Bob Barr of Georgia and Jim Sensenbrenner of Wisconsin, proposed to defend traditional, heterosexual marriage against any change in definition that would permit same-sex marriage. The act, first submitted on May 7, 1996, included two primary proposals: 1) no state would be forced to recognize a marriage of two people of the same sex, even if the same-sex couple were granted a marriage license in another state, and 2) marriage would be defined as involving one man and one woman only, to the exclusion of all other parties.

The federal DOMA passed both the Senate and the House of Representatives and was signed into law by President William J. Clinton on September 21, 1996. Same-sex marriage opponents believed that overall the federal DOMA would quell debate concerning same-sex marriage and safeguard state interests. It was understood that individual states might permit same-sex marriage at any point, but the purpose of the federal DOMA was to protect states from being forced to honor marriage licenses from out-of-state same-sex marriages.

Critics of the federal DOMA law state that the law goes too far concerning the Full Faith and Credit clause of the constitution and violates the Equal Protection clause of the constitution. These critics have pursued a U.S. Supreme Court review of the legislation since the bill was passed into law. The U.S. Supreme Court, however, has declined to hear these cases. As same-sex marriage supporters began to use the judicial system to file lawsuits against these laws and gained success in states such as Vermont, same-sex marriage opponents began to push for state legislatures to pass state DOMA laws.

■ PRIMARY SOURCE

A BILL

To amend section 3101.01 of the Revised Code to specifically declare that same-sex marriages are against the strong public policy of the state, to declare that the recognition or extension of the specific statutory benefits of legal marriage to nonmarital relationships is against the public policy of the state, and to make other declarations regarding same-sex marriages.

BE IT ENACTED BY THE GENERAL ASSEMBLY OF THE STATE OF OHIO:

Section 1. That section 3101.01 of the Revised Code be amended to read as follows:

Sec. 3101.01. (A) Male persons of the age of eighteen years, and female persons of the age of sixteen years, not nearer of kin than second cousins, and not having a husband or wife living, may be joined in marriage. A marriage may only be entered into by one man and one woman. A minor shall first obtain the consent of the minor's parents, surviving parent, parent who is designated the residential parent and legal custodian of the child minor by a court of competent jurisdiction, guardian, or any one of the following who has been awarded permanent custody of the minor by a court exercising juvenile jurisdiction:

(1) An adult person;

(2) The department of job and family services or any child welfare organization certified by such the department;

(3) A public children services agency.

(B) For the purposes of division (A) of this section, a minor shall not be required to obtain the consent of a parent who resides in a foreign country, has neglected or abandoned such the minor for a period of one year or longer immediately preceding the minor's application for a marriage license, has been adjudged incompetent, is an inmate of a state mental or correctional institution, has been permanently deprived of parental rights and responsibilities for the care of the child minor and the right to have the child minor live with the parent and to be the legal custodian of the child minor by a court exercising juvenile jurisdiction, or has been deprived of parental rights and responsibilities for the care of the child minor and the right to have the child minor live with the parent and to be the legal custodian of the child minor by the appointment of a guardian of the person of the minor by the probate court or by any other another court of competent jurisdiction.

(C)(1) Any marriage between persons of the same sex is against the strong public policy of this state. Any marriage between persons of the same sex shall have no legal force or effect in this state and, if attempted to be entered into in this state, is void ab initio and shall not be recognized by this state.

(2) Any marriage entered into by persons of the same sex in any other jurisdiction shall be considered and treated in all respects as having no legal force or effect in this state and shall not be recognized by this state.

(3) The recognition or extension of the specific statutory benefits of a legal marriage to nonmarital relationships between persons of the same sex or different sexes is against the strong public policy of this state. Any public act, record, or judicial proceeding of this state, as defined in section 9.82 of the Revised Code that extends the specific statutory benefits of legal marriage to nonmarital relationships between persons of the same sex or differ-

ent sexes is void ab initio. Nothing in division (C)(3) of this section prohibits the extension of specific benefits otherwise enjoyed by all persons, married or unmarried, to nonmarital relationships between persons of the same sex or different sexes.

(4) Any public act, record, or judicial proceeding of any other state, country, or other jurisdiction outside this state that extends the specific benefits of legal marriage to nonmarital relationships between persons of the same sex or different sexes shall be considered and treated in all respects as having no legal force or effect in this state and shall not be recognized by this state.

Section 2. That existing section 3101.01 of the Revised Code is hereby repealed.

Section 3. In enacting new division (C) of section 3101.01 of the Revised Code in this act, all the following apply:

(A) The General Assembly declares and reaffirms the state of Ohio's historical commitment to the institution of marriage as a union between a man and a woman as husband and wife.

(B) The General Assembly declares its intent to define marriage and clarify that relationships that are intended as substitutes for marriage, including but not limited to "civil unions" as provided for in 15 V.S.A. §1202 (2000), will not be recognized in this state. It is not the intent of the General Assembly to prohibit the extension of specific benefits otherwise enjoyed by all persons, married or unmarried, to relationships between persons of the same sex or different sexes.

(C) The General Assembly declares its intent not to make substantive changes in the law of this state that is in effect on the day prior to the effective date of this act with respect to the validity of marriages heretofore occurring within this state.

SIGNIFICANCE

Ohio's DOMA, considered to be the most restrictive of all such laws, goes much farther in restricting the rights of same-sex couples than the federal DOMA. Authored by state Representative Bill Seitz of Green Township, the act used language that appeared in the original federal DOMA, outlawing any extension of the benefits of marriage to non-married couples or same-sex couples. That language was removed from the federal bill before it was passed by the U.S. House and Senate.

The text of the act alarmed gay rights activists, for a strict interpretation of the law in court could lead to the stripping of all legal agreements made in lieu of marriage. Many same-sex couples use legal procedures to create the approximation of marital rights, such as medical powers of attorney or legal arrangements for guardianship of children. Under Ohio's DOMA, these legal procedures could be nullified, leaving same-sex couples with no way to provide domestic partner benefits and no legal protections for their relationships or the children of these relationships. In addition, not only does the act prevent the recognition of same-sex marriages made in other states or countries, it also voids legal arrangements made in other states, such as financial agreements or custodial arrangements.

On November 6, 2004, Ohio governor Robert Taft signed the Ohio Defensive of Marriage Act into law, making Ohio the thirty-eighth state in the United States to have a Defense of Marriage Act. The act, placed on the ballot during the 2004 presidential election, was overwhelmingly approved by voters in a sixty-two percent for, thirty-seven percent against, vote.

In January 2005, public defenders in Ohio's Cuyahoga County used the DOMA as a defense against domestic violence charges. Claiming that the 2004 DOMA invalidates domestic violence charges against unmarried cohabiting couples, the public defenders asked that the charges against their clients be reduced to that of assault. The difference between a "domestic violence" charge and an "assault" charge under Ohio law is significant. Assault carries a first-degree misdemeanor charge only, regardless of the number of times that a person is charged with the offense. Domestic violence charges, however, have escalating degrees; the first charge is a misdemeanor, but subsequent events can lead to felony charges.

Social service agencies, in many instances, are only permitted to provide counseling to victims of domestic violence vs. assault; funding for such agencies is tied to a domestic violence charge. This unintended consequence of the Ohio DOMA is one that state Representative William J. Healy of Canton proposes to change with House Bill 161, which would change Ohio law to allow for the domestic violence charges to be applied to unmarried couples.

Same-sex marriage opponents, such as the Family Research Council, call Ohio's act a "Super-DOMA." FRC considers the Ohio act to be a model for other states to follow; as the thirty-eighth state to pass a DOMA, Ohio became a symbol of the country's ability to ratify an amendment to the U.S. constitution banning same-sex marriage.

Rev. Harvey Drake, left, of the Emerald City Bible Fellowship, who opposes gay marriage, talks with Ryan Olson, right, a student who supports gay marriage, before a rally at the state Capitol in Olympia, Wash, March 8, 2005. AP IMAGES

FURTHER RESOURCES

Books

Dobson, James. *Marriage Under Fire: Why We Must Win This Battle*. Sisters, Ore.: Multnomah, 2004.

Gerstmann, Evan. *Same-Sex Marriage and the Constitution*. New York: Cambridge University Press, 2003.

Periodicals

Adam, Barry D. "The Defense of Marriage Act and American Exceptionalism: The 'Gay Marriage' Panic in the United States." *Journal of the History of Sexuality* 12 (April 2003): 259–276.

Web sites

DOMA Watch. <http://www.domawatch.org> (accessed February 15, 2006).

Lambda Legal. "Marriage Project." <http://www.lambdalegal.org/cgi-bin/iowa/issues/record?record=9> (accessed February 20, 2006).

National Organization for Women. "Same Sex Marriage is a Feminist Issue." <http://www.now.org/issues/lgbi/marr-rep.html> (accessed February 15, 2006).

NPR.org. "Calif. Judge Rejects Ban on Same-Sex Marriage." <http://www.npr.org/templates/story/story.php/> (accessed February 15, 2006).

Thomas.gov. "Defense of Marriage Act." <http://thomas.loc.gov/cgi-bin/query/z?c104:H.R.3396.ENR:> (accessed February 15, 2006).

Second-Class Survivors

Newspaper article

By: Andy Humm

Date: November 2001

Source: *The Village Voice*

About the Author: Andy Humm is a veteran gay journalist based in New York City. He is a former member of the City Commission on Human Rights and served as the Director of Education at the Hetrick-Martin Institute for Lesbian and Gay Youth, starting an AIDS education program. Humm is also currently the co-host and producer of the New York based television show "Gay USA."

INTRODUCTION

The terror attacks of September 11, 2001 left thousands of victims in the rubble of the World Trade Center and Pentagon. In an effort to assist the families of those victims, the federal and state governments along with charity organizations began to offer financial assistance. As part of the September 11th Victim Compensation Fund, representatives of married victims or those with children were eligible to receive at least $500,000 in total compensation—an amount that included contributions from both state and federal funds and life insurance. Representatives of unmarried victims were eligible to receive at least $300,000. Although the federal government deferred to state laws to define the victim's representation, many charity organizations, such as the American Red Cross and United Way, also began to offer assistance to victims' domestic partners.

"Domestic partners" are unmarried cohabiting same-sex and heterosexual couples. Each state defines domestic partnerships differently; some offer a civil union registry. However, the federal government provides certain rights only to spouses and not to domestic partners, including automatic inheritance, child custody, domestic violence protection, insurance and tax considerations, immigration rights, and survivor benefits.

According to the Human Rights Campaign—a national gay, lesbian, bisexual, and transgender political action organization—only five employers offered domestic partner benefits in 1989. This number, as well as public perception, has risen in recent years. An Associated Press poll of 1,012 Americans in 2000 showed that at least half supported domestic partnership benefits that included health insurance, social security benefits, and inheritance. Employers that do offer benefits to domestic partners often require documentation, such as a municipal certificate of domestic partnership, evidence of an established relationship, or cohabitation for six to twelve months. Other than a marriage certificate, none of these criteria is required of married employees.

Paul Holm stands in front of a collage of photographs he put together in memory of his late partner Mark Bingham, in his San Francisco home on October 18, 2006. Bingham was killed in the 9-11 terrorist attacks. AP IMAGES

Between 1997 and 2003, the number of Fortune 500 employers who offer domestic partner benefits quadrupled to 190. Activists believe that this attracts a broader base of employees. Of *Fortune* magazine's "100 Best Companies to Work For," at least sixty-seven offer benefits to domestic partners. In addition, in April 2000, Vermont became the first state to grant civil unions the same rights as marriages.

Although many states have antidiscrimination laws enacted to protect individuals in the workplace, gay rights activists assert that without domestic partner benefits homosexual employees do not receive equal pay for equal work. For those employees who accept benefits for their domestic partners, the Internal Revenue Service considers company payments for domestic partners taxable income. If the partner is not covered under his or her own workplace insurance, the value of accepting the benefits and paying additional taxes must be compared to purchasing an independent health insurance.

■ PRIMARY SOURCE

George Cuellar lost the love of his life on September 11—"a nightmare," he says. Had Cuellar been able to marry his partner, he would now be entitled to a wide array of government and private benefits. But because his partner, Luke Dudek, was another man, their 20 years together counts for nothing to the federal government.

Cuellar says the people at the Family Assistance Center have been "wonderful. They treated me with nothing but respect. But when I went for Social Security, they looked at me and said, 'Don't even think about it.'"

No federal program benefits domestic partners. But the 9-11 disaster has changed a lot of things. Whether the new spirit of unity will apply to gay and lesbian survivors depends largely on John Ashcroft. The attorney general will decide, reportedly over the next few weeks, which survivors are entitled to relief under the Airline Stabilization Act. Congress put up $15 billion to sustain the industry and offer settlements—probably $1 million—to each survivor who forgoes a lawsuit against the airlines. As of now, the wording of the resolution leaves the fate of gay and lesbian survivors unclear.

"I let everyone out there interpret the phrase 'families of victims' accordingly," says Justice Department spokesperson Charles Miller. He refused to state explicitly that domestic partners were welcome to apply to the September 11th Victim Compensation Fund.

The late Luke Dudek, who was food and beverage controller for Windows on the World, spent the last week of his life helping Cuellar with their flower shop in Cedar Grove, New Jersey. Now trying to put together the pieces of his life, Cuellar faces a mixed and shifting landscape, especially if he tries to access programs funded by Washington. He will fare better as he navigates the various relief agencies.

For the first time since it was founded in 1881, the American Red Cross is explicitly offering disaster relief to domestic partners left behind. Gay groups like New York's Empire State Pride Agenda immediately lobbied the agency. "The minute it happened, we knew there would be surviving partners," says Matt Foreman, ESPA's executive director.

Gay groups also lobbied Governor George Pataki, who was about to keynote ESPA's annual dinner, to amend his September 11 emergency executive order by redefining a "dependent person" eligible for relief from the Crime Victims Board—up to $600 a week with a cap

of $30,000—to include those showing "mutual interdependence." Only a few years ago, the state-run board had fought successfully in court for the right not to treat domestic partners the same as spouses, as city law would require. "We can learn a little bit from September 11," Pataki told the ESPA crowd.

State Senator Tom Duane, a leader of the gay community, has written Pataki asking him to go further and make domestic partners of uniformed workers who were killed eligible for pensions and other benefits. Edgar Rodriguez, a gay cop, asked the governor's counsel about this at the ESPA dinner and was told that Pataki "wanted to work on it."

Things are clearer when it comes to city benefits. Safe Horizon, the new name for the city's Victim Services Agency, offers survivors, including domestic partners, up to $1500 every two weeks, to a maximum of $10,000. A spokesperson for the group said they can even help unrelated roommates who have proof of interdependency.

As the partner of someone who worked in the food, beverage, or hospitality businesses at the twin towers, Cuellar can also apply to the Windows of Hope Family Relief Fund. However, like most charities set up by Trade Center firms, it does not specify coverage for domestic partners.

Voice calls to the scores of funds listed at the World Trade Center Relief Web site found that most—like Cantor Fitzgerald, Carr Futures, and Marsh & McLennan—will cover unmarried partners. But this arrangement isn't mentioned on any of their Web sites. And while domestic partners in New York City have certificates as proof, those who did not or could not register—like the suburban Cuellar—will have to negotiate over the legitimacy of their relationships. "We're setting up guidelines," says Darlene Dwyer of Windows of Hope.

The most sustaining forms of relief are the fed's Social Security and state pensions and worker's compensation, all of which would require new legislation to include domestic partners. Gay lobby groups are not seriously attempting to lobby for this change now. "We don't even have civil rights protections in New York," notes Foreman. Neither Pataki nor state senate leader Joe Bruno's office returned calls asking whether they would support new legislation on gay rights.

However, the House of Representatives did take a small step toward equality when it voted recently to allow the District of Columbia to implement domestic-partner benefits for some employees. Gay activists are buoyed by the vote, but they are not optimistic when it comes to securing benefits nationwide. Right-wing leaders like the Reverend Lou Sheldon of the Traditional Values Coalition have already charged that gays "are taking advantage of this national tragedy to promote their agenda." It seems unlikely that conservatives will stand for a redefinition of the family, despite the plight of survivors like Cuellar.

The Human Rights Campaign is lobbying the administration to include domestic partners. "The fact that the language of the relief bill is open is helpful," says Barney Frank, the House's senior gay member. But expecting Congress to pass gay-inclusive language is "wildly optimistic." His strategy: "I will focus on the attorney general."

Senator John McCain wept as he eulogized his former campaign volunteer Mark Bingham, the gay rugby player who went down with United flight 93 in Pennsylvania, and may have helped bring down the plane before it could hit Washington. "I may very well owe my life to Mark," McCain said. But he did not return calls about whether Bingham's partner would deserve any consideration as a spouse.

New York senators Hillary Clinton and Chuck Schumer support gay partnership rights, especially for September 11 survivors. Schumer wrote to Ashcroft urging compensation for domestic partners. "Preliminary vibes are not as bad as we'd think," the senator told the Voice. But Clinton is concerned about "political blowback" from "the more ideological House GOP leadership."

There was one piece of good news last week: Gerald Ford became the highest-ranking Republican to endorse equal treatment for gay couples. "People are more receptive to the basic human story of gay and lesbian families after 9-11," says Evan Wolfson, a longtime advocate for equal marriage rights. But survivors like Cuellar are still far from being treated equally when they need it most.

SIGNIFICANCE

In the aftermath of September 11th, public perception of domestic partnership survivor benefits for gay and lesbian couples began to shift. In a speech to New York's Empire State Pride Agenda, Governor George Pataki offered to extend crime fund benefits to domestic partners of victims of the attack. In addition, former President Gerald Ford expressed his support for equal treatment of domestic partners within federal tax policies and Social Security benefits.

Businesses have also begun to adopt more domestic partner–friendly policies. In 2002, the District of Columbia finally granted benefits after rejecting the proposal for ten years. In New York City, more than 225 city employers provided domestic partner benefits in 2004, up from the 163 in 2000.

FURTHER RESOURCES

Periodicals

Barton, Mary Ann. "Who Should Reap the Benefits?" *American City and County* (December 1, 2003).

Marshall, Samantha. "More Benefits for Gays." *Crain's New York Busines* (June 27, 2005).

Ghent, Bill. "Lobbying: Tragedy Changed Gay Climate." *National Journal* (January 12, 2002).

Web sites

National Lesbian and Gay Journalists Association. "Domestic Partnerships." <http://www.nlgja.org/pubs/DP/DPovrvw.html> (accessed March 13, 2006).

Lawrence et al. v. Texas

Legal decision

By: United States Supreme Court

Date: June 26, 2003

Source: *Lawrence et al. v. Texas.* 539 U.S. 558 (2003). <http://caselaw.lp.findlaw.com/scripts/> (accessed March 27, 2006).

About the Author: Justice Anthony M. Kennedy of the United States Supreme Court wrote the majority decision in the Lawrence case. By law, the individual justice who prepares the written judgment is deemed to speak for the entire majority side, which in turn represents the binding ruling of the Supreme Court on the case that was the subject of the appeal. In *Lawrence et al. v. Texas*, Justice Kennedy was joined by Justices John Paul Stevens, David Souter, Ruth Bader Ginsberg, and Stephen Breyer; Justice Sandra Day O'Connor delivered her own judgment that concurred with the majority. Chief Justice William Rehnquist and Justices Antonin Scalia and Clarence Thomas dissented from the majority ruling.

INTRODUCTION

The Texas legal prohibition against homosexual practices that culminated in the 2003 Unites States Supreme Court ruling in *Lawrence et al. v. Texas* has deeper roots in the soils of the Anglo-American legal traditions than was credited in the court's decision. The shared legal history of England, Canada, and the United States has numerous instances of prosecutorial action directed against homosexuals.

The first sodomy trial in America took place in the colony of Virginia in 1624, when a sea captain named Richard Cornish was executed at Jamestown for alleged "unnatural acts." Five years later, a group of young men accused of sodomy were returned to England from the Virginia colony for execution. In the most famous of all criminal proceedings aimed at a homosexual, novelist and playwright Oscar Wilde was prosecuted and convicted of sodomy in London in 1895. In both England and Canada into the 1980s, there was significant police action taken against bathhouse inmates in various cities, places where gay men often met for consensual sexual purposes.

The trend in the United States regarding the prosecution of certain types of sexual acts performed by homosexual persons was consistent with these common law countries. In 1921, a Florida court characterized homosexuals as "creatures," not humans. The 1986 decision of the United States Supreme Court in the case of *Bowers v. Hardwick* upheld as constitutional a Georgia law that was virtually identical in its language to that of the Texas statute that was the subject of the *Lawrence* appeal. At the time that *Lawrence* was argued in 2003, thirteen American states had laws in force that prohibited sodomy or other sexual acts between homosexual persons.

Although the number of sodomy prosecutions in the United States has been comparatively few, these are proceedings that when initiated tend to galvanize public opinion. These cases do not represent a continuum of prosecutorial activity so much as they constitute a series of legal flashpoints, which engage the polar opposites of the conservative religious elements of American society and secular liberal groups.

Terminology is important in various aspects of how the reasoning of the Supreme Court in *Lawrence* bears upon wider societal issues. The prosecution in *Lawrence*, *Bowers*, and all earlier cases dealt with the sexual acts and homosexual practices in a clinical fashion, addressing the physical nature of the act. Modern consideration of these issues occurs within the multidimensional concept of gay rights, the term "gay" now broadly accepted as an omnibus covering all aspects of same-sex orientation.

In the seventeen years that passed between the *Bowers* decision and that of *Lawrence*, a number of different points of contention had arisen with respect to gay rights generally across America. The determination of questions such as gay marriage, adoption, discrimination against gay persons in a variety of circumstances, and pension rights and survivorship rights between gay partners all centered on the central issues at stake in "equality under the law and the right to privacy between consenting adults to act as they may choose."

The importance of each issue is also a function of the size of the American homosexual population. There is significant conflict in the estimates as to its precise size, but it is very likely that three to six percent of the American population is homosexual.

PRIMARY SOURCE

Responding to a reported weapons disturbance in a private residence, Houston police entered petitioner Lawrence's apartment and saw him and another adult man, petitioner Garner, engaging in a private, consensual sexual act. Petitioners were arrested and convicted of deviate sexual intercourse in violation of a Texas statute forbidding two persons of the same sex to engage in certain intimate sexual conduct. In affirming, the State Court of Appeals held, *inter alia*, that the statute was not unconstitutional under the Due Process Clause of the Fourteenth Amendment. The court considered *Bowers v. Hardwick*, 478 U.S. 186, controlling on that point.

Held: The Texas statute making it a crime for two persons of the same sex to engage in certain intimate sexual conduct violates the Due Process Clause. Pp. 3–18.

(a) Resolution of this case depends on whether petitioners were free as adults to engage in private conduct in the exercise of their liberty under the Due Process Clause. For this inquiry the Court deems it necessary to reconsider its *Bowers* holding. The *Bowers* Court's initial substantive statement—"The issue presented is whether the Federal Constitution confers a fundamental right upon homosexuals to engage in sodomy..." 478 U.S., at 190—discloses the Court's failure to appreciate the extent of the liberty at stake. To say that the issue in *Bowers* was simply the right to engage in certain sexual conduct demeans the claim the individual put forward, just as it would demean a married couple were it said that marriage is just about the right to have sexual intercourse. Although the laws involved in *Bowers* and here purport to do not more than prohibit a particular sexual act, their penalties and purposes have more far-reaching consequences, touching upon the most private human conduct, sexual behavior, and in the most private of places, the home. They seek to control a personal relationship that, whether or not entitled to formal recognition in the law, is within the liberty of persons to choose without being punished as criminals. The liberty protected by the Constitution allows homosexual persons the right to choose to enter upon relationships in the confines of their homes and their own private lives and still retain their dignity as free persons. Pp. 3–6.

(b) Having misapprehended the liberty claim presented to it, the *Bowers* Court stated that proscriptions against sodomy have ancient roots. 478 U.S., at 192. It should be noted, however, that there is no longstanding history in this country of laws directed at homosexual conduct as a distinct matter. Early American sodomy laws were not directed at homosexuals as such but instead sought to prohibit nonprocreative sexual activity more generally, whether between men and women or men and men. Moreover, early sodomy laws seem not to have been enforced against consenting adults acting in private. Instead, sodomy prosecutions often involved predatory acts against those who could not or did not consent: relations between men and minor girls or boys, between adults involving force, between adults implicating disparity in status, or between men and animals. The longstanding criminal prohibition of homosexual sodomy upon which *Bowers* placed such reliance is as consistent with a general condemnation of nonprocreative sex as it is with an established tradition of prosecuting acts because of their homosexual character. Far from possessing "ancient roots," *ibid.*, American laws targeting same-sex couples did not develop until the last third of the 20th century. Even now, only nine States have singled out same-sex relations for criminal prosecution. Thus, the historical grounds relied upon in *Bowers* are more complex than the majority opinion and the concurring opinion by Chief Justice Burger there indicated. They are not without doubt and, at the very least, are overstated. The *Bowers* Court was, of course, making the broader point that for centuries there have been powerful voices to condemn homosexual conduct as immoral, but this Court's obligation is to define the liberty of all, not to mandate its own moral code, *Planned Parenthood of Southeastern Pa. v. Casey*, 505 U.S. 833, 850. The Nation's laws and traditions in the past half century are most relevant here. They show an emerging awareness that liberty gives substantial protection to adult persons in deciding how to conduct their private lives in matters pertaining to sex. See *County of Sacramento v. Lewis*, 523 U.S. 833, 857. Pp. 6–12.

(c) *Bowers'* deficiencies became even more apparent in the years following its announcement. The 25 States with laws prohibiting the conduct referenced in *Bowers* are reduced now to 13, of which 4 enforce their laws only against homosexual conduct. In those States, including Texas, that still proscribe sodomy (whether for same-sex or heterosexual conduct), there is a pattern of nonenforcement with respect to consenting adults acting in private. *Casey, supra,* at 851—which confirmed that the Due Process Clause protects personal decisions relat-

ing to marriage, procreation, contraception, family relationships, child rearing, and education—and *Romer v. Evans*, 517 U.S. 620, 624—which struck down class-based legislation directed at homosexuals—cast *Bowers'* holding into even more doubt. The stigma the Texas criminal statute imposes, moreover, is not trivial. Although the offense is but a minor misdemeanor, it remains a criminal offense with all that imports for the dignity of the persons charged, including notation of convictions on their records and on job application forms, and registration as sex offenders under state law. Where a case's foundations have sustained serious erosion, criticism from other sources is of greater significance. In the United States, criticism of *Bowers* has been substantial and continuing, disapproving of its reasoning in all respects, not just as to its historical assumptions. And, to the extent *Bowers* relied on values shared with a wider civilization, the case's reasoning and holding have been rejected by the European Court of Human Rights, and that other nations have taken action consistent with an affirmation of the protected right of homosexual adults to engage in intimate, consensual conduct. There has been no showing that in this country the governmental interest in circumscribing personal choice is somehow more legitimate or urgent. *Stare decisis* is not an inexorable command. *Payne v. Tennessee*, 501 U.S. 808, 828. *Bowers'* holding has not induced detrimental reliance of the sort that could counsel against overturning it once there are compelling reasons to do so. *Casey, supra,* at 855–856. *Bowers* causes uncertainty, for the precedents before and after it contradict its central holding. Pp. 12–17.

(d) *Bowers'* rationale does not withstand careful analysis. In his dissenting opinion in *Bowers* Justice *Stevens* concluded that (1) the fact a State's governing majority has traditionally viewed a particular practice as immoral is not a sufficient reason for upholding a law prohibiting the practice, and (2) individual decisions concerning the intimacies of physical relationships, even when not intended to produce offspring, are a form of "liberty" protected by due process. That analysis should have controlled *Bowers*, and it controls here. *Bowers* was not correct when it was decided, is not correct today, and is hereby overruled. This case does not involve minors, persons who might be injured or coerced, those who might not easily refuse consent, or public conduct or prostitution. It does involve two adults who, with full and mutual consent, engaged in sexual practices common to a homosexual lifestyle. Petitioners' right to liberty under the Due Process Clause gives them the full right to engage in private conduct without government intervention. *Casey, supra,* at 847. The Texas statute furthers no legitimate state interest which can justify its intrusion into the individual's personal and private life. Pp. 17–18.

41 S. W. 3d 349, reversed and remanded.

Kennedy, J., delivered the opinion of the Court, in which Stevens, Souter, Ginsburg, and Breyer, JJ., joined. O'Connor, J., filed an opinion concurring in the judgment. Scalia, J., filed a dissenting opinion, in which Rehnquist, C. J., and Thomas, J., joined. Thomas, J., filed a dissenting opinion.

SIGNIFICANCE

On a literal reading of the facts of the case, *Lawrence* deals with whether consensual sexual acts between homosexual adults are protected by the Constitution. On a broader view, *Lawrence* is the most significant decision ever rendered by the United States Supreme Court with respect to the modern concept of gay rights.

At the heart of the Supreme Court's ruling is the examination of what constitutes *due process*, a multidimensional legal concept that includes the protection for both the rights of individuals to equality before the law, as well as the right to privacy. The definition of due process is not always capable of dictionary-style precision, as each case will present unique features that may affect the application of the due process doctrine. Due process is a template within which all laws must fit; Daniel Webster (1782–1852), the noted American statesman and lawyer, defined due process as a law that is not unreasonable, arbitrary, or capricious, one that "hears before it condemns."

The Fourteenth Amendment to the United States Constitution codifies due process as a prohibition against any state from depriving any citizen of life, liberty, or property, without due process, or to deny such persons equal protection under the law. The Texas statute examined in *Lawrence* specified a variety of homosexual practices as deviant sexual intercourse and thus illegal; such acts were not prohibited if the acts were engaged in by consenting heterosexuals. There was evidence before the court that the Texas statute was rarely enforced; the accused parties in *Lawrence* seem to have been the subject of a selective investigation by the Houston police, given that there was no evidence of any other criminal conduct to require the attendance of the police at the defendant's residence at the time that the sexual activity was observed.

It is significant that through the *Lawrence* ruling, the Supreme Court emphatically overruled its own decision from only seventeen years before, *Bowers*. *Bowers* was a similar appeal which considered the application of a Georgia state prohibition against homosexual acts that was virtually identical to that of

Supporters of civil rights for homosexuals rally at Republic Square in downtown Austin, in reaction to the United States Supreme Court Ruling to strike down the Texas sodomy laws. © BOB DAEMMRICH/CORBIS

the Texas statute. It is common for courts in the Anglo-American tradition, when faced with legal issues that are substantially the same as those determined in a prior case, to invoke the principle of *stare decisis*, a Latin maxim that is a legal short form for a court's ability to stand by an earlier precedent, and to not disturb a settled legal point. The Supreme Court's willingness to depart from the ruling in *Bowers* is as much a testament to changing American public opinion between 1986 and 2003 regarding the rights of anyone, including gay persons to live as they choose, as it is any other legal principle. It is rare for a court, as the Supreme Court did in *Lawrence*, to state that *Bowers* was not only wrongly decided as of 2003, it was wrongly decided when the Supreme Court made its ruling in 1986.

It is of interest that while many elements of the various conservative religious movements of the United States denounced *Lawrence* as permitting wickedness to occur in any community, the Court does not attempt to define moral or immoral conduct in its judgment. It is also evident from the ruling that as with any other freedom, there are limits presumed in law while permitting the conduct; predatory persons, non-consensual acts, and sexual acts with minors would never be protected under the language of the 14th Amendment.

The *Lawrence* decision carried special significance for Lambda Legal, the organization that provided the legal counsel who represented the accused appellants in all appeal proceedings. Lambda Legal is a national legal advocacy organization created in 1973 with a specialty in the pursuit of civil rights for lesbians and gays. Lambda Legal took the *Lawrence* appeal as a test case through which to advance its wider philosophical position regarding equal rights.

Given the strong language in the *Lawrence* decision regarding equality and privacy, one may question whether this particular moral battle is now exhausted. It seems likely that organizations such as Lambda Legal and the forces of American religious conservatism will each turn their attention to the more impactful issues arising from the sanction and extension of gay marriage, the availability of adoption to gay couples, and the ability of gay partners to advance survivor and estate claims.

The *Lawrence* decision echoes the famous utterance of former Canadian prime minister Pierre Trudeau, who said in 1968 that "The state has no business in the nation's bedrooms." Given the temper of modern American society, it is doubtful that the Supreme Court would ever permit the future enforcement of any legislation that was enacted to differentiate between the consensual sexual practices of any American citizens.

FURTHER RESOURCES
Books

Burgwinkle, William. *Sodomy, Masculinity and Law in Medieval Literature*. Cambridge, U.K.: Cambridge University Press, 2004.

Holland, Merlin. *The Real Trial of Oscar Wilde*. New York: HarperCollins, 2004.

Web sites

The History of Lambda Legal <http//:www.lambdalegal.org/cgi-bin/iowa/cases/record?record=93>(accessed March 27, 2006).

SodomyLaws.org. <http://www.sodomylaws.org/lawrence/lawrence.htm>(accessed March 27, 2006).

Ads by the Nonprofit Group Parents and Friends of Ex-Gays and Gays

Photograph

By: Anonymous

Date: October 30, 2003

Source: The Associated Press

About the Photographer: This photograph was taken by an unknown photographer for The Associated Press, a worldwide news agency based in New York.

INTRODUCTION

Parents and Friends of Ex-Gays (PFOX) is an organization advocating the view that homosexuality is not an innate condition but a chosen or curable pathological condition. PFOX also maintains that homosexuals are deliberately recruiting young people to be gay rather than straight; the group's website stated in 2006 that there is a "massive cultural campaign to promote homosexuality to kids." PFOX first placed ads in stations of the Washington, D.C.–area commuter rail system or "Metro" in October, 2002. The ads featured photographs of smiling, handsome individuals accompanied by text testifying that the persons pictured had made a "choice" to change from homosexuality to heterosexuality. Similar ads, including the one shown here, were placed by PFOX in about 10 Metro stations in and near Washington, D.C. in October 2003, to run for one month. "…I realized there was a choice—and I chose to change from gay to straight," reads the ad. Its text alleges that "thousands" of persons have already done so and concludes, "Please respect our choice."

Placing the ads was cost-free because at the time, the Washington Metro system had a policy of placing public service ads at no charge. The ads were highly controversial. The executive director of the local chapter of Parents, Families & Friends of Lesbians and Gays, an area organization, said, "I think they're creating a false sense of hope for people who have not come to acceptance [of their own homosexuality], both the GLBT [gay, lesbian, bisexual, transgender] people and their families who think that this is really based on sound research, and we know it's not." The chair of the Metro board, a gay D.C. city council member, said that "we're exploring ways in which we can legally and constitutionally extricate ourselves from the dilemma of having advertising in the subway system which is open not only to substantial controversy—which is of course what the First Amendment is all about—but it's also the truth in advertising issue, the extent to which whether [sic] their claims are in fact truthful."

Shortly after the PFOX ads appeared, the Washington Metro Operations Committee voted to permanently halt free public service ads as of January 1, 2004. Under the new system, it would cost PFOX over $12,000 to run similar ads, which the group has said it cannot afford. The Human Rights Campaign Foundation, which states that it is "working for lesbian, gay, bisexual, and transgender rights," developed a series of counter-ads that ran for free in the Metro public-service spaces in December, 2003, immediately after the PFOX ads. "The PFOX ads were deceptive and untrue," said the organization's education director. "We know that gay, lesbian, bisexual and transgender people cannot 'change' their identities, and the discredited techniques that purport to change them are damaging." The reply ads did not directly address the question of whether homosexuality is a "choice," but did say, "If you're gay, lesbian, bisexual or transgender, live your life honestly…. It's how we change hearts and minds."

PFOX's ads were not the first time public-service ads on the Metro about homosexuality had caused controversy. In 1978, the Gay Activists Alliance launched a public-service Metro ads saying "Someone In Your Life Is Gay." The ads ran only after the Alliance won a lawsuit against the Metro system, which had refused the ads.

Although the PFOX Metro ad shown here asks readers to "respect our choice" (to become heterosexual), it may be noted that PFOX explicitly rejects the legitimacy of what it believes to be the opposite choice: that is, to be homosexual. In 2006, the PFOX website asserted that there is "no doubt that homosexual activists are recruiting kids into homosexual sex and a 'gay' identity, using 'tolerance' as a ruse."

PRIMARY SOURCE

ADS BY THE NONPROFIT GROUP PARENTS AND FRIENDS OF EX-GAYS AND GAYS

See primary source image.

SIGNIFICANCE

At the root of the controversy over the PFOX ads is the factual question of whether homosexuality is innate or a lifestyle choice. Attempts to "cure" homosexuality have been made for over a century. Nine-

teenth-century efforts at homosexual conversion sometimes included repeated drunken visits to female prostitutes (per doctor's orders); few if any conversions were achieved. Social and religious conservatives have in recent years been promoting a school of psychotherapy known as "conversion therapy" or "reparative therapy," which purports to be able to change the sexual orientation of a person from homosexual to heterosexual. A number of conservative Christian ministry groups are devoted to homosexual-to-heterosexual conversion, both psychotherapeutic and prayer-centered, as well as PFOX and a small group of mental health professionals, the National Association for Research and Treatment of Homosexuality. Almost all individuals associated with this school of thought are conservative Christians, who view homosexuality as a sin or illness. Modern conversion therapy may involve counseling, prayer, religious conversion, or the monitored formation of a close nonsexual relationship with an adult of one's own gender.

There is scientific evidence—including studies of identical twins raised in separate households—that support the view that homosexuality is genetically determined. Both major professional mental-health organizations have denounced conversion therapy: the American Psychiatric Association stated in 2000 that it "opposes any psychiatric treatment, such as 'reparative' or conversion therapy, which is based upon the assumption that homosexuality *per se* is a mental disorder or based upon the a priori assumption that a patient should change his/her sexual orientation." The American Psychological Association issued a policy statement in 1997 saying that "societal ignorance about same gender sexual orientation put some gay, lesbian, bisexual, and questioning individuals at risk for presenting for 'conversion' treatment due to family or social coercion and/or lack of information" and reiterating the APA's view that homosexuality is not a "mental illness."

As of 2006, no rigorously designed scientific studies on the efficacy of efforts to convert homosexuals to heterosexuals appeared to have been performed, but what studies were available indicated success rates for conversion or reparative therapy of between 0% and 0.5%. Some higher figures have been cited, but scientific critics note that these figures are based on populations including large or unknown numbers of bisexual patients and that enabling bisexual patients to concentrate on heterosexual activity does not count as conversion of a homosexual person to heterosexuality. Persons formerly identifying themselves as homosexual but now identifying themselves as heterosexual do exist but are a very small fraction of those who have attempted to make such a transition.

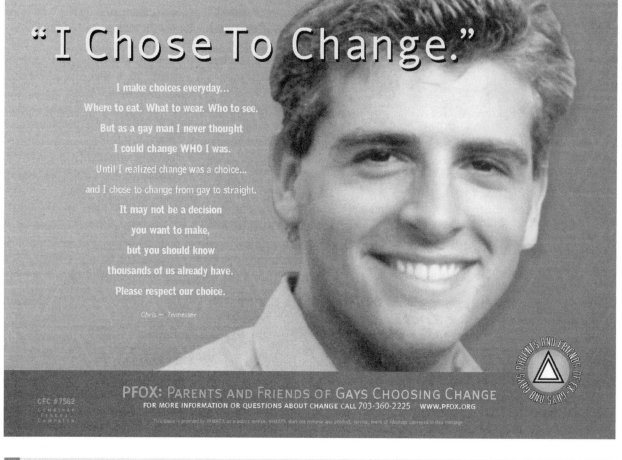

"I Chose To Change."

I make choices everyday...

Where to eat. What to wear. Who to see.

But as a gay man I never thought
I could change WHO I was.

Until I realized change was a choice...
and I chose to change from gay to straight.

It may not be a decision
you want to make,
but you should know
thousands of us already have.

Please respect our choice.

Chris – Tennessee

PFOX: PARENTS AND FRIENDS OF GAYS CHOOSING CHANGE

CFC #7562
COMBINED
FEDERAL
CAMPAIGN

FOR MORE INFORMATION OR QUESTIONS ABOUT CHANGE CALL 703-360-2225   WWW.PFOX.ORG

This space is provided by WMATA as a public service. WMATA does not endorse any product, service, event or ideology conveyed in this message.

PRIMARY SOURCE

Ads by the Nonprofit Group Parents and Friends of Ex-Gays and Gays: One of the ads that the group Parents and Friends of Ex-Gays and Gays sought to run as a public service advertisement in the Washington Metro system in 2003.
AP IMAGES

FURTHER RESOURCES

Periodicals

Anderton, Bryan. 'Ex-Gay' Ads Reappear in Metro Stations." *The Washington Blade.* Oct. 24, 2003. <http://www.washblade.com/2003/10-24/news/localnews/exgayad.cfm> (accessed April 6, 2006).

Web sites

American Psychiatric Association. "COPP Position Statement on Therapies Focused on Attempts to Change Sexual Orientation (Reparative or Conversion Therapies)." March, 2000. <http://www.psych.org/psych_pract/copptherapyaddendum83100.cfm> (accessed April 6, 2006).

American Psychological Association. "Appropriate Therapeutic Responses to Sexual Orientation." August 14, 1997. Available at <http://www.apa.org/pi/lgbc/policy/appropriate.html> (accessed April 6, 2006).

Human Rights Council. "HRC Places Public Service Ads in Washington's Subway System to Counter Anti-Gay Messages." Press release, Dec. 12, 2003. <http://www.hrc.org/Template/> (accessed April 6, 2006).

President Calls for Constitutional Amendment Protecting Marriage

Speech

By: George W. Bush

Date: February 24, 2004

Source: Bush, George W. "President Calls for Constitutional Amendment Protecting Marriage." Speech delivered in the Roosevelt Room of the White House, Washington, D.C., February 24, 2004. Available at: <http://www.whitehouse.gov/news/releases/2004/02/20040224-2.html> (accessed February 15, 2006).

About the Author: George W. Bush is the forty-third president of the United States.

INTRODUCTION

In the early 1990s, homosexual couples in America began gaining rights held previously only by heterosexual, married couples. Domestic partner benefits, designed to aid unmarried couples who wanted to access a partner's health or life insurance benefits through employers, were used by same-sex couples in increasing numbers throughout the late 1980s and early 1990s.

In 1993, the Hawaii Supreme Court, in the case of *Baehr vs. Levin*, placed the burden on the state to show a compelling reason for prohibiting same-sex marriage. Gay marriage opponents in the United States, including Christian conservatives and groups such as Focus on the Family, claim that same-sex marriage would threaten traditional, heterosexual marriage by changing the definition of marriage, and opening the institution to court challenges for polygamy and other nontraditional couplings.

The Hawaii Supreme Court's decision concerned lawmakers in other states, for if Hawaii legalized gay marriage, the Full Faith and Credit clause of the Constitution could, theoretically, have forced other states to accept as valid the marriages performed in Hawaii. This reciprocity had extended for traditional heterosexual marriages.

The Defense of Marriage Act, passed by Congress in 1996, defined marriage as a union between "one man and one woman." The bill, signed by President William J. Clinton on September 21, 1996, was part of a drive by Republican members of Congress and religious conservatives to use policy to maintain traditional heterosexual marriage. The act allowed any state to deny recognition to any marriage from another state that involves a same-sex couple and also allows states to deny recognition of marriages that do not involve "one man and one woman."

In 1999, Vermont became the first state in the United States to offer same-sex partners a civil union—a legally binding ceremony that carried most of the rights of marriage. In the Vermont state Supreme Court decision *Baker v. Vermont*, the court compelled the state legislature to grant same-sex cou-

Demonstrator Jim Thompson holds a sign with an image of George W. Bush during a rally outside City Hall in Chicago, Illinois on May 17, 2004. Supporters and non-supporters of equal marriage rights gathered outside in reaction to the state of Massachuetts legalizing same sex marriage. PHOTO BY TIM BOYLE/GETTY IMAGES

ples the same rights afforded married heterosexual couples. The result, civil unions, was signed into law by Vermont Governor Howard Dean.

In 2003, Massachusetts became the first state in the United States to grant full marriage rights to same-sex couples. In the case of *Goodridge v. Department of Public Health*, the Massachusetts Supreme Judicial Court ruled that denying marriage to same-sex couples was a violation of the Equal Protection Clause in the state's constitution. Effective May 17, 2004, same-sex couples were permitted full marriage rights in Massachusetts.

Canada made civil marriage of any two persons, to the exclusion of all others, legal in July 2005. These actions caused a flurry of activity on the part of same-sex marriage opponents. Representative Marilyn Musgrave, a Republican from Colorado, introduced a "Federal Marriage Amendment" that would take the heart of the Defense of Marriage Act and turn it into an amendment to the Constitution. This amendment, reworded and submitted in 2004 shortly after the city of San Francisco began illegally offering marriage licenses to same-sex couples, gained support from conservative groups such as the Alliance for Marriage, the Family Research Council, and Focus on the Family.

Gay marriage became an issue in the 2004 presidential campaign, and President George W. Bush campaigned on a promise to maintain marriage as a heterosexual institution. In this speech, President Bush outlines his support for the Federal Marriage Amendment.

■ PRIMARY SOURCE

Remarks by the President
The Roosevelt Room
10:43 A.M. EST

THE PRESIDENT: Good morning. Eight years ago, Congress passed, and President Clinton signed, the Defense of Marriage Act, which defined marriage for purposes of federal law as the legal union between one man and one woman as husband and wife.

The Act passed the House of Representatives by a vote of 342 to 67, and the Senate by a vote of 85 to 14. Those congressional votes and the passage of similar defensive marriage laws in 38 states express an overwhelming consensus in our country for protecting the institution of marriage.

In recent months, however, some activist judges and local officials have made an aggressive attempt to redefine marriage. In Massachusetts, four judges on the highest court have indicated they will order the issuance of marriage licenses to applicants of the same gender in May of this year. In San Francisco, city officials have issued thousands of marriage licenses to people of the same gender, contrary to the California family code. That code, which clearly defines marriage as the union of a man and a woman, was approved overwhelmingly by the voters of California. A county in New Mexico has also issued marriage licenses to applicants of the same gender. And unless action is taken, we can expect more arbitrary court decisions, more litigation, more defiance of the law by local officials, all of which adds to uncertainty.

After more than two centuries of American jurisprudence, and millennia of human experience, a few judges and local authorities are presuming to change the most fundamental institution of civilization. Their actions have created confusion on an issue that requires clarity.

On a matter of such importance, the voice of the people must be heard. Activist courts have left the people with one recourse. If we are to prevent the meaning of marriage from being changed forever, our nation must enact a constitutional amendment to protect marriage in America. Decisive and democratic action is needed, because attempts to redefine marriage in a single state or city could have serious consequences throughout the country.

The Constitution says that full faith and credit shall be given in each state to the public acts and records and judicial proceedings of every other state. Those who want to change the meaning of marriage will claim that this provision requires all states and cities to recognize same-sex marriages performed anywhere in America. Congress attempted to address this problem in the Defense of Marriage Act, by declaring that no state must accept another state's definition of marriage. My administration will vigorously defend this act of Congress.

Yet there is no assurance that the Defense of Marriage Act will not, itself, be struck down by activist courts. In that event, every state would be forced to recognize any relationship that judges in Boston or officials in San Francisco choose to call a marriage. Furthermore, even if the Defense of Marriage Act is upheld, the law does not protect marriage within any state or city.

For all these reasons, the Defense of Marriage requires a constitutional amendment. An amendment to the Constitution is never to be undertaken lightly. The amendment process has addressed many serious matters of national concern. And the preservation of marriage rises to this level of national importance. The union of a man and woman is the most enduring human institution, honoring—honored and encouraged in all cultures and by every religious faith. Ages of experience have taught humanity that the commitment of a husband and wife to love and to serve one another promotes the welfare of children and the stability of society.

Marriage cannot be severed from its cultural, religious and natural roots without weakening the good influence of society. Government, by recognizing and protecting marriage, serves the interests of all. Today I call upon the Congress to promptly pass, and to send to the states for ratification, an amendment to our Constitution defining and protecting marriage as a union of man and woman as husband and wife. The amendment should fully protect marriage, while leaving the state legislatures free to make their own choices in defining legal arrangements other than marriage.

America is a free society, which limits the role of government in the lives of our citizens. This commitment of freedom, however, does not require the redefinition of one of our most basic social institutions. Our government should respect every person, and protect the institution of marriage. There is no contradiction between these responsibilities. We should also conduct this difficult debate in a manner worthy of our country, without bitterness or anger.

In all that lies ahead, let us match strong convictions with kindness and goodwill and decency.

Thank you very much.

END 10:48 A.M. EST

SIGNIFICANCE

On February 12, 2004, Mayor Gavin Newsom of San Francisco permitted city hall to issue and recognize marriage licenses for same-sex couples. Nearly 4,000 couples were married before the California Supreme Court ruled in August 2004 that the mayor had overstepped his authority. All same-sex marriages were declared invalid and annulled. In New Mexico and Oregon, similar events took place. Based on the San Francisco events and the Massachusetts Supreme Judicial Court ruling, same-sex marriage activists throughout the United States began to bring lawsuits through the court system requesting equal rights.

In response, same-sex marriage opponents pushed for the constitutional amendment declaring marriage to be between "one man and one woman." On July 14, 2004, the U.S. Senate voted fifty to forty-eight to close debate on the issue. A sixty vote majority would have been needed to pass the amendment. The two senators abstaining were John Kerry and John Edwards, who did not want to vote on an issue that was so contentious during the 2004 presidential election. Both men at the time were running for the Democratic nomination for the presidential election. In the House of Representatives, a vote took place on September 30, 2004; the vote was 227–186, sixty-three votes shy of the 290 required for a two-thirds majority.

President Bush's speech was viewed by his advisors as a political necessity; as much as thirty percent of his support base was comprised of conservative Christian voters who viewed same-sex marriage as a threat to traditional Christian values and morality. By addressing what he termed "activist judges" and "activist courts", Bush used buzzwords that opponents of same-sex marriage had used in airing concerns that the courts—and not legislatures—were setting policy. Laws, such as the Defense of Marriage Act and the Federal Marriage Amendment, were designed, from the viewpoint of same-sex marriage opponents, to prevent judicial rulings from carrying the weight of law.

As of this writing, Belgium, Canada, the Netherlands, Spain, and the state of Massachusetts in the United States legally permit gay marriage. Seventeen other countries (including certain states in the United States) offer civil unions or other rights to same-sex couples who choose to form a union that resembles marriage. South Africa will extend same-sex marriage legal protections to its citizens in December 2006.

FURTHER RESOURCES

Books

Dobson, James. *Marriage Under Fire: Why We Must Win This Battle.* Sisters, Ore.: Multnomah, 2004.

Gerstmann, Evan. *Same-Sex Marriage and the Constitution.* New York: Cambridge University Press, 2003.

Periodicals

Adam, Barry D. "The Defense of Marriage Act and American Exceptionalism: The 'Gay Marriage' Panic in the United States." *Journal of the History of Sexuality* 12 (April 2003): 259–276.

Web sites

National Organization for Women. "Same Sex Marriage is a Feminist Issue." <http://www.now.org/issues/lgbi/marr-rep.html> (accessed February 15, 2006).

NPR.org. "Calif. Judge Rejects Ban on Same-Sex Marriage." <http://www.npr.org/templates/story/story/> (accessed February 15, 2006).

Thomas.gov. "Defense of Marriage Act." <http://thomas.loc.gov/cgi-bin/query/z?c104:H.R.3396.ENR:> (accessed February 15, 2006).

Lofton v. Secretary of the Florida Department of Children and Families

Legal decision

By: Judges of the United States Court of Appeals for the Eleventh Circuit

Date: July 21, 2004

Source: Lofton v. Secretary of the Florida Department of Children and Families. In the United States Court of Appeals for the Eleventh Circuit. No. 01-16723, D. C. Docket No. 99-10058-CV-JLK, On Petition for Rehearing En Banc. Available at: <http://www.ca11.uscourts.gov/opinions/ops/200116723ord.pdf> (accessed March 8, 2006).

About the Author: The twelve justices of the Eleventh Circuit of the U.S. Court of Appeals issued this opinion denying a rehearing of a decision by a three-judge panel of federal appellate court judges in the case *Lofton v. Secretary of the Florida Department of Children and Families.*

INTRODUCTION

In 1977, Florida enacted a law (Ch. 77-140, §1, 1977 Fla. Laws, 466) that explicitly banned the adoption of children by homosexual couples: "[n]o person [otherwise] eligible to adopt under this statute may adopt if that person is a homosexual." The same day, a bill was signed into law restricting marriage to heterosexual couples (Ch. 77-139, §1, 1977 Fla. Laws, 465). Florida's gay adoption ban has been repeatedly challenged in court, but never successfully. The most recent challenge, and the first to seek relief under the United States rather than the Florida Constitution, was a suit brought by Florida pediatric nurse Steven Lofton and several other plaintiffs against the Secretary of the Florida Department of Children and Family Services (Kathleen Kearney) and the District Administrator of District Eleven of Florida's Department of Children and Families (Charles Auslander). The case is sometimes referred to simply as *Lofton v. Kearney* .

Steven Lofton became the foster parent of a male baby ("John Doe" in the court records) in 1991. In September 1994, Lofton filed an adoption application, but refused to answer question G, "Are you a homosexual?" This began years of legal wrangling between Lofton and the Florida Department of Children and Family Services. In 1999, the American Civil Liberties Union (ACLU) brought suit against Kearney and Auslander (in their official capacity only) on behalf of Lofton and three other gay men, all of whom had been denied petitions for adoption in Florida because of their homosexuality. This suit, *Lofton v. Kearney*, filed in a Federal Court in Miami, claimed that the Florida law violated the U.S. Constitution.

The court decided against Lofton and his fellow plaintiffs in 2001. The ACLU appealed to the United States Court of Appeals for the Eleventh Circuit. On Jan. 28, 2004, a panel of three judges from the court upheld the lower court's ruling. The plaintiffs then petitioned for an *en banc* rehearing of their case by the circuit court, that is, a hearing by all twelve of the circuit's judges at once. (*En banc* is French for "by the full court.") On July 21, 2004, in a six to six vote, the circuit judges denied the petition for rehearing (a majority would have been necessary to mandate a re-hearing). The excerpts reproduced here are from the July 21, 2004, document in which the court denies the requested rehearing en banc. The ACLU then

asked the U.S. Supreme Court to hear a further appeal in the case, but in January, 2005, the Court declined to hear the case.

▮ PRIMARY SOURCE

BIRCH, Circuit Judge, Specially Concurring in the Denial of Rehearing En Banc:

I will conclude on a purely personal note. If I were a legislator, rather than a judge, I would vote in favor of considering otherwise eligible homosexuals for adoptive parenthood. In reviewing the record in this case one can only be impressed by the courage, tenacity and devotion of Messrs. Lofton and Houghton for the children placed in their care. For these children, these men are the only parents they have ever known. Thus, I consider the policy decision of the Florida legislature to be misguided and trust that over time attitudes will change and it will see the best interest of these children in a different light. Nevertheless, as compelling as this perspective is to me, I will not allow my personal views to conflict with my judicial duty—conduct that apparently fewer and fewer citizens, commentators and Senators seem to understand or appreciate. And, I hasten to add, the vast majority of federal judges, including each and every judge of the Eleventh Circuit, are similarly sensitive to separate their personal preferences from their duty to follow precedent as they understand it.

ANDERSON, Circuit Judge, Dissenting from the Denial of Rehearing En Banc in Which DUBINA, Circuit Judge, joins:

I agree with Judge Barkett that the cases she discusses in Section I of her comprehensive dissent indicate that the challenged provision of the Florida statute violates the Equal Protection Clause. For this reason, and because the issue is of exceptional importance, Fed.R.App.P.35(a)(2), *en banc* rehearing should be granted.

BARKETT, Circuit Judge, Dissenting from the Denial of Rehearing En Banc:

Lofton v. Sec. Of Dep't of Children & Family Services, 358 F.3d 804 (11th Cir. 2004), finds constitutional 1977 Fla. Laws, ch. 77-140, §1, Fla. Stat §63.042(3) (2003), which provides that "[n]o person eligible to adopt under this statute may adopt if that person is a homosexual." Florida is the only state in the union to have such a categorical statutory prohibition targeted solely against homosexuals. This provision finds, as a matter of law, hundreds of thousands of Florida citizens unfit to serve as adoptive parents solely because of constitutionally protected conduct. There is no comparable bar in Florida's adoption statute that applies to any other group. Neither child molesters, drug addicts, nor domestic abusers are categorically barred by the statute from serving as adoptive parents. In a very real sense, Florida's adoption statute treats homosexuals less favorably than even those individuals with characteristics that may pose a threat to the well-being of children.

SIGNIFICANCE

Florida and Mississippi are the only U.S. states to explicitly forbid adoption by homosexual couples. The informal motivation for the law was expressed in 1977 by its sponsor, Florida state senator Curtis Peterson: "The problem in Florida has been that homosexuals are surfacing to such an extent that they're beginning to aggravate the ordinary folks. We're trying to send them a message, telling them: 'We're really tired of you. We wish you'd go back into the closet.'"

Formally, however, the state argued that its primary concern was the welfare of the children in its custody. Specifically, it contended that it wished children to be adopted into "mainstream American culture." The state's defense further argued that "the adoption law is rationally related to the best interests of children in being raised in homes with married mothers and fathers due to the stability provided by marriage and the contribution of male and female influences to childhood growth and development, including heterosexual role modeling and sexual and gender identity" (quotation from the denial of petition for rehearing en banc). While not all judges on the Eleventh Circuit agreed with the state's offered rationale—as the excerpt from the majority opinion by Judge Stanley Birch shown above makes clear—the majority reasoned that if a law passed by the Florida legislature could "arguably" have a rational basis, and if the law is not clearly unconstitutional, then the court is obliged to not overturn that law.

The opposition to homosexual adoption primarily comes from religiously conservative segments of society such as evangelical Christians and conservative Catholics. These groups tend to believe that homosexuality is sinful or pathological. The Vatican, for example, has recently described adoptions by gay couples as "gravely immoral." In 2006, the four Catholic bishops of Massachusetts petitioned the governor of that state to exempt Catholic social-service agencies from state anti-discrimination policies so that these church-based agencies could deny adoption to gay couples. (The state licenses the agencies to place children with adoptive parents.) As of mid-March 2006, the governor had not yet made a decision on the matter.

Partners Rob Flint and Kevin Burns spend time with their 5-month-old adopted daughter Autumn Hope. Because of Florida's 1977 ban on gay parent adoption, the couple, who are both Florida residents, established a residence in Vermont in order to adopt. PHOTO BY DAVID FRIEDMAN/GETTY IMAGES

Alabama, Mississippi, North Carolina, and Virginia all deny child custody based on sexual orientation; Florida denies adoption by homosexuals but allows foster care and custody. The general legal trend has been toward recognition of gay adoption. Nine U.S. states and the District of Columbia have explicitly legalized adoption by openly gay and lesbian couples. Most U.S. states neither forbid gay adoption nor explicitly establish a right to it. Gay adoption is legal in Belgium, England, the Netherlands, Spain, Sweden, most of Canada, and part of Australia; approximately equivalent arrangements are legal in a number of other countries. Medical and psychiatric opinion has recently tended to favor gay adoption. The American Academy of Pediatrics stated in 2002 that "children with parents who are homosexual have the same advantages and the same expectations for health, adjustment, and development as children whose parents are heterosexual." The American Psychiatric Association stated in 2002 that it "supports initiatives which allow same-sex couples to adopt and co-parent children." In 2004, an Arkansas court struck down a state regulation barring gay persons and persons sharing households with gay persons from being foster parents. *Lofton v. Kearney* is significant, in part, because it runs counter to this trend.

FURTHER RESOURCES

Web sites

American Psychiatric Association. "News Release: New Position Statement Adopted by the American Psychiatric Association (APA): Adoption and Co-parenting of Children by Same-Sex Couples, December 13, 2002." <http://www.psych.org/news_room/press_releases/adoption_coparenting121802.pdf> (accessed March 8, 2006).

American Academy of Pediatrics. "News Release: AAP Says Children of Same-Sex Couples Deserve Two Legally Recognized Parents, February 4, 2002." <http://www.aap.org/advocacy/archives/febsamesex.htm> (accessed March 8, 2006).

Burch v. Smarr

Legal decision

By: Judges of the Supreme Court of Appeals of West Virginia

Date: June 17, 2005

Source: *Burch v. Smarr*: Tina B., Appellant, v. Paul S., in His Official Capacity of Next Friend and Guardian of Z.B.S., an Infant, Appellee: Appeal from the Circuit Court of Clay County, Honorable Jack Alsop, Judge, Civil Action No. 02-D-100 REVERSED. Available at <http://www.aclu.org/lgbt/parenting/12260lgl20050617.html> (accessed March 9, 2006).

About the Author: The Supreme Court of Appeals is West Virginia's highest court and the court of last resort. The five Supreme Court justices hear appeals of decisions over all matters decided in the circuit courts, including criminal convictions affirmed on appeal from magistrate court and appeals from administrative agencies.

INTRODUCTION

The Supreme Court of West Virginia's 2005 decision in the case of *Burch v. Smarr* awarded custody of an infant, "Z.B.S.," to Tina Burch, a lesbian who had co-parented the child since birth. Custody was sought by the child's biological grandparents. The Family Court of Clay County, West Virginia, awarded custody to Burch in 2002, but a West Virginia Circuit Court of Appeals reversed the decision in 2003, awarding custody to the grandparents. Burch was allowed visitation rights. The West Virginia Supreme Court reversed the circuit court's opinion, finally awarding full custody to Burch.

Tina Burch and her lover, Christina Smarr, formed a committed partnership in the late 1990s and decided to have a child together. Smarr was impregnated by a man and gave birth to a son on Christmas Day, 1999. Burch and Smarr raised the child together until Smarr was killed in a car accident in 2002.

Smarr's parents then sought custody of their grandchild. The Family Court of Clay County awarded custody to Burch on the ground that she was the child's "psychological parent," that is, she had functioned as the child's parent in every respect since birth and was fully recognized by the child as his parent. Psychological parenthood had been recognized by West Virginia courts before, but not in a case involving a gay partner.

A state court of appeals reversed the lower court's decision and gave custody to the grandparents, stating that Burch "does not have standing to seek custody of the infant child" under West Virginia law because she "is not the legal parent of Z.B.S., [and] ... the concept of 'psychological parent' [has not been extended] to include the former same sex partner of a biological parent." In other words, the concept of psychological parenthood could not be extended to a lesbian because it had never been extended to a lesbian. The Supreme Court, while agreeing that Burch was not the child's legal parent, decided that the Family Court had been right to award her custody originally: "Simply stated," the court wrote, "the child's best interests would best be served by awarding permanent custody to Tina B."

■ PRIMARY SOURCE

Justice Davis delivered the Opinion of the Court.

The appellant herein and petitioner below, Tina B., appeals from an order entered December 2, 2003, by the Circuit Court of Clay County. By the terms of that order, the circuit court denied Tina B.'s petition for custody of the minor child, Z.B.S., who Tina B. had raised from infancy with her now-deceased partner, finding that Tina B. lacked standing to seek an award of custody under W. Va. Code 48-9-103 (2001) (Repl. Vol. 2004). Additionally, the circuit court granted temporary custody of Z.B.S. to his maternal grandfather, the appellee herein and respondent below, Paul S. On appeal to this Court, Tina B. complains that the circuit court erred by finding that she lacked standing to assert her status as Z.B.S.'s psychological parent and to seek his custody in such capacity. Upon a review of the parties' arguments, the record presented for appellate consideration, and the pertinent authorities, we conclude that Tina B. is a proper party to seek custody of Z.B.S. Accordingly, we reverse the contrary decision of the Clay County Circuit Court.

Having established Tina B.'s relationship to the subject child, we next must determine whether her status as a psychological parent entitles her to intervene in proceedings seeking a determination of his custody. Under the unique facts and circumstances of this case, we agree with the family court's conclusion that Tina B. is a proper party to these proceedings and disagree with the contrary decision reached by the circuit court. Although we caution that not every psychological parent is, by virtue of such status, entitled to intervene in custodial proceedings pursuant to W.Va. Code 48-9-103(b), the very unusual and extraordinary facts of this case warrant extending that privilege to Tina B. Not only do the facts support such a finding herein, but the best interests of the subject child demand such a result. The best interests of Z.B.S. also militate in favor of an award of custody to Tina B., consistent with the result obtained by the Family Court of Clay County.

At the forefront of our decision is the counsel of the Legislature that the aim of the governing statute is to secure the best interests of the children whose custody is to be determined and to promote stability and certainty in their young lives. "The primary objective of this article is to serve the child's best interests, by facilitating [s]tability of the child [and] [c]continuity of existing parent-child attachments[.]" W.Va. Code §§ 48-9-1029(a)(1,3). This appreciation for stability in a child's life has also been a frequent refrain of this Court. "[S]tability in a child's life is a major concern when formulating custody arrangements." Snyder v. Scheerer, 190 W. Va. 64, 72-73, 436S.E.2d299,307-08 (1993) (per curiam) (citation omitted). Therefore, "in cases where a child has been in one home for a substantial period, [h]is environment and sense of security should not be disturbed without a clear showing of significant benefit to him." In re Brandon, 183 W. Va. at 121, 394S.E.2d at 523 (quoting Lemley v. Barr, 176 W. Va. 378, 386, 343 S.E.2d 101, 110 (1986) (internal quotations and citations omitted)). We would be remiss if we did not also reiterate that "[a] child has rights, too,

some of which are of a constitutional magnitude." Lemley, 176 W. Va. at 386, 343 S.E.2d at 109 (internal quotations and citations omitted). Among these, "[a] child has a right to continued association with individuals with whom he has formed a close emotional bond—provided that a determination is made that such continued contact is in the best interests of the child." Syl. pt. 11, in part, In re Jonathan, 198 W. Va. 716, 482 S.E.2d 893. Accord Snyder v. Scheerer, 190 W. Va. at 72, 436 S.E.2d at 307 (recognizing "the right of a child to continued association with those individuals to whom the child has formed an attachment"). In this regard, "[t]he length of time that the child has remained with [such individuals(s)] is a significant factor to consider in determining this issue." In re Jonathan, 198 W. Va. at 736 n.41, 482 S.E.2d at 913 n.41.

The tragic events that have led to the circumstances in which Z.B.S. currently finds himself have resulted in litigation over his permanent custodial placement only because too many people love this little boy. Oh that all of the children whose fates we must decide would be so fortunate as to be too loved. That said, it is now up to this Court to ascertain whether the family court correctly determined that Z.B.S.'s best interests would be served by awarding his custody to Tina B. first and foremost, we have determined that Tina B. is Z.B.S.'s psychological parent, with all the bonds, attachments, caretaking functions, and responsibilities that such status entails. In reaching this decision, we have found that both of the child's biological parents not only acquiesced, but actively fostered, the relationship that has developed between Tina B. and Z.B.S.

We are also persuaded by the current situation into which the child has been thrust upon the tragic death of his mother: the other parental figure with whom he has continuously resided, Tina B., is eager to legally assume his custody and to continue attending to his daily needs, and his biological father, his sole surviving legal parent, readily agrees and enthusiastically consents to such an arrangement. To reunite Tina B. and Z.B.S. through a formal custodial arrangement would be to secure the familial environment to which the child has become accustomed and to accord parental status to the adult he already views in this capacity. Simply stated, an award of custody to Tina B., having found no indication that she is unfit to serve as the minor's custodian, would promote Z.B.S.'s best interests by allowing continuity of care by the person whom he currently regards as his parent and would thus provide stability and certainty in his life.

For these reasons, then, we find that Tina B. was entitled to participate in Z.B.S.'s custodial proceedings. Accordingly, we reverse the December 2, 2003, ruling of the Clay County Circuit Court which denied Tina B. permission to participate in Z.B.S.'s custodial determination.

Furthermore, remanding this case for additional proceedings to determine Z.B.S.'s permanent custody would be futile. The family court has consistently held that the best interests of Z.B.S. dictate that his custody be awarded to Tina B., which finding is consistent with the guardian ad litem's recommendations and the psychological evidence presented below.

Simply stated, the child's best interests would best be served by awarding permanent custody of Z.B.S. to Tina B. Thus, we reinstate the July 25, 2003, decision of the Clay County Family Court awarding custody of the minor child Z.B.S. to Tina B.

SIGNIFICANCE

The West Virginia Supreme Court's decision in *Burch v. Smarr* is significant partly because of its contrast to a decision by a Virginia court in 1995, *Bottom v. Bottom*, which removed a child from the custody of his lesbian biological mother and put him in the custody of the child's grandmother (the biological mother's own mother). In that case, the state of Virginia's anti-sodomy law was invoked. The court made the distinction that while "a lesbian mother is not *per se* an unfit parent … Conduct inherent in lesbianism is punishable as a Class 6 felony in the Commonwealth [of Virginia]; thus, that conduct is another important consideration in determining custody." That is, the mother's private practice of oral sex with consenting adult women was presumed to make her guilty of a felony (although she had never been accused or convicted under the sodomy law), and it was this criminality that made her an unfit parent. Virginia sodomy laws criminalized all anal and oral sexual behaviors, not merely homosexual acts. Virginia also has laws criminalizing premarital sex. A view of lesbianism as inherently troubling was part of the court's rationale for removing the child from his mother's custody. The court said that the "moral climate in which the child is to be raised" is an "important consideration" in deciding custody. However, it also noted other factors, such as that the mother had "struck the child when it was merely one year old with such force as to leave her fingerprints on his person."

By the 1990s, Virginia was in the minority among U.S. states in retaining a sodomy law. Only fourteen U.S. states (plus Puerto Rico) retained laws outlawing sodomy as of 2003. All the other states had repealed these laws, mostly in the period 1960–1990. Thus, no mention was made of West Virginia's sodomy law in *Burch v. Smarr* because the law had been repealed in 1976. In 2003, the U.S. Supreme Court, which in 1986 had upheld the constitutionality of Georgia's anti-sodomy law, reversed itself and declared the anti-sodomy law of Texas (and, by implication, those of all other states) unconstitutional.

Burch v. Smarr reflects the ways in which the legal legitimacy of homosexuality has been increasing in U.S. society for the last several decades. However, this case was not decided on novel legal or technical grounds. The principle that a child's "psychological parent" might be properly designated the child's legal guardian had already been applied to heterosexual partners in West Virginia and to homosexual parents in other states. Further, the standard of the child's "best interests," also emphasized by the West Virginia Supreme Court, is simply the standard always cited by all courts rendering custody decisions. *Burch v. Smarr* thus typifies a trend in U.S. custody, foster-care, adoption, and parenting law toward recognizing the legitimacy of homosexuals as parents. Nevertheless, most states do not formally require equal treatment for homosexual custodians or adoptive parents, and individual family-court judges retain great power over particular decisions, often on a county-by-county basis. On-the-ground practice thus varies widely and in a patchwork way throughout the United States, despite high-profile decisions such as *Burch v. Smarr*.

FURTHER RESOURCES

Web sites

American Civil Liberties Union. "The Bigger Picture: Gay Parenting and the Law." <http://www.lethimstay.com/bigpicture_parenting.html> (accessed March 9, 2006).

American Psychological Association. "Lesbian and Gay Parenting." <http://www.apa.org/pi/parent.html> (accessed March 31, 2006).

Second-Parent Curbs Driving Same-Sex Couple from Arizona

Newspaper article

By: Stephanie Innes

Date: December 22, 2005

Source: Innes, Stephanie. "Second-Parent Curbs Driving Same-sex Couple from Arizona." *Arizona Daily Star* (December 22, 2005).

About the Author: Stephanie Innes is a newspaper reporter with the *Arizona Daily Star* and a professor of journalism at the University of Arizona. Her articles focus on faith and values.

INTRODUCTION

In the 1980s and 1990s, as same-sex couples worked toward gaining more civil and social rights in the United States, the issue of gay adoption presented a complex issue for courts, legislatures, and individuals and families. The topic of gay parenting is not new. As a result of social pressures to conform to a heterosexual ideal, gay men and women (or persons struggling with their sexual orientation) have historically entered into heterosexual marriages, had children, and later divorced, parenting their children as a "gay parent" without fanfare. Until the past two decades, gay parents generally kept their sexuality a secret or treated it as a very private matter disclosed only to close friends and family.

As homosexuality in the United States has gained greater acceptance, increasing numbers of gay couples openly choose to have children within a same-sex relationship. For lesbian couples this may involve artificial insemination of one of the partners, giving the child a biological mother with full parenting rights and a non-biological mother whose rights—depending on the state in which she resides—may vary from full parental rights to absolutely none.

Gay male couples generally use adoption of a non-biological child in their journey to parenthood, although surrogacy—hiring a woman to carry an egg fertilized with one male partner's sperm to term, at which time the baby is adopted by the male couple—is gaining popularity among gay male couples.

Each of these parenting processes presents legal and social challenges for the same-sex couples, the children in these families, and for society and government. Opponents of gay adoption claim that the children in these families suffer from social and sexual problems, as a result of being raised by two parents of the same gender. Some research studies indicate that, although being raised by gay parents does not lead to higher rates of homosexuality among offspring, the children of gay couples do experiment with homosexuality to a greater extent than do children of heterosexual parents.

Same-sex adoption proponents point to a larger (and growing) range of published research studies that show little or no difference in developmental and emotional health between children of gay parents and children of heterosexual parents. With endorsements from the American Psychiatric Association, American Academy of Pediatrics, American Academy of Family Physicians, and the American Psychological Association, gay parenting is gaining acceptance.

◼ PRIMARY SOURCE

Last week, Jeanine, Nichole and Isaac Soterwood left a home they loved, solid careers, and a wide circle of friends.

The state of Arizona does not allow them to be a legal family, so the Soterwoods moved from Tucson to California, where Nichole and Jeanine will file papers to become the legal parents of Isaac, who is 22 months old.

"This is tough for us. We love Tucson. And I had a great workplace and a promising, good career," said Nichole, 35, who was a systems engineer at Raytheon Missile Systems. "I was disappointed to leave and my co-workers at Raytheon were disappointed. But they understood that family comes first."

Like most other states, Arizona law does not allow unmarried couples to do what's known as second-parent adoption—when the non-biological parent adopts a partner's child. Stepparents in heterosexual unions can adopt the children of their spouses in Arizona. Gay couples can be foster parents. And gay people, as long as they are single, can adopt. But couples like the Soterwoods, who can't legally marry here, can't both be parents of a child.

SAME-SEX QUANDARY

Gay rights advocates say it's a growing issue because more same-sex couples are raising children. But challenging Arizona's law could backfire—lawmakers could react by passing laws prohibiting same-sex couples from adopting, as they did in Mississippi in 2000.

"Unfortunately, the political climate in Arizona is one that would not be welcoming of that change," said Amy Kobeta, director of public affairs for the Arizona Human Rights Fund. "We have a conservative Legislature, and the topic of gays and lesbians being parents is a very hot-button issue with the conservative movement."

Research by the city of Tucson's Urban Planning and Design Department, based on U.S. Census data, shows 1,253 same-sex male couples in Pima County, and 1,399 same-sex female couples, although many gay rights advocates believe those numbers are conservative because of underreporting.

At least one of three lesbian couples and one of five gay male couples are raising children nationwide, according to a 2004 research paper from the Washington, D.C.-based Urban Institute, based on an analysis of 2000

Census data. The research also says Pima County's numbers are higher than the national average for same-sex couples living with minor children.

The American Academy of Pediatrics issued a policy paper in 2002 endorsing second-parent adoption laws for same-sex couples, saying that children who are born to or adopted by one member of a same-sex couple deserve the security of two legally recognized parents.

Same-sex ballot measures

But at the moment, gay and lesbian rights advocates in Arizona are focused on preventing the passage of a proposed constitutional amendment that's slated to appear on the November 2006 general election ballot, rather than lobbying for second-parent adoption rights. The constitutional amendment, backed by a coalition that believes children should be raised in families with married, heterosexual parents, would prohibit same-sex couples from marrying and also would bar local governments from offering insurance benefits to domestic partners.

"I think the majority of Arizonans would agree that children being raised in a family of one man and one woman— a husband and a wife— is the environment we want to have in Arizona," said Nathan Sproul, a spokesman for Protect Marriage Arizona, the group backing the proposed amendment.

State Sen. Karen S. Johnson, the GOP chair of the Senate's Family Services Committee, did not return calls about second-parent adoption but sent a message through an assistant that she does not support same-sex couples. In her legislative biography, Johnson pledges to stand "resolutely against the homosexual agenda."

Kobeta noted there are alternatives same-sex parents in Arizona can use now to give the second parent power of attorney for emergency medical decisions and school record access. But she said the options are complicated and expensive, and schools and hospitals don't necessarily respect them.

Local attorney Amelia Craig Cramer knows the imperfection of those options too well. She is the former executive director of the Gay and Lesbian Alliance Against Defamation and former managing attorney for the Western office of Lambda Legal, a national group that works for the full recognition of the civil rights of lesbians, gay men, bisexuals and transgender people. She also is raising a 6-year-old child with her female partner.

"I'm the legal parent and it's in my will that my partner has guardianship, but that is not a guarantee," Craig Cramer said. "It terrifies me to think about what would happen if I were to die or become incapacitated."

2003 civil union in Vermont

The Soterwoods met as graduate students in applied mathematics at the University of Arizona in 1998. They had a commitment ceremony with 65 friends and family in 2001.

In 2003, they again exchanged vows, when they obtained a civil union in Vermont. That's when they also took the same last name, a combination of Nichole's surname, Soter, and Jeanine's last name, Smallwood.

They always knew they wanted a family and they wanted to live in Tucson, which they describe as a diverse and accepting community.

Nichole gave birth to Isaac in February 2004 and is his sole legal guardian. Every six months since his birth, she's had to fill out papers to give power of attorney to Jeanine, so Jeanine can legally make health and school decisions about Isaac.

"If, God forbid, we were to split up, I'd have no rights as a parent," said Jeanine, 31, who recently finished her doctorate at the UA, where she was an adjunct engineering instructor.

Jeanine and Nichole ultimately decided to move to Santa Clara, Calif., where Nichole already has a job and they will be near Jeanine's parents. One of the first things they'll do is sign on to California's domestic partner registry and find a lawyer to guide them through a second-parent adoption.

"I've heard of folks who have left Tucson and adopted children in another state. But they have to establish residency in that other state before they come back. It's a real hardship and it underscores the fact that we have a somewhat broken system in the United States," said Kent Burbank, executive director of Wingspan, Tucson's lesbian, gay, bisexual and transgender community center.

"If there are more people like Nichole and Jeanine leaving, it is a big loss, not just for the lesbian, gay, bisexual and transgender community, but for the community as a whole."

SIGNIFICANCE

In 1977, Florida's state legislature passed a law banning gay adoptions; in spite of recent challenges to the law, it stands, making Florida the only state in the United States to specifically ban gay adoption. Other states, including Mississippi, Oklahoma, and Utah, make it very difficult for same-sex couples to adopt. However, in all of these states, gay parents are permitted to act as foster parents. Gay adoption supporters point to this policy as hypocritical, asking why gay parents can act as substitute parents, but not as full legal parents.

More same-sex couples wishing to adopt and gain full legal protections are moving to the nine states that permit gay adoption. Part of a demographic shift, these gay couples seek out states with gay-friendly legal and social policies. While the raw number of gay couples who move for such reasons remains small as of 2006, the trend is of interest to sociologists, marketing experts, and economists, who point to a possible "brain drain" of mobile, higher-income couples with the means to move as needed and relocate based on gay-friendly policies.

At the same time, groups that oppose gay adoption, such as the Family Research Council, Concerned Women for America, and Focus on the Family, are working in sixteen states to put laws in place that would ban adoption by any gay person. The Ohio Restoration Project, a conservative Christian organization headed by Reverend Russell Johnson, seeks to ban all adoptions by gay individuals and families. Johnson is an activist who vigorously promoted passage of the Ohio Defense of Marriage Act ballot initiative in 2004. The Act defines marriage as a relationship between a man and a woman and makes any legal procedures created by same-sex couples in an imitation of marital rights (such as child custody or powers of attorney) illegal. Johnson currently is urging Ohio state legislators to pass a law banning gay adoption.

Gay rights groups, such as the Human Rights Council, claim that such laws punish many children within the foster care system, who are in need of loving, stable homes. The Child Welfare League of America, an umbrella organization representing more than 900 human services organizations, states that research shows gay parents to be as nurturing as heterosexual parents, and that decades of studies of gay parents and gay foster parents back up their claim. According to the CWLA, the crisis of the foster care system in the United States, with more than 500,000 children under state custody, would deepen if gay individuals and couples could no longer adopt or act as foster parents.

Adoptions by same-sex couples are currently legal in Andorra, Belgium, England, the Netherlands, Spain, Sweden, and Wales. Other countries permit "step-children" adoptions in which a partner in any couple can adopt a child.

FURTHER RESOURCES

Books

Gerstmann, Evan. *Same-Sex Marriage and the Constitution.* New York: Cambridge University Press, 2003.

Periodicals

Adam, Barry D. "The Defense of Marriage Act and American Exceptionalism: The 'Gay Marriage' Panic in the United States." *Journal of the History of Sexuality.* 12 (April 2003): 259–276.

Web sites

American Academy of Pediatrics. "AAP Says Children of Same-Sex Couples Deserve Two Legally Recognized Parents." <http://www.aap.org/advocacy/archives/feb-samesex.htm> (accessed February 28, 2006).

American Psychiatric Association. "Adoption and Co-Parenting of Children by Same-Sex Couples." <http://www.psych.org/news_room/press_releases/adoption_coparenting121802.pdf> (accessed February 28, 2006).

Child Welfare League of America. <http://www.cwla.org> (accessed February 28, 2006).

Ohio Restoration Project. <http://www.ohiorestorationproject.com> (accessed February 28, 2006).

4 Transgendereds and Transsexuals

Transgendereds and Transsexuals

Transgendered persons exemplify the fluidity of gender and complexity of sexuality. Transgendered individuals assume a different gender identity than that which corresponds to their physiological sex. They are men who live as women, women who live as men, and individuals who shift between genders. Transgendered persons often face a greater social stigma than their gay peers. Transgenderism is often misunderstood. Others may perceive a transgendered person as not fully masculine or feminine because they retain mannerisms and physical characteristics of their biological sex. For example, a transgendered women may retain a deeper voice and Adam's apple that many ascribe as masculine. Transgenderism is also commonly mistaken for transvestitism (dressing in the clothes of another gender). Transgendered persons do not merely changes their clothes. Many transgendered individuals feel a deep, and often life-long, psychological commitment to their assumed gender.

Transsexuals are individuals who have surgically altered their bodies to match their assumed gender identity. An article on penile reform discusses gender reassignment surgeries. Transgendered and transsexual persons typically shift genders in adulthood, meaning that friends, family, and coworkers must adjust to the individual's new gender identity. The article *Second Serve* chronicles Renee Richard's adjustment period before and after gender reassignment surgery.

Transgendereds and transsexuals can also exist in an awkward legal and social limbo. Some places do not recognize the ability of a person to change their gender or sex; others will permit altering a person's legal identification only after gender reassignment surgery. Even everyday concerns such as which restroom to use at work or a restaurant are burdened by legal and social constraints. California's efforts to aid nondiscrimination of transgendered persons are highlighted in this chapter.

By defining gender as more than the sum of genetics and genitals, and challenging social stereotypes, transgendered individuals profoundly question our assumptions of both gender and sexuality. However, questioning traditionally defined gender identities is not free of controversy.

The Intermediate Sex

A Study of Some Transitional Types of Men and Women

Book

By: Edward Carpenter

Date: 1908

Source: Carpenter, Edward. *The Intermediate Sex: A Study of Some Transitional Types of Men and Women.* 1908. Available at: <http://www.fordham.edu/halsall/pwh/carpenter-is.html> (accessed April 4, 2006).

About the Author: Edward Carpenter (1844–1929) is one of the best known of the English sexologists. A gay man and a socialist, Carpenter believed that romances that crossed class lines could break down the class barriers that plagued England. Carpenter lived with a series of working-class lovers until meeting his life partner, George Merrill, a young man from the Sheffield slums, in 1891. While he wrote widely on a range of subjects, his most influential work addressed the topic of homosexuality, especially *Love's Coming-of-Age* (1896) and *The Intermediate Sex* (1908).

INTRODUCTION

Edward Carpenter, a gay British writer, helped develop a positive sense of gay identity in the early twentieth century. At a time when Great Britain criminalized homosexual conduct, Carpenter portrayed gay men and lesbians as knowers, healers, and pioneers. He is one of the early leaders of the gay rights movement.

Carpenter is best known for his 1908 book *The Intermediate Sex*, which introduced the topic of "homogenic love." He coined and preferred the term "homogenic" rather than "homosexual" because of the latter's bizarre half-Greek, half-Latin derivation. Homogenic love was a spiritualized and altruistic attachment that owed much in conception to ancient Greek platonic love with its subordination of passion into finer emotions. People who engaged in homogenic love pointed the way through sexuality to a free society.

Carpenter saw the "intermediate sex" as a further state in human evolution. His conceptualization of the intermediate sex is derived from the idea of a third sex. Influenced by the "urning" (love between men with female souls) theories of German sexologist Karl Heinrich Ulrichs as well as the transgender figures of the berdache and shaman from Native American cultures, Carpenter identified some people as belonging to both genders. He argued that this double identity prepared such people to serve as reconcilers and interpreters between the two sexes.

PRIMARY SOURCE

More than thirty years ago, however, an Austrian writer, K. H. Ulrichs, drew attention in a series of pamphlets (Memnon, Ara Spei, Inclusa, etc.) to the existence of a class of people who strongly illustrate the above remarks, and with whom specially this paper is concerned. He pointed out that there were people born in such a position—as it were on the dividing line between the sexes—that while belonging distinctly to one sex as far as their bodies are concerned they may be said to belong mentally and emotionally to the other; that there were men, for instance, who might be described as of feminine soul enclosed in a male body (anima muliebris in corpore virili inclusa), or in other cases, women whose definition would be just the reverse. And he maintained that this doubleness of nature was to a great extent proved by the special direction of their love-sentiment. For in such cases, as indeed might be expected, the (apparently) masculine person instead of forming a love-union with a female tended to contract romantic friendships with one of his own sex; while the apparently feminine would, instead of marrying in the usual way, devote herself to the love of another feminine.

People of this kind (i.e., having this special variation of the love-sentiment) he called Urnings; [Note: From Uranos, heaven; his idea being that the Uranian love was of a higher order than the ordinary attachment. For further about Ulrichs and his theories see Appendix, pp. 157–159.] and though we are not obliged to accept his theory about the crosswise connexion between "soul" and "body," since at best these words are somewhat vague and indefinite; yet his work was important because it was one of the first attempts, in modern times, to recognise the existence of what might be called an Intermediate sex, and to give at any rate some explanation of it. [Note: Charles G. Leland ("Hans Breitmann") in his book "The Alternate Sex" (Wellby, 1904), insists much on the frequent combination of the characteristics of both sexes in remarkable men and women, and has a chapter on "The Female Mind in Man," and another on "The Male Intellect in Woman."]

Since that time the subject has been widely studied and written about by scientific men and others, especially on the Continent (though in England it is still comparatively unknown), and by means of an extended observation of present-day cases, as well as the indirect testimony of the history and literature of past times, quite a body of general conclusions has been arrived at—of which I propose in the following pages to give some slight account.

Contrary to the general impression, one of the first points that emerges from this study is that "Urnings," or Uranians, are by no means so very rare; but that they form, beneath the surface of society, a large class. It remains difficult, however, to get an exact statement of their numbers; and this for more than one reason: partly because, owing to the want of any general understanding of their case, these folk tend to conceal their true feelings from all but their own kind, and indeed often deliberately act in such a manner as to lead the world astray—(whence it arises that a normal man living in a certain society will often refuse to believe that there is a single Urning in the circle of his acquaintance, while one of the latter, or one that understands the nature, living in the same society, can count perhaps a score or more)—and partly because it is indubitable that the numbers do vary very greatly, not only in different countries but even in different classes in the same country. The consequence of all this being that we have estimates differing very widely from each other. Dr. Grabowsky, a well-known writer in Germany, quotes figures (which we think must be exaggerated) as high as one man in every 22, while Dr. Albert Moll (Die Conträre Sexualempfindung, chap. 3) gives estimates varying from 1 in every 50 to as low as 1 in every 500. [Note: Some late statistical inquiries (see Statistische Untersuchungen, by Dr. M. Hirschfeld, Leipzig, 1904) yield 1.5 to 2.0 per cent as a probable ratio. See also Appendix, pp. 134-136.] These figures apply to such as are exclusively of the said nature, i.e., to those whose deepest feelings of love and friendship go out only to persons of their own sex. Of course, if in addition are included those double-natured people (of whom there is a great number) who experience the normal attachment, with the homogenic tendency in less or greater degree superadded, the estimates must be greatly higher.

In the second place it emerges (also contrary to the general impression) that men and women of the exclusively Uranian type are by no means necessarily morbid in any way—unless, indeed, their peculiar temperament be pronounced in itself morbid. Formerly it was assumed, as a matter of course, that the type was merely a result of disease and degeneration; but now with the examination of the actual facts it appears that, on the contrary, many are fine, healthy specimens of their sex, muscular and well-developed in body, of powerful brain, high standard of conduct, and with nothing abnormal or morbid of any kind observable in their physical structure or constitution. This is of course not true of all, and there still remain a certain number of cases of weakly type to support the neuropathic view. Yet it is very noticeable that this view

is much less insisted on by the later writers than by the earlier. It is also worth noticing that it is now acknowledged that even in the most healthy cases the special affectional temperament of the "Intermediate" is, as a rule, ineradicable; so much so that when (as in not a few instances) such men and women, from social or other considerations, have forced themselves to marry and even have children, they have still not been able to overcome their own bias, or the leaning after all of their life-attachment to some friend of their own sex.

A few words may here be said about the legal aspect of this important question. It has to be remarked that the present state of the Law, both in Germany and Britain—arising as it does partly out of some of the misapprehensions above alluded to, and partly out of the sheer unwillingness of legislators to discuss the question—is really impracticable. While the Law rightly seeks to prevent acts of violence or public scandal, it may be argued that it is going beyond its province when it attempts to regulate the private and voluntary relations of adult persons to each other. The homogenic affection is a valuable social force, and in some cases a necessary element of noble human character—yet the Act of 1885 makes almost any familiarity in such cases the possible basis of a criminal charge. The Law has no doubt had substantial ground for previous statutes on this subject—dealing with a certain gross act; but in so severely condemning the least familiarity between male persons [Note: Though, inconsistently enough, making no mention of females.] we think it has gone too far. It has undertaken a censorship over private morals (entirely apart from social results) which is beyond its province, and which—even if it were its province—it could not possibly fulfil; [Note: Dr. Moll maintains (2nd ed., pp. 314, 315) that if familiarities between those of the same sex are made illegal, as immoral, self-abuse ought much more to be so made.] it has opened wider than ever before the door to a real, most serious social evil and crime—that of blackmailing; and it has thrown a shadow over even the simplest and most ordinary expressions of an attachment which may, as we have seen, be of great value in the national life.

That the homosexual feeling, like the heterosexual, may lead to public abuses of liberty and decency; that it needs a strict self-control; and that much teaching and instruction on the subject is needed; we of course do not deny. But as, in the case of persons of opposite sex, the law limits itself on the whole to a maintenance of public order, the protection of the weak from violence and insult, [Note: Though it is doubtful whether the marriage-laws even do this.] and of the young from their inexperience; so we think it should be here. The much-needed teaching and the true morality on the subject must be given—as it can only be given—by the spread of proper education and ideas, and not by the clumsy bludgeon of the statute-book. [Note: In France, since the adoption of the Code Napoleon, sexual inversion is tolerated under the same restrictions as normal sexuality; and according to Carlier, formerly Chief of the French Police, Paris is not more depraved in this matter than London. Italy in 1889 also adopted the principles of the Code Napoleon on this point. For further considerations with regard to the Law, see Appendix, pp. 164 and 165.]

Having thus shown the importance of the homogenic or comrade-attachment, in some form, in national life, it would seem high time now that the modern peoples should recognise this in their institutions, and endeavour at least in their public opinion and systems of education to understand this factor and give it its proper place. The undoubted evils which exist in relation to it, for instance in our public schools as well as in our public life, owe their existence largely to the fact that the whole subject is left in the gutter so to speak—in darkness and concealment. No one offers a clue of better things, nor to point a way out of the wilderness; and by this very non-recognition the passion is perverted into its least satisfactory channels. All love, one would say, must have its responsibilities, else it is liable to degenerate, and to dissipate itself in mere sentiment or sensuality. The normal marriage between man and woman leads up to the foundation of the household and the family; the love between parents and children implies duties and cares on both sides. The homogenic attachment, left unrecognised, easily loses some of its best quality and becomes an ephemeral or corrupt thing. Yet, as we have seen, and as I am pointing out in the following chapter, it may, when occurring between an elder and younger, prove to be an immense educational force; while, as between equals, it may be turned to social and heroic uses, such as can hardly be demanded or expected from the ordinary marriage. It would seem high time, I say, that public opinion should recognise these facts; and so give to this attachment the sanction and dignity which arise from public recognition, as well as the definite form and outline which would flow from the existence of an accepted ideal or standard in the matter. It is often said how necessary for the morality of the ordinary marriage is some public recognition of the relation, and some accepted standard of conduct in it. May not, to a lesser degree, something of the same kind (as suggested in the next chapter) be true of the homogenic attachment? It has had its place as a recognised and guarded institution in the elder and more primitive societies; and it seems quite probable that a similar place will be accorded to it in the societies of the future.

SIGNIFICANCE

Nowadays largely forgotten, British sexologist Edward Carpenter had a crucial influence on early twentieth century society. He was the best-known defender of homosexuality. Instead of seeing gay men and lesbians as demonized people, Carpenter celebrated them.

Carpenter's notion of a third sex was historically an important way of conceptualizing homosexuals. It allowed an argument to be made that homosexual traits were innate and inborn and that gay identity was as fixed and normal as heterosexual identity. Therefore, there could be no justification for condemning homosexuality. Harsh legal sanctions and religious condemnation could not change biology. Carpenter was one of the first to argue that sexual orientation is biological and not a choice.

Yet as advanced as Carpenter's theories were for the Edwardian era, he promoted stereotypes of women and gay men. Although he was a feminist, Carpenter was unable to see women outside of a maternal role and did not consider them to the extent that he focused on men. He viewed heterosexual women as participating in animalistic sex rather than the superior and spiritual homosexual sex that is divorced from reproduction. His writings are essentially the exploration of an argument between heterosexual and homosexual men. Carpenter separates homosexual desire from sexual promiscuity, but simultaneously fails to rescue homosexuality from the stereotype of effeminacy and supermasculinity.

Part of a group of theorists who sought physical causes for same-sex desire, Carpenter provided emotional support to a generation of gays and lesbians. By insisting that there was nothing wrong with homosexuality, he freed many people from self-condemnation. He influenced such writers as sexologist Havelock Ellis (1859–1939) and novelist E. M. Forster (1879–1970) and helped start the movement to liberate gays from repression.

FURTHER RESOURCES
Books

Fone, Byron R.S. *A Road to Stonewall: Male Homosexuality and Homophobia in English and American Literature, 1750–1969.* New York: Twayne, 1995.

Rowbotham, Sheila, and Jeffrey Weeks. *Socialism and the New Life: The Personal and Sexual Politics of Edward Carpenter and Havelock Ellis.* London: Pluto, 1977.

Rupp, Leila J. *A Desired Past: A Short History of Same-Sex Love in America.* Chicago: University of Chicago Press, 1999.

Transvestite

Magazine article

By: Anonymous

Date: March 18, 1929

Source: *Time* magazine, XIII, no. 11 (March 18, 1929).

About the Author: The author is a staff writer for *Time* magazine.

INTRODUCTION

Wearing the garb of the opposite sex has a long history. Records dating from the fifth century B.C. describe male cross-dressing. From the Native Amer-

ican *berdache* (a male who adopted the clothing and work of women) to the *hijra* community of India (a groups of eunuchs, transsexuals, and transvestites), some traditional cultures have invested cross-dressers with spiritual power. In other countries, however, cross-dressers have been condemned by the state, religious authorities, and medical professions. Transvestism became the term for cross-dressing in 1910, when pioneering sexologist Magnus Hirschfeld published his book *Transvestites.*

Cross-dressing became a concern in the nineteenth century as middle-class men in the U.S. and Europe began to suffer a growing anxiety about the meaning of masculinity. As they increasingly entered the professions, lived in urban environments, and sensed a loss of control with the rise of industrialization, men sought ways to bolster their masculine iden-

Marguerite Radclyffe Hall, a prizewinning writer whose novel *The Well of Loneliness* was originally banned in Britain for its sympathetic approach to female homosexuality. She is with Lady Una Trowbridge. PHOTO BY FOX PHOTOS/GETTY IMAGES

tities. The result was a new ideal of manliness that sharply distinguished men from women. Physical exertion, aggression, and martial discipline were celebrated. In this context, the 1929 discovery of an aggressive and athletic woman challenged core beliefs about the differences between men and women.

■ PRIMARY SOURCE

Transvestite

Monday, Mar. 18, 1929

Stationed in the trig military centre of Andover, Hampshire, are some of His Majesty's most gallant officers and whole regiments of British Tommies who have a cocky, engaging eye for women. Last week these connoisseurs were utterly flabbergasted when they learned that Captain Leslie Ivor Victor Gauntlett Slight Barker, D. S. O., who was universally regarded in Andover as "a gentleman, and by gad a sportsman, Sir!" is in fact a transvestite—one of the most remarkable of modern times.

Over the mantelpiece in the Officers' Club, there hangs a photograph showing several of its War-veteran members standing with their flag before the Empire's most sacred military shrine—the Cenotaph in Whitehall. Proudly erect and tall beside the flag bearer stands Captain Barker, wearing seven decorations, including the D. S. O. Last week in Andover the Captain's former valet, one Wrigley, exclaimed incredulously: "Why the Captain always left his razors and soap-filled brush for me to put away. And I used to take his boy for walks! A little tyke he was, and always talking about his daddy's exploits. I'm fair astonished! Blown, as you might say. How could anyone who wasn't at Mons know all the Captain knows about it?"

Many distinguished officers from Tidworth barracks had, it appeared, ridden to hounds and played cricket with Captain Barker. "He ascribed his difficulty in throwing the ball to War wounds," said Dr. Farr of the Cricket Club last week, "I may have sometimes thought, mind you, that Barker was built 'all wrong," He was. But there again, the poor feller was so terribly bashed in the War! Gad, I can't think of old Barker yet as a woman! The thing sticks and won't go down."

Even more remarkable was the statement of Mrs. Barker, the onetime Miss Alfreda Emma Howard, a country lass of Littlehampton, Sussex. She said last week that Transvestite Barker courted her "as any young man would"; and the Register of Brighton Parish Church reveals that they were married as man and wife on Nov. 14, 1923. "I am dazed, stunned!" exclaimed Mrs. Barker. "In our six years of married life I never once suspected

that dear Victor was a woman too!" Mrs. Barker's father, a venerable druggist, added his affirmations of astonishment.

The Captain's two children, a boy of nine and a girl of eight, are his by a previous marriage. She—"Captain" Barker"—was originally Miss Lilias Irma Valerie Barker, daughter of a rich, landed proprietor on the Isle of Jersey, Thomas William Barker, who died some 15 years ago. Miss Barker was in service at Mons and elsewhere in the War area as a Red Cross nurse and ambulance driver. In 1918 she married an Australian officer, Colonel Harold Arkell Smith, who begot her two children. Some five years later she discovered her tendency to transvestism, yielded to it, renounced home and family, courted and married Druggist's Daughter Alfreda Emma Howard, moved to the congenial military centre of Andover, and found apparent happiness.

Captain Barker's means were apparently derived at this time from the British Organization of Fascists. As secretary of these young, Conservative zealots she led them in numerous "Raids on Reds" during the British General Strike, and did valiant service in breaking up Communist mass meetings in Hyde Park.

With the recent disbandment of the British Fascists, Captain Barker, penniless, sent Mrs. Barker home to her druggist father, exchanged her military uniform for a sleek cutaway, and was employed early last week to welcome guests with unctuous politeness by London's irreproachable Regent's Palace Hotel.

Unable to pay a judgment assessed by a London court, last week, Reception Clerk Barker submitted quietly to arrest for "contempt of court," and was driven in a patrol wagon to Brixton Prison for males. After scrutinizing Transvestite Barker, the prison surgeon ordered her transferred to Holloway Jail for females. Some 24 hours later the Bankruptcy Court ordered her release, and she left Holloway Jail in women's clothes by a side entrance, thus escaping the peering eyes of a vulgar throng of at least 1,000 male and female Britons, most of whose vocabularies do not even yet contain the noun transvestite, the verb transvestize, the adjective transvestile, the adverb transvestily. Example: 'Transvestizing herself she became transvestile so transvestily that she may fairly be called a transvestite."

The newspaper of world's largest circulation, London's Daily Mail, presently presented its 2,000,000 readers with My Own Story by "Captain Barker." Excerpts:

"I was reared as a boy and always thought a boy had a jolly good time.

"The first tragedy of my life was when the man I loved and should have married was made a prisoner early in the War. Now I am fond of nobody and have no feelings—I only adore my son."

SIGNIFICANCE

To many people in the nineteenth and twentieth centuries, transvestism was a sexual perversion. The German neuropsychiatrist Richard von Krafft-Ebing first categorized it as a pathological behavior in 1886. By 1952, the American Psychiatric Association listed male, but not female, transvestism as an illness in its *Diagnostic and Statistical Manual.*

Only in the late twentieth century did this label come under attack. As part of the sexual revolution of the 1960s, transvestites began to organize. In 1961, Virginia Price, also known as Charles Price, founded Hose and Heels, the first support group for male cross-dressers; women cross-dressers tended to find support within the butch-femme lesbian community. In contrast, the vast majority of male transvestites are heterosexual. Hose and Heels (known after 1962 as Full Personality Expression) merged with Mamselle in 1976 to form the Society for the Second Self, the largest heterosexual transvestite organization to date. Studies of male transvestites have revealed that many dress in male clothing by day and wear women's clothing for the purpose of sexual arousal.

New definitions of masculinity that incorporate transvestism have not been widely accepted. For women, the situation is dramatically different. The general relaxation in clothing standards in the late twentieth century has made it acceptable for women to dress in many types of male attire. Additionally, the increasing opportunities available to women in employment and everyday life make it unnecessary for a woman to attempt to pass as a male to enjoy privileges once reserved only for men.

FURTHER RESOURCES
Books

Allen, J. J. *The Man in the Red Velvet Dress: Inside the World of Cross-Dressing.* New York: Carol Publishing Group, 1996.

Bullough, Vern L., and Bonnie Bullough. *Cross Dressing, Sex, and Gender.* Philadelphia: University of Pennsylvania Press, 1993.

Garber, Marjorie. *Vested Interests: Cross-Dressing and Cultural Anxiety.* New York: Harper Perennial, 1993.

Penile Reform

Journal article

By: Jack Penn

Date: July 1963

Source: Penn, Jack. "Penile Reform." *British Journal of Plastic Surgery* 16 (July 1963).

About the Author: Jack Penn was born in Cape Town, South Africa, in 1909. A plastic surgeon by training, he worked in South Africa, Scotland, Japan, Taiwan, Israel, and the United States. During World War II (1938–1945) he was a battlefield surgeon and later treated atomic bomb victims in Japan.

INTRODUCTION

The ritual of male circumcision predates the Bible; while Jewish men were circumcised as part of religious ritual, ancient Greeks and Romans specifically forbade circumcision in their respective societies. Muslims consider the procedure a part of Islam, although the Koran does not specifically mention it. Unlike Jewish males, who are circumcised on the eighth day after birth, Muslim boys experience the ritual at an older age, after they recite the Koran in full, around the onset of puberty.

European and United States physicians began to call for routine infant male circumcision in the mid-nineteenth century. Physicians such as Jonathan Hutchinson, a British doctor, proposed a connection between overexcitement of the sexual organs and maladies such as epilepsy, hysteria, and mental illness. According to Hutchinson's theory, overexcitement and stimulation, caused by the friction of the foreskin (or prepuce) against the glans of the penis, led to more frequent masturbation. Excessive masturbation, especially at a young age, led to an increased sexual appetite, which allegedly drove men to use prostitutes, leading to the spread of venereal disease.

Hutchinson used data on Jewish men, who were circumcised as part of their religious beliefs, to examine venereal disease rates in 1850s London. His research, later proven to be faulty, showed an alleged connection between circumcision and lower rates of sexually transmitted disease. By circumcising males in infancy, he theorized, mental illness as well as sexual disease could be curtailed.

Other physicians, such as gynecologist Isaac Baker Brown, proposed similar theories concerning

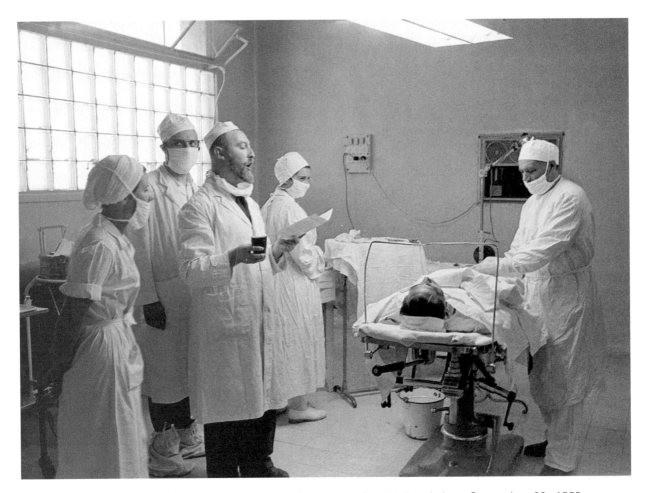

A Japanese convert to Judaism is circumcised in the Sha'are Tzedeq hospital on September 20, 1960. © DAVID RUBINGER/CORBIS

females and the clitoral hood, but female circumcision did not gain the popularity that secular male circumcision gained in the late 1800s and early 1900s. By the 1910s, female circumcision had been relegated to a tiny fraction of babies born with ambiguous genitalia, while increasing numbers of boys born in the United States and Britain were circumcised shortly after birth.

During World War II, the concept of foreskin restoration emerged as a protective measure for Jewish men attempting to conceal their religious identity. Fear of concentration camps in German-occupied areas fed an underground movement of foreskin restoration, though the method was crude and left the person vulnerable to infection.

By 1963, when South African plastic surgeon Jack Penn developed the surgical technique noted below, the circumcision rate in the United States was nearly 80 percent.

PRIMARY SOURCE

By Jack Penn, F.R.C.S.

Johannesburg

Mr. E., aged 35 years, was concerned about the fact that he had a circumcised penis and did not like it. He wished to have his prepuce replaced. He agreed to having psychological investigation. The report submitted indicated a markedly psychological disturbance due to his circumcision and that he was normal in every other way. Surgical repair was then offered.

The operation consisted of a "degloving" of the skin of the penis by means of a circumferential incision at the base of the penis with the skin pulled forward to cover the glans. A free graft was then applied to cover the entire new area from the tip of the new prepuce to the base of the glans. The result was satisfactory physically and the patient was completely rehabilitated psychologically.

SIGNIFICANCE

Foreskin restoration via surgery was uncommon in 1963, when Penn performed this operation, and the idea of "uncircumcision" was greeted with great skepticism in medical circles. The resulting foreskin reconstruction is not a true foreskin, in that the nerve endings present in the foreskin found in the frenar band and Meissner's corpuscles, which account for approximately 40 percent of penile nerve sensation and arousal, cannot be replicated or created via surgical or other methods.

Plastic surgeons in the U.S. perform foreskin restoration surgeries at a cost of between $10,000–$50,000. Three operations are often required, with a 70 percent success rate. Unlike Penn's technique, in most modern surgical restorations the surgeon removes a portion of the scrotum to sculpt a foreskin that has a mucosal quality to it.

Foreskin restoration via foreskin stretching is another technique that is used to create a foreskin. In Greek society, Jewish men used weights on the ends of their existing foreskin to stretch it; the process, called epispasm, helped to cover the exposed glans. By the mid 1970s, a small group of men in the United States began to self-restore, using complex stretching techniques. By applying a series of weights to the existing foreskin, these men slowly stretched the skin over a period of 1–3 years, eventually creating a sheath around the glans of the penis.

The National Organization of Restoring Men (NORM), an organization devoted to men who wish to restore their foreskins surgically or via stretching techniques, does not keep statistics on men who stretch their foreskins (labelled "tuggers"), but in 2000, the organization estimated that 20,000 men worldwide were actively stretching foreskins for restoration. Restorers claim that while they can never replicate the original foreskin, a restored foreskin can provide heightened sexual sensation and protect the glans, helping to undo keratinization, or the build up of skin cells in the glans that occurs over time when it is exposed by circumcision.

Routine infant circumcision ended in England in 1949, and the Canadian Academy of Pediatrics has not recommended the procedure since 1981. In 1999, the American Academy of Pediatrics issued a policy that routine infant circumcision holds no medical benefits.

From a high point of eighty-five percent in 1975, the circumcision rate in the United States steadily decreased to fifty-five percent in 2003. The circumcision rate in the United Kingdom was approximately four percent in 2003.

FURTHER RESOURCES

Books

Darby, Robert J. *A Surgical Temptation : The Demonization of the Foreskin and the Rise of Circumcision in Britain.* Chicago: University of Chicago Press, 2005.

Gollaher, David L. *Circumcision: A History of the World's Most Controversial Surgery.* Basic Books, 2000.

Periodicals

Dawson, Benjamin E. "Circumcision in the Female: Its Necessity and How to Perform It." *American Journal of Clinical Medicine* 22, no. 6 (June 1915).

Schultheiss, Dirk, M.D. "Uncircumcision: A Historical Review of Preputial Restoration." *Plastic and Reconstructive Surgery* 101, no. 7 (June 1998): 1990–1998.

Web sites

American Academy of Pediatrics. "Circumcision Policy Statement" <http://pediatrics.aappublications.org/cgi/content/abstract/103/3/686> (accessed March 22, 2006).

National Organization of Restoring Men <http://www.norm.org> (accessed March 22, 2006).

Second Serve

Book excerpt

By: Renee Richards

Date: 1983

Source: Richards, Renee. *Second Serve.* New York: Stein and Day, 1983.

About the Author: Richard Raskind, a naval officer, eye surgeon, and professional tennis player, sought gender reassignment surgery in 1975 at the age of forty. As a woman he chose the name Renee Richards, reestablished his medical practice in a different state, and went on to play professional women's tennis and coach players such as Martina Navratilova.

INTRODUCTION

Richard Raskind, born in 1934, was the captain of his tennis team at Yale and went on to become a

Renee Richards returns serve during the U.S. Open Competition at Forest Hills, New York, on September 1, 1977. AP/WIDE WORLD PHOTOS. REPRODUCED BY PERMISSION.

nationally ranked tennis player on the men's tennis circuit in the 1950s and early 1960s. An opthalmologist by training, Raskind served as an officer in the Navy, followed a traditional medical career path, and spent much of his first forty-one years in conflict about his gender identity.

Raskind, a male heterosexual by birth, felt compelled to become a female heterosexual. From the age of six Raskind felt different from other little boys, and as he hit puberty his gender identity confusion only deepened. In the 1950s in the United States, social sexual norms involved a strict dichotomy between male and female; in many states homosexual acts were criminal, and transsexuality was virtually unheard of. In 1952, American Christine Jorgensen became the first known American to undergo gender reassignment surgery, in Denmark. Her case made national headlines and was the first introduction to the concept

of transsexuality for most Americans. Raskind came of age during this time, secretly cross-dressed, and finally pursued treatments to change his gender. In the meantime, he lived a very conventional, successful life as a tennis player and accomplished eye surgeon.

In the late 1960s, Raskind used hormones to grow breasts and change his figure and appearance to be more feminine. He traveled to Europe for a complete sex change operation but stopped himself on the day of the surgery, unsure of his decision. He returned to the U.S., altered his appearance to resume life as a man, married a woman, and had a child. He also drank heavily and dealt with a wide range of psychological problems, which he detailed in his autobiography. In 1975, at the age of forty one, Richard Raskind underwent genital reassignment surgery and became Renee Richards, an alter-ego he had invented during his childhood and adolescence.

PRIMARY SOURCE

It was as if someone had slipped me a mood-elevating drug. The world seemed less antagonistic, more supportive; I had a sense of lightness as I moved through it. Dick had always been a presence of great density; many people found him aloof, superior. The burgeoning Renee found herself less inclined to isolation, more interested in the people around her. I suddenly began to feel more personally about people who had heretofore been defined primarily by my formal relations with them. So-and-so was my nurse. So-and-so was my anesthesiologist. My efforts in their behalf (and often I bent over backward) were in the line of duty. I went to the captain's mast to speak up for my corpsmen, not out of humanitarian feeling but because it was my duty; it was dictated by an abstract code of fair play. They did for me, and in return I did for them. It was all very civilized but, at the same time, distant. As treatment progressed, I found myself more and more interested in personal details. In some instances my friendships began to alter. One doctor and his wife who had been longtime associates of mine noticed a peculiar shift in my orientation. For most of our relationship I had treated the wife as a tolerable but fairly uninteresting part of the duo. Her conversation centered primarily around the kids and the intricacies of homemaking. I preferred to discuss medicine and tennis strategies with her husband rather than commiserate with her over her son's inability to master a two-wheeled bike. Slowly though I began to find myself more able to be concerned with the homey details of housewifery. If the husband left the room to go to the bathroom, on his return he might find me gone. Looked for, I could be found in the kitchen watching his wife do the dishes and savoring her chatty resume of the day's events. I know that they discussed this between themselves. She was impressed with how much more human I had become. He thought maybe I was planning a seduction. Years later they finally understood.

SIGNIFICANCE

Richards discusses her struggles to get medical doctors to approve her gender reassignment surgery; gender identity disorder is considered by many medical professionals to be a psychiatric disorder rather than a medical condition requiring hormonal and surgical treatment. After arguing with psychiatrists and surgeons, Raskind/Richards completed the transformation and attempted to get on with her new life.

An avid tennis player as Richard Raskind, Renee Richards wished to continue to play. On August 27, 1976, Renee Richards was barred from competing as a woman in the U.S. Tennis Open on the grounds that she would fail a chromosome test and therefore could not qualify as a woman. The story made the front page of newspapers worldwide; the U.S. Tennis Association expressed concerns that if Richards were permitted to play, it would open professional sports to male athletes who would change genders simply to gain a competitive advantage.

Richards sued for the right to play, and in 1977 the New York state Supreme Court found in Richards' favor. On the court, Richards lost her first round, but in later years won a title, coached Martina Navratilova for two years, and retired from tennis in 1981.

A 1986 television movie titled *Second Serve* and starring Vanessa Redgrave as Raskind/Richards brought Richards back into the spotlight briefly. In a 1999 interview, Richards expressed some ambiguity concerning the gender reassignment: "As far as being fulfilled as a woman, I'm not as fulfilled as I dreamed of being. I get a lot of letters from people who are considering having this operation… I say that you'd better get on Prozac or any other medication available, or get locked up or do whatever it takes to keep you from being allowed to do something like it."

A 2004 decision by the International Olympic Committee to permit transsexuals to compete in the Olympics cleared the way for transsexuals to compete in categories based on their gender reassignment rather than their chromosomes. Renee Richards, now a respected pediatric opthalmologist in New York City, publicly questioned the decision, citing concern that transsexuals should be considered on a case-by-case basis rather than opening Olympic sports to potential fraud.

FURTHER RESOURCES
Books

Lev, Arlene Ister. *Transgender Emergence: Therapeutic Guidelines for Working with Gender-Variant People and their Families*. New York: Haworth Press, 2004.

Levit, Nancy. *The Gender Line: Men, Women, and the Law*. New York: New York University Press, 1998.

Meyerowitz, Joanne. *How Sex Changed: A History of Transsexuality in the United States*. Cambridge, Mass.: Harvard University Press, 2002.

Periodicals

Pfafflin, Friedemann, and Astrid Junge. "Sex Reassignment: Thirty Years of International Follow-up: A Comprehensive Review, 1961–1991." *International Journal of Transgenderism* (1998).

Shmerler, Cindy. "Regrets, She's Had a Few." *Tennis* 35, 2 (March 1999).

The Hard Part

Book excerpt

By: Kate Bornstein

Date: 2005

Source: Bornstein, Kate. *Gender Outlaw: On Men, Women, and the Rest of Us.* New York: Routledge, 1995.

About the Author: Kate Bornstein is a transsexual author, gender theorist, performance artist, and author of numerous books and plays.

INTRODUCTION

Kate Bornstein was born Albert Bornstein to parents in North Dakota; his father was a Lutheran minister and his mother had been Miss Betty Crocker of 1939. Bornstein was aware from an early age that his sense of gender identity was not "normal," that is, in agreement with the male and female options—boy/girl, man/woman—that he perceived in the people around him. Bornstein eventually underwent sex-change surgery and hormone treatments to become physically female and became a performance artist and influential author of books on gender issues. Although the word "he" has been used here to refer to Bornstein prior to the sex-change surgery, Bornstein herself and many other transgender persons often prefer various newly coined gender-ambiguous pronouns such as "ze" (which substitutes for "he" or "she") and "hir" (which substitutes for "her" or "his").

Bornstein's books include *Hello, Cruel World: 101 Alternatives to Teen Suicide, My Gender Workbook, Nearly Roadkill, Kate Bornstein Is a Queer and Pleasant Danger,* and *Gender Outlaw* (the book from which the selection given here is taken). She has toured widely speaking on gender, sex, and teen suicide.

▮ PRIMARY SOURCE

Our Changing Sense of Self

The hard part was sorting it all out. The hard part was taking a good look at everyone else and the way they looked at the world, which was a lot different from the way *I* was looking at the world! ...

I know I'm not a man—about that much I'm very clear and I've come to the conclusion that I'm probably not a woman either, at least not according to a lot of people's rules on this sort of thing. The trouble is, we're liv-ing in a world that insists we be one or the other—a world that doesn't bother to tell us exactly what one or the other *is*....

All my life, my non-traditional gender identity had been my biggest secret, my deepest shame. It's not that I didn't want to talk about this with someone; it's just that I never saw anything in the culture that encouraged me to talk about my feeling that I was the wrong gender. When I was growing up, people who lived cross-gendered lives were pressured into hiding deep within the darkest closets they could find. Those who came out of their closets were either studied under a microscope, ridiculed in the tabloids, or made exotic in the porn books, so it paid to hide. It paid to lie. That was probably the most painful part of it: the lying to friends and family and lovers, the pretending to be someone I wasn't. Going through a gender change is not the easiest thing in the world to do, but I went through it because I was so tired of all the lies and secrets....

Nowadays, I try to make it easier for people to ask questions. I tell people that I've never been hurt by an honest question, and that's true: it's a cruel opinion that hurts, not a question. But people still don't ask questions easily; maybe that has something to do with manners or etiquette. Folks seem to naturally back off from inquiring as to the nature of someone's—my—gender. It seems to need some special setting. Like in my living room, or on television, or from behind a podium at some university. It's "good manners" to say and ask nothing, and that's sad. But the children still ask....

For the most part, people cautiously observe and don't ask questions, and there are plenty of opportunities in today's world to look at people like me. The talk show ratings go way up during sweeps month when they trot out the transsexuals and the cross-dressers. Then there are the drag shows and the female impersonator spectacles—even though we began them for our own entertainment and enjoyment, their widespread popularity seems to grow and grow; you've probably got one of those shows in your city, or in a nearby town. Comedy skits, like "It's Pat" (a skit based on a person whose gender is not clear) on *Saturday Night Live* are real popular....

If I look past the ghettos of the drag bars and standup joints, both popular music and cinema reflect my transsexual face back to me. Glance discreetly, if you will, at some of the brightest deities in our cultural heavens. At this writing, some friends of mine are truly interested in seeing if Michael Jackson (all his other issues aside) will actually become Diana Ross. I've heard bets being placed on the gender of some of Madonna's lovers in some of her videos. And what really made *The Crying Game* the smash hit that it was? It's interesting that we can ask questions about transgender issues when there's some distance between us and the person we're asking about—we just don't ask directly.

There's a lot of writing bout gender now. I keep reading the magazine articles, the newspaper columns, and the text books, pre- and post-modern. I read, watch, and listen to all the ads and commercials. You can learn a lot about gender from those commercials. I've also been watching the talk shows, listening to the call-in programs, and browsing the electronic bulletin boards. When I was very young, growing up in the 50s, I read the medical texts, devoured the tabloids, and hoarded the pornography—because I was intensely interested in me and my people. I was scared, though, shaking scared, to see what I might actually find out. But I couldn't stop reading.

SIGNIFICANCE

Many thinkers have, in recent decades, distinguished between "sex" and "gender." Sex, in this view, refers to the physical "equipment" of sexuality: one can deduce the sex of most people by examining their bodies. About one person in 2,000, however, is born with both male and female sex organs. Such individuals are called "hermaphrodites" (a combination of the names Hermes and Aphrodite, male and female Greek gods) or "intersexed." Surgery and hormones can "correct" this condition, but such treatment is increasingly controversial: some argue that to not make intersexed children definitely male or female is cruel, others argue that to do so is cruel.

"Gender," meanwhile, is a more elusive or psychological concept. Gender is defined as a person's self-concept: male, female, or something else. This may or may not correspond with their sex. That is, people with male sex organs may view themselves as male, female, or both simultaneously. Persons whose genders do not match their physical sex, who are intersexed, or who have had surgery to make their physical sex conform approximately to their gender, are often termed "transgender" persons. They may or may not adopt the dress and mannerisms of the opposite sexuality (for example, a physically male person who considers his gender female may or may not dress as a woman). Transgender persons who have had their bodies transformed surgically are "transsexuals."

But this is only the beginning of the distinctions and categories that might be listed. Vocabulary proliferates with the varieties of human sexual desire and behavior. Kate Bornstein herself has argued that while there is a fixed list of human gender categories, there is a continuum of genders or sexual self-concepts. Moreover, she argues that gender is not fixed or static even for individuals. "I think we do change our gen-

Masae Torai, a Japanese transsexual who was born a woman and underwent a sex change in the United States, spoke outside parliament's Upper House in Tokyo on July 2, 2003 against the discrimination towards Japanese transexuals. Soon after, parliament's Upper House approved a bill allowing Japanese transexuals to change their gender. © REUTERS/CORBIS

ders all the time … In response to each interaction we have with a new or different person, we subtly shift the kind of man or woman, boy or girl, or whatever gender we're being at the moment."

A loosely unified transgender movement has come into being over the last few decades; as Bornstein puts it, this movement "seeks to position gender as an identity we build for ourselves, rather than something we're born with." It is closely associated with the gay and lesbian liberation movements, which in turn have modeled themselves after the feminist and civil rights movements.

The transgender movement advocates the passage of two types of laws: those that protect them from discrimination in housing and employment, and hate crime laws, which specify specific penalties for violent crimes motivated by the victim's gender. As of February 2006, eight states—California, Hawaii, Illinois,

Maine, Minnesota, New Mexico, Rhode Island, and Washington—have statewide transgender-inclusive antidiscrimination laws. At least seven states—California, Hawaii, Minnesota, Missouri, New Mexico, Pennsylvania, and Vermont—have transgender-inclusive hate crime laws. The "hate crime" concept, however, is controversial in legal circles: it is defended by many experts, but others argue that it criminalizes motives rather than actions.

The transgender movement's fluid views of gender are not commonly accepted. Many religious and social conservatives assert that sex should directly determine gender, and that persons whose sexual self-concepts and behaviors do not match their physical sex are guilty of a morally reprehensible choice or, possibly, victims of a psychological disorder.

FURTHER RESOURCES

Web sites

Public Broadcasting System. "Georgie Girl: An Interview with Kate Bornstein" (June 20, 2003). Available at <http://www.pbs.org/pov/pov2003/georgiegirl/special_quiz_kate.html> (accessed March 19, 2006).

National Gay and Lesbian Task Force. "Transgender Civil Rights Project" (2005). Available at <http://www.thetaskforce.org/ourprojects/tcrp/index.cfm> (accessed March 19, 2006).

American Medical Student Association. "Transgender and Transsexuality" <http://www.amsa.org/advocacy/lgbtpm/> (accessed March 19, 2006).

Hijras Are Women: Third Gender Rights in India

Photograph

By: Indranil Mukherjee

Date: June 23, 2004

Source: AFP/Getty Images

About the Photographer: Indranil Mukherjee is a staff photographer for AFP/Getty Images. Her portfolio includes thousands of published photographs across a broad spectrum of news and feature stories.

INTRODUCTION

Hijras occupy a third-gender role and are considered a sub-caste throughout Indian culture. They reside largely in secretive subcultures located in Bombay, Hydrabad, Ahmedabad, Delhi, Southern India, Pakistan, and Bangladesh. Hijras are primarily defined as men who dress and act like women. However, the definition is deeper. These men wear women's jewelry and brightly adorned saris. They refer to themselves with the feminine pronoun and expect others to do so as well. Ideally, hijras renounce sexual desires and practices by undergoing castration in order to be reborn as hijras. The term hijras derives from the Urdu word meaning "impotent ones" and they claim ancient lineages. Some are born with deformed or missing genitalia, while others optionally become castrated in their youth. Although true hijras are eunuchs, a significant proportion participate in sexual activities, either in the form of prostitution or in relations with their husbands.

Through the ambiguous gender identification of the hijras and confrontational practices of the group, they are viewed by many in their native countries as dirty outcasts with no shame, or social pariahs. However, the group has been institutionalized into the culture through tradition. There is a religious context for the hijras within Indian culture. In one tale, after the god Siva is asked to create the world, he disappears for 1,000 years. In his absence, the gods Vishnu and Brahma become impatient and create other gods and beings. Siva reappears ready to perform his creation and is angered by the actions of Vishnu and Brahma. He brakes off his linga, or phallus, and throws it to earth where it becomes a source of universal fertility. In the same context, as a hijras relinquishes his own fertility, he becomes gifted with universal procreative powers. As a result, many hijras derive their social and religious legitimacy from this tradition. Believed to possess the power to bestow fertility on a newly wed couple or on children, hijras often appear uninvited to weddings or birth parties. They perform dances and demand gifts or threaten the couple or child with curses. If a gratuity is not offered to the hijras, they will threaten to expose themselves. Hijras are also known to beg for money and engage in prostitution.

Hijras live in a communal setting under the guidance of a "guru." The hijras, upon entrance into the guru's household, takes the guru's surname and receives training in the activities of the household and culture. The hijras becomes a "chelas," or disciple and is supervised by the guru. They are expected to relinquish earnings, from performances at weddings and birth parties, begging, or prostitution, to their guru. The guru is expected to meet the chelas basic needs of food, clothing, and shelter.

PRIMARY SOURCE

HIJRAS ARE WOMEN: THIRD GENDER RIGHTS IN INDIA

See primary source image.

SIGNIFICANCE

An estimated two million hijras live in India. Although many occupy a marginalized minority within the country, many are becoming politically active. Since 1998, hijras have won local, state, and national elections, sometimes outperforming the prevailing political parties. In 2001, the All-India convention of Hijras met in Rohtak, a farming town northwest of Dehli. Over 1,000 hijras met to create a political strategy. One slogan of the hijras political campaigns states, "You don't need genitals for politics; you need brains and integrity."

Beginning in 1998, Shobha Nehru won a city council seat in Hissor, located in the Northern Indian state of Haryana. In 2000, "Aunt" Shabnam won a state legislative assembly position. Also in 2000, Kamla Jaan was elected mayor of Katni, a prosperous mining town in central Madhya Pradesh. Asha Devi was also elected to a mayoral position. Remarkably, these candidates ran as hijras. They identified themselves as genderless, without ties to tradition, families, and castes. As a result, they were able to promote a platform free from corruption within prevailing Indian politics. Even still, politicians use the label of "hijras" to call opponents who appear to be impotent of power or political will.

In addition to political power, hijras have been instrumental in the creation of HIV/AIDS awareness and human rights organizations such as Dai Welfare Society and the Hijra Kalyan Sabha.

PRIMARY SOURCE

Hijras Are Women: Third Gender Rights in India: An individual calls for equal rights for hijras with a poster in Bangalore, India on June 23, 2004. INDRANIL MUKHERJEE/AFP/GETTY IMAGES

Indian hijras pose for photos during a meeting to discuss a High Court Judgement in Madras, on March 25, 2004. DIBYAN-SHU SARKAR/AFP/GETTY IMAGES

FURTHER RESOURCES

Periodicals

Reddy, Gayatry. "'Men Who Would be Kings: Celibacy, Emasculation, and the Re-Production of Hijras in Contemporary Indian Politics". *Social Research* (Spring, 2003): 70, 1.

Web Sites

Worldpress.org. "Pakistan's Hijras: Feminine Soul, Masculine Body." <http://www.worldpress.org/Asia/845.cfm> (accessed April 10, 2006).

Custody Case Turns to Anatomy

Newspaper article

By: Alicia Caldwell

Date: January 26, 2002

Source: Caldwell, Alicia. "Custody Case Turns to Anatomy." *St. Petersburg Times* (January 29, 2002).

About the Author: Alicia Caldwell is a reporter for the Associated Press.

INTRODUCTION

Since the first successful gender reassignment surgery in Germany in 1931, transsexuals—people who choose to modify their bodies through surgery, hormones, or both, to become the opposite sex—have been a small, but growing, portion of Western society.

In many cultures, some form of transsexuality has been documented. In India, the Hijra, boys of the lower caste who choose to be castrated before puberty and live life as a woman, are a small sector of society that defies gender dichotomy. In the 1600s, Europeans came in contact with male Illini Indians in North America who dressed as women and openly acted out the role of women in their culture. Most recently in Western society, transsexuals undergo extensive psychiatric testing, surgical sexual reassignment surgery, and hormone treatments to accomplish the conversion from the body of the sex into which they were born to the body of the opposite sex.

Many transsexuals are parents long before deciding to undergo a surgical change from one sex to the other. When a mother or a father makes the decision to change his or her gender, the impact on the transsexual's partner and children can be complicated and challenging. If the partner is heterosexual, will the transsexual's change make the partner "gay"? How do children deal with having Mommy become a male, both biologically and legally? If the transsexual person decides to change his or her name, how do children handle the change in identity or the parent's birth name?

Current law, both at the state and federal level, was not designed to handle sex changes. Family law courts have had to face questions about adoptions and custody issues, addressing questions such as: Is transsexuality itself a sign of psychological disturbance? If so, should children be placed in the care of transsexuals? If a child was adopted by a man and a woman in a U.S. state where gay adoption is illegal (such as Florida), and one partner undergoes sexual reassignment surgery, is the adoption invalid?

The following article addresses the child custody battle between Michael Kantaras and Linda Kantaras for legal custody of their two children. Michael Kantaras, born Margo Kantaras, was a female-to-male transsexual. He underwent gender reassignment surgery before meeting Linda and Linda knew about his transsexuality before marrying him.

■ PRIMARY SOURCE

CLEARWATER— The issue would seem to have little relevance in a child custody dispute: The definition of masculinity.

But it was a central topic in hours of testimony Monday as transsexual Michael Kantaras continued his battle in Pinellas-Pasco Circuit Court to get custody of his two children from his ex-wife, Linda Kantaras.

It was a day filled with explicit testimony about the anatomy of people who have undergone sexual reassignment surgery and the resulting sexual and psychological function. No question, it seemed, was too intrusive.

"It is horrifying to us to have to delve into this level of detail about Michael's treatment," said Shannon Minter, a lawyer from the National Center for Lesbian Rights, who is serving on Michael Kantaras' legal team. "The only reason we are doing so is because we have to

protect his relationship with his children. She (Linda Kantaras) is forcing him to prove he is male. It is very embarrassing."

Michael Kantaras, 42, of Holiday, began life as Margo Kantaras, but was overwhelmed with feelings that she ought to be a man. In 1986, she underwent sexual reassignment surgery: surgeons removed her breasts and reproductive organs and prescribed hormone therapy to help in the transition from Margo to Michael. The resulting physique, and the effect of the absence of a penis, was something Claudia Wheeler, Linda Kantaras' lawyer, asked numerous questions about.

"This is a world where a lot of things aren't perfect," said Collier Cole, a psychologist from Galveston, Texas, who treated Michael Kantaras before and after surgery. "It doesn't make anybody less of a parent."

Cole said in his years of treating people who have undergone sexual reassignment surgery, he has seen many transsexuals go on to have productive lives with partners, marrying and raising children. The children involved in the dispute are a 10-year-old girl the couple conceived through artificial insemination with sperm from Michael Kantaras' brother, and a 12-year-old boy whom Linda Kantaras conceived in another relationship, but whom Michael Kantaras adopted shortly after birth.

Linda and Michael Kantaras separated in 1998 after Michael became attracted to another woman and had an affair.

■

SIGNIFICANCE

Part of the focus of the Kantaras' custody dispute became Michael Kantaras' sexuality and the effect it had on his ability to parent in a psychologically healthy fashion. In traditional child custody conflicts between the legal parents of minor children, the psychological health of the parents can be used in court as a mitigating factor in examining which parent is best suited to act as primary guardian for the children. At times in family court and custody issues, sexuality can come into play as well, in terms of the romantic partners a parent may choose to have enter into their children's lives.

As experts from gay rights organizations such as the National Center for Lesbian Rights and the Human Rights Campaign note, when transsexuals are involved in child custody hearings, the transsexual's choice to undergo gender reassignment surgery itself is often used against the transsexual. Gender identity disorder is considered to be a diagnosable psychiatric condition in the *Diagnostic and Statistical Manual of Mental Disorders-IV*, the manual used by psychiatrists and psychologists to diagnose mental illness. Lawyers for the opposing parent, like Linda Kantaras' lawyer, can use the transsexual's choice to make surgical and hormonal changes to convert to the opposite sex against the transsexual.

The Kantaras' custody battle, however, involved more than Michael Kantaras' transsexualism. Under Florida state law, same-sex marriage is illegal. Linda Kantaras' lawyers argued that Michael Kantaras was a woman, in spite of his sex change operation. In court, the lawyers used detailed evidence and asked intimate questions about Michael Kantaras' anatomy and his sex life with Linda to prove that he was not fully male and therefore the marriage was between two women rather than between a man and a woman. Adoption by gay partners is illegal under Florida law; therefore, had Linda Kantaras' lawyers been successful in their claim that Michael was not a man, the marriage would have potentially been invalid, as well as his adoption of the two children. Linda Kantaras, as the biological mother of the two children, would have been granted custody.

The Kantaras' case garnered headlines, was the subject of talk shows such as *Dr. Phil* and brought the subject of transsexualism and parenting into the media spotlight. In 2001, Michael Kantaras was granted temporary custody of the children; the judge stated that Linda Kantaras had unfairly used Michael Kantaras' transsexuality as a wedge between her children and their father. In February 2003, a Florida judge granted Michael Kantaras primary custody. In the ruling, the judge said that Michael Kantaras' sexual self-identity as a man, as well as the surgical and hormonal changes Kantaras went through, were sufficient for him to be considered a man according to the law, therefore making the Kantaras' marriage and Michael Kantaras' adoption of the children legal.

FURTHER RESOURCES

Books

Lev, Arlene Ister. *Transgender Emergence: Therapeutic Guidelines for Working with Gender-Variant People and their Families.* Binghamton, N.Y.: Haworth Press, 2004.

Levit, Nancy. *The Gender Line: Men, Women, and the Law.* New York: New York University Press, 1998.

Meyerowitz, Joanne. *How Sex Changed: A History of Transsexuality in the United States.* Cambridge, Mass.: Harvard University Press, 2002.

Pfäfflin, Friedemann, and Astrid Junge. *Sex Reassignment: Thirty years of International Follow up: A Comprehensive Review, 1961–1991.* (International Journal of Transgenderism electronic book, 1998), <http://www.symposion.com/ijt/pfaefflin/1000.htm> (accessed March 31, 2006).

Web sites

TransParentcy. <http://www.transparentcy.org/index.htm> (accessed March 12, 2006).

In re Jose Mauricio LOVO-Lara, Beneficiary of a Visa Petition

Legal decision

By: U.S. Department of Justice, Executive Office for Immigration Review, Board of Immigration Appeals

Date: May 18, 2005

Source: "In re Jose Mauricio LOVO-Lara, Beneficiary of a Visa Petition filed by Gia Teresa LOVO-Ciccone, Petitioner." Board of Immigration Appeals, U.S. Department of Justice, May 18, 2005.

About the Author: The Executive Office for Immigration Review (EOIR) was created on January 9, 1983. It is not charged with enforcing immigration laws. The agency is simply responsible for interpreting and administering federal immigration laws. The Board of Immigration Appeals (BIA), an appellate body within EOIR, is charged with hearing visa petition appeals from the Department of Homeland Security's Citizenship and Immigration Services division. BIA decisions are effective as precedent that must be recognized by federal immigration-related agencies.

INTRODUCTION

The definition of marriage has been the subject of enormous political debate. While gays and lesbians seek formal recognition of their partnerships, others have argued that acknowledging such relationships threatens the institution of marriage. Opponents of gay marriage succeeded in passing the Defense of Marriage Act (DOMA) in 1996, which defined marriage as a union between a man and a woman.

In 2005, the marriage debate became more complicated when a man and a woman who had formerly been a biological man attempted to obtain the protection of marriage on the grounds that they were an opposite sex couple. The Lovo case involved the validity of an immigrant visa petition filed by an American citizen, Gia Teresa Lovo-Ciccone, who was born male in North Carolina in 1973. Lovo-Ciccone underwent a sex reassignment operation to become female in

Jiffy Javenella and his wife, Donita Ganzon at home, in Los Angeles. Ganzon was born a male and underwent a sex change operation. Marriages involving someone who has had a sex change pose many legal questions. AP IMAGES

allows a person to change their sex designation after an operation, the petitioner is legally a woman and the marriage is between partners of opposite sexes.

▌ PRIMARY SOURCE

IN RE JOSE MAURICIO LOVO-LARA, BENEFICIARY OF A VISA PETITION FILED BY GIA TERESA LOVO-CICCONE, PETITIONER

File A95 076 067 - Nebraska Service Center

Decided May 18, 2005

U.S. Department of Justice
Executive Office for Immigration Review
Board of Immigration Appeals

(1) The Defense of Marriage Act, Pub. L. No. 104–199, 110 Stat. 2419 (1996), does not preclude, for purposes of Federal law, recognition of a marriage involving a postoperative transsexual, where the marriage is considered by the State in which it was performed as one between two individuals of the opposite sex.

(2) A marriage between a postoperative transsexual and a person of the opposite sex may be the basis for benefits under section 201(b)(2)(A)(i) of the Immigration and Nationality Act, 8 U.S.C. § 1151(b)(2)(A)(i) (2000), where the State in which the marriage occurred recognizes the change in sex of the postoperative transsexual and considers the marriage a valid heterosexual marriage.

FOR PETITIONER: Sharon M. McGowan, Esquire, New York, New York

FOR THE DEPARTMENT OF HOMELAND SECURITY: Allen Kenny, Service Center Counsel

BEFORE: Board Panel: GRANT, HESS and PAULEY, Board Members.

GRANT, Board Member:

In a decision dated August 3, 2004, the Nebraska Service Center ("NSC") director denied the visa petition filed by the petitioner to accord the beneficiary immediate relative status as her husband pursuant to section 201(b)(2)(A)(i) of the Immigration and Nationality Act, 8 U.S.C. § 1151(b)(2)(A)(i) (2000). The petitioner has appealed from that decision. The appeal will be sustained.

I. FACTUAL AND PROCEDURAL HISTORY

The petitioner, a United States citizen, married the beneficiary, a native and citizen of El Salvador, in North Carolina on September 1, 2002. On November 20, 2002, the petitioner filed the instant visa petition on behalf of the beneficiary based on their marriage. The record reflects that when the petitioner was born in North Carolina on April 16, 1973, she was of the male sex. How-

2001 and received a new birth certificate from North Carolina that designated her as female. She married a man from El Salvador, Jose Mauricio Lovo-Lara on September 1, 2002 and filed a visa petition on his behalf in November 2002. The federal government opposed the petition on the grounds that DOMA precluded the recognition of this marriage. Jose Lovo-Lara remained in the U.S. legally under a temporary protected immigration status while the case proceeded.

On May 18, a BIA panel consisting of judges Edward R. Grant, Frederick D. Hess, and Roger Pauley decided that recognizing transgendered marriage for immigration purposes was not forbidden by DOMA. A review of DOMA indicated that the legislation was intended by Congress to forbid federal recognition of marriages between homosexuals with the terms "same sex" and "homosexual" used throughout the congressional debate. Since North Carolina

ever, an affidavit from a physician reflects that on September 14, 2001, the petitioner had surgery that changed her sex designation completely from male to female.

In support of the visa petition, the petitioner submitted, among other documents, her North Carolina birth certificate, which lists her current name and indicates that her sex is female; the affidavit from the physician verifying the surgery that changed the petitioner's sex designation; a North Carolina court order changing the petitioner's name to her current name; the North Carolina Register of Deeds marriage record reflecting the marriage of the petitioner and the beneficiary; and a North Carolina driver's license listing the petitioner's current name and indicating that her sex is female.

On August 3, 2004, the NSC director issued his decision denying the instant visa petition. In support of his denial, the NSC director stated that defining marriage under the immigration laws is a question of Federal law, which Congress clarified in 1996 by enacting the Defense of Marriage Act, Pub. L. No. 104–199, 110 Stat. 2419 (1996) ("DOMA"). Pursuant to the DOMA, in order to qualify as a marriage for purposes of Federal law, one partner to the marriage must be a man and the other partner must be a woman. In his decision the NSC director stated as follows:

> While some states and countries have enacted laws that permit a person who has undergone sex change surgery to legally change the person's sex from one to the other, Congress has not addressed the issue. Consequently, without legislation from Congress officially recognizing a marriage where one of the parties has undergone sex change surgery... this Service has no legal basis on which to recognize a change of sex so that a marriage between two persons born of the same sex can be recognized.

The NSC director concluded that "since the petitioner and beneficiary were born of the same sex, their marriage is not considered valid for immigration purposes and the beneficiary is not eligible to be classified as the spouse of the petitioner under section 201(b) of the Act."

The petitioner filed a timely Notice of Appeal (Form EOIR-29) and subsequently filed a brief in support of her appeal. The Department of Homeland Security ("DHS") Service Center Counsel also filed a brief in support of the NSC director's decision.

II. ISSUE

The issue presented by this case is whether a marriage between a postoperative male-to-female transsexual and a male can be the basis for benefits under section 201(b)(2)(A)(i) of the Act, where the State in which the marriage occurred recognizes the change in sex of the

postoperative transsexual and considers the marriage valid.

III. ANALYSIS

In order to determine whether a marriage is valid for immigration purposes, the relevant analysis involves determining first whether the marriage is valid under State law and then whether the marriage qualifies under the Act.

We find that the petitioner's marriage to the beneficiary is considered valid under the laws of the State of North Carolina. We also note that neither the NSC director nor the DHS counsel has asserted anything to the contrary on this point.

The dispositive issue in this case, therefore, is whether the marriage of the petitioner and the beneficiary qualifies as a valid marriage under the Act. Section 201(b)(2)(A)(i) of the Act provides for immediate relative classification for the "children, spouses, and parents of a citizen of the United States." The Act does not define the word "spouse" in terms of the sex of the parties. However, the DOMA did provide a Federal definition of the terms "marriage" and "spouse" as follows:

> In determining the meaning of any Act of Congress, or of any ruling, regulation, or interpretation of the various administrative bureaus and agencies of the United States, the word 'marriage' means only a legal union between one man and one woman as husband and wife, and the word 'spouse' refers only to a person of the opposite sex who is a husband or a wife.

Neither the DOMA nor any other Federal law addresses the issue of how to define the sex of a postoperative transsexual or such designation's effect on a subsequent marriage of that individual. The failure of Federal law to address this issue formed the main basis for the NSC director's conclusion that this marriage cannot be found valid for immigration purposes. As stated above, the NSC director found that because Congress had not addressed the issue whether sex reassignment surgery serves to change an individual's sex, there was no legal basis on which to recognize a change of sex. Accordingly, he concluded that he must consider the marriage between the petitioner and the beneficiary to be a marriage between two persons of the same sex, which is expressly prohibited by the DOMA.

In determining the effect of the DOMA on this case, we look to the rules of statutory construction. The starting point in statutory construction is the language of the statute. See INS v. Cardoza-Fonseca, 480 U.S. 421, 431 (1987); INS v. Phinpathya, 464 U.S. 183, 189 (1984). If the language of the statute is clear and unambiguous, judicial inquiry is complete, as we clearly "must give effect to the unambiguously expressed intent of Congress." Chevron,

U.S.A., Inc. v. Natural Resources Defense Council, Inc., 467 U.S. 837, 843 (1984). We find that the language of section 3(a) of the DOMA, which provides that "the word 'marriage' means only a legal union between one man and one woman as husband and wife, and the word 'spouse' refers only to a person of the opposite sex who is a husband or a wife," is clear on its face. There is no question that a valid marriage can only be one between a man and a woman. Marriages between same-sex couples are clearly excluded.

We therefore conclude that the legislative history of the DOMA indicates that in enacting that statute, Congress *only* intended to restrict marriages between persons of the same sex. There is no indication that the DOMA was meant to apply to a marriage involving a post-operative transsexual where the marriage is considered by the State in which it was performed as one between two individuals of the opposite sex.

There is also nothing in the legislative history to indicate that, other than in the limited area of same-sex marriages, Congress sought to overrule our long-standing case law holding that there is no Federal definition of marriage and that the validity of a particular marriage is determined by the law of the State where the marriage was celebrated. *See Matter of Hosseinian*, 19 I& N Dec. 453, 455 (BIA 1987). While we recognize, of course, that the ultimate issue of the validity of a marriage for immigration purposes is one of Federal law, that law has, from the inception of our nation, recognized that the regulation of marriage is almost exclusively a State matter. *See, e.g., Boddie v. Connecticut*, 401 U.S. 371 (1971); *Sherrer v. Sherrer*, 334 U.S. 343 (1948)

The DHS counsel appears to argue that in determining whether a particular marriage is valid under the DOMA, we must look to the common meanings of the terms "man" and "woman," as they are used in the DOMA. Counsel asserts that these terms can be conclusively defined by an individual's chromosomal pattern, i.e., XX for female and XY for male, because such chromosomal patterns are immutable. However, this claim is subject to much debate within the medical community. According to medical experts, there are actually eight criteria that are typically used to determine an individual's sex. They are as follows:

1. Genetic or chromosomal sex—XX or XY;
2. Gonadal sex—testes or ovaries;
3. Internal morphologic sex—seminal vesicles/prostate or vagina/uterus/fallopian tubes;
4. External morphologic sex—penis/scrotum or clitoris/labia;
5. Hormonal sex—androgens or estrogens;
6. Phenotypic sex (secondary sexual features)—facial and chest hair or breasts;

7. Assigned sex and gender of rearing; and
8. Sexual identity.

See Julie A. Greenberg, *Defining Male and Female: Intersexuality and the Collision Between Law and Biology*, 41 Ariz. L. Rev. 265, 278 (1999).

While most individuals are born with 46 XX or XY chromosomes and all of the other factors listed above are congruent with their chromosomal pattern, there are certain individuals who have what is termed an "intersexual condition," where some of the above factors may be incongruent, or where an ambiguity within a factor may exist. *Id.* at 281. For example, there are individuals with a chromosomal ambiguity who do not have the typical 46 XX or XY chromosomal pattern but instead have the chromosomal patterns of XXX, XXY, XXXY, XYY, XYYY, XYYYY, or XO. *Id.* Therefore, because a chromosomal pattern is not always the most accurate determination of an individual's gender, the DHS counsel's reliance on chromosomal patterns as the ultimate determinative factor is questionable.

Moreover, contrary to the suggestion of the DHS counsel, reliance on the sex designation provided on an individual's original birth certificate is not an accurate way to determine a person's gender. Typically, such a determination is made by the birth attendant based on the appearance of the external genitalia. However, intersexed individuals may have the normal-appearing external genitalia of one sex, but have the chromosomal sex of the opposite gender. *Greenberg, supra*, at 283–92. Moreover, many incongruities between the above-noted factors for determining a person's sex, and even some ambiguities within a factor, are not discovered until the affected individuals reach the age of puberty and their bodies develop differently from what would be expected from their assigned gender. *Id.* at 281–92.

We are not persuaded by the assertions of the DHS counsel that we should rely on a person's chromosomal pattern or the original birth record's gender designation in determining whether a marriage is between persons of the opposite sex. Consequently, for immigration purposes, we find it appropriate to determine an individual's gender based on the designation appearing on the current birth certificate issued to that person by the State in which he or she was born.

IV. CONCLUSION

We have long held that the validity of a marriage is determined by the law of the State where the marriage was celebrated. The State of North Carolina considers the petitioner to be a female under the law and deems her marriage to the beneficiary to be a valid opposite-sex marriage. We find that the DOMA does not preclude our recognition of this marriage for purposes of Federal law. As the NSC director did not raise any other issues regarding the validity of the marriage, we conclude that the marriage between the petitioner and the beneficiary may be the basis for benefits under section 201(b)(2)(A)(i) of the Act. Accordingly, the petitioner's appeal will be sustained, and the visa petition will be approved.

ORDER:

The petitioner's appeal is sustained, and the visa petition is approved.

SIGNIFICANCE

The Lovo decision reaffirmed that the federal government will defer to the states to define marriage. The BIA concluded that if a marriage is valid in the state in which it is entered into, it should be recognized for immigration purposes. Such a decision overturned a memorandum issued on April 14, 2004 by the Citizenship and Immigration Services (CIS). The memorandum stated that all marriage-based immigration petitions would be denied where one spouse was a transsexual.

For most of U.S. history, immigration law forbade the granting of legal status to immigrants who exhibited "sexual deviation." In 1990, the phrase was eliminated from immigration laws as a basis for keeping gays and lesbians from entering the country. In 1994, Attorney General Janet Reno directed the Immigration and Naturalization Service to consider sexual orientation as a legitimate basis for political asylum. Gays and lesbians could gain asylum if they could prove that they had suffered persecution in their native countries or could document a well-founded fear of future persecution.

The first person in the U.S. to benefit from the United Nations Convention Against Torture and Other Cruel, Inhuman, or Degrading Treatment or Punishment was a transgendered man from Nicaragua. Oscar Serrano, also known as Amanda DuValle, was tortured and raped in 1996 by Nicaraguan immigration officers because she was a transsexual. She had just been deported by the U.S. for immigrating illegally. DuValle returned illegally to the U.S. and escaped deportation a second time in 1999 by invoking the torture convention.

As the Lovo matter went through the legal system, a transgender man who fled Jose Lovo-Lara's home of El Salvador was trying to remain in the U.S. Luis Reyes-Reyes did not have a sex change operation but lived as a woman. For being transgendered, he was tortured by the El Salvador police. He was the victim of officially tolerated gay-bashing. He immigrated illegally to Los Angeles to avoid further abuse. In 2002, immigration judges ordered him to be deported. In 2004, the Ninth U.S. Circuit Court of Appeals overturned the decision because U.S. law bars deportation of illegal immigrants to countries in which they would face torture.

The CIS memorandum that was overturned in the Lovo case had the potential to cause significant harm because of the dangers of being gay in other nations. While Lovo did not address the risk of torture, the subject was raised by gay activists who celebrated the decision.

FURTHER RESOURCES

Books

I Do/I Don't: Queers on Marriage, edited by Greg Wharton and Ian Philips. San Francisco: Suspect Thoughts Press, 2004.

Same-Sex Marriage: The Moral and Legal Debate, edited by Robert M. Baird and Stuart E. Rosenbaum. Amherst, N.Y.: Prometheus Books, 2004.

Periodicals

Leonard, Arthur S. "Panel OKs Transgendered Marriage." *Gay City News* 4, 21 (June 1, 2005): 1–2.

AB 1586 California's Anti-Discrimination Law for Transgendered Persons

Legislation

By: California State Legislature

Date: September 29, 2005

Source: California State Legislature. "AB 1586 Anti-Discrimination Law for Transgendered Persons." (September 29, 2005): 1283–1297.

About the Author: The California State Legislature has a tradition of being the among most progressive legislative bodies in the United States on social policies involving equal rights for minorities.

INTRODUCTION

California's Anti-Discrimination for Transgendered Persons law (also known as the Insurance Gender Non-Discrimination Act), was introduced by

Sue Upmeyer, center, holds up a sign in protest, during a Westminster School Board meeting. Westminster is the only school in the state of California that has not signed off on the new state directive that would protect the rights of transgender students. AP IMAGES

Assembly member Paul Koretz (D-West Hollywood) and signed into law by Governor Arnold Schwarzenegger on September 29, 2005. The law was the first effort by any state to protect transgendered people from discrimination in health care coverage. It added gender and gender identity to existing anti-discrimination provisions in California laws regulating insurance companies and health care service plans. Despite existing anti-discrimination statutes, many transgendered people in California suffered health care discrimination. They were either denied the option to purchase insurance or denied coverage for medically necessary procedures.

Transgender people may have undergone sex reassignment surgery to go from male-to-female or female-to-male, or altered their bodies with hormones. Transition-related health care and services can include blood work, hormones, mental health therapy,

surgical removal of the breasts and chest reconstruction, breast augmentation, and genital reconstruction. People who have the legal gender of the opposite sex may also need medical care appropriate to their original sex. For example, a female-to-male transgender person may now be legally male, but may still have need for gynecological care. Additionally, transgender people often suffer substance abuse issues that relate both to their gender identity problems and to widespread discrimination against the transgendered.

In 2002, the Transgender Law Center released a report, "Trans Realities: A Legal Needs Assessment of San Francisco's Transgender Communities," that stated that ninety-three percent of the transgender people surveyed had utilized medical services as part of their transition to the other sex. Nearly one in three respondents experienced some form of health care-related gender identity discrimination, including routine denial of coverage by health insurers and discriminatory behavior by health care providers and office staff. A 1999 Transgender Community Health Project study discovered that over half of transgender people were uninsured, while thirteen percent of male-to-female transgenders and thirty-nine percent of female-to-male respondents reported being denied or experiencing difficulties in obtaining health care.

PRIMARY SOURCE

THE PEOPLE OF THE STATE OF CALIFORNIA DO ENACT AS FOLLOWS:

SECTION 1. Section 1365.5 of the Health and Safety Code is amended to read:

1365.5.

(a) No health care service plan or specialized health care service plan shall refuse to enter into any contract or shall cancel or decline to renew or reinstate any contract because of the race, color, national origin, ancestry, religion, sex, marital status, sexual orientation, or age of any contracting party, prospective contracting party, or person reasonably expected to benefit from that contract as a subscriber, enrollee, member, or otherwise.

(b) The terms of any contract shall not be modified, and the benefits or coverage of any contract shall not be subject to any limitations, exceptions, exclusions, reductions, copayments, coinsurance, deductibles, reservations, or premium, price, or charge differentials, or other modifications because of the race, color, national origin, ancestry, religion, sex, marital status, sexual orientation, or age of any contracting party, potential contracting party, or person reasonably expected to benefit from that contract as a subscriber, enrollee, member, or otherwise; except that premium, price, or charge differentials because of the sex or age of any individual when based on objective, valid, and up-to-date statistical and actuarial data are not prohibited. Nothing in this section shall be construed to permit a health care service plan to charge different premium rates to individual enrollees within the same group solely on the basis of the enrollee's sex.

(c) It shall be deemed a violation of subdivision (a) for any health care service plan to utilize marital status, living arrangements, occupation, sex, beneficiary designation, ZIP Codes or other territorial classification, or any combination thereof for the purpose of establishing sexual orientation. Nothing in this section shall be construed to alter in any manner the existing law prohibiting health care service plans from conducting tests for the presence of human immunodeficiency virus or evidence thereof.

(d) This section shall not be construed to limit the authority of the director to adopt or enforce regulations prohibiting discrimination because of sex, marital status, or sexual orientation.

SEC. 2. Section 10140 of the Insurance Code is amended to read:

10140.

(a) No admitted insurer, licensed to issue life or disability insurance, shall fail or refuse to accept an application for that insurance, to issue that insurance to an applicant therefore, or issue or cancel that insurance, under conditions less favorable to the insured than in other comparable cases, except for reasons applicable alike to persons of every race, color, religion, sex, national origin, ancestry, or sexual orientation. Race, color, religion, national origin, ancestry, or sexual orientation shall not, of itself, constitute a condition or risk for which a higher rate, premium, or charge may be required of the insured for that insurance. Unless otherwise prohibited by law, premium, price, or charge differentials because of the sex of any individual when based on objective, valid, and up-to-date statistical and actuarial data or sound underwriting practices are not prohibited.

(b) Except as otherwise permitted by law, no admitted insurer, licensed to issue disability insurance policies for hospital, medical, and surgical expenses, shall fail or refuse to accept an application for that insurance, fail or refuse to issue that insurance to an applicant therefore, cancel that insurance, refuse to renew that insurance, charge a higher rate or premium for that insurance, or offer or provide different terms, conditions, or benefits, or place a limitation on coverage under that insurance, on the basis of a person's genetic characteristics that may, under some circumstances, be associated with disability in that person or that person's offspring.

(c) No admitted insurer, licensed to issue disability insurance for hospital, medical, and surgical expenses, shall seek information about a person's genetic characteristics for any nontherapeutic purpose.

(d) No discrimination shall be made in the fees or commissions of agents or brokers for writing or renewing a policy of disability insurance, other than disability income, on the basis of a person's genetic characteristics that may, under some circumstances, be associated with disability in that person or that person's offspring.

(e) It shall be deemed a violation of subdivision (a) for any insurer to consider sexual orientation in its underwriting criteria or to utilize marital status, living arrangements, occupation, sex, beneficiary designation, ZIP Codes or other territorial classification within this state, or any combination thereof for the purpose of establishing sexual orientation or determining whether to require a test for the presence of the human immunodeficiency virus or antibodies to that virus, where that testing is otherwise permitted by law. Nothing in this section shall be construed to alter, expand, or limit in any manner the existing law respecting the authority of insurers to conduct tests for the presence of human immunodeficiency virus or evidence thereof.

(f) This section shall not be construed to limit the authority of the commissioner to adopt regulations prohibiting discrimination because of sex, marital status, or sexual orientation or to enforce these regulations, whether adopted before or on or after January 1, 1991.

SEC. 3. This act is not intended to mandate that health care service plans or insurers must provide coverage for any particular benefit, nor is it intended to prohibit sound underwriting practices or criteria based on objective, valid, and up-to-date statistical and actuarial data. Rather, the purpose of this act is to prohibit plans and insurers from denying an individual a plan contract or policy, or coverage for a benefit included in the contract or policy, based on the person's sex, as defined.

SIGNIFICANCE

On January 1, 2006, two new California laws took effect that marked the first state efforts to ban all forms of transgender discrimination. AB 1586, the Insurance Gender Non-Discrimination Act, combined with AB 1400, the Civil Rights Act of 2005, to make California into the most protective state for transgender rights in the nation. Transgender people obtained legal safeguards against discrimination in health care coverage, education, employment, housing, foster care, and public accommodation.

In the past, a number of California localities, including Oakland, San Francisco, and San Jose passed ordinances protecting transgender people from discrimination. The ordinances covered all city facilities as well as all business establishments that were open to the general public, such as restaurants, cafes, and shops. Of particular value and in answer to a long-standing complaint, the laws allowed transgendered people access to restrooms and dressing rooms appropriate for the gender that they identified with, even if it is different from their biological gender. The ordinances were not prompted by any one particular instance, although transgendered people had long complained about harassment by police. The laws also did not immediately transform hostile attitudes toward transgendered people, with discrimination remaining enough of a concern to prompt the statewide protective legislation.

The California laws were an attempt to provide a powerful tool for creating lasting social change. It will take some time for the effects of the laws to be fully felt. However, their symbolic value is already being felt by transgendered people who have been told that their well-being is a matter of public policy concern.

FURTHER RESOURCES
Books

Lev, Arlene Istar. *Transgender Emergence: Therapeutic Guidelines for Working with Gender-Variant People and Their Families* . New York: Haworth, 2004.

Rice, Califia-Patrick. *Sex Changes: The Politics of Transgenderism*. San Francisco: Cleis, 2003.

Web sites

Transgender Law Center. <http://www.transgenderlaw.org> (accessed March 26, 2006).

Why Be Just One Sex?

Magazine article

By: Gloria Kim

Date: September 12, 2005

Source: Kim, Gloria. "Why Be Just One Sex?" *MacLean's* 118, no. 37 (September 12, 2005): 52–53.

About the Author: Gloria Kim is a staff writer for *MacLean's* magazine.

INTRODUCTION

Transsexuality, in which members of one biological sex adopt the physical attributes of the other, emerged as an independent sexual orientation in the mid-twentieth century, distinct from homosexuality and transvestism. In an attempt to maintain the gender norms considered necessary to social order, however, physicians and psychologists defined transsexuality in negative terms.

The growth of medical technology did little to change negative attitudes towards transsexuals, but did make it possible for such individuals to change their anatomy. The earliest case of sex reassignment surgery (SRS) apparently occurred in Germany in 1930 when a hermaphrodite designated to be male received ovaries. By midcentury, Scandinavia led the world in SRSs. The first known American transsexual, Christine Jorgensen (formerly known as George W. Jorgensen, Jr.) traveled to Denmark in 1952 for the surgery. The publicity surrounding Jorgensen's operation helped educate the public about the differences between homosexuality, transvestism, and transsexuality.

After the Jorgensen case, American physicians began to offer SRS to men. Women seeking SRS continued to face strong opposition, a difference due in part not only to the difficulties of constructing an artificial penis, but also a cultural resistance to allowing women to claim masculinity and its privileged status. The best-known transsexuals have received male-to-female surgery, including mountain climber Jan Mor-

The "Miss International Queen" pageant celebrates transvestite and transgender contestants from 10 different countries. The winner of 'Miss International 2005' Mimi Mark (center) is photographed with runner up Yu Ri (left) and second runner up Tiptantree Rujiranon, in Pattaya, Thailand on October 29, 2004. AP IMAGES

ris (James Morris) and tennis player Renee Richards (Richard Raskin) in the 1970s.

PRIMARY SOURCE

THE FIRST THING THAT strikes you about Sally is her eyes. Bright blue, they're the kind that inspire songs. The next thing you notice is how she moves. Sally is poised the way dancers are, the result of taking movement classes with a runway model. She inspires courtliness from those around her, including the waiter who helps her into her chair. By the time you notice her muscular build and she tells you she was born in a male body and lives about half the time as a man, it's too late. You already think of this 45-year-old as a woman.

Sally (not her real name) is one of a growing group of people who identify not as male or female, but as trans-

gendered. It's an umbrella term that describes people who are born of one biological sex but feel they belong to the other, or both, and don't necessarily want sex reassignment surgery. "There's definitely a social movement of transgendered people trying to break down the binary system and expressing themselves in whatever way they want," says Lukas Walther, a counselor at the Vancouver-based Transgender Health Program and a female-to-male transsexual. "There's more fluidity with bodies and gender and freedom of expression."

"They even have new terms, "gender-queer' or 'gender-fluid,'" says Rupert Raj, counselor at the Toronto-based Sherbourne Health Centre, and himself a transsexual who was born female. "They mean an openness to not being boxed in to either sexual orientation or gender identity. Sometimes they want hormones and no surgery. Sometimes they want surgery and no hormones. Sometimes they don't want either."

Most people are familiar with transsexuals, who have had sex-change operations, such as much-publicized individuals Christine Jorgensen (the ex-GI turned blond bombshell performer in the 1950s), Tula (actress Caroline Cossey), a Bond girl in *For Your Eyes Only,* and tennis star Renee Richards. But society and the medical community are just learning about transgendered people. The American Psychiatric Association's Diagnostic and Statistical Manual of Mental Disorders IV classifies transgenderism and transsexualism as disorders (in much the same way homosexuality was considered a mental illness before it was de-listed in 1973), and estimates that "roughly 1 per 30,000 adult males and 1 per 100,000 adult females seek sex-reassignment surgery." But many health care professionals believe a substantial number of cases are not reported, because of a lingering social stigma and the fact that many transgendered people don't seek surgery.

GROWING UP as a boy, Sally had no words to describe what she felt. "Harry," as we'll call him, just knew he was different. He was always more comfortable with his mother than his aggressive father, and he enjoyed trying on his sister's clothes. His dad "wanted me to play hockey and be a man's man," Sally recalls, "and I just couldn't be that for him." During puberty, Harry found out about cross-dressers or transvestites. This, he thought, must be him. After all, he didn't want a sex-change operation, so he wasn't a transsexual. Besides, he was attracted to women. He married and went on to run his own business. Privately, with his wife's support, he indulged in cross-dressing. Then one summer, while they were vacationing in California, a salesgirl in a fetish store gave him an entire makeover—hair, clothes and makeup. Harry walked out of the store as Sally, knowing there was something more to his feelings than just having fun wearing his wife's panties.

Many people like Sally consider themselves gender outlaws, playing outside the standard definitions of man and woman. But current thinking on gender is coming around to the concept that sex, like sexual preference, isn't an either/or proposition, but rather a continuum. Transgender studies have become a hot new area of scholarship as more transgendered academics come out and publish. Philosophy professor Michael Gilbert of Toronto's York University is a "committed cross-dresser" who started teaching periodically as Miqqi Alicia Gilbert in 1996, after he received tenure. "When we're born, the doctor takes a peek between our legs and says, 'Oh, it's a boy or girl,' and that's the end of it," Gilbert notes. "But there are a huge number of people who are not comfortable with that. Not all are cross-dressers or transsexuals. Some are tomboys who resent having to play a feminine role. Some are 'sissies' who didn't want to play sports

but were forced to. I think of gender as analogous to eyesight—there are many different prescriptions."

Scientists are learning there's much more to sexual differentiation than just what's between our legs. First comes chromosomal differentiation—XY for men, XX for women. Then we develop either ovaries or testes. Next comes the difference in genitalia and, finally, the differentiation of the brain into male and female. In 1995, scientists at the Netherlands Institute for Brain Research and Amsterdam's Free University Hospital found there's one brain structure essential to sexual behaviour that develops between the ages of 2 and 4, as a result of interaction between the developing brain and sex hormones. When they are examined this area of the brain in male-to-female transsexuals, they found it matched those of females more than males.

Nature furnishes multiple examples of gender variation. Stanford University biologist Joan Roughgarden, herself a transsexual, shows in her book *Evolution's Rainbow: Diversity, Gender and Sexuality in Nature and People* that in plants and about half of the animal world, the most common body form is both male and female, either simultaneously or at different times of life. Many species have three or more genders. Roughgarden challenges the prevailing notion that diversity in biology is a deviation from an ideal "norm." Instead, she suggests diversity is the norm. She cites data indicating the incidence of male-to-female transsexualism in the U.S. is close to one in 500.

And ambiguous gender identity among humans isn't just a modern Western phenomenon. Various societies have traditions of transgendered people. In Polynesia, the transgendered are often called *mahu* (half-man, half-woman), and are identified before the onset of puberty. Among North American First Nations, transgendered people—known as "two-spirited"—have been held in high esteem, serving as religious leaders or warriors.

OF MI'KMAQ heritage, Alec Butler, born Audrey, identifies as two-spirited. He's a playwright, filmmaker and "trans" policy adviser at the 519 Church Street Community Centre in Toronto. At 46, without having had surgery or hormone treatment, he looks like a stocky, grey-bearded male rocker. "It's not that I felt that I was a guy," he says, "it's just that from an early age, I knew that I wasn't a girl. I was always getting mistaken for a boy, even when I was little." When puberty hit and Audrey started growing facial hair, her alarmed parents took her to see a slew of doctors, all of whom were puzzled. Eventually, she moved to Toronto from Cape Breton Island and started to grow a beard. She was spat on and called names because she had breasts she didn't bind. At 40, Audrey took the final step, changed her name to Alex and assumed a male identity.

Such indignities are not uncommon. "Trans people are one of the only groups left that people feel they have the right to insult to their faces," says Walther in Vancouver. "I have clients come in regularly who've had coffee thrown on them." The discrimination extends to the medical community, where many believe either that cross-gender behaviour can be corrected, or that the transgendered should be encouraged to get a full sex-change operation.

Vancouver MP Bill Siksay sees a need for better legal protection for people caught up in gender issues. The NDPer has introduced a private member's bill, given first reading in May, that would amend the Human Rights Act to include gender identity and gender expression as prohibited grounds of discrimination. "In terms of formal or legislative equality, trans rights are the next frontier," says Gilles Marchildon, executive director of Egale Canada, a gay, lesbian, bi, and trans advocacy group in Ottawa. "Trans people are where the gay and lesbian rights movement was a couple decades ago."

Unemployment, homelessness, suicidal tendencies, and self-harm—all are issues health care workers cite as commonplace among trans people. Even the simplest pleasures, like going to the gym or swimming pool, are out for someone like Alec Butler, Still, trans people like Sally and Alex prefer not to have surgery. "I don't have a penis," says Alec, "but I have a penis in my head. I don't think genitals make gender." For Sally, who runs her business as a man, surgery could mean losing her livelihood.

But she'd never want to give up her female persona. Once, she met a man in the cafeteria of a department store where a friend worked. Afterwards, the man told her friend that he had fallen in love with the most beautiful girl—it was her eyes that haunted him. The only thing was, he said, he had to know if she wanted children, because having a family was so important to him. "I said to my girlfriend, 'Don't you dare tell him,'" says Sally. "I couldn't break his heart."

SIGNIFICANCE

In contrast to Native American societies that recognize a third gender, Western society defines an individual as either male or female, with a sharp, distinguishing differences between the sexes. This social system has created inequalities that place men and masculinity above women and femininity. It also stigmatizes transsexuals who threaten male power by challenging the system.

Even at the beginning of the twenty-first century transsexuals frequently suffer discrimination in employment and housing as well as public harassment. Opponents of transsexuality, who support conservative definitions of gender, question whether transsexuals should be able to teach school, marry, and adopt children.

To cope with such widespread public hostility, transsexuals established dozens of support and advocacy organizations, including the American Educational Gender Information Service in 1990 and the Transgender Law and Policy Institute in 1991. These organizations promote legal protections for transsexuals, although only a handful of states, including California, Minnesota, New Mexico, and Rhode Island, have passed laws prohibiting discrimination against transgendered people. As SRS becomes more common, howver, Americans are less likely to see transsexuals as a menace.

FURTHER RESOURCES
Books

Bullough, Bonnie, Vern L. Bullough, and James Elias, eds. *Gender Blending*. Amherst, NY: Prometheus Books, 1997.

Califia-Rice, Patrick. *Sex Changes: The Politics of Transgenderism*. San Francisco: Cleis Press, 2003.

Hausman, Bernice L. *Changing Sex: Transsexualism, Technology, and the Idea of Gender*. Durham, NC: Duke University Press, 1995.

Lev, Arlene Istar. *Transgender Emergence: Therapeutic Guidelines for Working with Gender-Variant People and Their Families*. New York: Haworth Clinical Practice Press, 2004.

Web sites

Transgender Law and Policy Institute. "News" <http://www.transgenderlaw.org> (accessed March 26, 2006).

Gender and Sexuality Issues in Medicine and Public Health

5

Gender and Sexuality Issues in Medicine and Public Health

Sex behaviors affect personal and public health. Without antibiotics or effective prophylactics, it was once difficult to treat and contain the spread of venereal diseases (VD). Noting the increased incidence of venereal disease during World War I, posters, flyers, and pamphlets instructed soldiers to abstain from sex with prostitutes. Inadequate means of diagnosis, as well as shame and embarrassment, kept many infected persons from seeking medical attention. Women, and sometimes children, were disproportionately affected by VD. In some locations, there was a greater social stigma—and even legal consequences—for women with VD. By the time of the Sexual Revolution in the 1960s, both treatment and prophylactics had greatly improved, but the problem had shifted to being one of the proliferation of individual sex partners and a lack of established "safe-sex" practices. The liberated sexual climate of the 1960s and 1970s abruptly ended with the discovery of AIDS in the early 1980s.

While to some extent sexually transmitted diseases had always been intertwined with issues of sex and sexuality, the AIDS crisis brought these issues to the forefront. AIDS first appeared in gay men—many of whom had numerous sexual partners. It was derided in early media reports as a "gay cancer." Even as AIDS reached an increasing number of people in heterosexual population, the disease retained its association with the gay community. Indeed, the community the disease first devastated embraced the struggle against AIDS as a unifying cause, raising money for research, sponsoring awareness campaigns, and forcing AIDS into the spotlight of the mainstream media.

The intersection of sex, gender, and sexuality is not limited to sexually transmitted diseases. Gender and sexuality issues arise everyday healthcare. Since 1980, there has been significant growth in healthcare directed specifically towards women. From childbirth to breast cancer, health care providers have invested in woman-centered facilities and patient care strategies. Part of this institutional response is driven at the grassroots level by women themselves. Women's groups have heavily funded research and treatment, and conducted international breast cancer awareness campaigns. Similarly, sexuality issues are also driving patient care. This chapter features two articles that discuss specific health issues that gay and lesbian patients should discuss with their health care providers.

First Annual Report of the Ladies' Association for Soldiers' Relief of the United States

Report

By: Ladies' Association for Soldiers' Relief of the United States

Date: July 28, 1863

Source: *First and Second Annual Reports of the Ladies' Association for Soldiers' Relief of the United States.* Philadelphia: Sherman & Co., Printers, 1863. Available at <http://www.gettysburg.edu/library/specoll/ 19thcentdocs/ladiesassoctitle.html> (accessed March 28, 2006).

About the Author: In 1862, a group of ladies organized themselves as the Ladies' Association for Soldiers' Relief, based in Philadelphia, Pennsylvania. Their objectives were to give aid to sick and wounded soldiers, visit hospitals housing soldiers, and provide financial support for soldiers—if needed and available.

INTRODUCTION

The U.S. Civil War shocked and divided the nation on personal and political levels. Although slavery ended with the conclusion of the war, other national reforms, campaigns, and social agendas arose from the conflict. One group that was organized as a direct result of the war is the Ladies' Association for Soldiers' Relief in Philadelphia, Pennsylvania.

The Ladies' Association for Soldiers' Relief was not a unique organization for Philadelphia, nor was it a new area in the activities of women. During the American Revolutionary War, the Ladies Association of Philadelphia, active from about 1780 to 1781, helped organize women's activities for the revolutionary cause. During the Revolution, women's organizations were responsible for boycotting of British goods, reporting and hounding merchants for hoarding goods, and creating "sewing circles." These sewing groups gave women a chance to gather and socialize, but they also made clothing for the troops. Philadelphia was not the only city with such an organization, and similar women's groups could be found in almost every area of the country.

Other women's groups, pre-Reconstruction, fought for abolitionism (the ending of slavery), demanded labor law reforms, argued for prohibition,

Clara Barton served as a battlefield nurse during the U.S. Civil War and went on to found the American Red Cross.
NATIONAL ARCHIVES AND RECORDS ADMINISTRATION.

started the campaign for equal rights, and helped continue the fight for female suffrage.

These women's groups aided society, while also celebrating its social norms. These groups brought women together outside the home, but their actions still occurred within the "cult of domesticity." The cult of domesticity refers to the social theory that women should center their lives around raising happy and healthy families, and creating productive members of society. Thus, these groups continued the Christian tradition of charitable work for women in a way that made working outside the home acceptable and respectable.

The Civil War-era Ladies' Association for Soldiers' Relief continued in the same tradition as its predecessors; however, in addition, the actions of these women focused on sanitary aid, the medical needs of soldiers, and obtaining food, shelter, and transportation for discharged and injured troops.

PRIMARY SOURCE

July 28, 1862. A number of ladies met together at No. 135 South Fifth Street, Philadelphia, and formed themselves into a Ladies' Association for Soldiers' Relief of U.S., the principal objects contemplated being,

1. That the members, with the sole exception of an Honorary Secretary, shall consist of ladies only.
2. That committees of members shall, *for the present,* visit the different wards of the U.S.A. General Hospital, West Philadelphia, for the purpose of ameliorating the condition of the sick and wounded soldiers; and
3. To make visits, for the above purpose, to the sick and wounded soldiers of the Army of the Potomac in the field, as soon as, and as often as, occasion may render the same advisable.
4. That the Ladies' Association for Soldiers' Relief of U.S. will receive for distribution from time to time, money and such sanitary stores as may be donated by their friends and by the public.
5. That the Ladies' Association and its officers may be officially recognized by the Government, the military and medical authorities of the United States, and by the State of Pennsylvania, as well as by the public generally.
6. That the services, of whatsoever kind, of the officers and members of the Association, shall be wholly voluntary and entirely gratuitous without any pay or pecuniary recompense, other than the necessary traveling and other expenses incurred by them.
7. That every member shall subscribe one dollar per month, for the incidental advertising expenses of the Association, in addition to an entrance fee of one dollar on her being elevated a member.

BY_LAWS were also duly adopted.

July 30, 1862. A letter of recognition of the Ladies' Association was received from Dr. I. I. Hayes, Surgeon-in-charge of U.S.A. General Hospital, West Philadelphia; and committees of ladies were at once organized, who visited daily, during a period of many months, the various wards of this extensive and well-managed hospital.

Large quantities of delicacies, etc., were distributed by the ladies among the three thousand sick and wounded soldiers in the Satterlee hospital, by the hands of the several committees, facilities being granted to them by Dr. Hayes, and by all the ward surgeons, and the exertions of the ladies being appreciated by the brave sick and wounded patients.

During the fruit season, peaches, apples, etc. were often distributed at the hospital by the President and members of the Association.

Acknowledgements frequently appeared in the public newspapers of large quantities of sanitary stores donated by the public to the Ladies' Association, for distribution.

Occasionally, it would happen that sick soldiers, either on furlough or discharged, would be assisted by the Association with money, or with tickets on the railroads, to their homes in distant states. Sometimes, the Association would detail a nurse, hired by them, to accompany a sick or wounded soldier, who was otherwise too feeble, or crippled, to travel by himself, all the way home to his family, in the interior of the State.

The Association has constantly been in receipt of letters, such as the following, expressive of gratitude to the members, for attentions shown to the patriotic men and who have fought and bled for our country.

SIGNIFICANCE

After the U.S. Civil War, the actions of groups like the Ladies' Association for Soldiers' Relief of Philadelphia did not go unnoticed. While their predecessors from the American Revolution saw themselves celebrated in patriotic literature for nearly a decade, civil war women also saw themselves honored in print and fiction. In the decades following the Civil War, women's organizations continued to grow, expand, and confront issues of social justice, community safety, and national prosperity.

Ladies groups providing relief to soldiers encouraged the U.S. Congress to release old-age pensions to veterans of the Civil War once the hostilities ended. Initially, these pensions were only granted to Union soldiers, but eventually Confederate soldiers received some assistance. Another important outgrowth of the Civil War women's organizations can be seen in the creation of the American Red Cross. Although Clara Barton (1821–1912) is often credited with "single-handedly" founding the organization by carrying medical supplies to the front lines and aiding wounded troops, her actions coincided with, and encouraged, those of other women's organizations. These groups may have worked independently from one another, but their common causes ultimately aligned for the benefit of the larger society.

FURTHER RESOURCES
Books

Clinton, Catherine. *The Other Civil War: American Women in the Nineteenth Century.* New York: Hill and Wang, 1999.

Cott, Nancy F. *The Bonds of Womanhood: "Woman's Sphere" in New England, 1780–1835.* 2nd edition. New Haven, Conn.: Yale University Press, 1997.

Web sites

The Library of Congress. American Memory. "Women's History." <http://memory.loc.gov/ammem/mcchtml/womhm.html> (accessed March 28, 2006).

Living the Legacy: The Women's Rights Movement, 1848–1998. "History of the Movement." <http://www.legacy98.org/move-hist.html> (accessed March 28, 2006).

Maryland State Archives. "Patterns of Patriotism." <http://www.mdarchives.state.md.us/msa/speccol/sc5400/sc5494/html/early_efforts.html> (accessed March 28, 2006).

Clitoridectomy and Medical Ethics

Journal article

By: Anonymous

Date: April 13, 1867

Source: *Medical Times and Gazette* (London) 1 (Saturday, April 13, 1867).

About the Author: This editorial in the *Medical Times and Gazette* was written by members of the publication's editorial board, and as such the author is undisclosed.

INTRODUCTION

The history of secular male circumcision in the United States traces its history to the 1850s. While members of certain religions, such as Judaism and Islam, have removed the foreskin as part of religious ceremonies, secular circumcision developed as a result of medical theories concerning masturbation, sexually transmitted disease, and mental illness.

Jonathan Hutchinson, a London physician, first connected male circumcision to lower rates of venereal disease in 1854, using poorly manipulated data. His conclusion—that venereal disease rates were lower for Jewish men vs. gentiles—led to his theory that circumcised men were less vulnerable to venereal disease.

In the 1880s and 1890s, Hutchinson published articles and lectured on the topic of routine male circumcision in infancy as a method to reduce masturbation; removal of the foreskin would reduce physical stimulation. Other researchers applied the same concept to

girls and women; clitoridectomy was introduced as a cure for various female ailments, including masturbation, hysteria, overexcitement, aggression, "the whites" (yeast infections), incontinence, and more.

Dr. Isaac Baker Brown, president of the Medical Society of London, proposed a theory in 1858 on the evils of masturbation in young women, which he believed created circumstances for eight stages of progressive illness: hysteria, spinal irritation, hysterical epilepsy, cataleptic fits, epileptic fits, idiocy, mania, and death. Removal of the clitoris, Baker Brown believed, could prevent masturbation, which would prevent disease.

The operation Baker Brown initiated involved the excision of the clitoris; the wound was packed, opium administered rectally, and the patient required one month to recover. Baker Brown's operation was used in England, and by the 1860s in the United States, to cure hysteria, nymphomania, and in younger girls, rebellion or "unfeminine" aggression.

Baker Brown's stature in the medical community, as well as an increased interest in routine male circumcision, kept the topic of clitoridectomy in medical journals throughout the 1860s. However, the medical community did not unanimously adopt the procedure or the rationale behind its use.

■ PRIMARY SOURCE

MEDICAL TIMES AND GAZETTE.

SATURDAY, APRIL 13, 1867.

CLITORIDECTOMY AND MEDICAL ETHICS

THE operation of clitoridectomy, as performed under the conditions described in Mr. Baker Brown's writings and denounced in Dr. West's lectures, is an offence against Medical science and Medical ethics.

1. It is an offence against Medical science in the first place, that it should be described as a mere circumcision (a) Instead of taking away a loose fold of skin, it removes a rudimentary organ of exquisite sensitiveness, well supplied with blood vessels and nerves, and the operation is described by the author as occasionally attended with serious bleeding; in these respects it differs widely from circumcision.

It is a second error to assume that if a woman desired to continue filthy habits this operation would stop her. The organ removed is but one amongst many susceptible of intense excitement.(b)

In the third place, it is against all Medical science to remove such a part because "subject" (or subjected?—

see note) " to unbearable irritation." Intense itching is a common malady, but this itching does not depend on local causes, and it may generally be relieved by proper measures. To cut off part of the body because it itches is monstrous.

If indeed the clitoris be diseased, that is another thing; but as clitoridectomy is practised, the part is cut off without any signs of disease in it.

It is nothing to the purpose to affirm that clitoridectomy may have been successful in postponing epileptic fits or lengthening their interval. Any positive line of treatment will do that for a time. Many young men believe for three months that they have found a specific treatment for epilepsy. An intimate friend lately thought he had found one in colchinum [autumn crocus]. Give enough of any potent drug to make the patient ill, break a leg, or cut off the clitoris, and the fits will probably be interrupted for a time.

Neither is it to the purpose to accuse Mr. Brown of having performed an operation rashly, groundlessly, and unsuccessfully. Many such operations have been performed in the best faith. Marshall Hall used to propose tracheotomy for epilepsy; a living Surgeon once performed castration for the same malady; each operation thoroughly unsuccessful, and not to be defended, save on the ground of the good faith of the proposers, and of an enthusiasm which had carried them beyond the bounds of sound discretion.

Although, then, clitoridectomy must be condemned as an offence against Medical science, if that were all, it might let pass into oblivion without further notice. It is the offence against Medical ethics which it involves, which has secured for it the reprobation of the Profession.

2. It is an ethical offence, in the first place, if the Practitioner who is consulted for any common complaint, say hysteria, or fissure of the rectum, set himself to consider whether or not the patient is guilty of immoral practices, which have nothing to do with the case before him. Thus, as we said in our last number, and as we implied in the Med. Times and Gaz. June 4, 1864, if the clitoridectoral theory and practice were established, no parent who sent a daughter to any Medical man for any complaint whatever, could be sure that she might not return tainted with filthy inquiries, or branded by filthy suspicions—a thing incompatible with the honour of the Profession, and the possibility of that unrestrained frank intercourse between Practitioner and patient that happily exists now.

As an illustration of this kind of breach of Professional honour and its consequences, we will mention a case which was shortly touched on in our first article in the number for June 4, 1864.

A young lady was brought by her friends, ten or twelve years ago, to a Surgeon practising specially on the

rectum, for a fistula. He did not content himself with exploring the fistula, but ascertained that she had lost her virginity, and told her father so. The consequences were frightful, including a painful trial, and loss of honour, character, and position to the parties concerned. All this, because the Surgeon had gone out of the path of his duty, and, instead, of confining himself to the malady for which he was consulted, had gratuitously imported into it certain moral considerations with which he had nothing to do. If this were a habit with Medical men, there would be an end to the present free and honourable intercourse with their patients. We should be accused, and justly, of making prurient, or indecent, or degrading inquiries, and of bringing a knowledge of evil to minds from which it had been absent.

Affirming then, in the first place, that the very entry of thoughts of pollution into the Practitioner's mind respecting his patients is an offence of the deepest dye, this offence is aggravated by the kind of evidence which the clitoridectomist is taught to accept as proof of his patient's guilt. That evidence consists, partly, in certain physical signs detailed in Mr. Baker Brown's book—a "peculiar straight and coarse hirsute growth," a peculiar follicular secretion, and other phenomena detected by inspection, which are as frivolous as they are disgusting. It is said by credible witnesses, that at a clitoridectomical operation nose as well as eyes were called into requisition, and that a respectable Practitioner was invited to apply his nose to the parts implicated, in order to satisfy his mind, by this test, that these parts had been subjected to abnormal irritation. The thing is almost too beastly to tell of, but we want to deal with this subject once for all, and to let our readers know why clitoridectomy does not stand in the same category as any other unsuccessful operation.

But says Mr. Brown, "before commencing treatment, I have always made a point of having my diagnosis confirmed by the patient or her friends." And this brings us to what we may call the moral evidence on which the patient's guilt is assumed, the process of obtaining which is one of the most heinous offences against good sense and Professional ethics that can be conceived.

We have heard of questions put (not by Mr. Brown) to female out-patients after the following fashion:—"Do you feel any irritation in certain organs?" "Is it very bad?" "Does it induce you to rub them?" "Does the rubbing ever make you feel faint?" And if the patient answers these questions affirmatively it is said that the evidence of unnaturally excitation is regarded as complete.

Nervous young women, as it is well known, may be profoundly ignorant of the nature and drift of such questions. They delight to magnify their own sensations, they enjoy the Physician's sympathy and are sure to answer " yes " to any leading question whatever. But we say that if young women are subjected to such inquiries as these in out-patient rooms at Hospitals and Dispensaries, or by private Practitioners, the sooner the Profession speaks out the better. A Medical consultation may involve the worst contamination to the patient. We think we are justified in saying that the kind of evidence on which the guilt of the woman is assumed is itself an ethical offence.

That the performance of clitoridectomy on a woman without her knowledge and consent, as detailed by Dr. West, is an offence against Medical ethics, needs not to be said. We suspect it is amenable to the criminal law of the land.

It is an offence against Medical ethics, also, to obtain the woman's consent, nominally, while she is left in ignorance of the real scope and nature of the mutilation, and of the moral imputations which it involves. Consent to a thing whose nature is not known, is like the consent of an infant or lunatic—null and void. Equally do we repudiate, as an offence against Medical ethics, the performance of such an operation, even with the consent, nominal or real, of the patient, but without the full knowledge and consent of the persons on whom she is dependent, as wife or daughter. As the woman's character affects theirs, they have a right to decide whether a female relative should undergo this operation, with the disgrace it involves, or whether relief shall be sought from other means.

We may be pardoned for adding that not one of the supposititious cases alleged by Dr. Routh at the late meeting of the Obstetrical Society has the least bearing on or analogy with the performance of clitoridectomy without the knowledge of the patient or her friends. Dr. Routh argued that all the details of every operation cannot be described to patients. But it is not the details—it is the moral questions involved in clitoridectomy, which ought not to be kept secret. Dr. Routh argued, also, that there are cases in which a Practitioner is bound to keep a patient's secrets from her husband; but in cases before us, it is not secrets imparted by the patient, but dishonourable surmises and filthy imputations generated in the mind of the Practititioner—the nature of the mutilation and its disgrace—that are kept secret.

Thus, then, we have shown, as shortly as possible, the real position of clitoridectomy as an offence against science and morality, and the reasons why the Medical Profession, as an honourable, moral Profession, whose members have free and familial access to families, must repudiate and utterly reject it.

(a) "Let it be known, once for all, that clitoridectomy is neither more nor less than circumcision of the female; and as certainly as that no man who has been circumcised has been injured in his natural functions, so it is equally certain that no woman who has undergone the operation of exci-

sion of the clitoris has lost one particle of the natural functions of her organs. I would here protest against the cruel insinuation made against me by my accusers, that my reasons for performing the operation are because women are subjected to immoral habits; when, as I have distinctly again and again asserted, I operation because there is undue and unbearable irritation of the clitoris, and in such cases alone is the operation likely to be successful."—(Mr. Baker Brown's "Replies to the Remarks of the Council," Nos. 12 and 13.)

(b) For evidence, see Baker Brown on Curability, etc., pp. 12, 18, etc.

SIGNIFICANCE

This editorial continued a strong debate in academic and medical circles as the specialty of Gynecology emerged in western medicine in the 1850s and 1860s. This debate, during the heart of the sexually restrained Victorian Era, divided gynecologists. The idea that women could be convinced to give consent via leading questions from the practitioner was an affront to some doctors who considered women to be unable to understand the medical procedure and its effects. As this editorial notes, "Consent to a thing whose nature is not known, is like the consent of an infant or lunatic—null and void. Equally do we repudiate, as an offence against Medical ethics, the performance of such an operation, even with the consent, nominal or real, of the patient, but without the full knowledge and consent of the persons on whom she is dependent, as wife or daughter. As the woman's character affects theirs, they have a right to decide whether a female relative should undergo this operation, with the disgrace it involves, or whether relief shall be sought from other means."

The frank discussion of clitoridectomy with the father or husband of a potential candidate for clitoridectomy, as a vehicle for gaining informed consent, was controversial. Under the sexual mores of the time such a discussion would have been difficult at best. In addition, the clitoris was one of "many organs" used for masturbation; if the goal of clitoridectomy was to end masturbation, it would not succeed.

In the 1880s, American doctor John Harvey Kellogg, inventor of Corn Flakes cereal and a health and hygiene advocate, theorized that masturbation was best curbed by circumcising young infant boys and applying carbolic acid to the clitoris of young girls to prevent overexcitement of the genitals. Clitoridectomy and variations of clitoral suppression remained part of the medical literature and practice for decades after Baker Brown's first writings on the issue.

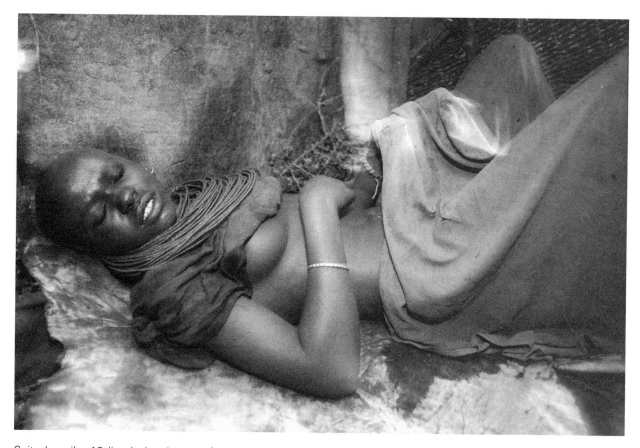

Seita Lengila, 16 lies in her house after undergoing a ritual femal circumcision in Kenya, 1995. PHOTO BY STEPHANIE WELSH/GETTY IMAGES

In a 1915 article by Dr. Benjamin Dawson, President of the Eclectic medical University, the clitoris and the foreskin are described as being the source of "convulsions, eczema, paralysis, constipation, tuberculosis, locomotor ataxia, rheumatism, idiocy, insanity, lust and all its consequences" in the body. Removal of the clitoris or the foreskin removes the "nerve-waste" that causes the medical and psychological conditions listed. Dawson's 1915 article revisits Baker Brown's original theory while adding new, systemic diseases and complications attributed to the sexual organs. Dawson, like Baker Brown, advocated clitoridectomy and male circumcision as remedies.

Britain outlawed female circumcision or clitoridectomy in the 1860s. Female circumcision, routinely described as "female genital mutilation" by the United Nations and non-governmental organizations that promote women's health and women's rights, continues in many sections of Africa. An estimated 130 million African women have experienced clitoridectomy or infibulation, in while the clitoris and the labia are removed and the wound stitched together, leaving a small hole for urine and menstrual blood to exit.

The practice of clitoridectomy and infibulation worldwide continues, and is part of modern western medicine in the 21st century, though in a different form than that practiced by Baker Brown. Clitoridectomy in modern, western terms involves the removal of the clitoris or the reduction of the organ when gender anomalies are present; each year 2,000 surgeries—including clitoridectomies—are performed on such children in the United States.

FURTHER RESOURCES

Books

Groneman, Carol. *Nymphomania: A History.* New York: W.W. Norton, 2000.

Periodicals

Dawson, Benjamin E. "Circumcision in the Female: Its Necessity and How to Perform It." *American Journal of Clinical Medicine* vol. 22, no. 6, June 1915.

Leonard, Lori. "We did it for pleasure only." *Qualitative Inquiry* vol. 6, no. 2, November 2, 2000.

Sheehan,E. "Victorian Clitoridectomy: Isaac Baker Brown and his harmless operative procedure." *Medical Anthropology Newsletter* vol. 12, no. 4, August 1981.

Web Sites

Amnesty International. "Female Genital Mutilation—A Human Rights Information Pack." < http://www. amnesty.org/ailib/intcam/femgen/fgm1.htm> (accessed March 20, 2006).

Eighty Years and More

Photograph

By: Elizabeth Cady Stanton

Date: 1898

Source: Elizabeth Cady Stanton, from *Eighty Years And More; Reminiscences 1815–1897*. New York: European Publishing Company, 1898.

About the Author: Elizabeth Cady Stanton (1815–1902), along with her close friend Susan B. Anthony (1820–1906), was a leader of the women's rights movement in the nineteenth century. She was a cosponsor of the 1848 Seneca Falls Convention, a landmark meeting that laid out a women's rights agenda. Primarily an advocate for women's suffrage, Stanton also supported more liberal divorce laws and coeducation.

INTRODUCTION

Elizabeth Cady Stanton may well have been the most influential supporter of the American women's rights in the nineteenth century. Chiefly a theorist, she authored a number of books that challenged the low status of women.

Born in upstate New York on November 12, 1815, Elizabeth Cady came from a well-to-do family.

A cartoon depicting a feminist speaker denouncing men at the first Women's Rights Convention, held at Seneca Falls, New York, July 19–20, 1848. © CORBIS-BETTMANN. REPRODUCED BY PERMISSION.

EIGHTY YEARS AND MORE

(1815–1897)

REMINISCENCES

OF

ELIZABETH CADY STANTON

"Social science affirms that woman's place in society marks the level of civilization."

NEW YORK
EUROPEAN PUBLISHING COMPANY
1898

PRIMARY SOURCE

Eighty Years and More: The frontispiece and title page of the book *Eighty Years and More,* by Elizabeth Cady Stanton.
PUBLIC DOMAIN.

Her father, a judge, once told her it was a shame that she was not born a boy because she had a fine mind. As a girl, however, she was expected to only keep house and raise children. When her brother died shortly after graduating from college, she vowed to ease her father's sorrow by becoming all that he had hoped for his son.

After graduating from Troy Female Seminary in 1832, she became active in both the temperance and antislavery movements. When she married abolitionist Henry B. Stanton in 1840, the couple chose to delete the word "obey" from their marriage vows. They honeymooned at the World's Anti-Slavery Convention in London, where some American delegates were refused entry because they were women. One of these, Lucretia Mott, introduced Stanton to emerging ideas about women's equality.

Stanton began her women's rights career by lobbying the state legislature of New York for married women's property rights. A voracious reader, she had studied her father's law books and became adept at crafting legal arguments. However, Stanton gave birth to seven children, and her increasing family obligation left little time to travel. So she organized the Seneca Falls convention in her hometown of Johnstown, New York. The first women's rights convention in the United States, the meeting called for social, religious, economic, professional, and political equality for women.

In 1869, Stanton and Susan B. Anthony founded the National Woman Suffrage Association. The two also collaborated to write the three-volume *History of Woman Suffrage* in 1888. Stanton argued that women's equality was based on the political philosophy of natural rights. Believing that religion was largely to blame for women's oppression, she wrote the enormously controversial *Woman's Bible* (1895) to challenge biblical and clerical authority. Stanton continued to advocate for women's rights until her death in 1902.

PRIMARY SOURCE

EIGHTY YEARS AND MORE

See primary source image.

SIGNIFICANCE

In the nineteenth century the world was clearly divided into separate spheres for men and women. While men were engaged in business and politics, women were expected solely to be keepers of the home and children. Masculine privilege included controlling property in marriage, sole custody of children after divorce, the right to serve in public office, and the right to vote.

Woman suffrage, with temperance and abolition, was a major nineteenth-century reform movement. Initially, women sought only to reform property, divorce, and child custody laws. Stanton and other activists soon realized that suffrage would give women access to the public arena and help them fight injustices protected by unfair laws. She challenged male domination in a manner that set the stage for greater equality between the sexes in the twentieth century.

Women in the United States fought for seventy-five years to gain the right to vote. Although she died before seeing victory, Elizabeth Cady Stanton began this struggle and ably led the woman suffrage movement for decades.

FURTHER RESOURCES

Books

DuBois, Ellen Carol. *Feminism and Suffrage: The Emergence of an Independent Women's Movement in America, 1848–1869.* Ithaca, NY: Cornell University Press, 1978.

Wellman, Judith. *Road to Seneca Falls: Elizabeth Cady Stanton and the First Women's Rights Convention.* Urbana: University of Illinois Press, 2004.

The Women's Court in its Relation to Venereal Diseases

Journal article excerpt

By: W. Bruce Cobb

Date: 1920

Source: Cobb, W. Bruce. "The Women's Court in its Relation to Venereal Disease." *Journal of Social Hygiene* January, 1920 (Volume 6, Number 1).

About the Author: W. Bruce Cobb was the City Magistrate for New York City in the early 1920s.

INTRODUCTION

Prostitution and the continued spread of venereal disease was a major public health issue for urban areas in Western Europe and the United States from the mid-1800s on. Before the widespread availability of antibiotics to treat conditions such as syphilis and gonorrhea, venereal disease generated severe morbidity and mortality issues for the men who frequented prostitutes, the prostitutes themselves, the clients' wives, and sometimes the clients' children, who could be born with disabilities or stillborn as a result of venereal disease contracted during pregnancy.

Britain and France enacted a series of laws to control prostitutes. In 1823, the Gendarmerie Royale in Paris required prostitutes to be registered, arresting those who refused. All brothels were registered as well. Registration was a simple process, involving basic questions about the person's life, whether she had children or a spouse (in which case she needed her spouse's permission), and why she was in the trade. A large number of prostitutes remained unregistered, however; the stigma attached to the trade was too great for many to wish to be on the official lists.

In Britain, the Contagious Disease Acts of the 1860s involved a greater degree of government involvement in the bodies of prostitutes. Prostitutes were required to register and undergo a physical exam; if they carried a venereal disease they were quarantined to a government hospital until declared "clean." Male clients of prostitutes, however, were not required to register or undergo exams of any kind. The police in Britain had wide latitude in determining which women were prostitutes; no probable cause was needed. The law lent itself to abuse by police, spurned lovers, or dissatisfied clients.

A poster publicizing a sanitarium for people suffering from syphilis, by Ramon Casas Carbo. © ARCHIVO ICONOGRAFICO, S.A./CORBIS.

Middle and upper class women in Britain, in a rare social movement, came to the defense of lower class prostitutes by fighting against the Contagious Disease Acts. In 1886, Britain repealed the Contagious Disease Acts, though venereal disease remained a public health problem.

In the United States, prostitution itself was not illegal on a federal level; interstate prostitution, governed by the 1910 Mann Act, prohibits interstate commerce, but states regulate prostitution. As of 2006, prostitution is illegal in all states except portions of Nevada. In the early part of the twentieth century, cities and states slowly made the solicitation of a client by a prostitute illegal; only later was the act of engaging a prostitute made a crime.

In New York City, the Women's Court processed prostitution cases for the first three decades of the twentieth century. In this excerpt below, W. Bruce Cobb, the City Magistrate for New York City in 1920, discusses the role of World War I (1915–1918) in understanding the public health crisis involved with the spread of venereal diseases.

PRIMARY SOURCE
CITY MAGISTRATE, NEW YORK CITY

In civil life, just as in the army, the threat of the so-called "social evil" is ever with us. According to many opinions it ever will be, just as it has continued throughout the ages, as the necessary accompaniment of indiscriminate sex relations.

But of this let us take note: that never before in the world's history have venereal disease and its great productive cause, commercialized vice, been so closely or scientifically studied or with better promise of definite results. Not only has medical science furnished marvelous methods of cure, but the world war has yielded a wealth of data that is a revelation, not only in its relation to military affairs but to our normal, everyday civil population.

From the vantage point we now occupy there opens up a vista of probably amelioration, not only for future generations, but even for the present one, to an extent which would have been regarded as unbelievable ten years ago.

Conceding the traditional conservatism of courts of law, I should be ashamed to be compelled to admit that they had not shared in this progress and awakening. Happily, however, I can say that the Women's Court of this city has done a great deal to keep pace with the onward march. If one familiar with the workings of this court ten years ago were to go there and study them now, a great change would be observed.

Ten years ago we were hardly out of the stage when prostitutes were merely fined—a method quite ineffectual to lessen their activities even in the slightest degree. Then came the cry to keep our streets clean—"outward order and decency." Then the cry to keep our tenements clean—a form of "inward order and decency"—all of which was the forerunner of "inward order and decency" not only in the tenements and homes of our people, but in their very bodies.

Of course, whatever restricts or lessens prostitution tends to combat venereal disease—if not to eradicate it, at least to keep it in bounds or diminish it. This may be done by long imprisonment for the hardened offender and by probation or reformative processes for the less hardened.

These methods will doubtless be necessary for a long time to come but without the helping hand of medical science they are bound to be ineffectual in achieving the best that can be achieved. Actual medical treatment for both body and mind is essential. Indeed, feeble-mindedness and venereal disease offer a doubly dangerous combination as a source of contamination.

In 1910 there was passed in New York state a law which provided that women found guilty in the Women's Night Court (now fortunately a day court) of prostitutional offenses were to be forthwith examined by a woman physician in an adjacent room. The physician then made a written report to the magistrate and, if infected, the offender was committed to a public hospital for a minimum period and a maximum of not more than one year. If cured before the minimum period, the prisoner was transferred to the workhouse for the rest of her term. If not cured she remained not only for the minimum term but as long thereafter, up to one year, as might be necessary to complete her cure.

This law, however, was destined to early failure since it was declared unconstitutional by the Court of Appeals in June, 1911, in the case of *People ex. rel. Barone, r. Fox* (202 N.Y. 616). The Court of Appeals thereby reversed the decision of the Appellate Division of the Supreme Court, adopting the dissenting opinion of Mr. Justice John Proctor Clarke (144 App. Div. 649), who said:

"I cannot avoid the conclusion that a woman coming within the provisions of the section receives a sentence not for the offense for which she was brought into court and upon which she has been convicted, but based upon her condition of health, in regard to which she has not had a hearing."

It would not be of interest here to follow from that time the various changes of laws and policy of the Women's Court with respect to sentences or other treatment. It is enough to say that after a scheme of an auto-

matic indeterminate sentence, the law again vested in the magistrates the usual discretion as to length of sentence. These sentences, graded by agreement among the four magistrates rotating in the court, were in proportion to the number of times the offender had been previously convicted. They greatly held in check the evil of prostitution and earned New York the title of the "cleanest city."

So much was this so that in time it became possible to be more lenient and also to give increased attention to individual treatment, especially in probation work, without allowing the evil to gain headway.

In 1915 came the parole Commission Law, which has been upheld by the courts in a series of interesting decisions (e.g. see *People ex. rel. Berger v. the Warden*, 176 App. Div. 602 and cases there cited). This law is still in full force and vigor. So far as it relates to prostitutional offenses, it provides that one who offends twice in two years, previous to the present conviction, or three times during any time previous thereto, may be sentenced to an indeterminate period not to exceed two years in the workhouse. It gives full scope to the finger-printing system, as a means of proving previous convictions. Finger-printing was, in fact, provided for in 1910 for the Women's Court and has at all times been of extraordinary value in ascertaining a defendant's previous record. Indeed, it has become indispensable to the work of the court, which could only function in the lamest fashion without it.

The Parole Commission Law is preeminently a reformative measure, though at the same time it makes possible a lengthy period of detention and removal from society of the hardened offender. Through a system of study of the character and environment of the individual, coupled with good behavior marks while in the workhouse, a prisoner may earn parole or even discharge, according to what she seems to merit.

At the time this law went into effect it was predicted that a possible two-year detention would deter from a second offense or drive from the city, many of these offenders. For a short time this seemed to be the case, though no permanent decrease has been established.

That the Parole Commission Law possesses splendid features is not to be gainsaid. And just stated, it keeps the hardened offender from contaminating society for a considerable period, and it gives wide opportunity for reformative measures for those susceptible of reform. Lastly it gives a splendid opportunity to rehabilitate them all physically and to cure them of venereal disease.

It may now be asked what facilities for cure were afforded before and at the time the Parole Commission Law went into effect. They were and still are as follows:

at the workhouse scientific modern hospital treatment is given those who are convicted there and prove to be infected. Workhouse statistics show upwards of eighty percent to be so infected. This treatment is excellent for those who are committed long enough to be cured, but short-term prisoners often have to be freed before the cure is complete or, sometimes, even fairly begun.

As to those sent to Bedford State Reformatory and to certain of the semi-private institutions, adequate treatment was and is furnished. On the other hand, other semi-private or charitable institutions have to rely on the public hospitals to care for such cases. This leaves much to be desired, especially as only the very active cases are apt to be so sent.

As to those placed on probation, no means of cure were afforded up to very recently. Indeed it often was unknown whether they were, or were not, victims of disease. Up to recently, it was rarely known whether a person was infected until she reached the workhouse or reformatory, since there was no physician to examine after conviction and sentence. With affairs in this state, it can readily be seen that medical treatment was accorded to only part of those convicted.

In 1917 came our entry into the great world war and with it the training camp activities and the wonderful efforts put forth to keep the army "clean." As New York City became more and more thronged with solders and sailors it became apparent that the Women's Court had an increasing amount of work and that the prisoners comprised an appalling number of first offenders. These were drawn to New York partly through the lure of the uniform and partly through the workings of the law of supply and demand. The girls came from all parts of the country and their earnings were vastly greater than in pre-war times. It was soon seen that the policy of comparative leniency which had, up to the war, kept the streets and tenements in fair order, would not do any longer, and the court realized it must adjust its policies to meet new conditions.

When the federal authorities made clear the immensity and seriousness of the problem—from the army viewpoint—a close cooperation was established. Lines were drawn more strictly on probation, and workhouse sentences were lengthened so as to increase detention, complete cures, and at the same time to keep the offender from her prey. Even the Parole Commissioner was appealed to, so as to prevent the possible release of old-time offenders.

Close on this came the demand for legislation, not only to secure proper medical treatment of convicted prostitutes, but of all that class generally and of men guilty of kindred offenses under the law. It was early realized that, due to the Barone case, declaring the law of 1910 unconstitutional, any such legislation must be in the form of a health measure pure and simple, so that a person's punishment or incarceration might not be measured primarily by his or her condition of health. In other words, compulsory treatment must be in a hospital or by a private physician and for the disease and not as the result of a court commitment.

We had long had a provision of the vagrancy law that permitted commitment of those suffering from an infectious disease acquired through debauchery and requiring charitable means to restore them to health. But this had failed utterly in practice, as defendants generally were able to prove that they did not require charitable aid.

On April 17, 1918, a new article for "the regulation of certain contagious diseases" was added to the state public health laws. Thus the health aspect of commercialized vice came to take its true place in law enforcement. Not only is this law a legal measure designed primarily to combat venereal disease, but it operates largely through the medium of the magistrates' courts, especially the Women's Court. By its terms both men and women who are reasonably open to suspicion of disease may be examined and treated either by the board of health or, at the option of the suspect, by a licensed physician. Women convicted of prostitutional offenses, as well as men guilty of related delinquencies known to the law, must be examined by a board of health physician immediately on conviction and may not be released until this is done.

By an amendment made in 1919 even those *arrested* for such offenses must be reported by the court for the purpose of examination, on the theory that they are reasonably subject to suspicion by the fact of arrest. This latter has seemed to some of us a dangerous extension of power and one which the board of health may well hesitate to exercise. In theory of law, a person is not only presumed innocent until convicted, but in like theory he or she may well be the victim of mistaken or unjustified arrest. To subject a possibly decent man or pure woman to what is to many a humiliating experience in being so examined, would possibly stir a revulsion of public feeling that would undo much of the good this beneficent legislation would otherwise accomplish. Such an exercise of the police or health power may indeed be of doubtful constitutionality. At least the health officer acts at his peril in a given case, even though we bear in mind that decent men or pure women are rarely, if ever, arrested. Again, the medical examination of those actually convicted reveals a positive reaction in only a little over fifty percent of all cases, so that on the face of it, it is safe to say that perhaps less than half of those merely arrested would show signs of disease. Consequently, at least half would prove to have been erroneously subjected to suspicion. It would seem that until the time when we shall all be examined, as part of a general clinical examination imposed upon all members of society, it is going pretty far to uphold this amendment.

SIGNIFICANCE

Thirty years after Britain repealed its Contagious Disease Acts, New York City imposed a similar law; the April 17, 1918 article titled the Page Bill permitting "the regulation of certain contagious diseases" and the 1919 addition permitting for the examination of anyone arrested on prostitution or "delinquency" charges (the male client's charge) echoed the British law that middle class female reform had fought so hard against.

While Cobb praises the public health components of such laws, he too finds the law's ambiguity and potential for abuse to be excessive. While the 1910 law providing for punishment based on disease status was unconstitutional, requiring an exam in and of itself was considered a part of public health law. Purity crusaders shifted their view of prostitution as a "fallen woman" or one who made an immoral choice to that of a medical or scientific problem to be solved, via legislation, examination, and criminalization.

In 1936, Dorothy Kenyon, a female lawyer who was active in social causes and women's rights, chaired a committee that investigated the Women's Court system. Arguing that prostitutes needed social services and social support rather than punishment and criminal prosecution, Kenyon helped once again shift this view of the prostitute from that of a public health menace to a person with a need for a social safety net, access to services, and one for whom prostitution was a desperate choice.

Military public service campaigns during World War I and World War II (1938–1941) served to combat the spread of venereal disease. In June 1944, the use of penicillin for syphilis became available, and it nearly eradicated all forms of venereal disease in treated soldiers. Within a short time, penicillin was available to the public and largely ended the plague of venereal disease that officials had worked to contain with such measures as the Mann Act, the 1918 Page Bill in New York, and the Women's Court.

FURTHER RESOURCES

Books

Brandt, Alan. *No Magic Bullet: A Social History of Venereal Disease in the United States Since 1880.* Oxford University Press. 1987.

Gilfoyle, Timothy. *City of Eros: New York City, Prostitution, and the Commercialization of Sex, 1790–1920.* W.W. Norton & Co. 1994.

Ringdal, Nils Johan. *Love For Sale: A World History of Prostitution.* Grove Press. 2004.

Periodicals

Wahab, Stephanie. "For Their Own Good?: Sex Work, Social Control and Social Workers, a Historical Perspective." *Journal of Sociology and Social Welfare.* December 2002.

She May Look Clean But

Poster

By: Anonymous

Date: early 1940s

Source: National Library of Medicine

About the Author: This poster was produced by the United States government during World War II (1938–1945) as part of its campaign against venereal disease among troops.

INTRODUCTION

This poster was one of a large number of propaganda posters produced by the U.S. Government and other governments, especially during the first and second World Wars, to warn military personnel about the dangers of contracting venereal diseases (now called sexually-transmitted diseases, STDS) from prostitutes or, in this case, "pick-ups [and] good-time girls." The Axis, referred to at the bottom of the poster ("You can't beat the Axis if you get VD") was the enemy alliance of fascist states comprising Nazi Germany, Italy, and Japan. The poster warns explicitly of syphilis and gonorrhea, both sexually transmitted diseases. As both of these diseases are caused by bacteria, they can be treated by antibiotics, such as penicillin; however, supplies of penicillin were very limited during World War II, and the drug was reserved mostly for combat injuries during the early years of the war. By 1944, penicillin was mass-produced and more available for the treatment of STDs.

This particular poster is typical in that it shows an attractive woman and identifies her as a possible source of infection. It was also commonplace for such posters to appeal to patriotism, as this one does (another typi-

PRIMARY SOURCE

She May Look Clean But: A World War II era public health poster warns men against the dangers of casual sex and prostitution. COURTESY OF THE NATIONAL LIBRARY OF MEDICINE.

cal poster says "Venereal disease helps the enemy"). It is unusual, however, in that the woman portrayed is an idealized "girl next door," not highly sexualized in appearance, who "looks clean" (i.e., free from venereal disease). Most posters warning servicemen against venereal disease portrayed women instantly identifiable as prostitutes in the visual code of the day: wearing heavy make-up, smoking cigarettes, leaning against the outsides of buildings at night.

■ PRIMARY SOURCE

SHE MAY LOOK CLEAN BUT

See primary source image.

SIGNIFICANCE

Understanding of the mechanisms of infectious disease only became scientifically possible during the mid to late nineteenth century. By World War I (1915–1918), the bacterial causes of STDs such as syphilis and gonorrhea—the two most serious common STDs—were well understood, but treatment lagged. Tuberculosis was also on the rise due to rabid urbanization with attended poor housing, water, and sanitation. Tuberculosis was the first infectious disease to be targeted by a national coordinated education and propaganda campaign, and this was the first time public-health officials availed themselves of the technique of the poster. The poster form had first been developed in the late nineteenth century for commercial advertising. During World Wars I and II, it was used extensively by the Allies and Germany for a variety of propaganda purposes; posters urged recycling, enlistment, caution when talking about defense-related information, job safety, general patriotism, and avoidance of venereal disease.

Posters are not the only method that has been employed by the military to raise anti-VD consciousness among troops. Films (including a famous 1973 Walt Disney short called "VD Attack Plan"), lectures, pamphlets, and distribution of free condoms to troops have also been used. The military opened free specialized treatment stations for military personnel in Europe during World War II.

The efficacy of posters and other education methods against the spread of STDs among troops, especially those stationed in countries where they can mingle freely with the population, must, however, be doubted. In 1967, during the Vietnam War, it was officially admitted that the rate of infection of troops by STDs was ten times higher than the civilian rate at home. Chairman of the Joint Chiefs of Staff General Earle Wheeler told Congress that "It must be admitted that VD prevention campaigns within the services are not eminently successful." A 1972 fact sheet for the Army's First Cavalry Division stated that the rate of STD infection was 226.3 soldiers per one thousand, about 3.75 times the sickness rate from all other causes combined. An Air Force document from 1966 put the rate in that branch of the service at 541 per one thousand.

STDs continue to be a major health-care concern of the U.S. military. A 1993 study of 1,744 male sailors found that forty-nine percent reported sexual contact with a prostitute before deployment on a six-month cruise and twenty-two percent reported a history of STDs; during the six-month deployment, forty-two percent reported sexual contact with a prostitute and ten percent acquired a new STD. The study concluded that "U.S. military personnel frequently engage in high-risk sexual behavior and that there is a continued need for comprehensive and culturally-sensitive STD prevention programs." A 2002 study of 1,028 U.S. Marines found that recent STDs were identified in 7.4 percent of subjects, and thirty-four percent reported a history of STDs.

FURTHER RESOURCES

Periodicals

Malone, J.D., et al. "Risk Factors for Sexually-Transmitted Diseases Among Deployed U.S. Military Personnel." *Sexually Transmitted Diseases.* 1993 Sep-Oct; 20(5):294-8.

Murphy, Clare. "Abortion Ship Makes Waves in Poland." *BBC News.* July 1, 2003. Available at <http://news.bbc.co.uk/1/hi/world/europe/3035540.stm> (accessed April 5, 2006).

Web sites

National Institutes of Health, National Library of Medicine, History of Medicine Division. "Visual Culture and Public Health Posters : Infectious Disease: Venereal Disease.". <http://www.nlm.nih.gov/exhibition/visualculture/venereal.html> (accessed April 5, 2006).

Birth Control Legislation

Photograph

By: Anonymous

Date: February 1945

Source: "Mrs. Thomas Hepburn Speaking to a House Committee." Corbis, February 1945.

About the Author: This photograph is part of the collection at Corbis Corporation headquartered in Seattle and provider of images for magazine, films, television, and advertisements.

INTRODUCTION

Birth control legislation is not a new factor in United States legislative history. State and local governments have continually enacted legislation regulating sex acts since the country's inception, and just as modernity forced some of these laws to be enacted or removed, similar motions have been taken with birth control legislation. In regard to sex laws, some of the laws that have been restructured and altered to suit the changing needs and expectations of society are those prohibiting marriage under a certain age (this minimum age still varies from state to state, but most states now have a minimum age requirement), not allowing individuals to be married to more than one person at the same time, and child pornography laws. But, unlike sexual acts that have been outlawed or restricted to marriage or age brackets, birth control legislation has not made the same strides within the U.S. legislative system.

In 1873, the U.S. Congress passed the Comstock Laws, which classified contraceptive devices and literature as obscene, making them illegal to be mailed. Before the Comstock Laws came into existence, however, many state and local governments had passed laws making the literature of or discussion of birth control illegal. Additionally, local court records show that in the early colonies (circa late 1600s), the legacy of prohibiting forms of birth control was well established in the American legislative system. Until *Roe v. Wade* in 1973, most states forbade a woman from having an abortion. By 1973, science and medicine had developed a fairly safe procedure to terminate a woman's pregnancy, but before modernized clinical procedures women used a variety of home remedies (the earlier colonial methods usually relied upon herbal tonics). Even though abortion is not considered, or recommended as, a standard method of birth control, it does remain within the birth control debate. This is because the basic premise of controlling a woman's body, controlling the population, and controlling a lifestyle reflect upon abortion in similar manners that are seen with birth control forms like "The Pill," abstinence, and other methods.

Even though women had been performing birth control methods on themselves for years, using communal knowledge to discuss practices like "withdrawal" and "the rhythm method," and the condom had been in use (for the select few who could afford it), large elements of society hesitated discussing birth control. Many believed that it was a taboo subject that should not be brought up in public. Larger world events, like World War I, sent the United States into a state of panic and thousands of radicals, subversives, and socialists were jailed and silenced for their beliefs. While birth control advocates may have not been members of these targeted groups, they were still silenced in the wake of the Red Scares in the United States in the early twentieth century. Hence, the movement to get birth control legislation and birth control discussions to the national level took considerably more effort because popular celebrities, politicians, and church leaders argued against birth control.

Father Charles Coughlin, a popular Roman Catholic priest who hosted his own radio program during the Great Depression, publicly spoke out against birth control by stating that it jeopardized the Nordic stock of the country. Coughlin is most often cited as the first evangelist preacher to convey his message over an electronic medium—the radio. Just as his popularity captivated many Americans, others who spoke for the support of birth control were women like Mrs. Thomas Hepburn. She was the mother of six children, and her notoriety came from her daughter Katharine Hepburn—a popular actress. Hepburn spoke before the U.S. Congress in 1945, and other leading women's rights and birth control activists supported her plea for birth control.

■ PRIMARY SOURCE

BIRTH CONTROL LEGISLATION

See primary source image.

■

SIGNIFICANCE

Mothers like Hepburn aligned in the fight for birth control, and their efforts helped elevate the already public struggle. Women like Margaret Sanger, who is often considered the leader of the birth control campaign, sent circulars about birth control, helped establish clinics, and in a "hands on approach" to the issue activists were able to bring affordable, safe, and reliable birth control to average women—not just the wealthy who had previously afforded it.

Hepburn's appeal before Congress in 1945 may not have brought forth national birth control legislation, but it did enable the next wave of public thinking

PRIMARY SOURCE

Birth Control Legislation Mrs. Thomas N. Hepburn, legislative chairman of the National Committee for Birth Control Legislation, speaks before the House Judiciary Committee. © BETTMANN/CORBIS

to occur. In 1954, the first human trials of "The Pill" began, which Sanger helped initiate, and by 1956 Envoid (the medically sanctioned form of a birth control pill) had been submitted before the Food and Drug Administration, and the FDA approved it for "therapeutic" purposes in 1957. By 1959, over half a million women in the United States were on it, and by 1968 seven different brands of the pill were on the market with sales reaching one hundred fifty million dollars.

Years before *Roe v. Wade* legalized abortions, the 1965 *Griswold v. Connecticut* decision paved the way for the 1973 abortion rights case. Justice William O. Douglas summed up the case by stating that neither Connecticut nor any other U.S. state could violate a person's "right to privacy." Hence, avenues were opened for the distribution of birth control, and to counter this legislative decision, some states rewrote their statues to prohibit unmarried women from obtaining birth control on the grounds of moral sanctity. Massachusetts was one of these states, but the

majority of these state laws were later over turned in the courts, on the local level, or the laws went dormant from lack of enforcement. Since Griswold and *Roe v. Wade*, the fight for women's reproductive rights has not ended. Modern legislative debates have seen public concern—both for and against—the reversal of the *Roe v. Wade* decision, restrictions on who can obtain birth control (i.e. most often teenagers, young adults, and unmarried women would be prevented from obtaining the prescription), and age and notification restrictions for abortion. These developments have all continued to color and change the birth control question.

FURTHER RESOURCES

Books

Critchlow, Donald T. *Intended Consequences: Birth Control, Abortion, and the Federal Government in Modern America.* Oxford and New York: Oxford University Press, 1999.

Dayton, Cornelia Hughes. "Taking the Trade: Abortion and Gender Relations in an Eighteenth-Century New England Village." In *Colonial America: Essays in Politics and Social Development* edited by Stanley Katz, et al. Boston: McGraw Hill, 1983.

Gordon, Linda. *Woman's Body, Woman's Right: Birth Control in America.* New York: Penguin Books, 1976.

Web sites

Time. "Leaders and Revolutionaries: Margaret Sanger." <http://www.time.com/time/time100/leaders/profile/sanger.html> (accessed April 1, 2006).

Yale-New Haven Teachers Institute. "History of Birth Control." <http://www.yale.edu/ynhti/curriculum/units/1982/6/82.06.03.x.html> (accessed April 1, 2006).

Not Just a Medical Procedure

Pamphlet

By: Health Organizing Collective of the Women's Health and Abortion Project

Date: May 1973

Source: *Vacuum Aspiration Abortion.* Brooklyn, N.Y.: Health Organizing Collective of the Women's Health and Abortion Project, May, 1973. Available at: <http://scriptorium.lib.duke.edu/wlm/abortion/> (accessed March 2, 2006).

About the Author: The Women's Health and Abortion Project, located in Brooklyn, New York, was a group of forty women that provided health and abortion care to other women.

INTRODUCTION

This document is the last page of a seven-page pamphlet entitled *Vacuum Aspiration Abortion* that was produced in 1973 by an organization called the Health Organizing Collective of the Women's Health and Abortion Project. The purpose of the pamphlet is to educate women about this abortion procedure. The first page of the pamphlet describes which abortion methods are suitable for which stages of pregnancy. The following pages describe how a woman can tell that she is pregnant, under what conditions a woman should have an abortion in a hospital rather than a clinic, how to seek counseling, what medical instruments are used, possible complications, and aftercare. The page reproduced below discusses the legal and political implications of abortion.

■ PRIMARY SOURCE

Abortion is more than a medical right. It's one of the ways we control our lives. It is a social and political issue.

As you know, on January 22, 1973, the U. S. Supreme Court ruled that women have a right to abortion. The court decided that:

- in the first 12 weeks of pregnancy, the state cannot restrict abortion. The decision to have an abortion is to be made by the woman and her doctor.
- in the second trimester (weeks 13–24), the state can impose restrictions in areas that are "reasonably related to maternal health," such as restrictions on medical facilities and persons that perform abortions and on abortion procedures.
- in the third trimester (24 weeks to term), the state can, if it chooses, prohibit or place restrictions on abortion. But the state cannot prevent an abortion if the physical or mental health of the woman is in jeopardy.

This argument is based on the 9th and 14th Amendments to the U.S. Constitution. The Court extended the "right to privacy" to include a woman's right to terminate her pregnancy.

There is no doubt that this decision is a victory for all women. But we have learned from our experience in New York City where abortion has been legal for several years that we must keep watch on the way abortions are provided.

- We must beware of unskilled abortionists.
- We must watch for restrictions that are built into state laws, into local regulations, or into hospital procedures. We must make sure that they are in the BEST INTERESTS OF WOMEN.
- We must be aware that businessmen (often doctors) in the multimillion dollar abortion business will use this law to make profits without necessarily meeting our needs as women. Vacuum aspiration abortions in New York cost between $100 and $200; saline abortions cost from $300 to $400, and they could cost much less. We must keep watch for profiteering of every sort. Report any abuses you encounter to your local Women's Liberation groups, Planned Parenthood, or Health Department.
- We must be aware that economists and population controllers may try to use legalized abortion to pressure women (especially poor women) who want babies to have abortions. For example, women have been led to believe that welfare departments can refuse aid to women who do not agree to an abortion. This is illegal. Any women who feels that an agency or institution is pressuring her to have an abortion against her will should contact a local Women's Liberation group, Welfare Rights Organization, or sympathetic consumer or legal group.
- We must see abortion as only one aspect of the quality health care we need to control our bodies.
- We must make it clear that control of our bodies means the RIGHT TO BEAR CHILDREN as well as the right not to, and that we need free maternity care, paid maternity leave, and free comprehensive day care.

The fact that there are unwanted pregnancies is only a symptom of how society has alienated us from our bodies. The fact that there is no truly adequate form of birth control and that we must keep such close watch on profiteering doctors are only two examples of how little the medical industry cares about our needs and rights.

It is not enough to have the "legal" right to abortion. It is not enough to lower slightly the price of abortion to any other medical procedure. These successes must be a part of an ongoing struggle by women to ensure that this society changes to meet everyone's needs.

■

SIGNIFICANCE

This pamphlet—already in its second revision—was produced immediately following the landmark U.S. Supreme Court Decision *Roe v. Wade*, 410 U.S. 113, January 22, 1973. In *Roe v. Wade*, a seven to two majority of the Court decided that U.S. states did not

NOT JUST A MEDICAL PROCEDURE

Abortion is more than a medical right, it's one of the ways we control our lives. It is a social and political issue.

As you know, on January 22, 1973, the U.S. Supreme Court ruled that women have a right to abortion. The Court decided that:

—in the first 12 weeks of pregnancy, the state cannot restrict abortion. The decision to have an abortion is to be made by the woman and her doctor.

—in the second trimester (weeks 13-24), the state can impose restrictions in areas that are "reasonably related to maternal health," such as restrictions on medical facilities and persons that perform abortions and on abortion procedures.

—in the third trimester (24 weeks to term), the state can, if it chooses, prohibit or place restrictions on abortion. But the state cannot prevent an abortion if the physical or mental health of the woman is in jeopardy.

This argument is based on the 9th and 14th Amendments to the U.S. Constitution. The Court extended the "right to privacy" to include a woman's right to terminate her pregnancy.

There is no doubt that this decision is a victory for all women. But we have learned from our experience in New York City where abortion has been legal for several years that we must keep watch on the way abortions are provided.

— We must beware of unskilled abortionists.

— We must watch for restrictions that are built into state laws, into local regulations, or into hospital procedures. We must make sure that they are in the BEST INTERESTS OF WOMEN.

— We must be aware that businessmen (often doctors) in the multimillion dollar abortion business will use this law to make profits without necessarily meeting our needs as women. Vacuum aspiration abortions in New York cost between $100 and $200; saline abortions cost from $300 to $400, and they could cost much less.

We must keep watch for profiteering of every sort. Report any abuses you encounter to your local Women's Liberation groups, Planned Parenthood, or Health Department.

— We must be aware that economists and population controllers may try to use legalized abortion to pressure women (especially poor women) who want babies to have abortions. For example, women have been led to believe that welfare departments can refuse aid to women who do not agree to an abortion. This is illegal. Any woman who feels that an agency or institution is pressuring her to have an abortion against her will should contact a local Women's Liberation group, Welfare Rights Organization, or sympathetic consumer or legal group.

— We must see abortion as only one aspect of the quality health care we need to control our bodies.

— We must make it clear that control of our bodies means the RIGHT TO BEAR CHILDREN as well as the right not to, and that we need free maternity care, paid maternity leave, and free comprehensive day care.

The fact that there are unwanted pregnancies is only a symptom of how society has alienated us from our bodies. The fact that there is no truly adequate form of birth control and that we must keep such close watch on profiteering doctors are only two examples of how little the medical industry cares about our needs and rights.

It is not enough to have the 'legal' right to abortion. It is not enough to lower slightly the price of abortion to any other medical procedure. These successes must be a part of an ongoing struggle by women to ensure that this society changes to meet everyone's needs.

Health Organizing Collective
of Women's Health & Abortion Project.
577 Sixth St.,
Brooklyn, N.Y. 11215

Second Revision 5/73
Copyright © Health Organizing Collective

Other pamphlets available.
Saline Abortions
The Gynecological Check Up
Infections of the Vagina
Venereal Disease

7

Part of a pamphlet put out by New York City abortion rights activists shortly after Roe v. Wade legalized abortion throughout the country. HEALTH ORGANIZING COLLECTIVE OF WOMEN'S HEALTH & ABORTION PROJECT

have the right to make abortion illegal during the first three months of pregnancy.

Feminism is a multifaceted movement that seeks equality for women and the revision of formerly basic assumptions about sexual behavior that began to develop during the nineteenth century. Progress for the evolving feminist agenda was relatively slow during the first half of the twentieth century, consisting primarily of women gaining the right to vote in a number of countries. The 1960s and 1970s, however, were a period of particularly intense political, cultural, and social ferment in many Western societies, including the United States. Feminism—which argues that the equality of men and women must be reflected in art, law, politics, personal and sexual relationships, language, technology, medicine, the workplace, etc.— was renewed by the success of popular movements such as the civil rights movement and the anti-Vietnam-War movement. In the 1970s it became a major force in academia, politics, and the arts. The feminist magazine *Ms.* was founded in 1972. It was the first journal to advocate the title "Ms." as an option for woman comparable to "Mr." for men, both without reference to marital status. Also, a number of women's health collectives were founded. A collective is a nonprofit organization of people who come together to work on a common project and who usually make decisions in a non-hierarchical or consensus-based way; some feminist thinkers have argued that consensus is a more inherently female way of making decisions than winner-takes-all democracy or top-down command by leaders.

The women's health collectives were devoted to empowering women by making accurate, useful information about medical and sexual subjects available to them. The pamphlet *Vacuum Aspiration Abortion*, produced by the apparently short-lived Health Organizing Collective of Brooklyn, New York, is one such effort. The foremost product of this type, however, is beyond doubt the book *Our Bodies, Ourselves* (1970; eighth edition, 2005), a project of the Boston Women's Health Book Collective, which remains active today.

In keeping with feminist thought, medical-empowerment documents like *Our Bodies, Ourselves* and *Vacuum Aspiration Abortion*, show frank illustrations of human bodies, medical tools, and other matters often avoided in polite conversation or media representations. Further, since 1970, one of the mottoes of the feminist movement has been "the personal is political"—meaning that sexual and private affairs cannot be isolated from the public realm of laws, politics, media, and money. This view is embodied in documents such as *Our Bodies, Ourselves* and *Vacuum Aspiration Abortion* by the inclusion of material not traditionally considered medical: personal stories, legal context, philosophy, ethics, and calls to political action. For example, on the final page of *Vacuum Aspiration Abortion* reproduced above, the Health Organizing Collective describes the main points of the *Roe v. Wade* decision and speaks of a number of other issues of concern to the writers: unskilled abortion doctors; the possibility that abortion foes will use state or local law to hamper access to abortion without actually banning it (in fact a successful tactic of anti-abortion activism since 1973); the possible use of abortion as a social engineering tool; the limited role of abortion ("only one aspect of the quality health care we need to control our bodies"); and the need to defend not only the right to abortion, but the right to bear children without being penalized by society.

The legality of abortion was politically and philosophically contentious before *Roe v. Wade* and remains so today.

FURTHER RESOURCES

Web sites

Boston Women's Health Book Collective. "Our Bodies, Ourselves." <http://www.ourbodiesourselves.org/> (accessed March 2, 2006).

CNN Interactive. "Roe v. Wade: 25 Years Later." <http://www.cnn.com/SPECIALS/1998/roe.wade/> (accessed March 29, 2006).

Oyez. "Roe v. Wade." <http://www.oyez.org/oyez/resource/case/334/> (accessed March 29, 2006).

Human T-Cell Leukemia Virus Linked to AIDS

Journal article

By: Jean L. Marx

Date: May 20, 1983

Source: Marx, Jean L. "Human T-Cell Leukemia Virus Linked to AIDS." *Science.* (May 20, 1983): 20, (4599) 806–809.

About the Author: Jean Marx is a regular contributor to the journal of *Science*, and is also the author of *A Revolution in Biotechnology*.

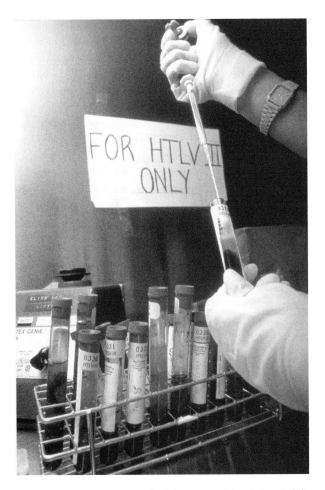

A health department technician tests blood for AIDS.
PHOTO BY JAMES POZARIK//TIME LIFE PICTURES/GETTY IMAGES

INTRODUCTION

Cells are the building blocks of all living organisms. The lifespan of cells partially depends on the functioning of organs. In a gradual process, the old cells perish and new ones are made. However, cells that lose the ability to die and continue to multiply at an abnormal rate give rise to the medical condition commonly known as cancer. A similar abnormal condition of blood cells is termed blood cancer, or leukemia. This disease afflicts human beings because of sudden mutations in blood cells or through a certain viral infection.

A virus known as the Human T-cell Leukemia Virus (HTLV) causes T-cell leukemia—a rare form of blood cancer that particularly affects T-cells. T-cells protect the body by tagging an outside object entering the body as foreign. Subsequently, the body would act against such foreign objects. In 1981, scientists pointed out that even if a person carries this virus from birth, the disease manifests only in adulthood. It is,

therefore, called Adult T-cell Leukemia (ATL). In the early 1980s, doctors treating some patients suffering from sexually transmitted diseases found that these patients also had high fever, sore throat, headaches, pneumonia, and swollen lymph nodes—symptoms indicating a suppressed immune system that was, at the time, thought to be caused by lack of T-cells. Research showed that this immune suppression could be transmitted from one person to another, and it was later termed the Acquired Immune Deficiency Syndrome (AIDS).

Further research on patients with ATL suggested a link between HTLV and AIDS. The American scientist Robert Gallo, along with his team from the National Cancer Institute (NCI) found a strong connection between HTLV infected people and those having AIDS. According to a report published by Gallo and his team, an important observation was that T-cells in patients showed abnormal behavior in both the diseases, and that the modes of viral transmission were similar. The team also discovered a single virus causing leukemia and suppression of the immune system in cats.

The following article excerpt was published in the journal *Science* in 1983, and discusses Robert Gallo's findings. The article, as its name suggests, reports that AIDS can be caused by the Human T-Cell Leukemia Virus.

■ PRIMARY SOURCE

Patients with the new immune disease show evidence of infection by human T-cell leukemia virus. Does the virus cause the disease?

Five reports in this issue of *Science* suggest a possible link between the serious new disease, acquired immune deficiency syndrome (AIDS) and human T-cell leukemia virus (HTLV), which has been associated with a rare type of human cancer. Investigators at the Harvard University School of Public Health, the National Cancer Institute, and the Pasteur Institute have fond evidence of HTLV infection in patients with AIDS or at high risk of developing the syndrome. The evidence includes isolation of the virus itself from a few patients, detection of the viral DNA in T cells from two cases, and also a much higher incidence of antibodies against HTLV in AIDS patients than in controls.

It is still too early to tell whether HTLV actually causes AIDS. The disease is characterized by immune suppression, which results in high susceptibility to opportunistic infections by agents that do not usually cause serious illnesses in healthy people but can prove devastating to individuals with defective immune responses. HTLV may be just another of these opportunistic pathogens, a consequence rather than a cause of AIDS. Max Essex of the Harvard group says, "I definitely do not want anyone to get the impression that we have proof of cause. What we do have is a good lead."

A good lead is much needed. Since AIDS first became manifest in 1981, more than 1350 cases have been reported to the Centers of Disease Control (CDC). The mortality rate may be 70 percent or higher, and the number of cases continues to grow by four to five per day. Epidemiological studies strongly suggest that AIDS is caused by an infectious agent, although other possibilities have not been conclusively ruled out. Efforts to identify the infectious agent have proved frustrating.

According to Robert Gallo of the National Cancer Institute (NCI), there are a number of reasons for taking a close look at HTLV as a possible cause of AIDS. First is the prevalence of HTLV in the Caribbean area and in Africa. The Caribbean area, especially Haiti, and equatorial Africa have been suggested as possible sources of the putative AIDS agent.

In the United States, Haitian immigrants constitute the third largest group of AIDS patients. The largest group consists of homosexual and bisexual men who have been extremely active sexually, and the second largest includes users of illegal intravenous drugs. Hemophiliacs are a fourth group with increased risk of AIDS.

AIDS has apparently spread among homosexuals by sexual contact and among drug users by contaminated needles. It is believed to have been transmitted to hemophiliacs by way of the blood clotting factor preparations that they must take. But the Haitians have always been a puzzle, because the vast majority deny both homosexual practices and drug use and they have not been exposed to clotting factor preparations. The identification of a causative virus in the Haitian population could help clear up this mystery.

Secondly, HTLV primarily infects T cells. As Gallo puts it, "HTLV is extraordinarily T-cell tropic." The primary AIDS defect also seems to be in the T lymphocytes, which are reduced in number in the patients and abnormal in composition. The helper T cells, which are needed to activate certain immune responses, including antibody production by the B-lymphocytes, are very low in number, whereas the killer-suppressor cells are much less affected. The loss of helpers, while the activities of suppressor T cells remain more or less intact, could produce the profound suppression of the immune response that is characteristic of AIDS.

A third point of similarity is mode of transmission. As noted previously, AIDS spreads by intimate contact and through blood products. "Everything we know about HTLV suggests that intimate contact is needed for transmission," Gallo remarks. He points out that the viral envelope, which is required for infectivity, is very fragile. It tends to come off when the virus buds from infected cells, thus rendering the particles incapable of infecting new cells. Gallo speculates that direct cell-to-cell contact may be required for the spread of HTLV.

Finally, there are the precedents for a virus causing both a leukemia and immunosuppression. This is true for feline leukemia virus, which has been studied for many years in the Essex laboratory. "More cats are killed as a result of feline leukemia virus causing immunosuppression than by feline leukemia virus causing leukemia," Essex says.

The virus generally impairs T-cell responses in the animals. Previous attempts to demonstrate an effect on antibody production had failed, but the Essex group now finds that natural infection by feline leukemia virus suppresses the antibody response to an antigen that normally requires the cooperation of helper T cells to elicit antibody production. Feline leukemia virus also has a preference for infecting T cells and produces primarily T cell leukemias. The antibody response may be deficient, Essex speculates, because of a problem with the helper T cells.

Previous failures to demonstrate a viral effect on antibody production may be attributable to the differing responses of cats to naturally occurring and laboratory-induced infections. The natural infections are more effective at suppressing the immune response of cats than infections induced by such laboratory methods as directly injecting the virus.

HTLV is one of the retroviruses, which have RNA as their genetic material. In infected cells, the RNA is copied into DNA, which may then become integrated into the DNA genome of the host cell and bring about the cell's cancerous transformation. To determine whether AIDS patients showed signs of infection by HTLV the Gallo group looked for viral DNA in the patients' T cells.

They detected the viral DNA in the cells of two of 33 patients, but did not find it in T cells from any of 25 healthy homosexual males. They were able to isolate infectious HTLV particles form the T cells of one of the two individuals who were positive for viral DNA and also from two additional patients. This is from a total of about 20 patients whose T cells were used in attempts to isolate HTLV. In addition, a French group, under the direction of Luc Montagnier of the Pasteur Institute in Paris, has isolated a related virus from the T cells of a homosexual male with lymphadenopathy, a condition that may be a mild form of AIDS or a forerunner of the full-blown disease.

There is more than one type of HTLV. About 35 isolates of the virus have been made throughout the world. Roughly 25 of these have been characterized and most are of the type designated HTLV-I, which was originally isolated by the Gallo group. A second type of the virus, which is designated HTLV-II, has been isolated from the cells of a patient with hairy cell leukemia.

The NCI workers have characterized one of their three HTLV isolates from AIDS patients and it is HTLV-I. The virus isolated by the French group is neither HTLV-I nor -II, but represents a third variant of the virus. Although the members of the HTLV family are distinguished on the basis of structural variations in one of the internal proteins of the viral particle, they have other features in common, including their preference for infecting T cells and the rather unusual properties of their enzyme for copying RNA into DNA.

Gallo suggests that logistical problems might explain why viral DNA could be detected in the cells of so few AIDS patients. "If infection leads to a decline in the population of infected cells, you may not be able to find them by the time you get frank disease," he explains. In fact, the NCI workers could not detect integrated viral DNA in T cells from blood samples taken at a later date from the two patients who had earlier given positive results. The same problem might affect attempts to isolate the virus itself. Lymphocytes from the spleen or lymph nodes might be a better source of virus than the peripheral blood cells used for the NCI studies. The French workers isolated their virus from lymph node cells….

If HTLV does cause AIDS then there must be a way of maintaining the immunosuppressed state even after the virus is no longer detectable. The immune systems of the patients do not appear to recover.

Simply finding HTLV or the DNA in AIDS patients does not mean that the virus caused the disease. "From our data it could be an opportunistic infection," Gallo concedes. "But Essex's data argue that it is more than opportunistic."

Essex and his Harvard and CDC collaborators detected antibodies against membrane-associated antigens of HTLV in at least 25 percent of 75 AIDS and 23 lymphadenopathy patients. Another 10 percent or so would be positive if the investigators used a somewhat less stringent criterion for a positive antibody test.

In contrast, only one of 81 homosexual controls who had been matched for age, race, and place of residence with 36 of the AIDS patients had the antibodies. The one positive individual was a friend, but not a sex partner, of one of the patients. Only two of an additional 305 controls, including homosexuals who had visited a venereal disease clinic, healthy blood donors, kidney dialysis and chronic hepatitis patients, had the antibodies. "The message is that 25 to 40 percent of AIDS cases have the antibodies and 1 percent or less of control groups do," Essex says.

Other attempts to identify differences in viral exposures between AIDS patients and controls have not turned up such a large discrepancy between the two groups. Nevertheless, some 50 percent of the patients did not have the antibodies, either because the test was not sensitive enough to detect them or because their immune systems failed to make the antibodies—or because they had not been infected by HTLV.

Militating against the possibility that HTLV causes AIDS, Gallo says, is the relatively short period of time required for the immune deficiency disease to develop. CDC officials have reported the latency period of AIDS to be several months to a year. The T-cell leukemia caused by HTLV may require years, if not decades, to develop after infection by the virus.

Perhaps more disconcerting than the discrepancies in the latency periods of the two conditions is the apparent lack of AIDS in southern Japan, an area where the rate of HTLV infection is very high. Some 25 percent of the population there have antibodies against the virus, compared to 4 to 5 percent in Haiti and 1 percent in the United States.

Either AIDS exists in that part of Japan but has not been diagnosed, which seems unlikely especially in view of the publicity AIDS has received during the past year, or the Japanese may respond differently to the infection. Another possibility, Gallo points out, is that a change occurred in the HTLV family in Africa or Haiti that conferred a new capability for immune suppression on the virus. Comparison of the nucleotide sequences of the DNA of viral isolates form the various sources may help to clarify this issue.

Why some people might develop AIDS as a consequence of HTLV infections while others get leukemia is unclear. It might be an as yet undetermined difference in the infecting HTLV or in the host response to the infection. It might depend on the site at which the viral DNA integrates in the genome of infected cells.

In any event, there are now a number of approaches that may be taken to clarify the relation between HTLV and AIDS. A prospective study of high-risk individuals to see whether HTLV infection precedes or follows development of AIDS is a possibility. Another is to look at people who have other types of immune suppression, children with congenital immunodeficiency diseases or kidney transplant patients, for example, to see if they too have an increased number of HTLV infections.

If HTLV does eventually prove to be the cause of AIDS, then a specific test for the early diagnosis of the condition may be feasible. Especially desirable is an assay for the AIDS agent in blood. The possibility that the condition may be transmitted in blood products has naturally generated a great deal of concern. Ultimately a vaccine may be developed to protect high-risk individuals. But that all awaits firm proof of the cause of AIDS.

SIGNIFICANCE

Gallo's above-mentioned report is one of the first scientific papers to be published on AIDS. In the early 1980s, considerable medical research was conducted to assimilate the root causes for AIDS. This was a period when no one was aware that infection with the Human Immunodeficiency Virus (HIV) eventually leads to AIDS.

Although Gallo's research indicated HTLV (or HTLV-I, as it is commonly known) as the most promising virus for causing AIDS, this was soon proven false. Further research revealed specific differences between HTLV I and the virus that actually causes AIDS. Researchers found that although the modes of transmission of both the viruses were similar, HTLV I was not as easily transmitted as the AIDS-causing virus. Moreover, while HTLV caused an abnormal increase in the number of T-cells, the AIDS-causing virus degenerated the defense mechanism. It was also found that HTLV maintained its genetic make-up, unlike the actual virus.

At the time, a team of French scientists, led by Luc Montagnier from the Pasteur Institute, also worked on isolating the AIDS virus. As mentioned above, they found that HTLV and the AIDS-causing virus had similar genetic make-up. However, the similarity ended there because both the viruses were found to operate inside the cell in distinct ways. Montagnier wanted the AIDS virus to be called HTLV III (due to its similarity to HTLV I and II), but the team termed it Lymphoadenopathy Associated Virus (LAV). At the same time, Gallo and his team published more papers in *Science* declaring HTLV III (now known as Human Immunodeficiency Virus or HIV) to be the cause of AIDS. This caused a legal conflict between the American and French scientists. The issue was resolved in 1987 by proclaiming both Gallo and Montagnier as co-discoverers of the AIDS virus, in an agreement signed by the respective scientists, then U.S. President Ronald Reagan (1911–2004) and French Prime Minister Jacques Chirac.

Although it reaches an erroneous conclusion, Gallo's report is considered a highly significant paper

by scientists, as it instigated exhaustive research and competition among scientists to find the cause of AIDS. Several viruses were initially and incorrectly linked to AIDS. For example, a *New York Times* article published in August 1985, stated that scientists assumed the Hepatitis B virus to be the basis of AIDS.

Since the 1980s, both HIV infection and AIDS have become a worldwide pandemic. There is also a common misconception that HIV and AIDS are identical conditions. Although HIV does eventually lead to AIDS, only when the numbers of the HIV virus are sufficient in the body to cause the symptoms characteristic of immune system compromise is AIDS diagnosed. According to a 2004 paper titled 'Human retroviruses in Leukemia and AIDS: reflections on their discovery, biology and epidemiology' by Abraham Karpas, ninety percent patients who are tested HIV positive develop AIDS in less than ten years. Medical research has also proved that HIV is a far more destructive virus compared to HTLV. The above-mentioned report suggests that only about one percent of those infected by HTLV eventually develop leukemia.

According to the United Nations, as of 2005, the number of people reportedly living with AIDS is 40.3 million.

FURTHER RESOURCES

Books

Gallo, Robert C. *Virus Hunting: AIDS, Cancer, and the Human Retrovirus: A Story of Scientific Discovery*. New York: Basic Books, 1993.

Web sites

Avert.org. "HIV & AIDS Statistics." <http://www.avert.org/statindx.htm> (accessed March 14, 2006).

Cambridge Journals Online. Karpas, Abraham. " Human Retroviruses in Leukemia and AIDS: Reflections on Their Discovery, Biology and Epidemiology." <http://journals.cambridge.org/> (accessed March 14, 2006).

Karen Carpenter's Death Draws Attention to Anorexia

Newspaper article

By: David Arnold

Date: February 8, 1983

Source: Arnold, David. "Karen Carpenter's Death Draws Attention to Anorexia." *Boston Globe*, February 8, 1983.

About the Author: David Arnold is a reporter who specializes in health issues with the *Boston Globe*, a daily newspaper with a circulation of over 500,000 based in Boston, Massachusetts.

INTRODUCTION

Eating disorders have been part of many cultures since antiquity. Ancient Romans invented the *vomitorium*, a place to purge bloated stomachs during multiday feasts so that celebrants could return to consume more food, while religious ascetics had long used fasting as a ritual to help gain spiritual purity. The eating disorder known as anorexia nervosa was given its name in 1868 by Sir William Whitney Gull, a British physician, who noted several cases of self-starvation in young girls. He ascribed the patients' "want of appetite" to "a morbid mental state…We might call the state hysterical" [*European Neurology* 55 (2006): 53–56].

At the same time, French physician Charles Lasègue found that girls suffering from anorexia went through three phases during their illness. First, they used alleged discomfort after eating as an excuse to reduce consumption. Second, they became preoccupied with weight loss and food. In the third stage, they entered into an emaciated and compromised state that led to death unless medical experts intervened. Despite the risk of death, Lasègue noted, the girls continued to starve themselves, against logic.

Jeff Everts, who is recovering from anorexia and bulimia, plays with his dog at his Albuquerque, N.M., home on April 29, 2004. AP IMAGES

In addition to self-starvation, Lasègue noted that patients who were force- fed as part of their treatment often vomited deliberately afterward. In the late 1860s, physicians referred to this as cynorexia; people who binged and then purged themselves by vomiting were called cynorexics; the modern term for this eating disorder is bulimia nervosa.

Cases of anorexia and bulimia dot medical literature from the late 1860s onward. Most patients were girls in their teens from middle and upper class families; most were treated in private hospitals. A handful of cases document the experiences of male anorectics or bulimics.

In the late 1970s in the United States, various dieting fads took hold; fashion magazines idolized rail-thin women as the female ideal. While this was not new—the 1960s had established the model Twiggy as an ideal—the trickle- down effect of these fashion trends to teen and preteen readers affected ideals of the female body. Books such as Hilde Bruch's *The Golden Cage: The Enigma of Anorexia Nervosa* came to public attention as mainstream newspapers began to review books on the issue and discuss this disturbing trend.

By the 1980s, eating disorders had become a major social and medical concern. A 1981 television movie, *The Best Little Girl in the World*, adapted from a 1978 novel by the New York psychotherapist Steven Levenkron, told the story of Kessie, the "perfect" daughter—straight-A student, happily involved in school activities, well liked by her peers. When her weight dropped to 98 pounds and her obsession with thinness put her life in jeopardy, her family was forced to confront their dysfunction.

Nor were celebrities immune from the pressure to be thin and perfect. Singer Karen Carpenter, half of the 1970s duo The Carpenters, whose hits such as "Close to You" and "We've Only Just Begun" have become pop classics, battled anorexia for sixteen years. Although she sought treatment after reading Levenkron's book, the disease had progressed too far, and she died on February 4, 1983.

PRIMARY SOURCE

Karen Carpenter's Death Draws Attention to Anorexia

The death of pop singer Karen Carpenter has again called attention to a compulsive dieting disease that can literally starve its victims.

Yesterday, a spokesman for the Los Angeles coroner said it would take several weeks for tests to determine if anorexia nervosa, for which Carpenter was being treated, has caused her heart to fail.

Dr. David Herzog, director of the Eating Disorders Clinic at Massachusetts General Hospital, said in a telephone interview yesterday that anorexia can cause problems such as coronary failure.

"I have had patients with a similar history," Herzog said, although he noted he was unfamiliar with Carpenter's case.

Anorexia afflicts women—the incidence among men is very rare—from their teens to their early 30s. It is self-induced starvation, driven by an obsession not to appear fat.

Victims usually are well-educated perfectionists from affluent families. They exercise often and have a distorted view that an emaciated body is beautiful.

Herzog said the incidence of anorexia is increasing; new cases at his clinic have soared from 30 to 150 annually in the past two years. The mortality rate is about 6 percent.

Recent reports indicate about 280,000 women between the ages of 12 to 25 suffer from anorexia in the United States.

Death may come from malnourishment leading to arrhythmia, or irregular heartbeats. Anorexics also are more vulnerable to other illnesses and often are depressed, making them more prone to suicide.

Carpenter was 32, recently divorced and living alone. She was visiting her family's home in Downey, Calif., when her heart stopped beating Friday morning.

One way anorexics lose weight is restricting food intake. A more severe method is by "gorging and purging," Herzog said, or going on eating binges and then expelling the food. Vomiting or taking laxatives, common means of purging, removes potassium that is vital to maintaining the body's electrical system. Erratic nerve pulses can retard or upset the heartbeat, withholding blood to the heart muscle, which will stop the heart.

SIGNIFICANCE

While psychologists and some physicians had known of anorexia and bulimia trends, the public was shocked by Karen Carpenter's death and the intricacies—as well as prevalence,—of eating disorders in the United States. Carpenter, a famous rock star with a string of hits in the early 1970s, had fought anorexia since the age of seventeen, when she developed a distorted sense of her body and self-image while performing on the national, and later, the international music scenes.

People with anorexia typically lose fifteen to sixty percent of their body weight; over time the body, needing protein from some source, begins to consume its own muscle mass, at times targeting even the heart. In Karen Carpenter, years of anorexia had weakened her heart. She had been under a physician's care but the damage done by years of anorexia were irreversible, and she died of cardiac arrest. Her mother found her naked and unconscious near a walk-in closet at their home.

Treatment for anorexia, which affects one percent of all females ages ten to twenty, and bulimia, which affects approximately four percent of all females ages ten to twenty, has changed since 1983, when Karen Carpenter's death brought the issue into the public spotlight. Public health campaigns aimed at healthy eating, improving body image and self-esteem, along with health curricula that discuss the dangers of anorexia and bulimia treat eating disorders as social and medical issues. Fashion magazines began to promote toned bodies with more athletic features in the mid 1980s, but in the late 1990s, extremely thin models and celebrities such as Kate Moss, Calista Flockhart, and Lara Flynn Boyle continued the emphasis on an unhealthy, unattainably thin ideal.

Approximately one in seven anorexia and bulimia patients is male; the disorders manifest in different ways with men. Male bulimics use obsessive exercise to hide purging, and many high school and college wrestlers use bulimia for weight class control. Male anorectics follow patterns that are similar to females'.

Researchers estimate that as many as one in four women exhibit some eating disorder behavior at some point in time, generally during the late teens and early twenties. While most pass through this phase quickly, six percent of all women develop a clinical eating disorder. Approximately twenty percent of all people with eating disorders die as a direct result of eating disorder behaviors or from medical complications related to anorexia or bulimia.

FURTHER RESOURCES
Books

Brumberg, Joan Jacobs. *Fasting Girls: The History of Anorexia Nervosa*. New York: Vintage, 2000.

Coleman, Ray. *The Carpenters: The Untold Story: An Authorized Biography*. New York: HarperCollins, 1994.

Stearns, Peter N. *Fat History: Bodies and Beauty in the Modern West*. New York: New York University Press, 2002.

Web sites

Eating Disorders Coaltition< httphttp://www.eatingdisorderscoalition.org> (accessed March 27, 2006).

National Association for the Mentally Ill "About Mental Illness: Anorexia Nervosa." < http://www.nami.org/Template/> (accessed March 27, 2006).

No Thanks For the Memories

Imagined Abuse

Magazine article

By: Anonymous

Source: "Imagined Abuse: No Thanks For the Memories." *Psychology Today*. vol. 26, no. 1, January/February 1993.

About the Author: *Psychology Today* is a widely distributed magazine focusing on the issues of the mind and body, the health of both, and the workings behind them.

INTRODUCTION

In the early 1980s, the topics of child abuse, child abductions, and child murders were the focus of newspaper articles, talk shows, and magazine pieces. High profile cases such as the 1979 disappearance of seven-year-old Etan Patz as he walked to school alone for the first time and the 1981 disappearance and murder of six-year-old Adam Walsh, lost during a shopping trip at a local Sears, fanned concerns about child safety outside of the home or school. The McMartin preschool case, which began in 1983 and involved hundreds of allegations of sexual abuse of children and the 1987 murder of Lisa Steinberg at the hands of her father, Joel Steinberg, reinforced fears about child safety in educational institutions and even in the child's own home.

As these events unfolded in American society, psychologists and psychiatrists worked with an increasing number of patients; the pursuit of therapy became more acceptable as a method for dealing with trauma and emotional problems. As more people sought therapy, more therapists dealt with stories from clients about childhood abuse. The Child Abuse Prevention and Treatment Act of 1974 had created a legal and social culture in which child abuse cases were taken seriously by law enforcement, social workers, and psychologists. By the 1980s, additional laws, such as mandated reporting for therapists and school officials, added to the goal of validating child abuse experiences and helping children and adults to heal from such abuse.

Holly Ramona testifies during a malpractice trial against her therapists. Her father, Gary Ramona, sued her thearpists for using the controversial technique of recovered-memory therapy to help her "remember" incidents of sexual abuse by him he claims never happened. Mr. Ramona won his suit in 1994. PHOTO BY JOHN STOREY//TIME LIFE PICTURES/GETTY IMAGES

Popular self-help books, written by psychologists, social workers, and victims gained bestseller status in the United States, with titles such as "Codependent No More," "The Courage to Heal," and "Toxic Parents." Psychological theories became part of common public discourse, therapy became more acceptable, and some psychologists began to focus on a new technique called Recovered Memory Therapy (RMT), also known as Repressed Memory Therapy.

RMT is based on the theory that certain dysfunctional behaviors and mental illnesses, such as depression, anxiety, bulimia, sexual inhibition, and anorexia, stem from childhood traumas such as physical or, more commonly, sexual abuse. In patients who exhibit no known history of trauma, but display severe behavior dysfunction, RMT uses a variety of techniques to "recover" a repressed memory of physical or sexual abuse.

These techniques include, but are not limited to hypnotherapy, art therapy, trance writing, and the use of "truth serum" medications such as sodium amytal. In a typical RMT session, the client is placed under hypnosis, the therapist administers sodium amytal, and the therapist proceeds to work with the client on a specific memory, asking the client to recall details, feelings, or events.

RMT, used extensively in the 1980s and into the early 1990s, was controversial during its peak. Based on the theory—later disproved—that all life experiences are dutifully recorded in the brain, and finding memories involves using the right technique to retrieve them, therapists who used RMT believed that these recovered memories were unadulterated truth.

In 1984 and 1985, magazines such as *Time* and *Newsweek* published in-depth stories on alleged ritual Satanic abuse. Many RMT clients recalled memories of being forced into sexual acts, engaging in cannibalism, brutally slaughtering of animals for sacrifice, and even being coerced into allegedly murdering children or babies as part of cult rituals. These "underground cults" allegedly included preschools, and these articles, along with talk shows and newsmagazine shows devoted to these subjects—were part of a national focus on child sexual abuse in homes and social institutions such as day care centers, schools and churches.

At the same time, tens of thousands of therapy clients, largely women, claimed to have recovered memories of abuse by fathers, uncles, grandparents, and other male adults in their lives. The typical accuser was between nineteen and fifty, female, suffered from depression and/or an eating disorder, and was high school educated; one third were college educated. RMT practitioners recommended that victims of recovered memories needed to confront their abusers with their stories, regardless of the harm that might come to family relationships, and regardless of lack of hard evidence, inconsistent memories, or lack of corroborating information from others.

PRIMARY SOURCE

Victims of childhood sexual abuse have long had support groups. Now there's an organization to aid the victims of imaginary memories of incest and abuse.

As the awareness of childhood sexual abuse has grown, so have false accusations of abuse—often the result of misguided therapeutic programs. Philadelphia psychologist Pam Freyd, Ph.D., decided to combat this trend and set up the False Memory Syndrome Foundation. In its first year alone, over 1,200 families made contact all with heartbreaking claims to defend themselves over accusations from one of their own.

Many psychologists have seen families torn apart by false memory syndrome and place much of the blame on a new type of therapist, the "traumatist." Encouraged by popular notions of victimization and prime-time disclosures of all kinds of abuse, the traumatist urges patients to remember sexual abuse or violence in childhood—whether it happened or not. False Memory Syndrome is now so prevalent that Paul McHugh, M.D., director of psychiatry at Johns Hopkins, compares the situation to the Salem witch trials.

At issue are the methods used to elicit memories, namely hypnosis and "narcoanalysis," employing agents like amobarbital sodium. Instead of unearthing genuine memories these therapies may make patients so suggestible that they misinterpret fantasy as reality. A therapist searching for clues of abuse could be planting the seeds of false memories.

The American Medical Association deems hypnosis a valid therapy—but not a reliable "means to refresh memory." In fact, the AMA declared hypnotic recall "less reliable 2than nonhypnotic recall," and cautioned that its use may result in "confabulations and pseudomemories."

All the traumatists are doing is spreading misery, says Freyd. Those accused face enormous emotional stresses and legal problems. Accusers risk losing their families and wasting time in misdirected and painful "therapy." And the genuine victims of abuse have a tougher time persuading others to believe their charges.

SIGNIFICANCE

The confrontations that were part of RMT shocked parents and grandparents; one such alleged abuser, Pam Freyd, created the False Memory Syndrome Foundation, as this article notes. In 1990, during a visit with their daughter Jennifer, she accused her father, Peter, of molesting her repeatedly throughout her childhood and adolescence. The Freyds created FMSF in part as a result of their experience. In 1993, their daughter, a tenured professor at the University of Oregon, made public remarks about her personal experience during a professional conference, describing years of molestation, exposure to her father's unwanted sexual advances, and his descriptions of having been molested himself by a gay man. Jennifer Freyd coined the term "betrayal trauma" in 1996 in her book titled *Betrayal Trauma*, describing the use of amnesia as a coping technique when a child experiences the betrayal of sexual abuse at the hands of a parent.

The very public conflict between the Freyds and their daughter played out in newspapers, magazine articles, and professional publications. As the head of the False Memory Syndrome Foundation, Pamela Freyd claimed to have received more than 1,200 contacts in the foundation's first year; within five years the Freyds stated that more than 17,000 families who experienced accusations based on recovered memories.

In the mid 1990s, some therapy clients, severely questioning their recovered memories, began to reconcile with their families and file lawsuits against therapists who used RMT. The FMSF works with families filing such lawsuits. The Canadian Psychiatric Association filed a position statement in 1996 which stated, in part: "Reports of recovered memories of sexual abuse may be true, but great caution should be exercised before acceptance in the absence of solid corroboration. Psychiatrists should be aware that excessive emphasis on recovering memories may lead to misdirection of the treatment process and unduly delay appropriate therapeutic measures." Paul McHugh, chair of the department of psychiatry at Johns Hopkins University School of Medicine, refers to RMT as "a shameful episode in the history of psychiatry." Psychologists and psychiatrists are quick to point out that there is a radical difference between recovering a memory spontaneously, though, and the techniques used in RMT, which many believe to be misleading.

In October 2005, Kyle Zirpolo, eight years old at the time of the alleged abuse against him in the McMartin preschool case, retracted his molestation accusation. In an interview he explained that "I remember telling them [interviewers] nothing happened to me. I remember them almost giggling and laughing, saying, "Oh, we know these things happened to you. Why don't you just go ahead and tell us? Use these dolls if you're scared. Anytime I would give them an answer that they didn't like, they would ask again and encourage me to give them the answer they were looking for."

Proponents of RMT say that Kyle's story does not negate the thousands of stories of repressed memories that are real, while opponents of RMT claim that his story is evidence that RMT, in a clinical or law enforcement setting, is invalid and misleading.

FURTHER RESOURCES

Books

Brainerd, C.J. and V.F. Reyna. *The Science of False Memory.* New York: Oxford University Press, 2005.

Freyd, Jennifer L. *Betrayal Trauma: The Logic of Forgetting Childhood Abuse.* Cambridge, Mass.: Harvard University Press, 1996.

Masson, Jeffrey. *The Assault on Truth: Freud's Suppression of the Seduction Theory.* New York: Pocket Books, 1998.

Spanos, Nicholas P. *Multiple Identities & False Memories: A Sociocognitive Perspective.* Washington, DC: American Psychological Association, 2001.

Web sites

False Memory Syndrome Foundation. <http://www.fmsfonline.org/> (accessed March 30, 2006).

L.A.Times.com. "McMartin Pre-Schooler: 'I Lied.'" <http://www.latimes.com/travel/destinations/pacific/la-tm-mcmartin44oct30,0,285518.story?coll=la-home-magazine> (accessed March 30, 2006).

Salon.com. "False Memory Syndrome: As Women Bring Lawsuits, Therapists are Having to Pay for Their Mistakes." <http://www.salon.com/health/feature/1999/12/22/false_memory/index.html> (accessed March 30, 2006).

Breast Cancer Awareness Stamp

Photograph

By: Tim Johnson

Date: June 17, 1996

Source: The Associated Press

About the Photographer: Tim Johnson is a regular contributor of photography to the Associated Press, a worldwide news agency based in New York.

INTRODUCTION

Breast cancer is the number one killer of women between the ages of fifteen and fifty-four in the United States. At least three million women in the United States are living with breast cancer. Of those, one million women have yet to be diagnosed with the disease. One in seven women will get breast cancer within her lifetime, and every two minutes, a woman is diagnosed with the disease. In 2005, an estimated 212,000 new cases of invasive breast cancer were diagnosed and 58,000 cases of non-invasive cancer were diagnosed. The disease claims the life of a woman in the United States every thirteen minutes and an estimated 40,000 women died from the disease in 2005. Early detection of the disease and early treatment are the only known factors in increasing a woman's survival rate.

In 1993, veteran postal worker Diane Sackett Nannery was diagnosed with breast cancer. She had spent the last fourteen years working in the Long Island Diversity Development Unit in the Hauppauge district office. Nannery began to use her position within the postal service to become the "stamp lady." She sent letters to newspapers and women's groups and organized petitions for the creation of a stamp regarding breast cancer awareness. With the assistance of former U.S. Senator Alfonse D'Amato, Nannery's goal for the creation of a stamp became a reality. For decades, the Citizen Stamp Advisory Committee had issued stamps on various health related issues. On June 15, 1996, the United States Postal Service (USPS) issued 100 million breast cancer awareness stamps. The stamp was to serve as the centerpiece for a national campaign launched with the National Cancer Institute to stress the importance of early detection and treatment of breast cancer. The USPS, National Cancer Institute, and Breast Cancer groups participated in a public service campaign intended to

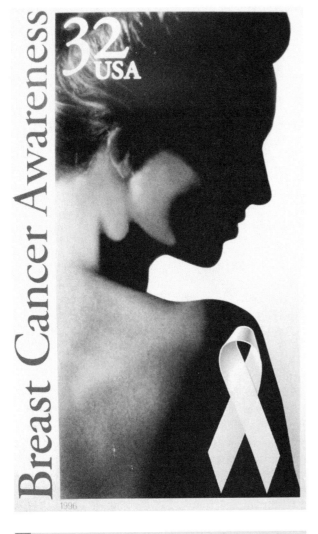

Breast Cancer Awareness Stamp The Breast Cancer Awareness Stamp was issued at the M.D. Anderson Cancer Center in Houston, on June 17, 1996, sending the message that the United States Postal Service and the National Cancer Institute have joined forces to spread the word about breast cancer. AP IMAGES

PRIMARY SOURCE

BREAST CANCER AWARENESS STAMP

See primary source image.

SIGNIFICANCE

Two years after the USPS issued the Breast Cancer Awareness Stamp, a new breast cancer stamp was unveiled. On July 29, 1998, the Breast Cancer Research semipostal stamp was issued at a White House ceremony. Semipostal stamps have been issued in France and Germany prior to World War I (1915–1918) and in Finland to benefit the Red Cross. However, this semipostal, or fundraising stamp, was the first of its kind issued in the United States. The stamp is priced twenty-five percent above the value of a first class stamp with the surplus revenues generated by its sale allocated to breast cancer research. Seventy percent of the proceeds are given to the National Institute of Health and the remaining thirty percent are given to the Department of Defense Army research project. The original legislation, authored by Senator Diane Feinstein of California, specifies that the federal government cannot reduce appropriations to the organizations in the amount of the raised funds.

In 2005, at the seventh anniversary of the stamps issue Senator Feinstein introduced legislation to reauthorize the stamps issue and continue the fundraising generated from its sale. By the end of 2005, over 678 million Breast Cancer Awareness semipostal stamps had been sold, resulting in $47.9 million raised for breast cancer research. The General Accounting Office also reported that the stamp was an effective fundraiser. As a result, the legislation passed to continue its sales.

The forty-five cent stamp was designed by Ethel Kessler, a breast cancer survivor. It features the phrases, "Fund the Fight" and "Find a Cure." The stamp has an illustration by Whitney Sherman of Diana, the Roman goddess of the hunt. Diana serves as a symbol of strength and independence who overcomes adversity. The goddess is reaching for an arrow, meant to signify the targeting of the disease. The placement of the arm is also a reminder for self-examinations. The background is a kaleidoscope of color meant to represent the spectrum of those affected by the disease.

In January 2005, the stamp reached international audiences when the Hungarian post office issued a surcharged stamp in the likeness of the U.S. Breast Cancer Stamp. The Hungarian stamp, called "Fight against breast cancer," benefits the Hungarian National Oncology Institute.

educate women about the importance of early detection of breast cancer. In addition, the stamp was issued in conjunction with the 1996 running of the Susan G. Komen Foundation National Run for the Cure five kilometer run/walk.

The thirty-two cent stamp, designed by Tom Mann, depicts the silhouette of a woman, intended to capture the personal and emotional trauma brought on by the disease. A pink ribbon rests over the woman's shoulder, signifying survival.

Participants in the Race for the Cure gather at the Washington Monument in Washington, DC , on June 3, 2000. The race raises funds for breast cancer research, and uses a pink ribbon as its symbol. NESHAN H. NALTCHAYAN/AFP/GETTY IMAGES

FURTHER RESOURCES
Periodicals
Josefah, Lisa. "Advertising and Marketing Briefs." *Long Island Business News.* (June 18, 1996) 43, 24.

Web sites
Ascribe: The Public Interest Newswire. "WIN Against Breast Cancer celebrates anniversary of historic Breast Cancer Research Stamp." <http://www.ascribe.org/cgi-bin/d?asid=20050729.162122> (accessed March 21, 2006).

Senator Diane Feinstein. "Breast Cancer Research Stamp." <http://www.senate.gov/~feinstein/breast_cancer_stamp.html> (accessed March 21, 2006).

United States Postal Service. "Breast Cancer Awareness Stamp." <http://www.usps.com/communications/community/semipostals.htm> (accessed March 21, 2006).

Focus on Women's Health Around the World

Article

By: Donna E. Shalala

Date: 2000

Source:

About the Author: Donna E. Shalala was born in Cleveland, Ohio, in 1941. She attended the Western College for Women and obtained her Ph.D from Syracuse University. She was one of the first U.S. Peace Corps volunteers, serving in Iran from 1962 to 1964. In 1993, President Bill Clinton appointed her as the U.S. Secretary of Health and Human Services, where she served for eight years.

INTRODUCTION

After the United Nations declared 1975 the International Women's Year, it sponsored a series of international conferences to address women's issues around the world. The first, which met that year in Mexico City, proclaimed 1976–1985 the United Nations Decade for Women: Equality, Development, and Peace. The next was held in 1980 in Copenhagen to assess progress made toward the goals identified in Mexico City. This gathering established the Programme of Action for the Second Half of the United Nations Decade for Women: Equality, Development and Peace, and featured a platform that identified additional obstacles toward women's equality and created an international agreement on the actions necessary to address those inequalities.

The Third World Conference for Women met July 1985 in Nairobi and produced "Nairobi Forward-Looking Strategies for the Advancement of Women," an agreement that addressed objectives for women's advancement from 1986–2000, and created concrete objectives—based on the UN charter, as well as other declarations and covenants—to address international cooperation toward the elimination of gender-based inequalities.

In 1995, the Fourth World Conference for Women convened in Beijing. Representatives from the 189 member nations discussed the inequalities that women faced throughout the world and published a declaration that focused on advancing the "goals of equality, development and peace for all women" and identified the United Nation's uneven progress toward

Zimbabwean women's pressure groups march in Harare, December 1, 2005, to bring awareness on World AIDS Day.
STR/AFP/GETTY IMAGES

universal women's rights. The declaration asserted that poverty affects women and children disproportionately and that "[t]he empowerment and advancement of women, including the right to freedom of thought, conscience, religion and belief, thus contributing to the moral, ethical, spiritual and intellectual needs of women and men, individually or in community with others and thereby guaranteeing them the possibility of realizing their full potential in society and shaping their lives in accordance with their own aspirations." The platform promoted women's issues by advancing their economic independence, ending violence against them, and ensuring equal medical access and treatment-including education and resources.

Five years later, the Women 2000: Gender Equality, Development, and Peace for the Twenty-First Century, dubbed the "Beijing +5 Conference," was held at Hunter College New York City, to review the progress made toward the goals established in Beijing.

PRIMARY SOURCE

Today, we're going to have what—in my younger days—would have been called a "teach-in."

We're here to talk as equals, to share what we know, and to learn from each other. I emphasize the word "equal." When it comes to women and women's health—no country, no leader, no researcher has a monopoly on the truth. So, although we're sitting together in a great lecture hall—I am not here to lecture. You, after all, have been on the frontlines of this battle for years.

You've been the voice for women's health and women's rights in the noisy halls of government, where—let's face it—women often have to fight their way in—just like we had to fight our way in to hear Mrs. Clinton speak in Beijing.

You've been the keepers of women's history—and the protector of women's health in your communities.

You've walked every mile you needed to walk to battle the major killers of women—from TB and malaria, to breast cancer, to HIV/AIDS to violence.

And now you've come here from every corner of the globe to make sure that five years from now—when we celebrate Beijing Plus Ten—we will look back at this moment and say: At Beijing we planted our cause—and at Hunter College our victory took root.

Before we go forward, I want to look back at how far our movement has come in the United States—in partnership with health ministries, non-governmental organizations, and individual women around the world.

Five years after Beijing, we're targeting young girls with powerful messages about staying in school, staying away from tobacco, alcohol, and drugs, and staying strong.

I'll go to almost any lengths to help girls make smart choices. I bring them into my office and say: Talk to me. Tell me what's on your mind. Tell what do you need to feel strong. I enlist their favorite sports stars as my allies. I even visit the writers and producers of their most-loved soap operas and talk shows—to make sure these programs are giving good public health messages. Those messages are getting through. Today, teen pregnancy rates in the United States are down for the seventh straight year—and overall drug use has leveled off or declined.

Five years after Beijing, our State Children's Health Insurance Program is up and running.

This is the largest expansion of health care in 30 years—and will help insure many young girls from low income working families.

Five years after Beijing, we've dramatically increased our funding for women's health research.

Today, we're learning invaluable information through the Women's Health Initiative—the largest clinical trial in history. It's a trial about the major causes of death and disability in older women, including heart disease, cancer, and osteoporosis. At the same time, we've drawn a line in the sand: No more federally funded research on diseases that affect women—unless that research includes women, and examines the differences and similarities between men and women.

Breast cancer is still the second leading cause of cancer death among women in the United States, and as we increase life expectancy in women around the world—breast cancer rates in other countries will likely go up too. That's why we're working overtime to beat this disease—with powerful new treatments, and by offering free mammograms to low-income women. We also support new legislation that will provide free breast cancer treatment for these same women. Better screening, early detection, and new treatments have brought down the breast cancer death rate in the United States. And the 5-year breast cancer survival rate is now over 90 percent when the disease is caught early.

But we are not about to declare victory against any cancer—or other disease which strikes women. All we are going to do is fight harder. Invest more. And raise the bar higher.

Five years after Beijing, we are building a seamless system that responds to the multiple needs of women who are victims of domestic violence. . . .

When a woman makes that first phone call following abuse—she must know that all of her legal and health needs are going to be met, quickly, completely, and with sensitivity.

Five years after Beijing we have an office of women's health inside every major health agency.

We have women's health centers in many large universities. . . .

These centers do not create new women's health programs. They create models for existing programs—models that demonstrate how to integrate services, build a seamless system of care, and address the health care needs of women holistically. In the twenty-first century, women's health must be defined as making sure that women always reach the highest attainable standards of physical and mental health.

That's what we said in Beijing. And that's what we're saying again this week.

The time has come to throw out the narrow view of women's health as simply reproduction, or preventing disease, or aging. Women's health must be woman-centered. Let me repeat that: Women's health must be woman-centered. That's where we should be headed five years after Beijing.

I want to be clear: Health—including reproductive health—must be integrated into our broader Beijing agenda. When we lift women out of poverty. When women have the power to make their own choices about family planning. When women have a full opportunity for an education. Then—and only then—will they have the tools they need to keep themselves and their families healthy.

That's why we must have a comprehensive woman-centered blueprint for health. But we won't get there unless we face up to several critical challenges—for women around the world.

First, we must expand access to health care across the globe.

In the United States alone, over 44 million people are still uninsured. We learned the hard way that this problem cannot be solved all at once. So we've taken a step-by-step approach: Making sure that changing jobs doesn't mean losing coverage. Expanding access for children. And proposing that older workers be allowed to buy into Medicare.

What sometimes gets lost in the numbers and proposals—is how the problem of access to health care directly affects women. Lack of access to health care keeps many women in India from seeking primary and preventive care. Lack of access to health care discourages women in the rural United States from going to work. Lack of access to health care in Africa increases maternal mortality. And lack of access to health care in nations around the world leads to chronic diseases associated with old age.

Which bring me to my second challenge: We must revolutionize long term care.

Some nations in Europe are at or near zero population growth—increasing the percentage of elderly. In Africa and Asia, where AIDS has been so devastating, working age adults are dying, leaving children and the elderly behind. Japan has one of the oldest societies on earth and is trying to encourage parenthood. In the United States, the number of Americans over 65 is expected to double in the next 30 years. A large majority of these older Americans will be women.

So there is no corner of the globe that does not face a crisis in long-term care—with the greatest burden falling on women—women who are elderly or caregivers. This is not a think-tank, academic issue. This is about life. This is about each one of us. My mother is healthy and active in her eighties. But I want my mother to have the care she will one day need. I am hardly alone in feeling this way. Being able to care for our parents—and other loved ones—is a very deep human need that we must never ignore.

Our third challenge is the long struggle against malaria, TB, AIDS, and other infectious diseases.

I mentioned the devastating impact AIDS is having in parts of Africa and Asia. India already has five million AIDS cases—and Africa is heading toward a generation of AIDS orphans. According to a recent World Bank study of 30 sub-Saharan countries, AIDS is likely to subtract up to 1.4 percent per year from GDP growth in these nations.

Ten years ago, many people in the United States thought of AIDS as a man's disease. Now we know better. In most of the world HIV/AIDS is a woman's disease. In this country, women are the fastest growing group of people living with HIV/AIDS. For African American women, the story is even worse. If you're an African American woman, you're almost 20 times more likely to have AIDS than a Caucasian woman.

My point is: HIV/AIDS is not a one-size fits all problem. Different countries have different needs and, frankly, different capabilities. So our approach is to make the solution fit the problem. In the United States, that means dramatically increasing our budget for both AIDS prevention—and

health services for people living with AIDS. It means setting a national goal of finding an AIDS vaccine by 2007. It means becoming partners with our diverse communities to address the changing face of AIDS. And it means mobilizing all of our health agencies to close the gaps in health outcomes, including HIV/AIDS, which is having such a disproportionate impact on women of color.

The United States also understands its role as an International partner in the fight against HIV/AIDS. That's why our budget to fight HIV/AIDS abroad is now over 300 million dollars. That's why we're testing nearly 60 microbicides in pre-clinical and clinical trials—compared to just a dozen in 1994. These microbicides will help put the health destiny of women back in women's hands—where it belongs!

Our role as your international partners is also why we're supporting the testing of drugs like nevirapine, which has been shown to be highly effective in preventing mother-to-child transmission, at a fraction of the cost of AZT. It's why we're investing 100 million dollars—along with funds from the United Nations and other donor countries—for the International Partnership for AIDS in Africa. It's why we're encouraging pharmaceutical companies to find new treatments—while reducing the cost of anti-viral drugs in the developing world. And it's why President Clinton is proposing a one billion dollar tax credit for companies that develop vaccines for TB, malaria, AIDS and other infectious diseases. The credit will have the effect of lowering the cost of vaccines for non-profits.

Our fourth challenge can be summed up in one word: Prevention.

I mentioned that breast cancer is the second leading cancer killer of women. The first is lung cancer. And the number one killer of women overall is heart disease. We can dramatically cut the rate of both lung cancer and heart disease—as well of stroke, osteoporosis and other public health risks to women—by changing our behavior.

First, stop smoking. Or, better yet, don't start! There are over 200 million women smokers—most in the developed world. The international marketing of tobacco, directed to women and children and without warning labels, is an outrage and it must stop! That's why the Kobe Declaration formulated at the World Health Organization Conference on Tobacco and Health is a strong message to the international negotiators now drafting the first "Tobacco Convention." That message is simple: Keep the health needs of women, at the top of your agenda. Second, stay physically active—which I've been doing since I was a kid. And third, eat a variety of healthy foods.

Sisterhood is still powerful. International sisterhood is even more powerful. But international sisterhood that takes our health into our own hands is unstoppable.

That's what prevention is all about. That's what the UN conference is all about. And that's why we're here today.

Which brings me to my fifth and last challenge: Working together.

Our fight for women's health did not begin in Beijing. It did not begin in 1975—which the United Nations declared the International Woman's Year. It did not even begin in the nineteenth century, when the cry heard throughout the land was: "Cast off your corsets!" Not only did our great-grandmothers fight this battle—their great grandmothers did too. How? By standing together. Learning together. And marching together.

We've come a long way since we hammered out our platform in Beijing. But as long as there is still one woman fighting breast cancer.

One woman being physically abused.

One woman being discriminated against.

One woman at risk for HIV/AIDS.

One woman dying from an unsafe abortion.

Or one woman unable to make her own choices, that is one woman too many and our work is not finished.

My nation is with you. And I am with you. But most important, we must be with each other. Holding on to our partnership. Staying unified. Staying strong. Sharing what we know. That is how we will advance the great cause of women's health and women's rights everywhere.

I know I'll see you many times between now and then—but I'll certainly see all of you when we take our next victory lap—at Hunter College Plus 5.

Thank you.

SIGNIFICANCE

The document that emerged from Women 2000: Gender Equality, Development and Peace for the Twenty-First Century, "Further Actions and Initiatives to Implement the Beijing Declaration and Platform for Action," reviewed the effectiveness of programs stemming from the Beijing Conference, including achievements and obstacles to reaching those goals. In the area of women's health, the declaration identified an increased life expectancy for women and girls and an improved concentration on sexual and reproductive health issues, as well as reproductive rights. The declaration also cited achievements in additional programs regarding contraception, education and family planning, HIV/AIDS, and increased awareness toward nutrition and breastfeeding.

In developing nations, however, women were still hampered by a lack of clean water, sanitation, and ade-

quate nutrition. A lack of gender-specific health research in certain countries further impedes women's health. The document calls for additional investment into obstetric care to reduce high infant and maternal mortality rates.

In 2001, the UN Millennium Summit was held in New York City. Over 150 member nations signed the Millennium Declaration and agreed to work toward the Millennium Development Goals, which include promoting gender equality and empowering women, reducing child mortality, and improving maternal health.

FURTHER RESOURCES
Web sites

Earth Summit 2002. Toolkit for Women. "Third World Conference on Women, Nairobi." <http://www.earth-summit2002.org/toolkits/Women/un-doku/un-conf/narirobi.htm> (accessed March 13, 2006).

United Nations. Division for the Advancement of Women. "Beijing +5: Women 2000—Gender Equality, Development for Peace in the Twenty-First Century" <http://www.un.org/womenwatch/daw/followup/beijing%2B5.htm> (accessed March 13, 2006).

United Nations. General Assembly. "Further Actions and Initiatives to Implement the Beijing Declaration and Platform for Action" <http://www.un.org/womenwatch/daw/followup/ress233e.pdf> (accessed March 13, 2006).

University of Minnesota. Human Rights Library. "Beijing Declaration and Platform for Action, Fourth World Conference on Women." <http://www1.umn.edu/humanrts/instree/e5dplw.htm> (accessed March 13, 2006).

Are Changes in Sexual Functioning During Midlife Due to Aging or Menopause?

Journal article abstract

By: Lorraine Dennerstein

Date: September 2001

Source: Dennerstein, L., E. Dudley, and H. Burger. "Are Changes in Sexual Functioning During Midlife due to Aging or Menopause?" *Fertility and Sterility.* 2001;76(3): 456–460.

About the Author: Lorraine Dennerstein is the chief investigator of The Melbourne Women's Midlife Health Project, a study of Australian-born women who have made the transition through menopause. She is the director of the Office for Gender and Health in the Department of Psychiatry at the University of Melbourne in Melbourne, Australia. From 1988–1993, she served as director of the department of psychological medicine at Mercy Hospital for Women, also in Melbourne. The professor is the former and first female president of the International Society of Psychosomatic Obstetrics and Gynecology. Professor Dennerstein is on the editorial board of three international journals and has authored more than twenty books. Her research interests include gender and mental health.

INTRODUCTION

Women often face a significant decline in sexual function during their midlife years. As a woman grows older, the female menstrual cycle (period or menses) slows down and eventually stops, an event called menopause. This typically occurs between ages forty-five to fifty-five. This transition disrupts the balance of hormones in the female body. The woman begins to produce less of the hormones estrogen and progesterone.

Menopause is a time of transition, and can be grouped into three phases. Perimenopause, the first phase, is when the menstrual cycle begins to slow down. Some women may notice changes; others may not. Perimenopause can begin as early as ten years before actual menopause. Menopause is an event and refers to the date a woman's menstrual cycle ceases. A woman is said to reach menopause when she has not menstruated within twelve consecutive months and no other reason can explain the absent menses. On average, menopause occurs naturally around age 51.2, according to the American Menopause Foundation. Menopause is sometimes called the "change of life." Postmenopause is the time after menstruation has stopped, and lasts the rest of a woman's life.

Medical research has suggested that hormonal changes in menopause negatively impact sexual interest and contribute to vaginal dryness, vaginal pain, and arousal difficulties. However, there has been some question whether these symptoms are due to menopause itself, or a combination of aging and the cessation of menstruation.

The following abstract outlines Dennerstien's 2001 study, which points to both aging and the menopausal transition as a contributor to at least a temporary decreased sexual response for both a menopausal woman and her partner.

■ PRIMARY SOURCE

ABSTRACT

OBJECTIVE: To determine whether changes in women's sexual functioning during midlife are due to aging or menopause. DESIGN: Prospective, observational study. SETTING: Population-based sample assessed in own homes. PATIENT(S): Four hundred thirty-eight Australian-born women aged 45–55 years and still menstruating at baseline. One hundred ninety-seven were studied for effects of the natural menopausal transition. Control group A (n = 44) remained premenopausal or early perimenopausal for 7 years. Control group B (n = 42) remained postmenopausal over 5 years. INTERVENTION(S): Nil; questionnaires and blood sampling annually. MAIN OUTCOME MEASURE(S): Shortened version of the Personal Experiences Questionnaire. RESULT(S): By the late perimenopause, there was a significant decline in the factors we had derived of sexual responsivity and total score, and there was an increase in the partner's problems factor. By the postmenopausal phase, there was a further decline in the factors sexual responsivity, frequency of sexual activities, libido, and in the total score, and a significant increase in vaginal dyspareunia and partner's problems. Sexual responsivity significantly declined in both control groups. CONCLUSION(S): Sexual responsivity is adversely affected by both aging and the menopausal transition. Other domains of female sexual functioning were significantly adversely affected when the women became postmenopausal. The relationship with the partner and his ability to perform sexually is adversely affected by the menopausal transition.

■

SIGNIFICANCE

Lorraine Dennestein, chief investigator of the Women's Midlife Health Project at the University of Melbourne in Melbourne, Australia, followed hundreds of women through the menopausal transition, documenting the biological and psychological changes they experienced along the way. Dennestein established the Project in 1991 because of a lack of adequate Australian data regarding the impact of menopause and aging on a woman's sexual functioning. The Project is the first to follow a population of women through this phase of life while rating their sexual function and linking it to body chemistry. Researchers involved in the Project have published a

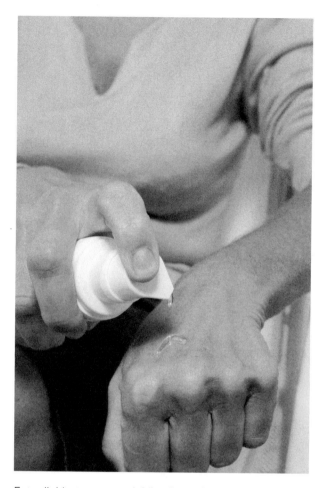

Estradiol (estrogen sterioid) gel, used in hormone replacement therapy. © T & L/IMAGE POINT FR/CORBIS

number of papers regarding sexual health, mood, and hormonal changes.

For the study, Professor Dennestein and her team conducted surveys every year for thirteen years, questioning the women's sexual patterns, feelings for their partners, and vaginal problems such as dryness and pain during intercourse. Most studies show that most aspects of a woman's sexual function decrease with age and decline further with the advent of menopause. The Melbourne project found that a woman generally becomes more symptomatic as she moved toward menopause, and that her sexual function can significantly decline with the transition through menopause. As the women in the study reached menopause they reported less sexual activity, greater decreases in arousal, a drop in sexual interest, and an increase in vaginal dryness and pain. Hot flashes increased in the late perimenopause phase, a symptom that the researchers theorize could impact a woman's desire to have sex.

The study also revealed that problems in a woman's romantic relationship, including changes in her partner's health and status, could instigate sexual dysfunction and override hormonal effects. This finding emphasizes the fact that partner relationships and psychology have powerful effects on midlife sexual function. While mood changes are said to be a common symptom of menopausal women, those who participated in the study did not report any significant mood changes during the menopausal transition.

In the United States, Australia, and Western Europe, the number of women either entering menopause or who are post-menopausal is steadily increasing, as women of the post World War II "baby boom" generation (those born between 1946 and 1964) approach and pass age fifty. With life expectancy also increasing, the average woman will now spend over one third of her life after menopause. Women of the baby boomer generation, who were responsible for the sexual revolution of the 1960s and the women's movements of the 1970s, are remaining vocal about their sexual issues as they age. The American writer Gail Sheehy noted in her book *The Silent Passage: Menopause*, "As the pacesetters among baby boom-generation women discover menopause on their horizon, they will bring it out of the closet."

FURTHER RESOURCES

Web sites

American Menopause Foundation. <http://www.american-menopause.org> (accessed March 14, 2006).

The Hormone Foundation. <http://www.hormone.org> (accessed March 14, 2006).

National Women's Health Information Center. <http://www.womenshealth.gov>(accessed March 14, 2006).

North American Menopause Society. <http://www.menopause.org>(accessed March 14, 2006).

Ten Things Lesbians Should Discuss with Their Health Care Providers

Press release

By: Katherine A. O'Hanlan

Date: July 17, 2002

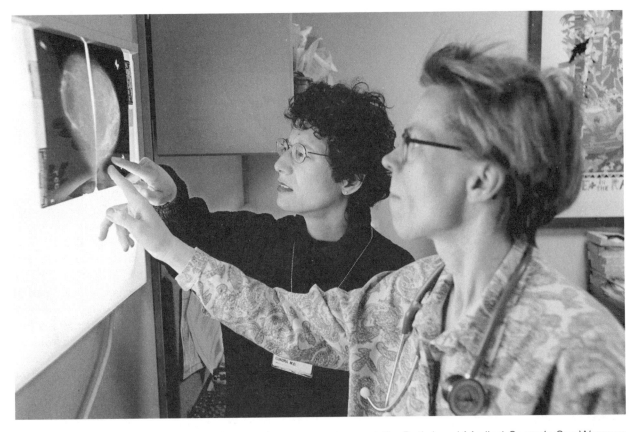

Dr. Teresa Cuadra and Dr. Joan Waitkevicz examine a mammogram at the Beth Israel Medical Center's Gay Womens Focus in New York. It is the first hospital-based health-care provider in the country for lesbians. AP IMAGES

Source: O'Hanlan, Katherine A. "Ten Things Lesbians Should Discuss With Their Health Care Provider." Gay and Lesbian Medical Association, July 17, 2002.

About the Author: Dr. Katherine A. (Kate) O'Hanlan is an oncological gynecologist affiliated with the Stanford University Medical Center as well as the past president of the Gay and Lesbian Medical Association. In the 1990s, she joined the National Center for Lesbian Rights in a letter-writing campaign urging researchers to include lesbians in their studies.

INTRODUCTION

To a large extent, lesbians have been an invisible population in the health care system. Although the health care needs of lesbians are the same as those of all women in most cases, lesbians have not attracted as much attention as heterosexual women. Meanwhile, health care in the gay community has focused on gay men.

The particular health needs of lesbians were first addressed by the women's liberation movement. *Our Bodies, Ourselves*, the landmark 1970 book about women's health and sexuality, was produced by the Boston Women's Health Book Collective because women had experienced doctors who were condescending, judgmental, and uninformative. The book briefly addressed lesbian health issues, but it was aimed at laypeople. Most health care providers remained unaware of lesbian health concerns while the women's health movement focused on the concerns that primarily affected straight women, such as abortion and birth control.

Most of the clinics that emerged in the 1970s and 1980s to serve homosexual populations focused on gay men. Only a handful of health clinics developed specifically for lesbians appeared at this time and these were limited to large cities such as San Francisco and New York. Lesbian-specific mental health, gynecological, and substance abuse services were generally absent. In 1987, the National Gay and Lesbian Health Foundation attempted to address lesbian needs by publishing "The National Lesbian Health Care Survey." However, a dramatic increase in lesbian health research began only in 1999, following the publication of a major private report and the U.S. Department of

Health and Human Services Scientific Workshop on Lesbian Health. The increased number of articles about lesbians in health professional literature and in lay publications reflected increased tolerance, but prejudice and ignorance remained obstacles to good health care.

Lesbians have special barriers to health care that include homophobia from the health care provider; internalized homophobia; heterosexist assumptions; lack of knowledge about special risks and screening needs of lesbians by lesbians themselves; incorrect knowledge about health care needs of lesbians by health care providers; the false belief by lesbians and health care providers that lesbians are immune to sexually-transmitted diseases, cervical cancer, and HIV; preventive care sought less since lesbians need routine contraceptive and prenatal care less often; and a lack of insurance coverage.

■ PRIMARY SOURCE

TEN THINGS LESBIANS SHOULD DISCUSS WITH THEIR HEALTH CARE PROVIDERS

SAN FRANCISCO—A survey of members of the Gay and Lesbian Medical Association (GLMA) released today listed 10 health care concerns lesbians should include in discussions with their physicians or other health care providers.

"We did the survey," said GLMA Executive Director Maureen S. O'Leary, RN, "because many lesbians and far too many health professionals are not comfortable or do not know how to discuss health issues related to sexual orientation. Unfortunately, there are some health risks that are of greater concern to lesbians, and we need to make sure they are addressed."

Gynecologist and former GLMA President Kathleen O'Hanlan, MD, said that the medical community must look at all factors—gender, age, family history, and current health—but that there are cultural competence issues involved in treatment of lesbians that many do not understand.

"We in the medical community need to find remedies for all the factors that reduce utilization of medical services and screening compliance among lesbians," she said. "Short of changing the laws of the country to reduce the sting of ubiquitous disdain, clinicians need to provide a safe haven for medical care for all women.

"We know from research," said O'Hanlan, "that lesbians are less likely to seek medical care than other women because of the stigma they experience everywhere in society. They also experience it when they go for medical

care. Health care providers may feel uncomfortable asking questions they feel to be personal. They then limit their visit and dash out without counseling the patient.

"Although more research is needed to understand the prevalence and causes," O'Hanlan continued, "there is evidence that lesbians smoke more and drink more. It is also more likely they are overweight, which adds significant health risks. Unfortunately, some health care providers make the presumption of heterosexuality or they may offend the lesbian patient in their conversations since they lack understanding of the salient cultural issues. Either way, it reduces the likelihood that the lesbian patient will return for care."

"We need to get the discussions going," O'Leary said. "Most health care professionals understand that there are certain risks that come with being a woman or with the aging process. However, we need to make sure that lesbians get equal care and that means incorporating this kind of understanding into the regular approach to treatment."

Lesbian Health Concerns

1. Breast Cancer
2. Depression/Anxiety
3. Gynecological Cancer
4. Fitness (Diet and Exercise)
5. Substance Use
6. Tobacco
7. Alcohol
8. Domestic Violence
9. Osteoporosis
10. Heart Health

"Of course," O'Leary added, "and it is important to repeat—many of the health concerns for lesbians are the same as they are for other women. But we must have a medical community that understands that there are cultural issues—orientation, gender identity, ethnicity, race, economic status—that must be understood as well. For lesbians, the 'Ten Things' list is a place to start."

1. Breast Cancer—Lesbians have the richest concentration of risk factors for this cancer than any subset of women in the world. Combine this with the fact that many lesbians over 40 do not get routine mammograms, do breast self-exams, or have a clinical breast exam, and the cancer may not be diagnosed early when it is most curable.

2. Depression/Anxiety—Lesbians have been shown to experience chronic stress from homophobic discrimination. This stress is compounded by the need that some still have to hide their orientation from work colleagues, and by the fact that many lesbians have lost the important emotional support others get from their families

due to alienation stemming from their sexual orientation.

3. Gynecological Cancer—Lesbians have higher risks for some of the gynecologic cancers. What they may not know is that having a yearly exam by a gynecologist can significantly facilitate early diagnosis associated with higher rates of curability if they ever develop.

4. Fitness—Research confirms that lesbians have higher body mass than heterosexual women. Obesity is associated with higher rates of heart disease, cancers, and premature death. What lesbians need is competent advice about healthy living and healthy eating, as well as healthy exercise.

5. Substance Use—Research indicates that illicit drugs may be used more often among lesbians than heterosexual women. There may be added stressors in lesbian lives from homophobic discrimination, and lesbians need support from each other and from health care providers to find healthy releases, quality recreation, stress reduction, and coping techniques.

6. Tobacco—Research also indicates that tobacco and smoking products may be used more often by lesbians than by heterosexual women. Whether smoking is used as a tension reducer or for social interactions, addiction often follows and is associated with higher rates of cancers, heart disease, and emphysema—the three major causes of death among all women.

7. Alcohol—Alcohol use and abuse may be higher among lesbians. While one drink daily may be good for the heart and not increase cancer or osteoporosis risks, more than that can be a risk factor for disease.

8. Domestic Violence—Domestic violence is reported to occur in about 11 percent of lesbian homes, about half the rate of 20 percent reported by heterosexual women. But the question is where do lesbians go when they are battered? Shelters need to welcome and include battered lesbians, and offer counseling to the offending partners.

9. Osteoporosis—The rates and risks of osteoporosis among lesbians have not been well characterized yet. Calcium and weight-bearing exercise as well as the avoidance of tobacco and alcohol are the mainstays of prevention. Getting bone density tests every few years to see if medication is needed to prevent fracture is also important.

10. Heart Health—Smoking and obesity are the most prevalent risk factors for heart disease among lesbians; but all lesbians need to also get an annual clinical exam because this is when blood pressure is checked, cholesterol is measured, diabetes is diagnosed, and exercise is

discussed. Preventing heart disease, which kills 45 percent of women, should be paramount to every clinical visit.

SIGNIFICANCE

Lesbians were an integral part of both the women's and the gay health movements that emerged in the 1970s, but these movements did not specifically address lesbian health concerns. For the most part, lesbians are an invisible constituency in the health care system, either entering the system incognito or opting out of the system altogether.

In the 1990s, organized efforts to make lesbians visible to the medical community began to bear some fruit. The largest study of women, the Women's Health Initiative (163,000 women studied over a ten-year period), agreed to include questions about the gender of sexual partners. This allowed researchers to compare data among women with different sexual behavior. The Harvard Nurses Study, the longest ongoing study of women's health, agreed to ask their study participants (127,000 female nurses) about their sexual orientation.

Studies that include lesbians have revealed that lesbians do not receive as much care as their straight female or gay male counterparts. Most lesbians have regular health care providers but more than half seek care only if they have a problem. Of concern is the fact that care is often delayed and noncare (negative care) is common. Noncare occurs when lesbians sense a lack of respect from a health care provider, do not feel safe enough to continue with a particular provider, and generally feel that they receive poor care. Behaviors from providers that discourage lesbians from seeking health care include prejudicial language, clipped voice tones, roughness in handling, a hurried pace, and false endearments. The current problems of the health care system, notably the spiraling level of the uninsured, is likely to further increase the number of lesbians who receive inadequate medical care.

FURTHER RESOURCES
Books

Solarz, Andrea L. *Lesbian Health: Current Assessment and Directions for the Future*. Washington, D.C.: National Academy Press, 1999.

Stern, Phyllis Noerager. *Lesbian Health: What Are the Issues?* New York: Taylor and Francis, 1993.

Youngkin, Ellis Quinn, and Marcia Szmania Davis. *Women's Health: A Primary Care Clinical Guide*. Upper Saddle River, N.J.: Pearson Prentice Hall, 2004.

White, Jocelyn, and Marissa C. Martinez. *The Lesbian Health Book: Caring for Ourselves.* Seattle: Seal Press, 1997.

Ten Things Gay Men Should Discuss with Their Health Care Providers

Press release

By: Vincent M. Silenzio

Date: July 17, 2002

Source: Silenzio, Vincent M. "Ten Things Gay Men Should Discuss With Their Health Care Providers." Gay and Lesbian Medical Association, July 17, 2002.

About the Author: Dr. Vincent M. Silenzio graduated from the University of Pennsylvania, then completed his medical and public health studies at Rutgers University. After founding the Program in Sexuality and Health at Columbia University, he became the Director of Social and Community Medicine at the University of Rochester School of Medicine and Dentistry. He has served on the Board of the Gay and Lesbian Medical Association and as Co-Editor-in-Chief of the Association's journal.

INTRODUCTION

While straight men can turn to parents, a family physician, or the mass media for health care information, it is far more difficult for gay men to obtain health guidance. Gay clinics and openly gay therapists are rare with homophobia widespread among health care providers. There are few comprehensive resources available to give a gay man general information tailored specifically to his sexuality, his body, and his mental and emotional health.

Gay men are disproportionally affected by certain ills. In addition to all of the physical diseases that affect men more than women, there are diseases that spread differently among gay men than straight men. Transmission variables, quality of health care, discriminatory health care practices, misdiagnosis of illness based on presumptions about sexual identity, and higher levels of stress combine to increase health risks for gay men. Additionally, some of the health care issues that affect gay men are political, including lack of insurance coverage for services related to same-sex activity, lack of coverage for same-sex partners, bias,

and violence as well as homophobia among health care providers.

In response to the problems specific to gay men's health care, activists in the gay male community began in the 1980s to provide health care information for gays. They believe that gay male wellness includes the development of individual skills and techniques for coping with health care issues.

■ PRIMARY SOURCE

TEN THINGS GAY MEN SHOULD DISCUSS WITH THEIR HEALTH CARE PROVIDERS

SAN FRANCISCO—A survey of members of the Gay and Lesbian Medical Association (GLMA) released today listed 10 health care concerns men who have sex with men (MSM) should include in discussions with their physicians or other health care providers.

"Clinicians providing health care to gay and bisexual men may not be aware of all of the things that should be discussed during the visit," said GLMA President Christopher E. Harris, MD. "We are concerned that physicians and other health care providers who do not understand the health risks in the gay community cannot provide competent care. This is why we asked our members to help us define the health care concerns most relevant to MSM. Our purpose is to inform health providers and allow patients to be proactive in their relationship by knowing what questions to ask."

"Naturally, not everyone has the same set of risks," said educator and medical journal editor Vincent M. B. Silenzio, MD, MPH. "But after we look at gender (men in general are increased risk of heart disease, for example) age, family history, and other basic factors, we need to consider issues that relate to the culture or subculture. We know that gay men face greater discrimination than their heterosexual counterparts, for example. Family pressures, combined with social pressure, cause significant stress. It might be important to discuss depression or anxiety, and possibly substance use. If you know that someone is sexually active, it is important to talk about safe sex, the need for hepatitis immunization, or periodic tests for anal papiloma."

Both Harris and Silenzio stress that this list broadens previously held views about appropriate treatment for gay men. They indicated this doesn't represent special treatment for gay or bisexual men, but appropriate treatment. Patients often don't know what they should ask their health care provider. And worse, many providers don't know what to look for. To effectively provide the best in health care, knowledge and honesty are essential.

"Both the provider and the patient should be aware of these concerns and they should be addressed non-judgmentally as part of a patient's regular health care program," Harris said.

Gay Men and MSM Health Concerns

1. HIV/AIDS, Safe Sex
2. Substance Use
3. Depression/Anxiety
4. Hepatitis Immunization
5. STDs
6. Prostate/Testicular/Colon Cancer
7. Alcohol
8. Tobacco
9. Fitness (Diet & Exercise)
10. Anal Papiloma

"Certainly, there are other health concerns that gay men and MSM face," Harris added. "And there are other cultural competence issues—gender identity, race, ethnicity, economic status, for example. But the 'Ten Things' list is a way to get the discussions started. Every physician and every health care professional—gay or straight—should know these things. And they should provide an open, comfortable environment in which these issues can be discussed."

1. HIV/AIDS, Safe Sex—That men who have sex with men are at an increased risk of HIV infection is well known, but the effectiveness of safe sex in reducing the rate of HIV infection is one of the gay community's great success stories. However, the last few years have seen the return of many unsafe sex practices. While effective HIV treatments may be on the horizon, there is no substitute for preventing infection. Safe sex is proven to reduce the risk of receiving or transmitting HIV. All health care professionals should be aware of how to counsel and support maintenance of safe sex practices.

2. Substance Use—Gay men use substances at a higher rate than the general population, and not just in larger communities such as New York, San Francisco, and Los Angeles. These include a number of substances ranging from amyl nitrate ("poppers"), to marijuana, Ecstasy, and amphetamines. The long-term effects of many of these substances are unknown; however current wisdom suggests potentially serious consequences as we age.

3. Depression/Anxiety—Depression and anxiety appear to affect gay men at a higher rate than in the general population. The likelihood of depression or anxiety may be greater, and the problem may be more severe for those men who remain in the closet or who do not have adequate social supports. Adolescents and young adults may be at particularly high risk of suicide because of

these concerns. Culturally sensitive mental health services targeted specifically at gay men may be more effective in the prevention, early detection, and treatment of these conditions.

4. Hepatitis Immunization—Men who have sex with men are at an increased risk of sexually transmitted infection with the viruses that cause the serious condition of the liver known as hepatitis. These infections can be potentially fatal, and can lead to very serious long-term issues such as cirrhosis and liver cancer. Fortunately, immunizations are available to prevent two of the three most serious viruses. Universal immunization for Hepatitis A Virus and Hepatitis B Virus is recommended for all men who have sex with men. Safe sex is effective at reducing the risk of viral hepatitis, and is currently the only means of prevention for the very serious Hepatitis C Virus.

5. STDs—Sexually transmitted diseases (STDs) occur in sexually active gay men at a high rate. This includes STD infections for which effective treatment is available (syphilis, gonorrhea, chlamydia, pubic lice, and others), and for which no cure is available (HIV, Hepatitis A, B, or C virus, Human Papilloma Virus, etc.). There is absolutely no doubt that safe sex reduces the risk of sexually transmitted diseases, and prevention of these infections through safe sex is key.

6. Prostate, Testicular, and Colon Cancer—Gay men may be at risk for death by prostate, testicular, or colon cancer. Screening for these cancers occurs at different times across the life cycle, and access to screening services may be negatively impacted because of issues and challenges in receiving culturally sensitive care for gay men. All gay men should undergo these screenings routinely as recommended for the general population.

7. Alcohol—Although more recent studies have improved our understanding of alcohol use in the gay community, it is still thought that gay men have higher rates of alcohol dependence and abuse than straight men. One drink daily may not adversely affect health, however alcohol-related illnesses can occur with low levels of consumption. Culturally sensitive services targeted to gay men are important in successful prevention and treatment programs.

8. Tobacco—Recent studies seem to support the notion that gay men use tobacco at much higher rates than straight men, reaching nearly 50 percent in several studies. Tobacco-related health problems include lung disease and lung cancer, heart disease, high blood pressure, and a whole host of other serious problems. All gay men should be screened for and offered cultur-

ally sensitive prevention and cessation programs for tobacco use.

9. Fitness (Diet and Exercise)—Problems with body image are more common among gay men than their straight counterparts, and gay men are much more likely to experience an eating disorder such as bulimia or anorexia nervosa. While regular exercise is very good for cardiovascular health and in other areas, too much of a good thing can be harmful. The use of substances such as anabolic steroids and certain supplements can adversely affect health. At the opposite end of the spectrum, overweight and obesity are problems that also affect a large subset of the gay community. This can cause a number of health problems, including diabetes, high blood pressure, and heart disease.

10. Anal Papilloma—Of all the sexually transmitted infections gay men are at risk for, human papilloma virus—which cause anal and genital warts—is often thought to be little more than an unsightly inconvenience. However, these infections may play a role in the increased rates of anal cancers in gay men. Some health professionals now recommend routine screening with anal Pap Smears, similar to the test done for women to detect early cancers. Safe sex should be emphasized. Treatments for HPV do exist, but recurrences of the warts are very common, and the rate at which the infection can be spread between partners is very high.

SIGNIFICANCE

The education of gay men about health issues specific to the gay community has bettered the lives of gay men. However, many factors restrict the ability of gays to get adequate health care, including negative attitudes toward homosexuality held by health care providers.

Health care providers are not immune to homophobia and are typically not educated about gay and lesbian health issues in their medical training, with the exception of HIV. In a 1994 survey of the membership

San Francisco Director of Health, Mitchell Katz, stands near a welcome sign during the opening of Magnet, a sexual health clinic for gay men, on July 1, 2003 in San Francisco, California. PHOTO BY JUSTIN SULLIVAN/GETTY IMAGES

of the Gay and Lesbian Medical Association (GLMA), over half of the respondents reported observing heterosexual colleagues deny care or provide reduced or substandard care to gay or lesbian patients because of their sexual orientation, with eighty-eight percent reporting that their physician colleagues made disparaging remarks in public about gay patients. While the overwhelming majority of GLMA members believed that it was medically important for patients to inform their physicians of their orientation, sixty-four percent believed that in doing so, patients risked receiving substandard care. Surveys of nurses and medical students have also discovered that many of these health care providers hold hostile attitudes toward gays.

The attitudes of nurses, medical students, and physicians are perceived by patients and can negatively affect their health care. Many gay patients report experiencing ostracism, rough treatment, and derogatory comments, as well as disrespect for their partners from their medical practitioners. Many gay men withhold information about their sexual behavior from their health care providers, fearing repercussions if they reveal their sexual orientation. As a result, some gays are hesitant to return to their physician's offices for new complaints and are less likely to receive medical screening tests.

Lastly, although substance use is listed as one of the major items that gay men should discuss with health care providers, little support is available for gay men with substance abuse issues. Detoxification and rehabilitation programs often show little sensitivity to issues of sexual orientation and generally do not encourage disclosure. It has been shown that failure to acknowledge gay identity issues in alcoholism treatment makes recovery more difficult and increases the likelihood of relapse.

FURTHER RESOURCES

Books

Eliason, Michele J. *Who Cares?: Institutional Barriers to Health Care for Lesbians, Gays, and Bisexual Persons.* New York: NLN Press, 1996.

Penn, Robert E. *The Gay Men's Wellness Guide: The National Lesbian and Gay Health Association's Complete Book of Physical, Emotional, and Mental Health and Well-Being for Every Gay Male.* New York: Henry Holt, 1997.

Peterkin, Allan D., and Cathy Risdon. *Caring for Lesbian and Gay People: A Clinical Guide.* Toronto: University of Toronto Press, 2003.

Hillary Goodridge vs. Department of Public Health

Legal decision

By: Massachusetts Supreme Judicial Court

Date: November 18, 2003

Source: Hillary Coodridge & others vs. Department of Public Health & another. SJC-08860. Available at: *The Massachusetts Court System.* <http://www.mass.gov/courts/courtsandjudges/courts/supremejudicial-court/goodridge.html> (accessed March 14, 2006).

About the Author: The Massachusetts Court System is the judicial network for the state of Massachusetts, United States. It comprises a network of courts arranged in order of hierarchy. At the bottom of the pyramid are the trial courts, followed by the Appeals courts, and then the Supreme Judicial Court. The trial court is a group of various courts that includes the Superior Court, District Court, Juvenile Court, Probate and Family Court, Housing Court, Land Court, and the Boston Municipal Court. Cases that are not settled at the trial courts are referred to the Appeals courts. The Supreme Judicial Court is the highest court in the state of Massachusetts. Established in 1692, it is the oldest operating court in the Western Hemisphere.

INTRODUCTION

According to legal norms and traditions worldwide, marriage usually means a union between a man and a woman. The institution of marriage endows significant social and legal responsibilities upon the husband and wife toward the society and the state. The definition of marriage varies for legal and social reasons across different cultures and societies. Marriage law in the United States is essentially a state matter, and the specifics of marriage law vary from state to state.

In the past few decades, the issue of same-sex marriage has gained considerable prominence in the United States and the world. Same-sex marriages in the United States face a fundamental battle of opinion between those who believe in traditional marriages and those who advocate basic liberties, such as civil rights, privacy, fair treatment of both sexes, and equality before law.

Although same-sex marriage has always faced stiff opposition, there have been cases in which some rights were granted to gay and lesbian couples. However, in most cases these rights were later revoked. For instance, in 1975, two men in Phoenix, Arizona, were

Penny Gardner, right and William Colburn talk outside a courthouse during a rally supporting domestic partner benefits in Lansing, Mich., on August 16, 2005. AP IMAGES

granted a marriage license. The license was later withdrawn. At the same time, Arizona laws were tightened to prohibit marriage between same-sex couples.

In 1993, the Hawaii Supreme Court ruled that the legislature could not stop gay and lesbian couples from marrying unless it found a convincing reason against such unions. In 1998, the Hawaii constitution was amended restricting marriage to the union of a man and a woman. Also in 1998, a similar issue was referred to the Supreme Court of Alaska; the court decided in favor of the plaintiff, declaring that the state must show a compelling reason for declining a same-sex marriage license to the plaintiffs. Later that year, the Alaska constitution also was amended by voters to prohibit same-sex marriages.

In September 1996, then U.S. President Bill Clinton signed a federal law called the Defense of Marriage Act (DOMA). According to this law, marriage is a legal union between a man and a woman. The law further defines a spouse as a person of the opposite sex bound in the union of marriage. This Act gave states

the power to deny the status of marriage to same-sex couples who entered into a union in other states.

Subsequently, gay marriage activists have filed lawsuits against government organizations and other institutions, seeking legalization of gay marriage. As mentioned earlier, these lawsuits were largely unsuccessful. An exception was the lawsuit filed in Massachusetts, in April 2001, by the Gay & Lesbian Advocates and Defenders (GLAD)—a rights organization representing seven gay and lesbian couples.

The primary source reproduced below is a synopsis prepared by the court reporter, detailing the decision taken by the Massachusetts Supreme Judicial Court in this lawsuit—*Hillary Goodridge & others vs. Department of Public Health and another.* It describes the court's ruling on the issue, based on the provisions of the Massachusetts Constitution. The Massachusetts Supreme Judicial Court ruled in favor of same-sex civil marriages in the state of Massachusetts. It also entitled people of the same gender to obtain civil marriage licenses. Following this ruling, Massachusetts became the only state in the United States to allow gay and lesbian couples to marry.

▌PRIMARY SOURCE

The Supreme Judicial Court held today that "barring an individual from the protections, benefits, and obligations of civil marriage solely because that person would marry a person of the same sex violates the Massachusetts Constitution." The court stayed the entry of judgment for 180 days "to permit the Legislature to take such action as it may deem appropriate in light of this opinion."

"Marriage is a vital social institution," wrote Chief Justice Margaret H. Marshall for the majority of the Justices. "The exclusive commitment of two individuals to each other nurtures love and mutual support; it brings stability to our society. For those who choose to marry, and for their children, marriage provides an abundance of legal, financial, and social benefits. In turn it imposes weighty legal, financial, and social obligations." The question before the court was "whether, consistent with the Massachusetts Constitution," the Commonwealth could deny those protections, benefits, and obligations to two individuals of the same sex who wish to marry.

In ruling that the Commonwealth could not do so, the court observed that the Massachusetts Constitution "affirms the dignity and equality of all individuals," and "forbids the creation of second-class citizens." It reaches its conclusion, the court said, giving "full deference to the arguments made by the Commonwealth." The Commonwealth, the court ruled, "has failed to identify any constitutionality adequate reason for denying civil marriage to same-sex couples."

The court affirmed that it owes "great deference to the Legislature to decide social and policy issues." Where, as here, the constitutionality of a law is challenged, it is the "traditional and settled role" of courts to decide the constitutional question. The "marriage ban" the court held, "works a deep and scarring hardship" on same-sex families "for no rational reason." It prevents children of same-sex couples "from enjoying the immeasurable advantages that flow from the assurance of 'a stable family structure in which children will be reared, educated, and socialized.'" "It cannot be rational under our laws," the court held, "to penalize children by depriving them of State benefits" because of their parents' sexual orientation.

The court rejected the Commonwealth's claim that the primary purpose of marriage was procreation. Rather, the history of the marriage laws in the Commonwealth demonstrates that "it is the exclusive and permanent commitment of the marriage partners to one another, not

the begetting of children, that is the sine qua non of marriage."

The court remarked that its decision "does not disturb the fundamental value of marriage in our society." "That same-sex couples are willing to embrace marriage's solemn obligations of exclusivity, mutual support, and commitment to one another is a testament to the enduring place of marriage in our laws and in the human spirit," the court stated.

The opinion reformulates the common-law definition of civil marriage to mean "the voluntary union of two persons as spouses, to the exclusion of all others." Noting that "civil marriage has long been termed a 'civil right,'" the court concluded that "the right to marry means little if it does not include the right to marry the person of one's choice, subject to appropriate government restrictions in the interests of public health, safety, and welfare."

Justices John M. Greaney, Roderick L. Ireland, and Judith A. Cowin joined in the court's opinion. Justice Greaney also filed a separate concurring opinion.

Justices Francis X. Spina, Martha B. Sosman, and Robert J. Cordy each filed separate dissenting opinions.

Justice Greaney concurred "with the result reached by the court, the remedy ordered, and much of the reasoning in the court's opinion," but expressed the view that "the case is more directly resolved using traditional equal protection analysis." He stated that to withhold "relief from the plaintiffs, who wish to marry, and are otherwise eligible to marry, on the ground that the couples are of the same gender, constitutes a categorical restriction of a fundamental right." Moreover, Justice Greaney concluded that such a restriction is impermissible under art. 1 of the Massachusetts Declaration of Rights. In so doing, Justice Greaney did not rely on art. 1, as amended in 1976, because the voters' intent in passing the amendment was clearly not to approve gay marriage, but he relied on well-established principles of equal protection that antedated the amendment.

Justice Cordy, with whom Justice Spina and Justice Sosman joined, dissented on the ground that the marriage statute, as historically interpreted to mean the union of one man and one woman, does not violate the Massachusetts Constitution because "the Legislature could rationally conclude that it furthers the legitimate State purpose of ensuring, promoting, and supporting an optimal social structure for the bearing and raising of children." Justice Cordy stated that the court's conclusions to the contrary are unsupportable in light of "the presumption of constitutional validity and significant deference afforded to legislative enactments, and the undesirability of the judiciary substituting its notion of correct policy for that of a popularly elected legislature responsible for making it." Further, Justice Cordy stated that "[w]hile the Massachusetts Constitution protects matters of personal liberty against government intrusion at least as zealously and often more so than does the Federal Constitution, this case is not about government intrusions into matters of personal liberty," but "about whether the State must endorse and support [the choices of same-sex couples] by changing the institution of civil marriage to make its benefits, obligations, and responsibilities applicable to them." Justice Cordy concluded that, although the plaintiffs had made a powerful case for the extension of the benefits and burdens of civil marriage to same-sex couples, the issue "is one deeply rooted in social policy" and "that decision must be made by the Legislature, not the court."

Justice Spina, in a separately filed dissenting opinion, stated that "[W]hat is at stake in this case is not the unequal treatment of individuals or whether individuals' rights have been impermissibly burdened, but the power of the Legislature to effectuate social change without interference from the courts, pursuant to art. 30 of the Massachusetts Declaration of Rights." He emphasized that the "power to regulate marriage lies with the Legislature, not with the judiciary."

Justice Sosman, in a separately filed dissenting opinion, stated that "the issue is not whether the Legislature's rationale behind [the statutory scheme being challenged] is persuasive to [the court]," but whether it is "rational" for the Legislature to "reserve judgment" on whether changing the definition of marriage "can be made at this time without damaging the institution of marriage or adversely affecting the critical role it has played in our society." She concluded that, "[a]bsent consensus on the issue (which obviously does not exist), or unanimity amongst scientists studying the issue (which also does not exist), or a more prolonged period of observation of this new family structure (which has not yet been possible), it is rational for the Legislature to postpone any redefinition of marriage that would include same-sex couples until such time as it is certain that redefinition will not have unintended and undesirable social consequences."

SIGNIFICANCE

In the United States, as in many countries worldwide, the issue of same-sex marriage has been increasingly in the public eye and, since the 1970s, there has been a movement seeking legal and social benefits for same-sex couples. Proponents of same-sex marriage state that it should be constituted as a fundamental civil right, whereas critics argue that marriage should

be only between two people of the opposite sex. Although the Supreme Judicial Court of Massachusetts ruling is a legal landmark, since it legalized same-sex marriages in the state, not much has changed in other parts of the U.S. since the ruling was handed down. As of 2006, Massachusetts is still the only state to allow same-sex marriages. In addition, legal experts maintain that the future of same-sex marriage in Massachusetts is uncertain, since there has been intense lobbying to ban it.

Since the early 2000s, more states have passed laws preventing gay and lesbian marriages. Despite this fact, there have been instances when these laws have been ignored. In February 2004, under the direction of San Francisco's mayor to bypass the state law, hundreds of same sex couples from all over the United States obtained marriage licenses. Subsequently, however, the Supreme Court of California revoked these licenses, citing the illegal nature of the action.

Many individuals, civil rights groups, and politicians have taken sides on the issue of same-sex marriage. Major civil rights organizations like the Partners Task Force for Gay & Lesbian Couples, the Lambda Legal Defense and Education Fund, and Gay & Lesbian Advocates and Defenders have been campaigning vigorously to legalize same-sex marriages. Federal and state laws make more than 1,000 statutory rights and benefits available to married couples. These rights include the application of federal inheritance laws, social security benefits, the right to unpaid leave to care for a family member, the ability to file joint tax return, and so on. Various groups and individuals, such as those mentioned above, have been pressing for these rights to be extended to gay and lesbian couples.

On the other hand, many prominent individuals and religious organizations are against same-sex marriages. In his presidential campaign of 2004, President George W. Bush endorsed a constitutional amendment banning same sex marriages, but left it on the states to decide on civil unions and domestic partnerships. Civil unions, which were first legalized in Vermont (in 2000) and later in Connecticut (in 2005), provide same-sex couples with some of the rights enjoyed by heterosexual married couples. However, as of 2006, civil unions have yet to be approved and accepted by other states.

According to a survey by CNN, younger Americans tend to favor the legalization of same-sex marriages, whereas older Americans and the residents of more conservative states are against same-sex marriages. This issue remains a controversial social and political topic in the United States with nearly half of the population reportedly against such marriages and the other half in favor of them.

FURTHER RESOURCES

Web sites

BBC News. "The Gay Marriage Map." <http://news.bbc.co.uk/2/hi/americas/3516551.stm> (accessed March 14, 2006).

Center for Health Statistics. "California Marriage License, Registration and Ceremony Information." <http://www.dhs.ca.gov/hisp/chs/OVR/Marriage/General-Info.htm> (accessed March 14, 2006).

CNN.com. "Same-sex Marriage Laws Across the United States." <http://archives.cnn.com/2000/LAW/05/25/same.sex.marriages/> (accessed March 14, 2006).

———. "Massachusetts Court Rules Ban on Gay Marriage Unconstitutional." <http://edition.cnn.com/2003/LAW/11/18/samesex.marriage.ruling/> (accessed March 14, 2006).

———. "States Determine Marriage Laws." <http://edition.cnn.com/2003/LAW/11/18/states.marriage.laws/> (accessed March 14, 2006).

Human Rights Campaign. "Frequently Asked Questions: Goodridge et al. v. The Department of Public Health." <http://www.hrc.org/Content/ContentGroups/Issues1/Marriage/FAQ_Goodridge.htm> (accessed March 14, 2006).

Thomas.gov. "Proposing an Amendment to the Constitution of the United States Relating to Marriage. (Introduced in Senate)" <http://thomas.loc.gov/cgi-bin/query/D?c109:3:./temp/~c1098H0WZa::> (accessed March 14, 2006).

U.S. Congress. "The Defense of Marriage Act/Public Law 104–199 Defense of Marriage Act (Enrolled Bill (Sent to President))." <http://www.indiana.edu/~glbtpol/doma.html> (accessed March 14, 2006).

Two Abortion Supporters Covered in Red Paint Thrown at Them by Anti-Abortion Protestors

Photograph

By: Eryk Puchala

Date: June 22, 2003

Source: The Associated Press

About the Photographer: Eryk Puchala is a photographer in Poland and contributed this photo to the Associated Press, a worldwide news agency based in New York.

INTRODUCTION

Women on Waves is a pro-abortion-rights organization headquartered in the Netherlands. It was founded in 1999 by Rebecca Gomperts, a medical doctor and artist. Gomperts's experience as physician for the Greenpeace protest vessel *Rainbow Warrior* led her to conceive of using vessels to bring attention to the illegality of abortion in some countries. Women on Waves has rented a vessel three times for pro-abortion campaigns in European countries where abortion is illegal. The ship is equipped as an abortion clinic and education center. Before arriving in a country, Women on Waves establishes a local hotline service and distributes free phone cards; while their vessel is in-country, women can make an appointment by calling, e-mailing, or showing up. Although it is equipped and licensed by the Dutch Ministry of Health for actual medical services, the goal of the campaign is not to provide abortions for large numbers of women—which is physically impractical—but to provoke public debate about legal abortion.

The ship chartered for the Poland campaign, the *Langenort* , arrived in Polish waters on June 20, 2003. The ship was met at dockside on June 22 by supporters welcoming it, and by protestors from the political party League of Polish Families, who threw eggs and red paint at the ship. The women shown here are splattered with some of the paint.

Upon arrival, the supply of RU-486 abortion pills aboard the ship, in the medicine chest, was sealed by customs officials to prevent its distribution in Poland. The distinction between national and international waters became important for the project at this point; Polish women desiring abortions were taken aboard the ship into international waters three times. The medical staff on board the ship unsealed the medicine chest, gave the abortion pill to the women, and then returned to Polish waters. By providing abortion services only outside the country, Women on Waves and the women receiving the abortions avoided breaking Polish law.

The Women on Waves ship stayed in Poland for two weeks. It received hundreds of calls and a number of women came to the ship. Media coverage and public debate were intense. According to Women on Waves, a July 12, 2003 survey commissioned by the Polish journal *Polityka* found that 65 percent of the Polish population supported the project. Moreover,

PRIMARY SOURCE

Two Abortion Supporters Covered in Red Paint Thrown at Them by Anti-Abortion Protestors: Two abortion supporters greet the ship "Langenort" in Poland on June 22, 2003. They are covered in paint thrown at them by anti-abortionist activists. The ship brought activists from the "Women on Waves" feminist organization to Poland offering counseling and abortion pills, amid protests from the Catholic Church and rightist groups. AP IMAGES

the official Polish polling bureau, Opinii Spolecznej, found that before the ship's visit, in Fall 2002, 44 percent of those polled thought Polish abortion law should be liberalized, while afterward, in Fall 2003, the percentage was 56 percent. The bureau speculated that the 12 percent increase, from minority to majority opinion, might have been a result of the Women on Waves visit.

PRIMARY SOURCE

TWO ABORTION SUPPORTERS COVERED IN RED PAINT THROWN AT THEM BY ANTI-ABORTION PROTESTORS

See primary source image.

SIGNIFICANCE

Women on Waves has made abortion-ship journeys not only to Poland, but also to Ireland (2001) and Portugal (2004), all primarily Catholic countries where abortion is illegal. In Ireland, for example, abortion is illegal except to save the life of a woman; it is not legal even in cases where pregnancy has resulted from incest or rape, although Irish courts have allowed women whose pregnancies resulted from rape to get abortions in England.

Abortion was legal in Poland under Soviet governance. Approximately 180,000 legal abortions were performed yearly. When Communist rule collapsed, a pro-Catholic government came to power and in 1993 banned abortion except (a) to save the woman's life, (b) if the fetus is "irreparably damaged," or (c) the pregnancy is the result of rape or incest. In practice, according to the United Nations Human Rights Committee, even when these conditions are met "social factors did not allow for possibilities of carrying out abortion mostly due to political and religious ramifications." Only about 150 legal abortions are carried out every year in Poland today. However, the Polish Ministry of Health estimates that 50,000–70,000 illegal abortions are carried out yearly. The United Nations, citing nongovernmental organizations, estimates that the figure is 80,000–200,000. Sixty percent of Polish women are below the poverty line, and so cannot afford to travel abroad to get abortions or to pay the high fees for illegal abortions. In February 2006, a Polish woman who went blind after being refused an abortion took her case to the European Court of Human Rights, arguing that although several doctors had told her that she will go blind if she had another baby, she was nevertheless denied an abortion under Polish law. The Court cannot overturn Polish law but could rule that the woman's human rights are being violated. The case was still pending as of mid-2006.

In the United States, legal battles arising from actions by anti-abortion protestors (such as those that threw the paint in this photograph) have gone all the way to the Supreme Court. Throwing eggs or paint at persons is considered a form of assault, regardless of the circumstances; furthermore, the Court has approved eight-foot-radius "bubble zones" around patients approaching or leaving abortion or family-planning clinics. Protestors cannot legally approach any unwilling patient more closely than eight feet (though they are not required to move away if the patient approaches them). In 2005, the Pittsburgh City Council approved a rule barring protestors from within fifteen feet of the doorway of any health-care facility; no court has yet ruled on the constitutionality of this provision. In 1994, the U.S. Congress made it illegal to attack or blockade abortion clinics, their operators, or their clients. In 2006, however, the Supreme Court ruled that federal racketeering and extortion laws could not be applied to levy higher penalties against anti-abortion protestors who repeatedly violated the 1994 law.

FURTHER RESOURCES

Web sites

Murphy, Clare. "Abortion Ship Makes Waves in Poland." *BBC News.* July 1, 2003. <http://news.bbc.co.uk/1/hi/world/europe/3035540.stm> (accessed April 5, 2006).

Feminist Majority Foundation "Anti-Abortion Activists Protest Women on Waves." <http://www.feminist.org/news/newsbyte/uswirestory.asp?id=7875> (accessed April 5, 2006).

United Nations Office at Geneva. "Human Rights Committee Considers Report of [sic] Poland." October 28, 2004. <http://www2.unog.ch/news2/documents/newsen/ct04017e.htm> (accessed April 5, 2006).

Women on Waves: Campaigns. <http://www.womenonwaves.org/set-1020.38-en.html> (accessed April 5, 2006).

Druggists Refuse to Give Out Pill

Newspaper article

By: Charisse Jones

Date: November 9, 2004

Source: Jones, Charisse. "Druggists Refuse to Give Out Pill." *USA Today* (November 9, 2004): A3.

About the Author: Charisse Jones is a national correspondent for *USA Today* and is a former staff writer with the *New York Times*. She is the co-author of *Shifting: The Double Lives of Black Women in America*.

INTRODUCTION

After the Supreme Court's 1973 *Roe v. Wade* decision on abortion in the United States, many states adopted "refusal laws," laws that gave health care providers the right to refuse to perform an abortion or to assist in the performance of an abortion, and for hospitals to refuse to allow abortions to be performed on their premises. These laws gave healthcare providers a choice to act—or not act—based on their personal, religious, or philosophical beliefs.

In 1998, South Dakota became the first state in the nation to adopt a "conscience clause" for pharmacists who did not want to dispense birth control pills or emergency "morning after" pills. Like the refusal laws, conscience clauses are designed to give pharmacists a choice in administering medications that conflict with the pharmacists' personal, religious, or philosophical beliefs. Four states—Arkansas, Georgia, Mississippi, and South Dakota—now have laws that protect a pharmacist from liability associated with refusing to dispense medications based on personal choice.

More than thirty other states either have "conscience clause" bills or, on the other side of the debate,

A teenage girl is being counseled on the uses of birth control pills. © LWA-STEPHEN WELSTEAD/CORBIS

bills requiring pharmacists to dispense medication regardless of personal, religious, or philosophical belief. Throughout 2003, 2004, and 2005, news media outlets published increasing numbers of stories describing contraception prescriptions and "morning after" pill prescriptions that were denied by pharmacists on personal ethical grounds.

■ PRIMARY SOURCE

For a year, Julee Lacey stopped in a CVS pharmacy near her home in a Fort Worth suburb to get refills of her birth-control pills. Then one day last March, the pharmacist refused to fill Lacey's prescription because she did not believe in birth control.

"I was shocked," says Lacey, 33, who was not able to get her prescription until the next day and missed taking one of her pills. "Their job is not to regulate what peo-

ple take or do. It's just to fill the prescription that was ordered by my physician."

Some pharmacists, however, disagree and refuse on moral grounds to fill prescriptions for contraceptives. And states from Rhode Island to Washington have proposed laws that would protect such decisions. Mississippi enacted a sweeping statute that went into effect in July that allows health care providers, including pharmacists, to not participate in procedures that go against their conscience. South Dakota and Arkansas already had laws that protect a pharmacist's right to refuse to dispense medicines. Ten other states considered similar bills this year.

The American Pharmacists Association, with 50,000 members, has a policy that says druggists can refuse to fill prescriptions if they object on moral grounds, but they must make arrangements so a patient can still get the pills. Yet some pharmacists have refused to hand the prescription to another druggist to fill.

In Madison, Wis., a pharmacist faces possible disciplinary action by the state pharmacy board for refusing to transfer a woman's prescription for birth-control pills to another druggist or to give the slip back to her. He would not refill it because of his religious views.

Some advocates for women's reproductive rights are worried that such actions by pharmacists and legislatures are gaining momentum. The U.S. House of Representatives passed a provision in September that would block federal funds from local, state and federal authorities if they make health care workers perform, pay for or make referrals for abortions.

"We have always understood that the battles about abortion were just the tip of a larger ideological iceberg, and that it's really birth control that they're after also," says Gloria Feldt, president of Planned Parenthood Federation of America. "The explosion in the number of legislative initiatives and the number of individuals who are just saying, 'We're not going to fill that prescription for you because we don't believe in it' is astonishing," she said.

Pharmacists have moved to the front of the debate because of such drugs as the "morning-after" pill, which is emergency contraception that can prevent fertilization if taken within 120 hours of unprotected intercourse.

While some pharmacists cite religious reasons for opposing birth control, others believe life begins with fertilization and see hormonal contraceptives, and the morning-after pill in particular, as capable of causing an abortion.

"I refuse to dispense a drug with a significant mechanism to stop human life," says Karen Brauer, president of the 1,500-member Pharmacists for Life International. Brauer was fired in 1996 after she refused to refill a prescription for birth-control pills at a Kmart in the Cincinnati suburb of Delhi Township.

Lacey, of North Richland Hills, Texas, filed a complaint with the Texas Board of Pharmacy after her prescription was refused in March. In February, another Texas pharmacist at an Eckerd drug store in Denton wouldn't give contraceptives to a woman who was said to be a rape victim.

In the Madison case, pharmacist Neil Noesen, 30, after refusing to refill a birth-control prescription, did not transfer it to another pharmacist or return it to the woman. She was able to get her prescription refilled two days later at the same pharmacy, but she missed a pill because of the delay.

She filed a complaint after the incident occurred in the summer of 2002 in Menomonie, Wis. Christopher Klein, spokesman for Wisconsin's Department of Regulation and Licensing, says the issue is that Noesen didn't transfer or return the prescription. A hearing was held in October. The most severe punishment would be revoking Noesen's pharmacist license, but Klein says that is unlikely.

Susan Winckler, spokeswoman and staff counsel for the American Pharmacists Association, says it is rare that pharmacists refuse to fill a prescription for moral reasons. She says it is even less common for a pharmacist to refuse to provide a referral.

"The reality is every one of those instances is one too many," Winckler says. "Our policy supports stepping away but not obstructing." In the 1970s, because of abortion and sterilization, some states adopted refusal clauses to allow certain health care professionals to opt out of providing those services. The issue re-emerged in the 1990s, says Adam Sonfield of the Alan Guttmacher Institute, which researches reproductive issues.

Sonfield says medical workers, insurers and employers increasingly want the right to refuse certain services because of medical developments, such as the "morning-after" pill, embryonic stem-cell research and assisted suicide.

"The more health care items you have that people feel are controversial, some people are going to object and want to opt out of being a part of that," he says.

In Wisconsin, a petition drive is underway to revive a proposed law that would protect pharmacists who refuse to prescribe drugs they believe could cause an abortion or be used for assisted suicide. "It just recognizes that pharmacists should not be forced to choose between their consciences and their livelihoods," says Matt Sande of Pro-Life Wisconsin. "They should not be compelled to become parties to abortion."

SIGNIFICANCE

The question of pharmacists' ethical rights vs. women's right to access physician-prescribed contraception or "morning after" pills emerged at the beginning of the twenty-first century as a major tipping point in the pro-choice/anti-choice debates in the United States. The American Pharmacists Association, the national professional association for pharmacists, issued a statement of ethics in 1998 that supports the right of a pharmacist to refuse to dispense a drug that conflicts with his or her personal beliefs, but also assigns responsibility to the pharmacist to make certain the patient has access to the drug requested.

The clause states that "APhA recognizes the individual pharmacist's right to exercise conscientious refusal and supports the establishment of systems to ensure patient access to legally prescribed therapy without compromising the pharmacist's right of conscientious refusal." The American College of Clinical Pharmacists also developed a clause of conscience, adopted in August 2005, which puts forth similar statements and also adds the requirement that pharmacists be clear and open about their beliefs with employers and colleagues so that patients' needs can be met without the conflict of conscience hindering patient access to prescribed drugs.

Groups such as Planned Parenthood, the National Abortion Rights Action League (NARAL Pro-Choice America), and the National Organization for Women (NOW) all condemn the actions of pharmacists who refuse to dispense contraception and "morning after" pills to women. These groups argue that women in rural areas are unfairly penalized for their pharmacists' choices. Finding another pharmacy with the needed drug is not easy in areas where the nearest pharmacy could be 100 miles away or inaccessible by public transportation. In addition, the increasing reports of pharmacists who violate the standard that the pharmacist protect the patient's right to access—by transferring the prescription to a different drugstore or handing the prescription to an on-site colleague for dispensing—lead women's rights groups to charge that this "conscience clause" movement is a stealth attempt at eroding a woman's right to access birth control.

Planned Parenthood issued a press release on February 3, 2006, that focused on Wal-Mart, the largest supplier of pharmaceutical drugs in the United States. The press release calls on Wal-Mart to begin stocking the "morning after" pill in its pharmacies, and highlights a lawsuit by three Massachusetts women against Wal-Mart for failure to do so. A portion of the statement reads: "[t]o be most effective, emergency contraception should be taken within 72 hours of unprotected intercourse or contraceptive failure. Because Wal-Mart has put so many smaller stores out of business, in a number of areas it is the only pharmacy for miles." Women's health advocates counter the question of morality by pointing to economics and access; if Wal-Mart is the only pharmacy in town, and all the pharmacists refuse to dispense a particular birth control pill or emergency contraception, where does that leave patients?

Other groups such as Pharmacists for Life International, which claims to have over 1,600 members on six continents, state that pharmacists should have legal protections for their personal choices. Karen L. Brauer, president of Pharmacists for Life International, was fired from her job as a pharmacist at a K-Mart in Ohio for refusing to dispense the "morning after" pill. Her group claims that pharmacists should have the freedom not to participate in the dispensing of drugs that they believe to cause actions that violate their personal beliefs.

In addition, some proponents of pharmacists' right to choose which medications to dispense question whether conscience clauses go far enough. Peter Kreeft, a professor of philosophy at Boston College, has written on this subject in *Inside the Vatican* magazine. Kreeft argues that requiring the pharmacist to refer the patient elsewhere is a violation of conscience as well, since it forces the pharmacist to facilitate the patient's access to a drug that conflicts with the pharmacist's personal ethics.

On April 1, 2005, Illinois Gov. Rod R. Blagojevich issued an emergency ruling requiring Illinois pharmacies to fill all prescribed medications; if a pharmacist objects to filling a particular medication, there must be another pharmacist on site who will fill it. Pharmacists for Life International condemned the Illinois ruling. On April 14, 2005, the backers in both houses of the U.S. Congress put forth a bill dubbed the Access to Legal Pharmaceuticals Act (ALPhA), designed to make access to properly prescribed medications of all kinds federal law.

FURTHER RESOURCES

Periodicals

Kantor, Julie, and Ken Baum. "The Limits of Conscientious Objection—May Pharmacists Refuse to Fill Prescriptions for Emergency Contraception?" *New England Journal of Medicine* 351 (November 4, 2004): 2008–2012.

Stein, Rob. "Health Workers' Choice Debated." *Washington Post* (January 30, 2006): A01.

Web sites

American College of Clinical Pharmacists. "Prerogative of a Pharmacist to Decline to Provide Professional Services Based on Conscience." <http://www.accp.com/position/pos31_200508.pdf> (accessed February 6, 2006).

Inside the Vatican. "Conscience and the Dictatorship of Relativism." <http://www.insidethevatican.com/articles/conscience.htm> (accessed February 6, 2006).

National Conference of State Legislatures. "Pharmacist Conscience Clauses and Legislation 2005." <http://www.ncsl.org/programs/health/conscienceclauses.htm> (accessed February 6, 2006).

Pharmacists for Life International. <http://www.pfli.org> (accessed February 6, 2006).

Asexuality

Prevalence and Associated Factors in a National Probability Sample

Article

By: Anthony F. Bogaert

Date: August 2004

Source: Bogaert, Anthony F., "Aesexuality: Prevalence and Associated Factors in a National Probability Sample". *Journal of Sex Research* (August 2004).

About the Author: Anthony F. Bogaert is a professor of psychology at Brock University in Ontario, Canada. Bogaert's primary focus of research is human sexuality, including sexual orientation and what determines it, risky sexual behavior, sex offenses, and pornography. He is the author of numerous articles and academic papers on the subject.

INTRODUCTION

Asexuality is a sexual orientation, and unlike celibacy, is considered no more a matter of choice than heterosexuality, homosexuality, or bisexuality. People who are asexual share the same emotions and needs for relationships as other people but do not have the same need for sexual intimacy and have been known to forgo the sexual aspects of a relationship entirely. The characteristics of asexuality vary from person to person, similar to variance in sex drive for other orientations. As a percentage of the overall population, asexuality appears to manifest itself in approximately the same numbers as homosexuality, but according to the study quoted, the effect of this orientation on lifestyle appears to be noticeably different. Yet, despite the number of people calling themselves asexual, this orientation receives far less attention and study than other sexual lifestyles.

PRIMARY SOURCE

RESULTS

Of the participants, 195 or 1.05% reported being asexual. (1) This rate is very similar to the rate of same-sex attraction (both exclusive same-sex and bisexuality combined; 207 or 1.11%). However, binomial tests indicated that there were more gay and bisexual men than asexual men ($p < .001$) and more asexual women than lesbian and bisexual women ($p < .001$). (2)

Sexuality

As shown in Table 1, relative to sexual people, asexual people had fewer sexual partners, had a later onset of sexual activity (if it occurred), and had less frequent sexual activity with a partner currently. Overall, then, asexual people had less sexual experience with sexual partners, and this fact provides some validation of the concept of asexuality.

Demographics

As also shown in Table 1, some significant relationships occurred between asexuality and the demographics. Contrary to prediction, asexual people were not younger than sexual people; in fact, they were somewhat older. However, as predicted, more women than men reported being asexual. Not surprisingly, there were fewer asexual people than sexual people currently in (or having had) a long-term relationship. On the other hand, a significant minority of the asexual people, 85 of the 195 (44%), were currently in or had had long-term cohabiting or marital relationships, with 64 (33%) currently married or cohabiting (see Diamond, 2003, for a distinction between romantic and sexual desire/attraction). Asexual individuals were also more likely than sexual individuals to come from lower socioeconomic conditions. A higher percentage (13%) of asexual individuals were also non-White relative to the sexual individuals (4%). Finally, asexual individuals were less well educated than the sexual individuals.

Health, Physical Development, and Religiosity

Asexual people were more likely to have adverse health, and the asexual women had a later onset of menarche relative to the sexual women. Asexual people were also shorter and weighed less than the sexual people. Finally, there was some evidence that asexual people were more religious than sexual people, at least with regard to attendance at religious services....

DISCUSSION

This study investigated asexuality, defined as a lack of sexual attraction for either sex, in a national probability sample. A significant minority (1.05%) of people reported that they had never felt sexual attraction to anyone at all. This rate of asexuality was similar to the rate of same-sex attraction. It is interesting to speculate why asexual people have been overlooked when discussions of sexual variability are presented. Perhaps this group is relatively invisible because their inclinations do not lead to overt sociosexual activities that would bring attention to their activities. The absence of sexual activities and the inclinations that induce this absence are not likely to bring public attention or scrutiny, either positive or negative. Neither, of course, has it been illegal or perceived as morally wrong to have such inclinations. Therefore, unlike other sexual minorities (e.g., gay people), asexual individuals would not have had to face public scrutiny from the press, religious institutions, or the legal system. (This is not to say, of course, that in their private and family lives asexual people have not felt pressure to take on traditional sexual and reproductive roles.) In addition, until recently sexual surveys using national probability samples were not conducted, so the vast majority of sexual studies using convenience samples of volunteers probably did not include many asexual people. Research shows, for example, that those who choose to participate in a sexual study have more sexual experience (e.g., more partners) and are more interested in sexual activity than those who do not participate (Bogaert, 1996; Morokoff, 1986; Saunders, Fisher, Hewitt, & Clayton, 1985). Indeed, it is interesting to speculate about whether the rate of asexuality is actually higher than reported here given that some of the participants who declined to participate in this survey (about 30%) could also be asexual.

This study provided a preliminary examination of some of the factors associated with asexuality. A variety of demographic (gender, social class, education, and race-ethnicity), physical development (height and menarche onset), health, and religiosity variables predicted asexuality. It is interesting that many of these variables independently predicted asexuality. This suggests that there may be a number of independent developmental pathways, perhaps both biological and psychosocial, leading to asexuality.

Even the physical development and health variables—late menarche, a shorter stature, and health problems in women and a shorter stature and health problems in men—independently predicted asexuality. This suggests that physical development factors that are independent of general debilitating illnesses (which may lower sex drive or interest) may affect growth and development mechanisms related to sexual orientation (e.g., anterior hypothalamus; see LeVay, 1991). These findings also add to a growing body of literature showing that the development of sexual attraction to adult men and women along with some atypical sexual proclivities may be partly biologically based and determined prior to birth (e.g., Bogaert, 2001; Bogaert, 2003a; Ellis & Ames, 1987; Lalumiere, Blanchard, & Zucker, 2000; Williams et al., 2000).

The results regarding the demographic variables suggest that one pathway to asexuality may relate to an environment different from a traditional middle-class or upper-middle-class White home (e.g., one with fewer resources). I found large differences between asexual and sexual people in education and social class, with asexual people tending to score lower on these demographic variables. This suggests that the educational system and the home environment play fundamental roles in typical sexual development, and that alterations of these circumstances can have a profound effect on basic sexual attraction processes. Moreover, the fact that the social class–asexuality and education–asexuality relationships remained significant when I controlled for general physical health suggests that these relationships do not occur merely because people with serious health problems, which may contribute to asexuality, are less likely to be able to attain a higher education or improve their life circumstances. Rather, these results suggest that the health problems of some asexual people may be the result of disadvantaged economic and social conditions. It is difficult to know what aspects of the educational and home environments may contribute to asexuality. As mentioned earlier, perhaps processes related to exposure to and familiarity with peers (see Bem, 1996; Storms, 1981) are altered when the home and educational environment are atypical. It is also important to point out that an atypical home environment for asexual people may have occurred prior to childhood during gestation, as might be expected if an altered prenatal milieu (e.g., altered prenatal hormones) partly underlies asexuality and other atypical sexual inclinations (e.g., Bogaert, 2001; Ellis & Ames, 1987; Lalumiere et al., 2000; Williams et al., 2000).

Gender was also an important predictor of asexuality. More women than men reported being asexual. This difference may be a reflection of gender roles and/or sexual strategies in which men are or at least are expected to be more sexual than women. If so, perhaps some women have internalized to an extreme degree, and hence "overadapted" to, these feminine roles or strategies (e.g., Mazur, 1986). Some research has also suggested that women's sexuality (or at least their sex drive) is more "plastic" than men's sexuality (e.g., Baumeister, 2000). Thus, cultural influences may have a more profound effect on women's sexuality than on men's; as a result, more women than men may become asexual if life circumstances are atypical. A related explanation is that women relative to men may be less likely to label males or females as salient sexual objects and hence may report themselves as having no attraction to either sex because they may not be as aware of their own sexual arousal as men are, even under conditions when genital responses are occurring (e.g., Heimen, 1977; Laan et al., 1994). A third possibility is that women may have fewer conditioning experiences (e.g., masturbation) relevant to sexual orientation development and this may lead to an increased likelihood of asexuality, along with other conditions....

Contrary to prediction, a younger age was not related to asexuality. In fact, asexual people were slightly older than sexual people. This result does not give support to the idea that many asexual individuals are "presexual" or in an early developmental stage prior to adult-oriented sexual attraction. Thus, although adolescents and some young adults probably vary in their awareness or experience of first sexual attraction (with a variety of social and psychological circumstances and biological aspects contributing to such awareness or experience), it would seem that most of the asexual individuals in this sample probably had had enough time to encounter the necessary circumstances to initiate sexual attraction experiences. Either they did not want to enter into such circumstances because of their asexual natures, or they had passed a critical age window beyond which these social and psychological circumstances were no longer sufficient to initiate sexual attraction to others.

SIGNIFICANCE

Asexual individuals appear to have been affected by physical and genetic predetermining factors as well as culture and environment. A tendency toward late onset of puberty, shorter stature, and various health problems marked both men and women who were asexual, suggesting that the development of a more typical sex drive might have been affected by the same traits that caused these other characteristics. A greater percentage of women than men reported being asexual, which might have been due to cultural expectations placed on men to be sexual aggressors, or on women to deny experiencing sexual arousal or interest. However, the study also implies that asexuality is a condition that may stem from a lack of something in the individual, a failure to develop a physical and emotional interest in sexual intimacy. Despite this, many asexual individuals enjoy friendships and close relationships that are fulfilling, even though they do not need to express that closeness in a sexual way. In many cases, they are capable of having a sexual relationship but do not feel driven to do so.

An actor in a "SpongeBob Squarepants" costume in New York. After Christian conservative groups attacked the character as being gay, creator Stephen Hillenburg said the character is asexual, neither gay nor straight. © NANCY KASZERMAN/ZUMA/CORBIS

Various labels and characteristics are attached to asexual individuals in the study, including older, lighter, and more religious, but these only indicate into what demographic those asexual individuals happened to fall. They are not conclusive predictors of asexuality. More informative are the types and numbers of relationships that asexual individuals had compared to those participants that labeled themselves as sexual.

Fewer asexual individuals were in long-term committed relationships such as marriage and on the whole they had had fewer close relationships in general, statistics that are natural given their lack of interest in sexual intimacy. Yet most asexual people do not consider themselves to have a problem despite their lack of sexual interest. Instead, they consider their orientation a valid sexual persuasion and have built up a support network through associations both in person and on-line

that provide education and camaraderie. Some asexual individuals, in fact, refer to themselves as nonsexual, believing that asexual sounds like a term used to refer to single-celled organisms, such as amoebas.

There can be many causes for a reduced sex drive, such as stress, illness, or emotional detachment. However, asexuality, like other sexual orientations, is not something that a person either gets over or suddenly develops. It is not a gradual loss of interest in sexual intimacy, but lifelong lack of physical attraction to either sex. Although asexuality has only come into public discussion in recent years, it most likely always existed as a sexual orientation, but remained unexplored due to a combination of factors, including people's reluctance to discuss it; the lack of an obvious, physical behavior that would have brought it to society's attention; and the refusal of others to recognize and accept the existence of asexuality as a factor beyond individual choice. In light of modern acceptance of sexual preferences, it is logical that asexuality should receive greater attention, study, and acceptance.

FURTHER RESOURCES

Periodicals

Radford, Tim. "No Sex Please, We're Asexual." *The Guardian* (October 14, 2004).

Web sites

Asexual Visibility and Education Network (AVEN). "Asexual: A person who does not experience sexual attraction" <http://www.asexuality.org/home> (accessed March 13, 2006).

Harris, Lynn. "Asexual and Proud!" *Salon.com* <http://dir.salon.com/story/mwt/feature/2005/05/26/asexual/index.html> (accessed March 13, 2006).

Westphal, Sylvia Pagan. "Glad to be Asexual." *NewScientist.com* <http://www.newscientist.com/article.ns?id=dn6533> (accessed March 13, 2006).

After the Tsunami, A Drive to Reverse Tubal Ligations in Tamil Nadu

Internet article

By: Margot Cohen

Date: July 2005

Source: Cohen, Margot. "After the Tsunami: A Drive to Reverse Tubal Ligations in Tamil Nadu." *Population Reference Bureau,* <http://www.prb.org/> (accessed March 13, 2006).

About the Author: Margot Cohen is a staff reporter for the *Wall Street Journal* based in Bangalore, India.

INTRODUCTION

In the early morning on December 26, 2004, an 8.9 magnitude undersea earthquake erupted off the coast of Indonesia, near Aceh province. The earthquake set in motion a series of tsunamis that struck the coastal regions of the Indian Ocean, including India's Tamil Nadu region. The devastation left by the sixty-foot waves affected over one million residents within the entire region, leaving approximately 200,000 dead.

The region of Tamil Nadu is located along the southern coast of India, on the shores of the Bay of Bengal and the Indian Ocean. With a history over 5,000 years old, the region is proud of being the birthplace of the Dravidian culture—the first settlers in ancient India. Largely a tourist destination and fishing community, the region was the most affected in India. The list of victims from India includes 10,749 dead and 5,640 still listed as missing. Within Tamil Nadu, 7,983 people lost their lives due to the tsunami and 350 children were orphaned.

PRIMARY SOURCE

(July 2005) When India accelerated its nationwide family planning program in the 1970s, the southern state of Tamil Nadu was quick to respond. Government officials set up a wide network of primary health centers and spread the message that tubal ligation (also known as tubectomy) meant permanent birth control with no fuss.

The campaign brought dramatic results: By 2002, nearly 44 percent of Tamil Nadu's women had borne two children and been sterilized before their 27th birthday. And the state's total fertility rate dropped from 3.8 in 1976 to 2.0 in 2002.

But after last December's Indian Ocean tsunami killed over 2,300 children under age 18 in Tamil Nadu, the state government began offering free reversals of tubal ligation for women there who wish to conceive again. So far, 189 women have signed up for the microsurgery, which is known as recanalization.

"In countering the depression of losing a child, this is a very intelligent option," says Dr. J. Radhakrishnan, the district collector (or top civil servant) of Nagapattinam, a coastal district of 1.4 million people where the tsunami left 6,065 dead, including 1,776 children. "They feel guilty that they survived but could not save the child," he says of the bereaved parents.

The issues raised by Tamil Nadu's recanalization program, however, reach well beyond parents directly affected by the tsunami. Nationwide, more than two-thirds of India's female contraceptive users rely on tubectomy. And for some family planning experts, the new initiative is a stark reminder that India's health bureaucracy has failed to devote sufficient counseling and other resources to promote easily reversible contraceptive methods such as pills, IUDs, and condoms—especially for young women in their 20s.

"Choice has been very limited for [India's] women," says Dr. Saroj Pachauri, regional director for South and East Asia at the New York-based Population Council.

NO HARD SELL NEEDED FOR TUBECTOMIES

In Tamil Nadu, just 3 percent of women are relying on IUDs, with 1 percent turning to the pill and 1.5 percent using condoms, according to a 2004 report from the Directorate of Family Welfare in Chennai, the state capital. But while annual targets for tubectomies have been officially abandoned, local governments such as Tamil Nadu's still strive to meet what they call each district's "expected demand" for sterilization. Between April 1, 2004 and April 1, 2005, doctors in Tamil Nadu performed more than 416,000 tubectomies, up from roughly 370,000 in the same period five years earlier.

Dr. G. Venkatachalam, joint director of medical services at the government hospital in Nagapattinam, says Indian women are advised to undergo a tubectomy immediately after delivering their second child. "If prolonged for two or three months, the mother might not come to the hospital for sterilization," he cautions. "Or she might conceive again."

After more than two decades of high-profile campaigns, though, the government no longer needs to make a hard sell for tubal ligation. "Women feel very comfortable with tubectomy," says Sheela Rani Chunkath, secretary of the Health and Family Welfare Department in Tamil Nadu. "They feel they don't want to mess with the hormones." Compounding the trend are continued complaints of excessive bleeding after IUD insertion and nationwide worries among women that pills bring side effects that include pronounced fatigue.

But Chunkath also emphasizes that the government is now seeking to promote vasectomies, which have only occurred sporadically in recent years due to broad male distaste for the method. "This gender imbalance, we really need to correct it," she says. "We think the man should also be responsible."

THE RIGHT OF A WOMAN TO CHOOSE, OR JUST MORE GENDER DISCRIMINATION?

More than a dozen tsunami survivors in Tamil Nadu have already had recanalization, but most of the other patients are expected to undergo the procedure in late June and July. Tamil Nadu's flamboyant chief minister, Selvi J. Jayalalithaa, added a political gloss to the drive by appearing on television to publicize an executive order that promised either free recanalizations at government hospitals or 25,000 rupees ($595) in compensation for those who opt for private clinics.

Some analysts think the initiative protects the reproductive rights of Tamil Nadu's women. "The recanalization approach is in fact in keeping with the right of women to choose the timing of the birth of their children as per their emotional needs," says Madhu Bala Nath, South Asia regional director of the International Planned Parenthood Federation.

But other observers are expressing concern that the high-profile program feeds into broad cultural biases that only validate women if they bear children. In India, childless women generally live in fear that their husbands will remarry in the search to continue the family line—often at the prodding of their own mothers. Economic dependence only deepens such fears.

"This is about societal pressure on a childless parent. And that's not the right reason to have a child," says Sujatha Natarajan, vice president of the Family Planning Association of India.

There is also no guarantee that all of these operations will result in healthy pregnancies: One public hospital in Chennai that specializes in the procedure reports that just 47 percent of its recanalization patients eventually gave birth again. In fact, Chunkath says that many reversals could be doomed because government doctors often cut too much of the fallopian tube during the original tubectomy in order to forestall legal claims of method failure.

"WITHOUT CHILDREN, WE FEEL SO LONELY AND LOST"

Still, officials believe that recanalization will bring fresh hope to bereaved couples. At Kilpauk Medical College Hospital in Chennai, surgeon A. Kalaichelvi considers 24-year old Sumathy, a fish vendor from the town of Mahabalipuram, one of the lucky ones. Sumathy, who lost her 7-year-old son to the tsunami, had her recanalization performed by Kalaichelvi a month ago.

"I feel at peace," says Sumathy, perched on a blue hospital mattress. "My mother-in-law said, in future, when you grow old, you need a child to be there."

Sumathy says she has no particular preference for a boy or a girl—feelings that are echoed by many other tsunami survivors, according to Dr. Pinagapany

Manorama, director of the Community Health Education Society, a Chennai-based NGO that conducted counseling in tsunami-affected villages. Such sentiments are unusual in a country where couples have long harbored a strong preference for boys, who ultimately inherit property and perform last rites for their parents.

Indeed, India appears to be fighting a losing battle against abortions of female fetuses, despite a measure that outlaws doctors from disclosing the sex of a fetus following prenatal scans. Tamil Nadu is no exception: The state's sex ratio among children up to 6 years old was 939 girls per 1,000 boys—a significant drop from the 948 females per 1,000 males recorded in 1991. In seven of the state's districts, the ratio has dipped below 930, with Salem district reaching an alarming 826 girls ages 6 and under for every 1,000 boys.

But in the ramshackle tsunami relief camps erected near the coast, some couples appear desperate for any sort of companionship. "Without children, we feel so lonely and lost," confesses Moorthy, a 29-year-old fisherman whose son and daughter died in the tsunami. His wife, 24-year old Indira, became in January one of the first survivors to undergo recanalization. But the couple is still restlessly awaiting pregnancy.

Like most other bereaved parents in this traditional coastal community, they have no interest in adopting any of the surviving orphans, reflecting the unpopularity of formal adoption in India. "It's nothing like having your own child," says Indira, who was feeding her toddlers when the waves swept over their coastal hut.

While many health experts doubt that the tsunami will significantly alter the Indian government's longstanding focus on tubectomy, they feel the disaster could prompt some second thoughts among coastal dwellers. Says Dr. Manorama: "They may think, why get sterilized? A tsunami might come again."

SIGNIFICANCE

India was one of the first countries to implement a government-sanctioned family planning program to combat population growth in developing nations. The program, which began in the 1950s, started as an educational program. In the 1960s, the Indian government began a formal effort to decrease the birth rate by instituting education into school curriculum. However, the results were minimal. In the 1980s, with financial assistance from the central government, state governments began to create public health centers that facilitated family planning programs. As part of this program, tubal ligation was offered as a means of birth control and local governments were given a tar-

In Matara, Sri Lanka, K.M.G Prinska works on homework with daughter Pujitha. Prinska is one of the many Sri Lankan women who have decided to have their tubal ligations reversed because of deaths from the December 26, 2004, tsunami in the Indian Ocean. Prinska's other two children died in the tsunami. AP IMAGES

get number of operations to perform. By the mid–1980s the government's family planning model seemed to have begun to work, since forty-three percent of couples were then using family planning. Over the last ten years over three million women have undergone tubal ligations.

The medical procedure called tubal ligation is a surgical sterilization operation. The procedure closes off the woman's fallopian tubes, thus preventing the egg from traveling to the uterus from the ovary and the sperm from reaching the fallopian tube to fertilize the egg. The procedure involves cutting, burning, or blocking the fallopian tubes with rings, bands, or clips and is 99.5 percent effective as birth control.

In a patriarchal culture, such as India's, there is pressure on women to marry young and to produce sons. In the *Indian Journal of Medical Ethics*, Malini Karkal asserts that women in Indian culture are dominated by men at every stage of their lives. She writes,

"The purpose of marriage is to transfer the dominance over the woman from the father to the husband. The girl is married off young to ensure that the domination is not questioned. Subjugation of the girl is also assured by marrying the girl to a man much older in age. Seniors in the family then decide on child bearing." The desire for a son is based on economic realities as well as cultural values. In rural areas, sons provide labor and supply security to parents in their old age. Even in urban communities, the preference is for sons. Sons carry on a family line in contrast to daughters who become part of their in-laws families. As a result, a deficiency in females has arisen within the Indian population and the government has made prenatal gender selection illegal. However, human rights groups estimate the annual incidence of female infanticide in India at 10,000 cases.

Nirmala Palanisamy, the head of a state nurses' group, visited the tsunami victims in Tamil Nadu. After meeting with the bereaved parents, she stated, "I could see their need was as acute as those in food queues in the relief camp." The Community Health Education Society, a nongovernmental organization aiding tsunami survivors, has cited at least 600 women and 100 men seeking to have their sterilization reversed. In a *Washington Times* article, Shaikh Azizur Rahman details the story of a woman who lost both of her children, a son and daughter, in the tsunami. She experienced deep depression from the loss, as well as the knowledge that her previous tubal ligation procedure made it impossible to have more children. Once she learned that the procedure is reversible, she began to emerge from her depression. As a result of stories such as these, the Indian government has offered to pay 25,000 rupees (approximately $575) for the procedure for those who have lost all their children. Women with surviving daughters are ineligible for the government-funded reversal.

FURTHER RESOURCES
Periodicals

Karkal, Malini. "Women's Sexuality Dominated by Men." *Indian Journal of Medical Ethics* (April-June 2006).

Web sites

Daily Times. "Indian State Offers to Reverse Sterilization of Tsunami Families." <http://www.dailytimes.com.pk/default.asp?page=story_3-3-2005_pg4_23> (accessed March 13, 2006).

Medical News Today. "Indian Province Offering Free Sterilization Reversal Surgeries to People Who Lost All Children in 2004 Tsunami." <http://www.medicalnewstoday.com/medicalnews.php?newsid=21276> (accessed March 13, 2006).

Washington Times. "Indians Reversing Sterilizations." <http://washtimes.com/world/20050311-093603-1520r.htm> (accessed March 13, 2006).

UNFPA Saddened by U.S. Decision Not to Rejoin Nations' Support For Multilateral Work to Protect Women's Health

Internet article

By: UNFPA, the United Nations Population Fund

Date: September 10, 2005

Source: *UNFPA.* "UNPFA Saddened by U.S. Decision Not to Rejoin Nations' Support For Multilateral

Work to Protect Women's Health." <http://www.unfpa.org/news/> (accessed February 14, 2006).

About the Author: UNFPA, the United Nations Population Fund, is an international development agency that focuses on women's reproductive health issues around the globe.

INTRODUCTION

In 1969, the United Nations created the United Nations Population Fund as a vehicle for promoting family planning and population control. The United States was instrumental in this agency's development. With a three-pronged approach—family planning, safe pregnancy and birth, and sexually-transmitted disease prevention—the UNFPA serves women and families in over 150 countries.

For the agency's first fifteen years, the United States was a strong supporter. In 1985, the U.S. passed the Kemp-Kasten Amendment, which barred U.S.

A family planning meeting for women in the densely populated impoverished area of Sangam Vihar of New Delhi, August 1999. AP IMAGES

funding for any agency that "supports or participates in the management of a program of coercive abortion or sterilization." President Ronald Reagan reduced UNFPA funding by $10 million in 1985—the exact amount spent in China. President Reagan, along with pro-life organizations in the United States, claimed that China's use of "coercive abortion" as part of its "One Child" population control effort, violated U.S. law preventing the use of taxpayer money for funding abortions. This U.S. action to reduce funding to the agency prompted sharp criticism from the UNFPA and from reproductive health organizations worldwide.

A 1985 review of the Kemp-Kasten Amendment demonstrated that the UNFPA activities were not in violation of or in conflict with the amendment, but, regardless of this finding, President Reagan suspended funding for the UNFPA by year's end. From 1985 through President George H. W. Bush's administration, which ended in early 1993, the United States withheld UNFPA funding.

When President William J. Clinton took office in early 1993, the new administration determined that UNFPA activities did not violate the Kemp-Kasten Amendment and restored funding, while simultaneously withholding the portion of funds that would be spent in China. In 1999, Congress withheld all funds when UNFPA renewed its work in China in full, although Congress appropriated $25 million for the program the following year. When President George W. Bush took office in January 2001, he continued funding for UNFPA. By January 2002, the United States, however, blocked the release of more than $34 million to the UNFPA, citing China as the reason. As of March 2006, the United States continues to withhold the funding from the UNFPA.

▮ PRIMARY SOURCE

UNITED NATIONS, New York— The United States Administration's decision for the fourth consecutive year not to release $34 million appropriated by Congress for UNFPA, the United Nations Population Fund, is regrettable, especially when leaders at the World Summit are stressing the need to act together on global concerns, the Fund said today. The funds are urgently needed for effective multilateral work in developing countries to prevent maternal and child deaths, stop the spread of HIV/AIDS, provide voluntary contraception and to support the work to end poverty.

The Administration's stated reason for continuing to withhold funds is simply incorrect, as an assessment team sent to China by the Administration itself found no evidence that UNFPA supports coercive abortions or sterilization, the Fund emphasized. To the contrary, it reported that UNFPA had registered its strong opposition to such practices. Other independent teams, from the British Parliament and a multi-faith panel of religious leaders, reached the same conclusion, some adding that UNFPA was a force for good, promoting positive change.

"This decision is disheartening because it contradicts clear evidence that UNFPA works hard to end coercion by proving the efficacy and superiority of the voluntary approach to family planning over any other alternative," said Thoraya Ahmed Obaid, UNFPA's Executive Director. "We receive funding from 166 nations that believe in strengthening UNFPA's role as a leading voice for human rights in family planning, safe motherhood and AIDS prevention."

"I hope the United States will rejoin the family of nations that support our multilateral work to eliminate maternal deaths, prevent HIV/AIDS, empower women and reduce poverty," said Ms. Obaid. "Our task is made more urgent by the fact that more than 300 million poor women in the world suffer from short- and long-term illnesses related to pregnancy or childbirth, with more than half a million of them dying each year."

The current Administration has, so far, withheld $127 million in funds appropriated by Congress. One year's withheld funding of $34 million could prevent as many as 2 million unwanted pregnancies and 4,700 maternal deaths in developing countries. The funds could also be used to scale up promising maternal health and HIV-prevention efforts, as well as to treat young women suffering from obstetric fistula.

UNFPA's pilot assistance in several China counties is proving that a client-oriented and quality-of-care approach to reproductive health and family planning is the superior alternative to a target-driven system. The Fund is pushing for Chinese women to have increased choice and access to quality, voluntary family planning and reproductive health. Abortions, surgical contraception and maternal deaths have dropped in the counties, while more women are choosing their own methods of contraception.

UNFPA helps approximately 146 countries and territories increase access to reproductive health care, including voluntary contraception; to promote safe motherhood; and to prevent unintended pregnancies, sexually transmitted infections and HIV/AIDS.

The United States is the only country to ever deny funding to UNFPA for non-budgetary reasons in the agency's entire 36 years of operation.

▮▮

SIGNIFICANCE

The United Nations Family planning agency does not restrict itself to contraceptive advice or abortions; services offered by UNFPA include a wide range of women's reproductive health measures including family planning, contraceptive supplies, prenatal and obstetric care, abortion services, obstetrical surgery, and more.

UNFPA supporters point to the agency's funding of obstetric fistula programs as a victim in the U.S. culture war over the issue of abortion. For many women in developing countries, fistula complications create an unbearable physical problem that leaves the woman an outcast. A fistula is a canal or hole that forms between the bladder and the vagina or the rectum and the vagina. Generally these fistulas form as a result of prolonged labor during childbirth or as a result of tearing during birth. Urine and feces leak into the vagina, leaving the woman prone to infection, incontinence, and unpleasant odors in public. The condition makes these women pariahs in their communities in the developing world.

According to UNFPA figures, more than 2 million women worldwide suffer from fistulas; most fistula complications can be corrected through basic surgery, which UNFPA offers. Recent campaigns in Chad, Sudan, and Pakistan elevated awareness of fistula and brought media attention to the medical problem as well as funding problems. UNFPA leader Thoraya Obaid points to the "end fistula" campaign as one of many that suffer from the U.S. funding decision.

Meanwhile, officials from the George W. Bush administration—in spite of the State Department's own finding in 2002 that UNFPA activities do not include any coercive elements and therefore do not violate the Kemp-Kasten Amendment—continue to hold the funding. The Bush administration points to the "compensation fee" charged to Chinese families who have more than one child as a policy that could coerce women into having abortions to avoid paying the fee. UNFPA has repeatedly ignored U.S. requests to suspend operations in China.

The U.S. policy has triggered sharp criticism worldwide, since its inception in 1985. In February 2006, Britain announced that it would devote three million pounds to replace withheld U.S. funding, with no restrictions on the use of funds for reproductive health services worldwide.

FURTHER RESOURCES

Periodicals

LaFraniere, Sharon. "Nightmare for African Women: Birthing Injury and Little Help." *New York Times* (September 28, 2005).

Boseley, Sarah. "Britain Defies U.S. With Funding to Boost Safe Abortion Services." *The Guardian* (February 6, 2006).

Web sites

House.gov. "Letter to George Bush Asking for UNFPA Funding." <http://www.house.gov/maloney/issues/UNFPA/unfpa22702.pdf> (accessed February 14, 2006).

Thomas.gov. "Repairing Young Women's Lives Around the World Act." <http://thomas.loc.gov/cgi-bin/query/z?c109:H.R.2811.IH:> (accessed February 14, 2006).

Audio and Visual Media

United Nations Children's Fund (UNICEF). *Protect Every Child.* Video tape number 390, 2002.

Early Sexual Intercourse, Condom Use and Sexually Transmitted Diseases

Newspaper article

By: Anonymous

Date: May 3, 2005

Source: "Early Sexual Intercourse, Condom Use and Sexually Transmitted Diseases." *The Daily* (May 3, 2005).

About the Author: This article was published without a byline and was contributed by a staff writer at *The Daily*, a Canadian English-language newspaper.

INTRODUCTION

This report on early sexual intercourse summarizes statistical data from two studies of young teens in Canada published in 2005. The first study, which focused on sexual intercourse, was based on surveys of 3,212 persons aged fourteen or fifteen in 1998–1999 or 2000–2001. The second, which focused on rates of diagnosis of sexually transmitted diseases (STDs), was based on a sample of 18,084 people aged fifteen to twenty-four surveyed in 2003.

A number of straightforward numerical data are presented. For example, the article notes that twelve percent of Canadian boys and thirteen percent of girls have had sexual intercourse by ages fourteen or fifteen, However, the data do not measure actual rates of sexual experience, but teens' unverified claims about their sexual experience (self-reported data). The article also reports the possibility that condom use is lower at older ages because "those in the older age group are more likely to be in a long-term relationship with one partner, and so perceive condom use as less of a concern." However, as the word choice makes clear, this is speculation, not a finding of the study.

The study on STDs reported here found that older young adults were more likely to report themselves as having been diagnosed with an STD, and that persons who started having sex at younger ages were more likely to report themselves as having had an STD than those who began having sex at older ages.

Finally, the article describes the statistical links found between certain factors and early commencement of sexual activity. Drinking and smoking were found to be associated with early sexual intercourse in girls: only smoking, not drinking, was associated with early sexual intercourse in boys. Lower incomes and poorer relations with parents were found to be associated with early intercourse in boys; if any association between these factors and early intercourse was found in girls, it is not mentioned here. None of these associations necessarily imply that one thing causes the other: that is, smoking does not necessarily lead to sex nor sex to smoking. Both may be caused by a third factor (or multiple factors).

▮ PRIMARY SOURCE

EARLY SEXUAL INTERCOURSE, CONDOM USE AND SEXUALLY TRANSMITTED DISEASES

An estimated 12% of boys and 13% of girls have had sexual intercourse by ages 14 or 15, according to a new study based on data that the teenagers reported to a national survey.

Using data from the National Longitudinal Survey of Children and Youth (NLSCY), the study found that characteristics associated with early sexual activity differed for boys and girls.

A separate study, also based on self-reported data, found that many young people may be putting their health at risk by having sex without a condom.

This second report is based on data from the 2003 Canadian Community Health Survey (CCHS). It examines sexual activity, number of partners and condom use among 15- to 24-year-olds, as well as their likelihood of reporting having been diagnosed with sexually transmitted diseases (STDs), now also referred to as "sexually transmitted infections."

In 2003, an estimated 28% of 15- to 17-year-olds reported having had sexual intercourse at least once in their lives. By ages 20 to 24, the proportion was 80%. One-third of sexually active 15- to 24-year-olds reported that they had had more than one sexual partner in the previous year.

In addition, about 3 in 10 young people who had sex with multiple partners in the past year had not used a condom the last time they had intercourse.

Multiple partners, condom use related to age

Young men were more likely than young women to report having had more than one sexual partner during the previous year. As well, 15- to 24-year-olds who had had intercourse by age 13 were significantly more likely to have had two or more sexual partners in the past year than were those whose first experience happened when they were older.

Sex without a condom was more common at older ages. Nearly 44% of sexually active 20- to 24-year-olds reported sex without a condom, compared with 33% of those aged 18 to 19, and 22% of those aged 15 to 17.

It is possible that those in the older age group are more likely to be in a long-term relationship with one partner, and so perceive condom use as less of a concern.

When the impact of other factors that might influence condom use (such as current age, age at first intercourse, marital status) was taken into account, young women in Quebec and New Brunswick emerged as being more likely to engage in sex without condoms than their counterparts in Ontario.

STD risk linked to age

According to CCHS data, 4% of 15- to 24-year-olds who had had sex at least once reported having been diagnosed with a STD. The true figure is likely higher than reported because of a possible lack of symptoms or awareness.

Young adults aged 20 to 24 were significantly more likely than 15- to 17-year-olds to have been diagnosed with an STD. This is probably because the older group has had more years of being sexually active.

Similarly, early age at first intercourse also increased the risk. Those who had had sexual intercourse by age 13 were more than twice as likely to report an STD than were those who had waited until they were older.

Factors differ for boys and girls

The factors related to early sexual intercourse differed for girls and boys, according to NLSCY data.

The odds of early intercourse among girls were high for those who, at ages 12 or 13, had reached puberty or were not overweight.

Also, girls whose self-concept was weak at ages 12 or 13 were more likely than those with a strong self-concept to have had sexual intercourse by 14 or 15. The opposite was true for boys.

An association between smoking and early sexual intercourse was strong for both sexes, even when the impact of the other factors was taken into account. At ages 12 or 13, 26% of boys and 31% of girls reported that they had tried smoking cigarettes. Within two years, over one-quarter of this group reported that they had had intercourse.

As well, for girls, having tried drinking by ages 12 or 13 was associated with reporting having had intercourse by ages 14 or 15.

Drinking was not associated with early sexual activity in boys. However, significantly high proportions of boys who had a poor relationship with their parents at ages 12 or 13, or who were in a low-income family, reported having had sex by ages 14 or 15.

Young girls in the eastern provinces and Quebec were more likely to report being sexually active than were those in Ontario.

NOTE TO READERS

The study on early sexual intercourse is based on data from the 1996/97, 1998/99 and 2000/01 National Longitudinal Survey of Children and Youth (NLSCY). It uses a sample of 3,212 youths who were aged 14 or 15 in 1998/99 or 2000/01.

A second study, on sexual intercourse, condom use and sexually transmitted diseases among older teens and young adults, is based on data from the 2003 Canadian Community Health Survey. It uses a sample of 18,084 youths aged 15 to 24 in 2003.

Some data limitations should be noted. For example, the term "sexual intercourse" was not defined in the survey questions. What one respondent considers "sexual intercourse" may differ from another's interpretation. Also, the answers that survey respondents give to questions about matters such as sexual activity, smoking or drinking may not accurately reflect their behaviour.

SIGNIFICANCE

Several large, government-funded studies have been devoted to the question of child and teen sexual

A teenage girl holds a condom. © ROYALTY FREE/CORBIS

activity, not only in Canada but in the United States and in other countries. There is ample public-health ground for this concern. Medical experts agree that there are a number of negative consequences for children and teens who begin to have sexual intercourse at early ages. Apart from pregnancy, an obvious risk for girls, multiple studies have found that teenagers who are sexually active are more likely to have been sexually or physically abused, to be depressed, to have STDs, to have contemplated suicide, to drink more, to get poorer grades, and to have poorer relationships with their parents. Not all these associations are causal, but some certainly are, partly or wholly. There is, then, science-based agreement across the ideological spectrum that early sexual activity is risky. The data supporting this belief are exemplified by the Canadian study described here. They confirm that sexual activity among young teens is not only risky but common and is even fairly common among children not yet in their teens. The American Academy of Pediatrics (AAP) said in 2001 that "Early sexual intercourse among American adolescents represents a major public health problem."

There is no universal agreement, however, on the causes of the high levels of sexual activity among young people. Social and religious conservatives tend to blame pornography, permissive parenting, permissive or no religious instruction, and the "sexual revolution" of the 1960s, which openly defied the traditional teaching that premarital sex is shameful.

The AAP points to media representations of sexuality as a major cause of early sexual activity: "Although early sexual activity may be caused by a variety of factors, the media are believed to play a significant role. In film, television, and music, sexual messages are becoming more explicit... these messages contain unrealistic, inaccurate, and misleading information that young people accept as fact." The average American teen views almost 14,000 sexual references on television per year, only one tenth of one percent of which deal with birth control, abstinence, or the risk of pregnancy or STDs. Some research finds that heavy exposure to sex in the media encourages an exaggerated idea of how much sex goes on in the real world; the AAP suggests that media may thus act as a "super peer" portraying highly active sexuality as normal and thus, almost by definition, desirable for teens.

Different ideological camps draw different conclusions from these facts. Social and religious conservatives often advocate abstinence-only sex education programs that explicitly encourage teens to not have sex at all: "[A]bstinence education programs are uniquely suited to meeting both the emotional and the physical needs of America's youth," concludes a review of the link between sex and teen depression by the conservative Heritage Foundation. Liberal groups urge the teaching of sexuality, STD, and birth control facts: a review by Planned Parenthood of data on the ills of early teen sexual activity concludes, in part, that teens should be provided with "responsible, medically accurate sexuality education." In 2001, the AAP bemoaned the "absence of effective, comprehensive sex education at home or in the schools."

FURTHER RESOURCES

Periodicals

American Academy of Pediatrics. "Sexuality, Contraception, and the Media." *Pediatrics* 107, 1 (January 2001): 191–194.

Web sites

Planned Parenthood. "White Paper: Adolescent Sexuality." <http://www.plannedparenthood.org/pp2/portal/files/portal/medicalinfo/teensexualhealth/white-adolescent-sexuality-02.xml> (accessed April 1, 2006).

Rector, Robert E., Kirk A. Johnson, and Lauren R. Noyes. *The Heritage Foundation.* "Sexually Active Teenagers Are More Likely to Be Depressed and to Attempt Suicide." <http://www.heritage.org/Research/Family/cda0304.cfm> (accessed April 1, 2006).

Midwife Assisting Home Birth

Photograph

By: Anonymous

Date: c. 2000

Source: Corbis Corporation

About the Photographer: This photograph is part of the collection of the Corbis Corporation, headquartered in Seattle, with a worldwide archive of over seventy million images.

INTRODUCTION

In the 1950s, most births occurred within the medical setting of the hospital. The rate of Cesarean sections (surgical birth) began to rise steadily, and medications for pain relief or even to induce amnesia were considered a normal part of the process. As the women's movement began to gain momentum in the 1960s and 1970s, interest in midwifery and home-births were rekindled as women began to challenge the obstetrical view that pregnancy was a sickness requiring medical procedures. Women began to assert that pregnancy and childbirth were a natural process. By the 1990s, some women began to choose to take the birthing process out of the hospital, out of the domain of the physician, and into birthing centers and homes. As a result, by 2002, the number of midwife-assisted births in the United States was over 328,000. Of those births, almost 14,500 of those births occurred outside of the medical community and in the private homes of the mothers. Many question the safety of home births, and in nine U.S. states, midwives who are not nurses and who assist in at home births can be arrested on felony charges. Supporters of hospital births suggest that lower infant and maternal mortality rates in recent decades are the result of medical intervention. Home birth practitioners, however, suggest that better prenatal care in the form of better nutrition, hygiene and disease control are the factors that have truly affected improved mortality rates.

Many cultures view home births as the norm. Traditionally, women, usually family members, have attended and assisted in the labor process. Home birth supporters assert that the creation of obstetrics relegated birth to the medical field. As women were limited in their ability to practice medicine, men became birth practitioners. As a result, childbirth became viewed as a medical procedure needing medical tech-

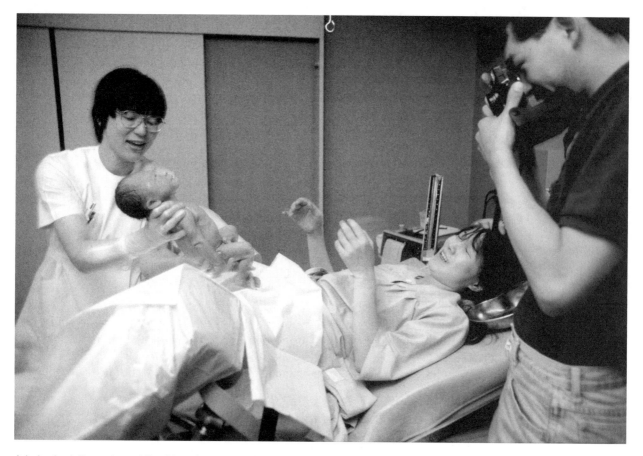

A baby is delivered at a Hiroshima hospital by Dr. Akiko Ahikatata, one of 4 female doctors in the OB-GYN section. © KAREN/CORBIS

niques and interventions. Women began to reassert themselves through the resurgence of midwifery.

The term midwife means "with woman" and there are several types of midwives: certified nurse midwife, certified professional midwife, direct-entry midwife, and lay midwife empirical. The certified nurse midwife (CNM) is a registered nurse who is educated in both nursing and midwifery. A CNM is also certified by the American College of Nurse-Midwives. Many CNMs perform home births with written collaboration with a physician. The certified professional midwife (CPM) has been educated either in schools or apprenticed. CPMs must pass a written and skills exam to be certified by the North American Registry of Midwives and work generally in birthing centers or at home births. Direct-entry midwives are considered independent practitioners who have been educated through self-study or apprenticeships. They may be educated through a school or university program, excluding nursing programs. The lay midwife empirical is an apprenticed midwife who chooses to not be certified.

She is usually apprenticed under an experienced midwife and focuses on home births or birthing centers.

Those choosing home births cite a range of benefits, beginning with the extreme personal attention received from the midwife during the prenatal care. The at home birthing experience allows the mother to be in control. She can choose to move around her own environment or deliver in whatever position she deems to be most comfortable. The experience can be as public or private as the family chooses.

PRIMARY SOURCE

MIDWIFE ASSISTING HOME BIRTH

See primary source image.

SIGNIFICANCE

The medical community offers somewhat contradictory opinions on the safety of at home births. The Society of Obstetricians and Gynecologists of Canada

Midwife Assisting Home Birth: A midwife assists with a home birth. © ROYALTY FREE/CORBIS

supports the practice of midwifery but has stated, "The SOGC is opposed to home births because of the potential risks to the mother and fetus." However, a February 2002 study published in the Canadian Medical Association Journal asserted that home births are no more dangerous than those that occur at hospitals. The University of Copenhagen reviewed six studies surrounding 24,000 planned home births and hospital births. The review revealed that mortality rates were not significantly different between the two experiences. However, home births resulted in fewer maternal lacerations and less general medical intervention. The study also discovered fewer low Apgar scores, the testing to identify the activity, pulse, grimace, appearance and respiration of the newborn. Supporters of home births assert that the home birth experience also lessens the occurrences of infections acquired during and after childbirth, as the mother is not exposed to bacteria present in the hospital setting.

There are risks involved with at home births. A 1997 study released by Midwifery and Childbirth in America states, "The available evidence indicates that births attended by either midwives or physicians in homes and birth centers in this country can be as safe as in hospital births provided the following conditions…" Those conditions include a competent midwife, good prenatal care, more than one knowledgeable caregiver present at the birth, a clear criteria for determining high-risk pregnancy, rapid means of and transportation to the hospital in case of complications. The most common complications for at home births are maternal bleeding and fetal distress, or when the baby has difficulty receiving oxygen. All midwives are expected to be fully trained in infant CPR.

FURTHER RESOURCES

Periodicals

Lees, Christopher MD, Karina Reynolds, MD, Grainne McCartan. "Preparing for a Home Birth." *Pregnancy and Birth* (November 1, 2004).

Reichert, Bonnie. "Home Delivery: Should You Give Birth on Your Own Turf?" *Today's Parent.* (July 1, 2002).

Webber, Tammy. "Trying to Boost At-Home Births." *Indianapolis Star* (March 3, 2006).

Web sites

Midwifery Today. "The Home Birth Choice." http://www.midwiferytoday.com/articles/homebirth-choice.asp (Accessed March 21, 2006).

Midwifery Coalition of Nova Scotia. "Is home birth safe?" http://mcns.chebucto.org/hmbrthsf.htm (Accessed March 21, 2006).

Prohibition on the Provision of Certain Intervening Medical Technology for Unmarried Women

Legislation

By: Robert G. Marshall

Date: January 11, 2006

Source: Virginia Assembly. Prohibition on the Provision of Certain Intervening Medical Technology for Unmarried Women. 2005–2006 reg. sess. HB 187.

Richmond. March 17, 2006. <http://leg1.state.va.us/cgi-bin/legp504.exe?061+sum+HB187> (accessed January 30, 2006).

About the Author: Robert G. Marshall is a delegate to the Virginia State Assembly from the thirteenth district. He is the patron, or author, of HB 187 and has served in the Virginia state legislature since 1992.

INTRODUCTION

Federal regulation of reproductive information and technology began with the 1873 Comstock Law. That law, named for Postmaster General of the United States Anthony Comstock prohibited the distribution of materials related to reproduction, including pamphlets, books, newsletters, or contraceptive devices. Condoms, which were manufactured shortly after Goodyear invented vulcanized rubber in the 1840s, were used in Europe and in high demand in countries such as France. By World War I, the European birthrate was half that of 1800, and American birthrates declined steadily as well.

The Comstock Law was repealed in 1936, but various laws regulating contraceptive devices remained on the books in many states. In the 1965 case *Griswold v. Connecticut*, the Supreme Court overturned an 1879 state law that banned the use of or aid in acquiring or using contraceptive devices and all such laws nationwide.

By the 1970s and 1980s, women in both the United States and Europe began, on average, to give birth at later and later ages. As a result, many women focused on college and career but postponed starting a family until their late thirties. In addition, research showing that men's sperm count has decreased worldwide since 1938 pointed to another possible explanation for the infertility problems that plague approximately 10 percent of all couples of childbearing age.

Access to reproductive technologies—medical procedures that can assist infertile women conceive a child—began to be requested by single women who wished to conceive and raise a child without a male partner and by lesbian couples as well. Usually this involves the use of anonymous donor sperm and artificial insemination, or IVF for donor eggs, unless there is a specific, identified infertility issue. The nineteenth and early twentieth century debate over access to reproductive information and contraceptives thus shifted, in the twenty-first century, to access to reproductive technologies.

Delegate Robert G. Marshall, of Virginia's thirteenth district, filed the following bill to amend the Code of Virginia regarding unmarried women's access to reproductive technologies.

■ PRIMARY SOURCE

HOUSE BILL NO. 187

Offered January 11, 2006

Prefiled January 2, 2006

A BILL to amend the Code of Virginia by adding a section numbered 54.1-2403.4, relating to prohibition on the provision of certain intervening medical technology to unmarried women....

Patron—Marshall, R.G.

...

Referred to Committee on Health, Welfare and Institutions

...

Be it enacted by the General Assembly of Virginia:

1. That the Code of Virginia is amended by adding a section numbered 54.1-2403.4 as follows:

§ 54.1-2403.4. Prohibition on the provision of certain intervening medical technology for unmarried women.

No individual licensed by a health regulatory board shall assist with or perform any intervening medical technology, whether in vivo or in vitro, for or on an unmarried woman that completely or partially replaces sexual intercourse as the means of conception, including, but not limited to, artificial insemination by donor, cryopreservation of gametes and embryos, in vitro fertilization, embryo transfer, gamete intrafallopian tube transfer, and low tubal ovum transfer.

■

SIGNIFICANCE

On the same day that Delegate Marshall proposed HB 187 he also proposed HB 412, titled "Gamete Donors; Anonymous Donations Thereof Prohibited in Medical Procedures," which "[p]rohibits the use of unrelated anonymous donor oocyte or sperm in the performance of intervening medical technology that completely or partially replaces sexual intercourse as a means of conception and requires, notwithstanding any traditional practice, agreement, regulation, or law to the contrary, the identity of any unrelated oocyte or sperm donor to be noted in the health record of any woman patient" whenever the woman uses any form of reproductive technology for conception.

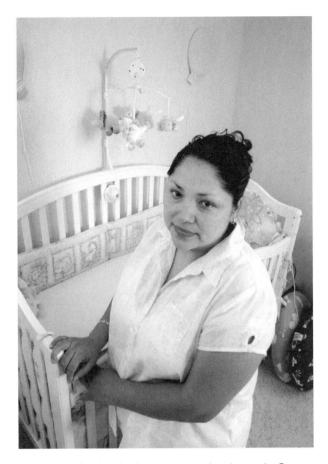

Guadalupe Benitez in the nursery at her home in Oceanside, Calif., October 11, 2005. Benitez, a lesbian, sued two of her former physicians for refusing to provide her with artificial insemination services on account of her sexual preferences. AP IMAGES

Taken together, the two bills restrict the rights of single women and gay couples while extending access to reproductive technologies to heterosexual married couples. Organizations such as Richmond Reproductive Freedom Project and Planned Parenthood Advocates of Virginia condemned Marshall's bills as assaults on women's rights and reproductive rights for all, including gay male couples who wish to have a child with the help of a surrogate mother.

Approximately 20 percent of all reproductive technology clinics refuse to treat single women; statis-tics on refusal rates for gay couples and individuals are not available. Each clinic sets its own policy concern-ing the patients it treats. In 2001, Guadalupe Benitez filed a lawsuit against a fertility clinic in California that refused to treat her and her lesbian partner; the doctors, both Christians, felt that working with Ben-itez would violate their personal beliefs. The lawsuit is pending as of March 2006 and has the careful atten-tion of women's rights groups, gay rights groups, and conservative religious groups.

Supporters of HB 187 point to a 2004 law in Italy that bans access to reproductive technologies to all but "stable heterosexual" couples as proof that other countries, concerned about the proliferation of chil-dren conceived without identified fathers who are involved in the child's life, have passed legislation sim-ilar to the Virginia bill.

HB 187 was tabled indefinitely in committee on January 17, 2006, and will not be considered by the Virginia legislature for further action.

FURTHER RESOURCES

Books

Inhorn, Marcia C., and Frank van Balen, eds. *Infertility Around the Globe: New Thinking on Childlessness, Gender, and Reproductive Technologies.* Berkeley: University of California Press, 2005.

Periodicals

Stern, J. E., C. P. Cramer, A. Garrod, and R. M. Green. "Access to Services at Assisted Reproductive Technol-ogy Clinics: A Survey of Policies and Practices." *American Journal of Obstetrics and Gynecology* 184, no. 4 (March 2001).

Swan, Shanna H., Eric P. Elkin, and Laura Fenster. "Have Sperm Densities Declined? A Reanalysis of Global Trend Data." *Environmental Health Perspectives* 105, no. 11 (November 1997).

Web sites

Michigan State University Libraries. "What Every Girl Should Know" < http://digital.lib.msu.edu/collections/index/> (accessed March 16, 2006).

Resolve. "Treatment Options for Non-Traditional Families." <http://www.resolve.org/site/> (accessed March 16, 2006).

6 Gender and Sexuality in School and the Workplace

Gender and Sexuality in School and the Workplace

This chapter begins by illustrating the expansion of the work world to include women. *Song of the Factory Girls* demonstrate's one attempt to draw women into the workplace. But as the workforce expanded, it did not always do so fairly. Women workers were often paid less, and were less secure in their employment, than male counterparts. Women also suffered employment discrimination based on age and marital status.

The women's movement pushed for equal pay and employment opportunities. These guarantees are now federal law, if not necessarily a reality, in the United States. However, some claim that the working world is not accommodating enough of working parents, especially women. The expansion of the workplace also included sexuality issues. Since 1990, many businesses, universities, and government employers have amended their nondiscrimination policies to include sexual orientation.

The editors have expanded the definition of workplace to include the home, religious orders, and the military. In the home, more fathers are raising children in the full-time profession of stay-at-home dads. In religious orders, the Roman Catholic Church continues to debate the merit of celibacy for priests and the role of women in the church. This chapter highlights the ordination of Gene Robinson as the first openly gay bishop in the Episcopal Church. While military service used to be exclusively reserved for men, there are expanding roles for women in the armed forces of many nations. The U.S. military continues to grapple with issue of openly gay servicemen and women, but many other nations have legalized gay members.

Schools also must cope with the impacts of gender and sexuality issues. Female students continue to push for equity in educational opportunities, and not without controversy. Several women challenged the admissions policies of traditionally male military academies to gain admissions. Their actions were both applauded and derided. Female students now receive equity in funding for sports teams, but the debate of whether boys or girls have more opportunities in the classroom has once again come to the forefront. Some public schools are even introducing single-sex classrooms to study the effects of gender segregation on academic achievement.

Since this chapter presents sources on gender and sexuality issues in schools, it also discusses those issues among students. Articles in this chapter highlight teen sexuality and sex education. One article discusses a controversial investigation of gender stereotypes and the quality of medical information contained in United States high school abstinence-only materials.

Household Hints

National Association OPPOSED to Women Suffrage

Pamphlet

By: Anonymous

Date: 1910s

Source: *Household Hints.* National Association OPPOSED to Women Suffrage, 1910s.

About the Author: The National Association OPPOSED to Women Suffrage, headquartered in New York City and later in Washington D.C., organized in response to groups such as the National Women's Party and the National American Women's Suffrage Association, which fought for women's right to vote in the United States. The National Association OPPOSED to Women Suffrage (NAOWS) included both men and women. It disbanded shortly after the Nineteenth Amendment to the Constitution, which granted women the right to vote, passed in 1919.

INTRODUCTION

The convention held in Seneca Falls, New York, in July 1848 marked the inception of the organized women's suffrage movement in the United States. More than 240 supporters of the right for women to vote gathered at the convention; forty were men, among them Frederick Douglass (1817?–1895), the former

Men read literature posted in the window of the headquarters of the National Association Opposed to Woman Suffrage as a woman stands off to the side, New York, New York, 1910s. THE LIBRARY OF CONGRESS.

slave and lecture circuit speaker devoted to the abolition cause. The convention was considered to be scandalous by opponents of female suffrage, who believed that any wife's viewpoint could be represented through her husband's vote. In addition, opponents argued, female nature was delicate, and politics was cruel and worldly. Permitting women the right to vote, they maintained, would place their femininity in jeopardy.

The Seneca Falls Convention produced the Declaration of Sentiments, which used the structure of the Declaration of Independence as a model and called for increased rights for women in the areas of property ownership, child custody, voting, and education. The Declaration of Sentiments became a rallying cry for the female suffrage movement.

With the passage of the Fifteenth Amendment to the Constitution, which extended the right to vote to all men, including African Americans, suffragettes increased their efforts to attain the vote for women as well. In 1890, two separate women's rights organizations merged to form the National American Women Suffrage Association (NAWSA), a group organized by middle-class women that appealed largely to women of the middle and upper classes.

By the early 1900s, another women's rights organization, the National Women's Party, emerged as a more radical group. Headed by Alice Paul (1885–1977), the NWP appealed to urban workers, women of the lower economic classes, and minority and immigrant women. Using tactics such as silent protests, marches, and hunger strikes when jailed, the NWP's actions angered NAWSA; the older organization believed that the radical tactics of the NWP would harm the suffrage cause.

In fact, NAWSA's concerns were valid. When the National Association OPPOSED to Women Suffrage formed in 1911, it used radical suffrage activities as a springboard for launching a campaign against female suffrage. Led by Josephine Dodge, NAOWS supporters included wealthy women, Catholic clergymen, and brewers and distillers; a motley crew, but one that gained national prominence as the tensions surrounding suffrage grew. The alcohol industry, concerned that women—the organizers behind the temperance movement—would vote in ways that would restrict alcohol access and production, supported NAOWS. As this pamphlet shows, NAOWS appealed to traditional ideas about womanhood and female roles in the household, while denigrating suffragette and activists' actions.

PRIMARY SOURCE

HOUSEWIVES!

You do not need a ballot to clean out your sink spout. A handful of potash and some boiling water is quicker and cheaper.

If new tinware be rubbed all over with fresh lard, then thoroughly heated before using, it will never rust.

Use oatmeal on a damp cloth to clean white paint.

Control of the temper makes a happier home than control of elections.

When boiling fish or fowls, add juice of half a lemon to the water to prevent discolorations.

Celery can be freshened by being left over night in a solution of salt and water.

Good cooking lessens alcoholic cravings quicker than a vote.

Why vote for pure food laws, when your husband does that, while you can purify your Ice-box with saleratus water?

Common sense and common salt applications stop hemorrhage quicker than ballots.

Clean your mirrors with water to which a little glycerine has been added. This prevents steaming and smoking.

Sulpho naphthol and elbow grease drive out bugs quicker than political hot air.

To drive out mice, scatter small pieces of camphor in cupboards and drawers. Peddlers and suffs are harder to scare.

To remove shine from serge, sponge with hot water and vinegar and press in usual manner.

Clean houses and good homes, which cannot be provided by legislation, keep children healthier and happier than any number of uplift laws.

Butter on a fresh burn takes out the sting. But what removes the sting of political defeat?

Clean dirty wall paper with fresh bread.

When washing colored hosiery, a little salt in the water will prevent colors from running.

If an Anti swallows bichloride, give her whites of eggs, but if it's a suff, give her a vote.

SPOT REMOVERS

The following methods for removing spots and stains will be found efficacious.

Grass stains may be removed from linen with alcohol.

Fruit stains may be removed in the same way, but
   hot alcohol works quicker.
To remove axle grease, soften first with lard.
Kerosene removes vaseline marks.
Sour milk removes ink spots.
Discolorations and stains on bath enamel may be
   removed by turpentine.
Leather stains on light colored hosiery may be
   removed by borax.

There is, however, no method known by which mud-
stained reputation may be cleaned after bitter political
campaigns.

VOTE NO ON WOMAN SUFFRAGE

BECAUSE 90% of the women either do not want it, or do
not care.

BECAUSE it means competition of women with men
instead of co-operation.

BECAUSE 80% of the women eligible to vote are married
and can only double or annul their husband's votes.

BECAUSE it can be of no benefit commensurate with the
additional expense involved.

BECAUSE in some States more voting women than voting men will place the Government under petticoat rule.

BECAUSE it is unwise to risk the good we already have
for the evil which may occur.

SIGNIFICANCE

By the time the National Association OPPOSED
to Women Suffrage formed in 1911, the women's
rights movement had more than seventy years of
organizing and lobbying behind it. Critics of
NAOWS charged that the brewers and distillers were
the primary force behind NAOWS. However,
Josephine Dodge's influence was key in the organization's development.

Dodge was instrumental in the day nursery movement in the late 1800s. Her work in creating day nurs-
eries, the precursors to modern day care centers,
centered on inner city immigrant families; in 1878 she
sponsored the Virginia Day Nursery in New York
City's East Side tenements. While the mothers
worked in the factories, nursery workers not only
cared for the children but were part of a plan to
"Americanize" the immigrants' children.

By 1899 Dodge viewed the growing suffrage
movement as a threat to women who worked on Progressive Era humanitarian issues. By 1911 she organized NAOWS, making use of the experience in

organizing and public relations she had gained
through her work in the nursery movement. She was
president of NAOWS until 1917, when the organization shifted its headquarters to Washington D.C.

NAOWS's primary message was acceptance of
women's role in the domestic sphere and insistence on
maintaining that tradition. As this pamphlet illustrates,
NAOWS blended political messages with practical
advice. In simple language interspersed with jokes and
light sarcasm, the theme is clear—women don't need
the vote. NAOWS organizers distributed pamphlets
such as this one, as well as a newsletter, *Women Protest*,
to convince women that having the vote was not only
superfluous (given the wife's representation through
her husband's vote) but could be damaging to their
children and the maintenance of their households.

Phrases such as "There is, however, no method
known by which mud-stained reputation may be
cleaned after bitter political campaigns" and concern
for "petticoat rule" zeroed in on the decade's concept
of femininity and delicacy. In black and white terms,
those opposed to suffrage painted voting rights supporters as unfeminine, poor mothers, derelict wives,
and as women of "loose" morals.

NAOWS, like NAWSA, organized supporters on
a state-by-state basis and used counter protest, as well
as pamphlet distribution, to sway public opinion.
When the Nineteenth Amendment passed both houses
of Congress and then was ratified by thirty-six states,
women received the vote in 1920. NAOWS continued
to publish messages through the mid–1920s, focusing
on anti-Equal Rights Amendment articles and pamphlets that criticized feminist activities.

FURTHER RESOURCES

Books

Clift, Eleanor. *Founding Sisters and the Nineteenth Amendment.* New York: Wiley, 2003.

Harrison, Patricia Greenwood. *Connecting Links: The British
   and American Woman Suffrage Movements, 1900–1914.*
   Westport, Conn.: Greenwood Press, 2000.

Web sites

PBS: The American Experience. "Wilson-A Portrait: Women's
   Suffrage." <http://www.pbs.org/wgbh/amex/wilson/
   portrait/wp_suffrage.html> (accessed March 23, 2006).

Audio and Visual Media

The American Experience. *One Woman, One Vote.* PBS,
   2005.

On the Path to a Great Emancipation

Newpaper article

By: Anonymous

Date: March 8, 1929

Source: "On The Path To A Great Emancipation." *Pravda* (March 8, 1929).

About the Author: This article was published without a byline in *Pravda* ("The Truth"), a leading Russian newspaper and official publication of the Communist Party between the years of 1918 and 1991. The author is not known.

INTRODUCTION

The 1920s are often dubbed as the "Roaring Twenties," and they are frequently celebrated as a decade of exuberance and decadence. Unfortunately, and as generally occurs, any decade, era, or event has many sides to its perception. The 1920s brought a decade of international labor strife, a new wave of feminism, and economic issues. The decade began with the 1919 Boston Police strike, the Red Scares of 1919–1920, and the Seattle General Strike.

The Boston Police Department strike saw about 1,100 officers momentarily leave their jobs to protest low wages, high uniform costs, vacation pay and leave, and sick pay. The Massachusetts National Guard was sent into Boston to restore order and the striking officers were replaced with new hires. This later decision was backed up with public statements saying that no one had the right to strike and put public safety in jeopardy. In contrast to the Boston walkout, the Seattle General Strike shut down the city for several days. Thousands of workers united to demand higher pay, leave time, and restricted workdays. This strike is the largest in United States history, and it also connects the plight of the worker to the social goals of the women's movement. The Seattle Strike saw the beginnings of a "buy union" campaign that urged women to only buy food, clothing, and other daily articles from union shops. This action mostly affected women because they were primarily responsible for the family's purchases. Aside from these significant strikes throughout the United States, other key events shaped the decade. One of these key events was the enactment of the Nineteenth amendment—also called the Susan B. Anthony Amendment.

The Nineteenth amendment granted women the right to vote, and Congress passed it in 1917. Three-fourths of the states ratified it in 1919, but the ratification of this amendment did not mean that a woman's traditional role in society changed. Rather, social expectations concerning a woman's place in the home and within the workforce stayed as it had been—she was considered a secondary worker with the primary role and job as that of mother and wife. Most unions did not allow women membership, and factory jobs that employed women were often segregated. In a segregated workplace, women and men were put in separate sections of the factory to work, and men often viewed women's labor as minimal. Women were viewed as temporary workers, even if they had been working at a plant for as long as or longer than men, because the social belief and hope reigned that a woman would stay home and take care of the family. Working class, working poor, and poor families could not always afford to have a woman stay home, but social precedent often prevailed over that truth of social reality.

"On the Path to Great Emancipation" captures these conflicting notions of a woman's role in society. It was first published in March 1929 in a Russian newspaper, but the message of the piece quickly spread throughout the world. Women in the United States have used this newspaper article as a key document to support their struggle for equal rights, equal pay, and equal treatment in labor unions and other avenues of life.

PRIMARY SOURCE

Today is international communist women's day, the international day for working women.

Our woman worker in the past...during the barbaric, savage, and blood stained tsarist regime. The heavy and hopeless fate of the woman worker—as mother, wife, and girl. All of the striving of the woman worker toward the light, toward freedom, and to a human existence were snuffed out by the criminal arm of the autocracy. The exploitation and debasement were tripled: in politics, in factory labor, and in daily life.

Working women in capitalist countries. Capitalist "democracy" has not and cannot give freedom to working and laboring women. Working women in all bourgeois countries are economically and politically enslaved. Middle class conventionality has a tenacious vice-grip on daily life. Advanced women workers and revolutionary women proletarians are persecuted. The most brutal blows of capitalist "rationalization," unemployment, and hunger in the midst of plenty descend upon the female half of the

Shakeli Omar Saraj celebrates the International Women's Day festivities on March 8, 2002 in Afghanistan. She and other women shed their burkhas during the celebration, but are putting them back on as they leave. This was the first time in 11 years that International Women's Day was celebrated in Afghanistan. AP IMAGES

proletariat. Fascism, Catholicism, and reformism with increasingly thoroughness exploit the historical backwardness of women workers in order to split apart the proletarian ranks and strengthen the position of imperialism. The temples of "national government"—what a thing to talk about!—are protected by stone walls which prevent the participation of working women....

The maximum activism of all women proletarians and conscientious working peasant women is one of the indispensable guarantees of our further successes and our victorious socialist growth. The greatest possible and most inexhaustible activism, the unceasingly creative work of the woman proletarian on all large and "small" fronts of our life, their rigid and total solidarity with the Party—these are the obligatory conditions for our creativity.

The struggle for a new cultured life—is this possible without the creative initiative of the woman worker? The struggle with alcoholism and disgusting drunken debauchery and the struggle to expel the green hydra

from the Soviet home—are these conceivable without the will and determination, without the intensive and constant force of the working woman? Could the struggle with such social ulcers as prostitution proceed successfully without arousing and involving hundreds of thousands of working women?

And the struggle to overcome difficulties, the struggle with our many-faceted class enemies, the struggle with anti-Semitism, with the priesthood, and with religious stupification—are these goals attainable if the campaign against these barbarisms does not include the millions of working women and if they are not advanced into the leading positions?

SIGNIFICANCE

As striking and labor demands increased throughout the 1920s, women gradually became more dominant in the picture. In the late 1920s and through the 1930s, many workers began organizing sit-down strikes, and women are often considered key components to keeping these strikes alive and forceful. One example is the General Motors sit-down strike of 1936–1937. Here, women brought food, clothing, and other staples into the plant to relieve the workers, and in post-strike accounts many workers remarked that the presence of the female encouraged them in their struggle.

The United States has not seen the creation of a true labor party, and after World War II labor unions took a serious decline in politics and life. The Equal Rights Amendment expired unratified in 1982, but issues concerning a woman's continual role in society have not left the public spotlight.

FURTHER RESOURCES

Books

Cohen, Lizabeth. *Making a New Deal: Industrial Workers in Chicago, 1919–1939*. Cambridge and New York: Cambridge University Press, 1990.

Frank, Dana. *Purchasing Power: Consumer Organizing, Gender, and the Seattle Labor Movement, 1919–1929*. Cambridge and New York: Cambridge University Press, 1994.

Zinn, Howard, Dana Frank, and D.G. Kelley. *Three Strikes: Miners, Musicians, Salesgirls, and the Fighting Spirit of Labor's Last Century*. Boston: Beacon Press, 2001.

Web sites

American Federation of State, County and Municipal Employees (AFSCME). "Women's Labor History." <http://www.afscme.org/otherlnk/whlinks.htm> (accessed April 1, 2006).

The Tamiment Library and Robert F. Wagner Labor Archives. "Sources in U.S. Women's Labor History." <http://www.nyu.edu/library/bobst/research/tam/women/cover.html> (accessed April 1, 2006).

President Kennedy Signs a Bill to Provide Equal Pay for Women

Photograph

By: Anonymous

Date: June 10, 1963

Source: Associated Press

About the Photographer: This photograph was taken by an unknown photographer for the Associated Press, a worldwide news agency based in New York.

INTRODUCTION

During World War II (1941–1945), women flocked to join the workforce as their patriotic duty. However, by the close of the war, women were pushed from the workplace in order for companies to be able to offer jobs to returning veterans. Through the 1950s, many women returned to the traditional role of homemaker and mother, but many other women continued to pursue employment. Women were also discouraged from pursing education and professions such as medicine, law, and business and were restricted from apprenticeships for skilled trades. In 1960, only 35.3 percent of bachelors and professional degrees were awarded to women. Women in the workplace at this time averaged 1.6 more years of education than men but were paid sixty-four percent of men's wages. By 1960, one quarter of married women with children worked. These women occupied traditionally female staffed positions such as secretaries, sales clerks, and teachers. And in 1963, women earned fifty-nine cents for every dollar earned by a man. Even employment advertisements were divided by gender, promoting men-wanted or women-wanted positions.

As the civil rights movement began to flourish across the United States, the concept of diversity in the workforce also began to flourish. In 1961, President John F. Kennedy (1917–1963) began to require federal contractors to take "affirmative action" to ensure individuals were treated without regard to race, color, or national origin. On June 10, 1963, President Kennedy signed into law the Equal Pay Act of 1963, which was enacted as Section 6(d) of the Fair Labor Standards Act. The Equal Pay Act was the first law to suggest that men and women should be paid equal amounts when their positions are equal. Its intent was to secure equal pay for similar jobs, eliminate discrimination, and end the depressing effects on living standards resulting from lower wages for female workers. The law supported women's economic rights and attempted to reverse the historical standard of paying women less than men for their work. The law requires equal pay for work requiring equal skill level, effort and responsibility performed by male and female employees. Equal work is expressed as positions requiring equal training, education, and over all ability required from employee. Equal effort is defined as the amount of mental and physical exertion demanded. The law prohibits labor unions from causing an employer to discriminate wages on the basis of gender. However, the

PRIMARY SOURCE

President Kennedy Signs a Bill to Provide Equal Pay for Women: President Kennedy after signing the Equal Pay Act into law on June 10, 1963. He is handing out ceremonial pens as souveniers to female lawmakers and equal rights activists who campaigned for passage of the law. © CORBIS-BETTMANN. REPROCUED BY PERMISSION.

Act does permit differential pay if it is based on something other than gender, such as seniority system, merit system, or a system of measuring earnings by quantity or quality of production. The burden of proof of discrimination lies on the woman. The female employee must prove in court that she received unequal pay for equal work and that the basis for the difference is gender. The Department of Labor was tasked with the authority to enforce the Equal Pay Act.

PRIMARY SOURCE

PRESIDENT KENNEDY SIGNS A BILL TO PROVIDE EQUAL PAY FOR WOMEN

See primary source image.

SIGNIFICANCE

In 1964, the year after the Equal Pay Act was signed into law, the Civil Rights Act of 1964 was passed. Title VII of the act provided additional protections to women and minorities in the workplace. The act prohibits discrimination on the job in the areas of hiring, firing, compensation, classification, and promotion on the basis of race, color, national origin, religion and gender. By 1965, the Equal Employment Opportunity Commission (EEOC) was started with an initial budget of $2.25 million and one hundred employees.

Women's participation in the labor force grew in years following the passage of the Equal Pay Act. By 1970, thirty-eight percent of the labor force was female. However, these women continued to face deflated salaries and earned, on average, sixty-five cents to each dollar earned by men. Because of the

PRIMARY SOURCE

People rally on the steps of the Statehouse in Montpelier, Vt., on April 8, 1999. They are marking National Equal Pay Day by holding signs that show how women earn 26 cents less than men who hold comparable jobs. AP IMAGES

Equal Pay Act and the Civil Rights Act, these women had recourse to challenge discrimination. In 1970, the US Court of Appeals for the Third Circuit ruled that jobs need not be identical to fall within the Equal Pay Act guidelines. Jobs that are "substantially equal" must be paid equal. In addition, in 1974, the US Supreme Court ruled in *Corning Glass Works v. Brennan* that the "going market rate" for salary is not sufficient reason for paying women less than men, "simply because men would not work at the low rates paid by women." Both of these rulings strengthened the standing of women in the workforce under the Equal Pay Act.

By the 1990s, outside factors began to affect the labor market. Union strength decreased while downsizing, outsourcing and the usage of temporary work-

ers was on the rise. By 1998, women were earning, on average 76.3 percent of men's wages, although the Labor Department cites a decline in men's wages as a reason for some of the income gap change.

FURTHER RESOURCES

Periodicals

Crampton, Suzanne M.; Hodge, John, W.; Mishra, Jitendra M. "The Equal Pay Act: The first 30 years." *Public Personnel Management.* (September 22, 1997).

Herman, Alexis M. "Equal Pay: A 35-Year Perspective." *US Department of Labor.* (June 10, 1998).

Stites, Janet. "Equal Pay for the Sexes." *HR Management.* (May 1, 2005).

Song of the Factory Girls

Song lyrics

By: Anonymous

Date: 1977

Source: "Song of the Factory Girls," in Foner, Philip S., ed. *The Factory Girls: A Collection of Writings on Life and Struggles in the New England Factories of the 1840's by the Factory Girls Themselves, and the Story, in Their Own Words, of the First Trade Unions of Women Workers in the United States.* Chicago: University of Illinois Press, 1977.

About the Author: Booming industries in the early nine-teenth century sought to create an army of regi-mented workers for their factories, most of whom were accustomed to regulating their own workplace on the farm, and many of whom were female. Indus-try glamorized factory work in songs such as "Song of the Factory Girls," which dates from this period in American history.

INTRODUCTION

The Industrial Revolution in the United States began in New England in the 1790s. Here, factory owners predominantly recruited young farm girls and girls from poorer families in order to staff the facto-ries. This kept the cost of factory employees low (because women's wages were considerably lower than men's), and the use of lower class females did not threaten existing social conventions, which held that women were supposed to work within the home.

Eleven-year-old Nannie Coleson sits at a sewing machine at Crescent Hoisery, where she receives three dollars a week making stockings. November 1914. © CORBIS

The average factory worker worked fourteen hours a day, sometimes seven days a week. Working conditions and pay were poor, and factories were often unsanitary and poorly ventilated; even if there were windows, for example, they were often covered with bars. To protest these working conditions, women (and other employees) began to strike. They fought against wage cuts, the loss of meal breaks (factory owners had a variety of reasons for ceasing meal breaks and the most common was the belief that workers got lazy after meals), and almost always to improve working conditions. The first recorded labor strike by female workers occurred in 1828 in Dover, New Hampshire.

To contrast the actual working conditions and the reality of the life of a factory worker, company owners subsidized booklets proclaiming factory life and work as happy, wholesome, and somewhat glamorous. In these accounts, factory girls were encouraged to highlight their conceptions of financial and personal independence. They did have some independence in the factories because they were not living in their father's homes, they could partially spend their money as they saw fit (after they paid boarding costs and sent money home, which happened frequently), and workers developed a sense of community with other females. Since many of these girls came from rural areas, their introduction to new people filled a sense of curiosity and longing for more experiences in life. In essence, stories attesting to freedom and independence tended to overshadow stories about horrible working and living conditions at the mills. Factory owners used these stories as propaganda to encourage new workers to come the mills.

PRIMARY SOURCE

Song of the Factory Girls

Oh, sing me the song of the Factory Girl!
So merry and glad and free
The bloom in her cheeks, of health how it
    speaks,
Oh! A happy creature is she!
She tends the loom, she watches the spindle,
And cheerfully toileth away,
Amid the din of wheels, how her bright eyes kin-
    dle,
And her bosom is ever gay.

Oh, sing me the song of the Factory Girl!
Who no titled lord doth own,
Who with treasures more rare, is more free
    from care
Than a queen upon her throne!
She tends the loom, she watches the spindle,

And she parts her glossy hair,
I know by her smile, as her bright eyes kindle,
That a cheerful spirit is there.

Oh, sing me the song of the Factory Girl!
Link not her name with the Slave's;
She is brave and free, as the old elm tree
Which over her homestead waves.
She ends the loom, she watches the spindle,
And scorns the laugh and the sneer,
I know by her lip, and her bright eyes kindle,
That a free born spirit is there.

Oh, sing me the song of the Factory Girl!
Whose fabric doth clothe the world,
From the king and his peers to the jolly tars
With our flag o'er all seas unfurled.
From the California's seas, to the tainted breeze
Which sweeps the smokened rooms,
Where "God save the Queen" to cry are seen
The slaves of the British looms.

SIGNIFICANCE

Poems and stories like "Song of the Factory Girls" celebrated the female worker for her independence, freedom, and wage earning ability. Phrases like "her bright eyes kindle" and "her bosom is ever gay" gave the impression that all factory girls were happy, and those workers who were not gleeful and happy to be there did not exist. But, the modern reader should remember that even though this piece depicts an enchanted girl, social dialect of the period held the underlying message that the factory worker (especially the female) was only temporary. The girl was always expected to eventually marry and stay home with her family to provide useful and needed labor within the home.

Female strikers continued to demand better pay, and as the factory system grew the life of the factory worker became more permanent. Technology increased production, the population grew, and men and women working in factories began to stay after marriage—and some never got married. Their labor became an intrinsic part of society's needs, and gradually their needs developed into unions and legislation restricting working hours, prohibiting children from working, and increasing pay.

FURTHER RESOURCES
Books

Kessler-Harris, Alice. *Out to Work: A History of Wage-Earning Women in the United States.* New York: Oxford University Press, 1982.

Kasserman, David Richard. *Fall River Outrage: Life, Murder, and Justice in Early Industrial New England.* Philadelphia: University of Pennsylvania Press, 1986.

Web sites

American Antiquarian Society. "A Woman's Work is Never Done." <http://www.americanantiquarian.org/Exhibitions/Womanswork/factory.htm> (accessed April 10, 2006).

Lavender, Katherine. Department of History. *College of Staten Island of The City University of New York.* "Lowell Mill Girls and the Rhetoric of Women's Labor Unrest." <http://www.library.csi.cuny.edu/dept/history/lavender/lowstr.html> (accessed April 12, 2006).

Division of Labor in Farming

Book excerpt

By: Heather M. Spiro

Date: 1985

Source: Spiro, Heather M.. "Division of Labor in Farming." *The Ilora Farm Settlement in Nigeria.* West Hartford, Conn.: Kumarian Press, 1985.

About the Author: Heather Spiro studied the Ilora Farm Settlement in Nigeria in 1977, and is also the author of an additional work on the subject, *The Fifth World: Women's Rural Activities and Time Budgets in Nigeria.*

INTRODUCTION

The Yoruba people have lived in West Africa for several thousand years, and are primarily found in western Nigeria, Benin, and Togo. Today's Yoruba are descendants of the powerful Oyo Kingdom, which broke up into smaller kingdoms following several wars, contributed to in part by the slave trade. Today, the Yoruba people live in many politically independent groups, but continue to share similar religious and cultural traditions. In Nigeria, a country with 128 million inhabitants, the Yoruba are the third largest ethnic group, with twelve million people. Yoruba women are held in rather high regard, particularly during a celebration called Gelede, when the ideals of patience, control, and reverence are personified as women. Yoruba women gain status by being known for their craftsmanship, trading abilities, and personal wealth.

Most Yoruba reside in rural areas, producing yams and corn as their staple crops. The Yoruba people

grow an important cash crop, cocoa, and are responsible for ninety percent of Nigeria's cocoa production. Nigerian women, including the Yoruba, are significantly involved with agriculture production. Similar findings have been noted throughout much of the developing world, indicating that women have traditionally played a crucial role in maintaining agricultural production. However, it was not until the 1970s and 1980s that the role of women in agriculture was truly quantified.

Women are said to be responsible for bush clearing, planting, fertilizing, harvesting, storing, processing, and marketing food. Women are also involved with raising livestock, managing fisheries, and collecting forest products such as mushrooms and snails in Nigeria. Additionally, women are often found to be decision makers regarding the farming activities of a community. Several studies have shown that men in rural areas have shorter working days than women, as men's duties are concentrated solely on agriculture and income generating activities, and men are rarely expected to take on housekeeping chores as well. The United Nations Food and Agriculture Organization (UNFAO) indicates that women in West Africa spend an equal amount of time performing household activities such as childcare, cleaning, and fetching water as they do on farming, processing, and marketing food. It is also reported that men spend twice as much time devoted toward leisure activities on a daily basis than women.

■ PRIMARY SOURCE

DIVISION OF LABOR IN FARMING

Among the Yoruba the majority of men farm and the majority of women trade. However, while women's role in trading has been described in the literature, their role in farming has been less clearly defined. It has been suggested on the one hand that women's only economic concern is with food processing and distribution, with some craft specialization; that women rarely take part in any phase of agriculture even though many of them live in the farmland area, and that women are almost completely excluded from agricultural work. On the other hand, it has also been reported that wives assist in reaping and preparing crops for the market, and in doing so form a single production unit with their husbands. Still other studies found that although very few women own farms, many of them work on their parents' or husbands' farms, or they are given the rights to use a piece of land.

Research for this study indicated that almost all women spend approximately 25 percent of their time in some farming activity. Table 1 shows the division of labor on both men's and women's farms under shifting cultivation methods used in the region. Men prepare the land through clearing and burning the forest or bush. Women help their husbands with planting, applying fertilizers, and weeding.

The source of required labor will vary somewhat on men's and women's farms. For example, women have to hire some male labor for their own farms to supplement their husband's contribution. In addition, women face compelling demands for their labor on their own farms and their husbands' farms, Given the Yoruba tradition of women having an independent income, they are often considered an "unreliable source of labor" on their husbands' farms, since they are unpaid for this work.

Women may be hired as labor (principally by men) for fertilizer application and harvesting, and occasionally for planting and carrying activities....

Goats, sheep, and poultry are owned by the majority of both men and women for household consumption and ceremonial purposes. Women are, however, responsible for looking after these animals.

Women's Economic Roles

Nigerian women generally, and Yoruba women in particular, plan their economic lives autonomously, separate from their husbands. Divorce is common and can be initiated by either party. Traditionally, income is not pooled or only incompletely pooled between husband and wife. Polygamy is practiced but is not widespread in the study villages. Therefore direct access to security assets is important for both women and men.

Ideally within the Yoruba culture husbands and wives have separate financial responsibilities. It is the husband's responsibility to provide staples such as maize, yam, and cassava from the farm or to provide money to buy them. Husbands are also expected to house their families and provide basic items of clothing. In addition, according to traditional standards which vary somewhat from practice, husbands are expected to pay for children's school and medical fees. They are also expected to give each wife her initial capital for trading or to provide land on which she can grow produce to sell.

Not every husband can meet all these obligations, and women generally contribute beyond their traditional requirements. Women are expected to supply the sauces, stews, and snacks eaten with the staples. Condiments are nutritionally significant components of the diet, often providing essential protein. They are also frequently the more costly items, and therefore women require a fairly constant cash flow to purchase the ingredients. Staples on the other hand are mostly provided in bulk and are preserved naturally. Women use their own money to buy clothes and luxury items for themselves and their children. In addition, both husband and wife have separate responsibilities to their own kin groups and are expected to contribute toward birth, death, and marriage ceremonies and other festivals, as well as to their own ceremonial funds.

A typical economic life of a Yoruba woman in western Nigeria might be sketched as follows. Yoruba women marry at about eighteen years of age and move to their husbands' village. During the early years of marriage women are economically subservient to their husbands. Their domestic duties also include extensive unpaid agricultural labor on their husband's holdings.

These early years are also devoted to organizing the household, and bearing and rearing children. Yorubas strive for a three-year space between children owing to traditional abstinence during an extended breast-feeding period. As children approach school age (age six) mothers start moving more seriously into trading enterprises. Children are net "dependents" on their parents between the ages of six and either fifteen or eighteen, depending on how much schooling they receive.

Women between the ages of 25 and 40 are in their prime years, since their economic authority grows with age and their status as mothers. Their economic responsibilities are increased because they usually need to "supplement" their husbands' income and help provide money for school fees, food and other family necessities. Initial trading capital most often comes from their husbands in the form of cash produce, as indicated above. It also comes from parents or money the women have saved, but rarely if ever from professional money lenders or from saving/loan societies.

As the children approach marriageable age and the women are old enough (in their husband's eyes) to be entrusted with land, some are given land that they farm on their own account. Women control this farming asset in case of divorce. Older women are supported principally by their own activities in trading or farming, and some also receive support from children.

Rural trading activities throughout western Nigeria are carried out through a system of periodic markets, a logical response by both traders and producer-sellers to the need to concentrate effective demand at particular points in time, namely at marketplaces on market day. This allows a rational division of time between production, processing, and trade, and is an advantage to many people carrying on several kinds of gainful activity, simultaneously or in alternation.

Oluwatedo's four-day market (it meets every four days) is open to any trader and is located in the center of the village. Trade is dominated by the local food crops, particularly maize, yam, cassava, and okra, which are destined for the markets in Oyo and Ibadan.

Women traders in Oluwatedo include farmer-traders who usually market their own farm produce on market days; a few wholesalers who buy and sell in bulk, and the retail traders, including those who trade cooked food and provisions on a daily basis. Retailers constitute the majority of grassroot traders in villages and small towns throughout Western Nigeria, selling a mixed portfolio of wares (cloth, plates, tinned food, and other miscellaneous items) and acting as intermediaries throughout the whole marketing chain.

Oluwatedo is like a big supermarket, except that products are not stored under one roof, but in separate households, and trading is not regulated by open and closing times, but by the availability of produce. Traders leave goods with neighbors and children, carrying on more than one activity at a time. They can be farming or traveling while their businesses are being looked after by someone else.

SIGNIFICANCE

Nigeria's Federal Agricultural Coordinating Unit, in the Department of Agriculture, began a program called Women In Agriculture (WIA) in 1991. The aim of WIA is to integrate women more fully into agricultural development by linking women to training, better sources of financial credit, and improved seed and fertilizer supplies. There are WIA women's groups throughout Nigeria, through which new technologies and agriculture training is distributed to women. There have been higher levels of agricultural output, and more food surplus and income for families involved with WIA groups. Reports have found though, that overall, women in Nigeria, including Yoruba women, continue to receive less farming assistance than men. Many believe gender discrimination continues to hamper the progress toward giving women access to agricultural support. Women generally have less access to land, loans, fertilizers, seeds, extension services, appropriate technology, and up-to-date training. These factors are known to decrease the efficiency and effectiveness of female farmers.

Yoruba Women in Nigeria, 1973. © OWEN FRANKEN/CORBIS

Many non-governmental agencies, and international agricultural development organizations such as UNFAO and the International Fund for Agricultural Development (IFAD), focus on the important role women play in rural farming communities. These organizations say that contributions of women are vital to the alleviation of poverty in many developing countries. The goal of many development projects is to foster the natural socio-economic potential women have, by providing better access to assets, services, knowledge, technology, and assisting women to become more active in decision-making processes. IFAD says gender equity allows women to express their potential, for the benefit of their families and communities. The World Bank and the UN Development Program have seen the benefits of supporting the training of female extension agents, who are able to successfully target female farmers. Also, these organizations focus on organizing women into cooperatives or other farming groups as a way to increase access to banking credit and marketing opportunities.

Governmental and non-governmental organizations say it is important for development projects to take into account the roles that men and women have in the communities where the projects are implemented. Not taking into account gender specificities may inadvertently increase the already stringent workload women have, disrupting the social systems that are already in place. Also, gender analyses are carried out to ensure a development project does not decrease the control women have over resources, technologies, and other assets.

FURTHER RESOURCES

Books

Olupona, Jacob K. *Kingship, Religion, and Rituals in a Nigerian Community : A Phenomenological Study of Ondo Yoruba Festivals.* Stockholm: Almqvist & Wiksell International, 1991.

Periodicals

Farinde, A. J., and A. O. Ajayi. "Training Needs of Women Farmers in Livestock Production: Implications for Rural Development in Oyo State of Nigeria." *Journal of Social Sciences* 10, 3 (2005): 159–164.

Web sites

Conner, Michael. *Henry Radford Hope School of Fine Arts, Indiana University.* "Cutting to the Essence." <http://www.fa.indiana.edu/~conner/yoruba/cut.html> (accessed April 1, 2006).

Das, Manju Dutta. *Food and Agriculture Organization of the United Nations.* "Improving the Relevance and Effectiveness of Agricultural Extension Activities for Women Farmers—An André Mayer Research Study." <http://www.fao.org/documents/show_cdr.asp?url_file =/docrep/V4805E/v4805e03.htm> (accessed April 1, 2006).

International Fund for Agricultural Devlopment. "Rural Women in IFAD's Projects: The Key to Poverty Alleviation." <http://www.ifad.org/pub/other/!brocsch.pdf> (accessed April 1, 2006).

International Fund for Agricultural Development. "Why Gender Matters." <http://www.ifad.org/gender/approach/gender/index.htm> (accessed April 1, 2006).

I Was a Playboy Bunny

Article

By: Gloria Steinem

Date: 1963

Source: Steinem, Gloria, "I Was a Playboy Bunny," from *Outrageous Acts and Everyday Rebellions*, by Gloria Steinem. New York: Holt, Rhinehart, and Winston, 1983.

About the Author: This essay by Gloria Steinem was first published in *Show* magazine in 1963.

INTRODUCTION

Gloria Steinem (1934–) is an influential feminist writer most famous for founding *Ms. Magazine* in 1972. She grew up in the American Midwest and earned a B.A. from Smith College in 1956, where she became a journalist. In the early 1960s, she went undercover as a Playboy Bunny at one of the chain of nightclubs owned by *Playboy* magazine founder Hugh Hefner (1926—). The clubs were nightclubs featuring drinks, live musical entertainment, and a staff of attractive young women called Playboy Bunnies who wore black bodysuits, puffy white tails, white collar and cuffs, and clip-on satin bunny ears. The clubs were not open to the general public but to paying members known as "keyholders;" The first Playboy Club opened in Chicago in 1960, and the last U.S. club closed in 1988. The last international Playboy Club closed in 1991.

Steinem became a Bunny when she was 28 and held the job for three weeks. Her article about the realities of life in the Playboy realm were published in *Show* magazine in 1963. The piece gained much attention, and after its appearance Steinem was able to launch a career as a freelance journalist. She eventually became one of the best-known figures in American feminism.

■ PRIMARY SOURCE

I Was a Playboy Bunny

FRIDAY, FEBRUARY 1ST

I was fitted for false eyelashes today at Larry Mathews's, a twenty-four-hour-a-day beauty salon in a West Side hotel. As a makeup expert feathered the eyelashes with a manicure scissors, she pointed out a girl who had just been fired from the club "because she wouldn't go out with a Number One keyholder." I said I thought we were forbidden to go out with customers. "You can go out with them if they've got Number One keys,' the makeup girl explained. "They're for club management and reporters and big shots like that." I explained that being fired for *not* going seemed like a very different thing. "Well," she said thoughtfully, "I guess it was the way she said it. She told him to go screw himself."

I paid the bill. $8.14 for the eyelashes and a cake of rouge, even after the 25-percent Bunny discount. I had refused to invest in darker lipstick even though "girls get fired for looking pale." I wondered how much the Bunny beauty concession was worth to Mr. Mathews. Had beauty salons sent in sealed bids for this lucrative business?

I am home now, and I have measured the lashes. Maybe I don't have to worry so much about being recognized in the club. They are three quarters of an inch long at their shortest point.

SUNDAY 3RD

I've spent an informative Sunday with the Bunny bible, or the *Playboy Club Bunny Manual,* as it is officially called. From introduction ("You are holding the top job in the country for a young girl) to appendix ("Sidecar: Rim glass with lime and frost with sugar"), it is a model of clarity.

Some dozen supplements accompany the bible. Altogether, they give a vivid picture of a Bunny's function. For instance:

. . . You . . . are the only direct contact most of the readers will ever have with *Playboy* personnel. . . . We depend on our Bunnies to express the personality of the magazine.

. . . Bunnies will be expected to contribute a fair share of personal appearances as part of their regular duties for the Club.

. . . Bunnies are reminded that there are many pleasing means they can employ to stimulate the club's liquor volume, thereby increasing their earnings significantly . . . . The key to selling more drinks is *Customer Contact* . . . they will respond particularly to your efforts to be friendly. . . . You should make it seem that [the customer's] opinions are very important. . . .

The Incentive System is a method devised to reward those table Bunnies who put forth an extra effort. . . . The Bunny whose [drink] average per person is highest will be the winner. . . . Prize money . . . will likewise be determined by over-all drink income.

There is a problem in being "friendly" and "pampering" the customer while refusing to go out with him or even give him your last name. The manual makes it abundantly clear that Bunnies must never go out with anyone met in the club—customer or employee—and adds that a detective agency called Willmark Service Systems, Inc., has been employed to make sure that they don't. ("Of course, you can never tell when you are being checked out by a Willmark Service representative.") The explanation written for the Bunnies is simple: Men are very excited about being in the company of Elizabeth Taylor, but they know they can't paw or proposition her. "The moment they felt they could become familiar with her, she would not have the aura of glamour that now surrounds her. The same must be true of our Bunnies." In an accompanying letter from Hugh Hefner to Willmark, the explanation is still simpler: "Our licenses are laid on the line any time any of our employees in any way engages, aids, or abets traffic in prostitution. . . ." Willmark is therefore instructed to "Use your most attractive and personable male representatives to proposition the Bunnies, and even offer . . . as high as $200 on this, 'right now,' for a promise of meeting you outside the Club later." Willmark representatives are told to ask a barman or other male employee "if any of the girls are available on a cash basis for a friendly evening. . . . Tell him you will pay the girls well or will pay him for the girls." If the employee does act "as a procurer," Willmark is to notify the club immediately. "We naturally do not tolerate any merchandising of the Bunnies," writes Mr. Hefner, "and are most anxious to know if any such thing is occurring."

If the idea of being merchandised isn't enough to unnerve a prospective Bunny, there are other directives that may. Willmark representatives are to check girls for heels that are too low, runs in their hose, jewelry, underwear that shows, crooked or unmatched ears, dirty costumes, absence of name tags, and "tails in good order." Further: "When a show is on, check to see if the Bunnies are reacting to the performers. When a comic is on, they are supposed to laugh." Big Brother Willmark is watching you.

In fact, Bunnies must *always* appear gay and cheerful. (". . . Think about something happy or funny . . . your most important commodity is personality") in spite of all worries, including the demerit system. Messy hair, bad nails, and bad makeup cost five demerits each. So does calling the room director by his first name, failing to keep a makeup appointment, or eating food in the Bunny Room. Chewing gum or eating while on duty is ten demerits for the first offense, twenty for the second, and dismissal for the third. A three-time loser for "failure to report for work without replacement" is not only dismissed but blacklisted from all other Playboy Clubs. Showing up late for work or after a break costs a demerit a minute, failure to follow a room director's instructions costs fifteen. "The dollar value of demerits," notes the Bunny bible, "shall be determined by the general manager of each club."

Once the system is mastered, there are still instructions for specific jobs. Door Bunnies greet customers and check their keys. Camera Bunnies must operate Polaroids. Cigarette Bunnies explain why a pack of cigarettes can't be bought without a Playboy lighter; hat-check Bunnies learn the checking system; gift-shop Bunnies sell Playboy products; mobile-gift-shop Bunnies carry Playboy products around in baskets, and table Bunnies memorize thirteen pages of drinks.

There's more to Bunnyhood than stuffing bosoms.

Note: Section 523 says: "Employees may enter and enjoy the facilities of the club as bona fide guests of 1 [Number One] keyholders." Are these the big shots my makeup expert had in mind?

MORNING, MONDAY 4th

At 11:00 A.M. I went to see the Playboy doctor ("Failure to keep doctor's appointment, twenty demerits") at his office in a nearby hotel. The nurse gave me a medical-history form to fill out. "Do you know this includes an internal physical? I've been trying to get Miss Shay to warn the girls." I said I knew, but that I didn't understand why it was required. "It's for your own good," she said, and led me into a narrow examining room containing a medicine chest, a scale, and a gynecological table. I put on a hospital robe and waited. It seemed I had spent a good deal of time lately either taking off clothes, waiting, or both.

The nurse came back with the doctor, a stout, sixtyish man with the pink and white skin of a baby. "So you're going to be a Bunny," he said heartily. "Just came back from Miami myself. Beautiful club down there. Beautiful Bunnies." I started to ask him if he had the coast-to-coast franchise, but he interrupted to ask how I liked Bunnyhood.

"Well, it's livelier than being a secretary," I said, and he told me to sit on the edge of the table. As he pounded my back and listened to me breathe, the thought crossed my mind that every Bunny in the New York club had rested on the same spot. "This is the part all the girls hate," said the doctor, and took blood from my arm for a Wassermann test. I told him that testing for venereal disease seemed a little ominous. "Don't be silly," he said, "all the employees have to do it. You'll know everyone in the club is clean." I said that their being clean didn't really affect me and that I objected to being put through these tests. Silence. He asked me to stand to "see if your legs are straight." "Okay," I said, "I have to have a Wassermann. But what about an internal examination? Is that required of waitresses in New York State?"

"What do you care?" he said. "It's free, and it's for everybody's good."

"How?" I asked.

"Look," he said impatiently, "we usually find that girls who object to it strenuously have some reason . . ." He paused significantly. I paused, too. I could either go through with it or I could march out in protest. But in protest of what?

Back in the reception room, the nurse gave me a note to show Miss Shay that I had, according to preliminary tests at least, passed. As I put on my coat, she phoned a laboratory to pick up "a blood sample and smear." I asked why those tests and no urine sample? Wasn't that the most common laboratory test of all? "It's for your own protection," she said firmly, "and anyway, the club pays."

Down in the lobby, I stopped in a telephone booth to call the board of health. I asked if a Wassermann test was required of waitresses in New York City? "No." Then what kind of physical examination *was* required? "None at all," they said.

SIGNIFICANCE

Steinem exposed the Playboy entertainment empire, which proclaimed itself part of the "sexual revolution," encouraging people to enjoy unmarried sex happily, freely, and without guilt, as part of a sexual-industrial complex in which women were expected to manage their appearance and behavior to please men for purely economic reasons. The Playboy Clubs presented sexually amplified but generally unavailable young women to male customers in a way that would stimulate sexual desire without satisfying it: The explicit goal was to sell more drinks, the highest-profit item in any nightclub or bar.

Gloria Steinem dressed as a Playboy Bunny, with a tray of drinks, August 8, 1960. © BETTMANN/CORBIS

Steinem went after the inside story on the Playboy Club because the behaviors demanded of a Playboy Bunny—smiling, dressing to emphasize one's sexual attractiveness, and reacting to male opinions as if they were "very important,"—were exaggerations of behaviors that feminists like Steineim had identified as standard for young women in American society. Dating manuals, for example, urged young women to smile, be agreeable, avoid offering strongly held opinions, and give male companions the impression that their views were important, just as the Playboy Club Bunny Manual did. The Playboy Club was, then, an employment setting where normal female behaviors were exaggerated, professionalized, packaged in Playboy mystique, and marketed to club customers as a product. Steinem's article illustrated some of the detailed quality-management efforts that went into the manufacture of that product.

Steinem's exposé is "feminist" journalism because it does not expose explicitly illegal workplace abuses such as rape, overwork, dangerous conditions, or the like, but brought to light other forms of exploitation and control inflicted on many women every day.

The primary form of labor performed by Steinem during her few weeks as a Playboy Bunny has been identified by feminist sociologists as "emotional labor," defined in 1983 by the inventor of the term, Arlie Russell Hochschild, as "the management of feeling to create a publicly observable facial and bodily display." Emotional labor may be performed for free, as when a worried or depressed family member pretends to be cheerful while guests are in the house, or for money, as when stewards and stewardesses, nurses, servers, salespeople, and others in service jobs must pretend to be welcoming, happy, concerned, fascinated, or the like.

Both men and women must perform emotional labor in various jobs, but a number of female-specific jobs exist in which women's sexuality is an integral part of the emotional performance. Apart from prostitution, in which employees (mostly women) must pretend to be sexually interested in and gratified by paying customers, a large number of waitressing positions, such as those held by the Playboy Bunnies, require sexualized emotional work. The burger-and-steak restaurant chain Hooters, for example, with over 350 locations in the U.S. today, employs a system similar to the now-defunct Playboy Bunny clubs. Hooters employs only attractive young women, called "Hooter Girls," as servers to give male customers the impression of encountering the "All-American Cheerleader, Surfer, Girl Next Door" (quoting the Hooters Employee Handbook). Hooter Girls, like the Playboy Bunnies, are required to provide sexualized emotional labor: Servers must sign a statement affirming their awareness that "my job duties require that I interact with and entertain the customers" and that "the Hooters concept is based on female sex appeal and the work environment is one in which joking and sexual innuendo based on female sex appeal is commonplace."

FURTHER RESOURCES
Websites

CBS News. CBS Sunday Morning. "No Slowdown for Gloria Steineim" <http://www.cbsnews.com/stories/2006/01/22/sunday/printable1227391.shtml> (accessed March 27, 2006).

The Smoking Gun. "Acknowldgement—Hooters Girl" <http://www.thesmokinggun.com/archive/0915051hooters8.html> (accessed March 27, 2006).

Educational Guidance in Human Love

Ecclesial Pronouncement excerpt

By: Pope John Paul II and the Congregation for Catholic Education

Date: November 1, 1983

Source: Pope John Paul II. Congregation on Catholic Education. "Educational Guidance on Human Love." (November 1, 1983).

About the Authors: Pope John Paul II (1920–2005), the former Karol Wojtyla, was born in Poland. Elected to the papacy in 1978, he was known for his strong opposition to communism and his staunch social conservatism. He also traveled more than any previous pope, which helped him become one of history's most popular Catholic leaders. The Congregation for Catholic Education, headquartered at the Vatican, is responsible for educational standards in Catholic Universities and schools.

INTRODUCTION

Sex education, historically a family matter, did not become a public concern until the late nineteenth century. Groups such as the American Purity Alliance and the Young Men's Christian Association sponsored lectures and panels on sex-related topics in the 1880s. A few grade school teachers discussed sexuality with their students in the 1890s, but sex education did not become a regular classroom topic until the early twentieth century.

Increasing fears of venereal disease and changing attitudes toward marriage led instructors to emphasize the importance of sexual hygiene and preparation for marriage. Still, by the 1920s, only tenty-six percent of the largest school districts in the United States offered sex education classes. The hesitance to address sexuality was based on a common belief that sex education merely meant instruction on the sexual organs. In 1940, the U.S. Public Health Service produced a pamphlet entitled "High Schools and Sex Education" that covered the methods, materials, planning, organization, and integration of sex education in many fields. This is the first government guide to sex education in the United States.

By the 1960s, government and educational leaders emphasized the importance of family life education at all grade levels. These programs were to focus on psy-chological, sociological, economic, and social factors that affect personality and individual adjustment. At the same time, conservative groups shocked by the sexual revolution and its liberal attitudes toward birth control, abortion, premarital sex, and homosexuality, rallied to oppose sex education. Over the next decades, conservative leaders and organizations, notably the Catholic Church under Pope John Paul II, called for a return to traditional sexual values.

■ PRIMARY SOURCE

The teacher may find that in carrying out his or her mission, he or she may be confronted by several particular problems, which we treat here.

94. Sex education must lead the young to take cognisance of the different expressions and dynamisms of sexuality and of the human values which must be respected. True love is the capacity to open oneself to one's neighbour in generosity, and in devotion to the other for the other's good; it knows how to respect the personality and the freedom of the other, (53) it is self giving, not possessive. The sex instinct, on the other hand, if abandoned to itself, is reduced to the merely genital, and tends to take possession of the other, immediately seeking personal gratification.

95. Relationships of sexual intimacy are reserved to marriage, because only then is the inseparable connection secured—which God wants—between the unitive and the procreative meaning of such matters, which are ordained to maintain, confirm, and express a definitive communion of life—"one flesh" (54)—mediating the realisation of a love that is "human," "total," "faithful," "creative" (55) which is marital love. Therefore, sexual relations outside the context of marriage constitute a grave disorder, because they are reserved to a reality which does not yet exist; (56) they are a language which is not found in the objective reality of the life of the two persons, not yet constituted in definitive community with the necessary recognition and guarantee of civil and, for catholic spouses, religious society.

96. It seems that there is a spread amongst adolescents and young adults of certain manifestations of a sexual kind which of themselves tend to complete encounter, though without reaching its realisation: manifestations of the merely genital which are a moral disorder because they are outside the matrimonial context of authentic love.

97. Sex education will help adolescents to discover the profound values of love, and to understand the harm which such manifestations do to their affective maturation, in as much as they lead to an encounter which is not

personal, but instinctive, often weakened by reservations and egoistic calculations, without therefore the character of true personal relationship and so much less definitive. An authentic education will lead the young towards maturity and self-control, the fruit of conscientious choice and personal effort.

98. It is the task of sex education to promote a continuous progress in the control of the impulses to effect an opening, in due course, to true and self giving love. A particularly complex and delicate problem which can be present is that of masturbation and of its repercussions on the integral growth of the person. Masturbation, according to catholic doctrine constitutes a grave moral disorder, (57) principally because it is the use of the sexual faculty in a way which essentially contradicts its finality, not being at the service of love and life according to the design of God. (58)

99. A teacher and perspicacious counsellor must endeavour to identify the causes of the deviation in order to help the adolescent to overcome the immaturity underlying this habit. From an educative point of view, it is necessary to consider masturbation and other forms of autoeroticism as symptoms of problems much more profound, which provoke sexual tension which the individual seeks to resolve by recourse to such behaviour. Pedagogic action, therefore, should be directed more to the causes than to the direct repression of the phenomenon. (59)

Whilst taking account of the objective gravity of masturbation, it is necessary to be cautious in evaluating the subjective responsibility of the person. (60)

100. In order that the adolescent be helped to feel accepted in a communion of charity and freed from self enclosure, the teacher "should undramatise masturbation and not reduce his or her esteem and benevolence for the pupil." (61) The teacher will help the pupil towards social integration, to be open and interested in others; to be able to be free from this form of autoeroticism, advancing towards self giving love, proper to mature affectivity; at the same time, the teacher will encourage the pupil to have recourse to the recommended means of Christian asceticism, such as prayer and the sacraments, and to be involved in works of justice and charity.

101. Homosexuality, which impedes the person's acquisition of sexual maturity, whether from the individual point of view, or the inter-personal, is a problem which must be faced in all objectivity by the pupil and the educator when the case presents itself.

"Pastorally, these homosexuals must be received with understanding and supported in the hope of overcoming their personal difficulties and their social maladaption, their culpability will be judged with prudence;

but no pastoral method can be used which, holding that these acts conform to the condition of these persons, accord them a moral justification.

"According to the objective moral order, homosexual relations are acts deprived of their essential and indispensable rule." (62)

102. It will be the duty of the family and the teacher to seek first of all to identify the factors which drive towards homosexuality: to see if it is a question of physiological or psychological factors; if it be the result of a false education or of the lack of normal sexual evolution; if it comes from a contracted habit or from bad example; (63) or from other factors. More particularly, in seeking the causes of this disorder, the family and the teacher will have to take account of the elements of judgement proposed by the ecclesiastical Magisterium, and be served by the contribution which various disciplines can offer. One must, in fact, investigate elements of diverse order: lack of affection, immaturity, obsessive impulses, seduction, social isolation, and other types of frustration, depravation in dress, license in shows and publications. In greater profundity lies the innate frailty of man and woman, the consequence of original sin; it can run to the loss of the sense of God and of man and woman, and have its repercussions in the sphere of sexuality. (64)

SIGNIFICANCE

In the 1960s and 1970s, Catholicism became more liberal as reflected in the reforms of Pope Paul VI and the Second Vatican Council, known as Vatican II. Upon taking office in 1978, Pope John Paul II repudiated many of these reforms. He wanted to restore Catholicism to its previous conservatism and strongly approved of an authoritarian church.

John Paul II made a number of pronouncements on sexual matters. In 1983, the Vatican issued a set of guidelines for sexual education. The thirty-six-page declaration "Educational Guidance in Human Love," was viewed in church circles as largely a stern restatement of the Roman Catholic Church's traditional attitudes. It was also an attack on the worldwide relaxation of sexual mores.

The statement, distributed to all bishops, strongly opposed the devaluation of sex. The Vatican stressed that sexual education is education in love and should never be separated from the morality of the Roman Catholic faith. While the government had an obligation to protect the citizens from pornography and prostitution, it was the family's responsibility to teach sexual education to children.

Margaret Hill and others take part in a rally on Capitol Hill, August 15, 1997. The rally was part of the Pure Love '97 national tour which promoted purity, fidelity and true love. AP IMAGES

It is not clear how much of an impact "Educational Guidance in Human Love" had upon Catholics and governments around the world. Europeans and Americans continued to practice liberal attitudes toward sexuality. Asia, Africa, and Latin America, historically more conservative than the industrialized West, may have been more influenced by the document, particularly since the Catholic church is increasing its influence in these regions.

FURTHER RESOURCES
Books

Eberwein, Robert. *Sex Ed: Film, Video, and the Framework of Desire*. New Brunswick, NJ: Rutgers University, 1999.

Melody, M.E., and Linda M. Peterson. *Teaching America about Sex: Marriage Guides and Sex Manuals from the Late Victorians to Dr. Ruth*. New York: New York University, 1999.

Pope John Paul II. *Pope John Paul II: In My Own Words*. New York: Gramercy, 2000.

Weigel, George. *Witness to Hope: The Biography of Pope John Paul II*. New York: Harper Perennial, 2005.

Should Your Wife Take a War Job?

Book excerpt

By: Sherna Berger Gluck

Date: 1987

Source: Gluck, Sherna Berger. *Rosie the Riveter Revisited: Women, the War, and Social Change.* Boston: Twayne Publishers, 1987.

About the Author: Sherna B. Gluck teaches women's studies at California State University. She is also the coordinator of the oral history program at the school. In addition to writing *Rosie the Riveter Revisited: Women, The War and Social Change*, Gluck also wrote *From Parlor to Prison : Five American Suffragists Talk about Their Lives.*New York: Octagon Books, 1976.

INTRODUCTION

Before America's entry into World War II in 1941, the Great Depression had created massive unemployment. As a result, more women joined the workforce during the 1930s but not in the most lucrative fields—manufacturing and professional jobs—which were reserved for men. Women took teaching positions, civil service and secretarial jobs, lower-scale factory work, and domestic positions. Cultural divisions were a factor as well. White middle-class women were expected to stay home; many of the twelve million women who occupied a quarter of the prewar workforce were minorities.

As Europe became embroiled in the war, American companies secured defense contracts for war equipment with the Allies. Auto factories were converted to build airplanes, shipyards were expanded, and new factories built. When the United States entered the war, the workforce shrank as men left to join the service. To fill the gap, the government launched a campaign to fill job vacancies with women. The ideal female worker was portrayed as loyal, efficient, patriotic, and pretty.

In 1942, the song "Rosie the Riveter" enjoyed enormous popularity, and Norman Rockwell created her famous "portrait" for the May 29, 1943 edition of the *Saturday Evening Post*. Companies began to recruit women when they graduated from high school. Demand for labor was so great, however, that even married women with children began to work, despite concern that this would contribute to social decline and juvenile delinquency. Of the six million war workers, most were married; 60 percent were over 35, and one-third had children under fourteen. Only three million war workers actually worked in defense factories; most filled traditional service sector jobs.

Half of the women who took war jobs were minority and lower-class women already in the workforce; many of them moved from lower-paying traditional jobs to higher paying worker jobs, although women were still paid only sixty percent of what men

One of the most famous symbols of World War II on the home front, "Rosie the Riveter" encouraged American women to show their strength and go to work for the war effort. © THE NATIONAL ARCHIVES/CORBIS

earned. The only true mixing of sexes in the workforce occurred in the blue-collar sector.

PRIMARY SOURCE

I started defense work in '42. I think a lot of it was because one of my neighbors found out about it, and she wanted me to go with her. I thought, "Well, now, this would take care of the situation." I still was getting along on next to nothing; it was still difficult. And my husband was talking about whether he should quit the school board or not. In those days, they didn't belong to any union, and they were paid a very small amount. As prices were going up it wasn't enough to cover our expenses. So I said, "No, I'll go see what I can do."

My husband didn't like it. He was one of these men that never wanted his wife to work. He was German and was brought up with the idea that the man made the living; the woman didn't do that. But he found that it was a pretty good idea at the time. It was a necessity, because he would have had to do something else. We couldn't live on what he was making, so that's the way it goes.

And my brother, especially my youngest brother, he thought it was terrible. My father, oh, he was very upset. He said, "You can't work amongst people like that." They were people just like me, but they thought it was people that were rough and not the same type I'm used to being with. They just couldn't see me going over and working in a factory and doing that type of work. And they were trying to protect me, I'm sure....

But I wasn't trained for just any type of work. See, most of the women I knew, they went into stores and into that type of work. It was easier to do. They wouldn't go into the war plants. My oldest sister worked at Lockheed and she was a drill press operator, but the sister right next to me, she was a waitress. When she looked at my wages and what she collected, she said, "No, no part of that." She was making more money by the time she figured her tips.

So, my family thought I was a little off for doing it. But if that's what I wanted to do, that's what I did. And my husband got used to the fact that his wife worked.

I went over and took tests to see about getting a job at Vultee. When I took the test, as far as using the hands and the eye and hand movements, I passed just about the highest. See, anything using my hands—I could take a little hand drill and go up and down these holes as fast as you could move, just go like that, where most people would break a drill. It was a very simple thing. The riveting is the same way. It's just a matter of rhythm. So it was easy to do.

They had a school set up in Downey to show us how to do assembly work and riveting and the reasons for things—what was a good rivet and what wasn't. We went there about two weeks before we started to work. It was mostly women on these jobs. See, so many young men were in the service that it didn't leave very many of them to do these types of jobs; the ones that were kept out of the service could do the more specialized work. They had to have men to make these jigs and to make the forms for the ribs. That was beyond us.

I was started on this job. The P-38 that Lockheed put out was a twin engine, and we worked on the center part between the two hulls. It was a much heavier rivet that went into this. It was what they call cold riveting; you took them out of the icebox real cold and riveted it....

But, of course, it was hard. I worked six days all the time and sometimes seven days—which was terrible. If I didn't have a family that supported me so much, I couldn't have managed it. I had a daughter that was very capable. She did all the shopping. See, by the time I got home

from work, the shops were closed. She took the ration books and she figured that all out....

My husband helped me a lot with the housework; he was always good about helping. He was very strong and could do his work and then help me with some of mine, too. So whoever had time to do that did it. Typically, what I'd do, I'd get up before 6:00 and get things going. I was ready to leave at 7:00 and I was picked up. Then we got off at 4:00 P.M. and came home. I had dinner to fix and what could be done around the place. So it was a full day. If it hadn't been for my family, though, it would have been much harder for me.

Then things began to slow down. We knew the war was about over. For that matter, I think the bomb had been dropped already and we were just kind of waiting. You could see the difference; it wasn't that push and the trying to do more all the time.

I was laid off in September of '45. I just got a slip of paper saying that I wouldn't be needed again....

The idea was for the women to go back home. The women understood that. And the men had been promised their jobs when they came back. I was ready to go home. I was tired. I had looked forward to it because there were too many things that I wanted to do with my daughter. I knew that it would be coming and I didn't feel any letdown. The experience was interesting, but I couldn't have kept it up forever. It was too hard....

The women got out and worked because they wanted to work. And they worked knowing full well that this was for a short time. We hoped the war would be over in a very short time and that we could go back home and do what we wanted to do. So that was what I felt.

SIGNIFICANCE

By the end of World War II in 1945, 18 million women occupied one-third of the U.S. workforce. Women were given economic incentives to work, and the government promoted the working woman as a patriotic, albeit a temporary solution to the job shortage. Having women work outside the home was accepted as a temporary solution but viewed as an undesirable permanent change because it was feared this would lead to a breakdown of family and social values. In addition, many feared that women would take returning soldier's jobs.

At the close of the war, most women were laid off and forced to return to their prewar occupations. Prewar domestic ideals were fostered with films like *Since You Went Away* and *Mrs. Miniver*, which showed faithful women tending the home front while their husbands were fighting. Cautionary tales such as *Double*

Indemnity and *Gilda* implied that the war had given women too much freedom. Although much of society reverted to earlier ideals of women in the home and the men in the workforce, society had been altered by the entrance of women workers into the war effort.

FURTHER RESOURCES

Web sites

Scholarly Technology Group: What Did You Do in the War, Grandma? "Women and World War II." <http://www.stg.brown.edu/projects/WWII_Women/WomenIn-WWII.html> (accessed March 18, 2006).

National Park Service—Rosie the Riveter: Women Working during World War II. "The Image and Reality of Women Who Worked During World War II." <http://www.nps.gov/pwro/collection/website/rosie.htm> (accessed March 18, 2006).

Gay Military Hero Buried

Photograph

By: Ira Schwartz

Date: 1988

Source: AP Worldwide Images

About the Photographer: This picture was taken in the Congressional Cemetery in Washington, D.C. on July 2, 1988, by Ira Schwartz, a staff photographer for the Associated Press.

INTRODUCTION

This photograph shows the burial of Leonard Matlovich (1943–1988), a former Air Force sergeant and Vietnam War veteran. His burial in the Congressional Cemetery in Washington, D.C. was an historic event, being the first burial of an openly homosexual person in an official government/military cemetery. The large print on his tombstone, legible in the photograph, conveys the message: "A GAY VIETNAM VETERAN." The text below, composed by Matlovich himself, reads: "When I was in the military they gave me a medal for killing two men and a discharge for loving one."

Matlovich was born into an Air Force family. From about the age of twelve, he was conscious of homosexual tendencies, but was not sexually active. He enlisted in the Air Force a year after he graduated from high school and volunteered for a tour of duty in Vietnam. While there he won a Bronze Star (1965), Purple Heart (1970), and Air Force Commendation Medal (1974). In later years he described his motivation for Vietnam service as wanting to "kill a Commie for Mommy," but also reflected that "I was so dissatisfied with being gay that in some ways, volunteering for duty in Vietnam was like a death wish or a suicide pact." Upon returning from Vietnam, Matlovich conducted racial sensitivity classes for enlisted personnel. While conducting research for his classes, he visited a gay bar in Pensacola, Florida. There he met another gay man and became sexually active with him. In doing so, he violated U.S. military policy, which then barred homosexual men and women from service.

Matlovich decided that given his distinguished record, he was well-positioned to challenge the military ban on homosexual personnel, so in 1975 he wrote a letter to Air Force Secretary John McLucas declaring that he, Matlovich, was a homosexual and asking for a waiver of the ban on homosexuals in the service. He was recommended by the Air Force's Office of Special Investigations for a general discharge, which is a form of separation from military service reserved for personnel who have established a record of poor conduct.

Matlovich fought the ruling. He became nationally known and appeared on the Sep. 8, 1975 cover of *Time* with the headline, "I am a homosexual." He was excommunicated by the Mormon Church in November 1975. In 1980, the U.S. Court of Appeals for the District of Columbia ruled that his discharge was illegal and ordered him reinstated with back pay; however, the Air Force persuaded Matlovich to take a $160,000 payment and an honorable discharge in exchange for not taking the case to the Supreme Court, which Matlovich considered would rule against him.

Matlovich publicly announced in 1987 that he had been diagnosed with acquired human immunodeficiency syndrome (AIDS). He died in 1988.

■ **PRIMARY SOURCE**

GAY MILITARY HERO BURIED

See primary source image.

■

SIGNIFICANCE

Matlovich's story illustrates the troubled history of homosexuality and the U.S. military. Homosexuality has been grounds for dishonorable discharge from

PRIMARY SOURCE

Gay Military Hero Buried: The body of Air Force Sgt. Leonard Matlovich is buried at the Congressional Cemetary on July 2, 1988. AP IMAGES

the U.S. military since Revolutionary times. The reason appears to be a general social abhorrence of homosexuality, rather than any specific set of experiences, which would establish that homosexual personnel are less able or willing to carry out their duties. In the post-World-War-II era, the military has sometimes argued that homosexuals are a higher security risk because they can be blackmailed, but as homosexuality has become socially more acceptable this argument has gradually lost force. Internal studies by the armed forces have not found, moreover, that homosexual personnel are more likely to constitute a security risk than heterosexual personnel. Another argument, still frequently adduced against acceptance of homosexual personnel in the military, is that their presence will diminish unit coherence by disturbing fellow service members.

During his campaign for the Presidency, Bill Clinton promised that if elected, he would change the gay-exclusion policy of the military, and that all Americans

regardless of sexual orientation would be welcome to serve. However, once in office he modified this policy under political pressure. The resulting compromise was the policy known as "Don't ask, don't tell." Under the policy, which is U.S. law, a person who reveals that they have had "any bodily contact, actively undertaken or passively permitted, between members of the same sex for the purpose of satisfying sexual desires" may be discharged dishonorably from the U.S. military. On the other hand, military commanders are barred from investigating the sexuality of individual members. Servicemembers will not be asked about their sexuality, and homosexual members may be discharged if they tell about their sexuality. Persons who have "married or attempted to marry a person known to be of the same biological sex" are also deemed unfit for service. As of 2006, the policy remained in effect, although widely criticized both by equal-rights advocates who say that it continues to discriminate against homosexuals and by social and religious conservatives who say that it compromises with a fundamentally pathological or sinful form of behavior that should be strictly barred from the armed forces.

FURTHER RESOURCES

Web sites

U.S. Code. "Policy Concerning Homsexuality in the Armed Forces." 10 U.S.C. Sec. 654. <http://www.law.cornell.edu/uscode/html/uscode10/usc_sec_10_00000654—000-.html> (accessed April 4, 2006).

Advocate. Kronenberg, Gail. "Leonard Matlovich September 1975." November 12, 2002. <http://www.findarticles.com/p/articles/mi_m1589/is_2002_Nov_12/ai_94598299> (accessed April 4, 2006).

Supreme Court Decides Not to Block First Woman Cadet at Citadel

Press release

By: Deval L. Patrick

Date: August 11, 1995

Source: Patrick, Deval L. *Statement by Assistant Attorney General for Civil Rights Deval L. Patrick on Today's Supreme Court Decision Not to Block Shannon Faulkner from Becoming a Cadet at the Citadel.* Washington, D.C.: U.S. Department of Justice, August 11, 1995. Available at: <http://www.usdoj.gov/opa/pr/Pre_96/August95/442.txt.html> (accessed April 5, 2006).

About the Author: Deval L. Patrick (1956–), a civil rights attorney, grew up on Chicago's South Side before graduating from Harvard University in 1978. He then earned a law degree from Harvard. After serving as a law clerk for a year to a federal appellate judge, Patrick joined the NAACP Legal Defense Fund in 1983 where he devoted most of his time to death penalty and voting rights cases. In 1994, President William J. Clinton appointed Patrick to be Assistant Attorney General for Civil Rights, the nation's top civil rights post. Patrick returned to private practice in 1997.

INTRODUCTION

In the 1970s and 1980s, many all-male organizations, including educational institutions, agreed to accept women. Yet a few schools, including The Citadel in South Carolina and Virginia Military Academy, steadfastly refused to join the coeducational movement.

A degree from The Citadel guaranteed success in the Carolinas. Graduates filled the highest ranks of politics and business. Officials of The Citadel, also known as the Military College of South Carolina, tolerated the often-brutal hazing of underclassmen in the belief that such abusive treatment built an elite breed of men. There was no place for women in such a system and The Citadel had long contended that there was no demand from women to enter the school.

When Shannon Faulkner applied to The Citadel in 1993, she deleted references to her gender. The school accepted her, thinking she was male, then withdrew the acceptance after realizing that she was a woman. Faulkner began attending classes at the school as a day student in January 1994. She was not permitted to take part in military training or to wear the distinctive gray uniform issued to cadets.

The Citadel is publicly funded by the state of South Carolina; it received $12 million from the state in 1995. As a state-supported school, it was legally required to admit women. Accordingly, Faulkner's effort gained the backing of the U.S. Justice Department, but it also stirred deep and bitter feelings in South Carolina. Faulkner received death threats, harassing phone calls, and was hissed at in restaurants. The school's alumni network lobbied hard to keep Faulkner out of The Citadel, even distributing bumper stickers reading "Save the Males." On April 13, 1995, the Fourth Circuit Court of Appeals said that The Citadel could not exclude Faulkner and other women from a program that had been exclusively male for 152 years. The Supreme Court refused to hear the appeal.

When the U.S. Military Academy at West Point went co-educational in 1976, 119 women entered as cadets at the same time. Faulkner entered The Citadel alone. She dropped out on August 18, 1995 after five days of training, unable to withstand the physical and psychological pressures. As word of Faulkner's departure spread across the school, cadets whooped and danced. A cadre of upperclassmen quickly created a chant: "Marching down the avenue/Now we know that Faulkner's through/I am happy and so are you!" Faulkner graduated from Anderson College in 1999 and became a public school teacher.

Nancy Ruth Mace (left) after her graduation ceremony, May 8, 1999. Mace was the first female graduate from the formerly all-male school The Citadel. Cadet Petra Lovetinska (right) became the first female four-year graduate from the school in 2000. AP IMAGES

PRIMARY SOURCE

WASHINGTON, D.C.— Today Chief Justice William Rehnquist cleared the way for Shannon Faulkner to become the first woman cadet at The Citadel by denying an emergency request to bar her entry. The Chief Justice's order follows more than two years of litigation by Faulkner and the Justice Department challenging the South Carolina school's all-male admissions policy. The Citadel is one of only two remaining all-male state schools in the nation.

After declaring the school's all-male admissions policy unconstitutional, the Court of Appeals for the 4th Circuit last April ordered state and school officials to admit

Faulkner if they had not established a legally-sufficient alternative program for women by tomorrow. The state waited until June to propose an alternative program, which has not yet been ruled on by the trial court.

Virginia Military Institute (VMI), the other all-male state school, has established an alternative program for women. In that case, the Justice Department has petitioned the U.S. Supreme Court, claiming the VMI alternative is not an adequate remedy for excluding women from VMI.

Deval L. Patrick, Assistant Attorney General for Civil Rights, issued the following statement today about the Citadel case:

"Today's action by the U.S. Supreme Court paves the way for Shannon Faulkner to become the first female cadet at The Citadel. Ms. Faulkner has shown tremendous courage in her fight for equal educational opportunity. She has opened the doors to one of the last all-male state schools in the nation.

Over three years ago Ms. Faulkner applied to The Citadel and got in, only to be later turned away because of her gender. Up to the very end, school officials fought the decisions of the courts that she was entitled to admission. The Justice Department will continue to support Ms. Faulkner and other women who seek to vindicate their right to equal educational opportunity."

SIGNIFICANCE

Women rarely received a formal education until the nineteenth century. As long as a woman knew how to cook and clean, the feeling was she did not need to know anything else. The aftermath of the American Revolution gave rise to the notion that citizens needed to be educated for the newly created democracy to succeed. One result of this belief was the education of girls. Educators introduced females to the subjects of science, history, government, and civic affairs.

Yet many people continued to regard women as constitutionally unfit to withstand the mental and physical demands of higher education. This attitude could be found well into the twentieth century. With the advance of the women's movement, attitudes shifted and such schools as Harvard University agreed to admit women in the 1970s. The Citadel's efforts to resist Faulkner were part of a wider resistance to social and cultural changes.

While Faulkner battled with The Citadel, another sex discrimination case wound its way through the courts. In 1990, the Bush administration filed a lawsuit on behalf of a woman denied admission to VMI on account of her sex. In July 1996, in a seven-to-one vote, the U.S. Supreme Court ruled that all-male admissions policies violate women's constitutional right to equal protection because the policies do nothing for women. The Court ordered VMI to admit women or give up state funding.

The decision ended any hopes that The Citadel would be able to remain all-male. In the wake of the Court's ruling, The Citadel's governing board voted unanimously to immediately accept qualified female applicants. By 2002, 97 women had enrolled, making up about five percent of the student body. Private women's colleges were not affected by the ruling since they

address economic disabilities particular to women and attempt to promote equal employment opportunity.

FURTHER RESOURCES

Books

Manegold, Catherine S. *In Glory's Shadow: Shannon Faulkner, the Citadel, and A Changing America.* New York: Alfred A. Knopf, 2000.

Sadker, Myra, and David Sadker. *Failing at Fairness: How America's Schools Cheat Girls.* New York: Charles Scribner's Sons, 1994.

Weis, Lois, and Michelle Fine, editors. *Beyond Silenced Voices: Class, Race, and Gender in U.S. Schools.* Albany: State University of New York Press, 2005.

A Solid Investment

Making Full Use of the Nation's Human Capital

Government report

By: U.S. Glass Ceiling Commission

Date: November 1995

Source: U.S. Glass Ceiling Commission. *A Solid Investment: Making Full Use of the Nation's Human Capital* (Final Report of the Commission). Washington, D.C.: U.S. Government Printing Office, 1995. Available at: <http://digitalcommons.ilr.cornell.edu/key_workplace/120/> (accessed April 11, 2006).

About the Author: The twenty-one member, bipartisan Federal Glass Ceiling Commission was created by Title II of the Civil Rights Act of 1991. The Commission's mandate was to study the barriers to the advancement of women and minorities within corporate hierarchies (the problem known as the glass ceiling), to issue a report on its findings and conclusions, and to make recommendations on ways to dismantle the glass ceiling.

INTRODUCTION

The Glass Ceiling Commission was created by the Civil Rights Act of 1991, which expanded upon previous civil rights legislation. The 1991 act redefined the language of existing statues, and it used newer terms from the civil rights, labor, and social literature. One of these terms refers to the "glass ceiling," a term that was frequently heard in the economic and labor debates of the late 1980s. Despite the term's novelty at the time, numerous studies show that a glass ceiling existed long before the 1980s. Glass ceiling refers to an invisible barrier faced by women and minorities in the business world that results in lower pay rates and fewer opportunities for promotion and managerial positions.

The commission operated under the auspices of the U.S. Department of Labor. René Redwood, an African American woman, served as the executive director of the commission. She guided the commission's reports and testimony before Congress and also acted as its spokesperson.

During the time of the commission's activities, women were attaining positions of greater influence and higher visibility in the federal government. Ruth Bader Ginsburg was nominated and confirmed as the second female justice of the U.S. Supreme Court, joining Sandra Day O'Connor. Justice Ginsburg is a well-known advocate of equality for women and minorities.

■ PRIMARY SOURCE

Workplace discrimination presents a significant glass ceiling barrier for minorities and women. The Commission recommends that Federal enforcement agencies increase their efforts to enforce existing laws by expanding efforts to end systemic discrimination and challenging multiple discrimination. The Commission also recommends evaluating effectiveness and efficiency and strengthening interagency coordination as a way off furthering the effort. Additionally, updating anti-discrimination regulations, strengthening and expanding corporate management reviews and improving the complaint processing system play major roles in ending discrimination. Finally, the Commission recommends making sure that enforcement agencies have adequate resources to enforce anti-discrimination laws.

The commissions' fact finding report makes clear that programs designed to expand equal employment opportunity, like affirmative action, work best when combined with real and vigorous enforcement. Strong enforcement efforts give employers an incentive to develop effective programs—like special outreach programs, mentoring and training programs, goals and timetables, and other affirmative action programs—that attack glass ceiling barriers by expanding employment opportunities for qualified minorities and women. Better interagency coordination will enable agencies to improve enforcement effectiveness and seek strong remedies, including affirmative action. Improving the enforcement of anti-discrimination laws is central to breaking the glass

ceiling. The Commission recommends the following actions be taken:

Expand efforts to end systemic discrimination

The paucity of minorities and women in managerial ranks serves as a compelling reminder of continued systemic and "pattern and practice" discrimination. Systemic discrimination is practiced against an entire class; pattern and practice discrimination is the regular, routine or standard practice of discrimination by an employer against a particular group. The commission recommends the continuation of efforts to end systemic discrimination through a variety of means, including bringing pattern and practice and class action cases and expanding systemic investigation of Federal contractors.

Challenge multiple discrimination

Discrimination affects different cultural groups differently. Research indicates and statistical data show that minority women face multiple burdens of race and gender discrimination in trying to break through glass ceiling barriers. The commission recommends government agencies recognize this phenomenon and develop enforcement, outreach and public education policies to target specific discriminatory employment practices that affect minority women.

Evaluate effectiveness and efficiency

To effectively enforce anti-discrimination laws, government anti-discrimination agencies must regularly evaluate and improve their existing program and policy systems. The Commission recommends that each agency review all programs and policies (both internally and with regulated groups), seek ways to improve operations and their effectiveness, and conduct regularly scheduled meetings to review the process and the outcomes. Viewed as a working partnership between regulators and those regulated, these consultations should improve fairness and effectiveness for affected parties, bolster public understanding and confidence, and assure that appropriated funds are spent in a cost-effective manner.

Strengthen interagency coordination

Strong interagency coordination—among the Department of Justice, the Department of Labor and the Equal Employment Opportunity Commission (EEOC)—promotes efficient and effective enforcement of anti-discrimination laws. While these agencies have some coordination of strategies in place, it is important to improve information sharing and ensure the best application of resources. The Commission recommends that Federal enforcement agencies responsible for enforcing anti-discrimination laws continue to explore new ways to coordinate.

Update anti-discrimination regulations

Over the last 15 years, key legal and legislative developments—such as the Americans with Disabilities Act, the Civil Rights Act of 1991, the Pregnancy Discrimination Act and the Family and Medical Leave Act—have impacted heavily upon minorities and women. The regulations and interpretations that agencies use to enforce anti-discrimination laws and executive orders must reflect current legal opinion and laws. The Commission recommends revision of regulations and compliance manuals to reflect changes in the workplace, and in society, and the law.

SIGNIFICANCE

Since the 1995 U.S. Glass Ceiling Commission's report, tangible evidence for the improvement and advancement of minorities and women is difficult to quantify. While strides have been made to increase the number of women in math and science, academia, and the legal profession, numerous lawsuits also have been brought by women claiming that they have been passed over for promotions or been sexually harassed in the workplace. Some of these cases have concerned discrimination against women who did not look "womanly enough", and other cases have concerned women who were deemed too forceful in their approach to business. Popular television shows and movies also have attempted to capture the sex-labor debate in their increased portrayals of women executives, business leaders, and educated females.

In 2004, the Institute for Women's Policy Research in Washington, D.C. issued a follow-up report on the glass ceiling entitled "Women's Economic Status in the States: Wide Disparities by Race, Ethnicity, and Region." The study showed that American women in the workforce continued to earn eighty cents for every dollar earned by their male counterparts. For African-American women, the gap is even wider, with a salary of twenty to fifty percent less, on average, than white males. Members of the U.S. House of Representatives John Dingell and Carolyn Maloney introduced legislation in December 2005 that would establish a national center that would

Jo-Ann C. Dixon, presidnet of Executive Women of New Jersey as well as regional director of the American Management Association, poses in her home office in West Caldwell, N.J., on June 23, 2004. AP IMAGES

examine the wage gap and make recommendations to businesses for combating it.

FURTHER RESOURCES

Books

Aptheker, Bettina. *Tapestries of Life: Women's Work, Women's Consciousness, and the Meaning of Daily Experience.* Amherst: University of Massachusetts Press, 1989.

Harvard Business Review on Work and Life Balance. Cambridge, Mass.: Harvard Business School Press, 2000.

Web sites

University of Massachusetts Lowell. The Center for Women and Work. <http://www.uml.edu/centers/women-work/> (accessed April 12, 2006).

Give a Poor Woman a Fish? No. A Fishing Pole? No. A Loan? Yes.

Newspaper article

By: Sheila Tefft

Date: September 13, 1995

Source: Tefft, Sheila. "Give a Poor Woman a Fish? No. A Fishing Pole? No. A Loan? Yes." *Christian Science Monitor.* (September 13, 1995).

About the Author: Shelia Tefft earned a bachelor's degree in journalism from the University of Wisconsin and a master's degree in economic history from the London School of Economics and Political Science. She has written for the *Chicago Tribune*, the *Atlantic, Business Week*, the *Washington Post* and the *Boston Globe*, as well as other publications. Tefft currently directs the journalism program at Emory University.

INTRODUCTION

In 1974, Muhammad Yunus was a young economics professor at Chittagong University in Bangladesh. He'd earned his Ph.D. in economics as a Fulbright Scholar at Vanderbilt University five years before and worked as an assistant professor at Middle Tennessee University. When he returned to Bangladesh, a poor nation on the Indian subcontinent, the country was in the midst of a famine.

Yunus was frustrated that the economics theories he taught had so little impact on the lives of his fellow citizens. As he sought to apply these principles to his stricken country, he found that several small businesses, such as artisans, fruit vendors, and rickshaw pullers, were tethered to local money lenders by high-interest loans. He discovered that $27 could release forty-two businesses from their debts. When local banks refused to assist his venture, Yunus bankrolled the effort himself, funding the area's first micro-credit loans. This allowed the business owners to break the cycle of debt and begin to profit from their businesses. Two years later, Yunus established the Grameen Bank to reach out small businesses; he has since provided loans to over five million clients.

Micro-credit can be as simple as a loan from friends or family or as official as one from agricultural, livestock, or fisheries banking programs. It is an alternative to conventional banks, which lend money to only those with adequate collateral. Because poverty, according to Yunus, is created by the institutions that surround the poor, he characterizes "Grameen Credit" as a social program based on the premise that the poor possess underutilized or unutilized skills.

Micro-credit requires no collateral. The participants do not enter into a legal contract and the family does not become responsible in the case of death or default. Instead, micro-credit is based on the goal of empowering the poor and the belief that charity creates dependence. Loans, generally less than $200, are provided to create self-employment for income-generating activities. The bank itself is considered a doorstep service; bankers go to the clients and provide additional services, such as education, savings accounts, insurance, and support—including business advice and counseling and, in some cases, help running the business if the owner is sick.

From its inception, the micro-credit program has sought women as clients. According to Yunus, they are more likely to repay loans on time, reinvest, and spend the profits to improve families' lives. As a result, approximately ninety-four percent of Grameen Bank's clients have been female. By targeting women in a traditionally male society, micro-credit has increased their leverage within family decision-making and also fostered self confidence. Of those clients, ninety-eight percent repay loans on time.

Balidawa Robinah stands in her backyard brick factory, as her employees lay out mud bricks. Robinah started her business from a loan she received from the Foundation for International Community Assistance Banking on the Poor (FINCA). AP IMAGES

■ PRIMARY SOURCE

GLOBAL REPORT

GIVE A POOR WOMAN A FISH? NO. A FISHING POLE? NO. A LOAN? YES.

A CAPITAL IDEA

DATELINE: BEIJING

ALICIA PAUCAR TAPIA knows the power of a $100 loan to buy a poor woman a sewing machine.

Three years ago, the veteran Nicaraguan aid worker overcame economic aftershocks of a civil war, government skepticism, and male resistance to [establish] a bank that grants small loans to aspiring women entrepreneurs in Managua's slums.

The program is part of a hot trend in economic development known as "micro-credit."

Micro-credit or small loans to the poor to help them earn on their own, is in vogue as cash-strapped governments cut poverty aid, socialism gives way to capitalism,

and the growing ranks of jobless worldwide seek new ways to survive.

This month, the UN Fourth World Conference on Women in Beijing was abuzz with an idea that has proved to be one of few success stories in fighting poverty.

The idea of micro-credit represents a major shift in helping uplift the world's poor. Frustrated by the failure of large loans and projects to ease destitution, Western governments are trying to find ways to get funds directly to the poor, in hopes of bypassing bureaucrats.

"I had worked with many [nongovernmental organizations, or NGOs], always giving out small charity grants that never amounted to much. I was frustrated because I just felt like I never really helped people get out of poverty," recalls Ms. Paucar Tapia. "I realized that what people need is not charity. What they need is to feel part of the system."

That first bank has now grown into a network of a hundred, and plans are under way to expand to 380 banks nationwide. But halfway through a three-year, $1.5 million United States Agency for International Development

(AID) grant, International Foundation for Community Assistance, a private aid group known as FINCA, worries that planned U.S. funding cuts could hurt the infant banking network as it nears self-sufficiency. The group is financially backed by the AID, Rotary Clubs, and some European governments.

"Eventually, we want to survive on our interest income. But now we still need seed capital," says Paucar Tapia, an economist who works with FINCA, which also hopes to eventually rise money from commercial banks. "What we are concerned about is sustaining the program when the donations end."

An alternative for the West

Even in developed countries like the United States, micro-credit is seen as a politically viable alternative to welfare and unemployment that has gained credence in recent years.

"As options for public and private employment have narrowed...everyone wants to have some say over their work," says Marie Wilson, a pioneer in micro-financing at Ms. Foundation for Women. "We know [the U.S.] is never going to be able to create enough jobs again."

The micro-credit method of helping poor women help themselves was pioneered almost two decades ago by Muhammad Yunus, a politically savvy economics professor from Bangladesh. Mr. Yunus was honored at the Beijing conference and even shared a podium with Hillary Rodham Clinton, an enthusiastic supporter. In a program that has since been used as a model worldwide, Yunus's Grameen Bank has shown that targeting women with small loans used to buy a cow, open a food stall, or launch a fishing boat is the best way to help a poor family.

While studies in Asia and Eastern Europe show that men tend to squander loans on drinking and gambling, women boast repayment rates of almost 100 percent when borrowing at market rates lower than extortionist interest charged by local moneylenders. Given enough financial support and time to develop, most Bangladeshi village banks have become self-sustaining in five years, advocates say.

"All we can do from our side is make credit available," says Yunus. "We say, 'We cannot change the world for you. But if you want to change the world, here is the money to help you do it.'"

"We have demonstrated that low-income women are the best credit risk in the world," says Nancy Barry, president of Women's World Banking in New York, a small loan specialist with affiliates in more than forty countries.

Although micro-credit currently reaches less than two percent of the world's 550 million poor, Ms. Barry, a former World Bank official, hopes to encompass 100 million poor women, half of the world's total, within the next ten years.

To do that, she says, governments would need to commit ten percent of total development aid to micro-lending organizations for seed capital, up from two percent currently. The money would be repaid as village banks loan enough to develop economies of scale and are eventually able to raise funds from commercial banks. "The beauty of this is that it pays for itself," she says.

But, expanding what are still small programs into a massive global initiative faces obstacles. Experts caution that micro-financing cannot be the panacea that some advocates hope for. While institutions like AID and the World Bank have jumped on the bandwagon, funding shortages will prevent aid-fatigued governments from making a huge commitment.

Since 1988, AID funding for small-scale lending has jumped to $140 million from $50 million. Currently, two-thirds of borrowers are women, up from thirty-five percent seven years ago. But micro-financing still represents only a small portion of the agency's seven-billion-dollar budget and could lose momentum next year as AID faces possible budget cuts of up to forty percent.

Women's activists are also at odds over the idea. Critics argue that credit programs cannot supplant more traditional aid for housing and education. The focus on small enterprise downplays the huge financial needs still facing women, they say.

At the women's conference, delegates from Africa and other developing countries have pushed for more funds to implement the "Plan of Action" now being drawn up at the conclave. But they have met resistance from Western donors who say the money just isn't available.

Micro-credit programs are "on a steep learning curve and will get significantly bigger over the next few years," says Beth Rhyne, head of Micro-enterprise Development at AID. "But it won't be the panacea for economic development."

As NGOs focusing on micro-credit have cropped up and grown, they have often encountered skepticism from governments and international institutions, advocates say. For example, in some countries like Bolivia, private groups are not allowed to collect deposits, a key step in building larger micro-financing programs that can stand on their own without subsidies.

This summer, the World Bank, which traditionally lends to governments, launched at $200 million micro-financing initiative through private organizations and special banks for the poor. The program was applauded as long-overdue recognition of this global lending force and the private organizations that are shaping it.

But bank critics contend there is still resistance within the staid institution, which is more comfortable dealing with governments than with grass-roots groups. In a recent report, the International Center for Research on Women in Washington, has criticized the World Bank for a reluctance to abandon its traditional emphasis on policy, rather than projects. The bank also has stuck to the belief that "women are not productive, that the things that women do do not contribute directly to economic growth, and that's wrong," says Mayra Buvinic, president of the research institute.

More talk than action

Despite World Bank rhetoric, there is little funding for micro-credit and a limited emphasis on women. "In fact, they should be paying more attention at a time when the [budget] pie is shrinking because this is an efficient way to deal with poverty," Ms. Buvinic adds.

"It is very difficult to get the World Bank to provide resources because the bank works through governments, and most governments are not good at providing credit," says Lawrence Yanovich of FINCA.

Minh Chau Nguyen, the World Bank's manager of gender analysis and policy, rejects the criticism as a red herring and says the bank is moving cautiously because of a shortage of micro-lenders that can handle expanded programs.

In trying to develop more viable private micro-credit organizations, the bank is pushing them to tighten up financial accounting, improve its financial management, and separate banking from social-welfare projects. Despite the bank's measured approach, she says "it comes out loud and clear that these intermediaries are the prime force in poverty reduction in the near term."

SIGNIFICANCE

Since its creation in 1976, the Grameen Bank has served over five million clients and has loaned over two billion dollars. Of these clients, ninety-four percent have been women, ninety-eight percent of whom have repaid their micro-credit loans on time. The bank operates 1,092 branches throughout Bangladesh, including 36,000 rural villages.

The theory of micro-credits, once called "banking for the poor," has developed into other forms of lending. Micro-finance institutions (MFIs) are frontline organizations that deliver services such as loans, education, savings accounts, insurance, and support. MFIs provide funds through direct loans, grants, and loan guarantees funded largely through governmental grants, international institutions like the World Bank, individual donations, philanthropists, and founda-

tions. Like micro-credit, they do not require collateral so that they can attract nontraditional clients, such as women. MFIs deliver services to their clients, many of whom are rural poor. Loans, which are generally less than $200, are repaid within six months to a year and are recycled to provide additional loans.

Critics of microfinance cite the high interest rate on these loans, ranging from fifteen to thirty-five percent. However, microfinance proponents suggest that the alternative is for businesses to reach out to exploitative local money lenders who charge 120 to 130 percent. In addition, although the repayment of loans is high, critics question the program's overall success, as only half of the participants succeed in staying out of poverty.

FURTHER RESOURCES

Web sites

Grameen Foundation USA. "Strategy." <http://www.grameenfoundation.org/strategy> (accessed March 13, 2006).

Grameen Bank. "Grameen Bank." <http://www.grameen-info.org/bank/index.html> (accessed March 13, 2006).

Public Broadcasting System. Online News Hour. "Banking on People." <http://www.pbs.org/newshour/bb/economy/jan-june01/grameen.html> (accessed March 13, 2006).

Your Job or Your Rights

Continued Sex Discrimination in Mexico's Maquiladora Sector

Report

By: Human Rights Watch

Date: December 1998

Source: *Humans Rights Watch.* "A Job or Your Rights." <http://www.hrw.org/reports98/women2/> (accessed March 14, 2006).

About the Author: Human Rights Watch is a non-government organization that aims to protect the rights of people around the world. Established in 1978, it was originally called the Helsinki Watch. With headquarters in New York, it has branches in Brussels, Bujumbura, Freetown (Sierra Leone), Kigali, Geneva, London, Los Angeles, Moscow, San Francisco, Santiago de Chile, Tashkent, Tbilisi, Toronto, and Washington. The group initially focused on upholding civil and political rights, but in the last few years it has also taken up financial, social, and cultural rights issues. Researchers affiliated with this group conduct investigations into abuses by governments and organizations and publish their findings. With the help of United Nations, the European Union, the U.S. government, and others, Human Rights Watch recommends changes in abusive laws and policies worldwide. Human Rights Watch is funded by private individuals and organizations.

INTRODUCTION

Discrimination based on an individual's sex accounts, at least in part, for an inequality in wages, benefits, and career opportunities for men and women all over the world. Occupational segregation is not only detrimental to the economy—in light of the waste of human resources—but it also has a negative impact on the status of women in society.

Women, especially in underdeveloped and developing countries, are often subject to discrimination because of a condition that is specific to them—their ability to get pregnant. Some employers attempt to justify such discriminatory practices by claiming that their cost of hiring and retaining a female employee is higher compared to male employees, since women receive paid maternity leave.

Reports from Human Rights Watch suggest that some companies urge female job applicants to provide urine and blood samples for pregnancy tests and to reveal their contraceptive usage, sexual activity pattern, and other such information that is deemed confidential under privacy laws. Using this information, employers are able to avoid hiring women who are pregnant or who are most likely to become pregnant. Discrimination against women in the workplace has been increasingly rampant in developing nations, including Mexico, Brazil, Guatemala, and South Africa.

In the late 1990s, media reports indicated widespread discrimination against pregnant women working in export processing factories (also known as *maquiladoras*) along the border of United States and Mexico. The Human Rights Watch report excerpted below discusses the discrimination prevalent in maquiladoras. This report follows a 1996 report published by the same organization describing the social injustice faced by women working in Mexican factories. Fifty percent of the 500,000 people working there are women. According to the report, companies in this region, some of which are U.S.-owned, have been following gender discriminatory policies targeting women.

■ PRIMARY SOURCE

In August 1996 Human Rights Watch released a report on labor force sex discrimination in Mexico. The report, "No Guarantees: Sex Discrimination in Mexico's Maquiladora Sector," showed that women applying for work in Mexico's export processing (maquiladora) sector along the U.S.-Mexico border were obliged to undergo mandatory, employment-related pregnancy testing as a condition for employment. The report also found that women who became pregnant soon after being hired risked mistreatment and forced resignation. "No Guarantees" condemned the government of Mexico for failing to protect female workers from these discriminatory practices and called on the government of Mexico to acknowledge and condemn pregnancy-based discrimination as discrimination based on sex; to uphold international human rights obligations to guarantee the rights to equality before the law and to nondiscrimination; and to investigate vigorously all allegations of sex-based discriminatory employment practices and punish those responsible. In the more than two years since our report's release, the Mexican government has yet to take any meaningful action to condemn, investigate, or punish this blatant sex discrimination. As a result, as this report documents, pregnancy-based sex discrimination persists both in places we had previously visited as well as in areas we had not visited before, like Ciudad Juárez, in the state of Chihuahua, across the border from El Paso, Texas.

Pregnancy as a condition is inextricably linked and specific to being female. Consequently, when women are treated in an adverse manner by their employers or potential employers because they are pregnant or because they may become pregnant, they are being subjected to a form of sex discrimination by targeting a condition only women experience. Pregnancy discrimination is not limited to the refusal to hire pregnant job applicants and the firing of pregnant workers but also includes any behavior or practice to determine pregnancy status, such as requiring information about women's sexual activity or contraceptive use.

During investigations conducted from May through November 1997, we found that in Tijuana, in the state of Baja California (south of San Diego, California); Reynosa and Rìo Bravo, in the state of Tamaulipas (opposite McAllen, Texas); and Ciudad Juárez (across the border from El Paso, Texas), corporations, the vast majority of which are U.S. owned, forced female applicants to undergo mandatory employment-related pregnancy testing in order to detect pregnancy and deny pregnant women work. In Ciudad Juárez, in particular, we also discovered disturbing means of implementing discriminatory policies: female employees are compelled to show their used sanitary napkins to verify nonpregnancy before they receive permanent contracts. In violation of Mexican federal labor law, maquiladora operators in Ciudad Juárez reportedly also refused to pay female employees their wages during maternity leave; threatened not to allow female employees to return to work after maternity leave; and, in one instance, retaliated against a woman who complained that pregnant co-workers were breathing in noxious fumes and fainting on the job by firing her.

Rather than condemn such practices, the Mexican government has taken every opportunity to interpret and apply labor law in a way that most favors the discriminatory practices of the corporations and affords women the least amount of protection. In fact, the government has even gone so far as to excuse publicly this discrimination. The Labor Department of the state of Baja California, which is charged with enforcing the federal labor code at the state level, issued a press release (see Appendix A for original press release in Spanish and an English translation) indicating that pregnancy testing in the hiring process was legal and was in fact a corporation's fulfillment of an authority granted to it by the labor law.

The Mexican government also initiated inspections of maquiladoras in response to our findings and convened a meeting between Mexican union representatives and the maquiladora trade association to discuss the findings of Human Rights Watch's report, encouraging them to investigate and change their practices regarding on-the-job pregnancy discrimination. However, since the Mexican government does not consider the determination and use of pregnancy status in the employment process to violate its federal labor code, the government in fact ignores the most pervasive and openly practiced type of sex discrimination that exists in that sector: hiring-process sex discrimination.

Female job seekers in Mexico cannot rely on the government for protection from discrimination in the workforce. They have few tenable options for legal redress. Several Mexican states have human rights commissions charged with investigating human rights abuses involving public officials (by omission and by commission). However, private-sector labor issues are outside the legal purview of these human rights commissions. Other government mechanisms include the Inspector of Labor Office, which is responsible for ensuring businesses' compliance with federal labor law; the Labor Rights Ombudsman Office, which is responsible for offering workers free legal advice and assisting them in the resolution of labor disputes through the conciliation and arbitration process; and the local Conciliation and Arbitration Board (cab), which adjudicates worker disputes and issues binding resolutions. However, these bodies maintain they are not legally empowered to address disputes involving job applicants, arguing that such individuals have not established a labor relationship with an employer. Female job applicants who are obliged to undergo pregnancy testing as a condition for employment fall within this category of people. Unless a victim files a complaint of on-the-job pregnancy-related sex discrimination, the cabs are not authorized to initiate investigations of these practices either. Furthermore, officials from Mexico's Ministry of Labor told us that in the absence of explicit prohibitions against pregnancy testing in the federal labor code as a type of sex discrimination, such treatment was in fact permissible under the law.

SIGNIFICANCE

The United Nations has always laid emphasis on equal rights for women. When the Charter of the United Nations was signed on June 26, 1945, it established "promoting and encouraging respect for human rights and for fundamental freedoms for all without distinction as to race, sex, language or religion" as one of the organization's three primary goals.

Although most countries have laws that prohibit inequality on the basis of gender, corporations around the world continue to circumvent the law in various ways. Discrimination against pregnant women has always been a common practice, and human rights organizations have frequently protested against such discrimination.

One of the regions known for widespread gender discrimination is the United States-Mexico border. Soon after Human Rights Watch published its initial report (in 1996), a petition was filed with the United States National Administrative Office (NAO). This petition contended that pregnancy-based discrimination existed in Mexico's export-processing factories and that this discrimination violated several provisions of national and international law. Several recommendations and appeals were made to the concerned corporations (both U.S.-owned and Mexican-owned), the Mexican government, and the U.S. government. Similar recommendations also were made in the 1998 Human Rights Watch report. However, these recommendations have failed to attract sufficient attention from the policy-makers to trigger effective action.

Mexico's Constitution and federal labor codes prohibit discrimination against women, and Mexico also is required to promote the elimination of sex discrimination by its participation in the North American Free Trade Agreement (NAFTA). However, despite these legal and regulatory prohibitions, gender-based discrimination seems only to have increased in Mexico in the past few years. Corporations and other employ-

At the Samsung Electromechanics plant, workers insert electronic components on an assembly line in Tijuana, Mexico on November 18, 1998. AP IMAGES

ers may use loopholes to circumvent the clear intent of the legislation or regulations. For example, if the law does not explicitly prohibit the use of pregnancy testing as a prerequisite for employment, an employer may claim he is entitled to use such testing. In the absence of clearly defined guidelines for determining gender discrimination policies, employers may interpret the existing laws to suit their own requirements and then use the law's lack of clarity as justification when confronted.

There are numerous cases of gender prejudice in the United States, too. The Pregnancy Discrimination Act, an amendment to Title VII of the Civil Rights Act of 1964, clearly states that discrimination on the basis of pregnancy, childbirth, or related medical conditions constitutes unlawful sex discrimination. Despite this clear legislative prohibition against pregnancy discrimination, in fiscal year 2005, the U.S. Equal Employment Opportunity Commission (EEOC) received 4,449 charges of pregnancy-based discrimination. Of these 4,449 charges, 4,321 were

resolved and $11.6 million in monetary benefits was recovered for the individuals who brought the charges and other injured parties.

According to human rights activists, although women constitute about forty percent of the total workforce worldwide, they experience higher unemployment rates and lower wages when compared to men. Although almost half of the world's population is female, women are responsible for only ten percent of the total income. These statistics graphically demonstrate the need to continue working vigorously toward an end to gender discrimination and true economic equality.

FURTHER RESOURCES

Web sites

Global Policy Forum. "Dominican Republic: U.S. Trade Pact Fails Pregnant Women—CAFTA Fails to Protect Against Rampant Job Discrimination." <http://www.globalpolicy.org/socecon/inequal/gender/2004/0422dominican.htm> (accessed March 14, 2006).

————. "Women Still Face Pay and Job Discrimination in the Global Workplace." <http://www.globalpolicy.org/socecon/inequal/gender/2004/0305ilo.htm> (accessed March 14, 2006).

Human Development Report. "Human Development Index." <http://hdr.undp.org/reports/global/2004/pdf/hdr04_HDI.pdf> (accessed March 14, 2006).

International Labour Review. "Theories of Occupational Segregation By Sex: An Overview." <http://www.ilo.org/public/english/support/publ/revue/articles/ank97-3.htm> (accessed March 14, 2006).

U.S. Equal Employment Opportunity Commission. "Pregnancy Discrimination." <http://www.eeoc.gov/types/pregnancy.html> (accessed April 12, 2006).

U.S. Equal Employment Opportunity Commission. "Sex-Based Discrimination." <http://www.eeoc.gov/types/sex.html> (accessed March 14, 2006).

U.S. Library of Congress. "The [Mexican] Constitution." <http://countrystudies.us/mexico/81.htm> (accessed March 14, 2006).

USA Today. "Pregnant Workers Report Growing Discrimination." <http://www.usatoday.com/money/workplace/2005-02-16-pregnancy-bias-usat_x.htm> (accessed March 14, 2006).

U.S. Department of Labor Equal Employment Opportunity Policy

Policy

By: Alexis M. Herman

Date: May 1998

Source: United States. Department of Labor. "Equal Employment Opportunity Policy." < http://www.fedglobe.org/issues/laborpolicy.htm> (accessed April 15, 2006).

About the Author: Alexis Herman, the first African American to become Secretary of Labor, served in the administration of President Bill Clinton from 1996 to 2000. Born in Alabama, Herman spent most of her career assisting minority women. After a stint as a social worker, she became the director of the Women's Bureau in 1976. She later headed the Minority Women Employment Program of R-T-P, Inc., where she established programs to place minority women in white collar and nontraditional jobs.

INTRODUCTION

Workplace discrimination has long been a matter of concern for gays and lesbians. The Civil Rights Act of 1964 prohibits workplace discrimination based on race, color, religion, sex, and national origin, but is silent on the matter of sexual orientation. Courts have consistently ruled that the act does not cover sexual orientation, leaving gays and lesbians vulnerable.

Some employers are open about their desire to exclude gays and lesbians from the workforce. Antigay discrimination has sometimes meant enduring daily harassment that includes name-calling, humiliation, and physical threats from coworkers and bosses alike. Most employers are more subtle, however. Policies rarely enforced against heterosexuals suddenly are invoked against employees perceived to be gay.

It is legal in a majority of states to fire a person because of his or her sexual orientation. In a well-known case, Cheryl Summerville, a cook in a suburban Atlanta Cracker Barrel restaurant, received a termination notice in 1991. The restaurant had adopted a policy of refusing to employ anyone who failed "to demonstrate normal heterosexual values." Summerville, who had earned excellent performance ratings, awards, and promotions, was fired for violating official company policy because she was gay. (Cracker Barrel has since changed its employment policies.)

In response to a campaign pledge to support gay rights, President Bill Clinton issued Executive Order 11478 on May 28, 1998, protecting federal employees from antigay workplace discrimination. However, the policy statement lacks any enforcement mechanism and employees who suspect discrimination can not bring their complaints to the Equal Employment Opportunity Commission. When he signed the executive order, Clinton urged Congress to pass the Employment Non-Discrimination Act.

▮ PRIMARY SOURCE

EQUAL EMPLOYMENT OPPORTUNITY POLICY

It is Department of Labor (DOL) policy to provide equal employment opportunity for all applicants for employment and employees of DOL. Therefore, discrimination, in any form, because of race, color, sex, national origin, religion, age, disability or sexual orientation, is prohibited.

Equal opportunity for all employees is an integral part of accomplishing the mission of DOL. As Secretary of Labor, I am committed to fostering a workplace that is free of discrimination in any form. I believe that the Department, as a model employer, should be committed to the principle that it not only preaches but practices inclusiveness, fairness, and the participation of all employees in all facets of the Department. This necessarily requires all of us to work together in creating a work environment that is perceived by all employees as fair and equitable.

Achieving this objective will require that each of us practice respect for one another, understanding that everyone employed here at DOL adds value to the work of this Department.

I expect every DOL manager and supervisor to be knowledgeable about and active in carrying out the Department's EEO policy, and to be rated annually, as part of their performance evaluations, on their ability to manage and develop people in keeping with this policy.

I expect every DOL employee to contribute to a work environment in which his or her coworkers can feel respected and valued.

I expect the Civil Rights Center, OASAM [Office of the Assistant Secretary for Administration and Management], to monitor compliance with this policy and the affirmative employment and nondiscrimination provisions of all applicable laws and regulations, and to assist me in promoting a dialogue to identify areas which serve to prevent us from achieving this policy.

/s/ AMH

Secretary of Labor

May 1998

Anne Conners, head of the New York City chapter of the National Organiztion for Women, speaks to reporters while leading a protest in front of the Bank of Tokyo branch in New York on June 27, 1996. The Japanese bank merged with the Mitsubishi Corp. that had been sued by the Equal Employment Opportunity Commision for sexual harassment. AP IMAGES

SIGNIFICANCE

The Employment Non-Discrimination Act (ENDA) would protect gay people from discrimination once they are employed. The act would make it a federal offense to discriminate against any individual because of actual or perceived sexual orientation and would cover any employer engaged in interstate commerce and who has fifteen or more employees. Religious organizations are exempt. It has been introduced in Congress repeatedly since 1995 by Senators Ted Kennedy (D–Massachusetts), Jim Jeffords (I–Vermont), and Joseph Lieberman (D–Connecticut), among others.

Supporters of ENDA argue that it is a logical extension of the Civil Rights Act. They believe that it is based on the American ideal of equal opportunity, a civil right from which gay men and lesbian women cannot be excluded. They argue that employment should be decided on the basis of merit, skills, and qualifications, not irrelevant characteristics unrelated to job performance such as sexuality.

Strong opposition from conservatives has blocked passage of ENDA. Some fear that adding federal workplace protections for gays and lesbians would be

a costly burden to small business owners. Others believe that the matter should not be handled at the federal level and instead should be left to the states. Social conservatives argue that legislation should not support a homosexual lifestyle, that it is an attack on the free exercise of religion, and that ENDA threatens freedom of association. They believe that an employment is a form of association that should freely be chosen by both sides.

Prospects for the ENDA's passage are not good. Other issues, notably that of gay marriage, have drawn attention away from the issue of antigay workplace discrimination. The General Accounting Office in 2000 found that there had been no marked increase in lawsuits in states that prohibit antigay workplace discrimination, perhaps indicating a shift in attitudes about gays and lesbians in the workplace.

FURTHER RESOURCES

Books

Friskopp, Annette, and Sharon Silverstein. *Straight Jobs, Gay Lives: Gay and Lesbian Professionals, the Harvard Business School and the American Workplace.* New York: Scribner's's, 1995.

Raeburn, Nicole C. *Changing Corporate America from Inside Out: Lesbian and Gay Workplace Rights.* Minneapolis: University of Minnesota Press, 2004.

Web sites

Office of Personnel Management, U.S. Government. "Addressing Sexual Orientation Discrimination in Federal Civilian Employment: A Guide to Employee's Rights." <http://www.opm.gov/er/address2/guide01.asp; (accessed March 15, 2006).

Audio and Visual Media

Anderson, Kelly, and Tami Gold *Out at Work.* Frameline, 1996.

Is Single Gender Schooling Viable in the Public Sector?

Internet article

By: Amanda Datnow, Lea Hubbard, and Elisabeth Woody

Date: May 20, 2001

Source: Datnow, Amanda, Lea Hubbard, and Elisabeth Woody. "Is Single Gender Schooling Viable in the Public Sector?" <http://www.oise.utoronto.ca/depts/tps/adatnow/final.pdf > (accessed March 14, 2006).

About the Authors: Dr. Amanda Datnow is a principal researcher with the department of theory and policy studies at the Ontario Institute for Studies in Education, University of Toronto. The primary focus of her research is school reform policies and politics. Dr. Datnow holds a B.A. in psychology from the University of California, San Diego and a Ph. D. in education from the University of California, Los Angeles. Dr. Lea Hubbard works with the Teacher Education Program at UC San Diego. She has studied educational inequalities as they exist across ethnic and gender lines. Dr. Hubbard holds a Ph. D. in sociology from UC San Diego. Dr. Elisabeth Woody is a principal research scientist at Policy Analysis for California

Education (PACE), University of California, Berkeley. Her research focuses on the impact of public school policies on students and teachers. Dr. Woody has a Ph. D. in Education from UC Berkeley.

INTRODUCTION

Private schools in the United States have some of the best reputations in the world, and their quality of education is considered second to none. Public school education in the United States, however, is an entirely different story. Over the years, its deterioration has been noticeable, and some experts believe that one reason for this is the prevalence of gender discrimination. The issue was widely publicized in a 1992 report by the American Association of University Women (AAUW) titled "How Schools Shortchange Girls."

The report concluded that girls received less attention in classrooms than boys, that few were encouraged to pursue math or science-related careers, that existing curricula stereotyped females, and that the testing system was significantly biased towards boys. The report fueled a debate among education policy makers about combating such discriminatory policies. Some educators proposed single-sex classes and schools as a way to eliminate gender bias.

In 1997, California became the first state to experiment with single-gender public schooling on a large scale. Under its pilot program, as many as six districts started single-gender public schools.

The article excerpted below, "Is Single Gender Schooling Viable in the Public Sector?" presents a three-year case study of all single-gender schools in California; it was published in May 2001.

PRIMARY SOURCE

Is Single Gender Schooling Viable in the Public Sector?

This report examines whether single gender schooling is a viable option in the public sector. Schools and districts throughout the nation are clamoring to adopt reforms to increase academic achievement and satisfy parents and community members. Single gender schooling, a relatively successful model from the private sector, has been considered as one possible remedy. Experiments with single gender schooling are occurring in public school districts across the U.S. Yet, very little systematic research has been conducted on these schools and little is known about their motivations, design, or outcomes with respect to students, teachers, and school systems.

In 1997, California became the first state to experiment with single gender public education on a large scale. Six districts opened single gender academies (both boys and girls) as a result of former California Governor Pete Wilson's legislation and funding for single gender academies pilot program in the public school system. This report presents findings from a three-year case study of these single gender academies in six districts in California. Our study involved 300+ extensive interviews with educators, policymakers, and students, and school and classroom observations. It is the most comprehensive study of single sex public schooling that has been conducted in the U.S. to date.

The purpose of this study was to assess the consequences of single gender schooling in the public sector. In doing so, we focused on the socio-political context of single gender public schooling in the state of California and in each community; the organization and implementation of single gender schooling in each district; and the policy implications regarding single gender academies as a school choice option. A major goal of our study was to examine the equity implications of single gender public schooling along these various dimensions.

A SUMMARY OF OUR MAJOR FINDINGS FOLLOWS:

Finding #1: For most administrators, single gender schooling was a vehicle for meeting at-risk students' needs and not an end in itself.

Instead of seeing the single gender academies as primarily an opportunity to address gender inequities for girls or boys (as one might predict), most educators saw the $500,000 state grant as a way to help address the more pressing educational and social problems of low achieving students. With the grant funding, educators developed social and academic support structures to address the needs of their particular student populations, such as low achievement, truancy, poverty, violence, or geographic isolation. To be sure, most of the educators did view the single gender schooling arrangement as a way to decrease distractions among boys and girls to improve students' self-esteem.

Finding #2: The success of California's pilot program was undermined by implementation challenges.

Educators were hampered at the outset by short timelines to propose and begin operation of the academies. They had very little time to think about and plan for the single gender academies, engage the support of constituencies, recruit qualified teachers, and advertise the new schooling option for students. These difficulties were compounded by an absence of legislated funding for state-level support and monitoring of the academies' progress. Once the academies were operational, they continued to suffer from implementation difficulties including staff and leadership turnover, a lack of political support, and funding problems.

Finding #3: Most of the single gender academies were, by design, not open to all students.

The California single-gender academies pilot program legislation was constructed primarily as a vehicle for expanding public school choice, not expressly for goals of gender equity or improving the education of "at risk" students. However, in the end, who enrolled was largely a matter that was determined by the design and target population of each district's single gender academies. In at least four of the six districts, "at-risk" students of color were recruited to join the single-gender academies. White, average, or high achieving students were more likely to freely choose to attend. In some districts, the academies operated under capacity due to insufficient public interest or to difficulties in advertising the choice option.

Finding #4: For most parents, California's single gender academies were seen as an opportunity for their children to benefit from special resources and to reduce distractions from the opposite sex.

Parents were attracted by the extra computers, field trips, small class sizes, and special opportunities offered in many of the academies, and they hoped that distractions among boys and girls would be decreased. Parents rarely mentioned that they chose to attend the single-gender academies because of their interest in empowerment or gender equity for their young boys and girls, except for some parents of white girls in a suburban district.

SIGNIFICANCE

A special report published by the National Center for Education Statistics (NCES) in 2002 stated that ninety percent of the children in America attend public schools. Despite heavy intake of students, public schools seldom offered single-gender opportunities until the late 1990s.

The report described in the primary source concluded that single-gender schools in California were not sustainable under the state's policy framework. As of the early 2000s, only one district out of six still had single-gender academies. The authors of the report stated that although the program was successful in attaining many of its objectives, various political, social, and economic reasons hampered its progress.

Nevertheless, according to experts, the pilot program proved that single-gender schooling is viable if the deficiencies found in the system are addressed.

A student at J. Hayden Johnson Junior High School in Washington takes notes during a single-sex class on January 30, 1996. AP IMAGES

One of the important reasons for launching single-sex schools was the belief among policy makers, educators, researchers, and parents that girls and boys learn differently in such an environment. Researchers found that when students were removed from social pressures and sexual biases inherent in co-ed schools, there was greater commitment to studies and higher achievement among both boys and girls. Benjamin Wright—a known proponent of single-gender schools who was instrumental in employing this approach in two urban Seattle schools, stated: "When you're having a conversation with boys about life issues, you can have a real, authentic conversation. When you have girls in the classroom with boys and talk about pregnancy and lifecycles, girls become embarrassed. When you separate them, you see both groups rise equally."

The U.S. government has also taken measures to encourage single-gender schooling. A CBS report in 2002 indicated that public schools could be given more freedom to establish single-sex classes by amending a 1972 law targeting gender bias in education. The Education Department announced its intention to propose changes to the Title IX statutes that ban sex discrimination in federally funded education programs:

"Our goal is to provide schools with as much flexibility as possible to offer students programs that meet their needs," said then–Education Secretary Rodney Paige. On January 8, 2002, President George W. Bush signed into law the No Child Left Behind Act of 2001, which allows local educational agencies to use their "Innovative Programs" funds for supporting same-gender schools and classrooms.

Consequently, since the early 2000s the number of single-gender schools in the United States has increased significantly. According to the National Association for Single Sex Public Education, as of

2006 there were more than 211 public schools that offer single-gender education opportunities. As many as forty-two of these are entirely single-gender schools.

Opponents of single-gender schools, however, claim single-sex schools are accessible only to affluent and better-educated communities. An American Association of University Women report, "Separated by Sex: A Critical Look at Single-Sex Education for Girls" concluded that "single-sex education is not necessarily better than co-education". The report states that better education is the key to improving the quality of public schools, and not the single-gender approach. Critics also believe that such measures violate basic civil rights. Emily J. Martin, an attorney for the Women's Rights Project of the American Civil Liberties Union, said, "I think that what our country has learned is, it's very dangerous to experiment with segregation to make our society better. I think we have too troubled a history to think that this is okay."

According to the U.S. Department of Education, many studies supporting single-gender schooling have been undertaken either in private schools or overseas. Officials argue that conclusions derived from such studies may not be valid for public schools in the United States. As of the 2000s, although many schools offer single-gender classes, there is still an extensive and sustained debate on whether such policies are viable for American schools.

FURTHER RESOURCES

Web sites

American Association of University Women. "How Schools Shortchange Girls: The AAUW Report (1992)" <http://www.aauw.org/research/girls_education/hssg.cfm> (accessed March 14, 2006).

Cornell University News Service. "Can Separate Ever be Equal in Public Single-Sex Schools? Cornell law Professor Says Issue Still Has to Be Resolved" <http://www.news.cornell.edu/stories/April05/Single.sex.schools.html> (accessed March 14, 2006).

Education World. "Single-Gender Classes: Are They Better?" <http://www.education-world.com/a_curr/curr215.shtml> (accessed March 14, 2006).

National Association for Single Sex Public Association. "Single-Sex Schools" <http://www.singlesexschools.org/schools.html> (accessed March 14, 2006).

U.S. Department of Education. "The Education Innovator" <http://www.ed.gov/news/newsletters/innovator/2005/1013.html> (accessed March 14, 2006).

———. "Guidelines Regarding Single Sex Classes and Schools" <http://www.ed.gov/about/offices/list/ocr/t9-guidelines-ss.html> (accessed March 14, 2006).

Washington Post. "Boy 'Tribes' on Frontier in Reading" <http://www.washingtonpost.com/wp-dyn/articles/A57611-2005Jan7.html> (accessed March 14, 2006).

The Content of Abstinence-Only Federally Funded Education Programs

Government report

By: Henry Waxman

Date: December 2004

Source: United States. "The Content of Abstinence-Only Federally Funded Education Programs." United States House of Representatives Committee on Government Reform, Minority Staff Special Investigations Division, December 2004.

About the Author: This report was prepared by the Special Investigations Division for the House of Representatives, at the request of Representative Henry Waxman, a Democrat serving California's 30th district.

INTRODUCTION

The National Education Association, in 1912, discussed the need for sexuality education programs in United States schools. At the time, the Comstock Law, which prohibited the dissemination of information on contraception and certain sexual acts, was still in place; this law constrained teachers and in effect made sexuality education illegal. The Comstock Law was repealed in 1936, and in 1940 the United States Public Health Service considered sexuality education an "urgent need" in public schools in the United States.

In 1953, the American Social Health Association developed and implemented a sexuality education curriculum for schools titled "Family Life Education." Two years later, the American Medical Association created a pamphlet series on sexuality education as well. These topics, taught in health and physical education classes or as pull-out seminars for sex-segregated learning, were designed to familiarize teens with basic reproductive biology.

Firmly in place by the 1960s, the issue of sexuality education in public schools has been a source of debate in the United States. Many sexuality education programs involved little more than a short movie about menstruation for young women and a pamphlet; young men watched a film on controlling sexual urges. As these programs evolved in the 1970s and early 1980s, the curriculum shifted to younger ages, such as fifth and sixth grade, and included discussions on emotions, self-esteem, sexually-transmitted diseases, and disease prevention.

For some parents, sex-ed programs go too far, teaching explicit details concerning anatomy and sexuality that parents do not feel to be age-appropriate or believe are private concerns for parents to teach. For other parents, religion plays a greater role; some religious conservatives who do not believe that premarital sex is moral condemn sexuality education that promotes condom use, for instance.

In 1986, the Surgeon General under President Ronald Reagan, General C. Everett Koop, called for expanding sexuality education to students in the third grade; the growing HIV/AIDS epidemic was considered a public health crisis, and Koop noted that disease prevention would be best initiated for children through a comprehensive sexuality education program. Koop advocated condom use as the primary means of preventing the spread of HIV/AIDS. At the time, eighty-six percent of Americans believed that sexuality education should be part of the public school curriculum.

By the 1990s, teenage pregnancy was at its peak in modern U.S. history; with a birth rate of 64.2 births per 1,000 females aged fifteen to nineteen in 1991, a twenty-year high, policymakers, educators, and public health specialists were concerned about the teen pregnancy increase. At the same time, HIV/AIDS infections among the heterosexual population were on the rise, with teen infection rates higher than average as well. Religious conservatives argued that the only way to prevent pregnancy and disease is to teach abstinence, which is one-hundred-percent effective against both.

Abstinence-only education programs teach abstinence as the only option; information on contraception and reducing or eliminating disease transmission is not available. In this excerpt below, taken from California Representative Henry Waxman's requested report on federally funded abstinence-only programs, the report discusses some of the messages taught to young men and women as part of the most popular abstinence-only curriculum packages.

PRIMARY SOURCE

THE CONTENT OF ABSTINENCE-ONLY FEDERALLY FUNDED EDUCATION PROGRAMS

E. Abstinence-Only Curricula Treat Stereotypes about Girls and Boys as Scientific Fact

Many abstinence-only curricula begin with a detailed discussion of differences between boys and girls. Some of the differences presented are simply biological. Several of the curricula, however, present stereotypes as scientific fact.

1. Stereotypes that Undermine Girls' Achievement

Several curricula teach that girls care less about achievement and their futures than do boys. One curriculum instructs: "Women gauge their happiness and judge their success by their relationships. Men's happiness and success hinge on their accomplishments." This curriculum also teaches:

Men tend to be more tuned in to what is happening today and what needs to be done for a secure future. When women began to enter the work force at an equal pace with men, companies noticed that women were not as concerned about preparing for retirement. This stems from the priority men and women place on the past, present, and future.

Another curriculum lists "Financial Support" as one of the "5 Major Needs of Women," and "Domestic Support" as one of the "5 Major Needs of Men." The curriculum states:

Just as a woman needs to feel a man's devotion to her, a man has a primary need to feel a woman's admiration. To admire a man is to regard him with wonder, delight, and approval. A man feels admired when his unique characteristics and talents happily amaze her.

A third curriculum depicts emotions as limiting girls' ability to focus. It states:

"Generally, guys are able to focus better on one activity at a time and may not connect feelings with actions. Girls access both sides of the brain at once, so they often experience feelings and emotions as part of every situation."

2. Stereotypes that Girls Are Weak and Need Protection

Some of the curricula describe girls as helpless or dependent upon men. In a discussion of wedding traditions, one curriculum writes: "Tell the class that the Bride price is actually an honor to the bride. It says she is valuable to the groom and he is willing to give something valuable for her."

The curriculum also teaches: "The father gives the bride to the groom because he is the one man who has had the responsibility of protecting her throughout her life. He is now giving his daughter to the only other man who will take over this protective role."

One book in the "Choosing the Best" series presents a story about a knight who saves a princess from a dragon. The next time the dragon arrives, the princess advises the knight to kill the dragon with a noose, and the following time with poison, both of which work but leave the knight feeling "ashamed." The knight eventually decides to marry a village maiden, but did so "only after making sure she knew nothing about nooses or poison." The curriculum concludes:

> Moral of the story: Occasional suggestions and assistance may be alright, but too much of it will lessen a man's confidence or even turn him away from his princess.

3. Stereotypes that Reinforce Male Sexual Aggressiveness

One curriculum teaches that men are sexually aggressive and lack deep emotions. In a chart of the top five women's and men's basic needs, the curriculum lists "sexual fulfillment" and "physical attractiveness" as two of the top five "needs" in the men's section. "Affection," "Conversation," "Honesty and Openness," and "Family Commitment" are listed only as women's needs. The curriculum teaches: "A male is usually less discriminating about those to whom he is sexually attracted... Women usually have greater intuitive awareness of how to develop a loving relationship."

The same curriculum tells participants: "While a man needs little or no preparation for sex, a woman often needs hours of emotional and mental preparation."

F. Abstinence-Only Curricula Contain False and Misleading Information about the Risks of Sexual Activity

Many of the curricula distort information about the risks of sexual activity. In the case of cervical cancer, the risk of disease is stressed, but simple prevention measures often go unmentioned. HIV exposure risks are discussed in confusing terms, and risks of substances and activities are exaggerated. Several curricula also present misleading information about the relationship between sexual activity and mental health, inaccurately suggesting that abstinence can solve all psychological problems.

SIGNIFICANCE

The first wave of abstinence-only sexuality education courses came in the early 1980s, when the U.S. Office of Population Affairs implemented standards from the Adolescent Family Life Act, which received $9 million in federal funds to promote sexuality edu-

cation that focused on abstinence. The programs often included religious lessons; in 1983 the American Civil Liberties union sued to have religious references removed. By 1993, when the suit was settled, the courts determined that abstinence-only programs must not have religious references, must teach medically correct information, and must conform to a variety of rules that separate church and state.

In August 1996, President Bill Clinton signed Public Law 104–193, part of a large welfare reform law. This law included a $350 million allocation for states that adopted abstinence-only curricula in sexuality education courses. The law stipulated that abstinence-only courses must meet eight criteria: "(A) has as its exclusive purpose, teaching the social, psychological, and health gains to be realized by abstaining from sexual activity; (B) teaches abstinence from sexual activity outside marriage as the expected standard for all school-age children; (C) teaches that abstinence from sexual activity is the only certain way to avoid out-of-wedlock pregnancy, sexually transmitted diseases, and other associated health problems; (D) teaches that a mutually faithful monogamous relationship in the context of marriage is the expected standard of human sexual activity; (E) teaches that sexual activity outside of the context of marriage is likely to have harmful psychological and physical effects; (F) teaches that bearing children out-of-wedlock is likely to have harmful consequences for the child, the child's parents, and society; (G) teaches young people how to reject sexual advances and how alcohol and drug use increases vulnerability to sexual advances; (H) teaches the importance of attaining self-sufficiency before engaging in sexual activity."

Representative Waxman's requested report systematically detailed violations of these eight criteria in sexuality education curricula across the board. In addition, a large-scale review of abstinence-only education by researchers at Columbia university found that while those who take an abstinence-only pledge tend to delay intercourse longer than those who do not pledge, when "pledgers" break their vow of abstinence, they are one-third less likely to use contraception, are equally likely to contract a sexually-transmitted disease, but are less likely to seek proper medical treatment for STDs.

Waxman's report notes that some curricula call a forty-three-day-old fetus a "thinking person," teach students that HIV/AIDS can be transmitted through sweat and tears, and that a fertilized egg receives twenty-four chromosomes from the mother and twenty-four chromosomes from the father. These

A billboard in downtown Baltimore, shown July 3 1997, displays a message of abstinence towards teens. AP IMAGES

inaccuracies constitute a serious problem in the quality of the information provided, according to Waxman; the Congressman points to inaccuracy of fact while questioning the abstinence-only approach.

Critics of Waxman's requested report accuse the Democratic Congressman of playing politics, and that many of the manuals reviewed by the report's investigators were outdated. Supporters of more comprehensive sexuality education claim that the $900 million spent on abstinence-only programs between 1996 and 2004 had not been justified.

Abstinence-only education is not federally mandated; state boards of education control curricula in public schools. Twenty-two states currently require some form of sexuality education programs in schools, and federal dollars for abstinence-only programs have grown at a far greater rate than allocations for comprehensive sexuality education programs since 1996.

FURTHER RESOURCES

Books

Luker, Kristin. *When Sex Goes to School: Warring Views on Sex—And Sex Education—Since the Sixties.* W.W. Norton, 2006.

Periodicals

Beh, Hazel Glenn, and Milton Diamond. "The Failure of Abstinence-only Education: Minors Have a Right to Honest Talk About Sex." *Columbia Journal of Gender and Law* 15, 1 (January 1, 2006).

Sanitelli, John, and Mary Ott. "Abstinence and Abstinence-only Programs: A Review of U.S Policies and Programs." *Journal of Adolescent Health* 38 (2006).

Wilson, Kelly L. "A Review of 21 Curricula for Abstinence-only-until-marriage Programs." *Journal of School Health* 75, 3 (March 1, 2005).

Web Sites

Justice Talking. "Abstinence-only Education." lt;http://www.justicetalking.org/viewprogram.asp?progID=426> (accessed March 27, 2006).

United States Department of Labor. "Public Law 104–193." <http://wdr.doleta.gov/readroom/legislation/pdf/104-193.pdf> (accessed March 27, 2006).

Stay-At-Home Parents Top Five Million

Press release

By: U. S. Census Bureau

Date: November 30, 2004

Source: *U.S. Census Bureau News.* "'Stay-At-Home' Parents Top 5 Million, Census Bureau Reports." <http://www.census.gov/Press-Release/www/releases/archives/families_households/003118.html> (accessed March 6, 2006).

About the Author: The first official census in the United States took place in 1790. In 1902, Congress created the United States Census Bureau. The U.S. Census Bureau maintains and distributes statistics related to the demographics in the United States.

INTRODUCTION

In 2003, the U.S. Census Bureau collected data on "stay-at-home" parents for the first time in the bureau's history. A stay-at-home parent is defined as a parent who does not work for income, but provides child care to his or her own children. Historically, in the United States, biological mothers fill this role, although a stay-at-home mother is largely a middle or upper class phenomenon.

Until industrialization took hold in the United States in the 1840s, most families worked on farms together, with the ebb and flow of daily life incorporating the work of the father, mother, and children. With the advent of factory work and rural to urban migration, the family unit and family roles changed. For workers who could obtain skills that provided a high enough wage to support a family on one income, or for the managerial class, industrialization created a new model—the single income family, in which the father worked and the mother stayed at home, raising the children and managing the domestic sphere.

For lower-income and working-class families, however, the mother's factory wages—and often those of the children as well—were critical for family survival. The concept of a stay-at-home parent, therefore, relied on a single income large enough to support a family and was within the reach of only a small sector of society—largely white, middle and upper class, Protestant, non-immigrant families. Within this narrow demographic, the ideal of the mother at home was glorified; the "cult of domesticity" declared a woman's place to be at home, managing a haven for her world-weary husband and nurturing her children so that they would become moral, upstanding citizens.

During World War II, the United States federal government used propaganda campaigns to change the idea of women's proper roles. With hundreds of thousands of men off to war in the Pacific or Europe, the war industries needed workers. African Americans migrated north for the higher paying war industry jobs, but to meet wartime need for munitions and machinery, the U.S. government appealed to women of all classes to work in the factories as well. Three thousand federally funded childcare centers, complete with laundry services and take-home dinners, were created between 1943 and 1944 to help support working mothers. Food, gasoline, car, and tire rationing meant that, while more people had more money, they had few places to spend it. Americans saved, wives worked, and wartime prosperity set the foundation for a new wave of women's domesticity in the 1950s.

When WWII ended, the need for women to work in the factories evaporated, as did the childcare centers and the federal propaganda campaigns. With marriage rates soaring and birth rates climbing, the late 1940s and 1950s saw a return to the cult of domesticity, revised. The wartime savings allowed couples to buy homes, cars, and durable goods, spurring production and economic progress. This financial security allowed more women to fill the role of stay-at-home parent.

The late 1960s and 1970s saw divorce rates climb, mothers entering the workforce in unprecedented numbers, and a wave of feminism that redefined a woman's role. Feminism encouraged a woman to have a career, an income, and an identity outside the home. Feminists such as former 1950s housewife Betty Friedan (1921–2006) and single career woman Gloria Steinem (1934–) put a face on this emerging movement.

By the 1990s, with a majority of mothers of small children in the workforce, questions about the quality of daycare, child development, marital happiness, and women's fulfillment raised the specter of work vs. home once more. The 2003 Census signaled a change in the government's interest in tracking the trend of stay-at-home parents.

PRIMARY SOURCE

The United States had an estimated 5.5 million "stay-at-home" parents last year—5.4 million moms and 98,000 dads, according to a report released today by the U.S. Census Bureau. It contains the Census Bureau's first-ever analysis of stay-at-home parents.

Among these stay-at-home parents, 42 percent of mothers and 29 percent of fathers had their own children under age 3 living with them. Thirty-nine percent of mothers and 30 percent of fathers were under age 35.

Other findings from the report, America's Families and Living Arrangements: 2003:

- After declining sharply between 1970 and 1995, the proportion of family groups with children that were married-couple families has remained stable, at about 68 percent. Since the mid–1990's, the percentages of single mothers and single fathers have also been fairly level. (Family groups are family units living in households; more than one unit may be included. A family group may include the householder and relatives.)

- The median ages at first marriage were 25.3 years for women and 27.1 years for men in 2003, up from 20.8 years and 23.2 years, respectively, in 1970. As a result, the proportion of young, never-married adults has risen dramatically. For women, ages 20 to 24, it more than doubled, from 36 percent to 75 percent; and for women, ages 30 to 34, it more than tripled, from 6 percent to 23 percent.

- Between 1970 and 2003, the average size of the nation's households declined from 3.14 people to 2.57 people.

- In 2003, 10 percent of the nation's households contained five or more people, down from 21 percent in 1970. Sixty percent of households had one or two people in 2003, up from 46 percent in 1970.

- The proportion of households consisting of one person living alone increased from 17 percent in 1970 to 26 percent in 2003.

- There were 4.6 million opposite-sex, unmarried-partner households in 2003. These households accounted for 4.2 percent of all households, up from 2.9 percent in 1996.

- In unmarried-partner households, 29 percent of women had higher levels of education than their partners, compared with 22 percent of wives in married-couple households.

The data are from the 2003 Current Population Survey's (CPS) Annual Social and Economic Supplement (ASEC). The ASEC supplement to the CPS is conducted in February, March and April at about 100,000 addresses nationwide. For further information on the source of the data and accuracy of the estimates, including standard errors and confidence intervals, go to Appendix G of <http://www.census.gov/apsd/techdoc/cps/cpsmar03.pdf>.

SIGNIFICANCE

By the late 1990s, the first generation of children raised by families affected by the demographic trends of the late 1960s and 1970s—including higher divorce rates, single parent households, mothers in the workforce, and daycare center care for small children—emerged as parents themselves. Two different ideals competed for attention in the media in the United States; the mother as career woman, managing children, marriage, and full-time professional work, vs. the stay-at-home mother, focused on the domestic sphere, raising children without child care.

The "Mommy Wars," a title given by the media to the alleged conflict between mothers who work outside the home and those who stay at home, painted each side as bitterly opposed to the other, alternately envious and dismissive of each other's choice. Critics charged mothers who worked with letting day care centers raise their children, while stay at home mothers—especially those with graduate or professional degrees—were allegedly shortchanging themselves and the feminists who worked hard for increased workplace rights and were harming their long-term financial prospects for retirement.

Stay-at-home fathers, representing a tiny portion of all stay-at-home parents, received spotty coverage from the media. The 1982 movie *Mr. Mom*, which depicted a stay-at-home father who came to the role via unemployment, created a comic stereotype for fathers who took on the traditional mother's role. According to the 2003 Census numbers, 98,000 fathers identify themselves as stay-at-home parents, though organizations, such as At Home Dad, state that between two and three million fathers spend more than thirty hours per week as their child's primary caregiver.

The inclusion of stay-at-home parents in the census relates to a political issue championed by activists in the United States—Social Security credits for stay-at-home parents. According to Mothers and More, an advocacy group, mothers spend an average of 11.5 years out of the workforce caring for children or other family members. This unpaid labor carries a collective economic impact of as much as forty-seven percent of GDP in Australia, forty-four percent of GDP in the United Kingdom, and nearly fifty percent of GDP in the United States.

Betty Mitas, a stay-at-home mom, spending time with her son and friends. © GAIL ALBERT HALABAN/CORBIS

Advocates for public policy recognition for stay-at-home parents and their contribution to the economy through unpaid labor argue that giving stay-at-home parents credits toward Social Security for their time spent at home would cut the "parent penalty" and give recognition to the economic role such parenting plays in society.

FURTHER RESOURCES

Books

Crittendon, Anne. *The Price of Motherhood.* New York: Owl Books, 2002.

Periodicals

Wallis, Claudia. "The Case for Staying Home." *Time* 163 (May 22, 2004): 259–276.

Web sites

At Home Dad. <http://www.athomedad.com> (accessed March 6, 2006).

Mothers And More. <http://www.mothersandmore.com> (accessed March 6, 2006).

World Illiteracy Rates by Region and Gender 2000–2004

Graph

By: UNESCO Institute for Statistics

Date: 2004

Source: UNESCO Institute for Statistics. "World Illiteracy Rates by Region and Gender 2000–2004." <http://www.uis.unesco.org/ev/> (accessed April 1, 2006).

About the Author: Established on November 16, 1945, the main objective of the United Nations Educational, Scientific and Cultural Organization (UNESCO) is to contribute to peace and security in the world through education, science, and culture. The UNESCO Institute for Statistics (UIS)—a statistical branch of the UNESCO—was formed in July 1999 to provide a wider range of policy-relevant, timely, and reliable statistics. The Institute collects and interprets statistical information on topics such as Technology, Communication, Education, and so forth. Such information is then used by member countries to assess their current programs and determine future policies. The UIS is located in Montreal, Canada.

INTRODUCTION

UNESCO has defined literacy as the ability of an individual to read, write, and understand simple statements pertaining to everyday life. However, this definition has broadened over a period of time. It is now commonly accepted that literacy should essentially mean functional skills that can be used in everyday life, such as the ability to read a bus schedule or to calcu-

late daily wages. Article 26 of the Universal Declaration of Human Rights, 1948, states that everyone has the right to education and that it shall be directed to the full development of the human personality and to the strengthening of respect for human rights and fundamental freedom. However, most regions of the world face gender discrimination in education.

A report published by the UNESCO Institute for Statistics (UIS) in 2006 stated that surveys conducted in the previous year indicated that two thirds of an estimated 771 million illiterate adults in the world are women. Over the years, there has been significant disparity between the literacy rates of men and women. According to UNESCO's World Education Report of 1995, the worldwide male literacy rate in 1985 was 72.2 percent as opposed to 61.9 percent for females. Although the literacy rates improved by 1995, the discrepancy between male and female literacy was similar. In 2005, the difference was almost the same with little or no progress made to ensure higher level of female literacy.

Past surveys suggest that a few regions have substantially higher disparity than others. These mainly

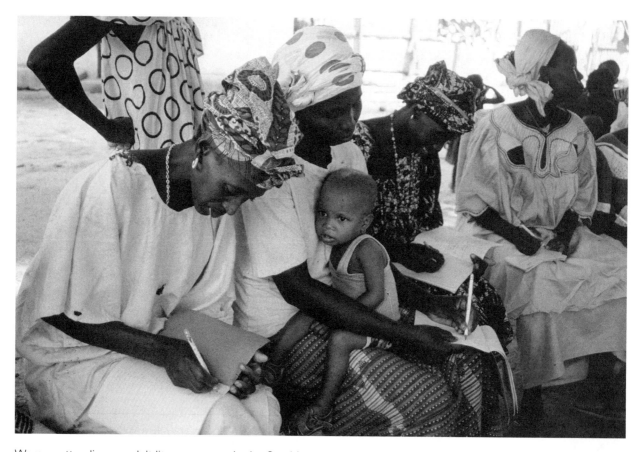

Women attending an adult literacy course in the Gambia. © LIBA TAYLOR/CORBIS

include Arab and Asian countries. For instance, according the above-mentioned report from UNESCO, in 1985, the male literacy rate in Arab countries was fifty-five percent as compared to a low 26.2 percent for women. In 1995, the literacy rates were 68.4 percent and 44.2 percent for men and women respectively. Similarly, Asian countries such as China and India also have low literacy rates for women—in 1995, the literacy rate for women was 37.7 percent compared to 65.5 percent for men.

Furthermore, half of the entire female population in South and West Asia, sub-Saharan Africa and the Arab States is illiterate. As of 2003, at least nine million more girls than boys are unable to get basic education.

The primary source is a UIS graph, for the years 2000 to 2004, signifying the disparity between the illiteracy rates of men and women. An important factor highlighted in this graph is the obvious gender disparity observed in terms of education in developing countries.

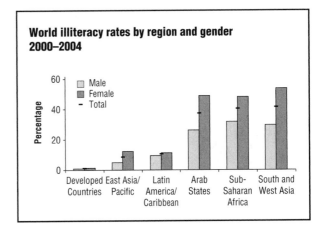

World Illiteracy Rates by Region and Gender 2000–2004: A bar graph from UNESCO showing the illiteracy rates by gender throughout the world. UNITED NATIONS EDUCATIONAL, SCIENTIFIC AND CULTURAL ORGANIZATION.

■ **PRIMARY SOURCE**

WORLD ILLITERACY RATES BY REGION AND GENDER 2000–2004

See primary source image.

■

SIGNIFICANCE

International development efforts have not been successful in ensuring basic primary education to girls in many countries. Despite several corrective measures and policies, government and non-governmental organizations the world over have found that gender disparity in education continues to grow at alarming rates, especially in developing countries.

An extensive study conducted by the Education Group of Food and Agricultural Organization (FAO) of the United Nations cites several reasons for the widening gap between male and female illiteracy. The report indicates that standard approach to achieving universal education has backfired because it assumed that common efforts to enroll more children would benefit all children equally. This assumption failed to take into consideration specific barriers faced by girls.

The report alludes to poverty as a primary reason for low literacy among women. In many under-developed or developing countries, children are not sent to school as parents can barely afford to provide them basic food and shelter. Moreover, conservative socio-economic outlook prevents them from sending girls to school, even if basic education is made affordable through government incentives.

Gender inequality typecasts females to be fit for household work and childcare. A male child is perceived as someone who would eventually provide financial support to the families. Consequently, more emphasis is placed on education of boys. Discriminatory policies by employers result in lower wages for women, further discouraging women to get educated. The report also mentions that organizational hurdles such as lack of female-only schools, or female instructors, prevent conservative parents from allowing their female children to go to school.

Educational inequality affects countries in more than one way. According to UIS, countries with low school enrollment ratio for girls have lower GDP per capita (lower income per person). Studies conducted by the World Bank, UNESCO, and the United Nations Development Program (UNDP) indicate lower fertility rates and higher family planning in families comprising women with at least basic education. With higher female literacy rate, infant mortality rates are also expected to go down as mothers who have even basic education are more likely to have healthy children. Moreover, education gives women greater earning power, which, in turn, translates into better living standards. Education of women in rural areas ensures higher productivity in traditional sectors such as agriculture.

A 12-year-old girl teaches other children how to read and write at during the Campaign for Elimination of Illiteracy in San Rafael. © MICHAEL PHILIPPOT/SYGMA/CORBIS

It is for these reasons, female education is critical. Elizabeth Dowdswell, then UN Under-Secretary General (UNEP-HABITAT) stated in 1995 that "Women are vital to our vision of a sustainable future. They are the guardians of natural wisdom in their societies; they are often the principal ecosystem managers of their communities. They are the first educators, and can do the most to change the habits and beliefs of a new generation… That is why the single most important step towards sustainable living that governments can take… is the education of women."

It is important that education is approached as a human right rather than a privilege or an expected outcome of economic progress. Over the years, several steps have been taken by the United Nations and policymakers all over the world to eradicate gender-based illiteracy. Most of the developed countries have invested millions of dollars to develop new educational assessment tools such as the Adult Literacy and Life Skills Survey (ALL). The UIS has developed the Literacy Assessment and Monitoring Program (LAMP) with international agencies and technical experts. By using customized assessment techniques that use local resources, participating countries can formulate an action plan that focuses on improvement of female literacy rates.

Although such programs have yielded some success, female literacy levels are almost stagnant in most countries. Experts say that the outcome could be a serious loss of human capital, and damage to the social and democratic framework, which in turn, would impair the health and education of the next generation. As UNICEF Executive Director, Carol Bellamy, at the time of releasing UNICEF's report—The State of the World's Children—stated, "We stand no chance of substantially reducing poverty, child mortality, HIV/AIDS and other diseases if we do not ensure that all girls can exercise their right to a basic education. In daily life, knowledge makes the crucial difference."

FURTHER RESOURCES

Web sites

Food and Agriculture Organization of the United States. "Higher Agricultural Education and Opportunities in Rural Development for Women—An Overview and Summary of Five Case-studies." <http://www.fao.org/documents/show_cdr.asp?url_file=/docrep/W6038E/W6038E00.htm> (accessed April 1, 2006).

Social Watch. "Unkept Promises." <http://www.globalpolicy.org/socecon/inequal/gender/2005/06unkept-promises.pdf> (accessed April 1, 2006).

UNESCO Institute for Statistics. "How Does Gender Inequity Relate to National Income?" <http://www.uis.unesco.org/ev./> (accessed April 1, 2006).

——— "Statistics Show Slow Progress Towards Universal Literacy." <http://www.uis.unesco.org/ev./> (accessed April 1, 2006).

UNICEF. "UNICEF Says Getting More Girls into School is First Step to Reaching Global Development Goals." <http://www.unicef.org/sowc04/sowc04_16165.html> (accessed April 1, 2006).

Gene Robinson Becomes First Openly Gay Episcopal Bishop

Photograph

By: Lee Marriner

Date: March 7, 2004

Source: The Associated Press

About the Photographer: Lee K. Marriner is a photojournalist based in Belmont, New Hampshire and makes frequent contributions of news and sports photographs to the Associated Press.

INTRODUCTION

The Episcopal or Anglican Church is a union of national churches forming the third largest Christian denomination in the world, with about seventy-seven million members. Anglicanism combines features of Protestantism and of Roman Catholicism and is governed primarily by its bishops, hence its name ("episcopal" means "of or having to do with bishops"). In March 2004, an openly homosexual priest of the Episcopal Church, U.S.A., Vicki Imogene Robinson ("Gene" Robinson) was consecrated as the ninth bishop of the Diocese of New Hampshire. The deci-

sion to consecrate Robinson aroused intense controversy among the Episcopal churches; conservative members, both in the United States and abroad, viewed the decision as an abandonment of traditional Christian doctrine, which has characterized homosexuality as sinful. The controversy threatened to split the church in two after almost 600 years of organizational unity.

Gene Robinson received a Master of Divinity degree from the Episcopal Church's theological seminary in New York in 1973. During his seminary time, he sought psychotherapy to cure himself of homosexual feelings. He married in 1972 and had two daughters with his wife before divorcing in 1986. Robinson is monogamously partnered with a New Hampshire man named Mark Andrews. He was elected bishop by the members of his New Hampshire diocese (a geographical unit of church organization) in 2003, but his election had to be ratified by the Episcopal General Convention, the governing body of the Episcopal Church U.S.A. (which meets every three years). Despite much controversy, the Convention voted to confirm Robinson. He became bishop of New Hampshire on March 7, 2004.

■ PRIMARY SOURCE

GENE ROBINSON BECOMES FIRST OPENLY GAY EPISCOPAL BISHOP

See primary source image.

■

SIGNIFICANCE

Robinson's consecration as bishop has threatened both the Episcopal Church U.S.A. and the larger global communion of which it is a part, the Anglican Church, with schism (religious division into separate churches). Many conservatives, both in the U.S. and elsewhere, do not accept the idea of an openly homosexual, noncelibate man being a bishop of the church. Particularly strong resistance to the acceptance of Robinson's appointment has been voiced by many of the Episcopal churches of Africa. In a historic reversal, the church that began as a strictly English institution has, as a result of its own missionary efforts, become a global institution, and the formerly majority-white, majority-European/American organization is now overwhelmingly Third World and nonwhite in membership. Moreover, these Third World churches tend to be much more theologically and socially conservative than the European and American churches from which they sprung.

PRIMARY SOURCE

Gene Robinson Becomes First Openly Gay Episcopal Bishop: Gene Robinson becomes the first openly gay bishop of the Episcopal Church, U.S.A. He is being given a crosier (shepherd's crook) carved by a Palestinian shepherd by the outgoing bishop of New Hampshire, Douglas E. Theuner (right). AP IMAGES

For example, the Bishops of the Anglican province of the Democratic Republic of Congo issued a statement on January 5, 2004 regarding "homosexuality and blessings of same-sex unions within the Anglican Communion." In the statement, the Congolese bishops specifically mentioned the consecration of Gene Robinson, along with the ordination to priesthood of "actively gay and lesbian people" and "the use of the newly devised Prayer Book published by the Diocese of New Westminster/Canada for the purpose of officiating the blessing of same-sex marriages." They stated that these acts "clearly and deliberately misrepresent the Word of God" and various resolutions and findings of the Anglican church and further declared that "the Anglican Province of Congo strongly condemns homosexuality and wishes to disassociate itself from relations with Dioceses and Parishes involved in homosexuality." The bishops stated their view that "active homosexuality" is "ravaging the western world." The Archbishop of Nigeria spoke separately of "the reality that a small, economically privileged group of people has sought to subvert the Christian faith and impose their new and false doctrine on the wider community of faithful believers." Nigeria alone has about eight times as many Episcopalians as does the United States.

In October, 2004, an official report was issued by a church commission, the Windsor Commission, which had been convened in an effort to stave off breakup of the global church. The church recommended a moratorium until at least 2006 on the consecration of gay bishops and on public ceremonies blessing or marrying same-sex couples. At a meeting held in February, 205, however, most of the heads of the thirty-eight Anglican Provinces (national churches) agreed in essence to reject the Windsor Report's wait-and-see approach and asked that the Episcopal Church, U.S.A. and the Anglican Church of Canada withdraw from the Anglican Consultative Council (a body through which the 38 national churches communicate) until at least 2008, when a conference of all bishops of the global Anglican church is scheduled to occur in England.

The Methodist Church and other "mainstream" churches are also afflicted by debate between liberal and conservative members over the permissibility of homosexuality. Homosexuality is not condoned by any Fundamentalist or Evangelical branches of Christianity, nor by the Roman Catholic or Orthodox churches.

FURTHER RESOURCES

Web sites

AmericanAnglican.org "A Statement from the Primates gathered at the first African Anglican Bishop's Conference held in Lagos, Nigeria, October 2004." <http://www.americananglican.org/site/apps/nl/> (accessed April 4, 2006).

Goodstein, Laurie. "Gay Episcopal Bishop Sees Glint of Hope in Church Report." *New York Times* . Oct. 21, 2004. Available at <http://www.americananglican.org/site/apps/nl/> (accessed April 4, 2006).

Public Broadcasting Service (PBS): Religion and Ethics Newsweekly. "Interview with Gene Robinson, Oct. 31, 2003." <http://www.pbs.org/wnet/religionandethics/week709/exclusive.html> (accessed April 4, 2006).

Only Fun For Stay-at-Home Dad

Internet article

By: Tracy Smith

Date: August 3, 2005

Source: Smith, Tracy. "Only Fun for Stay-at-Home Dad." *CBSNews*, August 3, 2005. <http://www.cbsnews.com/stories/2005/08/03/earlyshow/series/main713664.shtml> (accessed March 6, 2006).

About the Author: Tracy Smith is a correspondent with CBS News and a co-anchor for *The Saturday Early Show* and a national correspondent with *The Early Show* on CBS.

INTRODUCTION

While the concept of a stay-at-home mother—a mother who provides full-time childcare for her own children—has been a cultural norm for the middle and upper classes in the United States throughout the twentieth century, the idea of a stay-at-home father is new. Before industrialization, fathers presided over the family as head of household and was part of his children's daily life, as the family unit worked together and lived together in rural settings as an economic unit.

With industrialization and the concept of a "family wage," skilled workers and members of the managerial class were able to work in factory and office settings, earning enough with one income to support a wife who stayed at home to raise the children and manage the household. A stay-at-home father—one who nurtured and raised children while attending to and managing the domestic sphere—was an aberration or a role played by men who were temporarily out of work, filling this role while searching for another job.

In the United States, the first major public attention to the idea of a stay-at-home father came in 1983, with the release of the feature film *Mr. Mom.* Starring Terri Garr and Michael Keaton, the movie examined a family in which the father lost his engineering job, and the stay-at-home mother returned to full-time work, leaving the father in charge of three young children and the house.

The movie depicted the father as bumbling, inept, and incompetent, and a poor substitute for the mother's skill. By the end of the movie, the father had mastered the new role of stay-at-home parent and household manager, but the phrase "Mr. Mom" has become synonymous with a stay-at-home father as a comic figure who cannot manage.

There are no historical figures or estimates for numbers of stay-at-home fathers; the U.S. Census Bureau began recording self-reported stay-at-home fathers in 2003.

■ PRIMARY SOURCE

In this week's My New Life segment, National Correspondent Tracy Smith went to Bethesda, Md., to meet a dad who made the decision to quit his job and raise his children, even though he was making more money than his wife. This Mr. Mom has very specific ideas on how it's done.

Mike Paranzino used to wear a tie. But he's traded his high-powered job on Capitol Hill for racing cars with 4-

year-old son Cameron and changing the diapers of the lovely Emily, who is 4 months old.

"I had a happy childhood," Paranzino says, "I had a wonderful childhood. Close to my parents and close to my brothers. And I wanted to try and recreate that for my children."

Paranzino, who prefers the title "full-time father," says he is never home. While wife Heather goes off to her job as a scientist, he heads outdoors to playgrounds and parks, making friends with both moms and kids.

He says, "I stashed enough diapers, enough water, enough formula, enough snack. We've done six, we've done eight hours out straight."

His biggest stress, he says, is keeping it fresh till mommy gets home.

"You have ten hours a day you have to fill," he notes, "You have to keep it interesting. And original. So that can be stressful."

But Mike Paranzino's definition of full-time father-hood doesn't include cooking or cleaning. His entire day is spent with the kids.

He notes, "There's a Yellow Pages filled with companies that want to clean your house, cut your grass. They want to cook your food. I signed on to raise the kids, not to clean the house."

No sweeping? No laundry?

"Where can I sign up?" asks Jen Singer and her crew of stay-at-home moms. They applaud Mike Paranzino's choice. But isn't housework part of the gig?

"If I didn't have to think about the housework, this would be like a big vacation," Singer says. Paranzino says, "Maybe it's a giant ruse or hoax that the men over the centuries have foisted upon woman. But I don't buy it. I don't see any inherent reason, any natural reason why, because you're focused on raising the children during the day that also means you have to clean the toilets."

Laughing, stay-at-home mom Marybeth Vazquez says, "It would be wonderful. I would probably have more children."

At 39, Mike Paranzino has saved enough money to hire a maid service, and he says they are sacrificing fancy cars and vacations. But the group of stay-at-home moms says even if they had the money, they could never get away with it.

"When I see the mess, I will just naturally clean it up," Eisha Locascio says. "I notice when my husband comes home, and he sees the mess, he'll ask me to clean it up."

But Mike Paranzino says the mess is not important.

He advises, "Show him where the detergent is and say, 'You do it, because I'm focused on the kids. I'm going to go read the children a book instead of doing the laundry.'"

Singer says, "He's a trail blazer; but he's a trail blazer with a staff."

Trail blazer or not, Paranzino has had some uphill battles, especially early on.

"It took me about 14 months to really get comfortable in my skin," he says. "I did feel isolated for the first year, and I used to sort of feel a need to tell people: 'Well, I do some consulting.' I think it was a macho thing."

As for his friends that are not full-time dads, Paranzino says, "They think it is amusing: the play dates with all the moms. Even though I spend my days with beautiful moms and nannies, I mean, there are kids around. Let's just keep it clear."

So joking about the play date only goes so far.

He says, "There's more sexual tension on the metro than there is at playgrounds."

Paranzino does try to make time for his advocacy work, which he says keeps him sane. Otherwise it's 100 percent all kids all the time.

"Dads can do this," he says. "It doesn't have to be mom home with the kids. Dads can do it."

And as long as the kids like take-out food, life is good.

Before you send your e-mails, Smith notes that many stay-at-home dads do housework.

The census says that 98,000 dads make a deliberate decision to stay home, but there could be up to a million fathers home with the kids because they are unemployed or disabled, so there are more out there than you'd think.

SIGNIFICANCE

The 2003 figures reported by the U.S. Census Bureau show that 5.4 million parents in the U.S. identified themselves as stay-at-home parents; 5.3 million mothers and 98,000 fathers. Stay-at home-father groups, such as At Home Dad, estimate that as many as two to three million fathers spend more than thirty hours per week as their child's primary caregiver, an estimate far in excess of the official census count.

While unemployed fathers have entered into stay-at-home status temporarily in the past, more fathers in the post-Baby Boom generation are making stay-at-home parenting a valid choice when attempting to balance work/life issues. The archetype of the American stay-at-home mother includes a mom who per-

Travis Clubb, center, plays with his son Preston , 4, right, and daughter Jordan, 3. Clubb is a stay-at-home dad and his wife is a full-time attorney AP IMAGES

forms full-time childcare and all household cleaning and management; stay-at-home fathers, like Mike Paranzino in this article, often eschew the drudgery of the domestic sphere in an attempt to define stay-at-home parenting with the focus on parenting, rather than domestic life. Modern magazines such as *Ladies Home Journal*, *Redbook*, and *Family Circle*, as well as websites such as Organized Home, address at-home mothers with articles on housework, organization, decluttering, and a host of household management issues that imply—or overtly state—that a stay-at-home mother's job includes much more than child care and that these domestic issues come with the choice to remain at home.

Stay-at-home fathers, however, spend less time than stay-at-home mothers on household management and cleaning. Their wives, working full-time, spend more time on household and cleaning issues

than do their male full-time working counterparts in marriages with a stay-at-home wife.

According to media reports in 2004 and 2005, twenty-two percent of mothers with graduate and professional degrees choose to stay at home. Feminist groups point to this choice as a step backwards for women's rights, while fathers who choose to stay at home receive media coverage as oddities or as human interest stories. The disparity between the approaches, expectations, and assumptions about stay-at-home mothers vs. stay-at-home fathers rarely receives media coverage. As the number of fathers who stay at home increases, stay-at-home fathering becomes more mainstream, and census data track these social changes, stay-at-home fathers will contribute to the gender role debate in the United States.

FURTHER RESOURCES

Books

Crittendon, Anne. *The Price of Motherhood.* New York: Owl Books, 2002.

Peters, Elizabeth H., and Randal D. Day, editors. *Fatherhood: Research, Interventions, and Policies.* Binghamton, N.Y.: Haworth Press, 2000.

Periodicals

Wallis, Claudia. "The Case for Staying Home" *Time* 163 (May 22, 2004): 259–276.

Web sites

At Home Dad. <http://www.athomedad.com> (accessed March 6, 2006).

Mothers And More. <http://www.mothersandmore.com> (accessed March 6, 2006).

National Fatherhood Initiative. <http://www.fatherhood.org> (accessed March 6, 2006).

Controversy Colors Teen Book

Newspaper article

By: Carol Memmott

Date: May 22, 2005

Source: Memmott, Carol. "Controversy Colors Teen Book" *USA Today*, May 22, 2005. <http://www.usatoday.com/life/books/news/2005-05-22-rainbow-usat_x.htm> (accessed March 14, 2006).

About the Author: Carol Memmott is a staff writer for *USA Today*. Established in September 1982, *USA Today* is one of the most popular newspapers in the United States. It was started with a goal of providing entertaining news with colorful photographs and graphics. The newspaper established itself within a year, selling more than 1.3 million copies a day all across the nation. As of 2006, its daily circulation is approximately 2.3 million, making it the largest-selling daily newspaper in the United States.

INTRODUCTION

Since the 1970s and 1980s, numerous surveys have been conducted to gather diverse information about adolescent sexual activity in United States. Most of these studies reveal that children as young as ten or eleven years old become sexually active and indulge in unsafe sexual practices. Consequently, there has been an increase in pregnancy rate, sexually transmitted diseases, and other psychological as well as physical problems among teenagers.

An increasing number of teenagers are involved in oral sex as compared to intercourse. The National Center for Health Statistics (NHCS) states that about ten percent of females, between fifteen and nineteen years of age, have engaged in oral sex but not intercourse. Among the many reasons for such practices are instant thrill and gratification, peer pressure, and most commonly a misconception that oral sex is a safe alternative to intercourse, as it involves no risk of pregnancy. An April 1997 *New York Times* article noted that high school students who had been educated about sex, HIV, and pregnancy considered oral sex to be a safe option, in both physical and emotional terms. The *Washington Post* also published an article in a July 1999 issue that emphasized the high prevalence of oral sex among middle and high school students. According to a study conducted by the NHCS in 2005, more than half of teenagers, aged fifteen and above, have engaged in oral sex.

Medical experts state that although oral sex does not lead to pregnancy, it may expose teenagers to various sexually transmitted diseases (STDs). According to a survey by the Center for Disease Control and Prevention (CDC), at least one in twenty teenaged girls have chlamydia—an STD. In many cases, this infection has been transmitted by oral sex. Yet, most teens are completely unaware of the risks involved in unsafe oral sex. In addition, most parents find it difficult to discuss oral sex with their children, fearing that it would only add to their curiosity. On the other hand, there are some who feel that talking to children about general safe-sex guidelines and pregnancy should suffice.

Apart from newspaper articles, books about the hazards of sexual practices perceived to be safe have also been published. The *USA Today* article discusses one such book titled *Rainbow Party*. Written by young adult fiction writer Paul Ruditis in 2003, the novel is about teenage girls who plan to perform oral sex at a "rainbow party." The article discusses the controversy surrounding the book.

■ **PRIMARY SOURCE**

A battle could be brewing in the book stacks over a new novel about teens and oral sex.

Rainbow Party, aimed at the teen market (ages 14 and up), has some booksellers and librarians wondering whether author Paul Ruditis sensationalizes the subject—and, more significantly, whether they should carry it on their shelves.

"Parents count on us to have books that are appropriate for their children," says Monica Holmes of Hicklebee's Books in San Jose, Calif. "We're not a conservative group, but this one is outside our safe area."

Elly Gore, a buyer for Harry W. Schwartz Bookshops in Milwaukee, concedes that the book is "edgy" but will stock it mainly because, she says, "I knew that if I skipped it, I would have been censoring it. ... I couldn't do that."

Two of the large chains—Barnes & Noble and Borders—will sell the book online but not stock it in their stores.

"This was one our buyers thought wasn't likely to be of interest to the bulk of our customer base," says Borders spokeswoman Anne Roman.

Rainbow Party, (Simon & Schuster, $8.99) is about a group of teens who plan an oral-sex party at which each of the girls wears a different color of lipstick.

Ruditis says the book was never meant to sensationalize sex parties. "We just wanted to present an issue kids are dealing with," he says.

Bethany Buck, Ruditis' editor at Simon & Schuster, came up with the idea for the book and says she hopes it will "scare" young readers.

Suzanne Kelly, a buyer for the Chester County Book and Music Co. in West Chester, Pa., which will stock a limited number of *Rainbow*, agrees. She says the book's message that oral sex "really is sex" and that teens can contract STDs through such sexual practices far outweigh the controversial story line.

"I can't imagine anyone reading this book and saying, 'Hey, what a great idea. Let's send out invitations,'" Ruditis says.

Gillian Engburg, an editor at the American Library Association's *Booklist* magazine, says her publication will not review *Rainbow*. But the reason, she says, has nothing to do with the subject matter. "We just didn't feel the book had enough literary merit to justify purchase."

SIGNIFICANCE

The novel *Rainbow Party* is a fictional account of two fourteen-year-old girls who plan a "rainbow party," wherein girls wearing different colored lipsticks perform oral sex on several boys in sequence, thus leaving a "rainbow" of colors on the recipient's penis. However, as news of an epidemic of STDs creates mass panic in their school, the girls abandon their

plan to organize the party. The book attempts to portray the common notion existing among teenagers that oral sex is casual and safe. There is no evidence to suggest that teens actually participate in "rainbow parties," but, as mentioned earlier, the prevalence of oral sex among teenagers (and pre-teens) is much higher than sexual intercourse.

According to the author Paul Ruditis, this novel is designed to "scare" teenagers by showing them the "dangerous side" of oral sex. Moreover, the author also suggests that the book is an eye-opener and aimed at motivating parents and schools to educate teenagers about oral sex through constructive dialog. Soon after it was published, the book generated considerable controversy.

Rainbow Party received extensive media coverage after popular talk show host Oprah Winfrey included it in an October 2003 show on teenage sexual behavior in the United States. Some critics have condemned the book, stating that it did not successfully accomplish its educational purpose. Terming the incidents depicted as shocking and exaggerated, they questioned whether teenagers, after reading the book, would feel repulsed by oral sex. Atoosa Rubenstein, Editor-in-Chief of *Seventeen* magazine, in an interview with CNN stated that he had never heard of any girl attending a "rainbow party." He also suggested that parents should use such books as a reference for discussing oral sex with their teens instead of relying on books alone without discussion. Although the publisher recommends *Rainbow Party* for ages fourteen and up, many critics feel that the content is inappropriate for such young readers. Consequently, the book has not sold well, and some bookstores and libraries have refused to sell it or include it in their collections.

FURTHER RESOURCES
Web sites
About.com. "Teens and Oral Sex...There are Risks." <http://aids.about.com/od/childrenteens/a/teensoral.htm> (accessed March 14, 2006).

CNN.com. "Teens in America." <http://transcripts.cnn.com/TRANSCRIPTS/0407/08/i_ins.01.html> (accessed March 14, 2006).

Guttmacher Institute. "Oral Sex Among Adolescents: Is It Sex or Is It Abstinence?" <http://www.guttmacher.org/pubs/journals/3229800.html> (accessed March 14, 2006).

National Center for Health Statistics. "Sexual Behavior and Selected Health Measures: Men and Women 15–44 Years of Age, United States, 2002." <http://www.cdc.gov/nchs/products/pubs/pubd/ad/361-370/ad362.htm> (accessed March 14, 2006).

USA Today. "Teens Define Sex in New Ways." <http://www.usatoday.com/news/health/2005-10-18-teens-sex_x.htm> (accessed March 14, 2006).

Washington Post. "Study: Half of All Teens Have Had Oral Sex." <http://www.washingtonpost.com/wp-dyn/content/article/2005/09/15/AR2005091500915.html> (accessed March 14, 2006).

Soldiers in the Mixed Gender IDF Karakul Combat Infantry Brigade Complete Their Basic Training

Photograph

By: Anonymous

Date: December 15, 2005

Source: Getty Images

About the Photographer: This photograph is part of the collection at Getty Images, a worldwide provider of visual content materials to such communications groups as advertisers, broadcasters, designers, magazines, new media organizations, newspapers, and producers. The photographer is not known.

INTRODUCTION

In 1948, when Israel began to fight its War of Independence, the majority of the Jewish population of Palestine was mobilized to fight against surrounding Arab forces. The original military volunteer youth organization was called Palmach. A forerunner to the present day Israeli Defense Force (IDF), the organization was based on egalitarian and socialist principles. As a result, combat forces included both men and women. However, women began to be excluded from combat roles in 1950.

By 1959, the Defense Service Law was passed to regulate the obligation of service for all Israeli citizens and permanent residents of Israel. According to the law, all women between the ages of eighteen and twenty-six, who are physically fit, unmarried with no children, and without religious objections must serve one year and nine months in the IDF. Men serve three years.

In 1995, Alice Miller brought a suit to the Israeli Supreme Court petitioning for admittance into military flight school. As a result, the Defense Service Law was amended to enable women recruits to serve in combat related units. The law allows women to serve in the police force, border police, and paramilitary border police. In 1999, the IDF announced that women would begin serving as combat soldiers along the Egyptian and Jordanian borders. This unit, called the Karakal Company, serves as a border patrol company in search of drug smugglers and terrorist infiltrators. The mixed gender company operates under the Nahal Brigade.

The Nahal Brigade was established during the War of Independence in 1948 by David Ben-Gurion (1886–1973), leader of the struggle to establish the state of Israel, and Nahal is a Hebrew acronym for *Naor Halutzi Lohem*, or the Fighting Pioneer Youth. Ben-Gurion stated, "The Army is the supreme symbol of duty, and as long as women are not equal to men in performing this duty, they have not yet obtained true equality. If the daughters of Israel are absent from the army, then the character of the Yishuv (Jewish community in Israel) will be distorted." The mission of the Nahal Brigade is to ensure border and settlement security. By 2004, approximately 450 women were in combat units. Those recruited for combat units are required to serve thirty months rather than the twenty-one months required of non-combat female recruits.

PRIMARY SOURCE

SOLDIERS IN THE MIXED GENDER IDF KARAKUL COMBAT INFANTRY BRIGADE COMPLETE THEIR BASIC TRAINING
See primary source image.

SIGNIFICANCE

From 1950 through the 1990s, women in the Israeli Defense Force were relegated to instructor positions. Women served in non-combat related roles, conducting most of the training and served in the Mossad—the Israeli intelligence service. However, since the 1995 amendment of the Defense Service Law, female soldiers can also serve in combat status in mixed-gender units, such as artillery, anti aircraft corps in the Surface to Air Missiles (SAM) elements, Combat Engineering corps in the Atomic Biological Chemical (ABC) unit, military Police (Sachlav)— stationed in the Occupied Territories, usually in Hebron, in the border police, as air crew including fighter pilots, and as naval officers.

The presence of women in combat brigades and units has not been without controversy. In 2003, a report commissioned by the Israeli General Staff rec-

PRIMARY SOURCE

Soldiers in the Mixed Gender IDF Karakul Combat Infantry Brigade Complete Their Basic Training: During training male and female Israeli soldiers run through the night carrying a comrade on a stretcher during training in Negev Desert, Israel, on December 14, 2005. PHOTO BY IDF VIA GETTY IMAGES

ommended that women should be excluded from combat related fields. The study determined that women can safely carry around forty percent of their body weight, compared to men who are able to carry about fifty-five percent of their body weight. As women, on average, weigh thirty-three pounds less than men, men can usually carry forty-four pounds more than women. In addition, the amount of oxygen-carrying hemoglobin in the blood of men is usually up to ten percent higher than those found in women. This limits the amount of physical training possible for women. The study found that men could be trained on marches up to fifty-five miles, compared to women, who could train on marches up to thirty-two miles. The physicians that completed the study recommended that women be barred from front-line infantry units, tank crews, artillery units, and as combat engineers with heavy equipment. The physicians

offered no objections to women serving in light infantry units along peacetime borders (such as the Karakal unit), in anti-aircraft missile units, as air force pilots, or as naval officers.

Also in 2003, at a graduation for the Karakal (or Caracal) company, the company's platoon commander was a woman, Sergeant Annabelle. After leading her company through the training she was named "Best Platoon Commander." Upon her graduation she stated, "The exams I had to pass in order to get into the company were both physical and psychotechnic [a test that measures logic and intelligence]…Boys and girls in the mixed company undergo exactly the same training. Girls carry stretchers and water cans as well as their weapons during training. Some girls even have to help boys who find the training exercises difficult. I

Sgt. Leigh Ann Hester, vehicle commander, U.S. 617th Military Police Company stands at attention before receiving the Silver Star during an awards ceremony at Camp Liberty in Baghdad, Iraq on June 16, 2005. Hester was the first female to receive the Silver Star since World War II. AP IMAGES

am very happy with the level of equality in the company; the girls here prove their worth."

FURTHER RESOURCES

Web sites

Israeli Defense Force. "I Am Thrilled That the IDF Has Given Me the Opportunity to Give of Myself." <http://www1.idf.il/DOVER/site/> (accessed March 25, 2006).

Jewish Virtual Library. "Women and Special Forces." <http://www.jewishvirtuallibrary.org/jsource/Society_&_Culture/womidf.html> (accessed March 25, 2006).

Mahal 2000. "IDF Background information." <http://www.mahal2000.com/information/background/content.htm#women> (accessed March 25, 2006).

Washington Times. "Israeli Women Won't See Combat." <http://www.washingtontimes.com/world/20031020-122552-3754r.htm> (accessed March 25, 2006).

Strangers! Non-Members in the Parliamentary Chamber

Government report

By: Ian Holland

Date: April 15, 2003

Source: Holland, Ian. *Strangers! Non-Members in the Parliamentary Chamber.* Current Issues Brief no. 25 2002-03, April 15, 2003.

About the Author: Dr. Ian Holland earned the Richard Baker Senate Prize for 2005 for excellence in writing regarding the Australian Senate.

INTRODUCTION

Humans, as mammals, produce young who are completely dependent on human breast milk for survival. Until the invention of artificial baby milk in the 1860s in Switzerland, the only safe method for feeding infants was breastfeeding. While cow's milk, goat's milk, and other substitutes had been used to feed infants, artificial baby milk—commonly called "formula"—provided the closest nutritional approximation to breast milk.

Historically, infants received breast milk from their biological mothers or from substitute nurses, such as hired "wet nurses" who breastfed the babies of upper class women in Europe, or African slave women in the American antebellum South who served as wet nurses for the children of owners on plantations. Breast milk is nutritionally complete, containing a balance of fats, proteins, amino acids, and vitamins and minerals. The composition of breast milk changes to meet the baby's needs; at times the milk has less fat and more water, and as the baby ages the milk's balance of nutrients alters to meet the child's developmental requirements.

Before artificial baby milk was widely available in the West, and currently in areas where it is not available, the need to breastfeed infants was and is clear. Babies who do not receive breast milk or a nutritionally complete formula face nutritional deficiencies, growth problems, greater levels of illness, lower immunity, and the risk of death is high. In parts of the world where the water supply is contaminated, breast milk provides babies and toddlers with a filtered liquid that facilitates growth and development; the mother's body acts as a filtration system.

By the early 1900s, in the United States, the use of artificial baby milk became the preferred feeding mode for infants in upper class, and later middle class, families. The "scientific management" movement, which equated scientific methods and approaches with progress, embraced artificial baby milk as a better infant feeding method, largely because the amount consumed could be measured, and the nutritional content was testable. Breastfeeding fell out of fashion.

During the Baby Boom in the United States, breastfeeding rates at birth dropped to eighteen percent in 1956, the lowest point recorded. By 1973, the rate rose to twenty-five percent, and, in 2000, it was approximately sixty percent. The increase in breastfeeding comes, in part, from public health campaigns that point to studies linking artificial baby milk to higher rates of diabetes, childhood illness, and lower IQ scores in children.

As breastfeeding rates rose in the United States and other developed countries, the debate over breastfeeding in public surged as a topic of interest. In the 1980s, stories described women who were asked to nurse in a bathroom, who were asked to leave public establishments because they were breastfeeding, or who were denied breaks to use breast milk pumps while at work to pump and store breast milk for future feedings. State and federal legislation in the United States, Europe, Australia, and New Zealand granted varying degrees of protection for public breastfeeding and workplace breastfeeding rights.

In 2003, Kirstie Marshall, an Australian Member of Parliament, breastfed her eleven-day-old daughter on the floor of the parliament chamber. She was asked to leave by the Sergent-at-Arms. The incident sparked an international debate on public breastfeeding.

PRIMARY SOURCE

EXECUTIVE SUMMARY

On 26 February 2003, newly-elected Victorian MLA Kirstie Marshall rushed into Question Time in Parliament with her 11 day-old baby. Seated in the chamber, she was breastfeeding the child when the Serjeant-at-Arms approached her and apparently asked her to leave, because she was breaching standing orders by having the baby (a 'stranger') in the chamber.

The rules governing 'strangers' (non-members within the parliament) have distant origins, and have changed considerably over the last two centuries. Parliaments around Australia and overseas generally have standing orders which control access of non-members to areas of the parliament reserved for members when parliament is sitting. The question raised by the incident involving Kirstie Marshall is whether those rules are keeping pace with the changing nature of work in the parliamentary environment.

The central issues are that parliament is:

- a working environment, and it needs rules that ensure that it functions effectively, and
- a democratically elected body, and it needs rules that ensure its members can participate fully if their citizens have chosen them to be there.

If parliaments continue to become increasingly representative of the demographic profile of the populations of their countries and regions, if they are to continue to operate as what are effectively 'live-in' organisations when sitting, and if they are going to maintain procedural rules requiring, for example, the immediate presence of members on a division, then the appropriate accommodation of children in general, and breastfed babies in particular, will need to be considered by the chambers.

A survey of standing orders and parliamentary practice around jurisdictions reveals some divergence between the orders and actual practice. There is also a surprising degree of variation in the standing orders themselves.

How might a situation such as that faced by Kirstie Marshall and the Victorian Parliament be dealt with? The main point to recognise is that a chamber can suspend standing orders should it so wish. There is nothing to stop a parliament from passing a motion along the lines, for example, that 'so much of standing orders be suspended as would prevent a member from bringing their infant into the chamber'. Suspensions of standing orders designed to admit strangers have been implemented before, such as in Victoria in 2002 when the orders were suspended to allow several people to address the chamber on two different occasions.

Houses can also pass resolutions (not specifically suspending standing orders) that would then overrule something otherwise provided in the standing orders. Finally, it is possible to amend the standing orders. This was the approach taken in the Australian Capital Territory's Assembly in March 2003.

The means available to admit strangers without amending standing orders vary from place to place. In Canada, it would be possible for a stranger to stay as long as the House's attention was not drawn to their presence, and they were not being disorderly. In Western Australia, they could be brought into the chamber with the Speaker's approval. This would also be the case in New Zealand: in addition, in New Zealand the Speaker is granted the power to make more general rules, such as one regarding breastfeeding babies. In Queensland, it would appear that, if a member were to draw attention to a stranger in the chamber, the stranger could stay if a motion that strangers be required to withdraw failed.

Ultimately, the important issue will not be whether infants or children should ever be in the parliamentary chamber. Whether chambers learn to accept, for example, breastfeeding of babies may be seen as a key indicator of the extent to which parliament recognises that parenting is something MPs have a right to do. But the main issue will be whether parliaments are going to become more 'family-friendly' workplaces generally. Are they going to have hours of operation, facilities, procedures and a workplace culture that accepts that any person elected by citizens should not face further barriers to being able to represent those citizens effectively in the parliament?

INTRODUCTION

On 26 February 2003, newly-elected Victorian MLA Kirstie Marshall rushed into Question Time in Parliament with her 11 day-old baby. Seated in the chamber, she was breastfeeding the child when the Serjeant-at-Arms approached her and apparently asked her to leave, because she was breaching standing orders by having the baby (a 'stranger') in the chamber. The incident received extensive media coverage.

STRANGERS!

In the British Parliament the custom is that a member desiring that the chamber go into closed or secret session declares 'I spy strangers!'. The Speaker then puts, without debate, the question 'that strangers do withdraw'.

The rules governing 'strangers' have distant origins, and have changed considerably over the last two centuries. They reflect practice prior to the 19th century that there be no public access to the deliberations of parliament, an idea we would find quite alien now. Public access to proceedings of the House of Commons was introduced in 1845, and by the twentieth century, the practice of going into secret session was very unusual, taking place only during wartime. Chambers may still go into closed session, but Australia's House of Representatives has not gone into secret session since the Second World War, when on three occasions in 1940 and 1941 it ordered strangers to withdraw. This meant clearing the public galleries, and would have applied to Senators as well, had the House not also passed a motion inviting them to stay. The 'strangers'; motion did not however cover officers of the parliament (for example, clerks and the Hansard reporting staff). For the Second World War secret sessions, a separate motion was passed requiring the Parliamentary Reporting Staff also to withdraw. The staff of the parliamentary chamber, however, are normally not regarded as 'strangers'.

While 'strangers' are now admitted to public galleries of parliaments essentially all the time, the floor of the chambers is another matter.

POLICING THE CHAMBER

Parliaments around Australia and overseas generally have standing orders which control access of non-members to areas of the parliament reserved for members when parliament is sitting. This primarily means the floor of the chamber, though there are often areas of that floor where non-members routinely visit, such as the adviser's boxes in the House of Representatives.

Access to the floor of the chamber is jealously guarded by parliaments. The preoccupation with keeping strangers out has its roots in British democracy of the seventeenth century and earlier, when the relationship between the power of the monarch and the power of the parliament was hotly contested. At that time, the chamber was a refuge for members being persecuted by King Charles I, who, alone amongst the British monarchs, deigned to enter the floor of the chamber in pursuit of his critics.

Such dramatic clashes between legislative and executive power are no longer an issue, and the integrity of the parliamentary chamber may seem assured. The operations of parliament have changed considerably over the centuries since the confrontation with King Charles, and so has parliament's membership. The rules, however, have changed little.

The question raised by the incident involving Kirstie Marshall is whether those rules are keeping pace with the changing nature of work in the parliamentary environment. In particular, do the strangers' rules reflect outdated and unnecessary restrictions on members' children that reflect a time when the membership of parliament was unlikely to be caring for young children....

Andrea Dorlester, of Fairfax, Va., breastfeeds her son, in protest, on Capitol Hill during a news conference in response to a ban on women breastfeeding on federal property. KEN LAMBERT/WASHINGTON TIMES VIA NEWSMAKERS

SIGNIFICANCE

The initial reaction to the removal of Kirstie Marshall from the parliament chamber led to public statements of support from breastfeeding proponents for the right to breastfeed in public. The Australian Breastfeeding Association supported Ms. Marshall's decision to breastfeed in her workplace, and called for breastfeeding-friendly changes in Parliament rules concerning "strangers" in Parliament.

Opponents of Ms. Marshall's decision to breastfeed in Parliament stated that she failed to be respectful of parliamentary rules, and that the environment was unsuitable for an infant. In video clips of Ms. Marshall's time in the chamber breastfeeding, her entire shoulder and top of her breast is exposed, a position that many opponents outside of Australia found to be too revealing, though in Australia there was little commentary on the exposure.

The sexualization of breasts in Western society is an issue that breastfeeding proponents claim is at the heart of opponents' arguments. According to breastfeeding advocates, a naked breast in one context is a sexual object; a naked lactating breast, used as a nutritional source for a baby, is not. Breastfeeding advocates claim that it is the perception and cultural assumptions of those offended by public breastfeeding that need to change. As breastfeeding increasingly becomes a public health issue, with government campaigns promoting higher breastfeeding rates, breastfeeding advocates argue that public breastfeeding needs to be encouraged to support better public health for children and mothers.

Unlike other breastfeeding in public incidents, such as a 2001 incident in San Mateo, California, in which a nursing mother was asked to leave, or a 2005 incident in Fort Collins, Colorado, in which a nursing mother was ticketed for indecent exposure while breastfeeding under towels and two umbrellas, Kirstie Marshall's story involves both public breastfeeding and workplace breastfeeding rights. While Parliament's rule prohibiting strangers from the chamber's floor was written at a time when no Member of Parliament could imagine a nursing mother attending a session, Kirstie Marshall's choice to breastfeed in public and at work opened a critical issue that inspired international discussion on the issue.

FURTHER RESOURCES

Books

Stuart-Macadam, P., and K. Dettwyler. *Breastfeeding: Biocultural Perspectives.* Binghamton, N.Y.: Haworth Press, 1995.

Web sites

FindLaw.com. "Public Breastfeeding." <http://writ.news.findlaw.com/colb/20040714.html> (accessed March 7, 2006).

La Leche League. <http://www.lalecheleague.org/NB/NBpublic.html> (accessed March 7, 2006).

Sex, Gender, and Sexuality in the Media

Sex sells. It is ubiquitous in advertising. From the use of supermodels to innuendo, sexual and sensual images are a staple of commercials and print advertising. Sex also sells movies and television programs. Racy titles and plotlines capture both summer blockbuster crowds and television ratings. The pervasiveness of sex in popular media is subject of ongoing debate. Some argue that pop culture only reflects what most of society is willing to accept, others assert that the prevalence of sex and sexual themes in media deserves increased scrutiny, regulation, and perhaps even censorship. The article in this chapter on the Federal Communications Commission (FCC) imposing fines for the infamous Superbowl "wardrobe malfunction" illustrates these tensions.

In the last 50 years, the depiction of women in the media has changed dramatically. Once featured almost exclusively in the home setting, women are now prominently featured in a variety of roles and settings. Popular culture follows reality: the modern media age and the Feminist movement coincide. Like their real-life counterparts, female characters are doctors, housewives, lawyers, domestic workers, and writers. They are single, married, partnered, lesbian or heterosexual. For example, the 1990s television comedy *Murphy Brown's* title character, a news anchor, chose to be a single mother. Increasingly, lead female characters are ethnically and racially diverse. Yet many critics are quick to point out that women (and to some extent men) in media are overwhelmingly stylized and idealized depictions of their real-life counterparts.

Movies and television shows with female-targeted themes—derided as "chick flicks"—are increasingly popular, but may also play to stereotypes of gender roles and preconceived notions of women's desires.

This chapter also highlights two news stories that made headlines largely because the subjects were female: a woman sentenced to death and a female suicide bomber. Each article discusses the impact of the subject's gender on their plight and the media interest in their story.

Finally, gay characters are not new to cinema or television. In movies, gay characters were often depicted as effete "dandies." They were minor characters meant to draw laughs or act as bumbling foil. By 2005, cinema had embraced more realistic and nuanced depictions of gay individuals. Movies such as *Philadelphia*, *Boys Don't Cry*, and *Brokeback Mountain* received critical and popular acclaim for sensitive portrayals of gay characters and issues. Cable and some network shows featuring openly gay and lesbian lead characters thrived in Britain, the United States, and Canada in the 1990s. U.S. network television aired the first gay male kiss in primetime in 2000. By 2006, openly gay characters were prominently featured on television in Europe and America. Despite the seeming embrace of gay and lesbian lead characters, substantial criticism of the portrayal of gay characters remained. *Will and Grace* and *Queer Eye for the Straight Guy* were television successes in the United States, but some critics noted that the show leaned too heavily on often-negative stereotypes of gay males.

A Cartoon Depicting How Masculine Women Have Become by Wearing Bloomers

Cartoon

By: John Leech

Date: January 1, 1885

Source: Leech, John. "A Cartoon Depicting How Masculine Women Have Become by Wearing Bloomers." Getty Images, 1885.

About the Artist: John Leech (1817–1864) was a prominent British illustrator and caricaturist. Originally a student of medicine, Leech's talent for anatomical drawing eventually led to a career as an artist, most notably as a contributor to *Punch*, a British weekly magazine of humor and satire.

■ **PRIMARY SOURCE**

A Cartoon Depicting How Masculine Women Have Become by Wearing Bloomers: A cartoon from around 1855 that links the wearing of bloomers by women to other unladylike activities like smoking and reading the newspaper. PHOTO BY HULTON ARCHIVE/GETTY IMAGES

INTRODUCTION

In the mid-1800s, leaders of the American women's rights movement attempted to use women's clothing to achieve social and political change. Instead of helping to liberate women, however, dress reform led to such a backlash that most women abandoned the effort at a new style of clothing by 1860.

For a brief period at the start of the nineteenth century, women's clothing followed the relatively lightweight, high-waisted "classical" style. This more natural style allowed women more freedom of movement. The trend reversed itself in the 1810s as fashionable clothing began to incorporate a growing number of layers. Women's attire in this era included voluminous trailing skirts that picked up dust and all manner of filth from the street, a minimum of six full petticoats, and tightly laced whalebone corsets that occasionally damaged internal organs. The entire outfit weighed between twelve and fifteen pounds, made housework a challenge, and often left the wearer gasping for breath.

By the early 1850s, many Americans had come to believe that something needed to be done about women's dress. Religious leaders, the medical establishment, and women's rights advocates increasingly condemned women's fashions as immoral and dangerous. Flamboyant and impractical styles damaged the minds and bodies of women while encouraging the sins of vanity and pride.

In 1851 Elizabeth Smith Miller, daughter of Gerrit Smith, designed a new style, a skirt that reached just below the knee worn over moderately full trousers or pantaloons that gathered above the footwear. Impressed by the freedom of Miller's attire, Amelia Bloomer published patterns in her newspaper, the *Lily*, for the "Turkish costume." She printed daguerreotypes of herself and Elizabeth Cady Stanton wearing it. Other papers noted the design and attributed it to Bloomer, and women from around the country wrote to her asking for precise details on how to make it.

For a few years, the key leadership of the woman's rights movement, including Elizabeth Cady Stanton and Susan B. Anthony, wore bloomers and promoted dress reform. Nevertheless, bloomers proved to be a disastrous experiment and speakers at conventions were heckled simply for their appearance. Despite the eagerness of women to be rid of heavy skirts, the style lasted about three years and only enjoyed popularity among women in the more liberal Northeast and West.

PRIMARY SOURCE

A CARTOON DEPICTING HOW MASCULINE WOMEN HAVE BECOME BY WEARING BLOOMERS

See primary source image.

SIGNIFICANCE

Dress reform is the least influential social movement of the nineteenth century. Yet, if it had succeeded, it had the potential to greatly change the lives of women. Early feminists understood that women's restrictive clothing was both a cause and effect of larger societal limitations. Extremely burdensome clothing enforced passivity and helped to oppress women. Bloomers would leave women physically and intellectually free.

The leadership of the women's movement abandoned dress reform because public ridicule drew attention from other important issues such as suffrage, marriage reform, and education. As women like Stanton and Anthony returned to their long dresses, ordinary middle-class women hesitated to follow them. Dress reform had a passionate following among ordinary women who testified in women's magazines about how a fashion reform changed their lives. Many of the women stated that bloomers allowed them to perform traditionally male tasks. However, social and family pressure made it too difficult to continue dress reform.

In the 1870s, women's clubs in the urban Northeast revived interest in dress reform. The new generation of reformers discarded the short dress and pantaloons costume in favor of promoting relatively small changes in women's undergarments. Women in great numbers did not adopt short dresses until the 1920s, while women in pants shocked the general public until the 1950s.

FURTHER RESOURCES

Books

Fischer, Gayle V. *Pantaloons and Power: A Nineteenth-Century Dress Reform in the United States.* Kent, Ohio: Kent State University Press, 2001.

Steele, Valerie. *Fashion and Eroticism: Ideals of Feminine Beauty from the Victorian Era to the Jazz Age.* New York: Oxford University Press, 1985.

Web sites

National Women's Hall of Fame. "Women of the Hall: Amelia Bloomer." <http://www.greatwomen.org/women.php/> (accessed March 27, 2006).

Pageant Protest

Photograph

By: Anonymous

Date: September 7, 1968

Source: "Pageant Protest." Associated Press, September 7, 1968.

About the Photographer: This image was taken by a staff photographer for the Associated Press, an international news agency providing syndicated coverage to thousands of newspapers, television stations, and radio stations around the world.

INTRODUCTION

On September 7, 1968, over a hundred women—mostly middle-aged careerists and housewives—picketed the Miss America pageant in Atlantic City, New Jersey. The protesters denounced the racism of the show (since its 1921 creation the pageant had never had a black finalist) and spoke out against "objects of enslavement"—these articles were bras, girdles, false eyelashes, and various other women's accessories. The women claimed to deplore the commercialization and over extenuation of a woman's body. They refused to speak to men and male reporters, and when a protestor mistakenly did so she was jeered by the others until she ceased. Robin Morgan, an editor and one of the protest's leading organizers, coined the phrase "No More Miss America." Her agenda for this statement, as well as the other organizers', was to remove the fantasy-like image of the female and replace it with that of a real woman—that is, a woman with mussed hair, imperfect make-up, and a figure that has bumps and bulges.

These female protestors crowned a sheep as "Miss America" to show that the pageant denoted women as nothing more than animals, held up a poster of a naked woman with the labels "rump" and "loin," and provided a plethora of other antics to ensure their visibility to the crowd and media outlets covering the event. Throwing bottles of pink detergent into the "Freedom Trash Can," they denounced traditional household duties, declared their abhorrence of confections of cosmetics and nail polish, and relied upon the symbolic burning of the bra to focus the media's attention—particularly after the counter protestors arrived. One of the counter protestors was the 1967 Miss America runner-up, who wore a sign stating: "There's Only One Thing Wrong With Miss America. She's Beautiful."

Media accounts tended to focus on bra burning. The *New York Times* and various other media sources ran pieces discussing the bra industry's reaction to female protestors burning their bras. Even though little bra burning actually occurred during the height of the women's liberation movement, the media still made it a focus of public concern because it heightened viewer and reader appeal, brought about notions and images of women running amok by disregarding "good fashion and taste," and the footage of bra burning honed in on the standard image of the woman as prim, proper, and perfectly composed and constructed. This newspaper article discussed how the bra industry managed to deflect a potential loss in clientele by implementing an ad campaign showing women how to wear a bra while looking like they were not wearing one. These ads told women to convert to the unwire bras for a more natural look, choose one from a variety of colors, and wear a backless one for dresses that "leave little to the imagination." But, most importantly, women were encouraged to wear bras because the weight of their winter clothes would flatten their breasts, causing sagging and distortion over time, which would later make them unattractive. Attempts like this ad campaign sought to demoralize protestors and uphold standard social conceptions about the female's appearance.

▮ PRIMARY SOURCE

PAGEANT PROTEST

See primary source image.

SIGNIFICANCE

Even though the media focused on bra burning and other more radical actions from the Miss America protest, the event was considered a major victory for the women's movement. The protest received ample media coverage, and the following year women again staged a counter-display outside the competition. The second year proved more fundamental in obtaining national recognition for female activists because the protesting activities nearly caused the pageant to not be televised.

The 1968 Miss America protest is often cited as encouraging women to seek out nearby women's liberation organizations, and it brought beauty pageants under scrutiny for many years. Into the modern era, in various parts of the country, protestors still publicly

PRIMARY SOURCE

Pageant Protest: A member of the Women's Liberation Party drops a bra in the trash in protest of the Miss America pageant, September 7, 1968. AP IMAGES

state their dismay at beauty pageants. Oddly, as Miss America slowly lost her public appeal, other forms of beauty infiltrated visual culture. For instance, television shows focused on "making a person beautiful," and an increase in plastic surgeons and over-the-counter beauty fixes have (on some levels) changed the focus of beauty from the female to both the male and the female.

FURTHER RESOURCES

Books

Douglas, Susan J. *Where the Girls Are: Growing Up Female with the Mass Media.* New York: Three Rivers Press, 1994.

Riverol, A.R. *Live from Atlantic City: A History of the Miss America Pageant Before, After and in Spite of Television.* Bowling Green, Ky.: Bowling Green State University Popular Press, 1992.

Web sites

PBS.org. "Miss America People and Events: The 1968 Protest." <http://www.pbs.org/wgbh/amex/missamerica/peopleevents/e_feminists.html> (accessed April 1, 2006).

Women's e-News. "September 1968: Women Protest Miss America." <http://womensenews.org/article.cfm/dyn/aid/2433> (accessed April 1, 2006).

Gloria Steinem, Publisher of the Magazine *Ms. Magazine*

Photograph

By: Anonymous

Date: December 16, 1977

Source: "Gloria Steinem, Publisher of the Magazine *Ms. Magazine*." Associated Press, December 16, 1977.

About the Photographer: This image was taken by a staff photographer for the Associated Press, the world's largest newsgathering agency.

INTRODUCTION

Gloria Steinem was born on March 25, 1934 in Toledo, Ohio. Her father left home when she was about ten years old; from 1944 until 1951, she cared for her mentally unstable mother. In 1951, Steinem moved to Washington, D.C. to live with her older sis-

ter, where she attended high school and in 1956 graduated Magna Cum Laude from Smith College.

Gloria Steinem is a prominent women's activist who began writing political articles in college. A two-year internship to India after graduation was an inspiration for her first book, *The Thousand Indias*. Upon her return to the United States, Steinem moved to New York City to begin a journalism career—her first major article was entitled "The Moral Disarmament of Betty Coed." Like much of her later work, the piece remarked on changing social guidelines, the rise of females on college campuses, and evolving "rules" for dating. This latter phrase referred to previous generations courting their significant others at their homes. Dates usually met parents first, and much of a dating relationship occurred under the watchful eye of family, friends, and relatives. However, with the advent of the automobile and its ready availability to teenagers, along with increasing numbers of women at college and women staying, entering, and re-entering the workforce, social customs were forced to evolve. By the mid 1960s, it was not uncommon for a young woman to spend an evening with a man without a chaperone.

Four years after writing her first major article, Steinem co-founded *New York Magazine* in 1968, and in 1969 she wrote her first feminist article: "After Black Power, Women's Liberation." The story derived from a feminist convention she attended while on assignment for *New York Magazine*, and the piece won the 1970 Penney-Missouri Journalism Award. Then, a year later, she co-founded *Ms. Magazine*—a feminist counter to popular culture. The creation of *Ms.* reflected social trends as well as agendas of the feminist movement. Nearly all major publications had been attributing sections of their work to the feminist movement, but *Ms.* was the first magazine to solely devote itself to the causes and concerns of women.

In 1973, Steinem told a reporter for the American Newspaper Publishers Association that the press was letting down American women because "mundane" things like basketball scores appeared to take precedent over matters of national concern. She furthered her argument by stating that the lack of coverage concerning the ERA (Equal Rights Amendment) and the press' focus and manipulation of images reflected badly on the women's movement. Steinem took particular concern with the press' use of images because her looks were often focused on in pieces covering the women's movement. She—like many others—felt that a woman's appearance was her personal choice and not a statement about the movement.

and many others considered vital to women's liberation, and the magazine made its mark by consistently holding U.S. political leaders to higher standards.

By 1973, *Ms. Magazine* had a subscription rate of over 200,000, and its rise and social focus showed its importance on social and political fronts. More importantly, the name of the magazine made a social statement—that "Ms." is a sexist neutral name. Married women and single women could both use the title, and removing sexist social denominators was a central goal of the feminist movement.

FURTHER RESOURCES

Books

Douglas, Susan J. *Where the Girls Are: Growing Up Female with the Mass Media.* New York: Three Rivers Press, 1994.

Steinem, Gloria. *Outrageous Acts and Everyday Rebellions*, 2nd ed. New York: Owl Books, 1995.

Web sites

National Organization for Women. <http://www.now.org> (accessed March 27, 2006).

National Women's Hall of Fame. "Women of the Hall: Gloria Steinem." <http://www.greatwomen.org/women.php/> (accessed March 27, 2006).

PRIMARY SOURCE

Gloria Steinem, Publisher of the Magazine *Ms. Magazine*: Gloria Steinem poses in front of the White House on December 16, 1977. She is holding an oversized mock-up of the January 1978 cover of *Ms.* AP/WIDE WORLD PHOTOS. REPRODUCED BY PERMISSION.

PRIMARY SOURCE

GLORIA STEINEM, PUBLISHER OF THE MAGAZINE *MS. MAGAZINE*

See primary source image.

SIGNIFICANCE

Covers of *Ms. Magazine*, much like the one shown here, reflected current political trends and women's health concerns. These were the issues that Steinem

---

Opening Statement

Sexual Harassment Hearings Concerning Judge Clarence Thomas

Speech

By: Anita F. Hill

Date: 1991

Source: Hill, Anita F. "Opening Statement: Sexual Harassment Hearings Concerning Judge Clarence Thomas." U.S. Senate 102nd Congress, 1st Session; Nomination of Clarence Thomas to be Associate Justice of the Supreme Courts of the United States. Washington D.C.: U.S. Government Printing Office, 1993.

About the Author: Anita F. Hill was born in 1956 in Oklahoma. She is the youngest of thirteen children, reared in a religious household (Baptist faith), and has been a member of Antioch Baptist Church in Tulsa since 1983. In 1977, she earned her Bachelor of Arts degree from Oklahoma State University. In 1980, Yale Law

School awarded her a Juris Doctorate and, shortly after graduation from law school, she began working for a firm in Washington, D.C. As a result of her work with the law firm, she met Clarence Thomas, and she worked for him from 1981 until July 1983. During the trial, Hill taught law at the University of Oklahoma, and she is currently on the faculty of Brandeis University in Waltham, Massachusetts.

INTRODUCTION

In October 1991, Anita F. Hill, then a law professor at the University of Oklahoma, testified before the Senate Judiciary Committee about her claims of sexual harassment. In her testimony and pre-hearing statements, she reported that Clarence Thomas sexually harassed her a decade earlier while she was his aide. In her controversial testimony, she provided examples of several different occasions when the alleged misconduct occurred, but after three days of statements the U.S. Senate confirmed Thomas to the U.S. Supreme Court by a fifty-two to forty-eight vote.

When Hill worked for Thomas, he headed the U.S. Equal Employment Opportunity Commission (EEOC). Prior to working at the EEOC, Hill was his aide at the U.S. Department of Education. Thomas led the EEOC from 1982 until 1990, and no other public claims of harassment arose during that time. As a result, during her testimony Hill was closely questioned on how this level of harassment could have occurred, particularly if no other complainants had come forward. Hill persisted in her testimony and provided examples of Judge Thomas calling her into his office on the pretense of discussing work-related projects, but then asking her out to dinner. When she declined, he would ask for a reason for her refusal. In addition, Hill stated that Thomas would make sexually charged remarks about her clothes. Hill qualified her statements with assertions that she felt "extremely uncomfortable talking about sex with him" and that she felt "severe stress on the job." As a result, she began seeking other employment. In 1983, she began teaching at Oral Roberts University in Tulsa, Oklahoma.

Throughout his appointment process, Clarence Thomas was a controversial Supreme Court candidate. Thomas was appointed to replace Justice Thurgood Marshall—the first black justice of the Supreme Court. As a result, Thomas's appointment was already under intense scrutiny, the media coverage was heavy, and some critics viewed him as too conservative. Therefore, when Anita Hill came forward with her claims of sexual harassment, many surrounding Hill, Thomas, and the appointment process and proceedings were shocked. Hill said that she had discussed the

Anite Hill is sworn in during an October, 11, 1991, U.S. Senate hearing on whether or not to confirm Clarence Thomas's nomination to the Supreme Court. AP/WIDE WORLD PHOTOS. REPRODUCED BY PERMISSION.

matter with no one but her closest family members and friends in the years after leaving Thomas's employment, and he admittedly denied her accusations. During the hearings, a number of witnesses were called to support Thomas's good character. In addition, witnesses were called to denounce Hill's character, and U.S. media accounts heightened the attention that the issue received.

■ PRIMARY SOURCE

At this point, late 1982, I began to feel severe stress on the job. I began to be concerned that Clarence Thomas might take out his anger with me by degrading me or not giving me important assignments. I also thought that he might find an excuse for dismissing me.

In January of 1983, I began looking for another job. I was handicapped because I feared that, if he found out, he might make it difficult for me to find other employment and I might be dismissed from the job I had. Another factor that made my search more difficult was that there was a period—this was during a period of a hiring freeze in the government. In February of 1983, I was hospitalized for five days on an emergency basis for acute stomach pain which I attributed to stress on the job.

Once out of the hospital, I became more committed to find other employment and sought further to minimize my contact with Thomas. This became easier when Allison Duncan (sp) became office director, because most of my work was then funneled through her and I had contact with Clarence Thomas mostly in staff meetings.

In the spring of 1983, an opportunity to teach at Oral Roberts University opened up. I participated in a seminar—taught an afternoon session and seminar at Oral Roberts University. The dean of the university saw me teaching and inquired as to whether I would be interested in furthering—pursuing a career in teaching, beginning at Oral Roberts University. I agreed to take the job in large part because of my desire to escape the pressures I felt at the EEOC due to Judge Thomas.

When I informed him that I was leaving in July, I recall that his response was that now I would no longer have an excuse for not going out with him. I told him that I still preferred not to do so. At some time after that meeting, he asked if he could take me to dinner at the end of the term. When I declined, he assured me that the dinner was a professional courtesy only and not a social invitation. I reluctantly agreed to accept that invitation, but only if it was at the very end of a working day.

On, as I recall, the last day of my employment at the EEOC in the summer of 1983, I did have dinner with Clarence Thomas. We went directly from work to a restaurant near the office. We talked about the work I had done, both at education and at the EEOC. He told me that he was pleased with all of it except for an article and speech that I had done for him while we were at the Office for Civil Rights. Finally, he made a comment that I will vividly remember. He said that if I ever told anyone of his behavior that it would ruin his career. This was not an apology, nor was it an explanation. That was his last remark about the possibility of our going out or reference to his behavior.

SIGNIFICANCE

As stated earlier, the U.S. Senate confirmed Clarence Thomas's appointment to the Supreme Court, but the social ramifications of the Thomas-Hill hearings continued to resonate. Initial polls from media outlets and private companies found that women, men, whites, and blacks were divided about both sides of the testimony—many felt that neither Hill nor Thomas told the complete truth. Additionally,

a perpetual question arose about why Hill waited so long to come forward. She stated that the emotional effects of the events, her religious background and nature, and fear of losing respect in her work community prevented her from coming forward earlier. As a side note, some activist groups and media outlets added to the Thomas-Hill controversy by pointing out that Hill was questioned by an all-male panel and that the Senate remained a predominantly male body.

After the Thomas-Hill hearing, statistics show that more women reported sexual harassment claims. A number of famous, wealthy, and politically prominent men were accused, including President William Jefferson Clinton. (The accusations against President Clinton concerned alleged actions during his terms as governor of Arkansas and during his first presidential campaign.) These cases, as well as countless others, captivated the media's attention, and in the mid- to late 1990s Hollywood made several movies addressing sexual harassment issues—from the male and female perspectives. Corporate American also began to take the issue seriously, and many companies instituted strict policies against sexual harassment in the workplace.

FURTHER RESOURCES

Books

Hill, Anita. *Speaking Truth to Power*. New York: Anchor, 1998.

Saguy, Abigail Cope. *What Is Sexual Harassment?: From Capital Hill to the Sorbonne*. Berkeley: University of California Press, 2003.

Web sites

Palmer, Barbara. "Ten Years Later, Anita Hill Revisits the Clarence Thomas Controversy." *Stanford Report*. <http://news-service.stanford.edu/news/2002/april3/anitahill-43.html> (accessed March 24, 2006).

U.S. Equal Employment Opportunity Commission. "Facts About Sexual Harassment." <http://www.eeoc.gov/facts/fs-sex.html> (accessed March 24, 2006).

First Execution of a Woman in Texas Since 1863

Photograph

By: Anonymous

Date: December 8, 1997

Source: "First Execution of a Woman in Texas Since 1863." Associated Press, 1997.

About the Photographer: This image was taken by a staff photographer for the Associated Press, an international news agency providing syndicated coverage to thousands of newspapers, television stations, and radio stations around the world. The Associated Press is considered to be a global leader in news and information dissemination.

INTRODUCTION

Karla Faye Tucker Brown was convicted of two counts of murder in 1984 and sentenced to death. While in prison, she converted to Christianity and garnered much support from Christians in the United States and around the world. Her appeal for clemency came before George W. Bush, then Governor of Texas, and was denied. On February 3, 1998, Tucker Brown became the first woman to be executed in Texas since 1863 and only the second woman to be executed in the United States since the death penalty was reinstated in 1976.

PRIMARY SOURCE

FIRST EXECUTION OF A WOMAN IN TEXAS SINCE 1863

See primary source image.

SIGNIFICANCE

On June 13, 1983, Karla Faye Tucker and her then boyfriend, Daniel Ryan Garrett, entered the home of Jerry Lynn Dean and his companion Deborah Thornton and stabbed them to death with a pickaxe as they slept. Tucker confessed her role in the murders to police and even claimed to have experienced orgasm during the killings. Both Tucker and Garrett were sentenced to death in 1984 when Tucker was just 23 years old, but Garrett died in prison of liver disease in 1994.

While in prison, Tucker claimed to have become a "born-again Christian." She was a model prisoner with a spotless prison record and even worked for a prison-based ministry aimed at keeping young people from becoming involved in crime. In 1996 she married prison chaplain Dana Brown. She claimed to be a completely different person from the young woman who committed the heinous murders of Dean and Thornton. She asked for clemency from the state, requesting that her death penalty sentence be com-

muted to life in prison. Karla argued that she was no longer a threat to society.

Under Texas law, every death penalty case has the opportunity to be granted clemency by the governor of the state. At the time of Karla Faye Tucker Brown's application, George W. Bush was Governor of the state of Texas. Notably, Karla's application for clemency was supported by United Nations Commissioner on Summary and Arbitrary Executions Bacre Waly Ndiaye, the World Council of Churches, Pope John Paul II, and Prime Minister Romano Prodi of Italy. Most unusual was the support that came from typically conservative Americans, such as Republican politician Newt Gingrich and conservative Christian televangelist Pat Robertson. Tucker Brown's claim of religious conversion seemed to have struck a chord with some American Christians. However, George W. Bush was adamant that, in considering Tucker Brown's clemency request, he would look only at whether or not she was likely to be guilty of the crime and whether or not she received a fair trial. In Texas there have been only thirty-six successful appeals for clemency since 1976, and not one has been granted solely on humanitarian grounds. Never has a pardon been based on a religious conversion.

Tucker Brown's lawyers launched an appeal to the Texas Criminal Court of Appeals to halt her execution on January 20, 1997, challenging the constitutionality of the clemency appeals process in Texas. They argued that Texas law provides no guidelines for the parole board in considering death row appeals. The motion was denied on January 28, 1998. On February 2, 1998, the Texas Board of Pardons and Paroles rejected Karla's appeal to have her sentence commuted. The execution would go ahead as scheduled.

The controversy that surrounded Karla Faye Tucker Brown's impending execution made strange bedfellows of individuals and organizations normally at odds. Conservative Christians in the United States tend to be supporters of the death penalty, and their opposition to Tucker Brown's execution was decidedly out of character. George W. Bush was faced with a dilemma—should he risk alienating the support of his conservative Christian voters by denying clemency, or grant the appeal and risk being thought of as "soft on crime?" The unusual support for Tucker Brown that came from the Christian community was a product of her vocal religious convictions, but also possibly of her gender. Criminal justice systems in western countries have traditionally been chivalrous toward women, being less likely to convict and less likely to impose harsh sentences. Underlying this deferential treatment seems to be an idealistic and chauvinistic view of

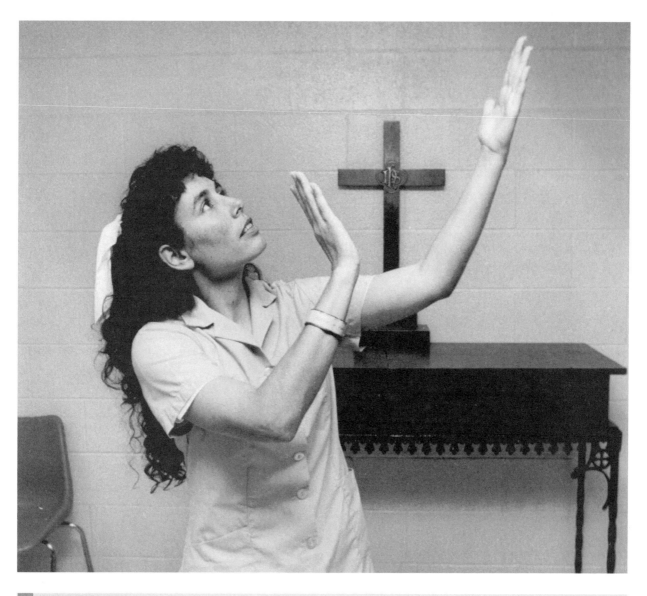

PRIMARY SOURCE

First Execution of a Woman in Texas Since 1863: Karla Faye Tucker. Tucker lost her appeal before the U.S. Supreme Court in Gatesville, Texas, on December 8, 1997, clearing the way for the first execution of a woman in Texas since 1863. AP IMAGES

women as incapable of being evil. Women are supposed to be kind and nurturing and a criminal woman is the antithesis of what is expected. Women who commit crimes are often viewed as "sick" or "mentally ill," rather than evil, and therefore are more worthy of mercy than men.

Karla Faye Tucker Brown's execution brought into question whether there is a gender bias in the application of the death penalty in the United States. Women are convicted of one in every eight murders in

the United States, yet only one in every seventy death row inmates is female. At the time of Tucker Brown's execution, there were seven women on death row in Texas and 437 men. Karla Faye Tucker Brown was executed by the state of Texas on February 3, 1998. Her story and her death brought national and international attention to the use of the death penalty. Following her execution, support for capital punishment in Texas dropped from eighty-five to sixty-eight percent.

FURTHER RESOURCES

Books

Strom, Linda. *Karla Faye Tucker Set Free: Life and Faith on Death Row*. New York: Random House, 2000.

Periodicals

Cruikshank, Barbara. "Feminism and Punishment." *Signs* 24, 4 (1999): 1113–1115.

Heberle, Renee. "Disciplining Gender; Or, Are Women Getting Away With Murder?" *Signs* 24, 4 (1999): 1103–1108.

Web sites

BBC News. "Governor Faces Death Row Dilemma." <http://news.bbc.co.uk/1/hi/special_report/1998/karla_faye_tucker/48851.stm> (accessed March 25, 2006).

BBC News. "Portrait of a Repentant Killer." <http://news.bbc.co.uk/1/hi/special_report/1998/karla_faye_tucker/48816.stm> (accessed March 25, 2006).

Miss Rosie Mae Watches Elvis Presley on the "Ed Sullivan" Show

Poem

By: Herbert Woodward Martin

Date: 2001

Source: Clemens, Will, ed. *All Shook Up: Collected Poems About Elvis*. Fayetteville, Ark.: University of Arkansas Press, 2001.

About the Author: Herbert Woodward Martin served as Poet-in-Residence and Professor of English at the University of Dayton. His published collections of poetry include *Galileo's Suns*, *The Forms of Silence*, and *The Log of the Vigilante*, a journal of slave captivity. He is best known for his portrayals of the African American poet and Dayton native, Paul Laurence Dunbar.

INTRODUCTION

Elvis Presley, the "King of Rock and Roll," became the symbol of youthful rebellion in the 1950s. He challenged the blandness and conformity of mainstream culture.

Born into poverty on January 8, 1935 in Tupelo, Mississippi to a truck driver and a housewife, Presley grew up in a racially mixed neighborhood. From birth, he heard gospel and spiritual music, Shakerag (Tupelo) black rhythm and blues, hillbilly, country, soul, and

Elvis Presley performing on the Ed Sullivan Show on January 6, 1957. During performances of Elvis Presley singing and gyrating on stage, the television audience only saw Presley from the waist up. © BETTMANN/CORBIS

jazz. Blending such musical influences, Presley made his first recordings in 1954 for Sun Records. Some of his songs were regional hits. In 1955, Presley's new manager, Colonel Tom Parker, negotiated a recording contract with RCA Records. With "Heartbreak Hotel," "Don't Be Cruel," and other number-one hits the following year, Presley became an international figure and the first major rock and roll star.

Bashful and awkward, Presley had no idea how his lascivious looks, impish grin, and sexy bump and grind would affect his fans as well as those who saw him as a bad influence. Lovelorn teenage girls did not just pine for Presley. Shockingly, they were uninhibited about their physical desire, something utterly removed from the realm of socially approved behavior. Reporters, teachers, preachers, and parents were appalled by "Elvis the Pelvis." As a white man who sounded like a black man, he also threatened the segregationist racial norms of the 1950s.

Presley's frequent appearances on television during the early part of his career culminated in his electrifying debut on the popular *The Ed Sullivan Show* on September 9, 1956. Sullivan did not like entertainment that went beyond the bounds of middle-class propriety. So his uneasy willingness to have Presley on the show was in a sense acknowledgment of the star's power to transgress social norms. Neither the guest nor the host failed to profit from the event: no television show up to that time had come close to attracting as large an audience. However, Presley was only shown from the waist up, with his swiveling hips deemed too sexy for the home viewers.

By the 1960s, Presley seemed increasingly irrelevant to those who wanted to push cultural boundaries further and to use music as a form of political protest. He turned his energies to making movies and doing concert tours. Presley died at Graceland, his Memphis home, on August 16, 1977 of various physical ailments that were exacerbated by drug abuse.

■ PRIMARY SOURCE

Miss Rosie Mae Watches Elvis Presley on the "Ed Sullivan" Show

Miss Rosie Mae,
sitting in her living room
watching "The Ed Sullivan Show,"
sucked in her pious lips,
smacked them clean as any sectarians',
watching from Los Angeles to the Adirondacks,
and uttered with her skeptical voice
of motherly concentration:
"Those little girls are too fast for words."
Every time his thigh would quiver,
as if he were writing
down some invisible numbers
or vast phrases to thrill the blood,
those tv girls would scream
a lightning jolt again and again.
Then Miss Rosie Mae would point to the screen
as if a million girls had, all of a sudden,
given up the privacy of their bodies wholly,
especially when Sullivan announced:
"For the first time on our stage,
here to perform for you this evening,
is the new singing sensation Elvis Presley."
The cheers never allowed us to hear again.
I never knew a guitar had so many seductive
    moves;

I never knew a guitar could win so many inno-
    cent lips.
They testified loudly when his guitar twitched;
they shivered, as if touched by the Holy Ghost,
when the chords tickled the loneliness
in their thighs.
"It is dangerous to watch that young man
from the waist down. He's pure sex,"
Miss Rosie Mae said.
"Somebody, somewhere needs to give those
little girls a pinch of saltpeter,
maybe a little more than a pinch if you ask me."
Elvis uttered his songs on a ledger of air;
he sang with such a vengeance
that every young girl felt
as if he were singing only to her,
that she had received her proper potion
and could cheer, unreservedly,
her blood into infinite hoarseness.

■ SIGNIFICANCE

The 1950s are often remembered as a time of political and cultural conformity. Yet an undercurrent of rebellion runs through the decade with the arts reflecting a sharp rejection of mainstream values. Music, in particular the rock and roll movement led by Elvis Presley, undermined the constraints of the 1950s. With roots in African American rhythm and blues, a raw sexuality, and cheerful rebelliousness, rock and roll exploded in the 1950s to threaten mainstream cultural mores.

Rock music combined a strong beat with off-beat accents and repeated harmonic patterns to produce its distinctive sound, with the electric guitar providing the basic instrument. It was once known as rhythm and blues, a black musical style. Radio disc jockey Alan Freed coined the term "rock 'n' roll" (a phrase used in black neighborhoods to refer to dancing and sex) to sell the songs to white audiences who would not otherwise listen to "race music." By blurring the divisions between blacks and whites, rock and roll music challenged the racial conformity of the 1950s. It promoted racial tolerance among the teenagers who formed its audience.

By the mid-1950s, rock had fully captured the imagination of young Americans. The music flourished as an expression for young people experiencing the turbulence of puberty. It gave adolescents a self-conscious sense of being a unique social group with distinctive characteristics. Teenagers used it to claim their own cultural style and to issue a message of resistance to authority figures. Rock music would continue through the subsequent decades as one of the major vehicles of youth revolt.

FURTHER RESOURCES
Books

Altschuler, Glenn C. *All Shook Up: How Rock 'n' Roll Changed America*. New York: Oxford University Press, 2003.

Mason, Bobbie Ann. *Elvis Presley*. New York: Viking, 2003.

Riley, Tim. *Fever: How Rock 'n' Roll Transformed Gender in America*. New York: St. Martin's Press, 2004.

Sexually Explicit Images in Advertising

Photograph

By: Tim Boyle

Date: December 8, 2003

Source: Getty Images

About the Photographer: Tim Boyle is a free-lance news and sports photographer based in Chicago.

INTRODUCTION

The exploitation of sex for advertising is a common criticism of the advertising industry. Women, and more recently men, are used to sell everything from toothpaste to beer, although women are featured much more often than men in advertising. Advertisers are taking advantage of the universal human need to feel sexually desirable, and one foundation of the modern consumer society has become human sexuality.

The use of sex to sell a product is a relatively recent phenomenon. In the 1960s, the French photographer Guy Bourdin used sexual and violent imagery in his photographs in French fashion magazines. Many of Bourdin's models were partially disrobed, with an atmosphere of sexual obsession and decadence pervading his photographs. American photographer Helmut Newton added fetishistic elements to sexually charged advertisements in the 1970s. By the millennium, some advertising photographs implied sadomaschochism, bondage, and lesbian sex.

The use of sexual images in television commercials and print advertisements has increased because they are effective tools for increasing sales. Sexual marketing has hidden costs, though. The exploitation of the body causes a sense of inadequacy among many women who do not have the thin bodies of models. As a result, rates of anorexia and other eating disorders have skyrocketed. More recently, men have fallen victim to the pressure to look like models, with steroid use and eating disorders rising among males.

PRIMARY SOURCE

SEXUALLY EXPLICIT IMAGES IN ADVERTISING
See primary source image.

SIGNIFICANCE

The use of sexually explicit images to sell goods and products has expanded to include the employment of sexually attractive personnel as a marketing strategy. Businesses from hotels to clothing stores are increasingly attempting to create a sexual atmosphere. In doing so, some of these companies have become the targets of a wave of private and government anti-discrimination lawsuits.

While it is not illegal to hire attractive people, it is illegal to discriminate on the basis of age, sex, disability or ethnicity. The Equal Opportunity Employment Commission has charged several companies, including retail giant Abercrombie & Fitch, of practicing race and age discrimination by favoring young white people in their hiring practices. Abercrombie & Fitch prefers a "classic American look" that is young, blond, blue-eyed, and preppy. The retailer finds such workers and models by concentrating it's hiring on certain colleges, fraternities, and sororities. Hispanic, Asian, and black job applicants were steered to jobs in Abercrombie's stockrooms. A federal lawsuit, settled in 2005 for $40 million, required Abercrombie to set up a diversity office and to cease the practice of limiting recruiting to particular fraternities and sororities.

While hiring by looks has a long history, the practice has increased at upscale businesses. Mass marketers, like Wal-Mart, do not typically use sex to sell their brands. Additionally, some clothing chains, notably the Gap and Benetton, encourage managers to build a staff that is filled with people of all ages from a range of different ethnic backgrounds.

FURTHER RESOURCES
Books

Berger, Arthur Asa. *Ads, Fads, and Consumer Culture: Advertising's Impact on American Character and Society*. Lanham, MD: Rowman and Littlefield, 2004.

McBride, Dwight. *Why I Hate Abercrombie & Fitch: Essays on Race and Sexuality in America*. New York: New York University Press, 2005.

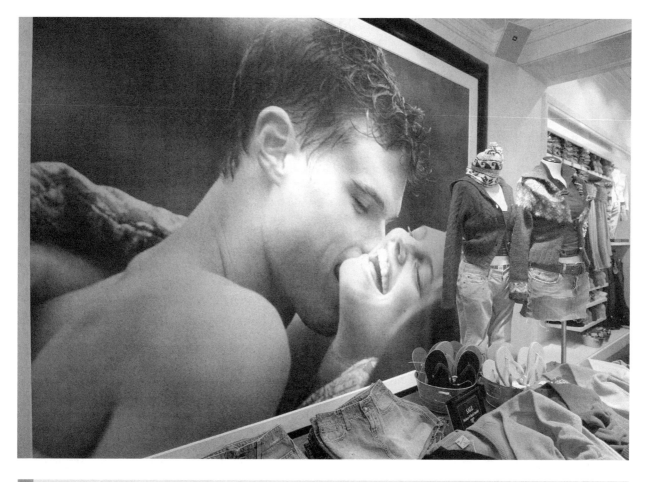

Sexually Explicit Images in Advertising: Abercrombie & Fitch clothing and advertising is displayed in one of its stores in Chicago on December 8, 2003. The company was forced to pull their controversial Christmas catalogs from the shelf in response to claims that they contained sexually explicit images. PHOTO BY TIM BOYLE/GETTY IMAGES

Web sites

Abercrombie & Fitch. <http://www.abercrombie.com> (accessed March 29, 2006).

Queer Eye for the Straight Guy

Photograph

By: Steve Azzara

Date: August 28, 2003

Source: This photograph is part of the collection of the Corbis Corporation, headquartered in Seattle, with a worldwide archive of over 70 million images.

About the Photographer: Steve Azzara is a professional photographer who has worked in a variety of modalities for nearly three decades. His photographs have appeared in numerous magazines, newspapers, and other print materials. He has produced a great deal of high fashion, modeling, and runway/ramp photography. He has also done photography for numerous book covers, CDs and other music media.

INTRODUCTION

"Queer Eye for the Straight Guy" premiered on Bravo—the American cable channel—in 2003. The show features five gay men, who have been labeled the "Fab Five," each of whom has a specific talent, who "make over" many aspects of the life of a straight man—from hairstyle and wardrobe to home decor and dining tendencies. The show achieved nearly instant success, and was among the summer buzz topics across the television watching subculture, both in the United States and countries abroad that access television broadcasts from the United States. The original cast included purported experts in the areas of interior design and efficient organization of living spaces; food preparation, spirits and wine selection; fashion and clothing styling; skin and hair care and attendant products, personal hygiene, contemporary culture, interpersonal communication and relationships, and social behavior. Each episode generally revolved around a lifestyle re-do in preparation for some seminal life event such as a large-scale house party, an introduction to the parents of a future spouse, or a proposal of marriage.

In an era fraught with reality television series, the unique aspect of this show was its portrayal of exceedingly unapologetically openly gay men who appeared to comfortably camp and clown with heterosexual men, while materially aiding them in the improvement of various aspects of their lives. One of the more poignant aspects of the show was the statements by the heterosexual subjects regarding commonalities they discovered with the "Fab Five," causing them to rethink their perceptions of cultural differences and feelings of homophobia. Interestingly, some of the most potent criticism of the show came from within the homosexual community, which raised concerns about generalized perceptions of gay men. A small cadre of non-homosexuals also critiqued what they termed the stereotypic presentation of heterosexual men as inept in the style and culture arenas. What has been particularly noteworthy about the program has been its wide and popular reception, both in the United States and elsewhere. There has been little conservative outcry, and the show has had a rather wide target audience. Several other countries attempted imitations of the series, few of which met with commercial success. As a result, the American series is broadcast and subtitled in many countries around the world.

PRIMARY SOURCE

QUEER EYE FOR THE STRAIGHT GUY

See primary source image.

SIGNIFICANCE

An interesting sidelight of the show's popularity has been the crossover of slang and colloquial vocabulary from a subculture to the mainstream of society. Many subcultures have within-group names that they have adopted from the larger society, as well as those they have invented for themselves, as a form of internal code, designed to insulate them from non-group members. As a group that has been routinely legislated against in nearly all parts of the world and has been, at various times in history, subject to harassment, arrest, and severe punishment (or death) simply for engaging in the mores and rituals associated with some aspects of the subculture (flamboyant behavior, obviously effeminate mannerisms and speech, engaging in same-sex affectionate behavior, etc.), it was deemed necessary by many members to create a safe distance in which to exist apart from mainstream cultures. The term "queer" has been somewhat politicized, and was used first by the GLBT communities to refer to a young radical group of GLBT people who were committed to being completely "out, loud, and proud" in society, using a self-styled confrontational presentation as a means of educating the public about what it means to be non-heterosexual in American society, which was considered by this group to be quite heterosexist in its belief system. Although much of contemporary slang is assumed to have originated in mainstream culture, a considerable amount of what has been termed queer language appears to have come from within the subculture itself.

There exists a mainstream social perception that there is a homogeneous culture among gay, lesbian, bisexual, and transgendered people. In fact, there are subcultures unique to each group, with one main unifying feature involving belonging to a sexual and cultural minority that lacks full civil rights in most contemporary societies. In smaller geographic areas, there may be no recognizable GLBT subculture, as individuals may be either too isolated or too scarce to develop a subgroup. In larger cities, there are often population pockets in which many GLBT people live and socialize. The subculture in one area may bear little or no resemblance to the way the GLBT subculture creates itself elsewhere: for example, the GLBT population in an area with a high density of Native American people will likely look quite different than that in a major urban area of the United States such as San Francisco or New York City.

Gay men appear to have crossed the cultural barriers to become a visible part of mainstream American culture in larger proportion than other segments of GLBT society. In part, that may be due to a percep-

PRIMARY SOURCE

Queer Eye for the Straight Guy: The cast of *Queer Eye for the Straight Guy* at the 2003 "MTV Music Video Awards." From left to right: Ted Allen, Carson Kressly, Jai Rodriguez, Thom Filicia, and Kyan Douglas. AP/WIDE WORLD PHOTOS. REPRODUCED BY PERMISSION.

tion of visibility, or a belief by heterosexual America that gay men as a whole can be accurately represented by effeminate, flighty, promiscuous, lisping, flamboyant, or other stereotypic mannerisms and behaviors. It is an interesting sociological commentary that gay male culture is not only better known and understood (and, sometimes, more readily accepted) by mainstream society than that for other factions of the GLBT world, but is also better understood within non-heterosexual culture than is lesbianism, bisexuality, and transgenderism. Many, many members of GLBT societies fit none of the alleged norms portrayed by the media and are simply individuals, as are members of any other cultural group. Nevertheless, many GLBT organizations hold that any positive visibility of GLBT people in mainstream society, no matter how edgy or tenuous, is better than none at all.

FURTHER RESOURCES
Books
Butler, Judith. *Undoing Gender*. New York: Routledge, 2004.

Jagose, Annamarie. *Queer Theory: An Introduction*. New York: New York University Press, 1997.

Kramer, Larry. *The Tragedy of Today's Gays*. New York: Jeremy P. Tarcher/Penguin Books, 2005.

Nestle, Joan, Riki Wilchins, and Clare Howell, eds. *Gender Queer: Voices from Beyond the Sexual Binary*. New York: Alyson Books, 2002.

Sullivan, Nikki. *A Critical Introduction to Queer Theory*. New York: New York University Press, 2003.

Wilchins, Ricki. *Queer Theory, Gender Theory: An Instant Primer*. New York: Alyson Books, 2004.

FCC Proposed Statutory Maximum Fine of $550,000 Against VIACOM-owned CBS Affiliates for Apparent

Violation of Indecency Rules During Broadcast of Super Bowl Halftime Show

Press release

By: Federal Communications Commission

Date: September 22, 2004

Source: "FCC Proposed Statutory Maximum Fine of $550,000 Against VIACOM-owned CBS Affiliated for Apparent Violation of Indecency Rules During Broadcast of Super Bowl Halftime Show." *FCC News* (September 22, 2004).

About the Author: The Federal Communications Commission, established in 1934 with the Communications Act, is a federal agency of the United States charged with regulating interstate and national communications.

INTRODUCTION

The Federal Communications Commission is responsible for regulating and managing communications across wire, radio, television, and the Internet in the United States. The FCC was created in 1934 and merged rules from the Federal Radio Commission, the Interstate Commerce Commission, and the Postmaster General.

Controlling and monitoring the content of information broadcast on radio and television stations and programs falls under the auspices of the FCC. The FCC restricts or prohibits the discussion or use of certain words deemed to be indecent and restricts nudity on network television. Cable programming and satellite radio, both subscription services, have far less restrictive FCC oversight and can broadcast nudity and profanity that does not cross the line into obscene material.

In addition, the FCC, in 2004, reaffirmed a 1995 rule concerning obscene and indecent material. The rule states that: "(a) No licensee of a radio or television broadcast station shall broadcast any material which is obscene. (b) No licensee of a radio or television broadcast station shall broadcast on any day between 6 A.M. and 10 P.M. any material which is indecent."

The definition of "indecent" material, according to the FCC, is material which "describe[s] or depict[s] sexual or excretory organs or activities. Once the Commission determines that the material aired falls within that definition, we must then evaluate whether the broadcast is patently offensive as measured by con-

Singer Janet Jackson covers her breasts after her outfit came undone during the halftime performance of Super Bowl XXXVIII in Houston, on February 1, 2004. Singer Justin Timberlake stands to her right. AP IMAGES

temporary community standards for the broadcast medium." The use of community standards refers to the 1973 United States Supreme Court case *Miller v. California*, in which the Supreme Court determined that the definition of obscene or indecent material is community-driven—what is acceptable for one community might not be acceptable for another.

In 1993, the first season of the television show *NYPD Blue* ushered in a new level of nudity on network television, showing a main character naked from behind. Words such as "bitch" were spoken on the show as well; because the show was in the 10 P.M. time slot, however, it was not affected by FCC rules about programming shown between 6 A.M. and 10 P.M.. Many conservative groups such as Reverend Donald Wildmon's American Family Association complained and protested that the nudity and use of profanity on *NYPD Blue* and other shows in 10 P.M. time slots crossed the line into indecency. The FCC permitted the shows to air as planned.

At the February 1, 2004 Super Bowl, during a halftime performance, singers Justin Timberlake and

Janet Jackson were in mid-performance when Timberlake, as part of a choreographed move, tore Jackson's costume. He unintentionally exposed the female singer's breast and nipple on live, national television.

PRIMARY SOURCE

Washington, D.C.: The Federal Communications Commission today issued a Notice of Apparent Liability for Forfeiture of $550,000 against various subsidiaries of Viacom Inc. for apparently willfully broadcasting indecent material during the February 1, 2004 Super Bowl XXXVIII halftime show. The show contained a musical performance that concluded with Justin Timberlake pulling off part of Janet Jackson's clothing, exposing her breast.

The Commission found that this partial nudity was, in the context of the broadcast, in apparent violation of the broadcast indecency standard. It proposed the statutory maximum amount against each of the Viacom-owned CBS licensees of the 20 television stations that aired the show due to the involvement of Viacom/CBS in the planning and approval of the telecast and the history of indecency violations committed by Viacom's Infinity Broadcasting Corporation subsidiaries. Although the Commission found that other, non-Viacom owned CBS affiliates also aired the material, it did not propose forfeitures against them because of the unexpected nature of the halftime show and the apparent lack of involvement in the selection, planning, and approval of the telecast by these non-Viacom owned affiliates.

Adopted by the Commission: August 31, 2004, Notice of Apparent Liability for Forfeiture (FCC 04-209). Chairman Powell, Commissioners Abernathy, Copps, Martin and Adelstein. Chairman Powell issuing separate statement; Commissioners Copps and Martin approving in part, concurring in part and issuing separate statements; and Commissioner Adelstein approving in part, dissenting in part and issuing separate statement.

SIGNIFICANCE

In the aftermath of the breast exposure, Janet Jackson and Justin Timberlake issued statements referring to the incident as a "wardrobe malfunction." The two performers claimed that the breast exposure was accidental and not part of any planned skit. Part of the lyrics to the song included Justin Timberlake singing "I'll have you naked by the end of this song." Janet Jackson later issued a statement saying that when Timberlake ripped her costume a red lace bra was supposed to remain in place; instead, her breast, nipple, and a metal nipple ring were displayed.

With an audience of more than 140 million worldwide, the incident gained immediate notoriety and was the subject of newscasts for the next few weeks. The National Football League, holding halftime show organizer MTV responsible, announced that MTV would no longer be involved with halftime shows. Groups such as the Parent Television Council filed complaints with the FCC; the PTC has a long history of filing indecency complaints regarding television content, and PTC reports account for 99.8% of all FCC indecency claims in 2003. In 2004, FCC officials estimated that complaints concerning the Super Bowl incident, numbering more than 500,000, accounted for more than half of all indecency complaints.

During the same Super Bowl, shortly after the Jackson-Timberlake incident, a male streaker ran onto the football field, wearing an advertisement for an online company as well as a g-string. Cameras did not broadcast the incident, however, and the streaker was quickly brought under control.

Many comments from the public centered around the fact that children were watching the halftime show, and that the incident occurred between the hours of 6 A.M. and 10 P.M. Critics of this viewpoint note that the Super Bowl has run commercials for erectile dysfunction medications and broadcast sexually suggestive advertisements in the past that were just short of the legal definition of indecent.

In the months following the incident, Howard Stern, a well-known radio talk show host, had his show taken off the air with Clear Channel Communications. Known for vulgar humor and indecent language bordering on obscenity, Stern moved to satellite operator Sirius, a subscription service that is held to a different standard than traditional radio. Stern alleges that Clear Channel dropped his show out of fear of receiving FCC violations and fines.

FCC fines at the time of the incident were $27,500. Congress passed bills that increased the per-violation fine to $375,000 in 2005.

FURTHER RESOURCES

Books

Obscenity and Pornography Decisions of the United States Supreme Court, edited by Maureen Harrison and Steve Gilbert. Carlsbad, Calif.: Excellent Books, 2000.

Wheeler, Lee Ann. *Against Obscenity: Reform and the Politics of Womanhood in America, 1873–1935*. Baltimore, Md.: The Johns Hopkins University Press, 2004.

Periodicals

Posner, Michael. "Both Chambers Act on Obscenity Curbs." *National Journal* (March 2004).

Web sites

Federal Communications Commission. "Regulation of Obscenity, Indecency, and Profanity." <http://www.fcc.gov/eb/oip> (accessed April 1, 2006).

The Media's Silence About Rampant Anal Sex

Newspaper article

By: William Saletan

Date: September 20, 2005

Source: William Saletan. "The Media's Silence About Rampant Anal Sex." *Slate.com* (September 20, 2005). <http://www.slate.com/id/2126643> (accessed April 1, 2006).

About the Author: William Saletan was a contributor to the online journal *Slate* when this essay was published as an installment of his column on science, technology, and society, "Human Nature." He has also contributed to *Mother Jones* magazine and was author of a book, *Bearing Right: How Conservatives Won the Abortion War* (2004).

INTRODUCTION

William Saletan devotes this essay to a study released on September 15, 2005 by the National Center for Health Statistics (NCHS, a division of the U.S. federal Centers for Disease Control or CDC), "Sexual Behavior and Selected Health Measures: Men and Women 15–44 Years of Age, United States, 2002." The survey gathered data in 2002 and 2003 by asking survey questions of 12,571 Americans aged fifteen to forty-four years about their sexual behaviors. Most coverage of the report focused on its finding that over half of U.S. teenagers (fifteen- to nineteen-year-olds) had engaged in oral sex, with male and female teenagers reporting about the same level of experience, and with the percentage increasing to about seventy percent among all eighteen- and nineteen-year-olds. According to the NCHS survey, one fourth of teens who had never had vaginal intercourse ("virgin" teens) had had oral sex. This was deemed surpris-

ing and disturbing by many commentators and was often assumed to be a large increase over earlier years. However, as Saletan notes, the NCHS report states that from 1995 to 2002, there was little or no increase in the proportion of males in the fifteen to nineteen age group who had had heterosexual oral or anal sex (for female teens, trend data were not available for these behaviors).

Many commentators interpreted the supposed increase in teen oral sexual activity as evidence that abstinence-only sex education programs in public schools, widely supported in the United States by religious and social conservatives, had moved teens to substitute oral sex (fellatio and cunnilingus) for vaginal intercourse. The *Washington Post*, typical of many news sources, opined on September 16, 2005 that "The new data tend to support this view." This was a controversial conclusion because such a result would be unwelcome to most of the persons who had supported abstinence-only sex education. Clinical studies have shown that oral sex can transmit gonorrhea, syphilis, herpes, human papillomavirus, and human immunodeficiency virus (HIV), the cause of acquired immunodeficiency syndrome (AIDS).

Saletan, however, focuses not on the teen-sex results of the study but on its little-reported numbers on the practice of anal sex among people aged twenty-two to twenty-four. The NCHS study found that thirty-two percent of females aged twenty-two to twenty-four self-reported as having had anal sex at least once, while thirty-four percent of men in the same age group reported likewise. (This single percentage point difference between men and women is not statistically significant.) Saletan makes the point that this result would have been more appropriate to highlight as a public concern, given that anal sex is more likely to result in the transmission of HIV than is oral sex—according to figures Saletan cites from the CDC, about fifty times more likely.

■ PRIMARY SOURCE

"Oral Sex Prevalent Among Teens," announced Friday's *Washington Post.* "A federal survey finds more than half of 15- to 19-year-olds have had oral sex," said the subhead in the *Los Angeles Times.* "Sex Survey Shocker; Concern as most American teens have had oral sex," cried the *Boston Herald.*

Across the United States—and beyond it—any newspaper that didn't focus on lesbianism in the sex survey (released last week by the National Center for Health Statistics) declared a crisis of oral sex among teens.

Experts and journalists, unwilling to express plain old moral dismay at the idea of their kids doing the deed, cited its health risks. "Oral sex has been associated in clinical studies with several infections, including gonorrhea, syphilis, herpes and the human papillomavirus," observed the *Post*. Teens "have not been given a strong enough message about the health risks of oral sex," an expert warned the *Times*. "We need to provide them with information about the public-health consequences," another expert told *Time*.

If only it were that simple. Talking to your kids about oral sex is the easy part. If you're going to be frank about the most dangerous widespread activity revealed in the survey, you're looking at the wrong end of the digestive tract.

There's no delicate way to put this, so I'll just quote the survey report: "For males, the proportion who have had anal sex with a female increases from 4.6 percent at age 15 to 34 percent at ages 22–24; for females, the proportion who have had anal sex with a male increases from 2.4 percent at age 15 to 32 percent at age 22–24." One in three women *admits* to having had anal sex by age 24. By ages 25 to 44, the percentages rise to 40 for men and 35 for women. And that's not counting the 3.7 percent of men aged 15 to 44 who've had anal sex with other men.

The last time major national surveys asked about this practice, in the early 1990s, only 20 percent of men aged 20 to 39 said they'd had anal sex with a woman in the preceding 10 years. Only 26 percent of men aged 18 to 59 said they'd ever done so. In the first survey, the 10-year limit excluded half the sexual career of half the sample, but that isn't enough to explain a doubling in the percentage saying yes. In the second survey, according to the current report, the inclusion of men aged 46 to 59 might have diluted the sample with "cohorts that were less likely to have had anal sex." But that's the point: Newer cohorts are more likely to have tried it.

Why does this matter? Because anal sex is far more dangerous than oral sex. According to data released earlier this year by the Centers for Disease Control, the probability of HIV acquisition by the receptive partner in unprotected oral sex with an HIV carrier is one per 10,000 acts. In vaginal sex, it's 10 per 10,000 acts. In anal sex, it's 50 per 10,000 acts. Do the math. Oral sex is 10 times safer than vaginal sex. Anal sex is five times more dangerous than vaginal sex and 50 times more dangerous than oral sex. Presumably, oral sex is far more frequent than anal sex. But are you confident it's 50 times more frequent?

A CDC fact sheet explains the risks of anal sex. First, "the lining of the rectum is thin and may allow the [HIV] virus to enter the body." Second, "condoms are more

likely to break during anal sex than during vaginal sex." These risks don't just apply to HIV. According to the new survey report, the risk of transmission of other sexually transmitted diseases is likewise "higher for anal than for oral sex," and the risk "from oral sex is also believed to be lower than for vaginal intercourse."

If you live in Bergen County, N.J., congratulations. You get the only newspaper in the world that mentioned heterosexual anal sex, albeit briefly, in its write-up of the survey. Two other papers buried it in lines of statistics below their articles; the rest completely ignored it. Evidently anal sex is too icky to mention in print. But not too icky to have been tried by 35 percent of young women and 40 to 44 percent of young men—or to have killed some of them.

Not that there's anything wrong with it, as Jerry Seinfeld might say. But if your moral standard for judging sex acts is the risk of disease, anal is worse than oral. The spin that activists, scholars, and journalists have put on the survey—that abstinence-only sex education is driving teenagers to an epidemic of oral sex—doesn't hold up. As the survey report notes, data "suggest that there was little or no change (accounting for sampling error) in the proportion of males 15–19 who had ever had heterosexual oral or anal sex between 1995 and 2002." The more interesting numbers are in the next age bracket up—and the next orifice down.

I understand why we fixate on the oral sex numbers. Even liberals can digest sexual revolutions only one taboo at a time. We think oral sex is the new frontier. We think talking about it in print and sex education classes makes us hip and candid. It doesn't.

SIGNIFICANCE

One can only speculate as to the cause for the relative silence in the media concerning the anal-sex results that Saletan highlights. First, it is possible that some journalists did not read the original report, but reported secondhand knowledge gained from earlier news reports that happened to emphasize the teen-oral-sex results. Second, commentators may have chosen to emphasize the teen results because teen sexuality and sex education are explosively political topics in U.S. society: the sexual behaviors of legal adults are much less politically controversial. Third, there is Saletan's theory that journalists think of anal sex as "too icky to mention in print." Some combination of these causes may also have been active.

Other than AIDS, all of the diseases that can be transmitted by oral sex can be readily treated. AIDS, however, is a life-threatening disease for which only partially effective treatments are available. Hence Saletan's emphasis on AIDS. As of 2003, according to the CDC, approximately 38,490 people in the United States between the ages of thirteen and twenty-four had contracted AIDS; 10,041 had died, accounting for about two percent of the 524,060 deaths of people in all age groups in the U.S. (Far greater numbers have died from AIDS worldwide, especially in Africa.) Further, the proportion of AIDS-diagnosed persons aged thirteen to fourteen was increasing: in 1999, only 3.9 percent of all persons diagnosed with AIDS were in this group, but by 2003 4.7 percent were.

The recent increase in AIDS infections among people aged thirteen to twenty-four might be related to the increase in anal sex found by the 2005 NCHS study and highlighted by Saletan—more anal sex, more AIDS cases—but this cannot be assumed. This depends partly on who young people are, on average, having anal sex with: anal sex with a person who does not have HIV cannot cause AIDS. The NCHS study, although intended to help identify U.S. populations at risk for AIDS, cautioned that it was "not an exhaustive analysis of either sexual behavior or of the risk of sexually transmitted infections." Great care should be taken in drawing any conclusions at all from the NCHS study, other than that certain sexual behaviors are probably prevalent at approximately the rates reported.

FURTHER RESOURCES

Periodicals

Heslam, Jessica. "Sex Survey Shocker: Concern as Most American Teens Have Had Oral Sex." *Boston Herald* (September 16, 2005). <http://news.bostonherald.com/national/view.bg?articleid=102800> (accessed April 1, 2006).

Stepp, Laura Sessions. "Study: Half of All Teens Have Had Oral Sex." *Washington Post* (September 16, 2005). <http://www.washingtonpost.com/wp-dyn/content/article/2005/09/15/AR2005091500915.html> (accessed April 1, 2006).

Mosher, William D., Anjani Chandra, and Jo Jones. "Sexual Behavior and Selected Health Measures: Men and Women 15–44 Years of Age, United States, 2002." *CDC: Advance Data for Vital and Health Statistics.* 362 (September 15, 2005). <http://www.cdc.gov/nchs/data/ad/ad362.pdf> (accessed April 1, 2006).

Palestinian Female Suicide Bomber Tries to Detonate Her Bomb

Photograph

By: Anonymous

Date: June 20, 2005

Source: "Palestinian Female Suicide Bomber Tries to Detonate Her Bomb." Getty Images, June 20, 2005.

About the Photographer: This photograph is part of collection at Getty Images, a worldwide provider of visual content materials to such communications groups as advertisers, broadcasters, designers, magazines, new media organizations, newspapers, and producers. The photographer is not known.

INTRODUCTION

The specter of suicide bombings is one that has come to be synonymous with the second Palestinian *Intifada* (uprising), which began in 2000, though the origin of such attacks long predates the Palestinian uprising. Moreover, while the use of female suicide bombers in the *intifada* has attracted worldwide public attention, women have accounted for only a small number of suicide attacks. Palestinian use of women as suicide bombers is comparatively small when compared to other nationalities that have carried out such attacks.

The notion of a suicide or suicidal mission is long enshrined in military culture. In the eighteenth-century British army, for instance, often the only way a low-ranking officer or private could rise quickly in rank was to volunteer for and survive a near suicidal mission. He would do so in the knowledge that the chances of him seeing that day were unlikely, but if that was the case he was sacrificing himself for some sort of greater cause. In the Second World War, around four thousand Japanese pilots volunteered for *Kamikaze* missions. Loaded into small planes packed with high explosives, they would attempt to destroy allied naval vessels by flying into them and detonating.

One of the most notorious and deadly suicide attacks in history occurred on September 11, 2001, when nineteen hijackers from Saudi Arabia, Lebanon, United Arab Emirates, and Egypt hijacked four passenger jets and flew them into the World Trade Center and the Pentagon, killing more than 3,000 people.

However, suicide bombings in their modern and most common form—namely when a protagonist straps explosives to their body, or drives a vehicle packed with explosives and detonates them in a crowded area—owe their origins to the Lebanese civil war. Hizbollah, then an Iranian-backed Shi'a insurgent group based largely in the south of the country, found such attacks an effective tactic in their brutal guerilla war against Israeli occupation, and their attack on United States Marine barracks in 1983, which killed 241 servicemen, effectively ended the U.S. peacekeeping operation in Lebanon. Suicide bombings would become features of the Sri Lankan civil war (1983—), Chechnya's break for secession from Russia (1994—), the second Palestinian *intifada* (2000—), and during the U.S. occupation of Iraq (2003—). Suicide bomb attacks have also taken place in Turkey, the United Kingdom, and Indonesia.

The use of women in these attacks varies from country to country. Hizbollah had no record of deploying them during its armed struggle, whereas women accounted for around a third of the Tamil Tigers (LTTE) suicide bombers in Sri Lanka. In 1991, Thenmuli Rajaratnam assassinated the Indian Prime Minister Rajiv Ghandi, instantly becoming the most notorious female suicide bomber in history. Chechen women, known as "Black Widows," have carried out suicide attacks in Chechnya and elsewhere. In Turkey, female members of the Kurdistan Workers Party (PKK) have carried out several suicide attacks against Turkish armed forces.

Yet suicide bombings only really attracted global attention during the second Palestinian *intifada*, from October 2000. Horrific attacks carried out primarily by Hamas and the al—Aqsa Martyrs Brigade killed large numbers of Israeli civilians and servicemen. Initially women were conspicuously absent in these attacks. Only at the end of January 2002 did Wafa Idris, a twenty-eight-year-old paramedic, become the first female Palestinian suicide bomber in an attack that killed one and wounded one hundred. According to the Israeli Ministry of Foreign Affairs, eight women have carried out suicide bomb attacks since then, and at least six more attacks by women suicide bombers have been stopped.

PRIMARY SOURCE

PALESTINIAN FEMALE SUICIDE BOMBER TRIES TO DETONATE HER BOMB

See primary source image.

SIGNIFICANCE

The use of suicide bombings as a tactic of insurgency has invariably attracted controversy and repulsion, but the very idea—particularly of female suicide bombers—has been further confused by misunderstandings of Islam in the West and also of the role of women in Arab society.

It is a frequent misconception of the Western media that Islamic law calls for martyrdom and holy war. While it is true that some extremist clerics have exploited the Koran's teaching on *jihad* (holy war) and occasionally *shahada* (martyrdom) to suit their own political ends and to even invoke suicide bomb attacks, most Islamic scholars define martyrdom as an historical issue, seeing it in terms of the death of Muslims in the religion's early years. Moreover, they do not see a close link between *jihad* and martyrdom. Instead, the majority of Islamic scholars teach that *jihad* can only be appreciated if the concept of enjoining right and discovering wrong (*al-amr bi'l-maruf*) is properly appreciated. They see such concepts as intrinsically linked. As such, it is wholly wrong to infer that suicide attacks are inherently Islamic or that *jihad* is as essential as teaching to the religion as, say, communion is to Catholics. The majority of Muslims abhor suicide bomb attacks, describing them as "unislamic."

When religion has been cited as a motivation for carrying out a suicide attack, the reason bombers have decided to carry out a suicide bomb attack can often be attributed to miscreant clerics striking a chord with suitably disaffected worshippers. In other cases, extreme nationalism or the desperation of a conflict have also been attributed as a cause. Sometimes it is a mixture of the three. The family of Wada Idris, the first female Palestinian suicide bomber, said that she was deeply affected by witnessing the iniquities of the Palestinian situation while serving as a paramedic in Israel's occupied territories and probably felt that volunteering to be a suicide bomber was the only path left open to her.

It has been suggested that the use of women as suicide bombers during the second Palestinian *intifada* was attributable to the rising status of women in Arab culture. This is often considered an outlandish notion that takes no account of the wide freedoms—in comparison to other Arab countries—long enjoyed by Palestinian women. Women in the occupied territories had long held important roles in Palestinian schools, hospitals, and even the media; almost uniquely in the Middle East, women are free to vote in Palestinian elections; and even casting an eye to terrorism, during Palestinian terrorism's 1970s heyday, its most famous and glamorous protagonist was a

■ **PRIMARY SOURCE**

Palestinian Female Suicide Bomber Tries to Detonate Her Bomb: Wafa Samir Ibrahim, a female Palestinian suicide bomber, tries to detonate her bomb after being discovered while trying to pass through Israel's Erez Checkpoint border crossing on the edge of the Gaza Strip, on June 20, 2005. PHOTO BY IDF VIA GETTY IMAGES

woman, Leila Khaled. Why then would women need to wait until 2002 to feel empowered enough to commit suicide bombing atrocities?

Instead, the role of women in Palestinian suicide bomb attacks can be viewed as a way of exploiting the small gaps that still exist in Israeli security arrangements. Put simply, men are easier to search than women, and a female suicide bomber is therefore harder to detect. An Israeli solider demanding a Muslim woman to lift her clothing to see if she was carrying an explosive belt would cause outrage in a way that doing the same to a man would patently not. Israeli Defense Force (IDF) procedures stipulate that a suspected woman be checked by a female soldier in a screened-off area. Given the usual stringency applied to Israeli security procedures, this was one of the few chinks in the armor still to exploit.

Conversely, fundamentalist groups who carry out suicide missions are usually unwilling to use women as bombers—hence the small numbers of female suicide bombers—as they alienate the conservative constituency from which they draw their support.

Suicide bomb attacks have nevertheless been used routinely by insurgents since the start of the U.S. occupation of Iraq in 2003. Again, women have been involved in several of these attacks, but as in Palestine they have accounted only for a small minority of them.

FURTHER RESOURCES

Books

Burke, Jason. *Al Qaeda*. London: Penguin Books, 2003.

Web sites

The Guardian. "From Angel of Mercy to Daughter of Death." <http://www.guardian.co.uk/israel/Story/> (accessed April 1, 2006).

The Jamestown Foundation. "Profile of a Female Suicide Bomber." <http://www.jamestown.org/publications_details/> (accessed April 1, 2006).

National Geographic. "Female Suicide Bombers: Dying to Kill." <http://news.nationalgeographic.com/news/2004/12/1213_041213_tv_suicide_bombers.html> (accessed April 1, 2006).

Obscenity, Pornography, and Sex Crimes

Obscenity, Pornography, and Sex Crimes

U.S. Supreme Court Justice Potter Stewart famously claimed in 1964 that he could not articulate adequate definitions for pornography or obscenity but that "I know it when I see it." While Justice Stewart's quip is not the legal benchmark for obscene material, it is certainly the most universally embraced social standard. Many people disagree on what constitutes pornography or what sexual images are too offensive for public (and even private) viewing. Sexually explicit images test the balance of free speech and press against public concerns of morality, exploitation, and decency.

While individuals may disagree over whether an advertisement featuring a nude model or the contents of a novel are pornographic or deserving of censor, most everyone agrees that its is acceptable to prohibit the creation and distribution of some explicit images, such as child pornography. Increasing attention has been paid to sex crimes in recent years as technology has enabled the wider distribution of pornographic materials and aided predators in finding victims. Articles in this chapter feature international efforts to curb the child sex trade and the distribution of child pornography. Often, the first stages of these investiga-tions involve surveillance of Internet sites and messaging and file transfer programs. Recent news articles on sex crimes such as molestation, sexual abuse, and rape, are featured in chapter entries. The chapter also features sex crime prevention measures such as Megan's Law, which requires the registration and public disclosure of sex offenders. An article on polygamy is included here because the practice is illegal in the United States and most other nations.

Articles in this chapter feature excerpts from the novels *Justine* and *Lolita*, both novels have been praised and alternatively reviled for their depictions of rape and sexual relations between an adult and child. At the respective times of their publication, both books were banned as pornographic or obscene. In some countries, *Lolita* was outright banned from sale, in other it was sold from shelves in a protective wrapper. Now, *Lolita* is a commonly assigned text in university English classes across Europe and North America, though it continues to shock readers. This example, like others featured in the chapter, illustrates the effect that changing mores have on our definition of pornography and obscenity.

Justine

Book excerpt

By: Marquis de Sade

Date: 1791

Source: de Sade, Marquis. *Justine.* New York: Globusz Publishing, 2004. Available online at <http://www.globusz.com/ebooks/Justine/> (accessed March 29, 2006).

About the Author: Comte Donatien Alphonse François de Sade, known as the Marquis de Sade, was born in France in 1740. A noble by birth, he wrote and published extensively on philosophical and sexual matters. He was imprisoned for a total of twenty-nine years on charges such as sodomy, poisoning, political disloyalty, and corrupting minors. He died in 1814 in France.

INTRODUCTION

The word "sadism," defined as deriving sexual pleasure or gratification from inflicting pain on another person, first made its way into dictionaries in the early 1830s. A sadist, by definition, enjoys inflicting pain on others; the Comte Donatien Alphonse François de Sade published a series of erotic books in which characters exhibited behaviors that came to be known as "Sadistic" behaviors, named for de Sade.

The Marquis de Sade was the only surviving child of noble parents with great wealth and aristocratic connections. Born in 1740 and given every advantage in terms of goods, education, and connections, de Sade chose to live a life as a libertine, pursuing hedonism, or pleasure, to the exclusion of all else. de Sade attended college and at the age of twenty-three married Renée-Pélagie de Montreuil; he maintained relationships with prostitutes throughout his marriage and was notoriously brutal in his sexual relations with them.

In 1768, de Sade captured and whipped a beggar, Rose Keller, for two days; he applied salve to her wounds, reopened them with a knife or whips, and then applied salve until she escaped, naked, into the streets. The incident shocked authorities and the public. In his defense, the marquis claimed he was testing a new salve; he served six weeks jail time and paid Rose Keller a small sum in damages. The Paris vice squad quickly warned sex trade workers of de Sade's proclivities, and his reputation spread. Seducing his wife's younger sister, Anne-Prospre, angered his mother-in-law and was part of his constellation of deviant sexual behaviors, which included extended orgies and use of pain for sexual pleasure.

In 1772, de Sade inserted "Spanish Fly," an aphrodisiac, into some candies he distributed to prostitutes whom he hired for an arranged orgy. According to various historical accounts, some prostitutes became sick from the drug; other accounts report that two women died. de Sade was tried and convicted on counts of sodomy and poisoning and sentenced to death. He escaped to Italy, where he lived for five years. The death sentence was removed, but in 1777, de Sade returned to France and immediately was jailed.

Between 1777 and 1814, de Sade spent a total of twenty-seven years in prison, for offenses ranging from sodomy to poisoning to political disloyalty. He began his writing career in prison, writing stories and plays to deal with the tedium of prison life.

Justine was the first of his published works, debuting in 1791.

■ PRIMARY SOURCE

"Oh by God!" quoth she, "here's an unhappy little one. What! you shudder before the obligation to serve four fine big boys one after another? Listen to me," she added, after some reflection, "my sway over these dear lads is sufficiently great for me to obtain a reprieve for you upon condition you render yourself worthy of it."

"Alas! Madame, what must I do?" I cried through my tears; "command me; I am ready."

"Join us, throw in your lot with us, and commit the same deeds, without show of the least repugnance; either that, or I cannot save you from the rest." I did not think myself in a position to hesitate; by accepting this cruel condition I exposed myself to further dangers, to be sure, but they were the less immediate; perhaps I might be able to avoid them, whereas nothing could save me from those with which I was actually menaced.

"I will go everywhere with you, Madame," was my prompt answer to Dubois, "everywhere, I promise you; shield me from the fury of these men and I shall never leave your side while I live."

"Children," Dubois said to the four bandits, "this girl is one of the company, I am taking her into it; I ask you to do her no ill, don't put her stomach off the métier during her first days in it; you see how useful her age and face can be to us; let's employ them to our advantage rather than sacrifice them to our pleasures."

But such is the degree of energy in man's passions nothing can subdue them. The persons I was dealing with were in no state to heed reason: all four surrounded me, devoured me with their fiery glances, menaced me in a still more terrible manner; they were about to lay hands on me, I was about to become their victim.

"She has got to go through with it," one of them declared, "it's too late for discussion: was she not told she must give proof of virtues in order to be admitted into a band of thieves? And once a little used, won't she be quite as serviceable as she is while a virgin?"

I am softening their expressions, you understand, Madame, I am sweetening the scene itself; alas! their obscenities were such that your modesty might suffer at least as much from beholding them unadorned as did my shyness.

A defenseless and trembling victim, I shuddered; I had barely strength to breathe; kneeling before the quartet, I raised my feeble arms as much to supplicate the men as to melt Dubois' heart....

The fourth attached strings to all parts of me to which it was possible to tie them, he held the ends in his hands and sat down seven or eight feet from my body; Dubois' touches and kisses excited him prodigiously; I was standing erect: 'twas by sharp tugs now on this string, now on some other that the savage irritated his pleasures; I swayed, I lost balance again and again, he flew into an ecstasy each time tottered; finally, he pulled all the cords at once, I fell to the floor in front of him: such was his design: and my fore-head, my breast, my cheeks received the proofs of a delirium he owed to none but this mania. That is what I suffered, Madame, but at least my honor was respected even though my modesty assuredly was not. Their calm restored, the bandits spoke of regaining the road, and that same night we reached Tremblai with the intention of approaching the woods of Chantilly, where it was thought a few good prizes might be awaiting us. Nothing equaled my despair at being obliged to accompany such persons, and I was determined to part with them as soon as I could do so without risk. The following day we fell hard by Louvres, sleeping under haystacks; I felt in need of Dubois' support and wanted to pass the night by her side; but it seemed she had planned to employ it otherwise than protecting my virtue from the attacks I dreaded; three of the thieves surrounded her and before my very eyes the abominable creature gave herself to all three simultaneously. The fourth approached me; it was the captain. "Lovely Therese," said he, "I hope you shall not refuse me at least the pleasure of spending the night with you?" and as he perceive my extreme unwillingness, "fear not," he went on; "we'll have a chat together, and I will attempt nothing without your consent. "O Therese," cried he, folding me in his arms, "'tis all foolishness, don't you know, to be so pretentious with us. Why are

you concerned to guard your purity in our midst? Even were we to agree to respect it, could it be compatible with the interests of the band? No need to hide it from you, my dear; for when we settle down in cities, we count on you to snare us some dupes."

"Why, Monsieur," I replied, "since it is certain I should prefer death to these horrors, of what use can I be to you, and why do you oppose my flight?"

"We certainly do oppose it, my girl," Coeur-de-fer rejoined, "you must serve either our pleasures or our interests; your poverty imposes the yoke upon you, and you have got to adapt to it. But, Therese, and well you know it, there is nothing in this world that cannot be somehow arranged: so listen to me, and accept the management of your own fate: agree to live with me, dear girl, consent to belong to me and be properly my own, and I will spare you the baneful role for which you are destined."

"I, Sir, I become the mistress of a—"

"Say the word, Therese, out with it: a scoundrel, eh? Oh, I admit it, but I have no other titles to offer you; that our sort does not marry you are doubtless well aware: marriage is one of the sacraments, Therese, and full of an undiscriminating contempt for them all, with none do we ever bother. However, be a little reasonable; that sooner or later you lose what is so dear to you is an indispensable necessity, hence would it not be better to sacrifice it to a single man who thereupon will become your support and protector, is that not better, I say, than to be prostituted to everyone?" "But why must it be," I replied, "that I have no other alternative?"

SIGNIFICANCE

Justine, or *Good Conduct Well Chastised*, caused a stir in 1791 in France. The book's protagonist, Justine, is a girl of twelve years old who, along with her sister Juliette, is set out into the world alone after their mother dies and their father disappears. As she travels throughout France, Justine finds herself tested by a variety of alluring settings. de Sade used Justine as a symbol of virtue violated; at one point she seeks help and shelter in a convent and is used repeatedly by a series of monks during an orgy. At other times, when presented with ethical dilemmas, she chooses the virtuous path, but suffers great injustices for it. In this passage quoted above, Justine has escaped prison with Madame DuBois, a notorious murderer. Asking Madame DuBois for help, Justine makes yet another foolish decision, one that leads her to being used by DuBois' henchmen for sexual purposes.

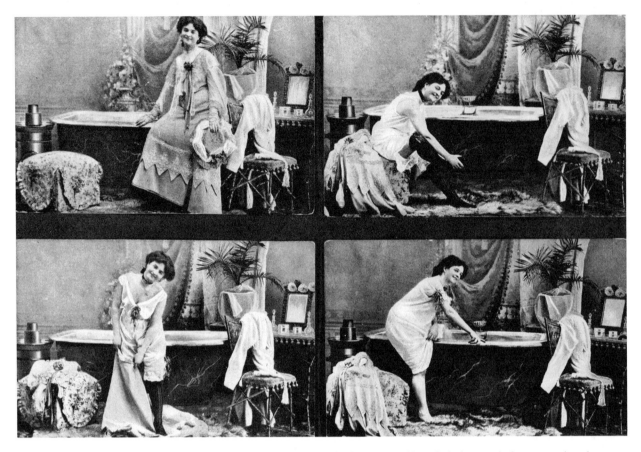

This series of late nineteenth century postcards would have been considered daring and risque at the time. © BETTMANN/CORBIS

By the end of the book, Justine, abused and near death, reunites with Juliette. While Justine has made life choices based on internal goodness and has been destroyed by it, Juliette has lived a life of vice and hedonism and has prospered.

This use of irony—that those most pious would be the most likely and willing to corrupt true virtue—and the direct attack on the Catholic Church led Napoleon to ban *Justine* and de Sade's story of Juliette, *The History of Juliette*, which was published in 1797. In 1801, de Sade was imprisoned once more, and contraband copies of *Justine* and *Juliette* were in high demand.

De Sade's works, starting with *Justine*, explore sexual themes in a literary fashion that had never been seen before in Western Europe. A philosopher at heart, de Sade used his works to detail sexual debauchery, to shock readers and the government, but also to communicate his central philosophical belief that man was governed by his inborn nature, however that may manifest itself, and that to fight such fatalism was folly. He separated natural law from social law; one was innate, the other created by man and highly subjective. Justine

follows her inborn nature, which is pious and chaste, and finds that the social laws that dictate the actions of others bring her nothing but sexual degradation and pain. De Sade used his writings as a vehicle for sexual gratification and philosophical expression.

The brutal experiences of such a young, innocent girl set the tone for the creation of the word "sadism," and its subsequent partner, "masochism," which is the quality of deriving sexual pleasure from receiving pain. Although the word "sadism" is named after de Sade, researchers believe that in fact de Sade was more than likely a masochist rather than a sadist.

The Marquis de Sade's works were banned in many countries; France banned his books until the 1960s and Britain did not decriminalize his works until 1983.

FURTHER RESOURCES
Books

Airaksinen, Timo. *The Philosophy of the Marquis De Sade.* London: Routledge, 1995.

Bongie, Laurence L. *Sade : A Biographical Essay.* University of Chicago Press, 1998.

Schaeffer, Neil. *The Marquis de Sade: A Life.* New York: Knopf, 1999.

Vice Resorts: Parlor Houses

Book excerpt

By: George J. Kneeland

Date: 1913

Source: Kneeland, George J. "Vice Resorts: Parlor Houses." *Commercialized Prostitution in New York City.* New York: Century, 1913.

About the Author: George Kneeland worked for the Bureau of Social Hygiene, whose aim was to study the social evil of prostitution, as it was called in New York City. Kneeland headed an investigation commission beginning in 1912, following his experience directing the Chicago Vice Commission in Chicago.

INTRODUCTION

During the eighteenth century, the United States experienced an increase in the number of prostitutes operating in port cities such as Boston and New York. The growth was attributed to the large number of immigrants settling in these communities, the significant presence of soldiers, and the many poor unmarried women who turned to prostitution to make money. The market for prostitutes expanded even further in the 1800s, along with the Industrial Revolution. Men were moving into cities to work in factories and live in boarding houses, releasing them from traditional family responsibilities. Male leisure time took on a new form of masculinity, as boxing matches, heavy drinking of alcohol, and promiscuous sexual behavior became the norm. This helped prostitution thrive.

Gender discrimination made it difficult for women to find well-paying jobs as easily as men in the 1800s, turning many women to prostitution as a means of survival. It was thought that five to ten percent of young women in New York City engaged in some type of prostitution, earning more than they would in a factory or other service-oriented job. Many landlords preferred to rent out their properties to prostitutes, as these women had stable sources of income, and could be charged more than other working-class tenants.

New York City had over five hundred brothels by the time of the Civil War, which routinely advertised their services in newspapers and guidebooks. Theatres, concert halls, saloons, cigar stores, restaurants, and cabarets normally supported prostitution to attract more business. By the 1850s, New York's red-light districts, which included Five Points and the Tenderloin, were well known for the prostitution they promoted. Throughout the U.S., the prostitution industry generated millions of dollars by the late 1800s, aided by an organized network of madams (who ran the brothels), municipal officials, doctors, and landlords.

Prostitution became an important social and political issue in the U.S. around 1810. However, it was not until the late 1800s and early 1900s that communities began to adopt laws concerning prostitution. As early as 1882, New York passed ordinances regulating prostitutes, saying they could be reprimanded if they disturbed the peace in any public area. Because of weak enforcement in urban areas, however, prostitution was rarely interrupted.

■ PRIMARY SOURCE

The actual business of prostitution in New York City is conducted in buildings which are designated in this report as vice resorts. These resorts are of several kinds. Most prominent are the so-called parlor house or brothel, the tenement house apartment, the furnished room house, the disorderly hotel, and the massage parlor. The present chapter deals only with the first named.

A parlor house or brothel is a building used exclusively for the business of prostitution. It derives its name from the fact that its inmates gather in the parlor to receive guests. There is, however, an exception to the definition, inasmuch as some parlor houses in New York City are situated on the upper floors of buildings, the ground floors of which are used for legitimate business enterprises.

During the period of this investigation, extending from January 24, 1912 to November 15, 1912, 142 parlor houses were visited in Manhattan. Though this number does not include all the places of this character in Manhattan, it may be said to approximate the total. It is improbable that many were overlooked. Every one of the establishments investigated was visited two or more times on different dates by different individuals who have made affidavits as to their findings; and the findings of different investigators working in ignorance of one another have been carefully compared. The date and hour of the observation are given in connection with each report.

Of the 142 parlor houses thus investigated, 20 are known to the trade as fifty-cent houses; 80 as one-dollar houses; 6 as two-dollar houses; and 34 as five- and ten-dollar houses. The prices charged in the remaining two houses are unknown.

The majority of these houses are situated in the business section of Manhattan, namely, on Sixth and Seventh Avenues from West 23rd to West 42nd Streets, and in residential sections on side streets from West 15th to West 54th Streets between Fifth and Eighth Avenues. A few of them are located on the East Side on residential streets east of Third Avenue, and on Second Avenue. A still smaller number were discovered on the extreme East Side near the river and below East 14th Street. Not a few of these houses are found in the vicinity of public schools, churches, and hotels; others occupy the upper floors over lunch rooms, jewelry shops, clothing stores, fur shops, and other business enterprises.

Private houses used exclusively for prostitution are usually three or four stories high; those of the cheaper type are in a dilapidated and unsanitary condition. For instance, the fifty-cent houses on the lower East Side are described as being practically unfit for human habitation. The rooms are dirty, the loose and creaking floors are covered with matting which is gradually rotting away, the ceilings are low, the windows small, the air heavy and filled with foul odors. The sanitary conditions in the majority of the one-dollar houses on the West Side streets between Sixth and Seventh Avenues are hardly less objectionable. No attempt is made to keep the houses clean. The floors are rotten and filthy; they sag as one walks across them. The small bedrooms are damp and unventilated; the atmosphere is heavy with odors of tobacco and perfumes, mingled with the fumes of medicine and cheap disinfectants.

Every step in the process of arranging for and conducting an establishment of this character is taken in the most businesslike fashion. Every detail is arranged in a cold, calculating spirit. It is first necessary to secure the consent of the owner or agent to use the property for the desired purpose. Negotiations may be conducted by the prospective keeper himself or through a go-between who is paid a bonus for securing a suitable building. In the majority of cases regular leases are drawn up and signed for stated periods. Usually two or more individuals enter into a regular partnership agreement to conduct parlor houses. In the course of this investigation interesting data were obtained respecting the purchase, sale, and value of these shares, which constantly fluctuate in value. Important factors in determining their value at a

particular time are public opinion and the attitude of the city authorities toward vice. If the law is rigidly enforced and frequent arrests are made, the shares depreciate and there is a scramble among the partners to dispose of their holdings. If the business is fairly undisturbed, the shares increase in value and can hardly be purchased.

The house once secured and the owners being ready to begin business, a madame or housekeeper is hired by the month or on a percentage basis to take personal charge of the enterprise. She is usually a former prostitute who has outlived her usefulness in that capacity. To her the owners look for results. Every day she reports to them when they call to "make up" the books after business is over—generally during the early morning hours.

Servants are employed to aid the madame: one or more cooks, according to the number of inmates boarding in the house; and maids, usually colored girls, who look after the rooms, tend the door, and aid in the sale of liquor to the customers during business hours. A porter is employed to care for the house and run errands, a "lighthouse," to stand on the street for the purpose of procuring "trade" and to give warning.

The prosperity of the business depends in the main upon the quality of the inmates. If they are young and attractive, and, as one madame was heard to say in another city, "especially womanly," success is assured. Thus the value of the manager depends in the first place on her ability to secure and hold the "right sort" of inmate. The girls must be contented; they must be stimulated to please; quarrels must be avoided, jealousies nipped in the bud. In the art of management, the madame must exercise all her ingenuity. If a girl is a good "money maker" the madame attaches her to herself in every possible way. Some of these unfortunate inmates become "house girls," remaining year after year, the unsuspecting victims of the madame's blandishments and exploitation.

Certain of the women are well known as "stars." Their reputation follows them wherever they go and madams vie with each other in securing them for their particular houses, in much the same way as a business firm is constantly looking for clever salesmen who have a reputation and a record for increasing business. The author has in mind a particular woman whose customers follow here wherever she goes. There are in this business many such "stars" or "big money makers," looked upon with envy by their less attractive and less prominent rivals. The secret of their popularity lies frequently in the perverse practices to which they resort.

An illustration depicting "Man-Fishers on Sixth Avenue, New York City—Siren Games They Play to Rope in Trade," circa 1885. The two women are dressed in provocative attire to entice male passengers. © BETTMANN/CORBIS

SIGNIFICANCE

During the 1800s, anti-vice movements arose, usually led by reformers, church leaders, and women's groups. These movements attempted to shut down brothels and assist prostitutes, but their early efforts were largely ineffective. However, by 1890, anti-vice movements grew more popular, with church leaders regularly voicing concern over the tolerance of prostitution in cities and towns. Progressive government officials began to follow suit, calling prostitution a social evil, and proposing measures to reduce its prevalence. The movement to end prostitution in urban areas throughout the U.S. gained steam in the first two decades of the 1900s, as it was recommended that sex districts be eliminated. Congress passed legislation in 1903 and 1907 that made it illegal to import new prostitutes, and illegal to deport immigrant prostitutes. The Mann Act of 1910 made it illegal to transport women across state lines for purposes of prostitution. Within the first six years of its existence, the Mann Act led to 1,537 convictions. The Commission on Training Camp Activities during World War I closed the sex districts in many of the nation's port cities, including New York, and vice police squads pressured many establishments to cease operations.

Significant changes to prostitution occurred over several decades starting in 1920. Brothels, parlor houses, and open prostitution were no longer tolerated. Prostitution became less conspicuous, with business conducted in hotels and low-profile massage parlors. Prostitution became associated with the alcohol trade and organized crime during the Prohibition period of the 1920s, with some prostitution businesses being protected by gangsters. By 1950, many prostitutes were forced to work alone, as the Federal Bureau of Investigation (FBI) and the congressional Kefauver committee cracked down on prostitution and other forms of organized crime.

The market for prostitution did not go away with further policing. A study in 1968 discovered there had been 95,550 arrests for prostitution around the United States, and that 286,650 men visited prostitutes every day. In the latter part of the twentieth and into the twenty-first centuries, there have been unsuccessful efforts to legalize prostitution throughout the United States, with groups saying it is legitimate work. However, feminists and other groups argue that prostitution exploits women and should remain illegal. There are estimates that between 10,000 and 50,000 women and girls are brought into the United States each year, many of whom are forced to work as prostitutes. Prostitution remains legal in certain districts of Nevada and Rhode Island, as well as in many other countries.

FURTHER RESOURCES

Books

Gilfoyle, Timothy J. *City of Eros: New York City, Prostitution, and the Commercialization of Sex, 1790–1920*. New York: W.W. Norton and Co., 1991.

Hill, Marilynn Wood. *Their Sisters' Keepers: Prostitution in New York City, 1830–1870*. Berkeley, Calif.: University of California Press, 1993.

Hobson, Barbara Meil. *Uneasy Virtue: The Politics of Prostitution and the American Reform Tradition*. Chicago: University of Chicago Press, 1987.

Rosen, Ruth. *The Lost Sisterhood: Prostitution in America, 1900–1918*. Baltimore, Md.: Johns Hopkins University Press, 1982.

Periodicals

"The Business of Vice." *The New York Times* (October 24, 1909): 12.

Landesman, Peter. "The Girls Next Door." *The New York Times* (January 25, 2004): 30.

Web sites

BBC News. "US Prostitution Traffic Revealed." (April 2, 2000). <http://news.bbc.co.uk/1/hi/world/americas/698537.stm> (accessed April 1, 2006).

Women's International Center. "Women's History in America Presented By Women's International Center." <http://www.wic.org/misc/history.htm> (accessed April 1, 2006).

Miller v. California

Legal decision

By: Supreme Court of the United States

Date: June 21, 1973

Source: *Miller v. California* 415 US 13 (1973).

About the Author: The Supreme Court is the highest judicial body in the United States, composed of eight justices and one chief justice. Chief Justice Warren Burger (1907–1995) delivered the opinion of the court in this case.

INTRODUCTION

Historically, American obscenity laws were designed to protect public morality, especially that of children, from exposure to materials that might prove psychologically or morally harmful. Definitions of "obscenity" were broad, and included anything deemed filthy, offensive to the senses, that violated biblical laws or social norms, and, especially, contained information about or descriptions of reproductive and sexual functions. Individual states passed their own obscenity laws. In 1842, the first federal law banned the importation of books that contained obscene content. The Comstock Law of 1873, named after the Postmaster General Anthony Comstock, prohibited the distribution or dissemination of information on contraception and abortion via picture or text through the postal service.

By the early twentieth century the concept of obscenity focused largely on whether material was designed to corrupt or incite depravity, a definition that was highly subjective. The 1957 Supreme Court case *Roth v. United States* produced the first true obscenity "test." The court determined that "[I]t is vital that the standards for judging obscenity safeguard the protection of freedom of speech and press for material which does not treat sex in a manner appealing to prurient [tending to incite lewd thoughts] interest....The standard for judging obscenity, adequate to withstand the charge of constitutional infirmity, is whether, to the average person, applying contemporary community standards, the dominant theme of the material, taken as a whole, appeals to prurient interest."

Whether an "average person" would deem that material "appealed to prurient interest," however, left unresolved problems in obscenity cases. Although the Roth decision had narrowed the definition, communities and states still wrestled with challenges posed by defendants who argued that their work was not obscene and therefore protected by the First Amendment. In 1973 the Supreme Court heard the case of *Miller v. California*, in which Marvin Miller, a distributor of sexually explicit materials, sent sales catalogs of adult publications by mail. He was charged with violating California law that prohibited distributing obscene material. The court addressed the question of how a community standard could be applied to determine obscenity.

■ PRIMARY SOURCE

The basic guidelines for the trier of fact must be: (a) whether "the average person, applying contemporary community standards" would find that the work, taken as a whole, appeals to the prurient interest, *Kois v. Wisconsin,* supra, at 230, quoting *Roth v. United States,* supra, at 489; (b) whether the work depicts or describes, in a patently offensive way, sexual conduct specifically defined by the applicable state law; and (c) whether the work, taken as a whole, lacks serious literary, artistic, political, or scientific value. We do not adopt as a constitutional standard the "utterly without redeeming social value" test of *Memoirs v. Massachusetts,* [413 U.S. 15, 25] 383 U.S., at 419 ; that concept has never commanded the adherence of more than three Justices at one time. 7 See supra, at 21. If a state law that regulates obscene material is thus limited, as written or construed, the First Amendment values applicable to the States through the Fourteenth Amendment are adequately protected by the ultimate power of appellate courts to conduct an independent review of constitutional claims when necessary.....

We emphasize that it is not our function to propose regulatory schemes for the States. That must await their concrete legislative efforts. It is possible, however, to give a few plain examples of what a state statute could define for regulation under part (b) of the standard announced in this opinion, supra:

(a) Patently offensive representations or descriptions of ultimate sexual acts, normal or perverted, actual or simulated.

(b) Patently offensive representations or descriptions of masturbation, excretory functions, and lewd exhibition of the genitals.

Sex and nudity may not be exploited without limit by films or pictures exhibited or sold in places of public accommodation any more than live sex and nudity can [413 U.S. 15, 26] be exhibited or sold without limit in such public places. 8 At a minimum, prurient, patently offensive depiction or description of sexual conduct must have

serious literary, artistic, political, or scientific value to merit First Amendment protection.... For example, medical books for the education of physicians and related personnel necessarily use graphic illustrations and descriptions of human anatomy. In resolving the inevitably sensitive questions of fact and law, we must continue to rely on the jury system, accompanied by the safeguards that judges, rules of evidence, presumption of innocence, and other protective features provide, as we do with rape, murder, and a host of other offenses against society and its individual members.

MR. JUSTICE BRENNAN, author of the opinions of the Court, or the plurality opinions, in *Roth v. United States,* supra; *Jacobellis v. Ohio,* supra; *Ginzburg v. United [413 U.S. 15, 27] States,* 383 U.S. 463 (1966), *Mishkin v. New York,* 383 U.S. 502 (1966); and *Memoirs v. Massachusetts,* supra, has abandoned his former position and now maintains that no formulation of this Court, the Congress, or the States can adequately distinguish obscene material unprotected by the First Amendment from protected expression.... Paradoxically, MR. JUSTICE BRENNAN indicates that suppression of unprotected obscene material is permissible to avoid exposure to unconsenting adults, as in this case, and to juveniles, although he gives no indication of how the division between protected and nonprotected materials may be drawn with greater precision for these purposes than for regulation of commercial exposure to consenting adults only. Nor does he indicate where in the Constitution he finds the authority to distinguish between a willing "adult" one month past the state law age of majority and a willing "juvenile" one month younger.

Under the holdings announced today, no one will be subject to prosecution for the sale or exposure of obscene materials unless these materials depict or describe patently offensive "hard core" sexual conduct specifically defined by the regulating state law, as written or construed. We are satisfied that these specific prerequisites will provide fair notice to a dealer in such materials that his public and commercial activities may bring prosecution.... The inability to define regulated materials with ultimate, god-like precision altogether removes the power of the States or the Congress to regulate, then "hard core" pornography may be exposed without limit to the juvenile, the passerby, and the consenting adult alike, as, indeed, MR. JUSTICE DOUGLAS contends.... In this belief, however, MR. JUSTICE DOUGLAS now stands alone.

MR. JUSTICE BRENNAN also emphasizes "institutional stress" in justification of his change of view. Noting that "[t]he number of obscenity cases on our docket gives ample testimony to the burden that has been placed upon this Court," he quite rightly remarks that the examination of contested materials "is hardly a source of edification to the members of this Court." Paris Adult [413 U.S. 15, 29] Theatre I v. Slaton, post, at 92, 93. He also notes, and we agree, that "uncertainty of the standards creates a continuing source of tension between state and federal courts …. The problem is…that one cannot say with certainty that material is obscene until at least five members of this Court, applying inevitably obscure standards, have pronounced it so." Id., at 93, 92.

It is certainly true that the absence, since Roth, of a single majority view of this Court as to proper standards for testing obscenity has placed a strain on both state and federal courts. But today, for the first time since Roth was decided in 1957, a majority of this Court has agreed on concrete guidelines to isolate "hard core" pornography from expression protected by the First Amendment. Now we may abandon the casual practice of Redrup v. New York, 386 U.S. 767 (1967), and attempt to provide positive guidance to federal and state courts alike.

This may not be an easy road, free from difficulty. But no amount of "fatigue" should lead us to adopt a convenient "institutional" rationale—an absolutist, "anything goes" view of the First Amendment—because it will lighten our burdens. 11 "Such an abnegation of judicial supervision in this field would be inconsistent with our duty to uphold the constitutional guarantees." Jacobellis v. Ohio, supra, at 187–188 (opinion of BRENNAN, J.). Nor should we remedy "tension between state and federal courts" by arbitrarily depriving the States of a power reserved to them under the Constitution, a power which they have enjoyed and exercised continuously from before the adoption of the First Amendment to this day. See Roth v. United States, supra, at 482–485. "Our duty admits of no 'substitute for facing up [413 U.S. 15, 30] to the tough individual problems of constitutional judgment involved in every obscenity case….'

III

Under a National Constitution, fundamental First Amendment limitations on the powers of the States do not vary from community to community, but this does not mean that there are, or should or can be, fixed, uniform national standards of precisely what appeals to the "prurient interest" or is "patently offensive." These are essentially questions of fact, and our Nation is simply too big and too diverse for this Court to reasonably expect that such standards could be articulated for all 50 States in a single formulation, even assuming the prerequisite consensus exists. When triers of fact are asked to decide whether "the average person, applying contemporary community standards" would consider certain materials "prurient," it would be unrealistic to require that the answer be based on some abstract formulation. The adversary system, with lay jurors as the usual ultimate factfinders in criminal prosecutions, has historically permitted triers of fact to draw on the standards of their community, guided always by limiting instructions on the law. To require a State to structure obscenity proceedings around evidence of a national "community standard" would be an exercise in futility.

As noted before, this case was tried on the theory that the California obscenity statute sought to incorporate the tripartite test of Memoirs. This, a "national" standard of First Amendment protection enumerated by a plurality of this Court, was correctly regarded at the time of trial as limiting state prosecution under the controlling case [413 U.S. 15, 31] law. The jury, however, was explicitly instructed that, in determining whether the "dominant theme of the material as a whole… appeals to the prurient interest" and in determining whether the material "goes substantially beyond customary limits of candor and affronts contemporary community standards of decency," it was to apply "contemporary community standards of the State of California."

During the trial, both the prosecution and the defense assumed that the relevant "community standards" in making the factual determination of obscenity were those of the State of California, not some hypothetical standard of the entire United States of America. Defense counsel at trial never objected to the testimony of the State's expert on community standards 12 or to the instructions of the trial judge on "statewide" standards. On appeal to the Appellate Department, Superior Court of California, County of Orange, appellant for the first time contended that application of state, rather than national, standards violated the First and Fourteenth Amendments.

We conclude that neither the State's alleged failure to offer evidence of "national standards," nor the trial court's charge that the jury consider state community standards, were constitutional errors. Nothing in the First Amendment requires that a jury must consider hypothetical and unascertainable "national standards" when attempting to determine whether certain materials are obscene as a matter [413 U.S. 15, 32] of fact. Mr. Chief Justice Warren pointedly commented in his dissent in Jacobellis v. Ohio, supra, at 200:

"It is my belief that when the Court said in Roth that obscenity is to be defined by reference to 'community standards,' it meant community standards—not a national standard, as is sometimes argued. I believe that there is no provable 'national standard.'…"At all events, this Court has not been able to enunciate one, and it would be unreasonable to expect local courts to divine one."

It is neither realistic nor constitutionally sound to read the First Amendment as requiring that the people of

Maine or Mississippi accept public depiction of conduct found tolerable in Las Vegas, or New York City....People in different States vary in their tastes and attitudes, and this diversity is not to be strangled by the absolutism of imposed uniformity. As the Court made clear in *Mishkin v. New York,* 383 U.S., at 508–509, the primary concern with requiring a jury to apply the standard of "the average person, applying contemporary community standards" is to be certain that, so far as material is not aimed at a deviant group, it will be judged by its impact on an average person, rather than a particularly susceptible or sensitive person - or indeed a totally insensitive one. See *Roth v. United States,* supra, at 489. Cf., the now discredited test in *Regina v. Hicklin,* 1868. L. R. 3 Q. B. 360. We hold that the requirement that the jury evaluate the materials with reference to "contemporary [413 U.S. 15, 34] standards of the State of California" serves this protective purpose and is constitutionally adequate.

SIGNIFICANCE

Miller v. California established the "three-prong obscenity test" for determining whether material is obscene: First, does "the average person, applying contemporary community standards" find the work obscene? Second, does the work depict or describe sexual conduct as defined by state law, in an offensive way? Third, does the work lack serious literary, artistic, political, or scientific value? By incorporating the Roth test into the Miller test, the Supreme Court narrowed the definition of obscenity and drastically reduced the number of obscenity case it heard.

In establishing this test, the Supreme Court provided an avenue for local communities, rather than states or the federal government, to decide whether material is obscene. Even within a community, however, the Miller test requires that the "average person" be the litmus test; this prevents extremists on either end from dictating standards.

Magazine publisher Larry Flynt answers questions from newsmen Februaury 9, 1977, after being convicted of pandering obscenity and engaging in orgazined crime in Cinncinnati. AP IMAGES

The third step, called the "SLAPS" test, examines whether the material has "serious literary, artistic, political, or scientific value." For instance, works by writers such as James Joyce, Henry Miller, Vladimir Nabakov, and others pass the test, in that their work has literary merit. The SLAPS test gave law enforcement officials an objective standard to use in evaluating allegedly obscene material.

The three-prong test was used by Congress to craft the 1996 Communications Decency Act (CDA), which prohibited the publication of "indecent" or "patently offensive" material on internet sites, especially the intentional transmittal of indecent or obscene materials to minors. Critics of the CDA argued that it violated Miller as well as the First Amendment. What constitutes "community standards" when electronic media broadens the "community" to include people from a wide range of states and countries? How much responsibility do content providers hold in regulating the information to which children are exposed?

The Supreme Court struck down the Communications Decency Act in 1997, declaring that it abridged the First Amendment and created a double standard in which print media could publish various materials that would be illegal for electronic media publishers.

The CDA sparked debate about the term "community" and the relevance of the Miller Test in modern electronic publishing. While child pornography and certain extreme forms of pornography are clearly defined "obscene" materials and remain illegal for all publishers, the juncture of *Miller v. California*, and the World Wide Web raises new questions about definitions of obscenity, indecency, community, and sexual standards.

FURTHER RESOURCES

Books

Harrison, Maureen, and Steve Gilbert, eds. *Obscenity and Pornography Decisions of the United States Supreme Court.* Carlsbad, Calif.: Excellent Books 2000.

Heins, Marjorie. *Not in Front of the Children: "Indecency," Censorship, and the Innocence of Youth.* New York: Hill and Wang 2001.

Wheeler, Lee Ann. *Against Obscenity : Reform and the Politics of Womanhood in America, 1873–1935.* Baltimore: The Johns Hopkins University Press. 2004.

Periodicals

Posner, Michael. "Both Chambers Act on Obscenity Curbs."*National Journal* (March 2004).

Web sites

Find Law "Roth v. United States." <http://caselaw.lp.find-law.com/scripts/getcase/> (accessed March 16, 2006).

Preschool Teacher May Have Molested 60 Young Children

Newspaper article

By: Anonymous

Date: March 7, 1984

Source: "Preschool Teacher May Have Molested 60 Young Children." *Boston Globe.* March 7, 1984.

About the Author: This article was written by an unnamed staff writer at the *Boston Globe*, a daily newspaper based in Boston, Massachusetts, with a circulation of over 500,000 worldwide.

INTRODUCTION

The McMartin preschool case was one of a series of cases centered on alleged ritual and sexual abuse in day care facilities in the 1980s. This primary source is an early report on the first arrests, searches, and allegations made by authorities against the owners and operators of the McMartin preschool in Manhattan Beach, California.

The author does not mention a feature of the case that was later to become central: The only evidence against the McMartins was the testimony of allegedly abused children. Although the article claims that photographs of "nude children performing sex acts," had been taken, no such pictures existed. Nor was any medical or other physical evidence ever produced. The prosecution's case was founded entirely on child testimony, much of it elicited by questionable interviewing methods.

Ray Buckey, a teacher at the preschool and grandson of the school's founder Virginia McMartin, was arrested in August 1983 and accused of sexually abusing a two-year-old boy. The charge was brought by Buckey's wife, from whom he was separated, and who the article identifies only as the "mother of a two-year-old." Buckey was released for lack of evidence, but police then contacted hundreds of parents whose children had attended the McMartin school.

Peggy McMartin Buckey testifies in her own defense in a Los Angeles courtroom on May 18, 1989. AP IMAGES

Under questioning by therapists and parents, children said that Ray, his mother Peggy, his grandmother Virginia, and other teachers had committed sex crimes and numerous bizarre acts against them. Some children described satanic animal sacrifices in tunnels beneath the school; others claimed that they had been led through underground tunnels to a crematorium where they beat dead bodies and watched them burn. Approximately 360 children were identified as abuse victims during the interviews.

The trial was the longest and most expensive in U.S. legal history; the preliminary hearings alone lasted 20 months. In 1989, Ray's mother was acquitted on all counts. Ray himself was acquitted on most counts, with the jury hung on others. In 1990, Buckey was tried again; the jury deadlocked on all counts. By the time he was finally released, he had spent five years in jail.

In 1990, efforts to find evidence of tunnels beneath the school found soil disturbances and objects that convinced some observers that filled-in tunnels had been found. Most observers viewed the evidence as insufficient to prove their existence. Skeptics pointed to the difficulty that the McMartins would have had in filling the tunnels with compacted soil while in jail.

■ PRIMARY SOURCE

Preschool Teacher May Have Molested 60 Young Children

MANHATTAN BEACH, Calif.—Photographs, weapons and records were seized in raids on 10 homes and now-closed school where authorities say up to 60 young children were bound, sexually abused, and forced to watch while pet rabbits and turtles were mutilated.

Today's raids came six months after a former teacher was arrested on suspicion of child molesting after the mother of a 2-year-old complained, authorities said.

Among the homes searched were those of Virginia McMartin, who ran the preschool for 30 years; her daughter, Peggy McMartin Buckey, who helped run the school; and Mrs. Buckey's son, Raymond C. Buckey, who had taught at the school.

Buckey, 25, was arrested Sept. 7 on suspicion of child molestation and released on $15,000 bail. However, the district attorney never filed charges against him, saying additional investigation was needed, and his bail was refunded.

The school voluntarily closed three months ago after parents began withdrawing their children.

The California Department of [Child Protection] Services complaint now alleges that for more than a year before his arrest, Buckey molested at least 25 boys and girls between the ages of 2 and 5 who were under the care of the preschool. Manhattan Beach police and the Los Angeles district attorney's office have said the number may be as high as 60.

Photographs allegedly were taken of nude children performing sex acts, although police Sgt. Jim Noble said boxes of evidence had yet to be examined.

In addition, police said, a former teacher tried to frighten the children into silence by maiming or killing pet animals while the children watched.

The teacher reportedly warned the children the same thing would happen to their parents if they talked, investigators have said.

SIGNIFICANCE

The belief that ritualistic sexual torture of children by day care providers was rampant swept the American public during the 1980s. The first notable case of this type occurred in 1983 in Kern County, California, where eight people were sent to prison on the basis of child testimony that they had abused their students in bizarre, ritualistic ways. All convictions were later overturned, but some were not freed until the mid-1990s. The McMartin case followed soon after and had some of the same features, especially the reliance of the prosecution on child testimony that bizarre ritualistic abuse had occurred. Several similar cases followed in the next several years. The McMartin case was unusual in that no convictions were obtained at all. Convictions were obtained in most of the other day care abuse cases but were later overturned.

Sexual abuse of children is not unusual. However, this does not mean that all claims of abuse are true. According to Dr. Stephen Ceci of Cornell University (interviewed by the Public Broadcasting System in 1998), a child can sometimes adopt a "false belief"—an inaccurate conviction about what they have witnessed, done, or experienced. "[K]ids are cooperative conversational partners," Ceci explained. "They believe that you're asking them about something because it probably happened. They want to please you, they want to give you the answer that they think will make you happiest." This opens the way to the formation of false beliefs, especially about persons who have been identified with "negative stereotyping," such as repeated assurances that the person in question is now in jail and cannot hurt the child.

Ceci and colleagues performed experiments in which they found that false beliefs about harmless events could easily be induced by questioning techniques similar to those used to obtain testimony in the day care abuse cases. For example, after repeated questioning about whether they had gone on a trip by hot-air balloon, children would eventually become convinced that they had done so. They would then resist suggestions that the trip was imaginary. A detailed, self-consistent narrative tends to develop in such cases, unlike the inconsistent, shifting, vague narratives that young children tend to construct when deliberately lying. The resulting testimony can be extremely convincing.

The McMartin case and other day care ritual abuse cases triggered a permanent heightening of legal skepticism child testimony. In 1994, the New Jersey State Supreme Court upheld a lower court's overturned conviction of a nursery-school teacher accused of abuse, saying that "the interviews of the children were highly improper and utilized coercive and unduly suggestive methods."

FURTHER RESOURCES

Web sites

Earl, John. "The Dark Truth About the 'Dark Tunnels of McMartin.'" *Issues in Child Abuse Accusations* 7 (1995) <http://www.geocities.com/kidhistory/mcmartin.htm> (accessed March 17, 2006).

Public Broadcasting System. "The Child Terror." Oct. 27, 1998. Available at <http://www.pbs.org/wgbh/pages/frontline/shows/terror/> (accessed March 17, 2006).

Summit, Roland C. "The Dark Tunnels of McMartin." *Journal of Psychohistory*, 21, no. 4 (Spring 1994) <http://www.geocities.com/kidhistory/mcmartin.htm> (accessed March 17, 2006).

Clergy Sexual Abuse: Dirty Secret Comes to Light

Newspaper article

By: Richard Higgins

Date: May 11, 1990

Source: Higgins, Richard. "Clergy Sexual Abuse: Dirty Secret Comes to Light." *Boston Globe* (May 11, 1990).

About the Author: Richard Higgins is a writer, book editor, and a former reporter for the *Boston Globe*. Higgins is a graduate of Holy Cross College in Indiana and has master's degrees from Columbia Journalism School and Harvard Divinity School.

INTRODUCTION

In 1985, the first allegations of sexual misconduct by Catholic priests emerged in a confidential memo written by Thomas Doyle, a cannon lawyer for the Vatican, to the bishops of the United States. The memo cited thirty cases and over one hundred victims of alleged sex crimes perpetrated by priests against parishioners and estimated a ten-year cost to the church of over $1 billion in settlements and legal fees. Also in 1985, Jason Berry, a journalist for the *National Catholic Reporter*, published an examination of nationwide allegations of sexual misconduct by priests. Four years later, in 1989, Joseph Ferrario became the first U.S. bishop accused of molestation charges, which were later dismissed by the court. The bishops agreed, in 1992, to a set of principles to govern the handling of accusations of sexual abuse by priests. Berry continued his investigations and by that same year had documented over four hundred cases of sexual misconduct by priests, many perpetrated against children.

In June of 2001, Cardinal Bernard Law, Archbishop of the Boston diocese, admitted in a routine court filing that he appointed defrocked priest John Geoghan to the position of vicar of a parochial school despite seventeen years of allegations of sexual abuse, including the molestation of seven boys. The archdiocese had received over 150 allegations of misconduct by Geoghan over his career and he was eventually defrocked in 1989. The admission opened a floodgate of charges against priests. Though claims of sex abuse by priests certainly did not begin in 2002, their number skyrocketed that year leading to a public outcry and eventually a response by the Vatican. Law's admission occurred during the trial of Geoghan, who faced charges of indecent assault and battery. He was con-

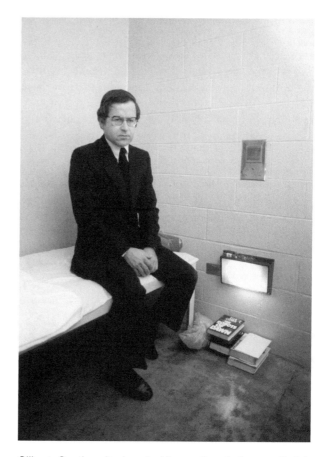

Gilbert Gauthe sits in a holding cell at Lafayette Parish Sheriff's Office, 1985. Father Gauthe was accused was sexually abusing dozens of altar boys. © PHILIP GOULD/CORBIS

victed of fondling a young boy at a pool and sentenced to nine to ten years in prison. The Boston Archdiocese eventually reached a $10 million settlement with eighty-six other alleged victims. While incarcerated, Geoghan awaited trial for child rape; however, he was killed by another inmate.

By 2002, the Boston Archdiocese received over five hundred allegations of sexual abuse perpetrated by priests and the church had paid out at least $40 million in settlements to victims. Some of the most notorious priests allegedly engaged in activities over decades and were shuffled from parish to parish once allegations arose regarding their conduct. Joseph Birmingham was one such priest. Birmingham, who died in 1989, allegedly abused over fifty boys in his twenty-nine years as a priest. According to the *Boston Globe*, the archdiocese ignored complaints against Birmingham.

Another example of the archdiocese's inaction against accusations of sexual abuse occurred in dealing with Paul Shanley. Shanley operated a street ministry program during the 1960s and 1970s to provide guidance and assistance to young runaways, drug addicts, and youths struggling with their sexual identity. According to reports, Shanley took advantage of those youths participating in the program. The archdiocese received complaints regarding Shanley's behavior and as a result, transferred him from parish to parish until he was finally transferred to California with the recommendation of Cardinal Law. Shanley, who publicly advocated sex with boys, was arrested in San Diego and returned to Boston to face ten counts of child rape charges and six counts of indecent assault and battery. In February 2005, he was sentenced to twelve to fifteen years in prison for two counts of child rape and two counts of indecent assault on a child under fourteen years of age.

■ PRIMARY SOURCE

Sexual misconduct among clergy, long a feared and fiercely kept secret within churches, is increasingly being reported by its victims. The complaints are forcing some churches and denominations to handle allegations of misconduct more openly and with more concern for its victims.

"The first step has been to break down the wall of silence and denial," said Rev. Marie M. Fortune, a specialist on sexual ethics within religion.

About "three to five" new allegations of misconduct by ministers, priests and rabbis are reported each week around the country, said Rev. Fortune of the United Church of Christ, the founder and executive director of the Center for the Prevention of Sexual and Domestic Violence.

The center, which focuses on the religious community, is based in Seattle.

Although there are no comprehensive national statistics, Rev. Fortune, who works with the victims and has served as a consultant to churches on the subject, said she knows of at least 250 misconduct cases in the last two years. The reported cases are "the tip of the iceberg," she said.

In the Boston area, Dr. Lawrence Kistler, clinical director of the Interfaith Counseling Center in Newton, reported "an upswing" in the number of victims of clergy misconduct coming to the center for counseling. He attributed that to "the increasing visibility of the issue."

The US Roman Catholic Church plans to spend hundreds of millions of dollars in settlements for cases of misconduct by its clergy, according to Rev. Fortune,

author of a new book, "Is Nothing Sacred: When Sex Invades the Pastoral Relationship."

Her estimate was based on a 1986 private report to the National Conference of Catholic Bishops by an advisory committee of two Roman Catholic priests and a lawyer.

The report, warning of insurance liability problems, said settlements costs for abuse cases "could reach $1 billion" by 1996. It was cited in "Psychotherapists: Sexual Involvement with Clients; Intervention and Prevention," published by the Walk-In Counseling Center in Minneapolis.

Rev. Kenneth Doyle, head of media relations for the United States Catholic Conference, said Rev. Fortune's estimate was "wildly speculative" and "sounds incredibly high."

Father Doyle said dioceses respond locally to any instances of misconduct but the Catholic Conference would give guidance if asked. "Our first interest is a pastoral one, to protect children, counsel families and, if there seems to be any basis for an allegation, to remove a priest from a situation. Even one case is a serious problem," Father Doyle said. But he said that given the 53,000 Roman Catholic priests in the country, the offenders are "numerically insignificant."

Rev Fortune, who led a two-day conference recently on the subject at Andover-Newton Theological School in Newton, said most misconduct cases involved male clergy abusing women but there was a substantial number of cases of abuse of boys as well.

Rev. Fortune described all the cases as "professional" misconduct. "It isn't a question of sex, it's a question of professional boundaries and professional trust," she said.

Two researches at the University of California who have studied the subject say the rate of sexual misconduct among the clergy is roughly the same as that for psychotherapists.

Studies have indicated that 10 percent of male therapists and 1 percent of female therapists have disclosed sexual contact with a client, she said. A mail survey of 80 pastors by the Center for Ethics and Social Policy at the University of California, Berkeley, found that 10 percent reported having a sexual relationship with a church member.

Complaints against the clergy are rising in part because of press attention on misconduct involving psychotherapists, said Rev. Ronald Barton of the Community Church of the Monterey Peninsula in Carmel, Calif.

"The current cultural environment is one in which victims of all kinds of abuse are ready to name the abuse and the abuser," said Rev. Barton, who helped conduct the Berkeley survey.

The victims of such abuse are particularly vulnerable because of the power vested in the clergy in many denominations as people whose moral and sacramental authority comes from God.

Despite the prevalence of psychotherapy in American society today, it is to the clergy that millions of Americans still turn in times of personal trouble. For many parishioners, a sexual violation by the minister or priest destroys a sacred trust.

"By authority of their position, ministers have a lot of sway over people coming to them seeking help," said Rev. Emilie M. Townes of the Saint Paul School of Theology in Kansas City, a Methodist seminary that recently held a conference on professional ethics for ministers.

"If the minister is always right, then anything he or she asks of them must not be out of line," Rev. Townes said.

Speaking at the Andover-Newton conference, Rev. Fortune said the problem is one of clergy "taking advantage of a situation in which the other person is vulnerable. And the meaning is intensified because it's a spiritual leader" sexualizing the relationship.

The "power imbalance" in such a relationship is so great, she said, that it is "inherently difficult" for clergy to be both pastor and sexual partner to a parishioner, especially outside of marriage. Spouses of clergy commonly seek other persons besides their spouse for spiritual direction.

The ecumenical conference at Andover Newton was designed to educate religious leaders on how to prevent and, if necessary, intervene when a worshiper reports abuse. Two Episcopal bishops, a Roman Catholic auxiliary bishop from Maine, a Roman Catholic priest from Worcester, local Congregational, Baptist and Lutheran denominational executives, pastoral counselors and parish pastors of various denominations registered for the conference.

"Some of us within the discipline of the church have become aware of the fact that the church is not effectively dealing with professional misconduct," said Rev. Dayl Hufford of the United Church of Christ and executive director of Foundations, a pastoral counseling center near the Newton school. Rev. Hufford said a number of the center's clients are clergy offenders who have been referred by their denominations or who have reported themselves to try to "get a handle" on their misconduct.

In response to the growing number of cases, some church groups are creating policies to respond openly and ethically to charges that clergy have sexually abused boys and women.

"The good news is that some denominations at the national level are moving swiftly and carefully to name the problem, to remove offending pastors so as to protect the church from further erosion of credibility and to bring healing to victims and survivors," Rev. Fortune said in a recent talk at the Harvard Divinity School in Cambridge.

Churches in Minnesota, for example, have set up a statewide interfaith committee to deal with the problem, and other churches around the nation are reviewing its guidelines.

At a conference on sexual misconduct earlier this year, Episcopal Bishop Harold A. Hopkins Jr., who directs pastoral development for the church headquarters in New York, said most churches are more willing to listen.

"The church has often looked the other way when inappropriate behavior occurs on the part of the clergy," said Bishop Hopkins. "Our commitment is not only to recognize the problem exists but to take preventative and educational steps."

On the other hand, said Rev. Fortune, "even when informed of the problem" some denominations are "continuing to hide their heads in the sand."

"Most judicatories don't want to deal with this kind of thing until it's too late and it lands in their lap," said one Boston-area church denominational executive who asked not to be identified.

Clergy misconduct has sometimes remained hidden behind the legal veil in common law that protects the clergy-parishioner relationship because of its confessional nature. Priests, for example, are not obliged to testify about matters disclosed to them during a confession.

More and more cases are coming to the courts, in part because victims are less willing to settle out of court.

Jeffrey W. Anderson, a St. Paul lawyer who specializes in clergy misconduct cases, said he has represented "about 60" people who have sued over sexual abuse by clergy in the last five years.

Massachusetts, Anderson noted, has a "charitable immunities" law that makes it difficult to hold churches financially accountable for personal injury and damages greater than $20,000.

"It may be true that percentage of clergy who engage in abuse or misconduct is small, but it's alarmingly prevalent," Anderson said. "The failure of the churches to deal with misconduct is why so many of these cases are winding up in court."

SIGNIFICANCE

In April 2002, Pope John Paul II called a conference of the United States cardinals and tasked them with the creation of a policy to handle allegations and prevent future cases from occurring. The pope stated, "There is no place in the priesthood and religious life for those who would harm the young." In response to the pope's admonishing, the U.S. bishops met in June of 2002 and agreed on a policy for handling allegations. The policy stated that an accused priest would be automatically removed from his position, but not automatically defrocked from the priesthood. Priests who have become, "notorious and [are] guilty of the serial, predatory sexual abuse of minors" would be submitted to a special course of action, with the role to defrock the priest. The Vatican initially rejected this document and in November of 2002, the bishops passed an amendment to immediately remove any priest who is convicted of engaging in sexual abuse of a minor. By this time, over 325 of the nation's 46,000 priests had been reassigned due to allegations of sexual misconduct. By December, the Vatican accepted the new policy toward sexual predators within the priesthood. In addition, Cardinal Bernard Law, of the Boston Archdiocese, resigned his position under pressure from the public.

FURTHER RESOURCES

Web sites

Boston Globe. "Spotlight Investigation: Abuse in the Catholic Church." <http://www.boston.com/globe/spotlight/abuse> (accessed April 1, 2006).

CBS News. "Instruction on the Manner of Proceeding in Cases of Solicitation." <http://www.cbsnews.com/htdocs/pdf/Criminales.pdf> (accessed April 1, 2006).

——— "Taint of Church Sex Scandal Lingers." <http://www.cbsnews.com/stories/2002/04/19/national/main506674.shtml> (accessed April 1, 2006).

Lolita

Book excerpt

By: Vladimir Nabokov

Date: 1955

Source: Nabokov, Vladimir. *Lolita.* Everyman's Library. New York: Knopf, 1992. Originally published in 1955.

About the Author: Vladimir Nabokov was born in St. Petersburg, Russia, in 1899. He was the oldest of five siblings and was raised in a wealthy, aristocratic family. After the Bolshevik Revolution in 1919, Nabokov and his family moved to England where he enrolled in Cambridge University to study French and Russian literature. After leaving England in 1922, Nabokov published his first Russian novel, *Mary*, in 1925; he continued to publish novels in Russian during the years before World War II, when he lived in Germany and France. *The Real Life of Sebastian Knight*, his first English novel, was published in 1941. In the 1950s, while pursuing another of his passions—the study of butterflys, Nabokov wrote his most famous work, *Lolita*. He died in 1977 having published several other works during the last sixteen years of his life, including *Pale Fire* and *Ada; or Ardor: A Family Chronicle*. None of them matched the notoriety of *Lolita*.

INTRODUCTION

After being rejected by four American publishers, *Lolita* was finally published in 1955 by a French publisher, Olympia Press. The book's first printing of 5,000 copies sold out quickly after author and critic Graham Greene hailed the work in the London *Times* as one of the best books of the year. *Lolita* also received other, less laudatory reviews as well. John Gordon of the *Sunday Express* called it "sheer unrestrained pornography"; the British Home Office confiscated all copies that entered the country. In 1956, the French interior minister banned the novel as well; it remained forbidden for two years. In 1958, the book was finally published in the United States and sold 100,000 copies in three weeks, the first novel to do so since *Gone with the Wind*.

The novel tells the story of Humbert Humbert, who is writing a novel from his jail cell, where he's being held while on trial for murder. His manuscript recounts his love affair with twelve-year-old Dolores Haze, or Lolita, the daughter of his landlady, Charlotte Haze, who rented a room to Humbert after his wife left him on the eve of their emigration to the United States.

Humbert, still recovering from an earlier, unrequited infatuation with Annabel, another "nymphet," soon becomes obsessed with Lolita. When her mother sends Lolita away to summer camp, Humbert marries Charlotte. After Charlotte discovers Humbert's journal documenting his obsession with Lolita, she is struck by a car.

Humbert picks up Lolita from her summer camp and tells her that her mother is at a hospital. The two have their first sexual encounter and then set out on a driving tour of the United States. As they travel for the next year, they continue the affair. They settle in the town of Beardsley, but their stay is short-lived. Lolita is pursued by Clare Quilty, a well-known writer and producer of pornography, who eventually bribes Lolita to leave Humbert and work for him. After years apart, Humbert receives word from Lolita, who is now eighteen, that she needs his help. Humbert finds Quilty and kills him, feeling justified that he did society a favor by killing a person with such perversions.

■ PRIMARY SOURCE

Now I wish to introduce the following idea. Between the age limits of nine and fourteen there occur maidens who, to certain bewitched travelers, twice or many times older than they, reveal their true nature which is not human, but nymphic (that is, demoniac); and these chosen creatures I propose to designate as "nymphets."

It would be marked that I substitute time terms for spatial ones. In fact, I would have the reader see "nine" and "fourteen" as the boundaries—the mirrory beaches and rosy rocks—of an enchanted island haunted by those nymphets of mine and surrounded by a vast, misty sea. Between those age limits, are all girl-children nymphets? Of course not. Otherwise, we who are in the know, we lone voyagers, we nympholepts, would have long gone insane. Neither are good looks any criterion; and vulgarity, or at least what a given community terms so, does not necessarily impair certain mysterious characteristics, the fey grace, the elusive, shifty, soul-shattering, insidious charm that separates the nymphet from such coevals of hers as are incomparably more dependent on the spatial world of synchronous phenomena than on that intangible island of entranced time where Lolita plays with her likes. Within the same age limits the number of true nymphets is strikingly inferior to that of provisionally plain, or just nice, or "cute," or even "sweet" and "attractive," ordinary, plumpish, formless, cold-skinned, essentially human little girls, with tummies and pigtails, who may or may not turn into adults of great beauty (look at the ugly dumplings in black stockings and white hats that are metamorphosed into stunning stars of the screen). A normal man given a group photograph of school girls or Girls Scouts and asked to point out the comeliest one will not necessarily choose the nymphet among them. You have to be an artist and a madman, a creature of infinite melancholy, with a bubble of hot poison in your loins and a super-voluptuous flame permanently aglow in your subtle spine (oh, how you have to cringe and hide!), in order to discern at once, by ineffable signs—the slightly feline outline of a cheekbone, the slenderness of a downy limb, and other indices which

despair and shame and tears of tenderness forbid me to tabulate—the little deadly demon among the wholesome children; *she* stands unrecognized by them and unconscious herself of her fantastic power.

Furthermore, since the idea of time plays such a magic part in the matter, the student should not be surprised to learn that there must be a gap of several years, never less than ten I should say, generally thirty or forty, and as many as ninety in a few known cases, between maiden and man to enable the latter to come under a nymphet's spell. It is a question of focal adjustment, of a certain distance that the inner eye thrills to surmount, and a certain contrast that the mind perceives with a grasp of perverse delight. When I was a child and she was a child, my little Annabel was no nymphet to me; I was her equal, a faunlet in my own right, on that same enchanted island of time; but today, in September 1952, after twenty-nine years have elapsed, I think I can distinguish in her the initial fateful elf in my life. We loved each other with a premature love, marked by a fierceness that so often destroys adult lives. I was a strong lad and survived; but the poison was in the wound, and the wound remained ever open, and soon I found myself maturing amid a civilization which allows a man of twenty-five to court a girl of sixteen but not a girl of twelve.

No wonder, then, that my adult life during the European period of my existence proved monstrously twofold. Overtly, I had so-called normal relationships with a number of terrestrial women having pumpkins or pears for breasts; only, I was consumed by a hell furnace of localized lust for every passing nymphet whom as a law-abiding poltroon I never dared approach. The human females I was allowed to wield were but palliative agents. I am ready to believe that the sensations I derived from natural fornication were much the same as those known to normal big males consorting with their normal big mates in that routine rhythm which shakes the world. The trouble was that those gentlemen had not, and I *had*, caught glimpses of an incomparably more poignant bliss. The dimmest of my pollutive dreams was a thousand times more dazzling than all the adultery the most virile writer of genius or the most talented impotent might imagine. My world was split. I was aware of not one but two sexes, neither of which was mine; both would be termed female by the anatomist. But to me, through the prism of my senses, "they were as different as mist and mast." All this I rationalize now. In my twenties and early thirties, I did not understand my throes quite so clearly. While my body knew what it craved for, my mind rejected my body's every plea. One moment I was ashamed and frightened, another recklessly optimistic. Taboos strangulated me. Psychoanalysts wooed me with pseudoliberations of pseudolibidoes. The fact that to me the only objects of amorous tremor were sisters of Annabel's, her handmaids and girl-pages, appeared to me at times as a forerunner of insanity. At other times I would tell myself that it was all a question of attitude, that there was really nothing wrong in being moved to distraction by girl-children.

SIGNIFICANCE

Nabokov's son Dmitri once noted that his father was more than "a person who wrote a very dirty book put out by a very dirty publisher." However, *Lolita*'s legacy overshadowed most of Nabokov's later literary works. Advocates and academics assert that the novel itself was benign, but that its legacy overtook the novel itself. The book was first translated to film in a 1962 version directed by Stanley Kubrick with a screenplay written by Nabokov himself. The film ran into the same problems that the book at first encountered. Kubrick was forced to deal with film industry censorship as well as powerful film rating groups who deemed it obscene. A 1997 film version received additional objections about the content.

Nabokov supporters suggest that the image of Lolita has been transformed by mass media. The book itself is not taught to high school students, not taught to many undergraduates, and has not been a best seller since it was first introduced. However, the idea of Lolita emerges in advertising; allusions—such as Amy Fisher's nickname "The Long Island Lolita"; and in music like the Police's "Don't Stand So Close to Me." Lolita branding covers anything from call girl services to underwear.

In August 1996, the First World Congress Against Commercial Exploitation of Children protested the release of the 1997 film version of *Lolita* and launched an attack on "Lolita imagery" in advertising. Regardless of academic acclaim of the book *Lolita*, much of society refuses to tolerate the depiction of pedophilia.

Customers at a London bookshop read *Lolita*. November 7, 1959. PHOTO BY KEYSTONE/GETTY IMAGES

FURTHER RESOURCES

Periodicals

Marks, John. "Lolita, a Girl for the '90s." *U.S. News and World Report* (October 14, 1996).

Schiff, Stacy. "Forever Young." *New York Times* (September 15, 2005).

Web sites

CNN In-Depth Reports. "Beyond Lolita: Rediscovering Nabokov on His Birth Centennial" <http://www.cnn.com/SPECIALS/books/1999/nabokov> (accessed March 20, 2006).

Megan's Law

Legislation

By: U.S. Congress

Date: May 17, 1996.

Source: "Megan's Law." Title 42 U.S. Code 14071(d), May 17, 1996.

About the Author: Congress is the legislative branch of the national government of the United States. It is made up of the Senate and the House of Representatives.

INTRODUCTION

On July 29, 1994, seven year old Megan Kanka was playing near her home in Hamilton Township, New Jersey. A neighbor who lived directly across the street, Jesse Timmendequas, lured her to his home by promising to show Megan his puppy. Timmendequas was a convicted sex offender, with convictions in 1979 and 1981 for aggravated sexual assault and attempted sexual conduct on two children ages seven and five. Megan's parents, Richard and Maureen Kanka, were unaware of Timmendequas' history.

According to Timmendequas' confession to police, he raped Megan, then covered her head with plastic bags and strangled her, to prevent her from telling her parents or authorities. He then dumped her body in the weeds at a nearby park. Megan's parents had alerted police to her disappearance after they went around the neighborhood, canvassing neighbors. Timmendequas spoke to them, telling the Kankas he had seen Megan earlier, playing outside. When police canvassed the neighborhood shortly after, Timmendequas appeared to be nervous in conversations with the officers. A police background check revealed his criminal record, along with the sex offender status of his two roommates, both convicted felons. Twenty-four hours after the police searches began, Timmendequas confessed to her murder and led authorities to Megan's body.

Richard and Maureen Kanka, in the aftermath of Megan's murder, began to advocate for sex offender registration laws that allowed the public to know where a sex offender lived and/or worked. The Kankas repeatedly stated in newspaper interviews that had they known about Timmendequas' convictions against children, and the sex offender status of his roommates, they would have been better able to assess risk in their neighborhood and protect their daughter.

Sex offender registry laws were not new; their genesis can be traced back to California in the 1940s. At the time of Megan's murder, Oregon had just passed a sex offender registry law. The Kankas petitioned the New Jersey legislature to pass a law similar to that in Oregon; in late 1994, Megan's Law legislation passed both houses of the New Jersey legislature and became law just eighty days after Megan's murder.

President William Clinton signed a federal version of Megan's Law in 1996. The federal Megan's Law was an amendment of the 1994 Jacob Wetterling Crimes Against Children and Sexually Violent Offender Registration Act, which had already mandated the creation of state sex offender registries. Under Megan's Law, the public now had the right to know about sex offenders, their names, addresses, and crimes committed. States that did not comply with the law risked losing federal funds for law enforcement.

PRIMARY SOURCE

An Act

To amend the Violent Crime Control and Law Enforcement Act of 1994 to require the release of relevant information to protect the public from sexually violent offenders. <<NOTE: May 17, 1996 - [H.R. 2137]>>

Be it enacted by the Senate and House of Representatives of the United States of America in Congress assembled, <<NOTE: Megan's Law.>>

SECTION 1. <<NOTE: 42 USC 13701 note.>> SHORT TITLE.

This Act may be cited as "Megan's Law".

SEC. 2. RELEASE OF INFORMATION AND CLARIFICATION OF PUBLIC NATURE OF INFORMATION.

Section 170101(d) of the Violent Crime Control and Law Enforcement Act of 1994 (42 U.S.C. 14071(d)) is amended to read as follows:

(d) Release of Information.—

1. The information collected under a State registration program may be disclosed for any purpose permitted under the laws of the State.

2. (2) The designated State law enforcement agency and any local law enforcement agency authorized by the State agency shall release relevant information that is necessary to protect the public concerning a specific person required to register under this section, except that the identity of a victim of an offense that requires registration under this section shall not be released.

Approved May 17, 1996.

SIGNIFICANCE

The Kankas promoted Megan's Law as a protective measure to promote public awareness of sex offenders in neighborhoods; current psychological research indicates that those who commit sex offenses against children have the highest recidivism rates among criminal populations.

Opponents of sex offender registry laws argue that these laws punish convicted offenders who served their sentence. By forcing the convicted sex offender to publicly announce his or her crime through registration, the offender faces a second sentence of sorts. In addition, a small percentage of sex offenders are charged with statutory rape, in cases where an eighteen year old perpetrator has sexual relations with a fif-

A sign warning of danger from a registered sex offender is posted in front of a house in Corpus Christi, Texas on May 22, 2001. Judge J. Manuel Banales ordered 15 Corpus Christi sex offenders to post signs in their yards. AP IMAGES

teen year old. In some of these cases, the fifteen year old gave verbal consent, but legally is under the age of consent, and rape charges applied. In addition, non-violent sex offenses, such as public indecency or lewd acts, require the convicted criminal to register as a sex offender; critics of this policy point to the destructive impact such registration has on the career, housing, and community involvement of such non-violent offenders.

In two 2003 United States Supreme Court decisions, Smith v. Doe, 01-729 and Connecticut Dept. of Public Safety v. Doe, 01-1231, the court determined that the laws do not violate the rights of offenders and do not constitute punishment after having served one's sentence. The laws are designed to regulate and to disseminate information of vital public important, the court said.

Police departments and states turned to the Internet as a vehicle for providing information about sex offender registries. The United States Department of Justice hosts the National Sex Offender Public Registry, in which users conduct searches by state and zip code. Each state sets different terms for the release of public information; some states provide public information on all sex offenders while others maintain registries for all, but release information to the public only for those offenders classified as likely to offend again.

On May 30, 1997, Jesse Timmendequas was convicted on counts of capital murder, kidnapping and aggravated sexual assault and sentenced to death. He remained on New Jersey's death row as of 2006.

Registries in the United States track more than 500,000 sex offenders nationwide.

FURTHER RESOURCES

Books

J. Craissati. *Managing High Risk Sex Offenders in the Community; A Psychological Approach.* Brunner-Routledge2000.

Periodicals

Brooks, Alexander D. "Megan's Law: Constitutionality and Policy." *Criminal Justice Ethics* vol. 15, 1996.

Web sites

Bureau of Justice Assistance. "Jacob Wetterling Crimes Against Children And Sexually Violent Offender Registration Act." <http://www.ojp.usdoj.gov/BJA/what/02ajwactcontents.html> (accessed March 27, 2006).

National Sex Offender Public Registry. <http://www.nsopr.gov/> (accessed March 27, 2006).

Child Prostitution Among Boys and Girls is on the Rise

Photograph

By: Anonymous

Date: February 1, 1999

Source: AFP/Getty Images

About the Photographer: This photograph is part of collection at Getty Images, a worldwide provider of visual content materials to such communications groups as advertisers, broadcasters, designers, magazines, new media organizations, newspapers, and producers. The photographer is not known.

INTRODUCTION

Child prostitution is an acknowledged and growing problem in Southeast Asia, particularly in the countries of Bangladesh, India, Nepal, Thailand, Taiwan, and the Philippines. The United Nations Children's Fund (UNICEF) estimates that nearly a million children in Asia (primarily girls, and some boys) are involved in the sex trade industry, whether by force and coercion or as a pragmatic alternative to dire poverty. Poor economic conditions, and the traditional marginalization and subjugation of females contribute to a cultural milieu that allows the proliferation of child exploitation to occur and links to international tourism perpetuate child prostitution as a financially lucrative activity.

PRIMARY SOURCE

CHILD PROSTITUTION AMONG BOYS AND GIRLS IS ON THE RISE

See primary source image.

SIGNIFICANCE

In much of Southeast Asia, female children are considered to be an economic and social liability. The parents of a female child must pay a dowry to the family of her future husband, and the girl then becomes the property of her husband's family. Given this cultural reality, combined with the prevalence of extreme poverty in that area of the world, parents are often enticed into selling their female children into sex slavery, either for a lump sum or for a monthly payment, thereby turning their female children into a financial

PRIMARY SOURCE

Child Prostitution Among Boys and Girls is on the Rise: Fourteen-year-old Reshma, a child prostitute, puts on make-up to attract clients in Dhaka, Bangladesh, February 2001. AFP/GETTY IMAGES

asset, rather than a liability. In some cases, an older child will be sold in order to pay for the education and dowries of younger children in the family. The children of adult prostitutes are also likely to become prostitutes themselves. Children living on the street may be enslaved by brothel owners in return for food and a place to live, or may choose to become involved in street prostitution as a means to make money for food, clothing and shelter.

In countries such as India and Nepal, there are established cultural traditions of ritualized and organ-

ized forms of prostitution, which normalize and perpetuate the sale of children into the sex trade. Girls who are trafficked into the sex trade also may fall prey to cultural and religious beliefs that justify their maltreatment. In one example given by Alice Leuchtag in her 2003 article "Human Rights, Sex Trafficking and Prostitution," a young Thai girl is convinced by her pimp that she must have been a bad person in a previous incarnation to have been born as a female and that she must also have a great deal of bad karma in her past to cause her to deserve the enslavement and poor treatment that she will have to endure.

Although there are laws against child prostitution and the sexual exploitation of children in many Asian countries, including Thailand, Cambodia and Bangladesh, law enforcement officers and officials in these countries are often corrupt and may have a vested interest in the brothels that pimp child prostitutes. The officers may collect a portion of the profits from the brothel owners in return for turning a blind eye to their illegal activities, or may in fact be part owners themselves.

Prostitution is a lucrative business in Asia. It is estimated that each year, sex slaves bring in profits of over ten and a half billion dollars to brothel owners worldwide. In Asia, vast amounts of money are brought into the country by men from developed countries who contribute to a growing "sex tourism" industry. In Thailand alone, millions of sex tourists from North America, Western Europe, Australia and Japan, visit each year, bringing billions of dollars into the local economy. According to Donna Hughes, who investigated the global sexual exploitation of women and children for the Coalition Against Trafficking in Women, men who engage in sex tourism seem to feel that they have a right to have sex with prostitutes, and with child prostitutes. These "sex tourists" commodify and objectify women [and children] of other cultures, nationalities and ethnic groups and seemingly have no awareness of the issues of racism, colonialism, global economic inequalities and sexism and the harm that it does.

Beyond the degradation and subjugation that child prostitutes are forced to endure, there are also significant risks to life and health associated with involvement in the sex trade. HIV infection is an epidemic and growing problem in southeast Asia. The girls who work as prostitutes cannot force their "customers" to wear condoms. The girls may be tested for HIV, often at their own expense, but their risk of contracting the disease is high. Once a prostitute has been diagnosed with HIV, she will no longer be able to work and will leave the brothel with no money, no job, and no place to live. Some may continue to work as prostitutes on the street in order to survive, placing their customers and others at risk. In fact, the World Health Organization has found that large numbers of new cases of HIV are occurring among the wives and girlfriends of men who purchase sex from prostitutes. Ironically, fear of HIV is actually contributing to the spread of child prostitution, as young girls (particularly virgins) are seen as desirable sexual partners because they are considered to be "cleaner" than older prostitutes. Men will pay a premium to a brothel to have sex with a young virgin. Examinations of one thousand children taken from brothels in Thailand revealed that twenty percent were infected with HIV and eighty-two percent had other sexually transmitted diseases.

Physical violence is another risk for child prostitutes in Asia. Young girls are often raped by their pimps as an initiation into the world of prostitution. They may also suffer violent sex and physical abuse at the hands of paying customers. Pimps and brothel owners may often use physical violence as a means of ensuring compliance and obedience from the girls.

The plight of child prostitutes has arisen on the world stage and has been under investigation by Human Rights Watch, the United Nations, and other concerned organizations. Regardless of whether children are sold into sexual slavery or choose to become prostitutes to escape poverty, the involvement of children in the sex trade is always exploitative and socially harmful. Asian governments are beginning to make changes to legislation to reduce child prostitution, and some western nations such as Sweden and Australia have pledged to prosecute those who abuse children abroad as a part of the sex tourism industry. Though much child prostitution can be linked to international tourism, there is also a domestic market for child prostitutes in Asia that is often overlooked. Sweeping cultural changes are necessary in the treatment of women and female children in Asia to eradicate the sexism and subjugation that allow widespread sexual exploitation to continue.

FURTHER RESOURCES

Periodicals

Banerjee, Upala Devi. "Globalization and its Links to Migration and Trafficking: The Crisis in India, Nepal and Bangladesh." *Canadian Woman Studies*. (2003) 22 (3–4):124–130.

Leuchtag, Alice. "Human Rights, Sex Trafficking and Prostitution." *The Humanist*. (2003) 63(1): 10–15.

Perrin, Andrew. "Shame: Asia's Child Sex Industry is Booming, Despite Tougher Laws and a Few High-Profile Deportation Cases." *Time International*. (2002) 160(10).

Web sites

Child Workers in Asia. "Working Children in the Service Sector." <http://www.cwa.tnet.co.th/Publications/Magazine/workingchildrenservicesector.html> (accessed April 10, 2006).

Is This Child Pornography?

Internet article

By: James R. Kincaid

Date: January 31, 2000

Source: Kincaid, James R. "Is This Child Pornography?" *Salon*, January 31, 2000. <http://www.salon.com/mwt/feature/2000/01/31/kincaid/index.html> (accessed March 7, 2006).

About the Author: James R. Kincaid is the Aerol Arnold Professor of English at the University of Southern California and has written extensively on the subject of sexuality in literature and in modern society.

INTRODUCTION

From Vladimir Nabakov's 1955 novel *Lolita* to Internet websites devoted to international child pornography trafficking, the topic of child pornography in the United States is a complex legal and social issue that carries taboo, disgust, and tense questions about the line between normal childhood sexuality and pornographic exploitation of children.

The reference guide to published articles, *The Reader's Guide to Periodical Literature*, began including the categories of "child pornography" and "child sexual abuse" in 1974. In the late 1970s and early 1980s, the issue of child pornography reached the public in the United States through a series of media exposés, in which pamphlets and materials depicting naked children in the Netherlands were investigated by the United States Senate. The Kildee-Murphy proposal, passed in 1977, made child pornography illegal in the United States. Until then, pornography depicting children engaged in sexual acts with other children or with adults was openly sold and traded. Most publishers of child pornography stopped voluntarily, but a small underground publishing enterprise continued.

Most American and European countries have enacted laws that make child pornography illegal. The age of consent often determines whether pornography is "child pornography" or legal pornography. In the United States, the age of consent is considered to be eighteen, and any depiction of a person under eighteen in pornographic photos or films is classified as child pornography and is, therefore, illegal. However, some states within the United States have set the age of consent at sixteen or seventeen; in these situations, would pornographic pictures of a sixteen- or seventeen-year-old legally be deemed child pornography?

This question—What constitutes child pornography?—created a series of laws and procedures that addressed particular situations as they came before the courts and the public, but which still, to this day, leave much to be interpreted. Is a picture of a child, alone and nude, pornography? Is a clothed child positioned in a sexually suggestive way in a movie being exploited, and, therefore, is the film child pornography?

Children, historically, have been held up as innocent, asexual creatures. Parents in the United States often snap photos of children in the bathtub, playing outdoors, or swimming, with the children in various states of undress. In Europe, where public nudity standards are more open than in the United States, naked toddlers and young children are a more common site on beaches and at lakes during vacation times. At what point do those family snapshots cross a legal line?

■ PRIMARY SOURCE

American photo labs are arresting parents as child pornographers for taking pictures of their kids in the bath.

Jan. 31, 2000—Picture this: A photo of a boy and girl—unmistakably naked, posed and giggling—holding two very large sausages (Italian?). The boy is maybe 8, the girl maybe 6. They are not touching each another, nor does the camera seem especially interested in their genitals. What catches the eye are those sausages, but not that they are involved in anything you or I would call, right off, sexual: They are not being licked, stroked or inserted. They are more atmospheric, I guess you could say.

Is this child pornography? Well, if you are a photo lab manager in Burbank, Calif., you follow the in-store policy and ask the store manager. The store manager, noticing the nudity and the meat, follows what he takes to be the law and calls the Burbank police. The police send two undercover cops out with instructions to nab the photographer. The cops then order the photo lab manager to phone the customer, tell him his prints are ready and instruct him to come pick them up right away.

The customer agrees to drop everything and run over, but then doesn't show, forcing the undercover police to cool their heels for six hours before giving up. Later the cops do nab the suspect, who says the photos were taken by the kids' uncle who thought the children's play with the sausages was "funny." The Burbank police decide to let it go with a warning laced with disgust: There's nothing "funny" about photos like these, photos that are indecent, degenerate and, *next time*, criminal.

As a script written for the Keystone Kops, this much ado about sausages scenario would be funny. But it is a true story. It is a sorry saga about our confused desires when it comes to kids and sex, and the way these collective desires are reflected in our failure to clearly define and execute the laws governing child pornography. This black comedy set in Burbank proves a scary point: At this time there is no way to differentiate—legally—between a family snapshot of a naked child and child pornography.

Not that photo labs don't try. They do, and every now and then they light upon (or concoct) what they take to be a case of child pornography. There are about 10 cases in the last dozen years that have emerged in the press. Some are worthy of mention here, mostly because they weren't worthy of attention when they occurred:

- William Kelly was arrested in Maryland in 1987 after dropping off a roll of film that included shots his 10-year-old daughter and younger children had taken of each other nude.
- David Urban in 1989 took photos of his wife and 15-month-old grandson, both nude, as she was giving him a bath. Kmart turned him in and he was convicted by a Missouri court (later overturned).
- A gay adult couple in Florida decided to shave their bodies and snap their lovemaking, convincing a Walgreens clerk that one of them was a child. They are suing the Fort Lauderdale police.
- More recently, Cynthia Stewart turned in bath-time pictures of her 8-year-old daughter to a Fuji film processing lab in Oberlin, Ohio. The lab contacted the local police, who found the pictures "over the line" and arrested the mother for, among other things, snapping in the same frame with her daughter a showerhead, which the prosecution apparently planned to relate somehow to hints of masturbation.

Even though the number of arrests is not large and the circumstances seem ridiculous, this photo lab idiocy is a serious matter: It puts all of us at risk, and it significantly erodes free speech protection by insisting that a photograph of a child is tantamount to molestation. Since it is what is outside the frame (the intention of the photographer, the reaction of the viewer) that counts legally, we are actually encouraged to fantasize an action in order to determine whether or not this is child pornography.

Every photo must pass this test: Can we create a sexual fantasy that includes it? Such directives seem an efficient means for manufacturing a whole nation of pedophiles.

The laws, whether state or federal, are inevitably firm-jawed when it comes to meting out punishment to child pornographers. But they seem uncertain both in what it is they want to put an end to and how far they want to reach into our home photo albums to do it.

In the great sausage caper, the photo lab operator and the Burbank police acted as our representatives to decide whether pictures of children and sausages constitute child pornography. This suggests that they have a clear idea of what a child is and that they know porn when they see it. What this also means is that we have a system that allows criminal conduct to be determined by just about anybody.

So, how do I know which kid pictures I can take to Wal-Mart, and how does the Wal-Mart photo guy know when to call the police about my pictures? The short answer is that there is no way I can know because there is no way he can know.

Some states require that photo labs report any photo that they deem suspicious to the police while others do not, but none give much help in explaining what suspicious photos of children actually look like. State law on child pornography is murky at best, and it varies from state to state. And when a photo lab sends its material to another state for developing, federal laws (which may differ from the state laws, but are equally murky) come into play.

In the absence of clear jurisdictional authority, much less clear laws, anyone snapping pictures of kids and wanting to avoid the slammer might decide to simply ask about the policies of their local labs and the corporations that direct them. How do they separate those who are simply charmed by their naked kids from those who seek to charm others for profit?

I expended no little energy trying to unearth the guidelines from the corporate headquarters of photo developing giants. I may as well have tried to get to the bottom of Cosa Nostra rub-out policies by making a few calls. I did discover that the world of photo developing is surprisingly small and, perhaps not so surprisingly, secretive.

When one talks to people at the top, as I did, one finds a penetrating and pervasive fear of public exposure. My sources promised to speak only on guarantee of anonymity. Too many lawsuits are pending and too many threats of others simmer to allow policy issues to be made public, said a top lawyer at one of the nation's largest photo developing companies.

Still, according to all my sources (which include executives on the corporate level and also five local photo-lab people incautious enough to spill the beans), the correct procedures for handling questionable photographs are never clear and they vary—even within the same corporation—according to state law. They do not pertain to erotic pictures of adults unless they appear to depict rape or some other illegal activity. (Or unless one of the adults could be mistaken for a child.)

Kids are different. Naked kids under the age of 5 or 6 are probably OK, so long as nothing else in the picture invites suspicion. Nudity in older children may be a problem—or maybe not. It is up to the lab person or a supervisor to consult his or her own sense of propriety and moral sensitivities, as well as any rough-and-ready training that has been given in how to determine whether a photo constitutes child pornography.

SIGNIFICANCE

In the 1994 United States Supreme Court case *United States of America v. Stephen A. Knox*, the "principal question presented by this appeal is whether videotapes that focus on the genitalia and pubic area of minor females constitute a 'lascivious exhibition of the genitals or pubic area' under the federal child pornography laws even though these body parts are covered by clothing."

The case garnered significant attention from child advocacy groups, such as The Center for Missing and Exploited Children and brought to the forefront of public attention the definition of child pornography. In that case the Supreme Court found for the plaintiff, declaring that "a 'lascivious exhibition of the genitals or pubic area'…encompasses visual depictions of a child's genitals or pubic area even when these areas are covered by an article of clothing and are not discernible."

As laws tightened in the U.S. concerning child pornography, photo labs faced a new challenge. Employees who worked in drugstores, retail establishments, and grocery stores faced the responsibility to report illegal photographs. Was a mother breastfeeding her three-year-old a pornographic scene? What about an eight-year-old in a bathtub? With no clearcut, objective guidelines for understanding what child pornography is, and what it is not, many parents and individuals who took pictures of children in various states of undress and had the film developed in a retail store found themselves in violation of a law that neither they—nor their accuser—fully understood.

Federal law in the United States defines child pornography as the visual depiction of a minor engaged in sexual acts, or in "lewd" or "lascivious" behavior or presentation. Simple nudity of a child in photographs or on film does not automatically constitute child pornography, though individual state statutes vary on the nudity issue. Because state law overlaps with federal law, the definition of child pornography—especially in photo lab cases where an employee must make a decision, on the spot, concerning a photograph's legality—creates serious questions about children's sexuality in modern American culture.

As Kincaid notes in this article, whether a photograph is child pornography depends largely on the point of view of the person examining the photo and

The reward poster was released on April 27, 2005. It shows a girl who may have a connection to another girl who has appeared in sexually graphic photos on the internet. AP IMAGES

deciding on the reason for the photo: "Since it is what is outside the frame (the intention of the photographer, the reaction of the viewer) that counts legally, we are actually encouraged to fantasize an action in order to determine whether or not this is child pornography." Because state and federal law are murky and contradictory at times, and because each individual brings a different set of cultural and sexual assumptions to the viewing of the photograph, the question "What constitutes child pornography?" remains difficult to answer.

FURTHER RESOURCES
Books

Sandfort, Theo G. M., and Jany Rademakers, editors. *Childhood Sexuality: Normal Sexual Behavior and Development.* Binghamton, N.Y.: Haworth Books, 2000.

Periodicals

Jackson, Judy, and Debbie Nathan. "The Hunting of Dr. Craft." *The Nation* (January 10, 2005).

Web sites

Findlaw.com "United States of America v. Stephen A. Knox." <http://laws.lp.findlaw.com/3rd/940734p.html> (accessed March 7, 2006).

Innocent Images National Initiative. <http://www.fbi.gov/innocent.htm> (accessed March 7, 2006).

Korosec, Thomas. "1-Hour Arrest." *Dallas Observer,* April 17, 2003. <http://www.dallasobserver.com/issues/2003-04–17/feature2.html> (accessed March 7, 2006).

Utah Polygamist Tom Green with Family of Five Wives

Photograph

By: Anonymous

Date: April 2000

Source: Getty Images.

About the Photographer: This photograph was submitted by the defense in the polygamy trial of Tom Green in May 2001, and is part of the archives of Getty Images, a provider of imagery and film to communications professionals around the world.

INTRODUCTION

Polygamy refers to the marriage of one person to more than one other person at the same time, or multiple, simultaneous marriages. Polyandry is the technical term for one woman who has more than one husband concurrently; polygny is the word used for one man with multiple wives. Polyamory is when one person has multiple significant relationship partners simultaneously, but is not necessarily married to any of them. Bigamy occurs when one person has two spouses at the same time, trigamy is the case when there are three concurrent spouses associated with one individual. Group marriage is said to occur when two or more couples marry one another and jointly manage a household, raise children and share responsibilities.

Historically, the state of Utah and the Mormon Church (correctly known as the Church of Jesus Christ of Latter-Day Saints, and also called LDS) are both associated with the concept of polygamy. How-ever, in 1890, the Mormon Church officially discontinued the practice of polygamy, and has been excommunicating members who practice it. In the state of Utah, legislation bans the practice, although there are numerous geographic areas in which groups of communities whose members practice polygamy quietly exist. It is not uncommon for members of some polygamous families to engage in criminal activities such as domestic, spousal, sexual, or child abuse.

One religious polygamist splinter group in Utah refers to itself as a Fundamentalist Mormon sect. This is emphatically denied by the mainstream Church of Jesus Christ of Latter-Day Saints, which asserts that there are no sects in which polygamy is allowed or condoned. Likewise, they deny the existence of any fundamentalists cadres within the main body of the LDS church. The Mormon church acknowledges that there are polygamous sects in society, and that there are factions that split off from the Church of Jesus Christ of Latter-Day Saints after the death of founder Joseph Smith, but assert that there are not connections, either spiritual or philosophic, between the smaller groups and the current LDS Church.

In recent years, the concept of polygamy has come to the attention of the American public both through the open admission and media attention of Tom Green, an admitted polygamist who has stated that he has five wives and at least thirty children, and through the fictional account of polygamy portrayed in the Home Box Office original television series *Big Love.* The latter describes the life and times of a contemporary (fictional) polygamist who lives in Salt Lake City, Utah, with three wives (who live, conveniently, in three adjacent houses) and seven children. His character is descended from polygamous parents who live in a polygamous community, and are members of a fundamentalist spiritual sect (one of the central tenets of which is the practice of polygamy).

PRIMARY SOURCE

UTAH POLYGAMIST TOM GREEN WITH FAMILY OF FIVE WIVES

See primary source image.

SIGNIFICANCE

In contemporary LDS culture, the practice of plural marriage (another term for polygamy) is referred to as "The Principle." A significant part of the reason that the contemporary practice of polygamy has achieved media status has had much to do with allega-

PRIMARY SOURCE

Utah Polygamist Tom Green With Family of Five Wives: This photo of Tom Green with his family was presented to the jury by the defense in Provo, Utah, on May 15, 2001. The photo shows Green with his five wives and some of his 29 children, taken in April 2000. PHOTO BY AFP/AFP/GETTY IMAGES

tions of criminal activity involving sexual relationships and marriage with underage individuals (typically females), incest, and child neglect or abuse in the polygamous community. Among the strongest allegations against Tom Green in his polygamy case had to do with engaging in "spiritual marriages" and sexual relationships with young girls who were below the legal age of consent in Utah. Others concerned his failure to adequately materially provide for all of the needs of his thirty children and several households (he and his large family lived on a compound in a remote area of Juab County, Utah, that he had dubbed "Greenhaven").

Among those who practice polygamy and speak openly about their lives, most consider it an integral part of their spiritual and religious belief system and, therefore, existing outside of the boundaries of legislation. It is difficult to obtain an accurate accounting of persons living in polygamous (including polyandry, polyamory and polygyny) relationships in America, as very few people are willing to openly admit being a part of a cultural group that is illegal across the country, but news reports published during the trial of Tom Green estimated that 20,000 to 40,000 people live in polygamous households, primarily located in Southwestern states, particularly Utah and Arizona.

As the Church of Jesus Christ of Latter-Day Saints was originally constituted and practiced by Brigham Young, plural marriages were condoned, and were, in fact, considered necessary for the achievement of the highest blessings of heaven, according to tenets espoused by Church founder Joseph Smith. The practice of polygamy was outlawed by the Church when the federal government legislated against it and made the banning of polygamy a requirement for all territories wishing to achieve statehood. In an effort to expedite admission to the Union, (then) Church President Wilford Woodruff declared polygamy against Mormon doctrine in 1890, several years before Utah was admitted to American statehood, and stated that the practice of polygamy would result in excommunication from the LDS Church.

Several anti-polygamy groups have been formed by former members of polygamous families. Former members related incidents to authorities of teenage boys being cast out of the group to make more young girls available for marriage to the group's older men. Girls are married as young as twelve years of age, and seldom are allowed to complete a high school education.

Tom Greene was eventually convicted of four counts of bigamy and one count of child rape for having sex with a thirteen-year-old girl who he claimed was his "spiritual wife." Green was sentenced to two five-year sentences in federal prison. In May 2006, the leader of a larger polygamist sect, Warren Jeff, was added to the Federal Bureau of Investigation's (FBI) Ten Most-Wanted List, amid charges of bigamy and sexual relations with children. The FBI has issued a $100,000 reward for information leading to his arrest.

FURTHER RESOURCES
Books

Bennion, Janet. *Women of Principle: Female Networking in Contemporary Mormon Polygyny*. New York: Oxford University Press, 1998.

Bradley, Martha Sonntag. *Kidnapped From That Land: The Government Raids on the Short Creek Polygamists*. Salt Lake City, Utah: University of Utah Press, 1993.

Gordon, Sarah Barringer. *The Mormon Question: Polygamy and Constitutional Conflict in Nineteenth-Century America*. Chapel Hill, North Carolina: University of North Carolina Press, 2002.

Kern, Louis J. *An Ordered Love: Sex Roles and Sexuality in Victorian Utopias— the Shakers, the Mormons, and the Oneida Community*. Chapel Hill, North Carolina: University of North Carolina Press, 1981.

Moore-Emmett, Andrea. *God's Brothel: The Extortion of Sex for Salvation in Contemporary Mormon and Christian Fundamentalist Polygamy and the Stories of 18 Women Who Escaped*. San Francisco: Pince-Nez Press, 2004.

Web sites

Polygamy.com. "Is Honeymoon Over for Bigamy?" April 23, 2000. <http://www.polygamy.com/articles/templates/> (accessed May 14, 2006).

Tapestry Against Polygamy. "Polygamy Background Information.". <http://www.polygamy.org/history.shtml> (accessed May 14, 2006).

The Principle. "Green Prosecutors Clash on Many Fronts." April 22, 2002. <http://www.polygamyinfo.com/plygmedia%2002%2040desnes.htm (verified link)> (accessed May 14, 2006).

Section 2423. Transportation of Minors

Legislation

By: United States Congress

Date: January 6, 2003

Source: "Section 2423. Transportation of Minors." Title 18, U.S. Code, Chapter 117, Section 2423, 2003.

About the Author: The 108th Congress passed the legislation that tightened laws against against transporting children out of state for the purpose of sexual activity.

INTRODUCTION

According to the U.S. Department of State, in 2003 between 600,000 and 800,000 children worldwide were transported between countries for the purposes of child labor and/or to be used as sex trade workers. Child trafficking within national borders, according to United Nations estimates, raises that number to 1.2 million.

In regions of the world where child poverty is endemic, as in parts of southeast Asia and Africa, traffickers use children as laborers, often paying parents a bounty to deliver the child to a factory or farm where the child receives food and shelter, but little if anything in wages. In other instances, parents are led to believe their child will be placed in such jobs, but the trafficker instead sells the child into sexual slavery. Child trafficking, according to UNICEF, is a $7 to $10 billion business annually.

International prohibitions on human trafficking date back from the 1910 International Convention for the Suppression of the White Slave Traffic. Subsequent agreements included the International Convention for the Suppression of the Traffic in Women and Children in 1921, and the International Convention for the Suppression of the Traffic in Women of Full Age in 1933; these conventions led to the United Nations Convention for the Suppression of the Traffic in Persons and of the Exploitation of the Prostitution of Others in 1949, which focused specifically on the prevention of human trafficking for the sex trade.

In December 2003, the United Nations updated its policy against child trafficking with the Protocol to Prevent, Suppress, and Punish Trafficking in Persons, Especially Women and Children, supplementing the United Nations Convention against Transnational Organized Crime. In the same year, the United States

Congress updated the U.S. Code to tighten laws against the transportation of minors within the United States for the purpose of sexual activity.

■ PRIMARY SOURCE

Section 2423. Transportation of Minors

(a) Transportation With Intent To Engage in Criminal Sexual Activity.—A person who knowingly transports an individual who has not attained the age of 18 years in interstate or foreign commerce, or in any commonwealth, territory or possession of the United States, with intent that the individual engage in prostitution, or in any sexual activity for which any person can be charged with a criminal offense, or attempts to do so, shall be fined under this title, imprisoned not more than 15 years, or both.

(b) Travel With Intent To Engage in Sexual Act With a Juvenile.—A person who travels in interstate commerce, or conspires to do so, or a United States citizen or an alien admitted for permanent residence in the United States who travels in foreign commerce, or conspires to do so, for the purpose of engaging in any sexual act (as defined in section 2246) with a person under 18 years of age that would be in violation of chapter 109A if the sexual act occurred in the special maritime and territorial jurisdiction of the United States shall be fined under this title, imprisoned not more than 15 years, or both.

SIGNIFICANCE

In the early twentieth century, China became a popular destination for sex tourism, defined as travel to a location for the sole purpose of engaging a prostitute or to engage in sexual activity. During World War II (1938–1941), the Japanese army captured Chinese, Korean, and Filippino women and forced them to work as sexual slaves for Japanese troops. By the 1950s, Vietnam had developed a large prostitution industry, and the Vietnam War in the 1960s and early 1970s fed the sex trade as well.

By the early 1980s, a new form of sexual tourism emerged: Wealthy Western men seeking children for sex. In countries such as Thailand, Malaysia, and Indonesia, foreign operators organized extended vacations with planned activities in brothels; clients could custom-design sexual experiences, asking for a particular age, race, gender, or fetish as part of their itinerary. Eastern bloc countries, including Czechoslovakia, Ukraine, and Poland, are the center of an increasing child sex trade, though Asia remains the primary destination. Ominously, as HIV/AIDS spread, the myth

that sex with a virgin could "cure" the disease fueled a bounty for virgins and led to the increased capture of young children.

The 2003 United Nations protocol, along with the U.S. Code tightening restraints on trafficking of minors, were part of a campaign to rein in sexual tourism. Section 2423 was part of the PROTECT (Prosecutorial Remedies and Other Tools to end the Exploitation of Children Today) Act of 2003, which also criminalized commercial sex with anyone under the age of eighteen anywhere in the world, regardless of the age of consent in the country in which the paid sex act takes place. Before the PROTECT Act, commercial sex was only illegal if the sex act involved a child younger than the host country's age of consent.

The transportation of minors within the United States for the purposes of child pornography or sexual activity was the center of a 2005 court case involving international chess star Alex Sherzer, a 32-year-old chess player from Hungary living in Maryland. Sherzer met a fifteen-year-old girl on the Internet and traveled to Alabama to meet her. He was arrested on charges of crossing state lines for a sexual encounter with a minor, but was later acquitted. "Internet predators"—adults who use message boards and chat rooms to find underage boys and girls for meetings involving sex—are targets of laws such as Section 2423.

FURTHER RESOURCES

Books

Barnitz, Laura A. *Commercial Sexual Exploitation of Children: Youth Involved in Prostitution, Pornography & Sex Trafficking.* Youth Advocate Program International: 1998.

Periodicals

Dessy, Sylvain E., and Stephane Pallage. "The Economics of Child Trafficking." Centre Interuniversitaire sur le Risques, les Politiques Economiques, et l'Emploi (CIRPEE) [Center for Research on Economic Flucutations and Employment]. Unpublished paper, August 2003.

Estes, Richard J., and Neil Alan Weiner. "The Commercial Sexual Exploitation of Children in the U.S., Canada, and Mexico." Center for the Study of Youth Policy, Full Report. February 2002.

Web sites

UNICEF. "Child Trafficking Research Hub" <http://www.childtrafficking.org> (accessed March 27, 2006).

United States Department of Justice. Child Exploitation and Obscenity Section (CEOS). "Child Prostitution." <http://www.usdoj.gov/criminal/ceos/prostitution_fed-efforts.html> (accessed March 27, 2006).

Innocent Images National Initiative

Congressional testimony

By: Keith L. Lourdeau

Date: May 6, 2004

Source: U.S. House of Representatives. Committee on Energy and Commerce. Subcommittee on Commerce, Trade, and Consumer Protection. *Online Pornography: Closing the Door on Pervasive Smut.* 108th Congress, 2nd session, May 6, 2004. Testimony of the Deputy Assistant Director of the Federal Bureau of Investigation Cyber Division, Keith L. Lourdeau. Available at: <http://energycommerce.house.gov/108/Hearings/05062004hearing1264/Lourdeau1970.htm> (accessed April 5, 2006).

About the Author: Keith L. Lourdeau is the Deputy Assistant Director of the Federal Bureau of Investigation Cyber Division.

INTRODUCTION

The 1970s and 1980s brought increased social awareness to the issues of child abuse and child pornography, and in response to public outcries almost every state enacted laws prohibiting the mistreatment of minors. The U.S. Congress also has taken action on this issue and has enacted laws that prohibit the making, selling, possession, and distribution of child pornography. The increasing use of the internet has added another element to the child pornography issue because, just as pornography seekers and makers use cyber space for personal gain, those fighting against sexually explicit material involving children use technology to locate pornography users.

The debate about child pornography is wide and multi-faceted, but a central consensus continues to emerge—that the proliferation of such material is harmful to children. Images of exploited children act like permanent records—those images are not erased, and once they are made the child retains the memory of their creation. More importantly, many psychological reports provide evidence that child pornography is not just a voyeuristic endeavor. Rather, its viewers frequently act out their fantasies upon children, turning into pedophiles, and sometimes these children are injured or killed. In additional, the scars that involvement in pornography leave on children have not been tallied because emotional trauma can not always be quantified into concrete numbers for statistical data.

The rise of "easy access" media portals has made the dissemination of child pornography much easier. No longer having to rely upon underground networks of bookstores, mail-order-catalogs, and networks of friends, those seeking child pornography can easily find it via the internet. In much the same way that people share information on free and illegal downloads of music, movies, and other data, those looking for child pornography obtain their information in the same way. File sharing software, internet chat sites, message boards, and other venues enable the seeker to easily find the desired information. In each of these situations, individuals establish a relationship—of sorts—with someone, and then "code words" are often used to start a conversation about the illegal topic. After a dialogue is begun then hidden sites are located, passwords shared, and files sent.

In conjunction with state and local governments, the Federal Bureau of Investigations has increased its child pornography task force to specifically target internet buyers, sellers, and transmitters of child pornography. This new task force, the Innocent Images National Initiative, seeks to locate online communities, organizations, and enterprises exploiting children for profit or personal gain. In addition to identifying these groups, the FBI's task force attempts to apprehend producers of child pornography, those willing to travel to engage in sexual activity with a minor, possessors of child pornography, and those who have transmitted large volumes of it.

■ PRIMARY SOURCE

FBI's Innocent Images National Initiative is comprised of twenty-eight Under-Cover Operations. These operations involve FBI Agents on-line in an undercover capacity to seek child predators and individuals responsible for the production, dissemination, and possession of child pornography. This is accomplished by using a variety of techniques, to include purchasing child pornography from commercial web sites, creating on-line personas to chat in predicated chat rooms, and co-opting predators' e-mail accounts. Innocent Images has grown exponentially between fiscal year 1996 and 2003 with a 2050% increase in cases opened (113 to 2430). Between fiscal year 1996 and 2003, Innocent Images has recorded over 10,510 cases opened.

Recently, Peer-to-Peer networks were identified as a growing problem in the dissemination of child pornography. A GAO report published in September of 2003 indi-

During the FBI's nationwide Operation Candyman crackdown on Internet-based child pornography, an unidentified suspect is led out of the Javits federal building on March 21, 2002 in New York. PHOTO BY ROBERT MECEA/GETTY IMAGES

cated a four-fold increase in reports complaining of child pornography in Peer-to-Peer networks. In 2001, the FBI received 156 complaints about child pornography in Peer-to-Peer networks. By 2002, the number of complaints had risen to 757. This increase may be attributable to, among other things, the popularity of Peer-to-Peer networks, as well as the overall increase in child pornography available on the Internet. These programs are free and are easy to install. In May of 2003, Sharman Networks, the developer of a very popular file sharing program, reported that their software had been downloaded more than 230 million times. This software and other file sharing programs like it, allow users to share files with anyone on the network. This creates an environment of relative anonymity amongst users however, this anonymity is only perceived, users are not truly anonymous.

Using Peer-to-Peer software, users' computers connect directly to one another to share files, without going through a central server. Nevertheless, each time a computer accesses the Internet, it is associated with an internet protocol, or "IP" address. Therefore, despite the fact that a Peer-to-Peer connection is not facilitated by a central server, users can still be identified in real time by the IP addresses associated with their computers.

IP addresses are the only way to definitively identify a particular user on a Peer-to-Peer network. In this environment, users of Peer-to-Peer often believe they are anonymous. There is some degree of truth in this assertion as peers in these networks are anonymous to each other. That being said, they are NOT anonymous to law enforcement. Through the use of covert investigative techniques and administrative subpoenas, Agents can determine which individual users possess and distribute child pornography over these networks. Utilizing search warrants, interviews, and computer forensic tools, Agents can strengthen their cases and these individuals are eventually indicted and prosecuted.

Agents have determined Peer-to Peer networks are one of many Internet havens for the open distribution of child pornography. Several of the individuals using Peer-to-Peer networks to distribute child pornography openly describe the content of the material they share as "illegal." This further contributes to the feeling of anonymity in these networks and leads users to become even more brazen in their conduct.

To combat this, the FBI has created an investigative protocol for Peer-to-Peer investigations to begin aggressively apprehending offenders. After developing a Peer-to-Peer investigative protocol with the Department of Justice's Child Exploitation and Obscenity Section, a number of cases were initiated to determine the technique's viability. Detailed discussion of these cases could possibly jeopardize ongoing investigations, however, I would like to assure this subcommittee that the FBI is aggressively pursuing the trading of child pornography on Peer-to-Peer networks.

In these investigations, Agents have found child pornography to be readily available using the most basic of search terms. Often, child pornography was easily available when innocuous search terms were used, such as 'Brittney Spears' or the word 'young'.

Additionally, the FBI is exploring the possibility of working with Peer-to-Peer software clients to allow them to more effectively warn users against the possession, distribution, or production of child pornography. These industry members may also be interested in placing icons or a pop-up link from their home page regarding subjects wanted by the FBI for exploitation of children by use of the Internet.

While these efforts may not prevent someone from downloading the material in question, it will put the user on notice that they are, more than likely, violating the law. These efforts will also assist investigations as it will eliminate the ability of the subject to claim ignorance of the law.

SIGNIFICANCE

The FBI's national initiative to stop child pornography, local and state governments' strengthening laws, and an increase in watch groups has brought much attention to efforts aimed at stopping child pornography. Nightly television news broadcasts, movies-of-the-week, and generalized heightened media coverage have helped the fight to end child pornography. Additionally, the Amber Alert system and legislative actions like Megan's Law continue to help protect children and stop the abuse of children. The Amber Alert system has been in effect since 2002;

Megan's Law requires police to keep databases of sex offenders and to notify communities of sex offenders in the area. These two laws are not directly related to child pornography, but they are part of the larger picture to prevent its continued proliferation.

The battle to stop child pornography is far from over. In 1996, the U.S. Supreme Court ruled that "virtual" child pornography is not illegal—that is, pornography that leads a viewer to believe that the person shown is a minor when he or she is older than eighteen. Activists against child pornography believe this ruling is a set back to the larger cause, while others interested in the issue continue to point out that First Amendment rights are involved. Thus, as governmental bodies strive to strengthen legislation against the sexual exploitation of children, they must do so within the context of First Amendment protections of free expression.

FURTHER RESOURCES
Books
Jenkins, Philip. *Beyond Tolerance: Child Pornography Online.* New York: New York University Press, 2001.

Tayler, Max, and Ethel Quayle. *Child Pornography; An Internet Crime.* New York: Brunner-Routledge, 2003.

Web sites
Anti-ChildPorn.org. <http://www.antichildporn.org/> (accessed April 5, 2006).

Association of Sites Advocating Child Protection. <http://www.asacp.org/index.php> (accessed April 5, 2006).

MSNBC. "'Legal Child Porn' Under Fire." <http://www.msnbc.com/news/730491.asp?cp1=1> (accessed April 5, 2006).

Sherri Williams v. Attorney General of Alabama

Legal decision

By: Judges of the U.S. Court of Appeals for the Eleventh Circuit

Date: July 28, 2004

Source: *Sherri Williams v. Attorney General of Alabama.* Sherri Williams, B. J. Bailey, Plaintiffs-Appellees, Bette Faye Haggermaker, et al., Plaintiffs, versus Attorney General of Alabama: Appeal from the

United States District Court for the Northern District of Alabama. July 28, 2004. Full text of second decision on this case by U.S. Court of Appeals for the 11th Circuit decision. Available at: <http://www.ca11.uscourts.gov/opinions/ops/200216135.pdf> (accessed March 9, 2006).

About the Author: A three-judge panel from the Eleventh Circuit of the U.S. Court of Appeals issued this opinion. Established by Congress in 1981, the U.S. Court of Appeals for the Eleventh Judicial Circuit has jurisdiction over federal cases originating in the states of Alabama, Florida, and Georgia.

INTRODUCTION

These excerpts are from the text of a two-to-one decision of a panel of three judges from the U.S. 11th Circuit Court of Appeals, issued July 28, 2004. The decision capped several years of convoluted litigation in which the American Civil Liberties Union (ACLU)

filed suit against the state of Alabama on behalf of several purchasers of "sex toys," defined by Alabama law as "any device designed or marketed as useful primarily for the stimulation of human genital organs." At issue was Alabama's 1998 Anti-Obscenity Enforcement Act, which made the sale of sex toys a crime. The ACLU argued that the law both lacked a rational basis and violated fundamental rights. The law banned only the sale of sex toys, not their possession or use. Georgia and Texas are the only other U.S. states banning the sale of sex toys.

In 1999, an Alabama federal district court decided against the state on the ground that the law lacked a rational basis. The judge declined to rule on whether the law violated fundamental rights, reasoning that the plaintiffs "had not presented an evidentiary basis for concluding that their asserted rights to sell, purchase, possess, and use sexual devices were among 'those fundamental rights and liberties which are, objectively, deeply rooted in this Nation's history and tradition ...'"

Katherine Williams holds a yellow ducky vibrating bath sponge outside the Spring Hill City Hall in Nashville, Tenn., October 12, 2004. Williams, who runs an adult lotions and novelties business, faced legal problems for trying to sell this item at a local flea market. AP IMAGES

Alabama appealed to the U.S. 11th Circuit Court, which on January 21, 2001, concluded that the district court had "erred when concluding that the Alabama statue's absolute ban on the sale of sexual devices was not rationally related to a proper governmental purpose" (in the words of the district court's case history). As the 11th Circuit put it, "The State's interest in public morality is a legitimate interest rationally served by the statute." Regarding the plaintiffs' argument that their fundamental rights were violated by the law, the 11th Circuit ruled that there was "no controlling precedent that specifically establishes the facial [i.e., obvious] unconstitutionality of this statue" and that the lower court had failed to address the plaintiffs' challenge to the law's constitutionality "as applied" to their particular persons. The 11th Circuit court remanded (sent back) the case to the district court for consideration of the fundamental-rights question.

In 2002, the district court held that the plaintiffs had "met their burden of showing that there is a 'history, legal tradition, and practice' in this country of deliberate state noninteference with private sexual relationships between married couples, and a contemporary practice of the same between unmarried couples." For a second time the district court had ruled against Alabama.

Alabama appealed again to the 11th Circuit, which in 2004 overturned the circuit court's second ruling and upheld Alabama's anti-sex-toys law. Yet in the meantime, the U.S. Supreme Court had overturned a Texas law banning oral and anal sexual acts (*Lawrence v. Texas*, 2003), holding that states have no legitimate rational grounds for criminalizing non-commercial sexual practices performed in private by consenting adults. This seemed, at least to some observers, to establish something like a right to sexual privacy. The 11th Circuit, therefore, remanded the case for a second time to the district court and asked it to rule again on the rational-basis issue in light of *Lawrence v. Texas*. The district court decided in February, 2006, that, in keeping with the opinions enforced earlier by the 11th Circuit, the Alabama law did have a rational basis. As of early 2006, Alabama had won.

PRIMARY SOURCE

Before Birch, Barkett, and Hill, Circuit Judges.

In this case, the American Civil Liberties Union ("ACLU") invites us to add a new right to the current catalogue of fundamental rights under the Constitution: a right to sexual privacy. It further asks us to declare Alabama's statute prohibiting the sale of "sex toys" to be

an impermissible burden on this right. Alabama responds that the statute exercises a time-honored use of state police power—restricting the sale of sex. We are compelled to agree with Alabama and must decline the ACLU's invitation....

The Alabama statute proscribes a relatively narrow bandwidth of activity. It prohibits only the sale—but not use, possession, or gratuitous distribution—of sexual devices (in fact, the users involved in this litigation acknowledge that they already possess multiple sex toys). The law does not affect the distribution of a number of other sexual products such as ribbed condoms or virility drugs. Nor does it prohibit Alabama residents from purchasing sexual devices out of state and bringing them back into Alabama. Moreover, the statute permits the sale of ordinary vibrators and body massagers that, although useful as sexual aids, are not "designed or marketed "primarily" for that particular purpose. Finally, the statute exempts sales of sexual devices "for a bona fide medical, scientific, educational, legislative, judicial, or law enforcement purpose....."

This case, which is now before us on appeal for the second time, involves a challenge to the constitutionality of the Alabama statute. The ACLU, on behalf of various individual users and vendors of sexual devices, initially filed suit seeking to enjoin the statute on 29 July 1998, a month after the statute took effect. The ACLU argued that the statute burdens and violates sexual-device users' right to privacy and personal autonomy under the Fourteenth Amendment to the United States Constitution....

The only question on this appeal is whether the statute, as applied to the involved users and vendors, violates any fundamental right protected under the Constitution. The proper analysis for evaluating this question turns on whether the right asserted by the ACLU falls within the parameters of any presently recognized fundamental right or whether it instead requires us to recognize a hitherto unarticulated fundamental right....

The ACLU invokes "privacy" and "personal autonomy" as if such phrases were constitutional talismans. In the abstract, however, there is no fundamental right to either. *See, e.g., Glucksberg,* 521 U.S. at 725, 117 S. Ct. at 2270 (fundamental rights are "not simply deduced from abstract concepts of personal autonomy"). Undoubtedly, many fundamental rights currently recognized under Supreme Court precedent touch on matters of personal autonomy and privacy. However, "[t]hat many of the rights and liberties protected by the Due Process Clause sound in personal autonomy does not warrant the sweeping conclusion that any and all important, intimate, and personal decisions are so protected." Such rights have been denominated "fundamental" not simply because they implicate deeply personal and private considerations, but because they have been identified as "deeply rooted in this Nation's history and tradition and implicit in the concept of ordered liberty, such that neither liberty nor justice would exist if they were sacrificed."

Nor, contrary to the ACLU's assertion, have the Supreme Court's substantive-due-process precedents recognized as free-standing "right to sexual privacy." The Court has been presented with repeated opportunities to identify a fundamental right to sexual privacy—and has invariably declined. ***See, e.g., Carey v. Population Servs. Int'l,*** 431 U.S. 678, 688 n.5, 97 S. Ct. 2010, 2018 n. 5 (1977) (noting that the Court "has not definitively answered the difficult question whether and to what extent the Constitution prohibits state statutes regulating private consensual sexual behavior among adults, and we do not purport to answer that question now") (internal citation and punctuation omitted). Although many of the Court's "privacy" decisions have implicated sexual matters, ***se, e.g. Planned Parenthood v. Casey,*** 505 U.S. 833, 112 S. Ct. 2791 (1992) (abortion); ***Carey,*** 431 U.S. at 678, 97 S. Ct. at 2010 (contraceptives), the Court has never indicated that the mere fact that an activity is sexual and private entitles it to protection as a fundamental right....

SIGNIFICANCE

At issue in this series of decisions is the existence of a Constitutional right to privacy. Generally speaking, social conservatives in the U.S. deny that such a right exists, while liberals tend to assert that it does. In *Williams v. Attorney General of Alabama*, both the majority opinion (by Judge Stanley Birch, a 1990 appointee of President George H. W. Bush) and the dissent (by Judge Rosemary Barkett, a 1994 appointee of President Bill Clinton) made impassioned arguments on the question of whether a right to privacy exists. Judge Birch wrote that the majority "decline[s] the ACLU's invitation" to "add a new right to the catalogue of fundamental rights under the Constitution: a right to sexual privacy…. Hunting expeditions that seek trophy game in the fundamental-rights forest … if embarked upon recklessly, endanger … our republican democracy. Once elevated to constitutional status, a right is effectively removed from the hands of the people and placed into the guardianship of unelected judges."

Judge Barkett wrote that the majority's assertions "directly conflict with the Supreme Court's holding in *Lawrence v. Texas* and that "This case is … about the tradition of American citizens from the inception of our democracy to value the constitutionally protected right to be left alone in the privacy of their bedrooms

and personal relationships…. Applying the analytical framework of *Lawrence* compels the conclusion that the Due Process Clause [of the Constitution] protects a right to sexual privacy that encompasses the use of sexual devices."

As the divergent outcomes in *Lawrence v. Texas* and *Williams v. Attorney General of Alabama* show, the question of a "right to privacy" is in dispute or flux in American jurisprudence. It is likely to remain so for the foreseeable future.

FURTHER RESOURCES

Web sites

Ringel, Jonathan. "11th Circuit Nixes Sex Toys, Sex Rights." *Fulton County Daily Report*, July 29, 2004. Available from *Law.com* at: <http://www.law.com/jsp/article.jsp?id=1090180191546> (accessed March 9, 2006).

Sherri Williams v. Attorney General of Alabama. Sherri Williams, B. J. Bailey, Plaintiffs-Appellees, Bette Faye Haggermaker, et al., Plaintiffs, versus Attorney General of Alabama: United States District Court, Northern District of Alabama, Northeastern Divison. Feb. 28, 2006. Full text of final U.S. District Court memorandum opinion on this case. Available at <http://legalaffairs.org/howappealing/WilliamsFeb28Order.pdf> (accessed March 9, 2006).

Videotapes Show Bestiality, Enumclaw Police Say

Newspaper article

By: Jennifer Sullivan

Date: July 16, 2005

Source: "Videotapes Show Bestiality, Enumclaw Police Say." *The Seattle Times* (July 16, 2005).

About the Author: This article was written by Jennifer Sullivan, a staff reporter at *The Seattle Times*

INTRODUCTION

On July 2, 2005, a forty-five-year-old man died on a farm near Seattle, Washington, after having sex with a stallion. The horse's penis caused the man severe internal injuries: Enumclaw Police Commander Eric Sortland told a reporter, "Basically, his colon was ruptured, along with his lower organs in that region, and he bled out." The man was dead on arrival at Enumclaw Community Hospital. Police found hundreds of videotapes of sex with livestock cached in a field on the farm. Other animals kept on the farm, apparently a destination for men around the United States seeking sex with livestock, were sheep, goats, ponies, and dogs.

The man's sexual act was not illegal because the state of Washington was, at the time of his death, one of the seventeen U.S. states in which bestiality (sex with animals, also known as zoophilia) was not forbidden by law. It was not found that other persons were criminally involved with the specific acts that led to the man's death, no evidence was found that the horse had suffered during the incident, and an animal cannot be charged with a crime, so despite the occurrence of the death no felony charges were brought in the case. A local truck driver who videotaped the fatal sex act, James Michael Tait, was charged in October 2005 with criminal trespass, a misdemeanor. In November 2005, Tait was given a one-year suspended sentence with eight hours of community service and a $778 fine ($300 fine plus court costs).

Reaction to the incident ranged from titillated fascination to disgust. A state senator, Pam Roach (R-Auburn), introduced a bill to ban bestiality in Washington, which passed in February 2006 with a 36–0 vote (thirteen lawmakers excused). Bestiality is now a Class C felony in Washington, punishable by up to five years in jail and a $10,000 fine.

▉ PRIMARY SOURCE

ENUMCLAW — Authorities are reviewing hundreds of hours of videotapes seized from a rural Enumclaw-area farm that police say is frequented by men who engage in sex acts with animals.

The videotapes police have viewed thus far depict men having sex with horses, including one that shows a Seattle man shortly before he died July 2, said Enumclaw police Cmdr. Eric Sortland. Police are reviewing the tapes to make sure no laws have been broken.

"Activities like these are often collateral sexual crimes beyond the animal aspect," said Sortland, adding that investigators want to make sure crimes such as child abuse or forcible rape were not occurring on the property.

Washington is one of 17 states that does not outlaw bestiality. Police are also investigating the farm and the two men who live on the property to determine whether animal cruelty—which is a crime—was committed by forcing sex on smaller, weaker animals. Investigators said that in addition to horses, they have found chickens, goats and sheep on the 40-acre property northwest of Enumclaw.

Officers talked with the two men, but neither has been arrested. Neither man could be reached yesterday for comment.

According to King County sheriff's spokesman John Urquhart, the farm is known in Internet chat rooms as a destination for people who want to have sex with livestock.

However, authorities didn't learn about the farm until a man drove up to Enumclaw Community Hospital on July 2 seeking medical assistance for a companion. Medics wheeled the man into an examination room before realizing he was dead. When hospital workers looked for the driver, he was gone.

Using the dead man's driver's license to track down relatives and acquaintances, authorities were led to the Enumclaw farm. Some earlier reports had said hospital-surveillance cameras were used to track down the driver.

The dead man was identified as a 45-year-old Seattle resident. According to the King County Medical Examiner's Office, he died of acute peritonitis due to perforation of the colon. The man's death is not being investigated because it did not result from a crime, Urquhart said.

The Seattle man's relatives said yesterday they never suspected he was involved in bestiality. They said they were surprised when they learned he had purchased a Thoroughbred stallion earlier this year. The man told his relatives he boarded the animal with some friends in Enumclaw.

While the man's relatives were unsure how many horses he had boarded at the property, one Enumclaw neighbor said the Seattle man was keeping two stallions there.

Police and neighbors said the people renting the property have also had dogs and bull calves on the farm. Yesterday there were several horses and ponies grazing near a barn.

Two neighbors, a married couple who declined to allow use of their names, said yesterday they had no idea what had been going on at the farm. They said they've known one of the men who lived on the farm for years.

On Thursday, police showed the couple videotape seized from the farm showing men having sex with horses. The couple identified one of the horses as belonging to them, Sortland said. The couple also said it appeared at least part of the tape was filmed in their barn, which left them shocked and angry.

"We couldn't believe what we were seeing," said Sortland. "In the rare, rare case this happens, it's the person doing the animal. I think that has led to the astonishment of all of the entities involved."

Thursday night, in reaction to the man's death, Susan Michaels, co-founder of Pasado's Safe Haven, posted a letter on the local animal-rights organization's Web site calling for people to e-mail legislators in an attempt to change state laws.

"This [the death] gives us credence of getting a bestiality law passed," said Michaels. "It's not natural for animals to do this."

State Sen. Pam Roach, R-Auburn, said she plans to draft legislation as early as next week making bestiality illegal in Washington.

"This is just disgusting," Roach said yesterday. "It's against the law to harm children; it should be against the law to violate an animal."

SIGNIFICANCE

The man who died in this incident was mentally ill by the standards of the Diagnostic and Statistical Manual of Mental Disorders (DSM-IV-TR, 2000, the American Psychiatric Association's authoritative list of all mental disorders). DSM-IV-TR states that bestiality or zoophilia, like other "paraphilias"—nonstandard sexual desires and practices—is a diagnosable disorder if it causes "clinically significant stress or impairment in social, occupational, or other important areas of functioning"—which was certainly the case with this fatality.

However, in the aftermath of the Seattle bestiality case, the public comments of legislators and others were focused not on the danger of zoophilia to mentally ill human beings, but on the sexual innocence of animals. "It's really a bill that will protect animals, who are innocent, by the fact that they can't consent," the bill's sponsor, Sen. Roach, said. She also said she felt it was important to ban the performance or video recording of what she termed "abhorrent" acts. As quoted in the primary source, a local animal-rights activist urged passage of an anti-bestiality law on the grounds that "It's not natural for animals to do this." No concern for the fate of the mentally ill man involved, or for others who might be injured by similar practices, appears to have been reported from any source.

Expressions of concern for animal "consent" do not seem to be consistent with the terms of U.S. law: the notion of animal "consent" does not appear anywhere in law. Animals may be legally castrated, hunted, or butchered, all without their consent, as long as animal-cruelty statutes are not violated. Furthermore, sex acts that cause pain to small or ill animals are illegal under those statutes even in the absence of special anti-bestiality laws. Because sex with animals does not necessarily cause physical pain or emotional distress to the animals involved, the Washington state law passed in the wake of Enumclaw had to make sexual contact with animals cruel by definition: "A person is guilty of animal cruelty in the first degree when he or she...[k]nowingly engages in any sexual conduct or sexual contact with an animal."

It is difficult to find any record of any expression of concern by legislators or others for the welfare of human beings involved in zoophilic acts. It may be concluded that many or all laws banning zoophilia are not primarily motivated by a concern to protect mentally ill humans from danger or to protect animals from pain. Many persons view zoophilic acts as immoral, unnatural, or offensive; it is these beliefs that are expressed in the laws banning such practices.

Sex with animals is forbidden in some of the world's earliest legal and behavioral codes. The biblical book of Leviticus, for example, immediately after forbidding homosexual intercourse as an "abomination," also forbids bestiality: "Neither shalt thou lie with any beast to defile thyself therewith: neither shall any woman stand before a beast to lie down thereto: it is confusion" (Leviticus 18:23, King James Version). Zoophilia and zoophilic pornography are banned in many countries. Yet sex with animals is not rare. While preferential or exclusive interest in sex with animals is, according to psychologists, an unusual condition, a 1991 study found that the prevalence of bestiality, defined as "actual sexual contacts and sexual fantasy" involving animals was ten percent among the general population of hospital in-patients, fifteen percent among professional psychiatric staff, and fifty-five percent among psychiatric patients.

FURTHER RESOURCES

Periodicals

Alvarez, W.A., and J.P. Freinhar. "A Prevalence Study of Bestiality (Zoophilia) in Psychiatric In-patients, Medical In-patients, and Psychiatric Staff." *International Journal of Psychosomatic Disorders*. 38 (1991): 45–47.

Web sites

Washington State Legislature. "SB 6417-2005-06: Prohibiting Sexual Conduct or Sexual Contact with an Animal." <http://apps.leg.wa.gov/billinfo/summary.aspx?bill=6417> (accessed April 1, 2006).

Sources Consulted

BOOKS AND WEBSITES

A Century of Lawmaking. "Library of Congress." <http://rs6. loc.gov/ammem/amlaw/lawhome.html> (accessed on April 30, 2006).

Adams, Abigail and John Adams. *The Letters of John and Abigail Adams*. New York: Penguin Classics, 2003.

Agency for Healthcare Research and Quality. "Agency for Healthcare Research and Quality." <http://www.ahrq. gov> (accessed on April 30, 2006).

AIDS Research Institute (ARI). "AIDS Research Institute (ARI)." <http://ari.ucsf.edu> (accessed on April 30, 2006).

Airaksinen, Timo. *The Philosophy of the Marquis De Sade*. London: Routledge, 1995.

Allen, J. J. *The Man in the Red Velvet Dress: Inside the World of Cross-Dressing*. New York: Carol Publishing Group, 1996.

Altschuler, Glenn C. *All Shook Up: How Rock 'n' Roll Changed America*. New York: Oxford University Press, 2003.

American Association for the Advancement of Science (AAAS). "American Association for the Advancement of Science (AAAS)." <http://www.aaas.org> (accessed on April 30, 2006).

American Association of University Women. "Equity in School Athletics." <http://www.aauw.org/issue_advocacy/ actionpages/positionpapers/titleix_athletics.cfm> (accessed March 14, 2006).

American Civil Liberties Union. "Lesbian and Gay Rights." <http://www.aclu.org/lgbt/index.html> (accessed April 10, 2006).

American Medical Student Association. "Transgender and Transsexuality." <http://www.amsa.org/advocacy/lgbtpm/> (accessed March 19, 2006).

American Memory. "Library of Congress." <http://memory. loc.gov/ammem/index.html> (accessed on April 30, 2006).

American Menopause Foundation. <http://www.american-menopause.org> (accessed March 14, 2006).

American Psychiatric Association. *Diagnostic and Statistical Manual of Mental Disorders*. 4th ed. Washington, D.C.: American Psychiatric Association, 1994.

American Rhetoric. "American Rhetoric." <http://www.americanrhetoric.com/> (accessed on April 30, 2006).

Amireh, Amil. *The Factory Girl and the Seamstress: Imaging Gender and Class in Nineteenth Century Fiction*. New York: Garland, 2000.

Amnesty International USA. "Women's Human Rights." <http://www.amnestyusa.org/women/index.do> (accessed April 13, 2006).

Amnesty International. "Amnesty International." <http:// www.amnesty.org/> (accessed on April 30, 2006).

Amnesty International. "Female Genital Mutilation—A Human Rights Information Pack." <http://www. amnesty.org/ailib/intcam/femgen/fgm1.htm> (accessed March 20, 2006).

Anderson, Kelly, and Tami Gold. *Out at Work*. Frameline, 1996.

Annual Review of Public Health. "Annual Review of Public Health." <http://arjournals.annualreviews.org/loi/pub-lhealth> (accessed on April 30, 2006).

Anti-Child Porn.org. <http://www.antichildporn.org/> (accessed April 5, 2006).

Aptheker, Bettina. *Tapestries of Life: Women's Work, Women's Consciousness, and the Meaning of Daily Experience*. Amherst: University of Massachusetts Press, 1989.

Association of Sites Advocating Child Protection. <http://www. asacp.org/index.php> (accessed April 5, 2006).

Baird, Robert M., and Stuart E. Rosenbaum, eds. *Same-Sex Marriage: The Moral and Legal Debate*. Amherst, N.Y.: Prometheus Books, 2004.

Baker, Robert A., ed. *Child Sexual Abuse and False Memory Syndrome*. Amherst, New York: Prometheus Books, 1998.

Barnitz, Laura A. *Commercial Sexual Exploitation of Children: Youth Involved in Prostitution, Pornography & Sex Trafficking*. Youth Advocate Program International: 1998.

Barry, Kathleen. *Susan B. Anthony: Biography of a Singular Feminist*. New York: New York University Press, 1988.

Bass, Ellen, and Laura Davis. *The Courage to Heal: A Guide for Women Survivors of Child Sexual Abuse*. New York: Collins Books, 1994.

Bauer, Nancy. *Simone de Beauvoir: Philosophy and Feminism*. New York: Columbia University Press, 2001.

Bayer, Ronald. *Homosexuality and American Psychiatry*. Princeton: Princeton University Press, 1987.

BBC News. "The Gay Marriage Map." <http://news.bbc.co.uk/2/hi/americas/3516551.stm> (accessed March 14, 2006).

Becker, Susan D. *The Origins of the Equal Rights Amendment: American Feminism Between the Wars*. Westport, Conn.: Greenwood Press, 1981.

Betts, Raymond F. *A History of Popular Culture: More of Everything, Faster, and Brighter*. New York: Routledge, 2004.

Blum, Virginia L. *Flesh Wounds: The Culture of Cosmetic Surgery*. Berkeley: University of California Press, 2003.

Bongie, Laurence L. *Sade : A Biographical Essay*. University of Chicago Press, 1998.

Brainerd, C.J. and V.F. Reyna. *The Science of False Memory*. New York: Oxford University Press, 2005.

Brandt, Alan. *No Magic Bullet: A Social History of Venereal Disease in the United States Since 1880*. Oxford University Press. 1987.

British Library "British Library Images Online." <http://www.imagesonline.bl.uk/britishlibrary/> (accessed on April 30, 2006).

British Medical Journal. "British Medical Journal." <http://bmj.bmjjournals.com> (accessed on April 30, 2006).

Brumberg, Joan Jacobs. *Fasting Girls: The History of Anorexia Nervosa*. New York: Vintage, 2000.

BUBL LINK Social Sciences. "Centre for Digital Library Research." <http://bubl.ac.uk/link/linkbrowse.cfm?menuid=2822> (accessed on April 30, 2006).

Buechler, Steven M. *Women's Movements in the United States: Woman Suffrage, Equal Rights, and Beyond*. New Brunswick, NJ: Rutgers University Press, 1990.

Bullough, Bonnie, Vern L. Bullough, and James Elias, eds. *Gender Blending*. Amherst, NY: Prometheus Books, 1997.

Bullough, Vern L., and Bonnie Bullough. *Cross Dressing, Sex, and Gender*. Philadelphia: University of Pennsylvania Press, 1993.

Burgwinkle, William. *Sodomy, Masculinity and Law in Medieval Literature*. Cambridge, U.K.: Cambridge University Press, 2004.

Burke, Jason. *Al Qaeda*. London: Penguin Books, 2003.

Burstein, Miriam Elizabeth. *Narrating Women's History in Britain, 1770–1902*. Burlington, VT: Ashgate, 2004.

Burton, Annie L. *Women's Slave Narratives*. Mineola, N.Y.: Dover Books, 2006.

Califia-Rice, Patrick. *Sex Changes: The Politics of Transgenderism*. San Francisco: Cleis Press, 2003.

Carter, David. *Stonewall: The Riots That Sparked the Gay Revolution*. New York: St. Martin's Press, 2004.

CDC (Centers for Disease Control and Prevention). "CDCSite Index A-Z." <http://www.cdc.gov/az.do> (accessed on April 30, 2006).

Census Bureau. "United States Census Bureau." <http://www.census.gov/> (accessed on April 30, 2006).

Clift, Eleanor. *Founding Sisters and the Nineteenth Amendment*. New York: Wiley, 2003.

Clinton, Catherine. *The Other Civil War: American Women in the Nineteenth Century*. New York: Hill and Wang, 1999.

Clinton, Hilary Rodham. *Living History*. New York: Scribner, 2004, reprint.

Cohen, Lizabeth. *Making a New Deal: Industrial Workers in Chicago, 1919–1939*. Cambridge and New York: Cambridge University Press, 1990.

Coleman, Ray. *The Carpenters: The Untold Story: An Authorized Biography*. New York: HarperCollins, 1994.

Cook, Rebecca J. *Human Rights of Women: National and International Perspectives*. Philidelphia: University of Pennsylvania Press, 1994.

Coontz, Stephanie. *Marriage, a History: From Obedience to Intimacy, or How Love Conquered Marriage*. New York, N.Y.: Viking, 2005.

Cott, Nancy F. *The Bonds of Womanhood: "Woman's Sphere" in New England, 1780–1835*. 2nd ed. New Haven, Conn.: Yale University Press, 1997.

Critchlow, Donald T. *Intended Consequences: Birth Control, Abortion, and the Federal Government in Modern America*. Oxford and New York: Oxford University Press, 1999.

Crittendon, Anne. *The Price of Motherhood*. New York: Owl Books, 2002.

Crompton, Louis. *Homosexuality and Civilization*. Belknap Press, 2003.

Daniels, Kay. *So Much Hard Work: Women and Prostitution in Australian History*. Sydney: Fontana, 1984.

Darby, Robert J. *A Surgical Temptation: The Demonization of the Foreskin and the Rise of Circumcision in Britain*. Chicago: University of Chicago Press, 2005.

Davis, Kathy. *Dubious Equalities and Embodied Differences: Cultural Studies on Cosmetic Surgery*. Lanham, MD: Rowman and Littlefield, 2003.

Day, Frances Ann. *Lesbian and Gay Voices: An Annotated Bibliography and Guide to Literature for Children and Young Adults*. Westport, Conn.: Greenwood Press, 1997.

de Beauvoir, Simone. *The Second Sex*. New York: Knopf, 1993.

Dobson, James. *Marriage Under Fire: Why We Must Win This Battle*. Sisters, Ore.: Multnomah, 2004.

DOMA Watch. <http://www.domawatch.org> (accessed February 15, 2006).

Dossey, Barbara Montgomery. *Florence Nightingale: Mystic, Visionary, Healer*. Springhouse, PA: Springhouse, 2000.

Douglas, Susan J. *Where the Girls Are: Growing up Female with the Mass Media*. New York: Three Rivers Press, 1994.

DuBois, Ellen Carol. *Feminism and Suffrage: The Emergence of an Independent Women's Movement in America, 1848–1869*. Ithaca, N.Y.: Cornell University Press, 1978.

Duran, Jane. *Eight Women Philosophers: Theory, Politics, and Feminism*. Urbana, Ill.: University of Illinois Press, 2006.

Earth Summit 2002. Toolkit for Women. "Third World Conference on Women, Nairobi." <http://www.earthsummit2002.org/toolkits/Women/un-doku/un-conf/narirobi.htm> (accessed March 13, 2006).

Eberwein, Robert. *Sex Ed: Film, Video, and the Framework of Desire*. New Brunswick, NJ: Rutgers University, 1999.

Echols, Alice. *Daring to Be Bad: Radical Feminism in America, 1967–1975*. Minneapolis: University of Minnesota Press, 1989.

Eliason, Michele J. *Who Cares?: Institutional Barriers to Health Care for Lesbians, Gays, and Bisexual Persons*. New York: NLN Press, 1996.

Evans, Sara M. *Born for Liberty: A History of Women in America*. New York and London: The Free Press, 1989.

Ezekiel, Judith. *Feminism in the Heartland*. Columbus, OH: Ohio State University Press, 2002.

Falco, Maria J., ed. *Feminist Interpretations of Mary Wollstonecraft*. University Park, Pa.: Pennsylvania State University Press, 1996.

Federal Bureau of Investigation. "Uniform Crime Reports: Hate Crime Statistics." <http://www.fbi.gov/ucr/ucr.htm> (accessed April 1, 2006).

Findlaw "Findlaw/West." <http://public.findlaw.com/library/> (accessed on April 30, 2006).

Fischer, Gayle V. *Pantaloons and Power: A Nineteenth-Century Dress Reform in the United States*. Kent, Ohio: Kent State University Press, 2001.

Florence Nightingale Museum. <http://www.florence-nightingale.co.uk/centre.htm> (accessed April 10, 2006).

Fone, Byron R.S. *A Road to Stonewall: Male Homosexuality and Homophobia in English and American Literature, 1750–1969*. New York: Twayne, 1995.

Frank, Dana. *Purchasing Power: Consumer Organizing, Gender, and the Seattle Labor Movement, 1919–1929*. Cambridge and New York: Cambridge University Press, 1994.

Fraser, Suzanne. *Cosmetic Surgery, Gender, and Culture*. New York: Palgrave Macmillan, 2003.

Friskopp, Annette, and Sharon Silverstein. *Straight Jobs, Gay Lives: Gay and Lesbian Professionals, the Harvard Business School and the American Workplace*. New York: Scribners's, 1995.

Gallo, Robert C. *Virus Hunting: AIDS, Cancer, and the Human Retrovirus: A Story of Scientific Discovery*. New York: Basic Books, 1993.

GAO (Government Account Office). "Site Map." <http://www.gao.gov/sitemap.html> (accessed on April 30, 2006).

Garber, Marjorie. *Vested Interests: Cross-Dressing and Cultural Anxiety*. New York: Harper Perennial, 1993.

Garrow, David J. *Liberty and Sexuality: The Making of Roe v. Wade*. Berkeley: University of California Press, 1998.

Gartrell, Nanette, and Esther Rothblum, eds. *Everyday Mutinies: Funding Lesbian Activism*. Binghamton, N.Y.: Haworth Press, 2002.

Gerstmann, Evan. *Same-Sex Marriage and the Constitution*. New York: Cambridge University Press, 2003.

Gilfoyle, Timothy J. *City of Eros: New York City, Prostitution, and the Commercialization of Sex, 1790–1920*. New York: W.W. Norton and Co., 1991.

Golden, Janet. *A Social History of Wet Nursing in America: From Breast to Bottle*. Cambridge, U.K.: Cambridge University Press, 1996.

Gollaher, David L. *Circumcision: A History of the World's Most Controversial Surgery*. Basic Books, 2000.

Gordon, Linda. *Woman's Body, Woman's Right: Birth Control in America*. New York: Penguin Books, 1976.

Groneman, Carol. *Nymphomania: A History*. New York: W.W. Norton, 2000.

Harrison, Maureen, and Steve Gilbert, eds. *Obscenity and Pornography Decisions of the United States Supreme Court*. Carlsbad, Calif.: Excellent Books 2000.

Harrison, Patricia Greenwood. *Connecting Links: The British and American Woman Suffrage Movements, 1900–1914*. Westport, Conn.: Greenwood Press, 2000.

Hausman, Bernice L. *Changing Sex: Transsexualism, Technology, and the Idea of Gender*. Durham, NC: Duke University Press, 1995.

Heins, Marjorie. *Not in Front of the Children: "Indecency," Censorship, and the Innocence of Youth*. New York: Hill and Wang 2001.

Hill, Anita. *Speaking Truth to Power*. New York: Anchor, 1998.

Hill, Marilynn Wood. *Their Sisters' Keepers: Prostitution in New York City, 1830–1870*. Berkeley, Calif.: University of California Press, 1993.

Hinkle, Warren. *Gayslayer!: The Story of How Dan White Killed Harvey Milk and George Moscone and Got Away With Murder*. Virginia City, NV: Silver Dollar, 1985.

Hobson, Barbara Meil. *Uneasy Virtue: The Politics of Prostitution and the American Reform Tradition*. Chicago: University of Chicago Press, 1987.

Holland, Merlin. *The Real Trial of Oscar Wilde*. New York: HarperCollins, 2004.

Hull, N. E. H. *Roe v. Wade: The Abortion Right Controversy in American History*. Lawrence, Kans.: University Press of Kansas, 2000.

Human Rights Watch. "Human Rights Watch." <http://www.hrw.org/> (accessed on April 30, 2006).

Ingebretsen, Edward J. *At Stake: Monsters and the Rhetoric of Fear in Public Culture*. Chicago: University of Chicago Press, 2001.

Inglehart, Ronald and Norris, Pippa. *Rising Tide: Gender Equality and Cultural Change Around the World*. New York: Cambridge University Press, 2003.

Inhorn, Marcia C., and Frank van Balen, eds. *Infertility Around the Globe: New Thinking on Childlessness, Gender, and Reproductive Technologies*. Berkeley: University of California Press, 2005.

International Women's Health Coalition. "Factsheet: Child Marriage." <http://www.iwhc.org/resources/childmarriagefacts.cfm> (accessed April 1, 2006).

Irvine, Janice M. *Disorders of Desire: Sexuality and Gender in Modern American Sexology*. Philadelphia: Temple University, 2005.

Isreal, Betsy. *Bachelor Girl: The Secret History of Single Women in the Twentieth Century*. New York: William Morrow, 2002.

Craissati, J. *Managing High Risk Sex Offenders in the Community; A Psychological Approach*. Brunner-Routledge, 2000.

Jacobs, Harriet. *Incidents in the Life of a Slave Girl*. Mineola, N.Y.: Dover Publications, 2001.

Jain, Devaki. *Women, Development, and the UN: A Sixty-Year Quest For Equality And Justice*. Bloomington: Indiana University Press, 2005.

Jenkins, Philip. *Beyond Tolerance: Child Pornography Online*. New York: New York University Press, 2001.

Jewish Virtual Library. "Women and Special Forces." <http://www.jewishvirtuallibrary.org/jsource/Society_&_Culture/womidf.html> (accessed March 25, 2006).

Jewish Women's Archive. "Exhibit: Women of Valor—Ray Frank." <http://www.jwa.org/exhibits/wov/frank> (accessed March 13, 2006).

Kasserman, David Richard. *Fall River Outrage: Life, Murder, and Justice in Early Industrial New England*. Philadelphia: University of Pennsylvania Press, 1986.

Kaufman, Moises. *The Laramie Project*. HBO Home Video, 2002.

Keen, Ian. *Aboriginal Economy and Society: Australia at the Threshold of Colonisation*. Oxford University Press, 2000.

Kelly, Gary. *Revolutionary Feminism: The Mind and Career of Mary Wollstonecraft*. New York: St. Martin's Press, 1995.

Kerber, Linda K. *No Constitutional Right to be Ladies: Women and the Obligations of Citizenship*. New York: Hill and Wang, 1999.

Kessler-Harris, Alice. *Out to Work: A History of Wage-Earning Women in the United States*. New York: Oxford University Press, 1982.

Ko, Dorothy. *Cinderella's Sisters: A Revisionist History of Footbinding*. Berkeley: University of California Press, 2005.

Koda, Harold. *Extreme Beauty: The Body Transformed*. New York: Metropolitan Museum of Art, 2004.

Koven, Seth. *Slumming: Sexual and Social Politics in Victorian London*. Princeton, NJ: Princeton University Press, 2004.

La Leche League. <http://www.lalecheleague.org/NB/NBpublic.html> (accessed March 7, 2006).

Lambda Legal. "Marriage Project." <http://www.lambdalegal.org/cgi-bin/iowa/issues/record?record=9> (accessed February 20, 2006).

Lawton, David A. *Blasphemy*. Philadelphia: University of Pennsylvania Press, 1993.

Legal Information Institute, Cornell University. "Code of Federal Regulations." <http://www4.law.cornell.edu/cfr/> (accessed on April 30, 2006).

LaHaye, Beverley and Tim LaHaye. *The Act of Marriage: The Beauty of Sexual Love*. Grand Rapids, Mich.: Zondervan, 1998.

Lenhart, Sharyn. *Sexual Harassment and Gender Discrimination: Psychological Consequences and Clinical Interpretations*. New York: Routledge, 2004.

Lev, Arlene Istar. *Transgender Emergence: Therapeutic Guidelines for Working with Gender-Variant People and Their Families*. New York: Haworth, 2004.

Levin, Phyllis Lee. *Abigail Adams: A Biography*. New York: St. Martin's Griffin, 2001.

Levit, Nancy. *The Gender Line: Men, Women, and the Law*. New York: New York University Press, 1998.

Library of Congress "Library of Congress Online Catalog." <http://catalog.loc.gov/cgi-bin/Pwebrecon.cgi?DB=local&PAGE=First> (accessed on April 30, 2006).

Loffreda, Beth. *Losing Matt Shepard: Life and Politics in the Aftermath of Anti-Gay Murder.* New York: Columbia University Press, 2000.

Making of America "Cornell University." <http://cdl.library.cornell.edu/moa/> (accessed on April 30, 2006).

Manegold, Catherine S. *In Glory's Shadow: Shannon Faulkner, the Citadel, and A Changing America.* New York: Alfred A. Knopf, 2000.

Masbridge, Jane J. *Why We Lost the ERA.* Urbana and Chicago, Ill.: University of Chicago Press, 1986.

Mason, Bobbie Ann. *Elvis Presley.* New York: Viking, 2003.

McBride, Dwight. *Why I Hate Abercrombie & Fitch: Essays on Race and Sexuality in America.* New York: New York University Press, 2005.

McKenna, Neil. *The Secret Life of Oscar Wilde.* New York: Basic Books, 2005.

MedWeb at Emory University. "MedWeb at Emory University search page." <http://170.140.250.52/MedWeb/> (accessed on April 30, 2006).

Melody, M.E., and Linda M. Peterson. *Teaching America about Sex: Marriage Guides and Sex Manuals from the Late Victorians to Dr. Ruth.* New York: New York University, 1999.

Meyerowitz, Joanne. *How Sex Changed: A History of Transsexuality in the United States.* Cambridge, Mass.: Harvard University Press, 2002.

Michigan State University Libraries. "What Every Girl Should Know." <http://digital.lib.msu.edu/collections/index/> (accessed February 6, 2005).

Millet, Kate. *Sexual Politics.* Champaign, Ill.: University of Illinois Press, 2000.

Moran, William. *The Belles of New England: The Women of the Textile Mills and the Families Whose Wealth They Wove.* New York: St. Martin's Griffin, 2004.

Morbidity and Mortality Weekly Report. "Morbidity and Mortality Weekly Report." <http://www.cdc.gov/mmwr> (accessed on April 30, 2006).

National Academy of Sciences. "National Academy of Sciences." <http://www.nas.edu> (accessed on April 30, 2006).

National Archives and Records Administration. "National Archives and Records Administration." <http://www.archives.gov/index.html> (accessed on April 30, 2006).

National Fatherhood Initiative. <http://www.fatherhood.org> (accessed March 6, 2006).

National Gay and Lesbian Task Force. "Transgender Civil Rights Project" (2005). Available at <http://www.thetaskforce.org/ourprojects/tcrp/index.cfm> (accessed March 19, 2006).

National Institutes of Health. "National Institutes of Health." <http://www.nih.gov> (accessed on April 30, 2006).

National Library of Medicine. "History of Medicine." <http://www.nlm.nih.gov/hmd/index.html> (accessed on April 30, 2006).

National Organization for Women. "Equal Rights Amendment." <http://www.now.org/issues/economic/eratext.html> (accessed March 18, 2006).

National Organization for Women. <http://www.now.org> (accessed March 27, 2006).

National Sex Offender Public Registry. <http://www.nsopr.gov/> (accessed March 27, 2006).

National Women's Hall of Fame. "Women of the Hall: Gloria Steinem." <http://www.greatwomen.org/women.php/> (accessed March 27, 2006).

National Women's Health Information Center. <http://www.womenshealth.gov>(accessed March 14, 2006).

National Women's Political Caucus. <http://www.nwpc.org> (accessed March 27, 2006).

Nature. "Nature." <http://www.nature.com> (accessed on April 30, 2006).

NICHD-National Institute of Child Health and Human Development. "NICHD -National Institute of Child Health and Human Development." <http://www.nichd.nih.gov> (accessed on April 30, 2006).

NIGMS-National Institute of General Medical Sciences. "NIGMS -National Institute of General Medical Sciences." <http://www.nigms.nih.gov> (accessed on April 30, 2006).

NLM-National Library of Medicine. "NLM -National Library of Medicine." <http://www.nlm.nih.gov/> (accessed on April 30, 2006).

Office of Research on Women's Health. "Office of Research on Women's Health." <http://www4.od.nih.gov/orwh> (accessed on April 30, 2006).

Olupona, Jacob K. *Kingship, Religion, and Rituals in a Nigerian Community: A Phenomenological Study of Ondo Yoruba Festivals.* Stockholm: Almqvist & Wiksell International, 1991.

Wilde, Oscar. *The Complete Works of Oscar Wilde.* New York: HarperCollins, 2003.

Patterson, Romaine. *The Whole World Was Watching: Living in the Light of Matthew Shepard.* New York: Advocate 2005.

Penn, Robert E. *The Gay Men's Wellness Guide: The National Lesbian and Gay Health Association's Complete Book of Physical, Emotional, and Mental Health and Well-Being for Every Gay Male.* New York: Henry Holt, 1997.

Perkins, Roberta, Garrett Prestage, Rachel Sharp, and Francis Lovejoy, eds. *The History of Female Prostitution in Australia.* Sydney: University of New South Wales, 1994.

Peterkin, Allan D., and Cathy Risdon. *Caring for Lesbian and Gay People: A Clinical Guide.* Toronto: University of Toronto Press, 2003.

Peters, Elizabeth H., and Randal D. Day, eds. *Fatherhood: Research, Interventions, and Policies.* Binghamton, N.Y.: Haworth Press, 2000.

Peters, Julie Stone and Andrea Wolper, eds. *Women's Rights, Human Rights; International Feminist Perspectives.* New York: Routledge, 1994.

Pharma-Lexicon International. "MediLexicon." <http://www.medilexicon.com/> (accessed on April 30, 2006).

Pinello, David R. *Gay Rights and American Law.* Cambridge and New York: Cambridge University Press, 2003.

Ping, Wang. *Aching for Beauty: Footbinding in China.* New York: Anchor, 2002.

Pomeroy, Wardell B. *Dr. Kinsey and the Institute for Sex Research.* London: Thomas Nelson and Sons, 1972.

Pope John Paul II. *Pope John Paul II: In My Own Words.* New York: Gramercy, 2000.

Project Gutenberg. "Online Book Catalog-Overview." <http://www.gutenberg.org/catalog/> (accessed on April 30, 2006).

Publiclibraries.com. "National Libraries of the World." <http://www.publiclibraries.com/world.htm> (accessed on April 30, 2006).

Purvis, June, ed. *Women's History: Britain, 1850–1945: An Introduction.* New York: St. Martin's Press: Ashgate, 1995.

Raeburn, Nicole C. *Changing Corporate America from Inside Out: Lesbian and Gay Workplace Rights.* Minneapolis: University of Minnesota Press, 2004.

Rice, Califia-Patrick. *Sex Changes: The Politics of Transgenderism.* San Francisco: Cleis, 2003.

Riley, Tim. *Fever: How Rock 'n' Roll Transformed Gender in America.* New York: St. Martin's Press, 2004.

Ringdal, Nils Johan. *Love For Sale: A World History of Prostitution.* Grove Press. 2004.

Riverol, A.R. *Live from Atlantic City: A History of the Miss America Pageant Before, After and in Spite of Television.* Bowling Green, Ky.: Bowling Green State University Popular Press, 1992.

Rosen, Ruth. *The Lost Sisterhood: Prostitution in America, 1900–1918.* Baltimore, Md.: Johns Hopkins University Press, 1982.

Rosen, Ruth. *The World Split Open: How the Modern Women's Movement Changed America.* New York: Viking, 2000.

Rowbotham, Sheila, and Jeffrey Weeks. *Socialism and the New Life: The Personal and Sexual Politics of Edward Carpenter and Havelock Ellis.* London: Pluto, 1977.

Royal Society, (UK). "Science Issues." <http://www.royalsoc.ac.uk/landing.asp?id=6> (accessed on April 30, 2006).

Rupp, Leila J. *A Desired Past: A Short History of Same-Sex Love in America.* Chicago: University of Chicago Press, 1999.

Sadker, Myra, and David Sadker. *Failing at Fairness: How America's Schools Cheat Girls.* New York: Charles Scribner's Sons, 1994.

Sagade, Jaya. *Child Marriage in India: Socio-Legal and Human Rights Dimensions.* Oxford, U.K.: Oxford University Press, 2005.

Saguy, Abigail Cope. *What Is Sexual Harassment?: From Capital Hill to the Sorbonne.* Berkeley: University of California Press, 2003.

Sandfort, Theo G. M., and Jany Rademakers, eds. *Childhood Sexuality: Normal Sexual Behavior and Development.* Binghamton, N.Y.: Haworth Books, 2000.

Sanger, Margaret. *The Autobiography of Margaret Sanger.* Mineola, N.Y.: Dover Publications, 2004.

Sanger, Margaret. *The Selected Papers of Margaret Sanger.* Champaign: University of Illinois Press, 2002.

Schaeffer, Neil. *The Marquis de Sade: A Life.* New York: Knopf, 1999.

Schulman, Sarah. *My American History: Lesbian and Gay Life During the Reagan/Bush Years.* New York: Routledge, 1994.

Selth, Jefferson P. *Alternative Lifestyles: A Guide to Research Collections on Intentional Communities, Nudism, and Sexual Freedom.* Wesport, Conn.: Greenwood, 1985.

Shilts, Randy. *Mayor of Castro Street: The Life and Times of Harvey Milk.* New York: St. Martin's Press, 1982.

Simon Wiesenthal Center "Simon Wiesenthal Center." <http://www.wiesenthal.com> (accessed on April 30, 2006).

Social Sciences Virtual Library. "Digilogical." <http://www.dialogical.net/socialsciences/index.html> (accessed on April 30, 2006).

SocioWeb. "Blairworks." <http://www.socioweb.com/> (accessed on April 30, 2006).

Solarz, Andrea L. *Lesbian Health: Current Assessment and Directions for the Future.* Washington, D.C.: National Academy Press, 1999.

Southern Poverty Law Center. "Southern Poverty Law Center." <http://www.splcenter.org/> (accessed on April 30, 2006).

Spanos, Nicholas P. *Multiple Identities & False Memories: A Sociocognitive Perspective.* Washington, D.C.: American Psychological Association, 2001.

Stearns, Peter N. *Fat History: Bodies and Beauty in the Modern West.* New York: New York University Press, 2002.

Steele, Valerie. *Fashion and Eroticism: Ideals of Feminine Beauty from the Victorian Era to the Jazz Age.* New York: Oxford University Press, 1985.

Steele, Valerie. *The Corset: A Cultural History*. New Haven, Conn. and London: Yale University Press, 2003.

Steinem, Gloria. *Outrageous Acts and Everyday Rebellions*, 2nd ed. New York: Owl Books, 1995.

Stephen, Lynn. *Women and Social Movements in Latin America: Power from Below*. Austin, Texas: University of Texas Press, 1997.

Stern, Phyllis Noerager. *Lesbian Health: What Are the Issues?* New York: Taylor and Francis, 1993.

Strom, Linda. *Karla Faye Tucker Set Free: Life and Faith on Death Row*. New York: Random House, 2000.

Stuart-Macadam, P., and K. Dettwyler. *Breastfeeding: Biocultural Perspectives*. Binghamton, N.Y.: Haworth Press, 1995.

Swigonski, Mary E., Robin S. Mama, and Kelly Ward, eds. *From Hate Crimes to Human Rights: A Tribute to Matthew Shepard*. New York: Harrington Park Press 2001.

Tayler, Max, and Ethel Quayle. *Child Pornography; An Internet Crime*. New York: Brunner-Routledge, 2003.

The Equal Rights Amendment. <http://www.equalrightsamendment.org> (accessed March 18, 2006).

The History of Lambda Legal. <http//:www.lambdalegal.org/cgi-bin/iowa/cases/record?record=93>(accessed March 27, 2006).

Thomas. "Library of Congress." <http://thomas.loc.gov/> (accessed on April 30, 2006).

Thompson, Mark, ed. *Long Road to Freedom: The Advocate History of the Gay and Lesbian Movement*. New York: St. Martin's Press, 1994.

Tidd, Ursula. *Simone de Beauvoir*. New York: Routledge, 2004.

Transgender Law and Policy Institute. "News" <http://www.transgenderlaw.org> (accessed March 26, 2006).

Transgender Law Center. <http://www.transgenderlaw.org> (accessed March 26, 2006).

Truth, Sojourner. *The Narrative of Sojourner Truth*. Mineola, N.Y.: Dover Publications, 1997.

U.S. Code. "Policy Concerning Homsexuality in the Armed Forces." 10 U.S.C. Sec. 654. <http://www.law.cornell.edu/uscode/html/uscode10/usc_sec_10_00000654---000-.html> (accessed April 4, 2006).

U.S. Equal Employment Opportunity Commission. "Facts About Sexual Harassment." <http://www.eeoc.gov/facts/fs-sex.html> (accessed March 24, 2006).

U.S. Equal Employment Opportunity Commission. "Pregnancy Discrimination." <http://www.eeoc.gov/types/pregnancy.html> (accessed April 12, 2006).

U.S. Equal Employment Opportunity Commission. "Sex-Based Discrimination." <http://www.eeoc.gov/types/sex.html> (accessed March 14, 2006).

United Nations Children's Fund (UNICEF). *Protect Every Child*. Video tape number 390, 2002.

United Nations Development Programme. "Gender Equality" <http://www.undp.org/gender> (accessed April 14, 2006).

United Nations Millennium Campaign. "Voices against Poverty" <http://www.millenniumcampaign.org/site/> (accessed April 14, 2006).

United States Department of Labor. "Public Law 104–193." <http://wdr.doleta.gov/readroom/legislation/pdf/104–193.pdf> (accessed March 27, 2006).

United States General Accounting Office. "Intercollegiate Athletics" <http://www.gao.gov/new.items/d01297.pdf> (accessed March 14, 2006).

Weigel, George. *Witness to Hope: The Biography of Pope John Paul II*. New York: Harper Perennial, 2005.

Weis, Lois, and Michelle Fine, eds. *Beyond Silenced Voices: Class, Race, and Gender in U.S. Schools*. Albany: State University of New York Press, 2005.

Weiss, Thomas G., David P. Forsythe, and Roger A. Coate. *United Nations and Changing World Politics*. Boulder, CO, and San Francisco: Westview Press, 2004.

Wellman, Judith. *Road to Seneca Falls: Elizabeth Cady Stanton and the First Women's Rights Convention*. Urbana: University of Illinois Press, 2004.

Wharton, Greg, and Ian Philips, eds. *I Do/I Don't: Queers on Marriage*. San Francisco: Suspect Thoughts Press, 2004.

Wheeler, Lee Ann. *Against Obscenity: Reform and the Politics of Womanhood in America, 1873–1935*. Baltimore, Md.: The Johns Hopkins University Press, 2004.

Wheeler, Marjorie Spruill, ed. *One Woman, One Vote: Rediscovering the Woman Suffrage Movement*. Troutdale, Ore.: New Sage Press, 1995.

White, Jocelyn, and Marissa C. Martinez. *The Lesbian Health Book: Caring for Ourselves*. Seattle: Seal Press, 1997.

Williams, B. *Women Out of Place: The Gender of Agency and the Race of Nationality*. New Brunswick, N.J.: Routledge, 1996.

World Health Organization. "WHO Statistical Information System (WHOSIS)." <http://www3.who.int/whosis/menu.cfm> (accessed on April 30, 2006).

Youngkin, Ellis Quinn, and Marcia Szmania Davis. *Women's Health: A Primary Care Clinical Guide*. Upper Saddle River, N.J.: Pearson Prentice Hall, 2004.

Zinn, Howard, Dana Frank, and D.G. Kelley. *Three Strikes: Miners, Musicians, Salesgirls, and the Fighting Spirit of Labor's Last Century*. Boston: Beacon Press, 2001.

Index

Boldface indicates a primary source.
Italics indicates an illustration on the page.